A map
William
Hon. W
Adapte

# YEOMEN AND COLLIERS
IN TELFORD

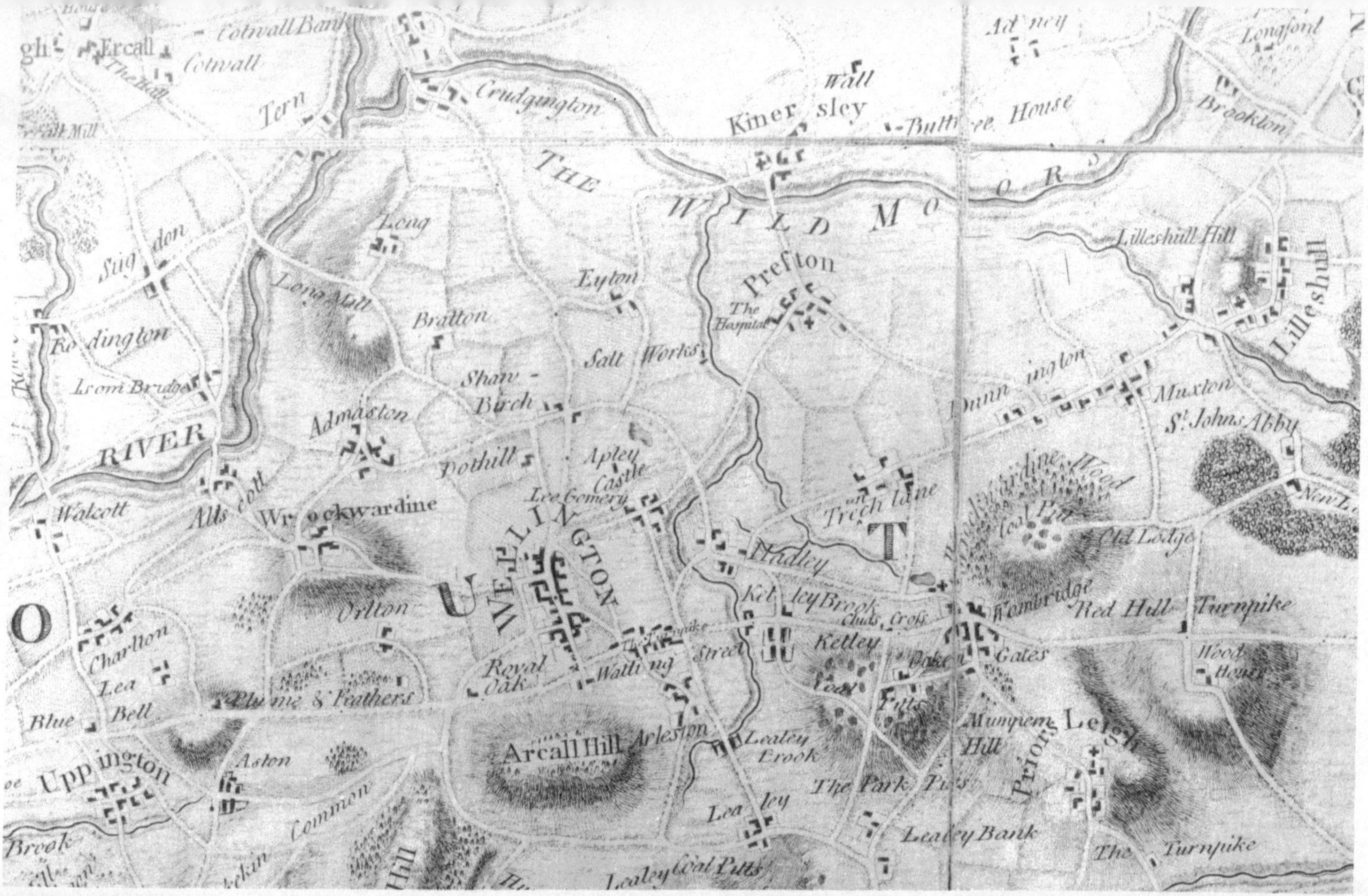

Ercall
Cotwall Bank
Cotwall
Tern
Crudgington
Kinersley
Wall
Butt ree House
Ad ney
Longford
Brookton
THE WILD MOORS
Long
Sugdon
Long Mall
Bratton
Eyton
Preston
The Hospital
Lilleshull Hill
Lilleshull
Rodington
Isom Bridge
Salt Works
Shaw - Birch
Admaston
RIVER
Dothill
Apley Castle
Lee Gomery
Dunnington
Muxton
St. Johns Abby
Trench lane
Walcott
Allscott
Wrockwardine
Hadley
Old Lodge
WELLINGTON
Orlton
Ketley Brook
Clubs Cross
Wombridge
Red Hill
Turnpike
Charlton
Lea
Royal Oak
Watling Street
Ketley
Gates
Wood House
Plume & Feathers
Blue Bell
Arleston
Leaky Brook
Arcall Hill
Mumpers Hill
Priors Leigh
Uppington
Aston
Common
The Park Pits
Lealey
Lealey Bank
Lealey Coal Pitts
The Turnpike
Brook

# YEOMEN AND COLLIERS IN TELFORD

Probate Inventories for Dawley, Lilleshall, Wellington and Wrockwardine, 1660-1750

*Edited by*

# Barrie Trinder & Jeff Cox

## PHILLIMORE

1980

Published by
PHILLIMORE & CO. LTD.
London and Chichester
*Head Office*: Shopwyke Hall,
Chichester, Sussex, England

© Barrie Trinder and Jeff Cox, 1980

ISBN 0 85033 282 2

The publication of this book
has been sponsored by
TELFORD DEVELOPMENT CORPORATION

Assistance from the parish councils of
LILLESHALL AND WROCKWARDINE
is gratefully acknowledged

The following members or ex-members of the Social History of Telford Research Class have contributed substantially to this study: Miss R. Alves, Mrs. J. Bearn, Miss J. Beddow, Mr. J. Bott, Mr. D. Boulton, the late Mr. F. Brown, Mrs. M. Brown, Dr. J. J. Cox, Mrs. N. C. Cox, Mr. P. Dunn, Mr. G. Evans, Mr. J. Fowler, Mr. G. Herbert, Miss R. Hollinsworth, Mrs. F. Jacobs, Mrs. M. Jelbart, Mr. K. B. Jones, Mr. J. Kennedy, Mrs. M. Kirby, Mr. J. Lenton, Mr. O. G. MacDonald, Miss A. Mapp, Mr. G. Muter, Mr. V. Needham, Mr. W. W. Norris, Mr. J. Pagett, Miss B. Pope, Miss U. Rayska, Mr. P. Tilley, Mr. T. Wastling, Mrs. M. Wilde, Mr. E. H. J. Wood. The tutor of the class was Barrie Trinder, Salop County Council Adult Education Tutor for Historical Studies.

Printed in Great Britain by
WHITSTABLE LITHO LTD
and bound by
THE NEWDIGATE PRESS, LTD

# CONTENTS

| | |
|---|---|
| Preface and Acknowledgements | vii |
| Introduction: | 1 |
| The four parishes | 10 |
| Houses | 14 |
| Money and Property | 17 |
| Trades and Professions | 19 |
| The Mercers | 20 |
| The Professions | 41 |
| The Leather Trades | 44 |
| The Dyers | 47 |
| Spinning and Weaving | 61 |
| Food and Clothing | 64 |
| Craftsmen in Metal | 65 |
| Craftsmen in Wood | 66 |
| Other Crafts | 67 |
| Innkeepers and Horsekeepers | 68 |
| The Colliers | 70 |
| Farming | 72 |
| Women in Society | 90 |
| Furnishings | 90 |
| The Kitchen | 103 |
| Water, Lighting and Heating | 108 |
| The Dairy | 109 |
| The Brewhouse | 111 |
| Conclusions | 113 |
| A List of people from the parishes of Dawley, Lilleshall, Wellington and Wrockwardine whose wills or administration bonds are recorded in the Calendar of Wills . . . at Lichfield, 1651-1750 | 119 |
| The Inventories of Dawley | 163 |
| The Inventories of Lilleshall | 193 |
| The Inventories of Wellington | 249 |
| The Inventories of Wrockwardine | 402 |

| | |
|---|---|
| Gazetteer of place names mentioned in the Inventories | 457 |
| General Glossary .. .. .. .. .. .. .. | 460 |
| Glossary of specialised terms used in mercers' inventories .. .. .. .. .. .. .. | 470 |
| Index of subjects and places .. .. .. .. .. | 477 |
| Index of names .. .. .. .. .. .. .. | 482 |

## LIST OF ILLUSTRATIONS

*Frontispiece*: John Rocque's Map of Shropshire, 1752

(*between pages 24/25*)

1. Lilleshall Lodge, *c.*1820
2. Ketley Bank House
3. Dyers at work
4. A tanner
5. A gardener
6. A smith
7. A table board and frame
8. A wainscott chair

# PREFACE AND ACKNOWLEDGEMENTS

THIS VOLUME is the largest of several projects undertaken by an adult education class organised by the Salop County Council Adult Education Service, which first met at Madeley Library, Telford, in the autumn of 1972. Since that time many people have made contributions to the work. In the nature of things the composition of such classes constantly changes, like that of a regiment in wartime, or the passenger complement of a stopping train. Over the years parenthood, marriage, death, departures from the district and the demands of full-time jobs have drawn away some students, but they have been replaced by others, and the class has always been a large one by the standards of other such groups.

We would like to record our gratitude to our two hosts, Mr. J. Kennedy, one-time librarian at Madeley, who first suggested the formation of the group, and was for two years a member of it, and Mr. V. Morris, principal of the Walker Technical College, who provided a home for the class when the consequences of the Yom Kippur War made it impossible to meet at Madeley. We would also like to thank Miss Jane Isaac, archivist at the Lichfield Joint Record Office for much helpful advice throughout the period of the project, and to her assistants for their patience in helping with photocopying. Mrs. M. Halford, the Shropshire County Archivist has also given useful professional advice and has provided a permanent home for the photocopies of the inventories used by the class.

The inventories in this collection were all photocopied at Lichfield, transcribed by class members, and typed, after which their contents were entered on 8in. x 5in. Copeland Chatterton punched cards, according to a system devised by Dr. J. J. Cox. The transcription and the punching of the cards were completed in 1977, and the analysis of the inventories was carried out by the class during the 1977-78 and 1978-79 sessions, although some sections not dependent on statistical data were begun much earlier. The introduction has been edited during the summer of 1979.

We are uneasily aware that there is much more to be extracted from the inventories of North Telford than we are able to discuss in this volume. We are able to say so much about mercers because one student has patiently teased information from the texts over several years, and compared it with that obtained from mercers' inventories from elsewhere. Similarly detailed treatment of other topics would doubtless have brought similar rewards. Nevertheless, the time has come to make the classes' work available to a wider public, and we hope that it will be the foundation on which other studies can be built. We hope also, in the not-too-distant future, to complete work on a parallel volume to this one, based on the inventories of the parishes bordering the Ironbridge Gorge.

Several historians have kindly provided information which has been used in this study, and we would like to thank in particular Dr. Malcolm Wanklyn of Wolverhampton Polytechnic for information from his work on the Forester Papers, and Dr. Peter Edwards of the Froebel College, Roehampton, for allowing us to refer to his thesis. The Shropshire Archaeological Society have kindly allowed the reproduction of a water colour in their possession, and we are grateful to Mr. James Lawson and the Shrewsbury Drapers Company for allowing the class to see and photograph 17th-century furniture in the Drapers' Hall. Mr. Tony Carr of the Salop Local Studies Library has helpfully provided assistance with illustrations, and Mr. Tim Bradburn of Wolverhampton Polytechnic kindly prepared the graph and sketch map.

An adult class is not the most rapid vehicle for completing an investigation of an historical topic. An industrious graduate student might have produced a work of a size comparable with this study in half the time, but such classes give to local history a dimension entirely lacking to the individual scholar. Any merits this study may have arise largely from the experience, the local knowledge and the highly varied expertise which students have brought to it, and to the ideas germinated during discussions as discoveries have been made and problems analysed. The group has benefited from a remarkable range of varied talents, and we hope that the publication of this volume will enable its members past and present to feel that their labours have been worthwhile.

*November 1980*  
BARRIE TRINDER  
JEFF COX

*Note.*—References to inventories in the introduction and elsewhere in the volume are indicated by the numbers of the inventories concerned in italics, thus:—Jane Hartshorne (*194*).

# INTRODUCTION

> It is an elementary life but neither entirely passive, nor, above all, completely static. It has moments of acceleration, and occasionally of surprise: new plants become acclimatised, techniques improve and spread, changes occur in processes employed by blacksmiths, weavers and still more by miners and shipbuilders. These changes take place slowly but steadily. Money and towns play a continually increasing part and some innovations are of decisive importance.[1]

MUSEUMS IN FIVE CONTINENTS testify to the ability of material objects to enlarge our understanding of the past. There are few more convincing ways of coming to terms with peasant culture than by absorbing the atmosphere of the open air museums of Scandinavia. A sense of living on the margin of subsistence, an awareness of man's dependence upon the seasons and the avoidance of plagues, above all a feeling of awed respect for the great multitude of skills which our ancestors had to practice in order to survive, all spring from a spell among the homes of farmers and craftsmen at Skansen in Stockholm, the Frilandmuseet near Copenhagen, or the Dutch Open Air Museum at Arnhem. Perhaps even more effective in recreating an awareness of the rhythms of past societies are smaller, less visited open-air museums, like that beside Lake Siljan at Mora. Lists of objects are inadequate substitutes for the objects themselves, but we shall never see an English weaver's or a husbandman's house as it was furnished in 1700, and probate inventories, available in thousands for most parts of England for the late 17th and early 18th centuries, offer perhaps the best substitute for the English folk museums whose potential exhibits were destroyed two centuries ago. The picture they give of English society is necessarily incomplete. We learn from them nothing of the music of Purcell, the deliberations of the Royal Society, the buildings of Nicholas Hawksmoor, the thoughts of John Locke, or the campaigns of Marlborough. Nevertheless, they provide perhaps the most vivid insights which we can now gain into the lives of most of our ancestors.

The Industrial Revolution is a great divide in our history. By the closing years of the 19th century, in consequence of changes extending over several previous generations, most people in Britain were buying clothes, shoes, beer, flour and household utensils made in factories by individuals with whom they were totally unacquainted. It requires a massive effort of imaginative understanding to conceive a world in which this was not so, in which people ate well or starved according to the local harvests, in which many of their clothes and household fabrics were of linen locally made from their own crops of hemp and flax, in which beer, butter and bread were largely produced in the homes where they were consumed, in which only a few luxuries, woollen and silk fabrics, sugar and raisins of the sun, prayer books and tobacco, were brought into the district from outside to be sold by the market town mercers. Mens' possessions, the furnishings of their homes, the clothes they wore, the tools and implements with which they made their livings, the stock they kept in their fields, offer one route towards a broader understanding of their lives, particularly when it is possible to study the possessions of large numbers of men over an extended period. The purpose of this study has been to attempt to gain some insights into the communities of an area which was to be profoundly affected by the Industrial Revolution, and which, like other such areas, was already considerably industrialised by the early 18th century.[2]

The town of Telford extends some eight miles from the fringe of Lilleshall village in the north to the Ironbridge Gorge in the south, and at its widest is about four miles from east to west. Its boundaries, except in the far south, roughly coincide with those of the Coalbrookdale coalfield. The Ironbridge Gorge is a district of well-recognised historical importance, the scene of numerous innovations in the manufacture and use of iron in the late 18th century. For about thirty years, following the construction of the Iron Bridge in 1779, it attracted artists and writers from all over the world.[3] The parishes in the north of the coalfield received much less attention in the Industrial Revolution period, and have been comparatively neglected by historians. Large parts of the area were considerably affected by the rapid expansion of coal and iron mining in the late 18th century, and by 1840 much of the surface of the land was covered with heaps of spoil from the mines and slag from the ironworks. Little is known of the social structure or the economy of the area before the Industrial Revolution, of the importance of mining, of the types of agriculture practised, or of the status of the market town of Wellington. Probate inventories provide an avenue which permits some of these problems to be explored, and the object of this study has been not just to make available to scholars and to local people an important range of sources, but to use the material gathered to attempt to answer certain basic questions about the social and economic history of the region in the period before the main onset of industrialisation.

The inventories studied have been those from the four parishes of Dawley, Lilleshall, Wellington, and Wrockwardine, which survive with grants of probate recorded in the three volumes of the Calendar of the Wills proved in the consistory Court of the Bishop of Lichfield and Coventry for the period 1651 to 1750. Probate records for the southern

# INTRODUCTION

## TABLE I

### North Telford Inventories: Distribution by parish and decade

|  | Dawley | Lilleshall | Wellington | Wrockwardine | Total |
|---|---|---|---|---|---|
| Pre-1660 | 1 | 1 | 3 | 2 | 7 |
| 1660-69 | 11 | 15 | 27 | 14 | 67 |
| 1670-79 | 6 | 22 | 46 | 16 | 90 |
| 1680-89 | 7 | 27 | 46 | 29 | 109 |
| 1690-99 | 7 | 9 | 47 | 21 | 84 |
| 1700-09 | 6 | 35 | 62 | 17 | 120 |
| 1710-19 | 9 | 32 | 44 | 8 | 93 |
| 1720-29 | 22 | 18 | 61 | 24 | 125 |
| 1730-39 | 11 | 19 | 44 | 20 | 94 |
| 1740-50 | 9 | 3 | 33 | 12 | 57 |
| Totals .. | 89 | 181 | 413 | 163 | 846 |
| Proportion of Total (%) | 10.52 | 21.39 | 48.82 | 19.27 |  |

part of Telford, the parishes of Benthall, Broseley, Madeley and Little Wenlock, which are in the Diocese of Hereford, were not available for study at the time the project began, but will be the subject of a further volume. The parishes of Dawley, Lilleshall, Wellington and Wrockwardine include most of the northern half of the Coalbrookdale coalfield, the only significant areas excepted being the small parish of Wombridge, which was a peculiar, and for which as far as is known no probate records survive for the period under review, other than one will with no inventory which is at Lichfield, and the chapelry of Priorslee in the large parish of Shifnal, which has been excluded because there was no way in which its inventories could have been studied without examining those for the whole parish.

The three volumes of the Calendar of Wills proved at Lichfield from 1651 to 1750 list 1,118 grants of probate or administration for the four parishes studied. All grants were made in or after 1660, but seven inventories were made some years earlier during the Interregnum. Some 846 of the grants are accompanied by inventories of which 89 (10.52 per cent.) were from Dawley, 181 (21.39 per cent.) from Lilleshall, 413 (48.82 per cent.) from Wellington, and 163 (19.27 per cent.) from Wrockwardine. These proportions tally well with other statistical comparisons between the parishes set out in Table IV. The proportion of inventories surviving from the 1740s is much less than for previous decades, and as in other areas, it seems that in Telford the practice of making, or at least of keeping inventories, was declining by the middle of the 18th century.

This study is based on an analysis of all 846 inventories, but to publish the full texts of so many documents was scarcely a practicable proposition. A selection of about a third has therefore been made, chosen to give a reasonable balance between parishes and values. In order to show the full variety of trades in the area, craftsmen are somewhat over-represented at the expense of farmers. Men are over-represented in relation to women, since a high proportion of womens' inventories contain very few details. Some inventories have been included to complete a sequence, where there are several surviving for one family.

TABLE II

North Telford Inventories: analysis of values (i)

|  | Dawley | Lilleshall | Wellington | Wrockwardine | Total | Proportion of total (%) |
|---|---|---|---|---|---|---|
| Under £10 | 16 | 32 | 112 | 29 | 189 | 22.34 |
| £10–£19 | 24 | 31 | 80 | 26 | 161 | 19.03 |
| £20–£49 | 25 | 38 | 87 | 31 | 181 | 21.39 |
| £50–£99 | 11 | 31 | 54 | 27 | 123 | 14.54 |
| £100–£199 | 11 | 27 | 43 | 37 | 118 | 13.95 |
| Over £200 | 2 | 22 | 37 | 13 | 74 | 8.75 |
| Total | 89 | 181 | 413 | 163 | 846 |  |

It was not necessary for anyone whose estate was worth less than £5 to make a will, but there are nevertheless in this collection several inventories of estates worth less than that sum. Wealthy people who had possessions located in more than one diocese were obliged to have their wills proved in the Prerogative Court of Canterbury, and it is likely that many of the rich whose property was concentrated in one place also preferred that court. Thirteen wills from the four parishes studied were proved in the Prerogative Court of Canterbury between 1700 and 1749.[4] Nevertheless the inventories of several people of considerable wealth appear in this collection, among them those of Richard Stanier of Aston (*154*) who had possessions worth £1,327, Robert Pemberton (*210*), whose goods were worth £1,112, and Jane (*194*), widow of the coalmaster Richard Hartshorne, whose estate was valued at £546. Her late husband's will was proved at the Prerogative Court of Canterbury in 1733.

In all collections of probate inventories it is likely that the middle ranks of society are over represented. There are, for example, only two inventories among the 846 representing the many domestic servants who worked in the area. There are nevertheless sufficient individual inventories

## TABLE III

North Telford Inventories: analysis of values (ii) (all figures are percentages)

|  | Dawley | Lilleshall | Wellington | Wrockwardine | Total |
|---|---|---|---|---|---|
| Under £10 | 17.98 | 17.68 | 27.12 | 17.79 | 22.34 |
| £10–£19 | 26.96 | 17.13 | 19.37 | 15.95 | 19.03 |
| £20–£49 | 28.09 | 20.99 | 21.07 | 19.28 | 21.39 |
| £50–£99 | 12.36 | 17.13 | 13.07 | 16.56 | 14.54 |
| £100–£199 | 12.36 | 14.92 | 10.41 | 22.70 | 13.95 |
| Over £200 | 2.35 | 12.15 | 8.96 | 7.98 | 8.75 |

to portray something of the way of life of the very rich in the area, and enough to throw some light on the living conditions of the poor. There can have been few other than outright paupers and vagrants who lived in harsher circumstances than some of the inhabitants of the two- and three-room cottages in Ketley and Trench Lane, whose inventories are in this collection. Table III shows that over three-quarters of the inventories from the four parishes were valued at less than £100, and over 40 per cent. at less than £20. The variations between the parishes are significant: Wellington had the highest proportion of inventories of low value, largely because of the high proportion of craftsmen who lived there. Wrockwardine had the lowest proportion of low value inventories. Among the inventories of the wealthy, Dawley had by far the lowest proportion of those valued at more than £100, and Wrockwardine the highest, over 30 per cent. of the inventories from the parish being so valued. The proportion from Lilleshall was only slightly lower, but the proportion from that parish valued at more than £200 was 12.15 per cent., significantly higher than the 7.98 per cent. of that value in Wrockwardine. Dawley with 73.03 per cent., had the highest proportion of inventories valued at less than £50, with Wellington recording slightly fewer, at 67.55 per cent., and the other two parishes being very similar, Lilleshall having 55.80 per cent., and Wrockwardine, in most respects the richest parish of the four, 53.02 per cent.

According to the a statute of 1529 (21 Hen. VIII 15) an inventory of the goods and chattels of a deceased person had to be exhibited at the time when probate of his will was granted, or when letters of administration were issued if he died intestate. As more collections of inventories have been studied and published,[5] so, gradually, more of the nature of the documents is coming to be understood. It becomes increasingly evident that there were considerable variations in practice between different areas, and many shades of meaning in the use of words and expressions which can be recognised only after the study of very large numbers of inventories. There are several items which occur on a high proportion of the inventories in this collection of which the use, purpose, shape or materials are defined in only one or two. It is clear from other, uncompleted studies, that practices differed in other parts of Shropshire. The inventories of the Royal Peculiar of Bridgnorth have many idiosyncracies which are not to be observed in North Telford, although Bridgnorth is only 12 miles from Wellington, and there were numerous links between the two towns.

The North Telford inventories are impressively consistent in their valuations.[6] Few items are appraised at values which are totally at variance with the general levels. A high proportion were made room by room, through the house of the deceased. Telford appraisers tended to neglect fuel, and in the 18th century often omitted to include poultry and bees. As in Essex, it seems likely that the inventories preserved in the Registry are copies of originals. The note at the bottom of the inventory of James Freeman (101) sets out the expenses involved in administering the estate, which includes a payment for copying the inventory. North Telford inventories are no more likely to be correctly totalled than those from any other area, and spellings are often phonetic, sometimes hilariously so. The item 'His ship' mentioned on the inventory of George Golbourne (104) needs to be pronounced several times in a local accent before its meaning becomes clear.

A probate inventory had to be made by 'honest and skillful' appraisers. It is virtually impossible to make an accurate assessment of how many people acted as appraisers in this period.[7] Eight hundred names appear in the inventories, just over half of them appearing only once. It cannot be assumed that each name always represents only one person. There were at least three people called Thomas Higgins who acted during the 1680s, one in Dawley and two in Lilleshall. There also appear to have been at least two men by the name of John Bradshaw at that time in Wellington, and several more later on. It has proved impossible on the evidence of handwriting alone to distinguish individual appraisers. Occasionally a signature is so distinctive that there can be no doubt that a series of inventories are the work of one man. William Newton had such a signature; so did Adam Wright, and 'R. Jones'. Even then one cannot say with certainty how often they acted since at times their names appear only in the preambles, and at others the scribe wrote them at the end in his own hand. Some men probably acted as appraisers on as many as a dozen occasions. William Icke is one example, and Thomas Windsor *alias* Winshurst ia another.

In general the appraiser came from the same social group as those whose wills found their way to Lichfield. This excludes both the very poor and those at the top of the social scale. The names of Eytons, Leveson Gowers and Forresters do not appear at all. Lower down the

# INTRODUCTION

social scale there appear to be differences between the parishes. In Wellington the incumbent was in no way involved with appraising, although William Langley probably wrote and certainly witnessed the will of Thomas Wright, dyer, in 1662. The minister would certainly have been a visitor to the homes of the dying and his services as scribe would no doubt have been called upon in times of need. Henry Haughton, vicar of Lilleshall, and William Cope, vicar of Wrockwardine each acted as an appraiser on several occasions, as did other, apparently unbeneficed clergymen resident in Wellington, John Field, Francis Ore, Robert Ore, and William Socket. George Arden, clerk, of Stirchley, appraised five Dawley inventories. It is evident that those whose riches came from trade rarely acted as appraisers, but wealthy farmers did so frequently. Rich yeoman like the Sheltons were much in demand. Members of the family acted on over thirty occasions, appraising both the rich and the poor in Lilleshall. Joshua Dunton the tanner seems to be an exception to the rule among tradesmen, both because Andrew Shelton came to Wellington to take his inventory, and because he himself acted on several occasions, mainly for business associates, his suppliers like William Bell of Kynnersley, one of the biggest cattle men in the district, and the users of his products like the shoemakers.

It is often possible to surmise why particular people were invited to act as appraisers. The highly technical inventories were usually done by experts, the mercers by other mercers, for instance. Alan Pickering was in much demand as an expert on horses. Over the period 1680–1742 four different men with that name acted as appraiser on at least twenty-three occasions in the four parishes, and doubtless went further afield for the same purpose. In all but four cases horses were involved. This use of experts is spelled out in the case of Anne Smaldridge of Lichfield whose inventory was taken in 1679 by three men 'except for the goods in the dyehouse taken by . . .'.[8] Sometimes the principal creditor carried out the appraisal. Thomas Harper acted both as appraiser and administrator to the estate of Robert Lanckyshire. The preamble to Ann Wright's inventory says that it was made by the churchwardens, verger and constable of Lilleshall. A study of the parish officers for each year would probably indicate more examples. Thomas Bradborne made three inventories in 1671 and never acted again, and Richard Crowther did four in 1676. Perhaps each was a parish officer in the year concerned, but none of the churchwardens listed in the Wellington parish register in the 17th century acted as an appraiser during his year of office.

Appraisers were most usually the relatives or neighbours of the deceased, although the connections are not always obvious. William Birch appraised the household of Joshua Johnson, who was probably his nephew. Birch's possessions were assessed by John Leake, a connection by marriage through Johnson's daughter. The 1672 Hearth Tax roll can be useful in indicating possible neighbours, even at a later date. An example is afforded by the estate of John Vickers of Wrockwardine Wood appraised in 1728 by Alan Fenn. Thirty-five years before Richard Vickers made the inventory of the possessions of Robert Fenn, and 20 years before that Robert Fenn and Richard Vickers appear to have lived on adjacent tenements.

Women frequently witnessed wills, doubtless because as servants and nurses they were readily available at the time wills were made, but appraising was almost exclusively the job of men. Only one woman, Jane Johnson, acted twice, seven acted once each, and two more witnessed inventories. One of these female appraisers, Elizabeth Langley, was dissatisfied with the inventory already produced of her husbands' goods, and made a long addendum to it. Four of the others made inventories of the possessions of deceased women. Elizabeth Wallis not only signed the inventory of William Fewtrell in 1693 but probably wrote it out herself. Other published collections of inventories show that women only rarely acted as appraisers.

TABLE IV

Comparisons between the four North Telford parishes

|  | Dawley | Lilleshall | Wellington | Wrockwardine | Totals |
|---|---|---|---|---|---|
| Proportion of inventories 1660–1750 (%) | 10.52 | 21.39 | 48.82 | 19.27 |  |
| Acreage | 2,633 | 6,111 | 9,184 | 4,630 | 22,558 |
| Proportion of acreage | 11.67 | 27.09 | 40.07 | 20.53 |  |
| Hearths in 1672 | 93 | 103 | 530 | 154 | 880 |
| Proportion of hearths in 1672 | 10.57 | 11.70 | 60.23 | 17.50 |  |
| Households in 1672 | 55 | 60 | 260 | 105 | 480 |
| Proportion of households in 1672 | 11.46 | 12.50 | 54.17 | 21.87 |  |
| Population 1676 | 216 | 428 | 1,544 | 507 | 2,695 |
| Proportion of population 1676 | 8.02 | 15.88 | 57.29 | 18.81 |  |
| Population 1801 | 3,869 | 2,060 | 7,531 | 1,913 | 15,373 |
| Proportion of population 1801 | 25.17 | 13.40 | 48,99 | 12.44 |  |
| Number of inventories of people engaged in trades other than farming | 8 | 18 | 117 | 15 | 158 |
| Proportion of traders among inventories of each parish | 8.99 | 9.94 | 28.33 | 9.20 |  |

# INTRODUCTION

## THE EXPERT APPRAISER

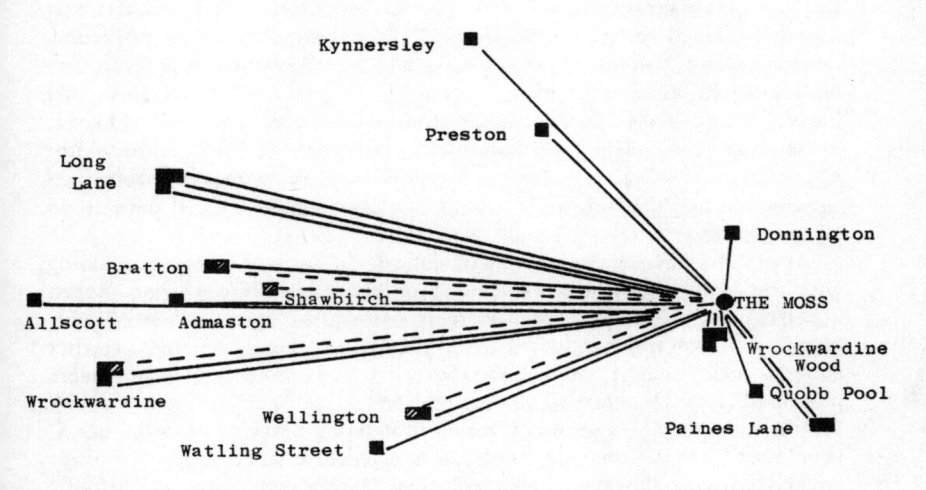

Alan Pickering I, II, and III were all carriers or horse dealers and were in wide demand as appraisers. For simplicity all three are represented as living at The Moss.

■ Inventory appraised involving horses or cattle
▨ Inventory appraised not involving horses or cattle

    The making of an inventory would appear to have required a degree of literacy and numeracy, but illiterate appraisers are not uncommon. In some cases none of the appraisers could sign his name and an unrecorded scribe must have been employed. At least one hundred and sixty appraisers made marks, but the real number of illiterates was certainly much higher since sometimes other appraisers signed for them. Usually the illiterate acted with another appraiser who could write, but it must not be assumed that the inability to sign went with a lack of efficiency. Thomas Windsor often worked with Richard Shelton and together they produced workmanlike if not highly detailed documents. Even when he worked with others, Windsor was characteristically efficient. Alan Pickering, an expert on horses and cattle was another illiterate whose skill outweighed his handicap. The typical illiterate was a man worth only a few pounds when he died, who appraised the estate of his neighbour or relative, and often did it badly, but of the 160 illiterate appraisers five had personal goods and chattels at their deaths worth over £150. Thomas Windsor was one of the richest men in the district with an estate worth £440, but Silvanus

Davis, Ralph Windsor, John Spearman and Richard Mountford had also administered considerable concerns without ever acquiring the skill of signing their own names. All five died before 1700. Later it seems that illiteracy ceased to be respectable. The number of illiterate appraisers declined sharply in the 18th century, and no 18th-century illiterate can be identified as a rich man. Several of the early illiterates like Alan Pickering and John Spearman had sons who could write. The practice of sending fair copies to Lichfield increased in the 18th century, but not enough to invalidate the conclusion that many more people, particularly among the well-to-do, could sign their name in 1750 than could do so a century before.

Appraisers have been studied particularly closely in Wellington. Starting with the hypothesis that a technical inventory was produced by an expert, a search was made for other mercers among the appraisers of Wright, Justice and Johnson, and they were there to be found. As a result other experts were sought, and Alan Pickering and Thomas Windsor were identified as such. Plotting the appraisers of all Wellington inventories for the 1680s on a map has revealed interesting patterns of communication, even though some of the detail is inaccurate since home townships are not always known. To search for reasons for anomalies among appraisers has proved a valuable source of questions about the workings of society during the period. There was a delay in 1689 between the death of William Embry and the taking of his inventory, by two men whose names do not appear on the Wellington Hearth Tax roll, and who appear to have come from Preston Boats, near Shrewsbury. Doubtless difficulties in communication caused the delay, but why they took the inventory remains unexplained. The inventory of Henry Stanworth (*103*), suggests that he was an unimportant, not very wealthy, shoemaker, yet it was appraised by four of the most prominent citizens of Wellington, three of them mercers, and the fourth Thomas Dicken, one whose name had the prefix 'Mr.' in the parish register. This is unique inventory. There is no other with such a disparity between the estate and the appraisers.

## The Four Parishes

The parishes considered in this study cover an area of 22,558 acres, and had a population of people over the age of 16 of 2,695 in 1676. In 1672 there were about 480 households in the region, excluding those of paupers. In 1801, half a century after the last of the inventories studied, the population was 15,373, but this followed a period of rapid industrial expansion when population grew much faster than the national average. A demographic study of the region[9] has suggested that growth between 1711 and 1760 was concentrated in the period 1716-25, 1731-40 and and 1756-55, and that there were spells of very high mortality in the 1720s and around 1740.

INTRODUCTION                                                                                                                       11

The parish of Dawley situated entirely within the productive coal measures was the smallest of the four studied, and on almost every reckoning the least wealthy. It comprised only 11.67 per cent. of the total area, and produced only 10.52 per cent. of the inventories. By 1801 more than a quarter of the inhabitants of the four parishes were resident in Dawley, but this increase was due to the building of large-scale ironworks in the 1750s and later. The parish consisted of three townships, Great Dawley, Little Dawley and Malins Lee, the two former often being known by Latinised names, Dawley Magna and Dawley Parva. Few records of any sort illuminate the history of Malins Lee. Maps of the two other townships[10] suggest that their medieval arable fields had been in close proximity to the parish church, and that traces of strip cultivation could still be seen in the late 18th century. From these twin nuclei the townships had steadily been colonised as woodland had been cleared through the centuries. The names of such farms as the Croppings and the Stocking are evidence of this work of clearance, and the numerous -hay place-names in the parish indicate the late survival of woodland. On its western fringe, where it adjoins Coalbrookdale in the ancient parish of Madeley, Little Dawley is still heavily wooded, the woodlands being interspersed with the remains of old shallow mine workings. Squatting was evident in the township by the middle of the 18th century in such places as Holywell Lane, a rambling road which led towards Little Wenlock. The centre of Great Dawley in the period of this study was around the parish church, but by 1800 it had shifted to Dawley Green along the turnpike road from Wellington to Bridgnorth and Dudley.

Lilleshall comprised just over a quarter of the area studied, and rather more than a fifth of the inventories came from the parish. It was owned almost entirely by the Leveson Gower family, to whom it had descended as a unit from the Augustinian Priory of Lilleshall. John Leveson Gower (1675–1709) was created Baron Gower in 1702, and his son, also John (d. 1754), became the first Earl Gower in 1746. Their descendants became successively Marquesses of Stafford in 1786 and Dukes of Sutherland in 1833. The Lilleshall Hall of this period was a relatively modest dwelling, and not the family's principal seat. The family's agent in the 19th century, the efficient James Loch, thought that the estate was laxly administered in the period under review, with farms let on uneconomically long leases, haphazardly arranged and ill-cultivated. The village of Lilleshall itself, under the lee of the volcanic outcrop of Lilleshall Hill, contained numerous farmsteads, but there are also several large isolated farms within the township, like those at Honnington and Cheshill which apparently originated as monastic granges. The fields of Lilleshall were apparently partially enclosed by the 1660s a process completed by 1717 if not earlier. Muxton and Donnington were the two other townships within the parish, the productive coal measures in the latter being sufficiently shallow to be mined during the period under review.

Wellington was by far the largest of the four parishes, producing nearly half of the inventories studied. It had half of the population recorded in 1676, and comprised 40 per cent. of the area of the four parishes. It consisted of 12 clearly-defined townships, Arleston, Aston, Apley, Dothill, Hadley, Horton, Ketley, Lawley, Leegomery, Wappenshall, Walcot, and Wellington, as well as the demesne of Watling Street and parts of Preston and Eyton. Field-name evidence suggests that each township had its own arable fields in the Middle Ages. Dothill and Apley had largely been destroyed by emparking, and only one dwelling in each was recorded in the 1672 Hearth Tax. Ketley, Hadley and Lawley were largely in the coalfield. Large tracts of common survived in Lawley until the mid-18th century. The manor of Ketley, which incorporated parts of Wombridge parish as well as the township in Wellington, belonged to the Leveson Gower family. It was thickly settled by industrial squatters during the 18th century. Walcot, four miles to the west of the parish church, was detached from the rest of the parish. Its mill on the River Tern had a far more reliable source of power than any of the other mills in the parish, built like those at Ketley and Leegomery, on small streams.

Wellington itself was fifth in order of size of the townships. Little is known of its early history, but place-name and topographical evidence suggest strongly that it was a town created by plantation in the Middle Ages. Grants of charters for markets and fairs are recorded in 1244 and 1283. The three rows of buildings between the Market Square and Walker Street have no land attached to them and show every appearance of having been encroachments within a large market place. To the west of the old town centre on either side of the present Haygate road are numerous fields with the element 'New Town' in their names. The inventories enable some assessment to be made of the trade of this little-documented market town.

The open fields of Wellington survived until the early 18th century, a detailed survey having been made of them in 1702 before enclosure, which lists the holdings of many of those whose inventories are in this collection. The three fields were then called Wrekin, Windmill and Smallbrook fields. Open fields in several Shropshire towns survived much later than the majority of village fields in the county, those at Ludlow, Bridgnorth, Market Drayton, and Shifnal all being enclosed later than those at Wellington.[14] The open fields of the outer townships of Wellington were probably all enclosed by 1700. The inventory of Thomas Lockley of Aston taken in 1659 (*81*) mentions his sheep on the Wrekin and cattle including 'his part of the wild beasts', suggesting that animals were grazed in common on the Wrekin, a subject on which little is currently known.

Wrockwardine parish comprised 20.52 per cent. of the district, provided 19.27 per cent. of the inventories, and included 18.81 per cent. of the population of the four parishes in 1676, a remarkably consistent group of figures. Like Wellington, it was a parish of many townships, consisting of Admaston, Allscott, Bratton, Burcote, Charlton, Clotley and Leaton, as well as Wrockwardine itself. Probably all had their own medieval open field systems, and all were recognisable if shrunken settlements in the period under review. Open fields survived in Wrockwardine and Leaton in 1674,[15] but it is doubtful whether there was much open land left in the parish by 1700. To the east of the parish is the parkland of Orleton which had formed part of Wellington in the early Middle Ages. Since the 14th century it had been the home of the Cludde family. In the parish documents of the early 18th century Orleton is always coupled with Nash or Ness, a deserted medieval village which was the home of Hercules Felton in 1668 (*212*), but of which only a barn survived by the mid-19th century. The men of Wrockwardine had since the Middle Ages enjoyed grazing rights on the Weald moors, with which the village was linked by a strakers' road,[16] the lower part of which, between Allscott and the moors, was lined with cottages built by squatters in slangs apparently enclosed from the verges, which, together with a cross-roads settlement on the Wellington–Whitchurch road, comprised a distinct settlement known as Long Lane. Investigations of the wills of several farmers in Wellington parish have shown that several also had land in Kynnersley, which they probably held in order to gain access to the Weald moors.

Wrockwardine Wood was an area of just over 500 acres detached from the rest of the parish and wholly within the coalfield. There is no evidence of open-field cultivation in the area, and in the Middle Ages it was doubtless woodland where the rest of the parish pastured their pigs and cut timber. Much of Wrockwardine Wood was still open heath or woodland in the period under review, and two large areas, the Nabb and Cockshut Piece remained open in the 19th century. At its south-eastern extremity Wrockwardine Wood was bounded by Watling Street, and part of the cross-roads settlement of Pains Lane (called St. George's since the 1850s) was situated within it. Its western boundary was Trench Lane, the road from Wellington to Newport where there was a considerable settlement of squatters.

The landscape of North Telford between 1660 and 1750 was varied and constantly changing. On the low and relatively flat lands of Lilleshall and Wrockwardine could be seen both open and enclosed fields in the 1660s, though the former had largely disappeared a century later. The inventories give no direct indications of crops growing in open strips, and only rarely identify fields of any kind. The town of Wellington stood amidst its open strips until after 1700. On the higher, more thickly wooded land of Dawley, Ketley, Hadley, and Wrockwardine Wood the open fields of the small townships had long since ceased to be worked, although some strips were still recognisable. To the north and west of Wellington was a belt of parkland encompassing Orleton, Dothill and Apley. Amidst the woods mining operations were steadily being extended, and in the first half of the 18th century wooden railway lines appeared in the district. Squatting could be observed in several areas alongside roads and on the open commons.

A dominant feature of the landscape was the Roman road, Watling Street, which for about half a mile formed the boundary between Lilleshall and Wrockwardine Wood on its northern side, and Shifnal to the south. It passed through what is now the centre of Oakengates, in Wombridge parish, became the boundary between Ketley and Hadley townships in Wellington, before crossing the Ketley brook to enter Arleston. At the Cock cross-roads it entered the Watling Street demesne, and then just east of the *Haygate* inn it passed into Wrockwardine parish, in which it remained until it went into Uppington west of the Bluebell cross-roads. The road, with its branches from Oakengates to Shifnal and Cotwall, and from Wellington to Crudgington, was the subject of a Turnpike Act in 1725-26, the first in Shropshire. It was commonly called the Street Way, and in one inventory (96) it is defined as 'the Streete Lane (alias) Watling Street Way'. Mention in the Wrockwardine parish registers of the early 18th century of John Lennox, an Irishman, John the Pepperman, a travelling man, and a 'strange Welch woman' witness to the variety of travellers using the road. Watling Street was lined with numerous inns as it passed through the district. There are inventories for the *Seven Stars* at Hadley, and the *Swan* in Wellington, which still survive, although both have been completely rebuilt. The construction of a new line of road around Overley Hill in Wrockwardine parish in the 1830s isolated two of the inns, the *Blue Bell*, which survives as a farmhouse, and the *Plume of Feathers*. The inventories abound in evidence of the thoroughfare trade which the road created, and of the blacksmiths, wheelwrights and innkeepers who gained their livings from it.

*Houses*

Probate inventories cannot be regarded as wholly reliable indicators of the numbers of rooms in houses, since there was no obligation on appraisers to make any mention of rooms which did not contain moveable objects. Nevertheless, the conclusions which can be drawn from a large sample do have some validity. In North Telford 484, or 57.2 per cent. of the inventories distinguish rooms, a high proportion by the standards of other areas which have been studied. In Telford it is extremely difficult to compare inventories with surviving houses. Industrial development on the coalfield, and James Loch's mania for rebuilding have destroyed a high proportion of the pre-18th-century buildings.

## TABLE V

### Size of houses as indicated in inventories (i)

|  | Total | Percentages in | | | | |
|---|---|---|---|---|---|---|
| Number of rooms | number of houses | Dawley | Lilleshall | Wellington | Wrock-wardine | All four parishes |
| 1 room | 11 | 1.96 | 3.57 | 1.96 | 2.13 | 2.27 |
| 2 rooms | 43 | 9.80 | 7.14 | 9.02 | 9.57 | 8.88 |
| 3 rooms | 61 | 11.76 | 17.86 | 11.37 | 11.70 | 12.60 |
| 4 rooms | 82 | 21.57 | 15.48 | 16.86 | 15.96 | 16.94 |
| 5 rooms | 85 | 17.65 | 14.29 | 17.25 | 21.28 | 17.56 |
| 6 rooms | 68 | 13.73 | 13.10 | 14.90 | 12.77 | 14.05 |
| 7 rooms | 48 | 11.76 | 9.52 | 10.98 | 6.38 | 9.92 |
| 8 rooms | 31 | 3.92 | 5.95 | 5.49 | 10.64 | 6.40 |
| 9 rooms | 19 | 1.96 | 8.33 | 3.14 | 3.19 | 3.93 |
| 10 rooms | 8 | 1.96 | 2.38 | 1.98 | nil | 1.65 |
| 11 rooms | 8 | 1.96 | 1.19 | 1.18 | 3.19 | 1.65 |
| 12 rooms | 5 | nil | nil | 1.96 | nil | 1.03 |
| More than 12 | 15 | 1.96 | 1.19 | 3.92 | 3.19 | 3.10 |

### Size of houses (ii) (figures quoted are number of houses)

| | | | | | | |
|---|---|---|---|---|---|---|
| 1–5 rooms | 282 | 32 | 49 | 144 | 57 | 282 |
| 6–10 rooms | 174 | 17 | 33 | 93 | 31 | 174 |
| More than 10 | 28 | 2 | 2 | 18 | 6 | 28 |

### Size of houses (iii) (figures quoted are percentages)

| | | | | | | |
|---|---|---|---|---|---|---|
| 1–5 rooms | | 62.75 | 58.33 | 56.47 | 60.64 | 58.26 |
| 6–10 rooms | | 33.33 | 39.39 | 36.47 | 32.98 | 35.95 |
| More than 10 | | 3.92 | 2.38 | 7.06 | 6.38 | 5.79 |

The word 'house' in the inventories normally means the 'house place' or the main living area of a dwelling. The commonest form of dwelling shown in Table V is that with five rooms, usually a house place, which included cooking facilities, a parlour and a buttery on the ground floor, and two chambers above. Nearly 60 per cent. of all the houses were five rooms or less, although the possibility that some of the one- or two-room houses were actually parts of larger dwellings must be a real one. One of the simplest and most typical dwellings is that of the weaver Edward Owen of Lilleshall (74), which consisted of a house place, a room above it, and a workshop, perhaps a lean-to, for his looms. The house of another weaver, Richard Adney (*97*) was very similar. He had a house place with a buttery and workshop on the ground floor, and a chamber, which was probably over the house place. This seems to have been the usual type of dwelling for the poorer craftsmen. William Davis, a Ketley weaver (*204*) had a house place and shop, and a room or rooms 'upstairs'. William Stanworth (*123*), a shoemaker, had a 'house or lower roomes', a buttery and workshop, and 'ye over rooms'. Richard Vickers of Wrockwardine Wood (*239*) who made his living from carrying coal, had a house place, parlour and buttery, and two chambers above. Edward Darrell (*21*), whose dwelling was probably one of the first squatter cottages in Holywell Lane, had a kitchen and a little room, and two chambers above. His contemporary and near neighbour, Michael Onions (*23*) had a three-cell dwelling, with a house place, buttery and brewhouse, and three chambers above. Sometimes craftsmen's houses, like those of the blacksmiths Thomas Bennett and John Peate (*90, 108*) seem to have consisted of intricately mixed working and living accommodation.

The houses of the poorer agriculturalists were basically similar. The dwelling of Edward Jones (*97*), a Wellington husbandman, is a good example of a four-room house, consisting of house place, parlour and two chambers above. The dwellings of labourers tended to be even smaller. John Handy (*153*), whose estate was worth only £1 16s. 11d., had a house place and a little room adjoining, and just one room above, and the dwelling of George Cleaton (*168*), whose possessions were valued at £3 5s. 7d. was virtually identical.

Over a third of the houses had between six and 10 rooms, and slightly less than six per cent. more than ten. The largest homes were those of Richard Stanier (*154*), who had 25 rooms, and William Cheshire (*249*), who had twenty-one. In the larger houses, particularly before 1700, the principal living room was often called the hall (*1, 4, 8, 9, 13, 32, 58, 81, 82, 83, 86, 87, 95, 100, 118, 147, 154, 199, 230, 249*). Often such houses had a kitchen separate from the hall or house place, additional parlours or butteries, and increased numbers of chambers above. Several inventories refer to new rooms, and a number distinguish the best chamber or room (e.g., *257*). Some distinguish rooms by colour. R. B. Leeke (*199*) had a green parlour and a 'blew room', while Thomas Lawrence (*226*) had a green chamber. The sleeping rooms in inns were normally distinguished by names or signs, and it seems to have been the usual practice to name the best room after the sign of the inn, and to list it first on the inventory. By the end of the 17th century new names were being used to describe rooms, which indicated increased standards of luxury and sophistication. Thomas Jones (*118*) of Wellington in 1692, and Walter Hartshorne (*12*) of Dawley in 1696 appear to have been the first in the district to have had dining-rooms. At least five dining-rooms are mentioned in 18th-century inventories, all in the homes of people of wealth. Thomas Calcott in

1744 (*264*) had a smoking-room, and R. B. Leeke (*199*) in 1739 a drawing-room. There was also growing sophistication in the service rooms of larger houses, shown by the appearance of sculleries (*26, 199, 249*), larders (*58, 65*), and pantries (*70, 196, 199, 258, 264*). Larger houses were also distinguished by their third storeys, the garretts or cocklofts as they were usually called. These were often used for storage, or for accommodation for servants. One inventory refers to 'the fellow's chamber' (*249*), while another distinguishes between the mens' chamber and the servant maids' chamber (*65*).

Many inventories list working-rooms, sometimes simply called the 'shop', the 'outbuildings', the 'outhouse', the 'back house', or on some inventories of men involved in trade on a considerable scale, 'the workhouse'. Sometimes they are more precisely defined as 'the weaver's rooms', the 'dye house' or the 'bakehouse'. Brewhouses, malt rooms or chambers, and milk houses were all relatively common. The word 'dairy' is used instead of the latter in a few 18th-century inventories of wealthy people (*199, 241*). Many inventories list stables and barns, a few mention cart houses, and there are several references to granaries (*154*). Cheese chambers occur in several of the larger farm houses (*66, 196, 257*), but rooms used for keeping cheese are more commonly called 'store chambers' (*216, 219, 223, 224*).

There are few references to building materials in the inventories. 'Saw'd boards' occur on several occasions. The Rev. William Langley (*110*) was the possessor of 'brick and tyle crests and gutters', and tiles are also found on the inventory of William Cheshire (*249*).

*Money and Property*

Landed property or real estate was not included in probate inventories, but leases which could be passed on to a descendant, often called *chattel leases*, were listed and appear on 61, or 7.2 per cent., of the inventories studied. In 1820 James Loch expressed his disapproval of the practice on the Leveson Gower estates of letting leases on three lives,[17] that is leases for a long, defined period, or for as long as three persons named within them were still living. There are numerous examples of such leases in these inventories, and not just on the Leveson Gower estate. Thomas Wright, the dyer, in 1662 (*83*) held leases from the Charlton and Corbett families, each for three lives. A widow in Wellington in 1705 held three cottages, a garden and backside 'by one old life about 50 years of age, valued at one year's value, £1'. Thomas Bennett (*90*) in 1676 held a lease 'during the life of John Bennett of Watling Street'. In 1699 Richard Jackson (*129*) held his own house on a lease on 'a very old life'. A Lilleshall man in 1682 held a chattel lease of a tenement under William Leveson Gower, Esq., 'for a number of years let to come determinable upon the life of Katherine ye deceased's relict'. John Smith in 1686 (*54*) held a lease of the Hinks farm for 80 years, depending on two lives, doubtless the same lease as that held by John Simons (*55*) in 1690 for 76 years, which also depended on two lives, Richard Mountford of Bratton in 1694, and Alice Mountford in 1699 (*231, 253*) both held a lease, the former dependent on 'an ancient life', and the latter on 'one old life'. The inventory of Walter Brodhurst (*65*) includes a lease 'held by only one infant life'.

There is evidence in the inventories of the sub-letting of leasehold land. William Minshall (*109*) held land by lease in both Leegomery and Little Wenlock, but that in the latter parish appears to have been let to tenants since his inventory includes rent due from it. Richard Beard of Lilleshall in 1704 (*62*) leased land well outside his own parish. Mortgages are mentioned on several inventories. William Charlton (*236*) in 1704 was owed £100 due upon a mortgage from William Pemberton, but in other cases no details are given. Two inventories list cottages and one a piece of land without reference to leases, but all three were of relatively poor men, and it is likely that they do in fact refer to leasehold property.

As in Dorset[18] substantial sums of cash rarely appear in the Telford probate inventories, although money in the pocket or the purse is usually mentioned. Two hundred and forty-one inventories, 28.49 per cent. of the total refer to debts, bonds or money out at interest. It is often difficult to distinguish between money which was invested and simple trade debts. Some inventories like those of Tryphosa Barnes and William Barker (*170, 173*), clearly define the latter as book debts, or, as in that of Francis Wright (*127*) as 'desperate debts by shop book'. *Desperate* debts were those of which there was little hope of recovery. *Sperate* debts or debts upon *sperialty* (often corrupted to *specialty*) were those which there was reason to hope might be paid. Very large sperate debts which appear on the inventories of people who show no sign of having been engaged in business at the time of their deaths were very probably investments. A widow from Wellington in 1672 had possessions worth £102 of which £60 comprised sperate debts. Another Wellington inventory of 1700 lists debts totalling £170 out of an estate worth £192. An inventory of 1666 includes £120 due by bond out of a total valuation of £142. None of these three appear to have been engaged in any sort of trading. A much richer man, Richard Stanier (*154*) left possessions worth £1,327, of which £710 comprised debts owing to him. While Stanier farmed on a considerable scale, his operations were not so large as to explain debts of this size, and it would seem possible that this money was invested. References to bonds appear usually to refer to invested money, although in some cases they may mean debts upon which the debtor had signed an obligation to pay. Joshua Johnson (*126*) had £410 due upon bond, distinguished from his book debts. Investments are sometimes referred to as securities as in the inventory of William Doughty in 1716 who had securities for £350 (*161*). In some cases invested money is described as 'out upon interest'. Elizabeth Blackshaw in 1727 (*250*) had £80 so invested. Some 92 inventories contain references to money upon bond, or at interest, or which there is some other reason to think was invested, comprising some 10.87 per cent. of the total. There were no banks in Shropshire in the period under review, but it is clear that there were ample opportunities for investing money, and that that traditional peasant's hoard of cash in a mattress was rarely to be found in the district.

Several inventories refer to monies owed by the deceased. George Golbourne (*104*) owed £82 to six listed people, while his possessions were valued at only £52. His appraisers noted hopefully 'So that his debts are £30 more than all his goods come to and therefore desireth to acquitted and discharged from any further trouble'. The Rev. John Field (*119*) died with assets worth over £20 less than his liabilities, and there are inventories for several other people who died in similar straits. John Peate in 1698 and Samuel Newnes in 1717 both owed considerable sums in rents to their landlords. The inventory of Robert Corbett listed debts which he owed to several people, including a mercer and a shoemaker, and also records the taking of a cow for a heriot, a feudal due paid to the lord of the manor on the death of a tenant.

## Trades and Professions

The figures relating to trades in Table IV clearly confirm the status of Wellington as the market centre of the district. In the parish of Wellington 28.33 per cent. of those for whom inventories were made were tradesmen other than farmers or colliers. In the other three parishes the proportion was in the region of nine per cent. The range of trades in Dawley, Wrockwardine and Lilleshall was limited to weavers, builders, occupations like milling directly related to agriculture, and the occasional shoemaker or tailor. In Wellington there were professional men like surgeons and a surveyor, large-scale retailers, dyers who were responsible for a range of cloth-finishing processes, a host of leather workers, butchers and bakers, and a small but varied community of metal workers. If Wellington's trades dominated the east Shropshire coalfield, they did not display the variety and sophistication of the more eminent West Midland market towns. In Lichfield there were attorneys, cutlers, musicians, and plumbers, for none of whom do inventories survive in Wellington. In Shrewsbury there were vintners, chapmen, brick-makers, comb-makers and a sword cutler, as well as vast numbers of cloth workers and leather workers. One street in Ludlow in the 1660s numbered among its inhabitants a brewer, an ironmonger, one of His Majesty's messengers, a 'clerk of the signet' and two 'distillers of hot waters'. In Bridgnorth there were haberdashers, clothiers and plasterers, and the town served as a base for crickers, who were itinerant sellers of pottery.[19] While the range of occupations revealed by the inventories is probably less than complete, the sample is sufficient to suggest that Wellington was by no means in the first rank of market towns. The range of its manufacturing trades is not unlike that of Bishop's Castle, but in retailing it was probably of the same order of importance as Bridgnorth or Ludlow. The inventories of Wellington's mercers are some indication of the town's status. They are also remarkable documents, the detail of which makes them of much more than regional significance.

## The Mercers[20]

The Wellington mercers' inventories have been compared with a selection of published and unpublished examples from elsewhere, a total of 40 in all, which are listed in Table VI. The published inventories of the early 17th century, with the exception of those of the two Sankeys from Ormskirk, came from widely separated places, and no attempt was made when they were published to judge the extent to which the mercers held monopolies in their own districts. The three highly detailed inventories of Wellington mercers are consequently particularly interesting, since they are nearly contemporaneous, and each describes a distinct business, unrelated to the others. Evidence from elsewhere suggests that two other mercers, William Phillips and Andrew Socket were probably operating at the same time. Each family and business merits individual examination.

Margaret Justice née Turner (*107*), whose inventory was made in 1687, was the widow of John Justice, shoemaker, constable and churchwarden of Newport, who died in 1680, when his wife was pregnant.[21] By 1682 the posthumous child, Elizabeth, and all of the couple's other children had died, and Margaret moved to Wellington. When she died in 1687 her body was returned to Newport for burial. She had married John in 1661, and quite probably came from Kynnersley, since Turner, and the names of her kinsmen, the Boulds, Freemans and Palins, all occur commonly in that parish.

The inventory of Margaret Justice shows that such documents can be highly misleading in individual cases. From it she appears to have been a widow struggling to make a living from a business which it might be supposed she inherited from her husband, and which might appear badly run down. She had several remnants and short lengths, and some odd parcels of garments, and her debts almost equalled the value of the business. This impression is totally false. She had been in business for only five years, and it was her own enterprise entirely, not her husband's. She specialised in expensive silks and quality cloth, and the remnants were probably what remained from special orders for wealthy customers. There cannot have been a high demand for Sarsnet and Persian silk, remnants of

# INTRODUCTION

## TABLE VI

Mercers and others whose inventories have been used for comparative purposes, in chronological order

| | Value of Inventory (to nearest £ below) | Date |
|---|---|---|
| | £ | |
| (1) Robert Sankey, gent., Ormskirk, Lancs. | 364 | 1613 |
| Kendricke Eyton, mercer, Chester | 213 | 1624 |
| (2) Thomas Harris, mercer, Charlbury, Oxon. | 109 | 1632 |
| Roger Burgess, mercer, Middlewich, Ches. | 1,277 | 1633 |
| Thomas Alsager, mercer, Nantwich, Ches. | 282 | 1634 |
| James Oldfield, mercer, Prestbury, Ches. | 270 | 1634 |
| (1) Richard Sankey, gent., Ormskirk, Lancs. | 814 | 1634 |
| John Johnson the elder, mercer, Northwich, Ches. | 182 | 1636 |
| John Bowland, haberdasher, Stockport, Ches. | 200 | 1638 |
| Hugh Blackburne, mercer, Wick Malbank, Ches. | 249 | 1639 |
| (3) Thomas Cowcher, mercer, Worcester (inventory of shop only) | 359 | 1643 |
| (4) Thomas Deakin, trade not given, Lichfield, Staffs. | 115 | 1659–60 |
| (4) Lawrence Clowes, mercer, Lichfield, Staffs. | 3 | n.d.c. 1660 |
| Josiah Willis, mercer, Shrewsbury | 156 | 1666 |
| John Hulme, draper, Stockport, Ches. | 223 | 1667 |
| William Bamford, mercer, Marchfield, Ches. | 245 | 1668 |
| Robert Greene, chapman, Shrewsbury | 306 | 1668 |
| John Glover, mercer, Congleton, Ches. | 52 | 1669 |
| Thomas Smith, no trade given, Shrewsbury | 80 | 1670 |
| Michael Wilding, mercer, Shrewsbury | 23 | 1672–73 |
| Lawrence Wozall, no trade given, Shrewsbury | 41 | n.d.c. 1672 |
| Nathaniel Clemson, mercer, Shrewsbury | 236 | 1676 |
| Margaret Justice, widow, Wellington, Salop. (107) | 21 | 1687 |
| Thomas Smith, junr., no trade given, Bridgnorth | 160 | 1688 |
| Robert Johnson, mercer, Wellington, Salop. (112) | 144 | 1690 |
| George Moore, tobacconist, Sandbach, Ches. | 1,656 | 1694 |
| Ann Lawrence, widow, Shrewsbury | 169 | 1694–95 |
| Joshua Johnson, mercer, Wellington, Salop. (126) | 768 | 1695 |
| Benjamin Wright, mercer, Wellington, Salop. (132) | 246 | 1700 |
| Richard Phillips, gent., Wellington, Salop. (144) | 277 | 1705 |
| William Corser, junr., mercer, Bridgnorth | 395 | 1710 |
| (5) John Coley, mercer, Middlewich, Ches. | 186 | 1713 |
| William Forster, mercer, Middlewich, Ches. | 67 | 1715 |
| William Doughty, gent., Wellington, Salop. (161) | 433 | 1716–17 |
| Tryphosa Barns, spinster, Wellington, Salop. (170) | 19 | 1723 |
| Andrew Sockett, mercer, Wellington, Salop. (174) | 51 | 1725 |
| Isaac Eaton, mercer, Northwich, Ches. | 1,250 | 1726 |
| Thomas Whittaker, tobacconist, Congleton, Ches. | 33 | 1728 |
| Robert Morris, no trade given, Wellington, Salop. | 72 | 1746 |
| (6) Thomas Kent, mercer, Church Hulme, Ches. | 112 | 1752 |

The names of all known North Telford mercers whose inventories are at Lichfield are on this list. Some are not so designated on their inventories and some have no evidence of their trade listed. There are other mercers known for the area whose inventories are not at Lichfield, and others suspected of being in the trade, so that the list must not be regarded as definite. For no other place is the list in any way complete or even necessarily representative.

NOTES

(1) *The Sankeys, mercers, of Ormskirk*, Pt. I, 1613, Pt. II, 1613-36. Lancashire Record Office *Reports*, 1965, pp. 37-45, 1966, pp. 12-13.
(2) 'A Charlbury Mercer's shop 1623', ed. D. G. Vaisey. *Oxoniensia*, XXI (1966), pp. 107-116.
(3) 'An Inventory of the goods and chattels of Thomas Cowcher, mercer, of Worcester', ed. R. G. Griffiths, *Transactions of the Worcestershire Archaeological Society*, XIV (1937), pp. 45-60.
(4) D. G. Vaisey, *op. cit.*, pp. 118-20, 123-24.
(5) In Hereford Record Office.
(6) All Cheshire inventories are in the Chester Records Office, and Shrewsbury inventories in the Lichfield Joint Record Office.

---

which were worth six shillings and eight shillings. Apart from small amounts owing to a whitesmith and another local mercer, most of her debts were to men of some standing who were given the title 'Mr.', and who lived outside Wellington. They were probably her suppliers. Her estate was larger than the inventory suggests. Before it was made, some of the best possessions had been removed, including her best castor hat (the inventory mentions one, but her will makes it clear that there were two), all her clothes, including two silk mantuas and a laced handkerchief, two gold rings, some silver spoons, and a big brass pot. The appraisers apparently omitted to list her possessions at Hadley and Crudgington. She had money which would accrue £10 of interest in five years. There seems to have been rather more wealth than one might expect of the widow of John Justice, a shoemaker with possessions worth only £38 at the time of his death, although his house included some fine possessions, among them a 'lampe'. Probably he had married well and Margaret had brought a good dowry, but if he had left a will it might have shown his inventory to be as deceptive as his wife's.[21]

Joshua Johnson (*126*) was one of three Johnsons who were mercers. Robert I (*112*) who died in 1690 was his father, and Robert II, who died in 1723 his son. Robert II's only child died before him so that the name died out. Joshua is the only one of the three for whom an informative inventory survives, so that his mercer's stock cannot be compared with that of his father or his son, but it is possible to build up a full picture of the family's business over 50 years. In 1672 Robert I had only two hearths and was probably not particularly wealthy. Eighteen years later it was the body of '*Mr.* Robert Johnson, mercer' that was buried in Wellington churchyard, and thereafter members of the family were usually so designated. His inventory totalled £144, but does not mention his mercer's shop nor his house and furniture, all of which had probably been handed over to his son. His will fails to mention his landed property. Joshua did not long survive his father. He was less than 30 when he died in 1695 and left a family of four young children. His early death resulted in a will and inventory which reflect the affairs of an active businessman worth in goods and chattels alone over £750. Robert II was six when his father died, but the business seems not to have declined during 15 years or so of minority management. As an adult he was accorded the same respect as his father, and at his death left considerable wealth, which following the death of his son and brother, went to the widower and son of his younger sister Mary Leake.

Johnson's inventory gives valuable insights into the mercery trade, but the mercer's shop was only a small part, about one-sixth, of Johnson's goods and chattels, and much less of his total wealth. His will is irritatingly vague about his landed property. The Forester rent rolls show Robert I in 1686 and Robert II in 1719 paying for properties in Wellington which Joshua doubtless possessed during his lifetime. The family almost certainly had land in the open fields of Wellington.[22] Joshua left all his real estate with the exception of 'the kitchen and backside lying on the backside of my new dwelling house' to his daughters, but some, as the rent book shows, went to Robert II, who acquired during his lifetime land at Walcot, Wem and Longdon-upon-Tern.

A substantial part of the family's business was in malting. Both Robert I and Joshua had large quantities of malt and barley, and Joshua possessed a malting house and a brewhouse with its equipment. If the process of brewing was on a household scale, the production of malt most certainly was not. He had 200 strikes of malt and 130 strikes of barley, more than practically anyone else in Wellington, and in March, quite late in the malting season.

The Johnsons were also investing money. Robert I had only £40 due to him, a reasonable amount for a tradesman. Joshua had a similar amount due, but also £410 due upon bond. Since his inventory does not survive, the full scale of Robert II's financial assets is unknown, but his will mentions a mortgage worth £235, plus interest, which may be a half-yearly charge of £2 10s. 0d. due to Mr. Robert Johnson mentioned in the Forester rent book of 1719.

Benjamin Wright (*132*) already holds a small place in the history of Wellington.[23] He was supposedly the son of Mr. Francis Wright, vicar of Wellington, a leading cleric during the Commonwealth, who died in 1659. Benjamin's daughter Anna married Robert Morris of Lutterworth, and persuaded him to settle in Shrewsbury where he became the first Baptist minister. Some of the legend is verifiable. Francis Wright and Robert Morris were both ministers. Benjamin was the son of Francis and Anna, the name of Benjamin's daughter. Francis left no will, but his wife Sara who died in 1662 left her estate to be divided between her son Benjamin and her brother. Benjamin was churchwarden in 1670, when presumably he had not broken with the Established Church, but his house was licenced for Dissenting worship in January 1694–95. He died intestate in 1700 and administration was granted to his children Kervin (not Reruin, as stated in the printed baptismal register), Benjamin and Anna, since his second wife, Margaret, was paralytic and incapable. Apart from the death of Margaret in 1702 there is no further record of the family in Wellington. Benjamin's business thus appears to have flourished for only one generation, since his father was not a mercer, and his children seem to have left the district. The business may possibly have passed to his son-in-law.

Since there is no will, the deductions which can be made about Wright's business are limited. He seems to have lived over the shop, since he had possessions in chambers over both shop and warehouse, each of which was furnished as a bedroom. He seems to have extended his house at some time, and to have moved into the new portion. He had brewing equipment and some furniture in a building over the road. His premises were extensive. The business quarters consisted of shop, warehouse, workhouse, and perhaps the tobacco room. The living-rooms were more in line with modern practice than was common among Wellington tradespeople. The parlour was furnished as a sitting-room and contained no bed. Since his books were worth only four shillings it appears that he did not retain many of the books 'in my library' mentioned in his uncle's will. Upstairs were five bedrooms, each with one bed. There was also a hall, and the passage chamber, a lumber room in 1700, but perhaps once a nursery or schoolroom, since there was still a child's chair in it. One could have hoped that the inventory might include the room used for worship, but it gives no indication of anywhere set aside for that purpose. Presumably when Wright's Dissenting friends met to worship they used the parlour or the hall.

Wright's inventory shows that he farmed some land, perhaps only a little, since he had few livestock, something which is confirmed in the account of the Wellington fields before enclosure, which lists land that had belonged to the late Benjamin Wright. He had £25 worth of corn and hay in September, just after the harvest. He had two malt mills, and some brewing equipment, but no malt.

He was owed £46, probably mostly trade debts, and if he had any money or bond or loan it is not recorded. Since the inventory was made with care he probably had none, but the Forester papers suggest he had lent money in the past since there is an aquittance for £150 paid to him in 1686. He also rented the tolls of Wellington market for £26 per annum in the 1680s, and possibly later.[24]

1. Lilleshall Lodge, c.1820

2. Ketley Bank House

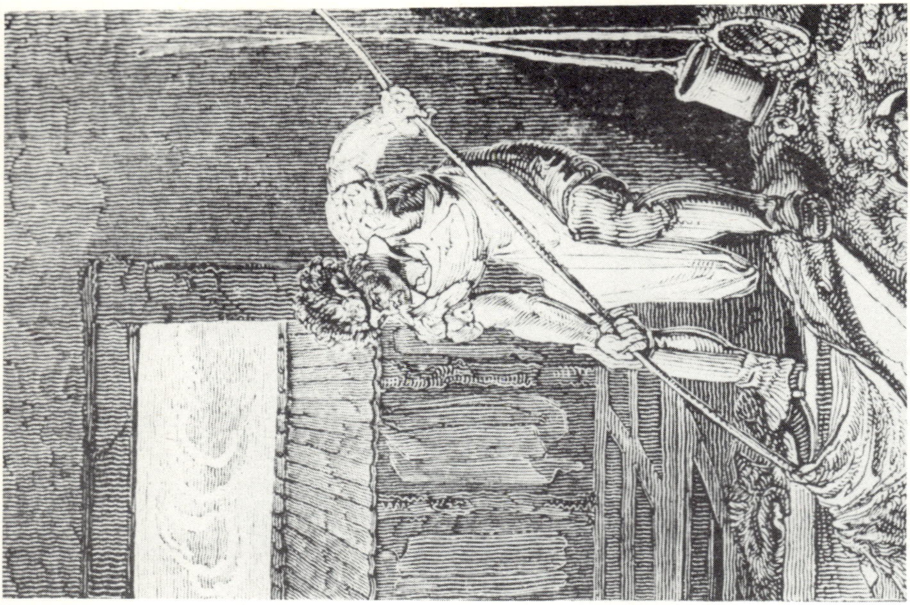

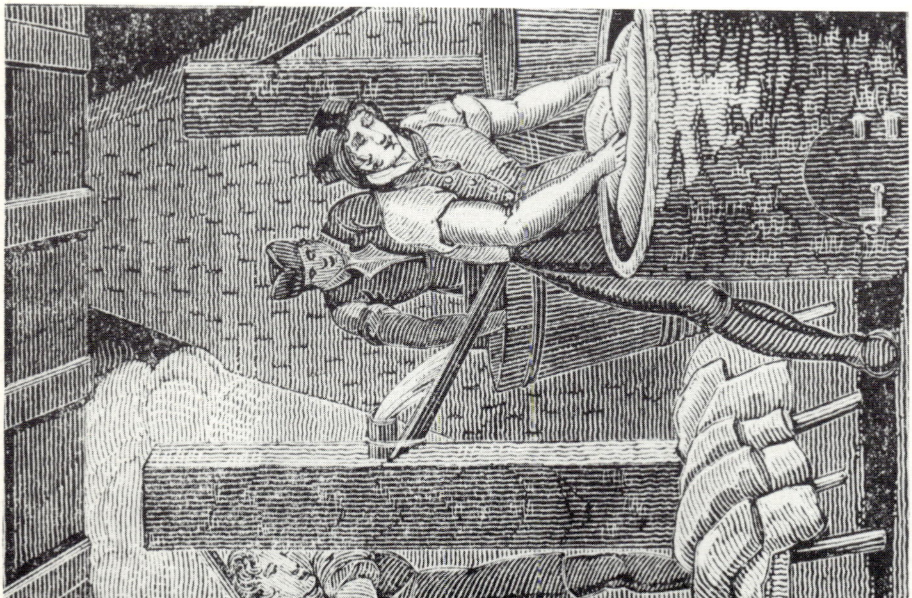

5. A gardener

6. A smith

7. A table board and frame

8. A wainscott chair

Benjamin Wright had connections which spread right across the Midlands[25] and even further afield. His wife, Ann Kervin, came from Coventry and probably belonged to a family of drapers. He had a cousin who was a grocer in Bewdley, an aunt whose husband was in business in the City of London, and another kinswoman who married a Birmingham draper. He had a cousin in Cocking, Sussex, and another in Shifnal. His pedigree has been studied more fully than most of other mercers, and it is not possible to say to what extent such widespread connections were typical either of mercers or Dissenters.

Richard Phillips (*144*) was described as a gentleman on his inventory in 1705, but the parish register records him as a mercer, and from at least the 1620s his family were called mercers. The will of William Phillips, Richard's father who died in 1685, was proved at Canterbury, and establishes that he had a shop on the east side of the market house in Wellington.[26] Richard was left the shop for his life only, and thereafter it was to pass to his two brothers, which explains why the shop and its stock do not feature in his will and inventory, which deal only with the possessions that he could leave as he wished, the value of which relative to his whole estate was probably quite small. The Phillips family was one of the most important in Wellington, and William's will indicates that they had connections with Shrewsbury, where one of his nephews was apprenticed to the Drapers' Company. The same man later settled in the City of London. The two wills show that the family had extensive property in Wellington and nearby villages, and Richard had a 'pitt' in Arleston for which he paid rent to the Foresters in the 1680s.[27] By the terms of William's will, Richard and Elinor, William's widow, had the use of the house, shop and contents for their joint lives and until the death of the longer lived, which explained why Elinor who died in 1692 had very few possessions, and why Richard's inventory, for all its length, obviously does not show a complete household.

The inventory of Andrew Sockett (*174*) made in 1725 suggests that he had largely retired from business and since he had been acting as an appraiser since 1702, and was probably born in 1668 this seems quite likely. His inventory describes him as a mercer, but the only indications of this trade are a few old grocery barrels and an empty shop, some fittings of which had been lent to a neighbour. He possessed equipment to process tobacco, which seems to have been out of use, but a third trade, that of chandlering or candlemaking was functioning. His father, Andrew Sockett I, died in 1721, but no will or inventory for him survives. The Socketts' business was of long standing. Andrew Sockett I must have been born about 1648, and could well be the same Andrew Sockett, mercer, to whom Robert Corbett of Lawley owed £1 in 1679, and the same one who was issuing token coins in 1666, bearing his name on one side and the mercers' arms on the other.[28] Andrew I had several sons, of whom Andrew II, William and Thomas appear to have lived into manhood. William was probably the Rev. William Sockett (*189*), and a Thomas Sockett was an industrious appraiser though he left no will.

The five mercers discussed above were all probably rich and successful. Wright and Justice were both able to start new businesses against the competition of the established families. All the evidence suggests that they did not take over existing mercer's shops from other people. Margaret Justice died childless and Benjamin Wright's children left the district so that newcomers could well have set up as mercers in Wellington in the 1690s and 1700s. One person who may have done so was Tryphosa Barnes, spinster and mercer (*170*) who died in 1723. Like Margaret Justice she conducted her own business, and was apparently wealthier than the inventory suggests. Her business assets were only £6, but her house was very well furnished and her possessions may have been undervalued. She was buried at High Ercall and administration went to her Aunt Sarah Podmore. William Doughty (*161*) and Robert Morris are both called 'gentlemen' on their inventories, but elsewhere both are called mercers.[29] They had family connections with each other and with Benjamin Wright, and one or other of them may have succeeded to Wright's business.

All five of the mercers' shops were probably within the township of Wellington and almost certainly they were near to the market house and within a short distance of each other. Phillips lived on the east side of the Market House. Wright must have lived close by since he managed the collection of the market tolls, and their names appear close together on the Hearth Tax roll. All five must have been competitors, but all seem to have prospered, probably because they practised a degree of specialisation. The detailed inventories of Johnson, Justice and Wright show considerable differences of emphasis. Justice stocked no woollens and clearly specialised in silks, fine linens, and women's and children's clothes. Goods of this sort are totally missing from the other two. We know nothing of Phillips's shop, but Richard Phillips's inventory show 14 pieces and 88 ells of hempen and linen cloth in his house, which is more than either Johnson or Wright had in their shops, and suggests that he specialised in linen. Evidence about Sockett is removed in time from the others, but it is doubtful whether he was without competition in selling tobacco, although he was the only person in the inventories to make candles or to sell them in large quantities.

Most mercers sold drugs and medicines, but these do not appear in the inventories of those from Wellington, probably because they were supplied in the town by William Birch (*160*), the apothecary, who was a kinsman of Johnson. The quantities of high quality groceries are small, and perhaps Phillips who had connections with London, the centre of the spice trade, specialised in this line. Dyestuffs, which were sold by mercers in some towns were not stocked in Wellington.

In Lichfield, where the inventories have been published, and in Shrewsbury, where they have been copied, there are none with detail to compare with those of Wright, Justice and Johnson. There is one at Lichfield and four at Shrewsbury with values over £100, though most Shrewsbury mercers' wills were proved at Canterbury. In Nantwich there were 11 families called mercers during the first decade of the 18th century, so that it is clear that, as in Wellington, several businesses were flourishing at the same time.

A superficial reading of a 17th-century mercer's inventory gives a picture of confusion, of an Aladdin's cave similar to the proverbial village shop, but in the inventory of Thomas Cowcher of Worcester the goods are divided into nine categories. After examining a considerable number of mercers' inventories it is clear that most were arranged in a systematic way, in what amounted almost to a standard format, doubtless reflecting arrangements in the shops. Nevertheless, several appear to have been quite chaotic. In Bamford's, 'candles, brown thread and white tape' are followed by 'loafe sugar and parchment'. The appraisers usually started with the fabrics, woollens, first, then linen, and finally silks. They continued with the silkware for embroidery, sewing and decoration, crewel (wool) and haberdashery (linen) in Cowcher's inventory, although these were usually stocked together. As technology changed the old distinctions lost their meanings, although usually all the laces are listed together, in a separate category from the ribbons and tapes. After haberdashery came hosiery, St. Martin's ware, and clothing, like bodices, sleeves, stomachers, and cravats. Most mercers, in the absence of specialist stationers, stocked paper and card, storing them in different sections according to use. The pasteboard was normally among the haberdashery since it was employed in making ladies' head dresses, and for the hot and the cold pressing of cloth. Capp paper was a form of wrapping paper, and was both sold and used to wrap other goods. Oldfield's inventory actually records 'odd paper with pepper in'. Some mercers kept capp paper near the scales, where Tryphosa Barnes had five paper boxes. Wright kept all his paper between the sugar and spices, convenient both for packaging and for sale. Writing paper was often kept with the books. Early mercers had quite large stocks of books. Oldfield in 1634 had £5 worth, including four copies of Ovid's 'De arte amandi', hardly the kind of volume one might expect on the shelves of a respectable merchant. By the end of the 17th century the Wellington mercers stocked only children's books, alphabets, hornbooks and primers, and religious books like psalters and catechisms, probably because there was a specialist bookseller in Shrewsbury, Rogers, the nephew of William Birch, and a kinsman of Johnson.

Grocery and saltery goods were often stored together. Sugar, originally the prerogative of apothecaries was stocked by all the general mercers in the 17th century. Some mercers were virtually grocers, and stocked practically nothing else, while others carried only a token, some sugar, raisins, and a few pounds of the common spices. Problems of contamination by strong-smelling articles must have been acute, and a good mercer probably arranged his goods to minimise the risks. The last section of Johnson's inventory seems to suggest this. He stocked his sugar and spices between the books and the hosiery. Past the stockings were the strongly smelling things, the herrings, the soap, the candles, and the tobacco, where they could do little harm.

Tobacco usually appears at the end of the list, often adjacent to the groceries. Pipes were normally stored with it, but the boxes to keep it in were regarded as haberdashery. Salt, earthenware and nails were stocked only by a few mercers, and usually only if they were not produced locally. Harris of Charlbury stocked all three, but all were made near Wellington, and none of the mercers sold them.

A mercer's stock was shaped by his market. The Sankeys and Cowcher were clearly catering for the wealthy, but Johnson and Wright were geared towards a wider and less affluent market, and so they stocked the cheaper ranges of cloth. The most expensive they had was priced at a few shillings a yard, and they had nothing like the 'Superfine Flanders Italiano serge' and the 'black silk grogram' purchased by Joyce Jeffreys in the 1630s. The same was true of food. None of the Wellington mercers stocked almonds, saffron, white powdered sugar or salad oil, but men like Sankey and Eyton did. Johnson probably served a richer class of customer than Wright. He had a brown sugar instead of bastard, the lowest grade, and he sold none of the cheap 'stems' of tobacco which formed a large part of Wright's stock. Wright kept no cloth or broadcloth and fewer serges or stuffs, but he did stock cheaper grades, even the poor quality Welsh plains.

The mercers were often affected by events abroad. Spermacetti and whalebone were frequently stocked in the period when the British successfully competed against the Dutch in the seas off Spitzbergen, but after 1660 supplies came entirely from foreign sources. In time of war they were almost unobtainable, and are not in Johnson's or Wright's shops. The absence of grains, nutmegs and cinnamon from these two inventories was also probably due to the effects of war.

Mercers' inventories were usually appraised by fellow tradesmen, and the values can be regarded with more confidence than those on inventories in general. It seems that goods were normally valued at wholesale prices. The retail prices paid by the Howard and Jeffrey households were consistently higher than those in contemporary inventories. Table VII shows prices from a selection of inventories, from the Howard and Jeffrey accounts, and those recorded by Beveridge, whose prices in general are higher than those in the other sources. There are some patterns which

## TABLE VII

Grocery prices: a comparison between the inventories, two household account books,† and sources quoted in Beveridge*

| | 1 | 2† | 3 | 4 | 5 | 6 | 7 | 8 | 9† | 10 | 11 | 12 | 13 | 14 | 15 |
|---|---|---|---|---|---|---|---|---|---|---|---|---|---|---|---|
| | 1613 | 1613 | 1624 | 1626 | 1632 | 1634 | 1634 | 1636 | 1640 | 1643 | 1669 | 1694 | 1695 | 1700 | 1752 |
| *Pepper* | 25 | — | 21 | 20 | 18 | 19½ | 16/18 | 20 | 32 | 22 | 16 | — | — | — | — |
| White | — | — | — | — | — | — | — | — | — | — | — | — | 96 | 28 | — |
| Westminster* | — | — | — | — | — | — | — | — | — | — | — | — | 60 | — | — |
| Lord Steward* | — | — | — | — | — | — | — | — | — | — | 11 | — | 64 | 14 | 42 |
| Black | — | — | — | — | — | — | — | — | — | — | — | — | 28 | — | — |
| *Ginger* | — | 12 | 12 | 10/15 | 11 | 13½ | 12 | — | 24 | 7–11 | — | — | 5–8 | 9 | — |
| Westminster* | — | — | — | — | — | — | — | — | — | — | — | — | 16 | 16 | 16 |
| Lord Steward* | — | — | — | — | — | — | — | — | — | — | 8 | — | 16 | 14 | 11 |
| *Cloves* | 88 | 96 | 80 | 103 | 126 | 132‡ | 128 | 88 | 112 | 60 | 144 | 96 | 168‡ | — | — |
| Westminster* | — | — | — | — | — | — | — | — | — | — | — | 144 | 176 | — | — |
| Lord Steward* | — | — | — | — | — | — | — | — | — | — | 180 | 192 | 192 | 168 | 126 |
| *Currants* | 4 | 4–6 | 4½ | 4½ | 3 | 4½ | 4 | — | 7 | 6½ | 5 | — | 5 | 7 | 7 |
| Westminster* | — | — | — | — | — | — | — | — | — | — | — | 6½ | 7 | — | 6 |
| Lord Steward* | — | — | — | — | — | — | — | — | — | — | 6 | 8 | 8 | 8 | 6 |
| Navy Plymouth* | — | — | — | — | — | — | — | — | — | — | — | — | — | 8 | — |
| *Raisins of the sun* | — | 5–6 | 3½ | 3½ | 3½ | 4½ | — | — | 7 | — | — | — | 4½ | 3½ | 3½ |
| Westminster* | — | — | — | — | — | — | — | — | — | — | — | 4½ | 4¾ | — | 5 |
| Lord Steward* | — | — | — | — | — | — | — | — | — | — | 5½ | 7 | 7 | 6 | 5½ |
| Navy Plymouth* | — | — | — | — | — | — | — | — | — | — | — | — | — | 4½ | — |

‡Includes mace.     Prices quoted are in pence per pound.

Sources for Table VII (for details see Table VI)

1. Sankey I.
2. The Household Book of Lord William Howard, op. cit.
3. Eyton.
4. Tench.
5. Harris.
6. Oldfield
7. Sankey II.
8. Robert Johnson.
9. R. G. Griffiths, *Joyce Jeffreys of Ham Castle*, op. cit.
10. Cowcher.
11. Glover.
12. Moore.
13. Joshua Johnson.
14. Wright.
15. Kent.

---

stand out. Pepper and ginger generally went down in price, while currants went up. Cloves fluctuated violently from year to year. As Beveridge shows, 1695 was a quite exceptional year in which many prices rocketted. If it had not been for the published series it might have seemed that Johnson's appraisers were unreliable, but the high values in his inventory show rather how war could affect the lives of the citizens of a remote provincial market town.

Mercers need warehouses for storing their goods as well as shops for selling them, and the preparation of some products required quite complex machinery. Johnson's inventory gives a detailed picture of the workings of a mercer's establishment, since there is a full list and valuation of the fittings and equipment. He had three counters, and the entries suggest that one was in a warehouse. This counter with three boards on the side and six drawers underneath would have been more suitable for selling small items than for lengths of cloth. He had three other sets of drawers, a press and 12 boxes. He had no means of grinding spices since his mortar was old and lacked a pestle, although based on the price of kettle brass quoted elsewhere in the inventory it must have weighed about 42lb. and so was quite large. Johnson had three sorts of scales, six ordinary counter scales for weighing groceries and the like, an iron beam for sacks, and the hop scales for bulky but light articles. He had pewter measures probably for liquids, although the only liquid actually in stock was brandy. It is likely that at certain times he might have stocked various sorts of oil, treacle, pitch and gum.

The other inventories listed in Table VI provide a useful supplement to the information in that of Johnson. Kent's inventory shows that he kept his cloth in the shop and the grocery in the warehouse, one definition of which is 'a tradesman's inner or back shop'. Scales were usually in the shop, however, and it was probably there that most materials were weighed out. Since Johnson's appraisers were unusually careful in itemising the scales, it is possible to make some calculations about his staff. If, as seems likely, he had one employee for each pair of scales he must have employed at least six people. Wright's scales and weights are valued

INTRODUCTION 31

more highly than Johnson's, which would suggest a slightly bigger staff. Both are near to the medium size of mercers' establishments, and shops like that of Moore with £10 worth of scales and £500 worth of stock must have been very large indeed. Before 1670 mercers usually had a heavy iron or brass mortar and pestle, but these become less common in the late 17th century, perhaps because some spices were processed by the wholesaler. There are no references to measures for cloth, or for tools to cut it, apart from 'ymplemets of cloth' worth 6d. on the inventory of Sankey I. Perhaps measures were set in the surface of the counter, and assistants were expected to provide their own shears.

In the diocese of Chester, but not in Lichfield, it was usual to itemise debts owing to the deceased. Eaton's appraisers wrote at the end of his inventory 'In regard ye Executrix has not yet had time to examine or extract and cast up ye deceased shop books (which are many and large), An exact account of ye debts standing out therein cannot be given at present'. They go on to estimate them at around £100, Johnson had £48 11s. 8d. of book debts which suggests that someone had 'examined, extracted and cast up' his books. It thus appears that a substantial part of his retail sales were by credit, which is consistent with the very small amounts of cash recorded in the mercers' shops. It is possible that shortage of small change obliged mercers to accept credit on small sales from regular customers, and that once a bill for a considerable sum had been run up it was settled in gold coin, which would explain the gold weights found in many shops. Tench's account book shows how one trader tried to cope with debts.[30] In 1615 he arranged for a debt for ribbons and lace to be paid off at 8d. a week. An alternative solution was for the mercer to issue his own token coins. Andrew Sockett I of Wellington did so in 1666, as did as least two other Shropshire mercers, John Shenton of Wem in 1666 and John Bowdler of Ludlow in 1664,[31] but such issues became illegal in the 1670s.

It is not possible to estimate turnover from any of the Wellington inventories, but in that of Moore of Sandbach, who had stock worth £500, £78 4s. 10d. appears for 'goods sold after his decease to this day as appear by book'. He was buried on 28 April, nine days before his inventory was made. Allowing for the possible closure of the shop from his death until after his funeral, and for one Sunday, that may represent seven days' trading, during which 15.6 per cent. of the stock was sold. If the shop were open for 300 days in the year, allowing for Sundays and holidays, his turnover would have been about £3,400, or nearly seven times the value of the stock. If these conclusions are correct and applicable to other mercers, Johnson had an annual turnover of about £1,200, Wright of £600, and Justice of £500. None of them had this quantity of capital available and so were obliged to work with small stocks, rapid turnover, frequent replacement, and extensive credit.

Mercers' inventories do not always list what they owed to their suppliers, but such sums, as in the case of Justice, could be considerable. Payment was probably always in arrears to the despatch of goods, for no instance has come to light of appraisers recording goods paid for but not yet delivered. Both Justice and Harris of Charlbury had debts which virtually balance their total stock. Tench's account book confirms that mercers generally ordered their stock in small quantities and frequently. His customers did not always find it easy to pay him, and he had to make complicated arrangements to satisfy his suppliers. The evidence from the Wellington inventories is consistent with this pattern, but as elsewhere, if the mercers suffered from cash problems, their sufferings were to some extent of their own making. Profits were not generally ploughed back into the business, but invested elsewhere. They were lent to landowners, spent on the purchase of property, or invested in parallel trades like candle-making. The Phillips family had a coal pit, and launched their sons on careers in the Shrewsbury Drapers Company and the City of London.

Virtually every mercer dealt in fabrics. Originally the mercer was concerned primarily with silks and velvets, but this was not so by the 17th century. Justice is the only mercer of the late 17th century in Table VI who offered any real choice in silk fabrics. With fine cottons and linens there was also a very limited choice. The Acts of 1701 and 1725 restricting the imports of printed cottons were still to come, but Johnson, Wright and Justice stocked very little of this sort. Materials like muslin, lawn and cambric were hard to find in a provincial town. In Wellington one bought muslin from Justice, went further afield, or went without, unless Phillips stocked such things. The heavier linens suitable for bedclothes, furnishings and clothing, buckram, canvas, fustian, holland, and some calico were all available throughout the period. Woollens were readily available, both the 'old draperies' like 'cloth', the coarse, cheap worsteds, and the new light 'stuffs'. To sort out their names is not easy. Fuller, writing in 1650, said:

> Expect not that I should reckon up their several names, because daily increasing, and many of them binominous, as which, when they began to tire in sale, are quickened with a new name. A pretty pleasing name, complying with the buyer's fancy, much befriendeth a stuff in the sale thereof.[32]

Through the welter of names it is possible to see some patterns, apart from the continuing dominance of cloth, kersey, frieze and serge. Of these heavy weights, Johnson stocked cloth, kersey and serge, whereas Wright, catering mainly for a cheaper market, replaced the cloth with Welsh plains and flannels. Bays, never widely stocked, and says, had disappeared by Johnson's time, although bays was still being made in 1720.[33] In the early 17th century it was stocked almost universally,

# INTRODUCTION

but apart from Lawrence in 1694, no mercer in Table VI had stocks of it after 1670. Many of the lighter woollen stocked by Johnson and Wright had been unknown a few years earlier. Crepe, once made of silk, but later a woollen, was generally stocked either bleached or dyed black, and the appraisers of Barnes actually state that she stocked it for shrouds.

Many fabrics, particularly woollens, were sold undyed and unbleached. Appraisers were generally consistent in mentioning colours. In the first 25 entries for Wright it is recorded that two were black, one red, one blue, and one dyed. They also noted fabrics that were mixed, milled, striped, spotted and flowered. What looks at first to be a list sadly lacking in detail turns out to be nothing of the sort, and it seems probable that the other 17 were unbleached and undyed. Entries in the Howard account book in 1613 suggest that it was common practice for cloth to be sold in this state. Woollens were found in all colours, though there is only one example of yellow and three of blue. Since these colours can be obtained easily, it may be assumed that the lack of them was a matter of fashion. Green was popular in the first half of the 17th century, but except for some say in the stocks of Lawrence in 1694, it is not to be found after 1650. It is the only colour that was apparently unobtainable in Wellington during the 1690s.

Linens, too, were frequently sold unbleached, and appraisers consequently noted when they had been whitened. The unbleached fabric is often called brown. Fine linens like Hollands were usually sold bleached, and some mercers stocked them with 'pinked' (scalloped) edges and embroidered, which put the price up so much that Wright and Johnson did not keep them. Fabrics of vegetable origin take blue dye very well, and it was a popular colour for coarse qualities. Nankeen, a naturally yellow fabric commanding a high price, was not found in any of the mercers' inventories, but yellow canvas, made in imitation of it was in several shops, including Johnson's. The terms 'dyed' and 'coloured' are each used at different times to mean different things. At times both mean 'as opposed to natural'. Wright had both black serge and dyed serge, and usually 'coloured' seems to mean checked or patterned.

Materials made of mixed fibres were used throughout the 17th century, but became much more common by 1700 than earlier. The cost of such fabrics, woven with stripes or patterns are indicated in the following examples, quoted in pence per yard. Prices of the basic fabrics are given, but they were not necessarily of comparable quality.

*Lawrence. 1694. Linen.*—Unspecified: 7. Black-and-blue: 10. Glazed and flowered: 12 and 13.
*Johnson. 1695. Linen.*—Unspecified: 9 and 10. Glazed: 12. Flowered: 12 and 13.
*Wright. 1700. Linen.*—Coloured: 8½. Blue. 12 and 13. Glazed: 13½.
*Wright. 1700. Buckram.*—Coloured: 11 and 13. Whitened: 14.

The appraisers of the Wellington mercers are reticent about the origins of fabrics, probably because they knew little of them. Many fabrics contained in their names an indication of their origins, but by the 1690s these rarely indicated where they were actually manufactured. Holland no longer came from the Netherlands, and Ozembrigs was more likely to be made in Montrose than in Osnabruck.

Haberdashery has been analysed less thoroughly than fabrics, but some trends have been noted. During the first half of the 17th century lace was available in great variety, Sankey II having at least 14 varieties, and Cowcher nine. After 1650 no mercer kept more than two or three varieties, and no new lace was introduced except for gymp lace in 1668 and perhaps filling lace in 1687. The place of lace was to some extent taken by galloons, which by the 1690s are listed in great variety. It was on one occasion called galloon lace, although it was more like a ribbon than a lace, but like lace it was used for decoration rather than for fastening. The range of tapes and ribbons increased enormously during the 17th century. Ribbon, inkle, binding and filleting, and ferrit were generally stocked and were invariably distinguished from each other, although it is no longer easy to say how they differed. The wider use of inkle was due to the introduction of the new inkle or engine looms which were common in Manchester by the 1680s.[34] Johnson in 1695 had blue inkle and striped tape, neither mentioned on earlier inventories, and Wright's inventory was the first to list blue and carnation tape. Johnson's appraisers recorded tapes and ribbons in dozens of yards, the usual practice in earlier years, but Wright's are recorded by the piece, probably of 36 yards, the length woven on the new looms.

There also seem to have been marked changes in the ways people fastened their clothes. In the early 17th century 'points' or laces and hooks and eyes were generally used. Buttons were available, but were used decoratively, as for a bailiff's new suit for which Joyce Jeffreys bought six dozen buttons. Coucher in 1643 had about eight pounds of hooks and eyes worth 15s. 2d., and five different sorts of points, but he also stocked many buttons. After this time the button rapidly replaced the old fastenings. By 1700 Wright had no points at all, and only 3s. worth of hooks and eyes, but his stock of buttons was worth three guineas. Johnson had no hooks and eyes, nor any points, but over £12 worth of buttons.

Few inventories list clothes or indicate the way in which the fabrics sold by the mercers were actually used. Most values given for clothes appear very low, and many of the wills suggest that the best garments were often the subject of individual bequests, and were removed before the inventory was taken. Ann Wright of Lilleshall in 1681 had 10 smocks and seven aprons apart from the usual linens and two hats. No gown or petticoat is listed, but the list is incomplete, and the best items had probably been removed. A better account of a female wardrobe is

# INTRODUCTION

provided by the inventory of Sarah Cornes (*228*) who died in 1691-92; she had three petticoats and a waistcoat made of cloth and stuff. She also had stockings and shoes worth a shilling. New stockings would have cost her anything from 3d. to 2s. if she wanted woollen ones, and silk ones were quite beyond her as they cost up to two pounds. The inventory of Mary Sockett (*142*) provides insight into a minimal female wardrobe. The writer noted that he had been forced to buy her a 'mant and petticoat' as her own were unfit to wear, but, unfortunately, did not give the price. The inventory of William Poyner (*16*) made in 1715 has a low value, but includes only his clothes and a few personal possessions. Doubtless he lived in someone else's house. His clothes, if old, were of good solid materials, and had held their value well. His complete suit, coat, breeches and waistcoat, would have needed about five yards of cloth which Johnson could have sold him at from 11d. to 18d. a yard. He would also have needed about 3½ yards of lining material, perhaps fustian at 14d. a yard, or something cheaper like the poorest stuff at 6d., or linsey at 9d., although neither would have lasted very well. With a yard of buckram or canvas for stiffening, at 14d., and thread and buttons it is unlikely that he would have bought the materials for less than half a guinea. When the Howards had clothes made for a farm labourer in 1618 they ordered grey cloth and hurden, but even then the materials cost 10s., and the materials for Poyner's suit probably cost rather more.

The inventory of John Eyton (*148*) made in 1708-9 itemises four articles of clothing: two mantles, valued at £4, and a petticoat and scarf, both of velvet. A similar garment to the mantles was bought by the Howards for £3 17s. 0d. in 1623. The velvet petticoat and scarf were normal garments for a man at the time, even though Eyton's were made of an unusually expensive cloth. Richard Phillips in 1704 (*144*) had a gown of silk and a hood which are not priced separately, and an old petticoat and a fur mantle worth 10s. in his attic, which had probably belonged to his mother who died in 1692.

While the fabrics, linings, fastenings and decorations for the clothes worn by the people of Telford could be obtained in Wellington, except for those used by the very rich, furnishing fabrics are conspicuously absent from the inventories. Kidderminster stuffs, Turkey work, huckaback and diaper, four fabrics in quite common use were not stocked by the mercers, and red and green, the most popular colours for furnishings, were difficult to find, the latter being almost unobtainable. While linen for bed clothes and table use were probably made locally, huckaback and diaper probably were not, since they involve a complex weaving process. Johnson had some diaper in his house, but none in his shop. It seems likely that furnishing fabrics were stocked by specialist merchants, but none have come to light in Telford. It is possible that such merchants were to be found in the county town.

Most linen fabrics seem to have been locally made,[35] but there are interesting variations of quality, both in the comparatively few references in the mercers' inventories and in the inventories of other households. Most, whether mentioning hemp, yarn or cloth, show at least two qualities.[36] Six entries that priced hemp yarn by the slippen give a mean value of 4.5d. but Peter Langley and Thomas Roe (26, 258) had some valued at 14.5d. and 15d. The difference is probably because the rich used 'hemp' to mean the fimble, or male plants, harvested first, and hurden to mean the carl, or steel hemp from the female plants. On the inventories of the poor, it seems likely that hempen meant the carl hemp, and hurden that made from the tow, the fibres extracted during the heckling process. This distinction is supported by the figures in Table VIII.

Even the poorest household had some bed linen. There is no example in the whole collection of North Telford inventories of a detailed inventory without linen, however poor the person concerned. Even Thomas Palmer of Lilleshall with possessions worth only £2 15s. 4d. had two pairs of sheets, one hempen and the other hurden, worth 4s. 6d. If he had grown and processed his own hemp he would have got some fimble, some carl and some tow. Unlike the rich, he could not afford to use the tow for stuffing mattresses or making ropes or sacks. He probably saved both the hemp and the hurden yarn until he had sufficient to make a sheet, and possibly disposed of the fimble as a cash crop. The only hemp recently grown legally in Shropshire produced three male plants out of twenty-four. If this is typical, the wealthy in the 17th century must have acquired extra supplies of fimble, as they often had equal quantities of the two grades of hempen sheets. About four ounces of fimble could have been sold for 2d., the cost of the annual rent of a poor person's tenement.

In the households of the wealthier classes the linen chest was filled up slowly over the years. Linen is hard wearing, and additions probably outweighed losses. A good quality sheet would last for at least two generations and was often the object of a specific bequest. Over the period studied, the number of sheets steadily rose. Table IX shows the number of sheets to each complete bed in a household, so far as it can accurately be estimated. The number of sheets is probably an underestimate, since such phrases as 'a bed and its furniture' could hide a pair of sheets in use. Probably by 1660 most people had a change of sheets for each bed, and by 1700 there were enough and to spare, one of the best indications the inventories give of steadily rising standards of comfort. An English visitor to north Germany in the 1840s described the linens in the housewife's press, together with the brass and tinware displayed on her shelves as 'locked-up capital, often worth a large sum . . . a stock as intangible amongst the middle classes and peasantry . . . as the jewels of noble families'.[37] The large stocks of sheets in the households

## TABLE VIII

### The value of hempen and hurden sheets

| Name | Date | Value of Inventory | Hempen sheets | Hurden coarse or canvas sheets |
|---|---|---|---|---|
|  |  | £ | s. d. | s. d. |
| Richard Shelton (48) | 1683 | 246 | 9s., 10s. | 3 0 |
| Joyce Bradshaw (106) | 1687 | 32* | 8 8 | 5 0 |
| Francis Bayley (130) | 1699 | 161 | 7 6 | 5 6 |
| Dorothy Followfield | 1700 | 100† | 4 0 | 2 0 |
| Richard Randle (137) | 1701 | 23 | 2 0 | 1 3 |
| John Duddell (24) | 1728 | 59 | 6 3 | 1 8 |
| Thomas Roe (26) | 1730 | 126 | 10 6 | 6 3 |
| Charles Stillgo | 1697 | 17 | 7 6 | — |
| Thomas Stanworth (157) | 1713 | 27 | 3s. (old) | — |
| Elinor Royston | 1716 | 26* | 5 0 | — |
| Richard Stanier (154) | 1711 | 1,327 | — | 6 0 |
| John Smith (254) | 1731–32 | 160 | — | 2 0 |

*Wealthy widows living in incomplete households of some comfort.
†A deceptively high value. The household goods are worth only £22 and the Forester rent books record continual late payment of rents.

## TABLE IX

### Numbers of pairs of sheets in relation to numbers of complete beds

| Decade | Numbers of inventories specifying sheets | Complete beds | Numbers of sheets | Ratio of sheets to beds |
|---|---|---|---|---|
| 1660–69 | 25 | 78 | 109.5 | 1.4 |
| 1670–79 | 20 | 53 | 84.5 | 1.6 |
| 1680–89 | 29 | 86 | 220.5 | 2.6 |
| 1690–99 | 21 | 60 | 110 | 1.9 |
| 1700–09 | 28 (27) | 86 (80) | 247 (207) | 2.9 (3.0) |
| 1710–19 | 17 | 54 | 135.5 | 2.5 |
| 1720–29 | 10 | 30 | 175.5 | 5.9 |
| 1730–39 | 14 | 35 | 125.5 | 3.6 |
| 1740–49 | 9 (7) | 39 (24) | 174 (168) | 4.8 (7.0) |

The figures in parenthesis are corrected figures when the three innkeepers are excluded.

of the yeoman and traders of Telford in the early 18th century were probably regarded in a similar light.

Tobacco[38] was stocked by most mercers. Smoking seems to have been almost an universal habit in the 17th century, when children were expected to take tobacco as a specific against infectious diseases. No inventory mentions tobacco or pipes, however, although Richard Stanier in 1711 (*154*) had 'tobacco tongues and stiller' worth 8s., and an inventory of 1730 lists a tin tobacco salver. Perhaps tobacco was so common, and pipes so cheap that they did not merit mention.

The three detailed mercers' inventories show that all the equipment necessary for a satisfactory smoke was available in Wellington in the late 17th century. Justice sold tobacco boxes, which are not priced on her inventory, although on other mercers' inventories they were valued at between 6d. and 1s. 6d. a dozen. Clearly most people would not have had a box valuable enough to be worth specific mention. Wright had pipes which would almost certainly have been of clay and locally made, perhaps by William Evans (*122*) the Wellington pipemaker who died in 1693. Both Wright and Johnson sold tobacco, and from their inventories and that of Sockett it is possible to understand a good deal about its processing and sale.

Tobacco was imported in large barrels holding about 1,000lbs. of ready-cured, 'bone dry' *hands*, or bundles of leaves. Johnson's inventory lists 'Best Bone', but if he had tobacco in this state it is surprising that he had no listed way of processing it. Wright had no bone-dry hands, but he did have equipment to deal with it. The hands were loosened and moistened, and it was for this purpose that he had a 'flatting trough'. The leaves were left in the trough in a cool cellar until the right condition was reached, when they were stripped from the main rib. The stems were supposed to be destroyed, but the high customs duty made this unlikely, and it was estimated that about one-fifth of the tobacco smoked consisted of stems. Over one-third of the tobacco sold by Wright is described as stems. The tobacco leaves were pressed into cakes and cut, an extremely onerous task for which an engine was used. In the early 19th century a blade would last only a few minutes before it needed re-grinding. This explains why uncut tobacco in Wright's shop cost 6½d. per pound, and the cut between 9d. and 1s. 6d. The dog-wheel in Sockett's inventory could not have been used to work his tobacco engine since the work was so heavy. The engines owned by Wright and Sockett are not defined by use, but that in Moore's inventory is called a cutting engine. Clearly such engines were in use long before the 1780s, the date given by Alford for their introduction.

The last two Stuart monarchs popularised snuff-taking among the upper classes, and before 1750 smoking was largely confined to the poor. There is no indication that the new fashion reached Shropshire until 1723 when Tryphosa Barnes had a pot of snuff among her stock.

# INTRODUCTION

Nor is there any indication of the growth of the separate trade of tobacconist in Shropshire. Moore of Sandbach was called a tobacconist in 1694, although his stock was similar to that of a mercer. Wright and Johnson together held about 4cwt. of tobacco when they died, enough to cater for about 200 people for a year. Sockett appears to have specialised in tobacco, together with candlemaking, and may, when his business was at its prime, have carried larger stocks.

Most mercers stocked candles or tallow, but the stocks were normally very small, and in some cases it is questionable whether they were for sale or for lighting the premises. Artificial light would obviously have been needed for reading scales and writing ledgers, and in nearly half the cases where candles are listed they are right at the end of the stock, just before the shop equipment. A dozen candles in the inventories means a dozen pounds, shown clearly in the case of Oldfield who had five dozen 9lb. of candles. Wright with 10½ dozen had more candles than most mercers, and Johnson with two dozen is more typical. This was clearly an inadequate stock of a commodity much in demand. Candles were quite expensive, however, the mean price being 4s. a dozen or 4d. per pound. Andrew Sockett II is the only mercer so far identified who made his own candles on a commercial scale. A modern candle weighs less than half an ounce, and on this basis his 4cwt. represented about 15,000 candles. His tallow, worth £6, works out at rather less than 3s. 3d. a dozen pounds. Since his candles were valued at 4s. 6d. a dozen, the wick, processing and profits added about a third to the cost of the tallow. His stock can be compared with that of Awkins and Moore, two 17th-century Lichfield chandlers. The former had similar equipment and a similar amount of tallow, both of which were valued more highly than Sockett's, and he also had candles in the making and wickyarn. Unlike Sockett, he had no furnace and so was unable to render his own tallow, a process which must have made Sockett an offensive neighbour in the centre of Wellington, where he had his premises. Moore had less equipment for making candles, but three furnaces for rendering, and it is possible that he was a specialist tallow renderer supplying material to other candlemakers.

In an age when most food is flavoured with sugar it is difficult to imagine a society where this was not so. It is probable that neither honey nor sugar, the two sweetening agents available in the period studied, were to be found in every household,[39] and they are rarely mentioned except as stock in mercers' inventories. Mercers invariably stocked sugar in variety, but many had no honey, perhaps because it was regarded as a medicine, and was stocked by apothecaries. John Hill in *The Virtue of Honey* said that if people kept their own bees, they could ensure that their honey was not adulterated with flour, which made it useless as a medicine, suggesting that many people neither kept bees nor had access to local supplies.

Only 16 inventories mentioned bees, and two of those are for the same household taken on the same day. Bees may have been ignored because hives were in the garden or further afield. The appraisers of Anthony Ellison of Lichfield[40] recorded that he had 'several stalls of bees in severall men's handes', apart from 'nine stalls of bees in the garden'. Beekeepers would certainly move their hives to orchards or beanfields at the appropriate times. Bees were expensive. A hive was comparable in value to a sheep, and so could hardly be included in that little-valued category of things forgotten. If they were generally ignored, one would expect that a few conscientious appraisers would provide the bulk of the references, but this is not so. Forty-three different appraisers are involved with the inventories that list bees, and only one of them more than once. The 43 include some of the most experienced and conscientious appraisers, and it seems reasonable to assume that if they did not list bees it was because normally they found none to list.

TABLE X

Beekeepers in North Telford, Lichfield and the Bristol region

|  | Telford | Lichfield | Bristol |
|---|---|---|---|
| Total number of inventories | 846 | 190 | — |
| Number of beekeepers | 15 (2%) | 7 (4%) | 13 |
| Number with inventories valued at more than £50 | 11 (73%) | 2 (29%) | 13 (100%) |
| Proportion of total with inventories valued at more than £50 | 27.35% | 44% | — |
| Number of inventories before 1700 | 357 (42%) | 190 (100% | — |
| Beekeepers before 1700 | 13 (87%) | 7 (100%) | 13 (100%) |
| Mean value of a hive | 3s. 4d. | 2s. 1d. | 3s. 8d. |
| Mean number of hives | 2 | 2 | 3 |

*Sources*—Lichfield: D G. Vaisey, *op. cit.*; Bristol: John Moore, *op. cit.*

The wealth of beekeepers varied from £9 (*236*) to £515 (*91*), but 11 of the 14 had inventories worth more than £50. For Daniel Pucksley (*236*) five shillings' worth of bees represents nearly 3 per cent. of his possessions, whereas for William Marigold (*91*) ten shillings' worth of bees represents only 0.1 per cent. of £515, and might justifiably have been ignored by his appraisers. For Pucksley, the bees were probably the source of a cash product. Marigold's bees can have played only a small part in his business, although they may have been useful in the household economy. Except for Francis Peate in 1746 (*208*), and three in the decade ending in 1710, all of the known beekeepers died before 1700. Bees were not unrecorded in the 18th century, because less care was taken with inventories (the long inventory of Thomas Calcott in 1744 [*264*] includes a watering can worth 2d.), but probably because there were none to list.

# INTRODUCTION

Table X compares Telford beekeepers with those in Lichfield and the Bristol area. In the latter, as in Telford, beekeepers were mainly rich; they had small numbers of hives, and records of bees after 1700 are sparse. In Lichfield beekeepers came mostly from the poorer classes, their hives are less highly valued, and there was one man, Anthony Ellison, who seems to have made his living from his hives.

Honey was probably used less because sugar was cheaper and more readily obtainable. Deere points out that in the 1570s honey cost about 3.4d. per pound, and that to be competitive, sugar, a more effective sweetener, would have had to cost no more than 4.9d. per pound, whereas in fact it cost 17p. Only two mercers' inventories give a price for honey: Oldfield at 5.5d., and Glover at 3.5d., both higher than Deere's figure. Table XI shows that apart from the disastrous year of 1695 (the year of Johnson's inventory), prices of sugar fell steadily. Household account books show that a rich family consumed quite large quantities of the better grades of sugar in the early 17th century. Most mercers stocked only small quantities in that period, but after 1650 it became usual for a good mercer to stock several different grades at a variety of prices. Moore in 1694 had seven hogsheads of powder and Jamaica sugar, as well as 5½cwt. of loaf sugar and six boxes of sugar candy. Since a hogshead of sugar contained over 10cwt., he had several tons in stock. Compared with this the stocks of Johnson were pathetically small, but hurricanes and the war with the French made 1694-95 a disastrous period for the sugar trade. The prices quoted by Beveridge for 1695 show a marked rise consistent with serious shortages.[41] By 1700 the situation had improved, and Wright had over a hundredweight of low-grade sugar, bastard and fine (this high-sounding word means once refined, and is a poor grade), not very suitable for crystallising fruits, but excellent for gingerbreads and mincemeats.

Mercers often kept beeswax which was used as a polish, in candles and as a constituent of sealing wax. The Wellington mercers did not supply wax candles, however, and the popularity of beekeeping among the wealthy may well have been because they wanted the wax. Schumpeter shows that the commerical production of wax candles, indicated in rising exports, greatly increased in the first half of the 18th century. If sugar became cheaper at the same time that wax candles became more generally available from shops, it becomes easier to understand why beekeeping declined.

## *The Professions*

There are three inventories for apothecaries and surgeons, or chirurgeons, all of them living in Wellington. Richard Hancox in 1728 (*180*) had possessions worth only a little over £9, and nothing among them to

## TABLE XI

Sugar price: a comparison between the inventories, two household account books,† and sources quoted in Beveridge*

| | 1 | 2† | 3 | 4 | 5† | 6 | 7 | 8 | 9 | 10 | 11 |
|---|---|---|---|---|---|---|---|---|---|---|---|
| | 1613 | 1613 | 1624 | 1632 | 1640 | 1643 | 1669 | 1694 | 1695 | 1700 | 1752 |
| *Sugar unspecified* | | | | | | | | | | | |
| Mercers | 15 | 11 | — | — | — | — | — | — | — | — | 3½ |
| Winchester* | — | — | 5¾ | — | — | — | — | — | — | — | — |
| Westminster* | — | — | — | — | — | — | — | 5¾ | 7¼ | 6 | 5½ |
| *Brown* | | | | | | | | | | | |
| Mercers* | — | — | — | — | — | — | — | 8½ | 7 | — | — |
| Navy Plymouth | — | — | — | — | — | — | — | — | — | 7½ | 5 |
| *Fine Powder* | | | | | | | | | | | |
| Mercers and Households | — | 14½ | — | 14 | 12½ | 14/16 | — | 8 | — | 4½/6½ | — |
| Lord Steward* | — | — | — | — | — | 14 | 10 | 10 | 16 | 10 | 9 |
| Westminster* | — | — | — | — | — | — | — | 8¾ | 12 | 9½ | 7½ |
| *Brown Candy* | | | | | | | | | | | |
| Mercers | 16 | — | 12 | 17 | — | — | 10 | — | — | 8 | — |
| *Treble fine/White Candy* | | | | | | | | | | | |
| Mercers and Households | 24 | 36 | 20 | — | — | — | — | — | 26 | 20 | — |
| Lord Steward* | — | — | — | — | — | — | 22 | 20 | — | — | 14 |

Prices quoted are in pence per pound

Sources (for details see Table VI)

1. Sankey I.
2. *The Household Book of Lord William Howard, op. cit.*
3. Eyton
4. Harris
5. R. G. Griffiths, *Joyce Jeffreys of Ham Castle, op. cit.*
6. Cowcher
7. Glover
8. Moore
9. Johnson
10. Wright
11. Kent

# INTRODUCTION

suggest that he was practicing medicine. John Walford three years later (*187*) had drugs, counters and instruments in his shop worth over £30, as well as a still, a boiler and pot, and a mare and colt, yet his possessions were valued at only £59 8s. 7d. William Birch in 1716 (*160*) was a much wealthier man with possessions worth £308 19s. 6d., and a 12-room house. The contents of his shop were worth £20, and he appears to have made malt and brewed beer on more than a purely domestic scale. He had married in 1672, and so was an old man at the time of his death, and the small volume of debts indicated in the inventory suggests that his business had probably contracted. Richard Johnson (*115*) had '2 Alkemmy dishes', but these were probably vessels made of antimony rather than receptacles for the elixir of life or the philosopher's stone.

There are inventories in the collection for seven clergymen, all but one of them resident in Wellington. Two are of quite exceptional quality, illustrating vividly the appearance of a late 17th-century parsonage. William Langley (*110*), whose inventory was taken in 1689 lived in a six-room house, which, from evidence in the inventory, he appears to have been extending at the time of his death. His growing crops were worth £10, suggesting that he worked a considerable acreage, but his only livestock were two pigs. His books were valued at £20, but some had been given to his sons before his death. He enjoyed many luxuries, pictures, china, Turkey work, and cushions of silk and gilt leather. John Field in 1693 (*119*) also lived in a house with six rooms and various outbuildings. He kept a cow and two pigs, brewed beer and made cheese, and had a pair of bowls in the room which served as his study. He had a 'desk upon a frame' and 131 books. He was in debt at the time of his death. Henry Haughton of Lilleshall (*70*) farmed on a considerable scale, with seven cattle, two pigs, and some corn. Henry Wood (*156*), vicar of Wellington, who died in 1712, had no livestock apart from a horse, but appears to have grown a considerable quantity of flax. His study of books worth £45 was more valuable than the total possessions of all but two of his fellow clergy. William Sockett (*189*), probably the 'Parson Sockett' who served the churches at Wombridge and Preston on the Wealdmoors,[42] had six pounds of flax in his home, but did not farm on a significant scale, his only livestock being two pigs, and two mares, one of which was blind.

There are inventories for two female school teachers from Wrockwardine, Elizabeth Bullock, who died in 1681 (*218*), and Jane Schofield, who died in 1705 (*237*). Curiously both amount to a little over £64. The former includes books worth £1, and the house included 'the loft which was the place where shee kept the schoole in'. In the latter the schoolroom was apparently on the ground floor and contained six benches and three stools. A school-house appropriately furnished is among the rooms listed in the inventory of John Smith (254), a wealthy Allscott farmer, in 1731-32.

One of the most remarkable inventories is that of William Cartwright (74) of Muxton, who died in 1718, and is described in his inventory as a 'mathematician'. His possessions were not especially valuable, the whole inventory being assessed at £17 0s. 4d., and while his house was comfortably furnished, it was not luxurious. The main interest in the inventory arises from the contents of a closet, which included 100 books, a three-legged staff and plane table, two quadrants, a pair of compasses, a spectacle glass, and a pair of globes, all valued at two guineas. In his will he left to his daughter, Elizabeth Boycott, a number of items, including 'my desk and map of Lilleshall Parke which hangs in the Kitchen Chamber'. The latter had been removed when the inventory was taken, but it was probably a version of a map of Lilleshall Park which Cartwright dedicated in 1679 to William Leveson Gower, which still survives.[43] It shows deer, drawn with a certain naive charm as if by a child, bounding through the woodland of the park, and is embellished with a quite magnificent cartouche and compass. His gloves and maps were left to his grandsons, William Boycott and John Walker, and he gave instructions that after his funeral a dole was to be given to the poor of Lilleshall, with Dick Jones, Ann Mason and Mary Bate receiving more than the rest. Thomas Woodhouse of Wellington, whose inventory was made in 1666, also had surveying instruments which appear to have been his only means of making a living.

## The Leather trades[44]

The leather trade flourished in all of the principal towns in Shropshire in the 17th and 18th centuries, nor was this surprising in a region where pastoral farming was widely practised, and where there were sufficient woodlands to bear considerable crops of bark. The inventories show not only that the primary process of tanning was carried on in Wellington, but that, as in Bishop's Castle, Bridgnorth and Ludlow, gloves were made from the tanner's products.

There are three tanners' inventories from Wellington, one of them, that of Walter Mansell, for a very poor man who died on the road outside the parish, and who may well have been a journeyman. The *Book of Trades*, published in 1821, remarked 'the trade of a tanner cannot be carried on without considerable capital: and a roomy yard, sheds and pits with plenty of water are indispensible requisites'.[45] Richard Jones (111) who died in 1689 was certainly wealthy. His estate was valued at £323 19s. 4d., and his house had 14 rooms, including a barn, a tanhouse, a brewhouse, and a malthouse. He must certainly have had ample capital. He had leather in the tanhouse worth £100, and 'all the barke about the tanhouse' was valued at £20. Layers of coarse-ground oak bark were put between prepared hides which were stacked in a pit and soaked for up to six weeks in the tanning lixivium or ooze, prepared from oak bark and water. Jones farmed on a considerable scale, with eight cattle, 26 sheep, five horses, and five pigs, and grew hard corn, barley, oats, beans, peas, flax and hay. He had brewing apparatus, 32 cheeses, and a spinning wheel, and his house was luxuriously furnished with two glass cases, carpets and wainscot panelling. Joshua Dunton (*95*), whose inventory was taken in 1686 had possessions worth £357 10s. 6d., including tanning equipment worth just over £200. He had bark worth £30, and a mill for grinding it. He had bulls' hides worth nearly £40, and 68 dozen calf skins worth £57. His farming interests were less extensive than those of Jones, but his house with livery cupboard, glass case, a cast-iron fire plate, and silver was clearly comfortably furnished. There were also two curriers in Wellington, men who prepared the skins from the tanneries for use by shoemakers. Both were poor men, one with possessions worth only just over £10, and the other, William Lloyd (*198*) with an estate valued at only £6 17s. 0d., of which 8s. 6d. was for a 'pin block and board and knives'.

Inventories survive for eight glovers who died in Wellington between 1660 and 1750. They are spread evenly throughout the period, which suggests that the trade was well established, and since most were poor, and the craft needed little equipment, it is probable that others had no inventories made, or had no items listed which reveal their occupation. None of the Wellington mercers sold gloves, which suggests that they were not brought into the town from elsewhere. Six of the eight glovers had estates valued at less than £50. The wealthiest was John Brown (*184*), who died in 1729, with possessions worth £129, but £100 of this was in money. None of the glovers lived in luxury, although two had looking glasses, and two possessed pictures. Most were partly self-sufficient. Three had cows, two had pigs, three possessed hay, two had corn, and three had hemp. One had wool in the house, one had milking pails, and one even had turnip seed. Three had equipment for brewing their own beer. The value of their stock and tools was generally low, with two exceptions, being appraised at between 10s. and £2 10s. 0d. John Brown had skins, pelts, hides, gloves and wool worth £22 17s. 0d. John Mansell's highly detailed list of stock in 1743 (*206*) amounted to £11 2s. 7½d. Thomas Howle (*89*), a skinner who was also involved in the glove trade, had a stock of gloves and leather worth five pounds. He may have been some kind of wholesaler.

Some of the inventories reveal the types of leather used in glovemaking. The *Book of Trades* noted that:

> All tanned leather is classed and universally known under two general denominations: namely hides and skins. The former being commonly applied

to the larger animals, as bulls, oxen, cows, &c. whose skins are chiefly intended for the soles of stout shoes . . . while the latter term is used for calves' seals' skins &c. which being thinner are more flexible.[46]

A reference in Mansell's inventory to '20 Shamey Linings' at 4d. per skin was probably not to real chamois skin as 'it is commonly counterfeited with common goats' and sheeps' skins'. In 1729 fourteen skins of tan leather were valued at 8s., nearly 7d. each. One horse hide was worth 3s., a 'wash lamb skin', 4d., and a 'wash leather shipskin' was worth 8d. Brown's inventory refers to '33 caslins', probably inferior calf skins, which were worth 4d. each. His inventory also includes '41 kyps', which were skins from large calves or small breeds of cattle. In 1743 a tanned sheepskin was worth 2½d., and a comparison of Brown's inventory with Mansell's suggests some decline in the cost of leather between 1729 and 1743.

The variety of gloves manufactured in Wellington was considerable. Brown's inventory included children's gloves at 3d. a pair, and children's mittens which were cheaper. Mittens for men and women were 6d. a pair, as were 'wash leather gloves', but ash-colour gloves were worth 8d. Mansell's gloves, like his leather, were valued rather lower than Brown's. One pair of 'woman's ordinary black gloves' was valued at just over 2d. 'Coarse mitts' were 3d. a pair, and 'hedge mittings', perhaps for hedging, 1¼d. a pair. 'Tandgloves' for women were 4d., as were 'women's black gloves' and 'white mitts'. White mitts for girls were worth 2d a pair. As in 1729 'ash coloured' gloves were among the most expensive. A pair of 'woman's coarse ash colour'd gloves' was worth 4¼d., and a pair of 'small men's ash colour'd gloves' just over 11d. There was clearly great variation in the type of gloves produced, those of lesser value being very cheap indeed, which perhaps explains the relative poverty of most of the glovers. It would seem that there was no specialisation, and that most of the Wellington glovers made a full range of products.

Some glovers did work which was normally that of a tanner or currier. John Mansell left '187 pelts in the limes' which refers to the process of working the hides in limewater to remove the outer and the inner layer ready for the tanning process:

> the hides are immersed in pits, containing a mixture of lime and water . . . being occasionally moved up and down that every part may be uniformly exposed to the action of the lime-water. . . . They are continued in the lime pits for ten or fifteen days; they are then deprived of their hair and washed in water, after which they are immersed in an infusion of pigeons' dung. called a grainer, having the property of an alkali. In this they remain for a week or ten days, according to the state of the atmosphere . . . during which time they are frequently handled and scraped on both sides upon a convex wooden beam.

The references to 'wash leather skins', 'rubbing skins' and 'black gloves' are explained in an account of the work of the currier, who in larger

## INTRODUCTION

towns was responsible for preparing tanned hides for the craftsmen who used them:

> ... the first operation is soaking the leather until it be thoroughly wet ... The hide is then conveyed to the shade, or drying place, where the oily substances are applied, which are put on both sides of the leather ... It is now fit for waxing, which is performed by rubbing it with a brush, dipped in a composition of oil and lamp-black on the flesh side, till it be thoroughly black ... leather ... termed black on the grain ... the black ... is a solution of copperas in bark liquor ... applied to it while wet.[47]

There were 15 shoemakers, corvisors or cordwainers in Telford during the period under review, the three terms having been used synonymously, although one corviser, John Taylor, who died in 1661, appears to have made his living from farming rather than making shoes. All but one of the shoemakers lived in Wellington parish, the exception being William Perkins of Dawley, whose inventory lacks interesting detail. The wealthiest was Miles Field (*94*) who died in 1680 with possessions worth £313 13s. 0d., £250 of which was accounted for by leasehold property in Lilleshall parish. Field's inventory indicates that he bought his leather untreated from a tanner, and then sent it to a currier to be dressed, and that he used hemp in shoemaking. He kept a cow, and had hard corn and barley in his house. Henry Adams (*183*), who died in 1728-29, had an estate worth £217, of which £130 was in money, and £12 in leather and shoes in his shop. He had five cows and two pigs, and a stock of malt and barley in his house. The inventory of Henry Stanworth (*103*) taken in 1684-85 is particularly detailed. It totals only £23 6s. 2d., but includes a Kidderminster carpet, two Turkey-work cushions and 22 glass bottles, which indicates that he lived in some comfort. No working tools are mentioned, and he may have retired from business. Seven of the 15 shoemakers kept animals of various kinds. Five had equipment for brewing and two had stocks of malt. Shoemaking was a trade in which only a moderate prosperity was generally possible, for nine of the inventories totalled less than £20, and only three exceeded £50.

The inventory of only one saddler survives. Saddlery was traditionally a trade which demanded considerable capital, but the inventory of Francis Puller of Wellington taken in 1721 totals only £17 12s. 6d., of which £5 was the value of three saddles, three collars, nine pads, and his tools. Unlike most of the shoemakers he had no animals other than a mare.

### *The Dyers*[48]

Dyeing was one of the most substantial trades in Wellington between 1660 and 1750. There are six inventories for dyers in the collection, one of whom seems no longer to have been in business at the time of his death, while another appears to have been an employee rather than the proprietor of a dye-house. The four others were among the most

## TABLE XII

Dyers whose inventories have been used for comparative purposes, in chronological order

|  | | Value of Inventory (to nearest £ below) | Date |
|---|---|---|---|
| | | £ | |
| (1) | John Robinson, dyer, Chester | — | 1598 |
| | Francis Wright, I, dyer, Wellington | 174 | 1625 |
| (1) | Reynold ap Robert, Ellesmere | 93 | 1634 |
| (2) | William Richardson, dyer, Newport, Salop. | 63 | 1637 |
| | Thomas Wright, dyer, Wellington (*83*) | 270 | 1662 |
| (1) | Urian Minshall, dyer, Chester | 72 | 1666 |
| (1) | Robert Maddock, dyer, Sandbach, Cheshire | 160 | 1666 |
| (1) | Nicholas Williams, dyer, Chester | 128 | 1667 |
| (3) | Laurence Wozall, St. Julian, Shrewsbury | 41 | c. 1672 |
| (4) | Anne Smaldridge, widow, Lichfield | 445 | 1679 |
| | John Smart, dyer, Wellington (*98*) | 172 | 1682 |
| (1) | Thomas Haddock, dyer, Chester | 124 | 1688 |
| (5) | Joseph Clarke, Grocer and draper, Roxwell, Essex | 145 | 1692 |
| | Alice Smart, widow, Wellington (*121*) | 25 | 1693–94 |
| | Francis Wright II, dyer, Wellington (*127*) | 288 | 1698 |
| (6) | John Taylor, dyer, Ludlow | 70 | 1713 |
| (1) | John Burroughs, Barthomley, Cheshire | 203 | 1717 |
| | Joshua Taylor, dyer, Wellington (*173*) | 29 | 1725 |
| | John Wright, dyer, Wellington (*193*) | 9 | 1737 |
| | John Cherrington, dyer, Wellington (*195*) | 230 | 1738 |
| (1) | John Prenton, dyer, Cheshire | 765 | 1738 |
| (2) | Thomas Phillips, dyer, Bridgnorth | — | 1739 |
| (7) | Charles Sturge, feltmaker, Frampton Cotterell, Glos. | 19 | 1754 |

### NOTES

(1) In Chester Record Office.
(2) In Lichfield Joint Record Office.
(3) In Lichfield Joint Record Office. Photocopy and transcript in Shropshire Record Office.
(4) D. G. Vaisey, *op. cit.*, pp. 280–83.
(5) F. W. Steer, *op. cit.*, pp. 212–13.
(6) In Hereford Record Office.
(7) John Moore, *op. cit.*, p. 265.

All the known North Telford dyers between 1660 and 1750 are included in this Table. For no other place is the list in any way complete or even necessarily representative.

substantial tradesmen in the town, their inventories having a mean value of £264 1s. 9d. All of the dyers' appraisers who can be identified were wealthy men, and the dyers' households were universally well-appointed, with silver, glassware, china, looking glasses, maps, pictures and books.

Several dyers were concerned with secondary enterprises. Francis Wright (*127*) had some £154 invested in farming. John Cherrington (*195*) had some £108 invested in malting, while John Smart (*98*) had more malt than might be supposed necessary for household purposes. Similarly Anne Smaldridge, dyer of Lichfield, had a malthouse with 400 strike of malt. Malting could logically have been combined with dyeing since the couching house used for processing woad would have been used only for a short season, and could well have been employed for malting for the rest of the year. Furthermore, it seems likely that dyers actually used some malt in their work, as a substrate in the woad-vat.

Dyeing was thus by no means a marginal trade in Wellington. The town supported at least two flourishing concerns for most of the period under review. The business of the Wright family, Francis I, who died in 1625, Thomas (*83*), who died in 1662, and Francis II (*127*), who died in 1698, must certainly have co-existed with that of John Smart (*98*), who died in 1682, and his step-son, Joshua Taylor (*173*). The latter seems to have ceased working the business before the time of his death in 1725, but unless he had given up long before, he must have overlapped with John Cherrington, who died in 1738 (*195*).

It is not immediately apparent from the Wellington inventories that small town dyers of this period carried out other finishing processes on the cloth they coloured, taking it from the fulling stage to completion ready for retailing. Comparison with the other dyers' inventories listed in Table XII makes this clear. Francis Wright I of Wellington had 'Cloth in his shop dyeinge and dressing undelivered £4.13.00d.; seven paire of sheares with handles and teasles and all other shop tooles £5.00.00d.'. William Richardson of Newport had 'Dyeing stuffe . . . w'th Sherman's tooles'. Robert Maddock of Sandbach had 'Sheares . . . belonging to the dye house'. John Burroughs of Barthomley in 1717 had 'Dying stuffe, other materials and Instruments belonging to the Trade of a Dyer and Shearman'. Thomas Phillips of Bridgnorth had '2 pair of dyers shears'. The processes to which most woollen cloths were subjected between fulling and retailing were the dressing or raising of the knap, in which the cloth was mounted on a *dubbing board* and stroked with increasing vigour with *teasles* (the burr-like heads of *Dipsacus Fullonum*) set in wooden *handles*; tentering in which the cloth was strained in both length and breadth using *tentering racks* and *tenter-hooks*; shearing, in which the knap was cut short with *shears* on a *shear board*, after which the cloth was brushed free of fluff and pressed, or more usually hot-pressed between paper to put on the final smooth finish. No single one of the Wellington dyers' inventories mentions equipment for all of these processes, but all list items concerned with some of them, and between them they include references to all of the tools listed above except for a dubbing board. One of the latter was part of the property of John Taylor of Ludlow who had 'the Racks and what belongs to them, 10 dozen Handells and 7 peare of Sheares, and . . . a sheare Bord a dobing Bord . . .'. Since the shear board and dubbing board were listed with other items making a total of only 19s. 6d., it seems likely that in other inventories they are covered by terms like 'other necessaries'. Many of the inventories that list a press or hot press mention also a 'crow' with it. This would have been a crowbar, used as a lever to exert extra pressure. Thomas Wright had, in addition to a 'standing Taintry' (or tenter-rack) a 'ffier Tantry', presumably one on which cloth could be heated to speed up the process.

In larger towns, particularly in Shrewsbury, the centre of the finishing trade in Welsh cloth, the trades of dyer and shearman seem to have been more sharply distinguished. In Lichfield, Ann Smaldridge, dyer, had no equipment for finishing cloth except for a press and hot press, nor was there any suggestion that William Meeson, shearman of that city was concerned with dyeing. It seems likely that the only way in which a dyer in a small town like Wellington could prosper was by vertically integrating his concern, becoming involved in finishing cloth and the associated trade of malting, as well as by investing in agriculture and property. There is no evidence, however, that the Wellington dyers concerned themselves with fulling, as did Uriah Minshall, dyer of Chester, who had a 'pcell of fullers earth' listed on his inventory. Any cloth which needed to be fulled in Wellington was probably processed at Allscott mill.

The inventories suggest that a dyer might ply his trade in several different but not mutually exclusive ways. Thomas Wright had 'the Collering of 140 yards of Glanion at £1.03.04d' and 'the Collering of 50 yards of Cloath at £1.00.00d'. John Smart had 'Lynnens and New Lynnen Cloth & Yearne at £13.06.06d', and 'Four ends of Lynsee and Woollen Cloth at £2.02.06d'. It would thus appear that Wright was dyeing someone elses's cloth and charging for the service, but that Smart had bought the cloth which he was dyeing before re-selling it. Nothing in the inventories shows that they did not act differently at different times. The word 'Glanion' is a corruption of the Welsh 'gwlanen', meaning woollen, from which the word flannel may be derived. This does not mean that Wright's cloth was what would now be called flannel, but its dyeing at 2d. per yard suggests that it was fairly cheap. It might have been dyed with Wright's madder, which was not of the best quality, to make the red cloth traditionally used for petticoats. Wright's broadcloth cost 4.8d.

per yard to dye. Broadcloth was valued at the time at begween 5s. and 11s. a yard, though it could be as cheap as 3s.[49] It was certainly a far more valuable cloth than the glanion, and was obviously intended for a different section of the market. There is no reason to think that the trade in Wellington had polarised into specialist linen, fustian and woollen dyers in the 17th century as had had happened in Lancashire. Such evidence as there is suggests that the Wellington dyers made their livings from a variety of activities. The linen cloth held by Smart was possibly locally produced. The broad cloth which Wright had would certainly have come from elsewhere, and he might have been dyeing it for a mercer. The glanion might have been work put out to Wright by a Shrewsbury draper, and may indicate that the Shrewsbury monopoly of this trade was less than complete. There is certainly no evidence that the Wellington dyers made their livings primarily as outposts of the extensive Shrewsbury finishing trade, or that they dealt principally with locally-produced linen cloth. It is more likely that they, like many other market town tradesmen, provided varied services for customers with a range of different demands.

Thomas Wright's inventory (*83*) is superbly detailed, listing many dyestuffs with both weights and values, so that prices can be deduced and compared with those on the similarly detailed and almost contemporaneous inventory of Anne Smaldridge of Lichfield. Both Thomas Wright and Anne Smaldridge died young so that each inventory is that of a working dyer, not that of an old person whose business had run down. Thomas Wright was almost certainly the son of Francis Wright I, dyer of Wellington, who died in 1625, although neither the death of Francis nor the birth of Thomas appears in the surviving parish register which was begun in 1625. The dynasty of dyers Wright does not appear to have been related to the dynasty of mercers which stemmed from the Rev. Francis Wright. Thomas married Magdalen Wright of Wroxeter in 1640, and they had 10 children, of whom only four survived at his death, two daughters and Francis II, aged 10, and Thomas II, aged two. His first son had also been named Francis but died in infancy, so that a later son was given the name. Magdalen survived her husband by 30 years. What happened to Thomas II is not known, since his burial is unrecorded in Wellington, but it is possible that he ultimately managed the business since a 'Thomas Wright, dyer' held land in the open fields of Wellington in 1702.[50] Francis II inherited the business from his father when he came of age. His inventory suggests that the business was still operating when he died, but there seems to have been less equipment and fewer dyestuffs than in the inventory of Thomas I. The will of Francis II suggests that he had moved to Leegomery, leasing out his house in Wellington. He may have moved merely to be nearer his farm, but since there was little access to running water in the centre of Wellington, he may have sought a site on the Ketley brook, which flows northwards through Leegomery. It drove a mill in the township, and in the 1750s provided enough water to power the large Ketley ironworks. Pressure of public opinion could also have provoked the move if Wright was generating the stench of couching woad in the centre of the town. Accounts of the 18th-century practice of 'streaming' cloth, suspending the 'piece' from a bridge into a rapid stream not less than 18ins. deep, and beating it until the water ran clean from each section, with perhaps three or four repetitions, leave no doubt of the heavy demand the dyer made on his water supply.[51]

In 1679 Francis Wright II married Mary Minshall, and at his death left a family of young children, his only son Minshall being then aged ten. By the time Mary died in 1718 Minshall seems also to have been dead, and her long and detailed will does not mention the business. Certainly the concern did not pass to John Wright, dyer (*193*), who had neither accommodation, equipment nor materials to work a dye-house. He may have worked for John Cherrington. He was born the son of Adam Wright, one of the most active appraisers in Wellington, in 1702. It is possible that his father died a pauper, and there is no evidence that this John Wright was related to the dynasty which sprang from Francis I, nor that he worked a dye-house.

John Smart (*98*) was the son of Richard and Jane. His first marriage in 1656 ended with the death of his wife within a year. His second union, which produced 10 children, ended when his wife died in 1676. He remarried almost at once, his third wife being Alice, widow of John Taylor of St. Martins-in-the-Field, London. The couple were in Wellington for the birth of their son John in October 1675, but it is not clear what children they had in London. In his will John Smart left to Joshua Taylor, his 'son-in-law' (i.e., step-son) and to his own son Richard, £20 and a bed apiece, the rest of the estate going to Alice his wife. When she died the property seems to have passed to her son Joshua, and although when he died in 1725 he had two furnaces, a dyer's press and other dyer's implements, they were in the brewhouse, and there is no indication in his inventory (*173*) that he was practising as a dyer.

John Cherrington probably came from one of the villages round the Weald moors, where the name is common. He married Magdalen Shakeshaft, widow of Shrewsbury, at Wroxeter in 1710. During the following decade when his name appears in the register with the baptisms of his children, he was perhaps a man of no great substance, but by the time of his death in 1738 he was accorded the title of 'Mr.'. He seems to have assumed from Francis Wright II the role of the most prominent dyer in Wellington, but whether he acquired the Wrights' business or moved into the gap left by its demise is uncertain. John Cherrington's inventory shows him a rich man, and his will reveals him as a man of property, who had already provided for his son, John II, in his lifetime.

His son, William, was to inherit the dyer's business. Both sons continued to live in Wellington, but neither was accorded the title 'Mr.'.

Most of the inventories reveal disappointingly little about the dyeing process, but they do show that the investment in equipment needed to practice dyeing was substantial. Francis Wright II had in his dye-house two furnaces and a winch valued at £4 15s. 0d., but his dyestuffs were dismissed as 'some collouring Stuffe'. The winch would have been situated above the vat to lift the wet and heavy 'pieces' of cloth, which would have been 24 yards long, or longer, depending on the material. John Smart had 'two ffurnaces and one Wadfat in the dyehouse' worth £8 10s. 4d. John Cherrington had '4 Furnices, 8 winces . . .' worth £14 4s. 0d., and Thomas Wright had 'two ffatts, two furnaces, One leade ffatt, two troughs and a Kindyr' in the dye-house, and in his 'Pressehouse', 'a furnace and a Leaden ffat' worth in all £15 5s. 0d. Partridge, writing of the late 18th century,[52] gave the dimensions of the English woad vat at 7ft. 6ins. deep, 7ft. 6ins. diameter at the bottom, 6ft. diameter at the top, and its capacity 1,640 gallons. It would work for about six months at a stretch, during which time it would consume 10cwt. of woad and 490lbs. of indigo, dyeing 5,720lbs. of wool, with an additional 400lbs. of dark blue, 200lbs. of half blue, and 200lbs. of very light blue during the six weeks of working down. The main methods of heating the vats were by transfer, portion by portion, from the wooden vat to a metal furnace for boiling, then returning to the vat, or by having a copper panel inserted in a wooden vat for the fires to play upon. On the inventories of the earlier dyers furnaces and vats are carefully distinguished, from which it appears that they favoured the former method. The latter ones seem not to have had vats as distinct from furnaces, which may reflect a change in practice, although the sample is too small to draw any firm conclusions. The inventory of Nicholas Williams of Chester in 1667 described 'one dying panne brasse in the bottom peiced on the top with lead, Iron barrs for a grate under it . . .'. Since the appraisers describe it in detail, it was presumably not a standard form of dyeing pan, and may reflect a trend towards metal vats. Since the practice with the woad vat was to set the fermentation going and run the vat for six months at a time, it is clear that Francis Wright II and John Smart had equipment to do little more than dye mixed colours or blue while the woad vat was running. Only Thomas Wright could operate on anything like the scale of Anne Smaldridge, who had three woad vats, enough to overlap the runs of the separate vats so as to have one permanently available.

Thomas Wright's inventory gives many details of his dyestuffs which can be compared with those of Cherrington, Francis Wright II and Smart, and with the detailed inventory of Anne Smaldridge. It seems that it was usual on dyers' inventories to calculate a hundredweight as 100lbs., not 112lbs. of dyestuffs.[53] Wright and Smaldridge each had, at least by

**PRICE OF INDIGO vs DATE**

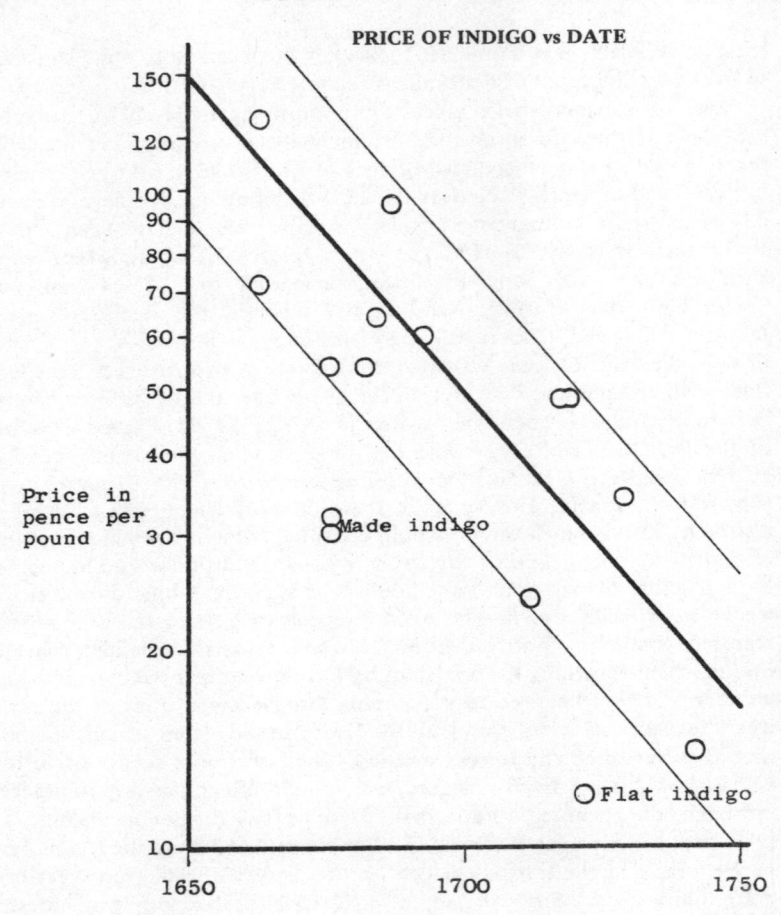

[Graph showing price in pence per pound vs date from 1650 to 1750, with data points labeled "Made indigo" and "Flat indigo"]

inference, both woad and 'indico' (i.e., exotic indigo). Wright had 6cwt. of woad (£4) and 10lbs. of indico (£1), while Smaldridge had '3 wodfats w'th all materialls to them . . . £6', amd 9lbs. of indico worth £1.5s. 6d. John Smart had a 'Wadfat' and John Cherrington had indico worth one pound. Both woad and indico contain the alkaloid dye indigo, $C_{16}H_{10}N_2O_2$, although this was not recognised at the time, and indico was used to supplement woad in the woad vat. This practice originated when indico was first imported into Europe on a significant scale, when in 1631 seven ships of the Durch East India Company brought in 580,345lbs., worth over five tons of gold. By the latter half of the 17th century a good deal was grown in the West Indies. The practice led to the retention of the term 'woad vat', especially in woollen dyeing, right up to the 1930s, by which time indico had been replaced by synthetic indigo, and the only function of the woad was to promote the fermentation process. The use of other synthetic dyes finally displaced indigo altogether, and the last woad farm in the world near Wisbech ceased work in the late 1920s. Woad was used with indico because it could initiate a fermentation process in the vat, ascribed to *desmobacterium hydrofenoferum* that reduced the indigo present (from whatever source) to the colourless leuco-form, while indico does not have this capacity, much less synthetic indigo. At the beginning of this century the equivalence between woad and indico was reckoned to be 4lbs. indico to the bale (210lbs.) of woad, or 1lb. of indico to 15lbs. of the best woad. Indigo is a vat dye, one which is applied by reducing it (in the chemical sense) to the colourless, soluble leuco-form. The material is then soaked in it, and exposed to the air to oxidise the leuco-form back to the insoluble, substantive form of the dye. Since the dye is thus generated within the structure of the fibres of the material rather than attached to their surface, it is extremely fast, and it was important for this reason, both in its own right and as the basis for mixed colours. Black was obtained from woad followed by alum, then madder and fustic, or (a cheaper but less durable process) from woad followed by alum then logwood. Green was obtained from woad followed by alum then fustic, and purples from woad followed by alum and cochineal, for expensive cloths, or madder, for cheap ones.

Besides her vats and indico Anne Smaldridge had a couching house, strongly suggesting that she processed her own woad. The procedure was to pluck the leaves from the growing plants, crush them, and drain them until they could be moulded by hand into balls about 6ins. in diameter, and dried on 'fleaks', which were wickerwork trays stacked in ventilated racks. In England the leaves could be picked up to three times a year. When all had been gathered it was combined, crumbled and watered in beds about 2ft. deep in the couching house, for the fermentation process which required a good deal of experience and close attention if the product was to be neither 'heavy' on the one hand nor 'foxy' on the other. After fermentation the dark, clay-like woad was packed into tuns ready for use in the vat. A yield of one part of woad from nine parts of the leaf was quoted in 1918.

Since the last woad imported came from Toulouse in 1638, the material used by the Wellington dyers was not imported, although it might have come from one of the celebrated woad-growing areas in England, like Lincolnshire or Somerset. The plant yielded from 1½ to 3 tons per acre about 1920, so that the 6cwt. held by Thomas Wright might have required between half an acre and one acre, allowing for lower yields in the 17th century. None of the North Telford inventories mentions woad growing, but since the acreage would have been small this is not surprising. Certainly the woad plant, *isatis tinctoria*, grows readily in Telford today. The dyers may have brought their material from travelling woadmen, who rented land for two or three years and moved on when it was exhausted. Arthur Young in 1805 recommended this practice to any young farmer as a lucrative letting for any suitable land.[54]

It is instructive to compare the quantities of materials in Wright's inventory with those of the standard formulations for the woad vat, in that the quantities he ordered and kept in stock may represent their rate of consumption. In Wright's time indico was used to supplement the woad, a current French formulation in 1705 recommending no more than 6lbs. of indico to the bale of woad (210lbs.). This proportion, 2.86 per cent., corresponds closely with Partridge's figures, published in 1823, but representing earlier practice. The madder in the formulations, a dyestuff in its own right, was often said to counteract any tendency towards a green tinge in natural indigo, but in reality it was rapidly consumed as a substrate in the bacterial action. The bran was the principle substrate for the process and the means of encouraging fermentation if it should slow down. Partridge gave bran and cornell as his main substrate (or ground grain of all kinds), but if an accelerator was needed, he advocated 'swill' from boiling, *inter alia*, malt. There is no indication in the inventories what substrate was used by the Wellington dyers, but any carbohydrate or sugary material would have served, and several of them had malt in plenty. The slaked lime was the retarding agent used to slow down the fermentation if it started running away, by controlling the pH with lime. No inventory in Wellington or elsewhere lists this labile material, but Francis Wright II regularly purchased lime from the kilns of Steeraway in 1685-87.[55]

An examination of the prices of indigo in a variety of sources shown in Fig. 2 shows the typical exponential fall in price of a new commodity, with a scatter falling into a band over the 17th century. No allowance has been made for wholesale and retail prices since there is no means of knowing which was quoted. The two points that fall markedly below the main band are respectively Tench's 'made' as opposed to his 'fine' indigo, and Wozall's 'flat' indigo. In the importing of indigo a distinction was always drawn between the 'rich' grade from Lahore, with its high tinctorial power, and the 'flat' from Gujerat. The distinction was reflected in the prices at the East India Co.'s annual sales. Even these two points outside the main band lie upon another, parallel line.

Beside the blue from woad, the Wellington dyers had available red from madder, yellow from fustic, another blue from logwood, another red from redwoods, and blacks from logwood, galls and sumach, with all the variants possible from mixtures and the use of different mordants. The only important colour for which no single dyestuff was available was green (and this is still true of natural dyestuffs), but combinations of blue and yellow made this no insuperable problem. The remaining

## TABLE XIII

**Wright's dyestuffs compared with standard formulations for the woad vat**

|  | 1662 Wright (83) | 1823 Partridge (1) | 1888 Hummel (2) | 1918 Martin (3) |
|---|---|---|---|---|
| Indigo | 4.5 | 8.4 | 15.25 | 12.2 |
| Woad | 305 | 305 | 305 | 305 |
| Madder | (152) | 2.7 | 2–15 | 4.3 |
| Bran | — | 10.8 | 10.2 | 12.2 |
| Dry slaked lime | — | 2.7 | 12.2 | 7.3 |
| Indigo as percentage of woad | 1.5 | 2.75 | 5 | 4 |

All weights were converted into kilos, but the figures quoted are ratios.

### NOTES

(1) William Partridge, *A Practical Treatise on Dyeing* (1823, rep. 1973).
(2) J. J. Hummel, *The Dyeing of Textile Fabrics* (3rd ed. 1888).
(3) G. Martin, *Industrial and Manufacturing Chemistry (Organic)*, (1918).

dyestuffs differ from woad in being mordant dyes. A mordant is required to make them fast upon the material. The mechanism of this process appears to be the attaching of a metal as its hydroxide or a basic salt to the fibre, then the formation of a coloured lake with the metal by the dye. It is for this reason that the colours of dyes differ with different mordants, and that without a mordant such a dye may act as no more than a rather feeble stain upon the material. In a few cases, principally with the dyewoods, it was necessary to use tannin, a natural polymer with aromatic carboxylic acids as its active sites, to bind the mordant more firmly on to the fibre.

Thomas Wright had madder at 3.2d. per lb.; John Smart had an unspecified amount, and Anne Smaldridge had madder at 3.6d. per lb., 2.76d. per lb., and 'a small parcell of mull madder". Surprisingly, none is listed in the detailed inventory of John Cherrington. In view of the different prices, and the implied distinction from 'mull madder' Smaldridge must have had three of the four commonly distinguished grades, in descending quality: bale, bunch, fat, and pipe, or in the Dutch notation, crop, umbro, gamene, and mull. Since she also had 'cuchineale' it is likely that the highest quality was missing since she would have used cochineal for dyeing high-grade cloths red. The main dye in madder is alizarin, 1, 2-dihydroxyanthraquinone, a secondary purpurin, 1, 2, 4-trihydroxy-anthraquinone, both present as glycoside, and both hydrolysed by the enzyme eythrozyme which is present, hence, no doubt, the maturing processes in the preparation of the dyestuff. Without a mordant madder merely stains wool a pale brown, but with alum it gives a colour between pink and scarlet, depending on the concentration, and with iron (i.e., copperas) a browner colour, ranging from maroon to red-brown. The colours with madder are not so bright as the scarlet obtained from cochineal, but are fast to light and to milling with soap. Madder is derived from the root of *rubia tinctoria*, which in the 17th century was imported, principally from Holland. The Wellington dyers probably got their supplies from London. Reynold ap Robert of Ellesmere in 1634 owed 'in London for Dying Stuffe, £3.05.00d'. The roots of two-year-old plants were dried, ground, and sieved to remove the epidermis and to separate the grades; then the powder was stored in barrels for three years before sale. Towards the end of the 18th century unsuccessful attempts were made to establish the growing of madder in England, but the Dutch monopoly was not broken until madder was displaced by synthetic alizarin in the 19th century.

Thomas Wright and John Cherrington both had fustic, but if Francis Wright or John Smart had any it was dismissed among the 'colouring stuffe' by their appraisers. Anne Smaldridge had 'halfe a hundred of shamesd fustic, 6s. 00d' in her dyehouse, and John Prenton of Chester had '2 loggs fusticke'. Old fustic was the wood of the tree *chlorophora tinctoria*, imported from the West Indies and South America. The Cuban was deemed the best, hence the alternative name, Cuba wood. For use it was chipped or rasped, so that John Prenton's logs and Anne Smaldridge's 'shamesd fustick' represent different stages in its preparation. Old fustic was the most important of the yellow dyestuffs. Its principle dye was morin, 3, 5, 7, 2', 4'-pentahydroxyflavone, and a minor one maclurin, 2, 4, 6, 3', 4'-pentahydroxybenzophenone. With an alum mordant morin gave yellow; with copperas, deep olive brown. Maclurin gave pale yellow, and a weak grey respectively, so that the overall effect of fustic was a yellow with alum, and a dark olive with copperas. The colours were fast to light and to milling with soap, although the yellow tended to go browner with light. Old fustic was much used in mixed colours, particularly to balance out the rusty colour of logwood mordanted with copperas to give a true black, but also for olives, browns and drabs. In the Stroud area it was used with indigo to give the green for billiards cloth.

Wright and Cherrington each had an unspecified weight of logwood. Anne Smaldridge had 200lbs. at £2, and Christopher Sturge of Frampton Cotterell, Gloucestershire, had half a hundredweight worth five shillings. The drop in price by a half between 1678 and 1754 no doubt reflects the increasing ease of importation. Logwood is the heartwood of *haematoxylon campechianum*, originally procured from Campeche Bay in Mexico by British privateers. It was claimed that the tree was established in Jamaica in 1715, and in later years this island with Honduras and San Domingo was the main source. The deep brown blocks of wood had to be chipped or rasped before use, and it was then watered and exposed to air to oxidise the haematoxylin present into the dye haematin, which is a pyran derivative. The last commercial load of logwood was imported from Jamaica in 1964.[56] With alum, logwood gave a blue, and with copperas grey to black. The black obtained with copperas was cheap, and had high tinctorial power and an even tone. It was widely used instead of the earlier copperas and galls as a cheap black, and it was less expensive if less durable than the black from woad, followed by an alum mordant, than madder and fustic. This was the main use of logwood until the 1960s. The use of logwood blues as a cheap rather unstable substitute for indigo, and attempts to pass off logwood blacks as woaded blacks led to a ban on its use, and various controls, the last of which were removed in 1662.

Wright had redwood at £1 per cwt.; Anne Smaldridge at £3 per cwt.; John Robinson of Chester in 1598 had 'Brassell' at £4, and John Prenton of Chester in 1638 'Brassell and Redwood at £4.06.08d' and a mill to grind Brassell at £2. Redwood was a term that encompassed the 'soluble' redwoods, brazilwood from *caesalpina braziliensis* (Brazil), peachwood, from *caesalpina echinata* (Mexico), and the 'insoluble' redwoods, sanderswood from *pterocarpus santalinus* (India and Madagascar), barwood from *baphia nitida* (Sierra Leone), and camwood from a similar species from West Africa. In the 17th century the term redwood was not used precisely, and usually referred to brazilwood, the only one distinguished apart from Anne Smaldridge's 'sanders'.

The main dye in soluble redwoods is brazilein, the same pyran derivative as the haematein in logwood, but with one phenolic group less. With alum as mordant a bluish-red is obtained, and with copperas, a more violet-grey colour, described as dark slate or claret. The colours were rather fugitive to soap and to light, and were principally used in mixtures, for example, with logwood and a mixed mordant of alum and copperas to give a dark purple, plum colour. The fastness could be improved by using a source of tannin (e.g., sumach) to fix the mordant to the cloth more firmly. The main dye of the insoluble redwoods was santalin, $C_{30}H_{24}O_9$, a pyran derivative related to brazilein and haematin, and with alum as mordant sanderswood gave an orange-red and with copperas maroon. These colours were rather faster to soap, but were fugitive to light, and again were used largely in mixtures. Two examples of the colours that could be produced are cinnamon from fustic and sanderswood with a little madder on an alum mordant, and dark brown from the same mixture with a mixed mordant of alum and copperas. Like logwood and fustic the dyestuffs were imported as logs and had to be chipped or rasped. In recent times this was done with a set of four blades mounted on a cast-iron disc, powered by a water-wheel. Without powered machinery chipping and rasping the very hard redwood must have been extremely heavy work.

Wright's appraisers listed 'Shumack and Galls' together. Cherrington's 'Sumack' was listed with his logwood, and his 'Gauls' with alum. Anne Smaldridge had 200lbs. of sumach at £1 4s. 0d. Thomas Haddock of Chester had galls at £3 8s. 0d. per hundredweight, and 70lbs. of 'Sumecke' at 9s. 3d. John Robinson of Chester had '1 quarter of gale . . .18s 08d.' Sumach is the tried and chopped leaves of *rhus* species. The preferred variety was Sicilian from *rhus coriaria*, which yielded up to 25 per cent. of tannin. A less satisfactory alternative was Venetian from *rhus cotinus*, yielding some 17 per cent. of tannin. The wood of *rhus cotinus* constituted the dyestuff young fustic.

Galls were a type of oak-apple, although the usual English variety was of little use. The best were Aleppo galls, which originated from insects of the *cynipidae* family puncturing the leaves and twigs of *quercus infectoria* and *quercus lusitanica*. The best blue galls yielded 50-60 per cent. gallotannic acid, which is a form of tannin. In each case the tannin was the material sought. Either material would give a black with copperas, and galls and copperas had been a source of cheap blacks long before the importation of logwood from America. The main use of both sumach and galls was to bind mordants more firmly to the cloth before the dye was applied, i.e., to improve the fastness, and this was principally necessary for the dyewoods. Thus sumach and copperas were used as a basis for a blue-black with logwood, a dark red drab with fustic, barwood, sanders and madder, and for a brownish drab with fustic.

Alum and copperas were the main mordants employed, the metal compounds used to form a coloured lake with the dye on the fibre. Alum is hydrated sodium (or potassium or ammonium) aluminium sulphate, and was obtained from aluminous shales worked for the purpose near Whitby (Yorkshire). The coal and iron pyrites ($FeS_2$) in the shales provided the heat and the source of oxides of sulphur respectively, to convert the alumino-silicate to aluminium sulphate. The heaps of many hundreds of tons were lixivated, ammonia in the form of stale urine added, and the alum crystallised out. For much of the period under review the manufacture was a royal monopoly and no alum was legally imported. In view of the importance of alum as a mordant, it is not surprising that all the detailed Wellington dyers' inventories list it, but it is remarkable that Ann Smalldridge had none.

Copperas is ferrous sulphate heptahydrate, $FeSO_4.7H_2O$, green vitriol, and, despite the name, nothing to do with copper. The term arose from the way that the word 'copperas' was used interchangeably with 'vitriol' for sulphates. 'English' copperas was ferrous sulphate, while 'Hungarian' was copper sulphate. Common usage degraded the term to refer only to the green copperas used for dyeing, tanning and making ink. Copperas was obtained particularly from North Kent where it was prepared by the 'ripening', i.e., the atmospheric oxidation and hydration of iron pyrites,

# INTRODUCTION

$FeS_2$, coal brasses, or fool's gold. The pyrites was laid some 2ft. deep in an open chamber 100ft. x 15ft. x 12ft. deep, and drained into a cistern with a capacity of 700 tuns. From time to time the liquor was evaporated to a small bulk and run into a cooler where twigs and branches were suspended, and as crystals formed on them they were lifted out and dried. Besides its use as a mordant, copperas was employed in the preparation of black ink.[57]

The only inventory to list 'pott ashes' is that of John Cherrington. Pott ash was a mild alkali used for scouring materials in cleansing, and for adjusting the pH of dye baths. It is a crude form of potassium carbonate obtained by extracting wood ash with water, filtering and evaporating the extract to dryness.[58]

## *Spinning and Weaving*[59]

'No country consumes more of the manufactures made of Hemp than our own', wrote John Campbell in 1774.[60] There were many parts of Britain which specialised in the manufacture of linen cloth of various kinds, among them the East Riding of Yorkshire, parts of Lincolnshire and Dorset, and the Warrington area. Some Shropshire linen was shipped down the Severn to Bristol,[61] although the extent of this trade is difficult to determine. It is clear from the evidence in this collection of inventories, however, that hemp and flax were grown on a considerable scale in North Telford, that spinning was a common occupation in many households, and that throughout the period there were weavers in the district who made into cloth the yarns spun in customers' homes.

Arthur Young noted when passing through Shropshire as late as 1776:

> Every cottager and every farmer has hemp: a farmer generally two acres, and a cottager all he can spare from potatoes and beans; they dress, spin, and weave it into cloth in the country.[62]

A map of Lilleshall of 1717 shows numerous hemp butts,[63] and there is abundant evidence in the inventories to show that both flax (*linum usitatissimum*) and hemp (*cannabis sativa*) were widely grown in North Telford. Some 156 inventories, 18.4 per cent. of the total, mention hemp, flax or tow, the latter being the short fibres separated out from the rest in the first stages of preparation. The growing of hemp and flax was spread evenly across the four parishes, but it appears that it was gradually diminishing during the period covered by the study. One hundred and sixteen of the inventories which mention hemp and flax were made before 1710, some 24.3 per cent. of those exhibited during that period. Only 40 were made between 1710 and 1750, a mere 10.8 per cent. of those appraised during those four decades.

Arthur Young suggested that most growers cultivated only small amounts of these crops, an impression confirmed by the inventories, although a few wealthy individuals were in possession of considerable quantities. Thomas Calcott in 1744 (*264*) had a growing crop of flax worth £30, and harvested hemp and flax worth £23, but these were quite exceptional amounts. Edward Harrington (*87*) in 1670 had 'hempe growing upon the ground', and an inventory of 1667 records hemp and flax both on the ground and in the house.

It is probable that flax was retted in pits on the holdings on which it was grown. John Stevenson (*58*) had 'hemp in watering'. It was then scutched by hand, probably with tools called tewtaws or tewtors, mentioned in several inventories. There is no evidence that there were ever any water-powered scutching mills in the district, as there were in Ulster and other specialist linen-producing regions. The fibres were then combed or heckled to separate the long, finer fibres from the short coarse ones. Several inventories among them that of Richard Darwall of Dawley (*4*) mention heckells or hackles, the comb-like tools used for this task. The short fibres when separated were called the *tow* yarns, and the hemp or flax from which they had been removed was said to have been *towed* or *dressed*. The inventory of William Minshall (*109*) mentions 30lbs. of 'drest' hemp worth 12s. 6d., and 40lbs. of 'drest' flax worth 7s. 8d., and that of Joseph Wolley (*68*) includes 'flax towed in ye House'. William Charlton (*235*) had 'hemp and flax, drest and undrest', and Richard Glover (*167*) had 'hemp in the rough, tewtored and untewtarded'. Carding was also carried on in some households. Richard Randle (*137*) had a pair of wool cards and also a pair for noggen or linen.

Spinning wheels were among the most common items of household equipment in the region. They are mentioned on 157, or 18.5 per cent. of the inventories, and appear to have become more common in the latter part of the period than earlier. They are recorded on 61 inventories, or 12.8 per cent. of the total, between 1660 and 1700, and on 96, or 26.0 per cent. of the total, in the first 50 years of the 18th century. They were to be found in the households of all social classes. Peter Langley, a rich gentleman, had 'two little wheels' with a quite exceptional value of £1 5s. 0d. Wheels are also mentioned in some of the poorest households in the district. They occur in the inventories of yeomen, dyers, wheelwrights, blacksmiths, carpenters, and colliers. It seems that the practice of raising small crops of hemp or flax, dressing it, and spinning yarn from it was common among all social groups. The inventory of Basil Richards (*1*) is one of many which includes 'flax and hempe in the house, spune and in yarne'. Many households had more than one wheel, and in some inventories a distinction is made between different types: long wheels, little wheels, short wheels, great wheels, and small wheels. It would appear that long, large or great wheels were used for spinning wool, and small, little or short wheels for spinning hemp or flax. Reels are mentioned, as on the inventory of Robert Shelton in 1717 (*73*), but it is uncertain whether they were spools, receptacles for yarn spun on wheels, or reels used as alternatives to the spinning wheel. *Yarwingles,* also called yarnwinds or earwingles, are mentioned on several inventories, and were used for winding skeins of yarn into balls. Catherine North in 1732 had 'two pairs off blades for winding yarn'. In the 17th century the value of a spinning wheel averaged 1s. 6d., with little difference between the two types, but after 1700 the larger wheels tended to be valued more highly.

Looms are almost unknown in the district except in the households of weavers, and it seems likely that the yarn woven by people in their own homes was normally taken to a specialist weaver to be woven into cloth. It should be noted that the word 'loom' sometimes means a bucket. One inventory (*37*) includes a loom among the coopery ware, and another (*95*) lists a 'brewing loom', and the meaning is usually obvious from the context. There are 23 inventories of weavers, websters or others who appear to have made their livings by weaving. They occur throughout the period covered by the inventories, and are to be found in all of the four parishes. Four were in Ketley and four in Hadley, and they tended to congregate in squatter settlements. Certainly weaving was not an essentially urban trade. There is no sign at all of concentration in the town of Wellington. Two of the weavers had equipment for working both wool and linen, and four for linen only, but the majority of inventories do not reveal the types of fabric made. Eleven weavers had two looms, two had only one, four had three, and one had six. Five do not specify the number. On some inventories other pieces of equipment are mentioned. A *warping bar* was a length of wood, usually with posts at each end, around which yarn was woven, and was used for measuring yarn when it was given to the weaver. *Gears* are mentioned on 15 of the weavers' inventories. They were small wires through which the warp was passed in a loom, which separated it into two sets to allow the shuttle to pass between alternate threads. John Smith of Admaston (*298*) had separate gears for woollen and linen weaving. Four inventories mention *warping troughs.* It is possble that these were used for scouring, for removing natural grease from the wool by steeping it in a mixture of soap and urine, but it is more likely that they were for sizing the warp, by dipping it in a solution of glue and water before fixing it to the loom. One weaver had treadles, which were foot peddles used to alter the pattern of the weave. Only five had spinning wheels.

Most weavers were quite poor. Nineteen of the 23 had possessions worth less than £20, and of 13 whose inventories specify the numbers of rooms in their houses, eight had four rooms or less. With such a small sample, it is difficult to make judgements about values at different periods, but it is interesting that values were lowest between 1690 and 1710, the period when wages in the West of England woollen industry were very depressed.[64] Fifteen weavers were concerned to a greater or lesser extent with farming, although seven of them had less than five animals each, and no crops. Only one appears to have been farming on any significant scale.

Richard Higgins of Ketley, who died in 1676 with possessions worth £45 6s. 2d., was described on his inventory as a clothier. He may have been some kind of wholesaler of locally-produced fabrics, but he had no stock of cloth, and his inventory suggests that he made his living chiefly by farming. He had only one hearth in 1672 which does not suggest great affluence.

*Food and Clothing*

Inventories survive for six millers or milners,[65] one of whom, Thomas Bickley (*139*) is described as a servant of the miller at Walcot, and had an estate worth less than five pounds. The other five all left possessions worth between £20 and £50. Three were from Lilleshall parish, where there were two water-mills on the brook which drained in a north-westerly direction from the vicinity of the abbey towards the River Strine.[66] The other two millers were both members of the Cope family from Allscott mill on the River Tern in Wrockwardine parish. This mill was in existence as early as the reign of Henry II. In 1719 a lease which involved a woollen draper and a cloth dresser from Manchester described it as a water corn-mill and fulling mill, and the parish register in 1700 describes John Cope of Allscott as a fuller. Deeds of the 1740s still refer to a fulling mill at Allscott, but by the end of the century it was used for dressing leather as well as for grinding grain.[67] All of the millers except Thomas Bickley were engaged in farming, five having cows, five keeping pigs, and three having growing corn. Their houses were generally well furnished, and Bickley even had some books.

All of the five butchers for whom inventories are available lived in Wellington. The value of their possessions ranged from £27 to £116, placing them well above the average level of wealth for tradesmen. Only one of them, John Steventon, who died in 1746-47, with six cows and 35 sheep among his possessions, seems to have been actively involved in farming. His seven sides of bacon appear to be the only possible reference in any of the inventories to butchers' stock. His tools were valued at 10s., but were not detailed. Thomas Reynolds (*113*) had tools worth only 3s., which included gambrells (or cambrels), bent pieces of iron used for hanging meat, knives, and settlesses, which in butchers' shops were probably benches used for cutting up meat.

There were inventories for only two bakers, both of whom lived in Wellington. Both appear to have made their livings entirely from their trade, and both were quite poor. The possessions of Abraham Gears, who died in 1691, were worth less than five pounds. John Hicks (*197*) had an estate worth £49 15s. 0d., but of that £40 was made up of debts. He appears to have used faggots as the fuel for his oven, even in a parish where coal was easily and cheaply obtainable.

The inventories of nine tailors survive, distributed evenly throughout the period. Seven lived in Wellington, and one of those who did not, John Key of Lilleshall, seems to have gained his living by farming rather than by making clothes. Three of the Wellington tailors were called Jackson and were probably related. None of the inventories mentions stocks of cloth, suggesting that customers usually provided their own materials. Apart from Key, the tailors seem to have gained their livings from their trade, and not to have been concerned on any significant scale with by-employments, although Richard Jackson the Elder (*129*) had two cows and crops of wheat and barley. Tools are rarely mentioned, but the inventory of William Jackson (*140*) itemises two pressing irons and two pairs of shears.

Inventories survive for three feltmakers, who produced materials for hat-making and possibly made hats themselves, and one hatter. The wealthiest was John Lodge (*134*) whose possessions were valued at £87 18s. 0d. He had debts totalling £65 owing to him, but the inventory gives no indications of how he worked. Thomas Lodge (*136*) had possessions worth only £9 18s. 0d., but these seem to have consisted entirely of his tools and stocks, except for a bed, trunk and chest. He had a brass pot and an old one-eyed horse with its gears, which were presumably used to grind wool to make felt. He had tools worth 14s., and a stock of wool-made hats worth four pounds. The hatter, Edward Jones, whose inventory was made in 1662–63, had 24 felt hats worth £2 8s. 0d., and basons and blocks which he used in his shop. The presence of wool and a mare suggest that he also may have made felt with horse-driven apparatus. With possessions valued at only £11 19s. 8d. he was obviously only moderately prosperous.

## *Craftsmen in Metal*[68]

There are inventories for 21 blacksmiths spread evenly throughout the period under review. Sixteen were from Wellington, many of them from premises alongside Watling Street. They were not men of great wealth, only one having an estate worth more than £100, and four having possessions worth less than ten pounds. John Bromley of Watling Street (*181*), who died in 1728 with possessions worth less than £7, had tools worth more than £2, a two-room house with an adjoining brewhouse, and a bed and two tables in 'the turnpike house'. It would seem likely that he was the first collector of tolls at the *Buck's Head* cross-roads, Watling

Street, after the road from Shrewsbury to Ivetsey Bank and Shifnal was brought under the control of a turnpike trust in 1725–26.[69] The inventory of Francis Ore (*116*) contains no household possessions but is simply a list of tools, worth less than two pounds. Among the obvious hammers, shears, files, and tongs, were a 'shoo box', which contained horseshoe nails, and would be used for holding tools when shoeing, and a rubber file, a tool used for rubbing scale off metal to see what colour it had turned in order to establish its temperature before working it. The two 'naile persors' were bradawls, used for starting screw-holes. A jack windlass was a pulley and tackle which enabled one person to lift heavy weights. A screw plate was used to put a thread on screws. A 'sette' was either a cold sett, which enabled a smith to cut a nick in cold metal prior to breaking it, or a hot sett, which enabled him to cut his metal when it was heated. The two 'blood strikes' for the time being defy definition. The inventory of William Cheese (*124*) reveals that his iron was obtained from a Mr. Boycott to whom he owed eighteen pounds. Silvenus Adams (*33*) of Lilleshall was one of the wealthier smiths, with possessions worth over sixty-three pounds. He had five cows and six sheep, as well as four horses and a house, with some indications of comfort. His tools and iron were worth £9, and included a beckhorn, the pointed end of an anvil, and three 'dizlees', which were possibly adzes. The Peate family of Watling Street appear to have been a dynasty of blacksmiths. The inventories of George, of 1686–87, and of John, of 1687, are of no particular interest, but that of Francis Peate (*208*), taken in 1746, is one of the few for which the house can be precisely identified. He lived at the *Seven Stars* inn alongside Watling Street in the township of Hadley. On what would appear to have been a quite sizeable farm, he kept eight cows, and grew wheat, oats and hay, as well as keeping a hive of bees. His house seems to have been too small to provide accommodation for travellers, but the presence of £3 worth of ale and beer confirms that he did keep an inn. His tools included two anvils, and two pairs of bellows, tongs, punches, hammers, pincers, a 'voice', presumably a vice, a 'boltsteet' or bolster, which was a wide-bladed chisel, a 'dogg', which was a type of clamp, and a bicken or beckhorn. James Morris (*131*) was a whitesmith, one who made highly finished or polished wrought-iron or steel goods. He had possessions worth £18 13s. 0d., among which were his tools and stock of unworked iron and steel assessed at £6, and finished goods in his shop worth one pound ten shillings.

## Craftsmen in Wood

There are inventories for eight carpenters and joiners, drawn from all four parishes. Half of them had estates worth between £20 and £50, and three left possessions worth less than ten pounds. The wealthiest was

John Duddell of Dawley (*24*), whose inventory is of quite exceptional interest for the wealth of detail it reveals on the furnishings of a tradesman's house. In his workshop Duddell had tools worth £6 and boards worth ten shillings. He probably farmed several acres since he kept five cows, two pigs, and four horses. Another John Duddell (*19*), who died in 1724, may have been his father, since the houses described on the two inventories are similar, and Pawn Hatch could well have been regarded as part of the loosely-defined area called Pool Hill. The elder Duddell's inventory includes three corves worth seven pounds. A corve was in origin a basket in which coal was lifted out of a pit, but in Shropshire well before the end of the 18th century it was a name applied to a railway wagon in which coal was carried. It is possible that Duddell built wagons for use on local colliery railways. Five of the carpenters kept cows, three had pigs, and one kept sheep. Robert Allen (*259*), a joiner who lived in the squatter settlement of Long Lane, whose goods were valued at nearly £35, occupied a tiny cottage with one room downstairs, a chamber above, and a small buttery adjoining. He had tools worth 10s., but grew corn, peas, oats and barley, kept nine cows, four horses, and two pigs, and had a cheese press in his house. Francis Light, of Lilleshall (*50*), had possessions worth less than £10, but he, too, was a farmer as well as a carpenter, having 'two poor old cows' and 'corn sowd on the ground'. William Minshall (*109*) was a wealthy farmer, but he had an interesting set of carpenters' tools: three axes, two bills, a hatchet, four augers, a pair of compasses, a gouge, three chisels, a spokeshave, a drawing knife, a whimble brace and bit, two pairs of pincers, three hammers, and a saw.

Barrels and 'coopery' or 'cowpery' ware are mentioned in most inventories, but only two inventories for coopers survive. John Beddow in 1733 was very wealthy, with possessions worth £244 16s. 0d., and much of his wealth was concentrated in his trade since he had wood and hoops worth £100, but the inventory is disappointingly lacking in detail. Richard Aston of Muxton in 1728 was by contrast very poor, with an estate worth just under £8, of which cattle comprised over seven pounds.

There are inventories for two wheelwrights, one of which, that of William Pearce, reveals little of interest. Humphrey Vernon (*57*) of Lilleshall, whose possessions were valued at £10 13s. 7d., lived in a cottage consisting of house place, chamber and buttery on the ground floor, with sufficient space 'above stairs' for only one bed. He had tools worth 10s., a pig and two cows, and two spinning wheels. Like many craftsmen in the district, he obviously made his living from a variety of sources.

## *Other Crafts*

The solitary ropemaker recorded in the district was Thomas Fletcher (*96*), whose estate was valued at £11 12s. 9d., of which £5 was made up of debts owing to him. His house consisted of one main room, with two chambers above. He had a workshop with tools worth 5s., and three and a half stone of hemp worth 7s. 6d., which was doubtless tow.

The making of clay tobacco pipes was well established in Broseley in the period under review, but there is only one inventory surviving for a pipemaker living in North Telford. William Evans (*122*) of Wellington, who died in 1692-93, had possessions worth just over £12, among which his working tools and clay were valued at just over one pound.

One inventory survives for a stone cutter, Robert Stanley (*202*) of Wellington, who had goods worth £6 9s. 0d. when he died. His unworked stone was worth 15s., but his working tools were worth only two shillings.

Edward Aston, whose inventory was made in 1708-9 (*67*), was a 'lymeman', one who tended a lime kiln. As might be expected he came from Lilleshall parish, but from Muxton at the opposite end of the parish from the limestone quarries. His estate was worth £12 15s. 6d., of which total nine guineas was the value of a small herd of cattle.

## Innkeepers and Horsekeepers

There are inventories for seven innkeepers, all of them in the parish of Wellington. They were all relatively wealthy, all having possessions worth more than £50, although debts owed by James Massey (*201*) brought the net value of his inventory below that figure. Rowland Goole (*147*), of Watling Street, whose inventory taken in 1703 included the 'Swan Chambre', probably kept the *Swan* inn, which apparently had 16 rooms. His goods were valued at over £700, by far the largest innkeepers's estate, although over £400 was in the form of debts. He was involved in farming on a considerable scale, growing wheat, oats, peas and beans, and keeping cows, horses, and pigs. The size and importance of the inn is indicated by the numbers of utensils in the kitchen; pewter worth £9 10s. 0d., including seven dozen plates, by the 16 hogsheads of beer in the cellar, worth £35, by the 40 pairs of sheets, worth £20, and by silverware valued at the same amount. The *Seven Stars*, the establishment of Francis Peate (*208*) was more modest, and Peate gained his living as a blacksmith as well as from keeping the inn. William Barker (*172*) of Watling Street had 14 horses with their gears, worth £38, but apart from growing a little corn, he was not involved in farming, so it would appear that he probably hired out the horses. James Massey (*201*) also of Watling Street, had corn worth £8, barley worth £11, and hay worth £20, which were doubtless for the sustenance of travellers' horses. Four of the innkeepers thus had establishments on Watling Street. The other three were all members of the Judgson family, and appear to have lived at the *Crown* inn, in the centre of Wellington.[70]

John Judgson I and his wife Elizabeth had two daughters and four sons, baptised between 1682 and 1697. John Judgson I (*146*) died in 1708, his possessions being valued at £65 10s. 8d. The *Crown* then consisted of a little parlour, a parlour chamber, kitchen chamber and the 'Crown Chamber', some lofts, some cellars, a room above them, and a kitchen. Judgson had a small collection of beasts, a bullock, a cow in calf, three old horses, and six pigs, with hay worth £7 in a barn. There were 12 beds in the house, and the 'drinke in the Cellar' was worth eight pounds. Elizabeth Judgson (*159*) survived her husband by seven years. Her inventory taken in January 1715-16 and valued at £79 13s. 4d., suggests that the inn had been extended. There was a parlour, probably the 'little parlour' of 1708, a parlour chamber, a kitchen chamber, the Crown Chamber, some garrets (doubtless the lofts of 1708), some cellars, and, in addition, a 'New Roome'. There was now hay worth £20 in the barns, but only one cow with a calf, one horse, and one mare. There were still 12 beds, but the value of linen in the house had increased from £5 to £15. The furnishings of the Crown Chamber had been improved. There were still, as in 1708, two beds, a looking-glass, two tables, two forms, and a chest, but the 10 stools had been replaced by six green cloth chairs. The *Crown* inn descended to Elizabeth's son, William, who had been baptised in 1691, and died in 1725, with an estate worth £109 18s. 6d. (*171*). The new room was known by 1725 as the 'New Parlour'. A closet had been constructed adjacent to the kitchen chamber, and a milkhouse and stable added to the outbuildings. There were now 11 beds in the house. The Crown Chamber was furnished in the same way as in 1715, but the New Chamber, previously sparsely equipped, was now the best room in the house, with a feather bed, a clock, a table, a screen, six leather chairs, two small tables, and a warming pan. The value of ale, beer and cider in the cellar was £15 10s. 0d., and the presence of bags of hops in two of the best rooms suggests that Judgson had been brewing on a considerable scale, and possibly that he lacked storage space, although guests may have welcomed the aroma of hops as they slept.

John Walker (*203*) is not described on his inventory as an innkeeper, but the Forester Accounts (*71*) show that he leased the *Talbot*. He brewed on a considerable scale, and seems to have been active in the cheese trade, but his inventory does not suggest that he provided accommodation for travellers.

There are two inventories for maltsters, one of which appears to be for a man who had given up the trade. The other maltster, Nicholas Broxton, of Wellington, was clearly still active, but since his total possessions were valued at only just over £17, and he had only 1½ strikes of grain in his malthouse, he was operating on a much smaller scale than many people who made malt in connection with other activities.

Ten inventories relate to people who seem to have been engaged in carrying goods in carts of wagons or on packhorses. William Smith of Watling Street (*81*) in 1659 had nine nags and mares with pack saddles, and 15 three-year-old colts, and while he also kept cattle and sheep and grew crops, it seems that part at least of his living came from haulage. Another William Smith, who died in 1680, was described as a carrier, and had 12 pack horses, and was perhaps his descendant. Thomas Fieldhouse (*143*) of Ketley had 15 horses worth, with their saddles, gears and backbands, a total of thirty-five pounds. Like Smith, he had cattle and crops, and it would seem that most of those who worked wagons or packhorses also farmed. A Wellington inventory of 1728 includes four cart mares worth £15, and a few cows and some grain. There were two carriers in Wrockwardine Wood, probably gaining their livings from the transport of coal. Richard Vickers in 1704 (*240*) had two aged horses and their gears to carry coal, while in 1714–15 Allen Pickering (*244*) appears to have made his living with a wagon. Pack-saddles appear on several other inventories, most of them those for wealthy farmers, but also on those of the more prosperous Wellington traders, two mercers, a maltster and a tanner.

## The Colliers[72]

Mining activities were established in the northern part of the Coalbrookdale coalfield well before 1660, but only 14 miners' inventories survive from the period under review, only three of them from before 1700, and none of them from the parish of Lilleshall. Although the study of the South Telford parishes is far from complete, it is already clear that there were many more miners in Madeley and Broseley in this period. It is probable that transport difficulties severely restricted the growth of mining in the northern part of the coalfield until the mid-18th century when there was a rapid expansion owing to the demands of the new ironworks at Ketley and Horsehay.[73]

The outstanding coalmaster of the period was Richard Hartshorne,[74] who leased mines in the manors of Ketley, Wombridge, Little Wenlock, Little Dawley and Great Dawley, built a railway from Little Wenlock to the Severn, was a pioneer in the use of iron railway wheels, operated the Kingley Wich salt works, and was one of the first users of steam engines in Shropshire. He died in 1733 and his will was proved at Canterbury,[75] but the inventory of his wife, Jane, who died in 1737 (*194*) provides important information on the family's fortunes. The Hartshornes had two houses less than three miles apart, Ketley Bank House, which bears their initials RJH and the date 1721, and a house in Watling Street, probably the Old Hall. Jane Hartshorne's inventory was valued at £546 14s. 0d. She was involved in coal and iron mining in Great Dawley where she controlled at least five pits in the Brandlee area, most of which appear to have taken their names from the charter masters or sub-contractors who operated them. The value of stock and equipment in the Brandlee area was a little over seventy pounds. In the manor of Ketley she was mining ore for

# INTRODUCTION

Mr. Ford, presumably Richard Ford of the Coalbrookdale, in Haines's wood. Elsewhere in Ketley were pits worked by five charter masters. Stock and equipment in the area was valued at £304 4s. 6d., of which £200 was the value of a Newcomen steam-pumping engine, the 'fire engine', one of at least two which the Coalbrookdale Company had supplied to Richard Hartshorne.[76] Jane Hartshorne also had mines at Snedshill and Hollinswood in the township of Priorslee on the manor of the Jerningham family, Earls of Stafford, but their value was rather less than that of the Dawley or Ketley mines. It is clear that she worked fewer mines than her husband had done at the height of his influence. The inventory reveals nothing that is remarkable about methods of mining, except for the existence of the steam engines, which was known from other sources, but which is, nevertheless, an unusual item on a probate inventory. Most of the pits were worked with horse gins, and the usual lamps, trunks, water buckets and ropes were to be found around the headstocks. Coal is rarely valued in Telford inventories, but that belonging to Jane Hartshorne was calculated to be worth 2s. 3d. or 2s. 6d. a stack, while iron ore was about £1 a dozen.

Richard Hartshorne's date and place of birth are unknown, but it is not unlikely that Walter Hartshorne of Malins Lee (*12*), whose will was proved in 1696 was his father. His inventory valued at £120 3s. 4d. was typical of that of a yeoman collier, working in a totally different way from his son. He had cows, sheep, horses, and pigs worth £49, farming implements worth £6, and growing crops of the same value. The 'tools and working gear' of his colliery were by contrast worth only £5, and the stock of coals on the pit bank, £20. He lived in a house with six rooms, a cellar and a cock loft, the 'dining room' perhaps indicating some pretensions to luxury. He had brewing vessels, a spinning wheel, and 20 small cheeses on shelves in a cheese chamber, where there were also four beds. His desk, where one may presume he kept his account books, was situated in the parlour chamber, which with its feather bed and joined hanging press appears to have been the best furnished room in the house.

Most other colliers were, like Walter Hartshorne, involved in dairy farming. Of the 14 whose inventories survive, 12 had dairy cows, 10 kept pigs, eight had sheep, and six were growing grain. Three had dairy equipment, five possessed brewing apparatus, and five had spinning wheels. Ten totalled less than fifty pounds. The wealthiest, if Jane Hartshorne is excluded, was George Hewlett of Dawley, who left an estate worth £365, of which £350 was out at interest. He could well have been an elderly man living on savings. Richard Lumas (*242*) left possessions worth £93 14s. 3d., with farming stock worth over £50, but although he is described as a master collier his inventory includes no mining equipment or stocks of coal or iron ore.

Edward Darrell of Holywell in Little Dawley (*21*), who died in 1726, was a ground collier. He had no mining equipment except a few 'working tools' itemised with household utensils. He had one cow, which probably found pasture in the 'slang' around his tiny cottage on Holywell Lane. It was probably this Edward Darrell from whom Abraham Darby I obtained coal in 1709 when he first began to use coke for smelting iron ore at the Coalbrookdale furnace. Darby's accounts show that Edward Darrell was also employed to 'charck' coals (i.e., to make coke) and to clear ditches.[77]

*Farming*

Agriculture was the dominant acitivy in North Telford in the period under review, but the word 'farmer' appears on none of the inventories for the district before 1750. Men engaged in agriculture were usually called 'yeomen' or 'husbandmen', or were not named as having any occupation. These terms like 'gentlemen', were apparently marks of social status rather than descriptions of economic functions. The values of the estates of gentlemen varied between £4 19s. 0d. and £1,327; of yeomen between £1 18s. 0d. and £1,032, and husbandmen between £1 10s. 0d. and £127. Husbandmen were in general less wealthy than yeoman, but there was a considerable overlap between the two groups. There are 17 inventories of men described as 'labourers'. The richest had possessions worth £28, and 11 were valued at less than ten pounds. One of them, William Bate (*51*) was described as a thatcher on his will. The labourers certainly did not rely entirely upon working for wages for their livings.[78] Six kept cattle, of whom three also had dairy equipment, four had a horse, three kept pigs, and one had sheep. Two grew corn, and one had a harrow for its cultivation. Two had spinning wheels, one had malt, and two had vessels for brewing. The term 'labourer' like 'yeoman' or 'gent' was a mark of status, not of occupation. A labourer was one below the grade of a husbandman, and was likely to be poorer, although he might well keep his own herds, grow his own crops and work at a trade.

Very many people in North Telford combined farming with some other activity. Some, like Walter Hartshorne the collier (*12*) farmed on a considerable scale, while very many weavers, miners or blacksmiths kept a pig or a cow and grew a little corn or flax. Agriculture was so much the basis of local economy that it is impossible in practice to separate 'farmers' from other sections of the community. The analysis which follows is based on agricultural activities rather than on a particular group of people.[79]

The most common agricultural activity was the keeping of cattle. Five hundred and sixteen, or 60.1 per cent. of the inventories include cattle of some kind, and on 466 of them it is possible to calculate the size of the herds. Table XV shows the sizes of herd revealed by these

## TABLE XIV

### Farming and status

|  | Dawley | Lilleshall | Wellington | Wrockwardine | Totals |
|---|---|---|---|---|---|
| Gentlemen and Esquires | 3 | 4 | 10 | 4 | 21 |
| Yeomen | 15 | 35 | 31 | 43 | 124 |
| Husbandmen | 4 | 2 | 5 | 7 | 18 |
| Men apparently making their livings primarily by farming | 12 | 40 | 57 | 42 | 151 |
| Women apparently making livings primarily by farming | 4 | 13 | 10 | 12 | 39 |
| Totals | 38 | 94 | 113 | 108 | 353 |

## TABLE XV

### Size of herds of cattle

|  | Dawley | Lilleshall | Wellington | Wrockwardine | Totals |
|---|---|---|---|---|---|
| (a) Cows in milk |  |  |  |  |  |
| 1660–9 | 4.8 | 4.4 | 3.47 | 3.62 | 3.94 |
| 1670–9 | 4.3 | 3.9 | 3.42 | 5.6 | 4.02 |
| 1680–9 | 4.3 | 5.4 | 3.6 | 4.5 | 4.53 |
| 1690–9 | 3.25 | 9.4 | 3.2 | 4.5 | 4.40 |
| 1700–9 | 2 | 6.7 | 2.8 | 5.3 | 4.59 |
| 1710–9 | 3.7 | 4.9 | 4.75 | 6.2 | 4.95 |
| 1720–9 | 3.3 | 3.25 | 3.9 | 4.1 | 3.78 |
| 1730–9 | 3.2 | 4.8 | 3.1 | 4.7 | 4.03 |
| 1740–9 | 2.9 | 6 | 3.2 | 7.6 | 4.49 |
| (b) All cattle |  |  |  |  |  |
| 1660–9 | 9.7 | 9.8 | 7.4 | 8.5 | 8.6 |
| 1670–9 | 12 | 7.6 | 7.75 | 14.0 | 9.09 |
| 1680–9 | 10.7 | 15.8 | 8.2 | 12.05 | 11.43 |
| 1690–9 | 15.75 | 23.4 | 8.3 | 11.9 | 12.38 |
| 1700–9 | 4.5 | 16.6 | 7.8 | 15.4 | 12.11 |
| 1710–9 | 5.7 | 10.9 | 9.0 | 14.5 | 10.05 |
| 1720–9 | 7.6 | 10.75 | 9.9 | 9.4 | 9.13 |
| 1730–9 | 7.0 | 11.1 | 6.7 | 11.3 | 9.25 |
| 1740–9 | 7.4 | 25.0 | 8.35 | 21.8 | 12.49 |

inventories. The numbers, both of cows in milk and of cattle of all sorts in each herd grew steadily between 1660 and 1710. The mean size of herds increased from 8.6 in the 1660s to 12.11 in the first decade of the 18th century. The median size of herds in the much wider region of north Shropshire was 9.0 in the 1690s.[80] The number of cows in milk rose from 3.94 to 4.59, and continued to rise to 4.95 in the second decade of the 18th century. There appears to have been a decline in the size of herds in the 1720s, when the mean size fell to 9.13, and the mean number of cows in milk to 3.78. Both the size of herds and the number of dairy cows rose again during the 1730s and 1740s. The large size of the samples suggests that this was a real fall. In the case of the dairy cows the fall occurs in each of the four parishes between the 1710s and the 1720s, although in the total size of herds, the decline is concentrated in Wrockwardine and Lilleshall where the farms appear to have been larger than in Dawley and Wellington. Table XV also demonstrates differences between the agriculture of the four parishes. In the 17th century herds in Wellington were appreciably smaller than those in the other three parishes, probably because a significant proportion of cows were kept by town tradesmen who had other sources of income. After 1700 the size of herds in Dawley dropped to levels similar to or below those in Wellington, perhaps reflecting a growth in mining activity in that parish.

Table XVI, which indicates the mean values of cows in milk, suggests a gradual upward movement over the period, from £2 7s. 1d. in the 1660s to a little over £3 in the 1730s, with a fall to slightly below £3 in the 1740s. There was a trough in the first decade of the 18th century when the lowest values of the whole 90 years were recorded. The highest values for individual cows recorded were in the region of £4 6s. 0d. Variations in prices between the parishes were not especially significant. The lowest values were recorded in Dawley, one of many indications that farming on the coal measures was less prosperous than elsewhere, but they are only slightly below those recorded in Wrockwardine and Lilleshall. Somewhat surprisingly the highest values were recorded in Wellington where the average size of herd was lowest.

Many inventories give interesting pictures of dairy herds, indicating the number of young cows and calves as well as the cows in milk. Of these 'followers' are simply categorised as 'young beasts' or 'the young cattle', but many inventories distinguish between the various groups. Among those which are of particular interest in this respect are *17, 25, 26, 31, 47, 48, 53, 55, 58, 72, 109, 130, 154, 169, 212, 221, 231, 232, 233, 236* and *243*. The word 'calf' could obviously mean a beast which had just been born or a weaned animal born in the year when the inventory was taken, possibly as old as 11 months. Values are thus of little consequence. Most calves were reckoned to be worth less than one pound, with

## TABLE XVI

### Mean values of dairy cows

|  | Dawley | Lilleshall | Welling-ton | Wrock-wardine | Mean | Number of herds |
|---|---|---|---|---|---|---|
|  | £ s. d. | £ s. d. | £ s. d. | £ s. d. | £ s. d. |  |
| 1660–9 | 1 15 0 | 2 15 7 | 2 4 2 | 2 4 9 | 2 7 1 | 19 |
| 1670–9 | 2 6 8 | 2 18 6 | 2 13 1 | 2 13 2 | 2 14 0 | 23 |
| 1680–9 | — | 2 4 4 | 2 4 4 | 2 3 2 | 2 4 0 | 37 |
| 1690–9 | 2 3 4 | 2 2 2 | 2 4 10 | 2 17 9 | 2 9 4 | 16 |
| 1700–9 | 2 6 8 | 2 3 6 | 2 8 6 | 2 1 11 | 2 4 6 | 22 |
| 1710–9 | 2 10 6 | 2 15 0 | 3 4 1 | 2 10 0 | 2 18 4 | 15 |
| 1720–9 | 2 7 10 | 2 7 6 | 2 14 9 | 2 10 6 | 2 11 5 | 23 |
| 1730–9 | 3 2 2 | 3 0 0 | 3 6 7 | 2 11 8 | 3 0 4 | 11 |
| 1740–9 | 2 13 4 | 3 10 0 | 2 19 5 | 2 16 8 | 2 18 4 | 14 |
| Parish mean | 2 7 11 | 2 9 6 | 2 12 9 | 2 8 8 | 2 10 5 |  |
| Herds | 19 | 46 | 70 | 45 | — | 180 |

## TABLE XVII

### Inventories listing cattle

|  | Dawley | Lilleshall | Welling-ton | Wrock-wardine | Total |
|---|---|---|---|---|---|
| 1660–9 | 11 | 10 | 18 | 15 | 54 |
| 1670–9 | 4 | 17 | 26 | 11 | 58 |
| 1680–9 | 3 | 25 | 24 | 25 | 77 |
| 1690–9 | 4 | 6 | 19 | 16 | 45 |
| 1700–9 | 4 | 25 | 31 | 13 | 73 |
| 1710–9 | 7 | 15 | 22 | 6 | — |
| 1720–9 | 18 | 12 | 26 | 21 | 77 |
| 1730–9 | 6 | 15 | 11 | 13 | 45 |
| 1740–9 | 6 | 2 | 18 | 11 | 37 |
| Totals | 63 | 127 | 192 | 131 | 516 |
| Number with hay and cattle | 25 | 66 | 97 | 55 | 243 |
| Proportion with hay as well well as cattle | 39.68 | 51.97 | 49.74 | 41.98 | 47.09 |

the lowest values recorded being 4s. 0d. in Dawley, 6s. 8d. in Lilleshall, 2s. 6d. in Wellington, and 3s. 4d. in Wrockwardine. Some inventories place an exceptional value on individual calves, with one being priced at £2 5s. 0d., and another at three pounds. Yearlings, cows born in the previous spring or summer are separately priced on 97 inventories, on which the mean value was £1 1s. 0d., with extremes of 10s. and £2 5s. 0d. Two-year-old cattle or twinters, those born in the season before the yearlings and which had been kept for two winters (hence, 'twinters') were naturally valued more highly. The mean value over the whole period based on 87 inventories was £1 14s. 5d. between extremes of 15s. and four pounds. The word 'heifer' is used less commonly than the terms yearling and twinter. Bulls appear on many inventories, but are individually appraised on only 12, on which the mean value is £1 16s. 0d., between extremes of £1 and £5. There are few indications that signficant numbers of cattle were kept for beef. Bullocks appear on some inventories, but the word was synonymous with oxen, and the high values of some of them suggest strongly that they were draught animals.

The inventories give only a few indications of the types of cattle kept in the district. Probably, as in the dairies of the Wheatland in the mid-19th century,[81] indifferent cattle predominated, cows which would produce the most butter or cheese at the least cost. Rowland Griffiths of Walcott (*85*) had black cows, probably of Welsh origin. John Hill (*155*) in 1712 had a white cow. Jane Eastop (*164*) of Ketley Wood had a red cow and a pied cow, perhaps typical of the mixed breeds of the district. There are few indications of the ages to which cattle were kept, but an inventory of 1703 lists a 13-year-old cow worth £2 10s. 0d., rather more than the mean value of dairy cows for the decade. Mary Cade (*35*) of Lilleshall in 1664 had let out one of her two cows, and interest was due upon it. Descriptions of the condition of cattle are rare, but in the bad year of 1685 one Wellington inventory included 'three cows being by reason of scarcity of fodder very poor'.

Hay was the normal winter fodder for cattle. It is recorded on 47 per cent. of the inventories which include cattle. The proportion is reasonably constant between 40 and 53 per cent. throughout the period, and there is little variation between the parishes (see Table XVII). In Lilleshall with its larger farms, 51.97 per cent. of the inventories with cattle have hay. The lowest proportion was in Dawley with 39.68 per. cent. Hay was often kept by those who farmed on a very small scale, as well as by substantial farmers like Robert Shelton (*73*), whose inventory included hay to the value of fifteen pounds. Rowland Goole (*147*), farmer and innkeeper had 14 trusses of hay worth £14 in 1703. Hay was usually kept in barns, often on tallants or tallets, lofts created with boards in barn roofs. James Spender (*80*) had 'hay in the Carthouse Tallant'. There are several references to ricks or stacks. Thomas Newell in 1731 had 'hay

## TABLE XVIII
### Inventories showing cattle, which also include cheese

| Value of cheese | Dawley | Lilleshall | Wellington | Wrockwardine | Total |
|---|---|---|---|---|---|
| Under £1 | 14 | 29 | 25 | 24 | 92 |
| £1–£5 | 5 | 26 | 19 | 18 | 68 |
| £5 or more | — | 9 | 5 | 10 | 24 |
| Equipment specifically for cheese making, but no cheese | 1 | 2 | 5 | 2 | 10 |
| Totals | 20 | 66 | 54 | 54 | 194 |
| Proportion of those with cows having cheese | 31.75 | 51.97 | 27.69 | 41.22 | 37.60 |

on stacks' worth £7 10s. 0d., and Edward Barker in 1729 had 'part of a rick of hay'. William Howle (*84*) in 1664 had both a 'hay reeke' and a bay of hay. Of only 16 inventories which record hay but no cattle, 14 (11 of them in the town of Wellington) itemise horses, apparently kept for riding or road haulage rather than for agricultural purposes.

Cheese was an important cash product for the dairy farmers of the district. Of the 516 inventories which record cows, 194, or 37.6 per cent. also record cheese, and only 13 inventories of people who did not have cattle mention cheese. When it was merely part of the provision of a household cheese seems rarely to have exceeded one pound in value, and provisions probably account for less than half of the references on the inventories. Cheese appears to have been made on a modest scale by people for whom farming was one of several occupations. Walter Hartshorne (*12*), the master collier, had six milking cows and stored 20 small cheeses in his house. Thomas Smith (*22*), a weaver, had some vessels for making cheese in a room adjoining his shop and a small parcel of new cheeses in a store chamber. Cheese was produced in considerable quantities by the larger farmers, presumably for sale elsewhere. A significant reference to cheese occurs in the inventory of William Webb of Wellington (*203*) taken in 1741. Webb kept no cows, and appears to have gained part of his living by brewing, but the presence of 23 cwt. of cheese worth £35 in his house suggests that he also worked as some kind of cheese factor. Apart from Webb everyone else who had substantial quantities of cheese also kept a dairy herd. Table XVIII shows that cheese was more commonly made in Lilleshall and Wrockwardine than in the other parishes. That only 27.7 per cent. of those who kept cows in Wellington made cheese, suggests that the milk produced by their cows

## TABLE XIX
### Prices of cheese

| (i) Value of 1cwt. of cheese: | | | (ii) Value of one cheese: | | |
|---|---|---|---|---|---|
| 1700 | .. | £0 16s. 0d. | 1681 | .. | 4.29 p. |
| 1707 | .. | £0 15s. 0d. | 1682 | .. | 5.17 p. |
| 1711 (a) | .. | £1 0s. 0d. | 1683 (a) | .. | 5.10 p. Old cheese |
| 1711 (b) | .. | £1 0s. 0d. | 1683 (b) | .. | 4.60 p. |
| 1732 | .. | £0 19s. 0d. | 1683 (c) | .. | 3.38 p. |
| 1741 | .. | £1 10s. 0d. | 1696 | .. | 8.40 p. Small cheese |
| | | | 1699 | .. | 2.78 p. Small cheese |
| | | | 1707 | .. | 11.11 p. Small cheese |
| | | | 1716 | .. | 7.50 p. |
| | | | 1725 | .. | 5.54 p. |
| | | | 1738 | .. | 8.13 p. |
| | | | 1744 (a) | .. | 12.20 p. Old cheese |
| | | | 1744 (b) | .. | 10.00 p. New cheese |
| | | | 1744 (c) | .. | 5.00 p. Small cheese |

was largely used for drinking or butter for local consumption. Nevertheless there were some farms in the parish where cheese was made on a considerable scale. The inventories of Joseph and Elizabeth Grice taken in 1665 and 1667 both record herds of six milking cows, with cheese worth respectively £5 10s. 0d. and £6. 10s. 0d. George Wilkes (*88*) in 1671 had a herd of 16 cows and butter and cheese worth £8. 10s. 0d. William Minshall of Leegomery (*109*) in 1687 had 175 cheeses and two steans of butter worth ten pounds. Richard Stanier (*154*) in 1711 had a herd of 11 milking cows and 5 cwt. of cheese worth five pounds. William Cleaton (*196*) in 1738 had only five cows, but 123 cheeses worth ten pounds. In Lilleshall the Shelton family were particularly active in cheesemaking. Richard Shelton in 1683 (*48*) had 13 cows and left 210 cheeses worth eight pounds. Andrew Shelton in 1690 had cheese and butter worth £10 6s. 8d., and milking cows and a bull worth thirty-seven pounds. Philippa Shelton (*66*) in 1700 left £7 worth of cheese, and Robert Shelton (*73*) in 1717 left cheese worth £10, nine cows and a bull. Thomas Cartwright (*32*) in 1661 left 70 cheeses, and 80 are mentioned in the inventory of John Minnion in 1716. In Wrockwardine, and particularly in the townships of Allscott, Admaston and Bratton, many farmhouses had store chambers for cheese and numerous inventories record large quantities kept in them. Thomas Lowe of Bratton had 'Cheese and other things in that chamber' worth nineteen pounds. Allen Pickering (*244*) of Bratton had cheese in a cheese chamber worth five pounds. Thomas Jebb of Allscott had 10 milking cows and £15 worth of cheese, and another Allscott farmer, Thomas Calcutt (*264*) had 18 cows and 141 cheeses worth fourteen pounds. The inventories thus show that cheese was made by a considerable

## TABLE XX
### Sheep: size of flocks

|  | 1660s | 1670s | 1680s | 1690s | 1700s | 1710s | 1720s | 1730s | 1740s |
|---|---|---|---|---|---|---|---|---|---|
| *Dawley* | | | | | | | | | |
| Total number of sheep | 154 | 29 | 46 | — | — | 10 | 36 | 15 | 27 |
| Number of flocks | 6 | 1 | 1 | — | — | 2 | 2 | 2 | 3 |
| Mean flock | 25.7 | 29 | 46 | — | — | 5 | 18 | 7.5 | 9 |
| Median flock | 17.5 | 29 | 46 | — | — | 5 | 18 | 7.5 | 9 |
| (Mean flock in Dawley, 1660–1750: 21.13) | | | | | | | | | |
| *Lilleshall* | | | | | | | | | |
| Total number of sheep | 112 | 46 | 127 | 16 | 346 | 24 | 26 | — | 19 |
| Number of flocks | 3 | 3 | 5 | 1 | 8 | 2 | 1 | — | 1 |
| Mean flock | 37.3 | 15.3 | 25.4 | 16 | 43.25 | 12 | 26 | — | 19 |
| Median flock | 40 | 12 | 9 | 16 | 44 | 12 | 26 | — | 19 |
| (Mean flock in Lilleshall, 1660–1750: 29.83) | | | | | | | | | |
| *Wellington* | | | | | | | | | |
| Total number of sheep | 221 | 165 | 99 | 182 | 112 | 226 | 207 | 94 | 208 |
| Number of flocks | 7 | 7 | 3 | 7 | 4 | 3 | 9 | 3 | 7 |
| Mean flock | 31.6 | 23.6 | 33 | 26 | 28 | 75.3 | 23 | 31.3 | 29.7 |
| Median flock | 30 | 20 | 21 | 28 | 25.5 | 27 | 18 | 41 | 29 |
| (Mean flock in Wellington, 1660–1750: 30.28) | | | | | | | | | |
| *Wrockwardine* | | | | | | | | | |
| Total number of sheep | 53 | 165 | 173 | 134 | 148 | 11 | 86 | 58 | 483 |
| Number of flocks | 4 | 7 | 7 | 8 | 4 | 1 | 5 | 3 | 5 |
| Mean flock | 13.25 | 23.6 | 24.7 | 16.78 | 37 | 11 | 17.2 | 19.3 | 96.6 |
| Median flock | 9 | 14 | 20 | 13 | 25 | 11 | 16 | 19 | 78 |
| (Mean flock in Wrockwardine, 1660–1750: 29.80) | | | | | | | | | |
| Overall mean | 27 | 22.5 | 27.8 | 20.75 | 37.9 | 33.8 | 20.9 | 20.9 | 46 |
| Overall median | 23.5 | 18 | 20.5 | 16 | 29 | 12 | 18 | 17 | 27 |

TABLE XXI

Sheep: size of flocks by months

|  | Number of flocks | Total number of sheep | Median | Mean |
|---|---|---|---|---|
| January | 11 | 299 | 25 | 27.2 |
| February | 7 | 119 | 15 | 17 |
| March | 16 | 311 | 18.5 | 19.4 |
| April | 12 | 251 | 13 | 20.9 |
| May | 15 | 561 | 25 | 37.4 |
| June | 12 | 363 | 29.5 | 30.3 |
| July | 8 | 269 | 16.5 | 33.6 |
| August | 7 | 171 | 16 | 24.4 |
| September | 15 | 475 | 22 | 31.7 |
| October | 9 | 505 | 25 | 56.1 |
| November | 13 | 259 | 16 | 19.9 |
| December | 6 | 129 | 23.5 | 21.5 |

number of farmers on the coalfield, but that it was a very important product of the larger farms on the better land in Lilleshall and Wrockwardine, which may be regarded as the southernmost extremity of the Cheshire cheese country. Daniel Defoe, about 1702, wrote that:

> though 'tis called by the name of Cheshire cheese, yet great quantities are made in Shropshire, Staffordshire and Lancashire, that is to say, in such parts of them as border upon Cheshire.[82]

If butter was manufactured as a cash product, it rarely appears in significant quantities in inventories. William Howle (84) had six steans of butter, but such quantities were probably for local rather than national markets. The inventories which provide information on the value of cheese, either by weight or by the price of individual cheeses, both suggest an upward movement of prices over the period, as shown in Table XIX.

Two hundred and eight inventories include references to sheep, of which 207 also itemise cattle. Only one, that of John Taylor of Wellington, who died in 1673, was first and foremost a sheep farmer. He had 44 old sheep and 24 lambs worth in all £6 4s. 0d., and wool worth £1 16s. 0d. He also had pigs and grew hemp, but apparently neither kept cattle nor grew grain. By no means all of the inventories which mention sheep indicate the sizes of flocks. On those which do, some 3,712 sheep are listed. The largest flocks were those of William Binnell (261) of Clotley in 1740, who had 160 sheep worth £23; Francis Wright (127) of Leegomery in 1698, who had 142 worth £25; and Richard Stanier of Leaton (154) in 1711, who had 178 worth £41 17s. 6d. No other flock exceeded

100 animals, and the average size was much lower. Table XX shows that the mean size of flocks was about 30 sheep in Lilleshall, Wellington and Wrockwardine, and a little over 20 in Dawley. It is doubtful whether the sample is large enough for the fluctuations of flock size by decades to be particularly significant. Table XXI demonstrates, what might well be expected, that the size of flocks was lowest in the winter months and at its highest in May and June following lambing. Analysis of the prices of sheep reveals no particularly striking patterns. Two groups of animals in Wrockwardine were valued at 9s. 1d. and 10s. each, but these were quite exceptional figures. Otherwise in all four parishes prices vary between 1s. 6d. and 6s. each. Fluctuations appear to be due more to the season or to the quality of the animals than to any recognisable economic factor. Twenty-eight of those who keep sheep, and seven others, had wool in their houses, the most considerable quantity, to the value of £5, being in the house of John Eyton (*148*). Three inventories list fleeces which ranged in value from 8¼d. to 2s. 3¾d. When wool was weighed its value was generally more consistent. One inventory priced it at five shillings a stone, but five give its value at between 10s. and 12s. 6d. a stone. The raising of sheep was not one of the chief agricultural activities in the region, but flocks of considerable size were kept by some of the farmers on the better land, both for their value in fertilising arable ground and for wool, while on the poorer soils of the coalfield sheep were doubtless a source of limited, but useful, additional income. Even the largest flocks in Telford, however, are of insignificant size compared with those to be found in the Bishop's Castle area in the same period.

Pigs were kept by a high proportion of the population of North Telford during the period under review. They are mentioned on 382 or 45.15 per cent. of the inventories. In Dawley there are 44 inventories with pigs, 49.44 per cent. of the total. The equivalent figures for the other parishes were 89, or 49.17 per cent. for Lilleshall, 160, or 38.74 per cent., for Wellington, and 89, or 54.60 per cent. in Wrockwardine. Keeping pigs was closely associated with other farming activities, even if the latter were on a small scale. Only 27 people who had no cattle kept pigs, and 295 of the 382 inventories which list pigs also mention grain. Details about pigs appear on only a few inventories. One of the most carefully categorised is that of Thomas Calcott (*264*), which lists 12 large pigs at 18s each, two lean sows, 10s. each, seven little pigs at 6s. 4d. each, and nine little pigs at 2s. 6d. each. More commonly the pigs are listed simply as 'the swine' or 'the swine young and old'. The word 'pig' is commonly used to mean piglet, and many inventories refer to 'a sow and nine pigs' or 'one sow and pigs'. There are several references to gilts, young female pigs, to shoats, shots or shuts, which were young weaned pigs, and to 'store' swine, pigs acquired for fattenings. One inventory mentions a 'porket', a young animal, rather bigger than a piglet. Pigs mature quickly, so that comparison of values means very little, but the vast majority are priced well below one pound. A few were exceedingly valuable beasts. Richard Stanier (*154*) had five swine worth £7 10s. 0d., or £1 10s. 0d. each. Edward Besford of Dawley had two fat hogs worth £1 15s. 0d. each, but the most highly rated pigs were three kept by Robert Shelton (*73*) in 1717, reckoned to be worth £3 each, as were two fat hogs owned by William Shelton in 1727. Such animals were of the same order of value as dairy cows.

Horses were listed in even more inventories than pigs. They are mentioned on 407, or 48.11 per cent. of the total. There are interesting contrasts between the parishes. In Wrockwardine, by most reckonings the richest parish, 65.03 per cent. of the inventories include horses, against a mean of 48.11 per cent. for all four parishes. Horses were closely associated with the practice of agriculture. Only 46 of the horse owners had no cattle. Horses were used for an infinite variety of purposes, from riding to the Assize to winding a pit, from heading a finely-fitted plough-team to working a mill for a poverty-stricken feltmaker. The values of horses thus vary enormously, and analysis over the whole period would mean little. Some individual examples indicate what particular types of horse were worth. The cheapest individual beast was an old mare belonging to Thomas Fieldhouse in 1688, valued at only 3s. 4d. An old horse worth 8s. 6d. is mentioned on an inventory of 1721, and an old mare worth 10s. is among the possessions of Bartholomew Wedge in the same year. Thomas Penson of Lilleshall in 1686 had an old lame mare worth 13s. 4d. The most valuable horse seems to be that of Henry Wood (*156*), vicar of Wellington, which was assessed at twelve pounds. Charles Eyton (*17*) had a black horse worth 7½ guineas, and the wealthy Thomas Calcott (*264*) a mare worth seven pounds. In several of the wealthiest households the horses were all assessed together, so that individual values cannot be ascertained. Richard Stanier (*154*) had a black mare, a schewed mare, a little bay mare, two colts, and seven cart-horses worth £63. The most thorough picture of a rich man's horses is to be seen in the inventory of Thomas Newell (*77*), of Donnington, which lists a black mare and colt at £7, an old chestnut mare at £3, a young chestnut mare at £7, a young black mare at £6, two two-year-old colts at £8, a two-year-old horse colt at £1 10s. 0d., and four yearling colts at ten pounds. A considerable number of inventories indicate the colourings of horses, bays, chestnuts, blacks, and greys all occurring quite commonly. A few indicate that particular animals were lame or old, but indications of condition are quite rare, few appraisers being as candid as those of the goods of Thomas Whittingham in 1711, who listed '4 Ould Sory horises and gears' at nine pounds. Types of horse are sometimes distinguished; there are many mares and nags, some geldings, and some stone or stoned horses, which were uncastrated males or stallions. In some cases the word 'horse' means specifically a male animal as distinct from a mare, as in an inventory of 1707 which distinguished a 'horse colt' from a 'filly colt'. The inventories reveal little of the extensive trade in horses which was carried on in Shropshire in this period, but Dr. Edwards has identified Thomas Windsor of Lilleshall (*41*), who died in 1673, as one of the principal dealers in the region.[83]

Poultry are mentioned on 75 inventories, a little less than 9 per cent. of the total. All but five of the references occur on inventories taken before 1710, which suggests either a substantial diminution in the stock of birds in the area in the early 18th century, or that the practice of listing them on inventories came to an end. Most inventories mention only poultry or 'pullen' without specifying what sort of birds were kept. Ten mention hens, four specify ducks, one of them listing a mallard, and 14 itemise geese. One inventory only, that of Thomasina Hawkins (*71*), taken in 1713, mentions turkeys. Poultry were rarely valued highly. In January 1660-61 three hens and a cock were reckoned to be worth 2s. 4d. Two pullets were valued at 8d. in May 1666, and two hens and a cock at 1s. in June 1671. In May 1676 nine young geese were estimated to be worth 3s., and three old geese five shillings. Nine geese in July 1694 were worth four shillings and sixpence. Six ducks in February 1713-14 were valued at two shillings. Poultry were most commonly listed on the inventories of the rich. Only 22 inventories with a total value of less than £50 mention poultry, while they appear on 36, with values of £100 or more.

Only one dog, a 'cur dog', worth a guinea in an inventory of 1747, is mentioned in the whole collection. It is beyond belief that only one out of 846 people owned a dog, particularly since the collection includes the inventories of sheep farmers, and game-keepers. Doubtless it was general practice not to include them. The 'dogg' mentioned on the inventory of Francis Peate, blacksmith (*208*) was a kind of clamp.

There are several pools in North Telford, which doubtless provided fish in the period under review, and several inventories must relate to properties bordering the River Tern, which was also an important source of fish for the table. Several inventories (*148, 162, 249, 258*), all of them of wealthy men, record fish nets, but no details are given of where they were used.

Wheat was by far the commonest grain crop in the region, although it is usually referred to as corn, and was commonly mixed with other grains.[84] Edward Besford in 1692 had a stack of wheat and rye. It is some indication of the mixed nature of farming in the area that only 14 of the inventories which list corn do not also mention cattle, and of those which include both corn and cattle, 171, or 52 per cent., also include sheep. The inventories give few indications of modes of cultivation. Wheat was principally an autumn-sown crop, and some inventories mention

## TABLE XXII

### The nature of farming

|  | Dawley | Lilleshall | Wellington | Wrockwardine | Total | Notes |
|---|---|---|---|---|---|---|
| Inventories with cattle | 63 | 127 | 195 | 131 | 516 |  |
| Inventories with cattle and corn | 29 | 94 | 110 | 94 | 327 |  |
| Proportion of those with cattle which have corn | 46.03 | 74.01 | 56.41 | 71.76 | 63.37 | Only 13 inventories have corn but no cattle |
| Inventories with cattle and corn which also have sheep | 14 | 29 | 63 | 65 | 171 |  |
| Proportion of those with cattle and corn which also have sheep | 48.27 | 30.85 | 57.27 | 69.15 | 52.29 |  |

sowings or 'seednesses' of corn upon the ground in the winter months. Many also mention *Lent Grain* or *Lent Tilling*, normally a crop of barley, mixed grain, oats, or peas. The inventory of Richard Beard (*62*) distinguished precisely between winter corn and Lent tilling. Mixed grain was grown quite commonly. Thomas Clare, a Dawley collier, had '4 thrave of mixt corn or muncorn' and *muncorn* is mentioned in 17 inventories. Mixed grain was also called *maslin*, 60 strikes of which are mentioned in the inventory of William Whitmore (*36*), or as *dredge*, nine strikes of which were among the possessions of Richard Shelton (*48*) in 1683. An inventory of 1664 refers to 'Dredge and other Lent Corn', indicating that mixed corn was a spring-planted crop. A mixture of wheat and rye was sometimes called *hard corn*. Thomas Harper in 1669 had 30 strikes of hard corn worth £14, and Thomas Hitchen (*99*) had five strikes sowing of hard corn worth two pounds. Buckwheat, or *French wheat*, as it is called in the inventories of Robert Ward in 1676, and Katherine Hall (*69*) in 1710 is mentioned on several occasions. Values of grain fluctuated considerably, and there is little consistency in units of measurement, so that it is difficult to ascertain movements of price over such a limited area. It is clear that wheat was always valued much more highly than the spring-grown crops. In 1749 Joseph Cleaton had corn worth 4s. a strike and Lent tilling worth 1s. 6d. a strike. An inventory of 1707 mentions 'bread corn', but there is otherwise little indication of precisely how grain was used. Harvested grain in some inventories is of such high value that it was probably a cash crop. Richard Phillips (*144*) had grain worth £35

## TABLE XXIII

### Crops other than wheat

|  | Barley | Oats | Rye | Clover | Peas | Beans | Vetches |
|---|---|---|---|---|---|---|---|
| 1660–9 | 6 | 4 | 1 | – | 2 | – | 3 |
| 1670–9 | 9 | 6 | 3 | – | 5 | – | – |
| 1680–9 | 18 | 10 | 5 | – | 8 | 1 | 1 |
| 1690–9 | 8 | 4 | 3 | – | 2 | – | 1 |
| 1700–9 | 8 | 11 | 1 | – | 10 | 2 | 2 |
| 1710–9 | 12 | 9 | 2 | – | 7 | – | – |
| 1720–9 | 11 | 13 | 2 | 4 | 7 | – | 3 |
| 1730–9 | 8 | 7 | – | 5 | 4 | 1 | 1 |
| 1740–9 | 11 | 10 | 1 | 3 | 6 | – | 1 |
| Totals | 91 | 74 | 18 | 12 | 51 | 4 | 12 |
| *Parish totals* | | | | | | | |
| Dawley | 12 | 14 | 3 | 3 | 4 | – | 3 |
| Lilleshall | 20 | 16 | 1 | 2 | 13 | 1 | 4 |
| Wellington | 31 | 25 | 8 | 3 | 16 | 2 | 4 |
| Wrockwardine | 28 | 19 | 6 | 4 | 18 | 1 | 1 |

in his granary. William Turner of Arleston had £50 worth of corn and hay in his barn. John Beddow of Wappenshall had corn and hay to the same value, and William Podmore of Arleston in 1734 had corn worth more than forty pounds.

Barley is mentioned on 91 inventories, some 23 of which do not include wheat or corn, but the majority of these are small households which probably kept a small quantity for brewing. Oats are mentioned on 74 inventories, 14 of which do not include wheat. Barley was probably grown principally for use in brewing. The inventory of John Smith (*254*) in 1732 shows that it was sometimes stored in bags. Some individuals possessed considerable quantities. Joshua Johnson (*126*) had 130 strikes worth £15 3s. 4d., while Robert Johnson (*112*) had 100 measures valued at ten pounds. Barley was generally worth less than wheat, and oats less than barley, but seasonal differences, and eccentricities of measurement make worthwhile comparisons impossible.

Rye is mentioned in 18 inventories, although it was frequently grown mixed with wheat and may have occurred more commonly than this figure suggests. Two-thirds of the references are on inventories made before 1700, and only one from the last two decades of the period under review, which suggests that its cultivation may slowly have been declining. Peas were commonly grown in the district throughout the period, being mentioned on 51 inventories, and they appear to have been especially favoured on the lighter soils of Lilleshall and Wrockwardine.

The inventory of William Cheshire (*249*) distinguishes between white and grey peas, and a Dawley inventory of 1692 mentions two ricks of peas. Beans require a heavier soil than peas, and are mentioned on only four inventories. A dozen include references to vetches, the bean-like fruits of the genus *vicia*. The most important new crop to appear during the period was clover, first mentioned in the 1720s, when it also first appeared in Essex, although elsewhere in North Shropshire it was being grown before 1700.[85] Thomas Roe and John Harris (*25, 26*), whose inventories were made in 1729-30, both had ricks of clover, and James Spender (*80*) in 1748 had clover stored over his horse tallant as well as in a rick.

Few inventories give any information about the threshing of grain after it had been harvested. John Smith (*254*) in 1732 had a fan, presumably a winnowing fan, and a sieve in his barn, and Thomas Roe (*26*) had 'a fan to winnow with' worth 10s., but flails are significantly absent from this collection.

Turnips are mentioned on two 17th-century inventories. That taken in 1664 of the goods of William Howle (*84*), a Wellington glover, whose farming activities appear to have been confined to keeping a cow and a horse, making some hay and growing hemp, includes '35 quarts of Turnip Seeds'. Such a large quantity suggests that the turnip may have been grown as a field crop, although there is no other evidence in the inventories that it was.. Eleanor Sandys (*128*), a widow not involved in farming, who died in 1698 had 'a pcell turnip seede', but it is itemised with other goods and it is not possible to deduce the quantity or the value.

Potatoes are mentioned on only two inventories. John Rowley (*185*) in 1728 had in his cellar 'potatoes with a few bottles' worth 15s. The inventory of Charles Stowers (*192*) gives a vivid picture of a small market garden in the 1730s. He cultivated 'pertaters' and 'kittney beans', and his tools included a 'watter pan', a rake and spade, flower pots, a garden line, an axe, and a hook, as well as 'glasses' worth 5s., which were perhaps some form of cloche.

Wagons or wains are noted on 71 inventories, and most of them were clearly intended for use on the land rather than for road transport. Carts are mentioned on 87 inventories, and tumbrels on 86, but it is difficult to distinguish between the two, although many inventories list both. Sometimes 'dung tumbrels' are specified. Wheels for both carts and tumbrels were often itemised separately from the vehicle bodies, and it would seem likely that bodies and wheels were often interchangeable. Old wheels seem to have littered many a farmyard. Iron-bound wheels are usually distinguished from those which were not, which were sometimes called *barefoot* or *naked* wheels, as on the inventory of Richard Goodales (*117*). Ploughs are mentioned on 84 inventories and harrows

## TABLE XXIV

### Farm implements and draught animals

|  | Wagons and wains | Carts | Tumbrels | Ploughs | Harrows | Draught oxen | Inventories with both corn and horses |
|---|---|---|---|---|---|---|---|
| 1660–9 | 14 | 9 | 10 | 15 | 10 | 11 | 32 |
| 1670–9 | 8 | 11 | 9 | 10 | 7 | 14 | 35 |
| 1680–9 | 10 | 10 | 13 | 13 | 10 | 14 | 42 |
| 1690–9 | 10 | 8 | 6 | 6 | 6 | 11 | 24 |
| 1700–9 | 10 | 12 | 13 | 9 | 12 | 12 | 43 |
| 1710–9 | 3 | 9 | 7 | 5 | 3 | 4 | 22 |
| 1720–9 | 6 | 13 | 12 | 11 | 14 | 12 | 36 |
| 1730–9 | 6 | 6 | 7 | 6 | 3 | 2 | 21 |
| 1740–9 | 4 | 9 | 9 | 99 | 10 | 5 | 16 |
| Totals | 71 | 87 | 86 | 84 | 75 | 85 | 271 |

*Parish totals*

| | | | | | | | |
|---|---|---|---|---|---|---|---|
| Dawley | 7 | 6 | 9 | 13 | 11 | 8 | 16 |
| Lilleshall | 17 | 27 | 22 | 23 | 18 | 19 | 83 |
| Wellington | 19 | 29 | 32 | 32 | 34 | 29 | 86 |
| Wrockwardine | 28 | 25 | 23 | 16 | 12 | 29 | 86 |

on seventy-five. Occasionally plough irons or timbers are listed, and several inventories mention copsoles, which were wedges for keeping the coulter of the plough in its place at the proper angle to the beam. A few inventories include sledges or sleds, including those of Charles Eyton (*17*) and Thomas Roe (*26*), both of which also list rolls or rollers.

One of the fullest accounts of a farm wagon and its accessories is in the inventory of Edward Harrington (*87*), who had a wain with wheels rimmed with iron, ripples, which were the rails added to increase the vehicle capacity when carrying such things as hay, a cop or cover for the wain, three ladders, and a pair of traces, the leather straps with which the collar of the animal pulling the wain was connected with the splinter bar. The inventory of William Cleaton (*196*) includes numerous wagon parts, among them felloes, the sections which made up the rims of the wheels, and raithes, the rails used to increase the capacity of a cart or wain.

An inventory which shows the range of implements on a large farm is that of William Minshall (*109*), who had a wain body with iron-bound sheels and ripples, a body with barefoot wheels, four caps or covers for wains, and three pairs of rathes. He had two tumbrel bodies, one with a pair of draught wheels, presumably for use in the fields, and the other with iron-bound wheels, perhaps for road work. He had four ploughs with three pairs of irons, four copsoles and two harrows.

Horses were the animals most commonly used for draught purposes in the fields of North Telford. They are listed on 271 of the 341 inventories which list corn, and appear on virtually every farm of any consequence. It is impossible, however, to distinguish which were used for draught purposes, and which for riding. Oxen were also employed as draught beasts, although on every farm where they were used there were also horses. The word 'oxen' and 'bullocks' were used synonymously, and it is sometimes uncertain whether the latter refers to draught animals or to those kept for beef. An inventory of 1693 refers to a yoke of 'bullox' and to '4 bullocks that were yoked', while that of Joshua Calcott (*243*) mentions 'six working bullocks'.

Draught oxen were valuable beasts, the mean value over the whole period being £4 0s. 10d. The cheapest were worth £2 10s. 0d., while the most valuable were the 12 kept by Richard Stanier (*154*), appraised at £6 10s. 0d. each in 1712. The values were lowest in Dawley, where the mean was £3 6s. 0d., and the highest in Wellington where dairy cattle were also valued most highly. Oxen were generally kept by the wealthier farmers. Only six of the 85 inventories which list them had a total value of less than £50, and only a further 17 were assessed between £50 and £100. It seems that the practice of keeping oxen slowly declined in the early 18th century, since only 23 of the 85 references occur after 1710, and

## TABLE XXV
### Inventories with horses

|  | Number of Inventories with horses | Proportion of total inventories | Number with horses but not cattle | Number with horses but no grain |
|---|---|---|---|---|
| Dawley | 39 | 43.82 | 2 | 14 |
| Lilleshall | 88 | 48.62 | 2 | 10 |
| Wellington | 174 | 42.13 | 38 | 86 |
| Wrockwardine | 106 | 65.03 | 4 | 22 |
| Totals | 407 | 48.11 | 46 | 122 |

there are no oxen at all listed in Lilleshall after that date, but they were by no means an unknown sight in the 1740s, and they were still in use in some parts of Shropshire in the 19th century.[86]

The expression 'implements' included hand tools as well as wheeled vehicles, although such tools are rarely itemised in detail. William Minshall's inventory (*109*) again illuminates many others. The commonest tools, as in Essex,[88] were axes, bill-hooks (often called just 'bills,) spades, pitch-fork (usually called pickells or pickerells in Shropshire), and mattocks, which were tools like pick axes with one end of the blade arched and flattened at right-angles to the handle. Minshall had two broom hooks, three spades, two mattocks, a pick, three axes, two bills and a hatchet. He had an iron for docking horses' tails, and a selection of carpenters' tools, as well as four augers, a maul, which was a very large hammer and two iron wedges, which might have been used in mining. For sowing there were two hoppers, which were large baskets used by the sower to hold the seed he was about to broadcast. There were two pairs of weeding tongs, a muck hook, and four muck forks. For use at haytime and harvest there were two drawing hooks, three hay rakes and 12 rick forks. He also had a hand barrow and a wheelbarrow. Some inventories list tools which Minshall did not have. Scythes are relatively common, William Cheshire (*249*) having two which were worth four shillings. They were probably used principally for haymaking, but were not the only tools so employed, since Humphrey Mansell (*46*) had a hay hook. For gathering grain, either sickles, of which Richard Bridgwood (*9*) had three, or reaping hooks which are listed in the inventories of Daniel Richards in 1669, and of Richard Randall (*137*) would have been employed.

Muck or compost is mentioned on 55 inventories, all but six of them from farms on which grain was grown. Often it was kept in a special enclosure, 'in ye fold', or 'a mixen of muck'. The value could be considerable. William Charlton (235) had muck and compost worth four pounds. Thomas Roe (26) had 'about 50 loads much' worth £2 10s. 0d., or a shilling a load. While lime was burned in the district, there are no references to it on any of the farms recorded in the inventories.

## Women in Society

Only 162, or 19.15 per cent., of the inventories studied relate to women. The proportion is highest in Lilleshall, where 25.97 list women's possessions, there being little variation between the other three parishes. Eighty-three of the 162 womens' inventories refer to widows, and it is likely that many of the rest also list widows' possessions. Only 16 are positively identified as spinsters.

The inventories show that women often carried on their husband's occupation after they had been widowed. Forty-five women, many of them identified as widows, were engaged in farming, some on a considerable scale (5, 34, 42, 66, 69, 71, 76, 100, 165, 233, 263). Three (including 76, 151) had looms in their homes, and may have made their livings by weaving. Elizabeth Judgson (159) kept an inn, which had belonged to her husband. Jane Hartshorne (194) maintained at least some of her husband's mining activities. In Wrockwardine there were two schoolmistresses (218, 238). The most interesting tradeswomen, however, were the two mercers, Margaret Justice (107), who set up business on her own account after the death of her shoemaker husband, and Tryphosa Barnes, who is positively identified as a spinster. There are in all, however, only 13 inventories of women who were engaged in particular occupations other than farming.

Many women's inventories are short, and appear to relate to elderly ladies living in other people's houses, probably, in many cases, mothers living with their offspring. Often such inventories are of low value, although the proportion of women's inventories worth less than £10 is, at 27.16 per cent., only slightly higher than the percentage for the whole collection. Many such short inventories include invested money. Eliza Darrall's (6) inventory appears to be concerned with rather less than a whole household. Some of her possessions are in 'her chamber', while the rest are 'above stairs in ye closet'. Ann Eastop (120) had a little farming stock, a few possessions in a house, and the remainder in 'ye old woman's chamber'. Elizabeth Blackshaw (250) had possessions 'In her own lodging room', with a few other pieces of furniture, her clothes, and £92 in money.

## Furnishings

The inventories provide a vivid impression of the domestic interiors of the period, and give some indication of changing fashions. Some are

# INTRODUCTION

outstanding in the amount of detail they reveal. Those of Richard Stanier (*154*) and Thomas Calcott (*243*) show very clearly the conditions in which a minor member of the gentry or a wealthy farmer lived in the early 18th century. William Langley's inventory (*110*) makes it easy to envisage a parsonage at the time of the Glorious Revolution. Few households can ever have been itemised more precisely than that of John Duddell (*24*), the Dawley carpenter, whose inventory was made in 1728. Few 17th-century houses can have contained such an extraordinary collection of items as that of Richard Clowes (*8*). The historical significance of an individual inventory, however fascinating it may be, is nevertheless limited. The value of an analysis of a very large collection is that each one throws light on the others. A single inventory of no great interest for what it reveals of a complete household, may, in its description of a single item, illuminate hundreds of others, by clarifying the purpose of a given object, or revealing the material from which it was made. Almost every inventory includes trunks, boxes and chests, but their uses are rarely defined. The inventory of Richard Phillips (*164*) makes it abundantly clear how they were utilised. The appraisers of inventories could assume an awareness of the nature and purpose of household objects which has disappeared during the last three centuries. Study of a large collection brings an awareness of the ways in which appraisers used words, of the common associations of objects. Much can be learned from the statistical analysis of inventories. They need also to be approached as linguistic creations, in the way that a critic would approach poetry or a Biblical scholar the Gospels. Appraisers, like poets or Evangelists, varied in their use of detail. One may describe an item as a chair worth one shilling and sixpence. Another might call it 'an elboe chair with red Turkey work on it'. In studying the households depicted in the inventories it is necessary to use the imaginative language of the latter to compensate for the taciturnity of the former.

Tables are found in almost every inventory which lists the contents of a household in any detail. The most common type was the long rectangular table, whose top rested on two solid trestles, usually described as a 'table and frame'. The better examples in these inventories probably resembled the one made in the 1630s for the Shrewsbury Drapers Company (Plate 8). Many inventories also list occasional or side tables, sometimes square, sometimes round, and sometimes oval. Such tables occur before 1700, but the great majority of them are on 18th-century inventories, usually those of wealthy people. Richard Stanier (*154*) had an 'oak oval table' John Eyton (*148*) had a large oval table as well as a long table in his hall. William Cleaton (*196*) in 1738 had an oval table worth eight shillings. Jane Hartshorne in 1737 (*194*) had large and small oval tables as well as a round table. John Duddell (*24*), the Dawley carpenter, had a round table in 1728, and most surprisingly, a round table also appears on the inventory of Edward Darrall, a very poor Dawley miner (*21*), which was taken in 1726.

*Livery tables* and *cupboards* occur on inventories throughout the period from 1660 to 1750. The former were small cupboards often with fronts and sides of turned balusters, originally used for the storage of liveries of bread and wine which people took to their sleeping rooms. A livery table was one on which such rations were placed, or alternatively one in which a livery cupboard might be put. Such tables and cupboards were often found in the sleeping rooms of the more comfortably furnished households. John Smith (*254*) in 1731-32 had a livery table worth 1s. in his best bedroom. The clergyman William Langley (*110*) in 1689 had two livery cupboards worth 6s. 8d. in his sumptuously furnished Great Chamber. William Pemberton (*230*) in 1693-94 had livery tables in three of his four sleeping rooms. They were found not only in the homes of the wealthy. William Cookson (*152*), a not very rich weaver from Hadley, had a livery table in one of his bedrooms in 1711.

Tables with leaves which drew out, sometimes called *drawing tables* are mentioned in several inventories, the earliest of them in 1672, the year after the first recorded in the Essex parishes examined by Mr. Steer.[88] The inventory of Richard Bridgwood (*9*) records two leaves of tables in different rooms. One *falling table*, probably of the gate-leg type, is recorded in the inventory of Nathan Peploe (*28*) in 1665. An inventory of 1662 refers to 'tables with cupboards in'; a 'folding table' is recorded in 1728, and three 'drinking tables' in 1747.

The most sophisticated tables are, not surprisingly, to be found on the inventories of some of the wealthier inhabitants of the district who died towards the end of the period under review. Richard Stanier (*254*) in 1711 had an inlaid table, and a dressing table. Thomas Calcott (*243*) in 1744 also had a dressing table. Jane Hartshorne (*194*) and Peter Langley (*258*) both had tea tables in their parlours in the mid-1730s, but the most exotic tables were perhaps in the dining-room of John Eyton (*148*) in 1708-9, where his appraisers found two 'Gapan Tables, one black and ye other white' which they valued at two pounds.

Tablecloths occur on inventories throughout the period and were usually made of some kind of linen. The 'fine flax table cloth fringed' mentioned on the inventory of Joyce Bradshaw (*106*) was perhaps one of the better examples. Tables were frequently covered with carpets. The inventory of Francis Richards (*2*) in 1666 includes a 'Carpet for a table'. That of Edward Harrington (*87*) mentions 'a carpett for the long table'. Benjamin Wright's (*132*) possessions included a 'table carpet'. Carpets are frequently mentioned in association with tables. The inventory of John Field (*119*) included 'one small side table and carpet' and that of Thomas Jones (*118*) in 1692 mentions 'One Long Table and frame and Carpett'. It would seem likely that most of the carpets mentioned in this collection

## INTRODUCTION

were table rather than floor coverings, and they are rarely itemised after 1710.

There are numerous references in the inventories to *Kidderminster*, the carpet-making town only 24 miles from Wellington. The earliest of them, that of Basil Richards (*1*) in 1659 predates the earliest use of the term to describe a carpet quoted in the *New English Dictionary*. Several inventories mention Kidderminster (or Ciddermist) carpets, but the name is also associated with other furnishing fabrics. William Langley (*110*) in 1689 had 'Curtains of Kederminster stuff', and Peter Langley (*258*) in 1735 owned 'a Pair of Green Kidderminster curtains'.

Chairs gradually came into common use in English homes during the 17th century, and are to be found in most of the households described in this collection. The older forms of seating remained in use. Benches or forms were the almost invariable accompaniment to a table, particularly in the period before 1700. The inventory of Joyce Acton in 1658 mentions the 'joyne form and bench belonging to ye table'. That of Basil Richards (*1*) made the following year includes 'One longe Table with too formes'. The possessions of the Rev. Henry Haughton (*70*) in 1711 include 'one Long Table with too Joyned forms'. William Dawes (*956*) in 1692 had '2 table boards and 4 forms belonging to them'. Forms are rarely described in detail, but an inventory of 1688 does mention a wainscott bench and back in association with a table.

Chairs are to be found in great variety and an increasing number during the period under review. The *Crown* inn, Wellington, in 1708 (*146*) contained numerous stools, but no chairs. By 1715 chairs, including a number covered with green cloth, were to be found there. There are many references to joined chairs, perhaps the Elizabethan type of box chair, but alternatively any chair made by a joiner. Some inventories mention wainscott chairs, which also occur in some of the Lichfield inventories of this period. These were armchairs with decorative carved panels forming the backs, rather like the chair made by Richard Ellis in 1662 which is still used by the Shrewsbury • Drapers' Company.[89] William Cheshire (*249*) had six wainscott chairs worth twelve shillings. Two inventories in 1679 and 1682 mention turned chairs, which also occur in the Lichfield inventories.

In the homes of the wealthy many chairs with padded seats are mentioned. Thomas Cartwright in 1661 (*32*) is recorded as having possessed three leather chairs. Joshua Johnson (*126*) had six worth 5s. each. Subsequent values tended to be lower. Richard Stanier's (*154*) four leather chairs in 1711 were worth 2s. 6d. each, the six owned by William Judgson (*171*) in 1725, 3s. 4d. each, and the six listed by Thomas Calcott's (*264*) appraisers in 1744 were valued at 2s. each. Only one inventory, that of John Binnell (*227*), which includes six chairs of calf skin, specifies any particular type of leather. Many chairs were covered with fabric. An inventory of 1685 mentions chairs 'bottomed with rugges'. There are many 'cloth chairs', and sometimes the colour of the fabric is specified. William Langley (*110*) had 'six red cloth chairs' worth 4s. each, as well as four 'blew chairs'. Elizabeth Judgson (*159*) had green cloth chairs. Sometimes the fabric was embroidered. Richard Stanier (*154*) had 12 tapestry chairs. Sometimes it was covered with *Turkey work*, a woollen material woven in the same way as a Turkish carpet. William Langley had 'six turkey work chairs' worth 6d. a piece more than his red cloth chairs.

Wickerwork chairs occur throughout the period although they are never so called. The earliest references are to 'twiggen chairs' which are found on inventories in 1659, 1688, and 1698. The inventory of Thomas Smith (*224*) in 1687 included two rush chairs. in 1700 Benjamin Wright (*132*) had 'Sedg bottomed chairs' and similar 'Seg' or 'Segg' chairs with bottoms made from coarse rushes are mentioned frequently right up to 1750. In 1744-45 William Keen (*30*) had 'two Seggen'd Bottomed Chairs'. Such chairs were sometimes very cheap. A widow in 1718 had 10 Segg chairs worth less than 6d. each. On an inventory of 1719 five were worth 8d. each. Richard Stanier (*154*) in 1711 had two elbow cane chairs in his parlour chamber and two elbow Segg chairs in his parlour. Cane as distinct from rush or Segg chairs were known in England before 1650, but it was not until after 1690 that they were recorded in rural Essex,[90] and Stanier's is the first Telford inventory to name them. Segg or cane chairs were thereafter frequently to be found in the parlours of the wealthy, sometimes with an elbow or armed chair forming a suite. John Eyton (*148*) had six Segg chairs and one with arms in his parlour. John Smith (*254*) had in his best room '6 Seg chairs . . . ye Elbow Chairs . . . and 4 cushions'. Peter Langley (*258*) had '1 Doz of Cane chairs 2 Elbow' in his parlour. Andrew Sockett (*174*) had in the chamber over his shop 20 cane chairs worth a little more than 3s. each, in the same room as cabinets, a table and a looking-glass. William Birch (*160*), the surgeon, had eight cane chairs in his elegant parlour. Jane Hartshorne (*194*) had six chairs worth 3s. 1d. each in the best room of her house in Wellington. It would seem, therefore, that while rush-bottomed chairs were used by the poor throughout the century after the Restoration, in the early 18th century cane or Segg chairs became fashionable in the most sumptuously furnished rooms of the wealthiest inhabitants of the district.

Some other types of chair are occasionally mentioned. William Cheshire (*249*) and Jane Hartshorne (*194*) both had 'easy' chairs, the one owned by the latter being worth ten shillings. One armchair, and several elbow chairs are listed. An inventory in 1700 mentioned a nursing chair worth 2s. 6d., and four, all of quite wealthy households, include chairs for children.

Stools occur on many inventories. Join stools are quite common, and it may be presumed that the 'yine stool' mentioned on a Dawley inventory referred to the same thing. An inventory of 1692 mentions leather stools, and there are numerous references to stools upholstered with fabrics. Thomas Cartwright (*32*) had six stools covered with cloth, and Richard Beard (*62*) had three of the same kind. William Langley (*110*) had six Turkey-work stools. An inventory of 1684–85 refers to three-footed stools. Buffet stools or foot stools occur on two inventories, one of them that of Elizabeth Bullock (*218*), who used them in her schoolroom. William Poyner (*16*) had a writing stool, which presumably fitted at a desk. Nursing stools are listed quite commonly in the period before 1700.

There are more than a dozen references to couches in the collection, evenly distributed over the period. William Langley (*110*) had a 'blew couch' and Henry Haughton (*70*) a couch chair. In 1707 a couch was listed with a table, chairs and a desk in the parlour of Walter Brodhurst (*65*) which, unlike many parlours, did not contain a bed. Thomas Calcott (*264*) had a couch in his smoking-room.

The 'chairs, stools and cushions' mentioned in the inventory of William Marigold (*91*) often go together, and it is apparent that cushions, or quishons or quishings as they were sometimes called, were often the only form of upholstery in a room. The majority were probably not especially decorative. An inventory of 1682 distinguishes between three wrought cushions and two plain ones. Henry Stanworth (*103*) had two Turkey-work cushions, Benjamin Wright (*132*) had six, and William Cartwright (*74*) four. The most ornate cushions seem to have been those of William Langley (*110*) which included three of silk and nine of gilt leather. Cushion covers are mentioned in the inventory of Joyce Bradshaw (*106*) but not elsewhere.

The condition of furnishings is rarely mentioned, although sometimes items are described simply as 'old' or 'overworn'. An inventory of 1737 mentions four old rotten chairs, but the most explicit is that of Mary Banger (*176*) which includes an old overworn couch and a table which was worm-eaten.

The distinctions between trunks, coffers, chests, boxes, cupboards, presses, desks, cages, shelves and dressers are bewilderingly uncertain. A *cupboard* was originally a flat board on which cups were stored, although the word was usually employed in the mid-17th century to mean shelves which were enclosed in a cabinet. There are several inventories in which the original meaning of the word is clear. William Cheshire (*249*) had two 'cupp-boards', while William Barker (*172*) had both a 'cupp-board' and a 'dish-board'. Thomas Lodge (*136*) also had a 'dish-board', and there are several references to dish benches. The inventory of Peter Langley (*258*) mentions the 'dish Bench and Pewter', while that of Jane Hartshorne (*194*) refers to '19 dishes on dish bench'. William Davis (*204*), a poor weaver from Ketley had 'One dish bench five small dishes one dozen plates' in his house place. John Harris (*25*) had a 'brass bench', an item on which to display brass rather than one constructed of that metal. It was therefore common practice to store dishes and plates of various materials on shelves which were called boards or benches, and cupboards might literally be cup-boards. Several corruptions of the word cupboard are indistinguishable, except by context, from corruptions of cob-iron. By the 1730s cupboards were becoming elegant items of furniture. Peter Langley (*258*) had a large glass corner cupboard, and Jane Hartshorne (*194*) a 'corner cupboard with drawers under'.

There are numerous references to standing or hanging cupboards or presses, which were receptacles in which to hang clothes, rather than pieces of furniture which hung on walls. They tend to be found in wealthier rather than poorer homes, and in the later rather than the earlier part of the period. The press cupboard owned by Thomas Wright (*83*) in 1662 was a kind of wardrobe with two doors.[91]

Glass cages or cases occur quite frequently throughout the period. The study of inventories in Lichfield raised doubts as to whether this term referred to a cupboard for the storage of glass objects or to one with a glass front.[92] The Telford inventories show clearly that such cupboards were used for the storage of items other than glassware, and suggest that the essential feature of a glass case or cage was probably that it had a glass front. Richard Jackson (*129*) had 'an old Glass cage with some tickney ware belonging to it'. John Field (*119*) had a 'Glass case with some white ware in it'. John Eyton (*148*) owned a 'Glass case with toys'. The one owned by William Cheshire (*249*) was nevertheless used for the storage of glassware, and was described as '1 Glass cage & glasses'.

Many inventories include chests, trunks, boxes and coffers, although they are rarely described in detail. In 1734 an 'Old Dutch Coffer' worth 4s. was mentioned, and William Langley (*110*) had an iron-bound trunk. Richard Stanier (*154*) had a portmanteau trunk. The meanest form of such receptacles was the dale (or deal) box, made of softwood. Elizabeth Bullock (*218*) had one in 1681. They were to be found in the kitchen of of John Eyton's (*148*) large house, and in the shops of mercers.

A desk was originally a portable and lockable box, and John Field's (*119*) 'desk upon a frame' recorded in 1693 evidences the transition from the original to the modern meaning. Desks were used throughout the period, and are mentioned on about a dozen inventories, principally those of people of wealth. Some are described as 'joyne' desks and two as writing desks. Walter Broadhurst (*65*) had a reading desk in his comfortably furnished parlour. John Eyton (*148*) had in his dining-room a 'scriptoire' (from the French 'escriptoire', a writing desk) which was valued at £1 10s. 0d. and was perhaps the best desk recorded in the collection.

The earliest reference to a *chest of drawers* is on the inventory of Richard Clowes (*8*) in 1679, and the inventories suggest that such items became relatively common during the period reviewed. An earlier form of the dresser was perhaps the 'box with drawers' among the possessions of William Whitmore (*36*) in 1667. John Eyton (*148*) had two chests of drawers in his own chamber, and there is a 'nest of drawers' in the 'Misstress's chamber'.

By the 1730s inventories begin to refer to *dressers of drawers*, and it would seem that the traditional Shropshire dresser, with shelves for household utensils mounted on a cabinet of drawers, evolved during the period under review. As early as 1679 Richard Clowes (*8*) had a dresser in his kitchen, and in 1690 John Simmonds (*55*) had two dressers in his dairy. In 1716 William Doughty (*161*) had in his buttery a dresser with wooden and earthenware on it. Robert Roe (*162*) the following year had a dresser with drawers and a pewter frame, the latter, presumably, a flight of shelves for the display of pewter mounted above the drawers. Most subsequent references to dressers, as well as items like 'a dish bench and drawers' can be interpreted as being similar pieces of furniture. In the inventory of Samuel Podmore in 1740 the dresser is itemised with the pewter in the kitchen, and in that of John Harrison (*31*) in 1746 there is a 'pewter frame and drawers'.

Few inventories describe the purposes to which the boxes, coffers, chests and trunks to be found in most households were put, but the few which do can be used to illuminate the many which do not. Sometimes such items were used for the storage of grain and other foods. In the barn of Richard Bridgwood (*9*) was 'one greate Corn Hutch'. In the kitchen of John Steventon (*58*) was 'one trunk with beans and pease'. Most boxes and coffers were employed for the storage of linen or clothing. Francis Wright (*127*) had a 'coofer' with some wheat in it, but also a coffer with a few linens. Edward Harrington (*87*) had among his possessions 'ye great truncke . . . (with) . . . . all sorts of linens with some of his wife's clothes'. William Icke (*177*) had '2 chests and 2 beds in them with some Linnen'. Francis Richards (*95*) had 'one trunk with linnens, table cloths and sheets'. John Eyton's (*148*) possessions in 1708-9 included a chest with coarse linen, a large trunk with fine linen, and a napkin press, which may have been a cupboard, or alternatively a screw-press for removing creases. Richard Stanier (*154*) also had one, as did Ralph Leeke (*199*) and Thomas Calcott (*264*). William Cheese (*124*) had a desk with linens in it, the term being used here in its original sense. Benjamin Wright (*132*) was keeping blankets in a coffer, and Benjamin Langley (*191*) was storing linen in a chest of drawers. The most illuminating inventory on the subject of household storage is that of Richard Philips (*144*) taken in 1705, which include '1 Small Chest marked EW with several small Remnants of Lynnen Cloth'. 'EW' represented the initials of his parents, Elinor and William.[93] He also had 'one small box Carved with several parcells of Lynnen in', 'One other great box with several sorts of Lynnen in', 'One Trunk marked 1661 of old cloths', 'One Chest of new Lynnen Cloth Containing 14 pieces with other wearing Lynnen', 'One Broad oak box with a Silk body of a gown and hood & skarf and several other pieces of Silk remants & Lynnens' and 'Two dale boxes with some Remnts of Callicoe & Severall old wearing Lynnens in'.

Beds were in most households the most valuable items of furniture, and in the homes of the wealthy they were, with their furnishings, often valued at more than £5, more than the total possessions of many of the poor. The many joyned bedsteads were probably of the rigid four-poster type illustrated by Mr. Steer.[94] Standing beds mentioned on several inventories were solidly built bedsteads sufficiently high off the ground for a smaller bed to be stored beneath them. Sometimes the word 'bed' is used to mean simply a mattress, in which case the bedsteads are usually separately mentioned. Across the frame of the *bedstead* were laced *cords*, which are mentioned on several inventories, and on them was placed a rush *mat*, on which rested the *bed* or mattress, filled with feathers, down, flock or chaff. With the bed went its 'appurtenances' or 'furniture', bolsters and pillows stuffed with the same kinds of materials as the beds, and covered with pillow *beers*. There were sheets on most beds, above which were *coverings, hillings,* blankets, and in some cases *quilts, rugs* or *counterpanes.* Above the bed might be a tester or canopy, or in some cases a half-tester, or half bed, and around it a range of curtains fringed with valences.

A typical bed which provides some of the details missing on other inventories was that of Joyce Bradshaw (*106*), described in 1687 as '1 p of Bedsteeds, a Sett of Green Curtains, one Cover lett, one Rugg, 1 Blankett, 1 under Bed, one Fither Bed, 3 pillows, a fither bolster', which was valued at £5 10s. 0d. A less luxurious bed was that of Thomas Stanworth (*157*), valued at £2 10s. 0d., described as 'The Bed Stides & Curtens & Vallins Cord & Matt 2 Blanketts & 1 old Rugg'. John Field (*119*) had 'one old Civerlett and blankett, one pair of bedsteds, Cover and Matt and cord', an item followed by three curtains and valence and three curtain rods which were doubtless part of the bed's furnishings. In another room iron curtain rods held up green curtains above a bed. Richard Philips (*144*) had a set of curtains on a bed 'with a silk fringe about ye vallence'. At the other end of the social scale, in the house of Richard Glover (*167*) was 'an old hurden chaff bed'. This is one of the few inventories to reveal the material from which the bed itself, the *tick* which contained the filling, was made. Eliza Darrall (*6*) had a canvas bed tick, and John Walford a coarse hempen one, but probably finer qualities of linen were used for the purpose in the homes of the rich.

Many households contained truckle, trickle, trundell, or low beds, which were usually set on casters, which enabled them to be rolled away under standing beds in day-time. Often such beds were used for servants, as in the inventory of John Binnell (*227*) or that of Richard Goodales (*117*) who had 'one lowe paire of bedsteads for a servant to lay in'.

Sheets are sometimes described as coarse or fine, but most commonly in terms of various grades of linen: Holland, flaxen, hempen, hurden, twill, canvas, huckaback and noggen.[95] Pillow beers or cases were made of similar materials and, like sheets, were sometimes ornamented. Joyce Bradshaw (*106*) had '7 lased pillow beers & 2 playne ones & a pr laced sheets'.

Blankets occur commonly throughout the period, but the inventories reveal little about them, and they were not stocked by the Wellington mercers. While *mats* were placed between the network of cords stretched between the bedsteads and the mattress, *rugs* were clearly among the clothes placed on the tops of beds. Nathan Peploe (*28*) had a rug with his blankets, while the inventory of Eliza Darrall (*6*) couples '1 Green rug and two blankets'. Ralph Barrett (*48*), Allen Adams (*102*), and William Cartwright (*74),* respectively had green, red and white rugs among the furnishings of their beds. Richard Bridgwood (*9*) had a thrum coverlett, either one with a shaggy tuft-covered surface, or one with a ring of tassels at the edge. Four inventories, all of them after 1700, mention quilts among the bed-clothes. Beds were heated with warming pans, which occur in many inventories. John Hampton (*169*) had a brass one. Cradles are frequently itemised, and there is one reference to a cradle cloth.

Hangings, tapestries, or other fabrics used to decorate walls occur in some inventories of the wealthy, like that of John Eyton (*148*). An inventory of 1682 refers to cloth hangings at the chimney, and the Rev. Henry Wood (*156*) had 'a sett of Hangings & Window Curtains'. Most references to curtains refer to those which hung around beds, and window curtains are normally distinguished. The earliest reference to window curtains is to the four made of calico which belonged to Joshua Johnson (*126*) in 1696.

Screens are mentioned in many households are are most commonly found in sleeping rooms. John Eyton (*148*) had a twiggen screen, and William Doughty (*161*) possessed large and lesser wainscot screens. It is usually possible to identify malt screens by the context. Wainscot or panelling was to be found in various forms, chiefly in the homes of the wealthy. It was used as chair or bench backs, screens or wall covering. Thomas Wright (*83*) had wainscot portals in the hall of his house and the chamber above.

Looking-glasses are listed in 90 households, and it is a sign of increasing levels of comfort that 56 of the references occur on inventories made after 1700. The values of looking-glasses varied from £2 10s. 0d. to 6d., but no distinction is made between hand-glasses and full-length standing mirrors, so that variations are not surprising. Pictures are listed on 31 inventories, 27 of them made after 1710. Four inventories mention maps, usually framed, and hanging on walls, and two, those of Richard Clowes (*8*) and William Langley (*110*) include coats of arms. There are three references to weather glasses, the earliest on the inventory of Richard Stanier (*154*) in 1711. The contents of only two picture frames are described. Richard Stanier had a portrait of Dr. Sacheverell, while William Cooper (*186*) in 1730 had a copy of a speech by King William III. Apart from hunting weapons, there are few indications of how people spent any leisure time they might have, but Richard Clowes (*8*) in 1679 had a chess board, the Rev. John Field (*119*) a pair of 'boules', and Ralph Barratt (*49*) a pair of skates.

Only four inventories mention musical instruments. Richard Clowes (*8*) had a pair of virginals, William Banks (*160*), the surgeon, possessed a spinet, and Thomas Cooper in 1684 (*222*) owned 'a treble vyall and case', worth ten shillings. The largest collection of instruments was that of Richard Phillips (*144*) which comprised three violins worth £1 2s. 6d., a steel bow, three flutes worth 2s. 9d., and five sets of chimes. This suggests a lower level of musical activity than in the cathedral city of Lichfield, which is hardly surprising, but it compares well with the parts of Essex studied by Mr. Steer, where only one person had an instrument.[96]

Books are mentioned on 97 inventories, 11.47 per cent. of the total, and the references are spread evenly throughout the period. The most valuable collection was that of the Rev. Henry Wood (*156*), who had a study of books worth forty-five pounds. John Eyton (*148*) had books in his study worth £38 12s. 6d., while the contents of the studies of the Rev. William Langley (*110*) and Ralph Leek (*199*) were both valued at twenty pounds. William Cartwright (*74*), the mathematician, had 100 books; the Rev. John Field (*119*) had 131, which were bound and 14 unbound; and Charles Eyton (*17*) had 20 old books worth one pound. Nineteen of the references to books are specifically to Bibles, several people had dictionaries and, intriguingly, Mary Sockett (*142*), who appears to have been little more than a poverty-stricken vagrant, had 'one old history book'. Peter Langley (*258*) in 1735 had two books valued at 4s., 'Dreclincourt upon Death and Beaumont psyche', which were probably the Huguenot Charles Drelincourt's *Christian's Defence against the Fears of Death*, published in 1675, and the epic poem *Psyche*, published in 1648 by Joseph Beaumont, the Royalist Master of Peterhouse.

Facilities for weighing whether in the household or the workplace were limited. Only five inventories, all of considerable total value, mention scales or beams for weighing. Thomas Jones (*118*) had brass and lead weights for use on scales. Several inventories (*194, 203*) mention steelyards used for weighing meat. There were more utensils for measuring volume. Pints and quarts for liquids, and strikes for measuring grain are frequently mentioned.

An increased awareness of clock time was one of the most marked changes in social habits during the Industrial Revolution.[97] The

# INTRODUCTION

inventories suggest that such awareness increased dramatically in the Shropshire coalfield in the half century before the great expansion of the iron industry in the 1750s. If an increased awareness of clock time was one of the preconditions for new forms of economic organisation, there is plentiful evidence that it existed in Shropshire. Watches were rarely used, only eight being itemised during the whole period, one of them a silver watch. Only seven clocks are recorded in inventories between 1660 and 1700, but six are itemised during the first decade of the 18th century, and no less than 74 in the ensuing 40 years. The costs of clocks fell steadily during this period. The mean value in the first decade of the 18th century was £3 10s. 0d., which in successive decades fell to £3 0s. 0d., £2 18s. 0d., £2 0s. 0d., until in the 1740s it was only £1.15s. 0d. In the early years of the 18th century most clocks were owned by yeomen farmers or innkeepers. By 1740 those who possessed them included a blacksmith, a collier, and a maltster. No inventory survives for a clockmaker, and William Webb, the only Wellington clockmaker, known to have been active in the period, only started work in 1750. There were, nevertheless, at least seven clockmakers in Shrewsbury in the first half of the 18th century, and nine in Ludlow, as well as individuals working in Ellesmere, Newport, Oswestry, Bishop's Castle, and Whitchurch.[98] Most of the timepieces listed were clocks with cases. The surgeon William Birch (*160*) had a clock with chimes, and in 1709 a German clock was recorded.

Guns are listed on 31 inventories. Most were fowling or birding weapons, doubtless used for hunting in the woodlands remaining in the area, or on the Weald moors. An inventory of 1660 includes 'one old carbine and one old sword', which may have been weapons once used in the Civil War, and several others refer to weapons like halberds, battle axes with pointed projections like spears, which could only have been used in wartime. A halberd worth a guinea is mentioned on an inventory of 1679, and Ralph Barrett (*49*) in 1683 had two halberds, a half-pike and a sword. Joshua Johnson (*126*) in 1696 had three old swords and a hanger. After 1700 only two inventories mention weapons which were not firearms. Six inventories mention pistols, and one a blunderbuss Weapons occur as might be expected, among the equipment of keepers. Lewis Dale (*44*) had three guns worth £2, and William Whitmore (*36*) in 1667 had 'bowes, Gunns and all manner of Keepers implements and Engines', as well as a stag skin and four buckskins. The pewter guns found in many diaries were not weapons but gauns.

Seventy-eight inventories mention gold or silver, 50 of them dating from the 17th century, about 14 per cent. of the total in that period, and 28 from the first half of the 18th century, just under six per cent. of the total. Gold was usually in the form of rings or coins, and silver usually meant spoons. In the 17th century silver spoons could be worth as much as £1 each, although some were valued at no more than five shillings. Eighteenth-century values tend to be much lower. The inventories reveal a great variety of individual items. Thomas Wright (*83*) had a silver bowl worth £1 10s. 0d., and Thomas Cartwright (*32*) in 1661 possessed 18 silver bowls. Mary Shelton (*42*) had spoons, two bowls, a seal, and perhaps the most unusual of all silver items, a bird-call. Richard Phillips's (*144*) silver included a cup with ears on, two bodkins, and a whistle. Mary Hunt (*100*) and Joyce Bradshaw (*106*) also had bodkins. One of the largest collections of silver was that of Rowland Goole (*147*), who had tankards, salts, a cup, spoons, forks, and tumblers worth twenty pounds. Two inventories list countersat or counterford dishes, which were probably of base metal made to look like gold or silver.

Fifty-three inventories, 6.9 per cent. of the total, refer to pottery.[99] Earthenware was manufactured in the Shropshire coalfield at Benthall, Jackfield, Little Wenlock, and possibly elsewhere. Mercers in most parts of the country stocked pottery, but the Wellington mercers had none, which suggests that the commoner wares were obtained locally, either direct from the potters, or from itinerant hawkers. The Rev. Richard Pococke, when visiting North Staffordshire in 1750, noted that imperfect wares were sold very cheaply to hawkers.[100] Many references are simply to earthenware, but 10 inventories, ranging in date from 1677 to 1739 mention *Tickneyware,* a type of pottery which took its name from the Derbyshire village of Ticknall, and which often had a black glaze. The term may have been used to denote a kind of pottery rather than its place of origin, and it is not unlikely that some of the Tickneyware in the inventories was a form of the fine black-glazed earthenware manufactured in the Severn Gorge, which is generally called Jackfield ware. Six inventories ranging from 1689 to 1732 refer to white ware. There is a reference in 1732 to 'blew plates' and an inventory of 1681 mentions jugs with blue spots. There are references to earthen steans, and earthen platters. Thomasin Hawkins (*71*) had 10 tickney milk-pans and some dishes of the same ware. The very large number of inventories on which wooden trenchers are listed, and the almost universal presence of pewter plates even in poor houses, suggests that even earthenware may not have been used in every home.

Five inventories refer to *china,* the earliest in 1682 and the last in 1737. It is likely that all of these relate to imported Oriental pottery of the kind generally called Nanking ware. The china was all located in the households of wealthy people like Jane Hartshorne (*194*) and William Langley (*110*).

Bottles were valued sufficiently highly to merit mention on a large number of inventories. Those of William Whitmore (*36*) and John Steventon (*58*) distinguish wooden from glass bottles. Joshua Dunton (*95*) had wooden and stone bottles. William Langley (*110*) had 20 wooden bottles worth a shilling. Glass bottles were generally more expensive.

Jane Schofield (237) had 24 worth a penny each. Joshua Johnson (126) had 96 worth twopence each. John Walker (86) had a rack for bottles. Glasses for drinking are listed in some of the more prosperous households. Peter Langley (258) kept flint glasses with his China Delf. Rowland Goole (147), the innkeeper, had three dozen glasses. Margaret Vickers in 1730 had a glass decanter, as did William Webb (203), who also had small glasses to accompany it.

## The Kitchen[101]

Foodstuffs were often omitted from probate inventories since they had no permanent value, but many inventories nevertheless record household provisions without going into detail. Meat and dairy produce which could be kept for long periods are listed with reasonable frequency. The latter is often called *whitemeat*, as on the inventory of Richard Hawkins (59). Beef or bacon or both are mentioned on 93 inventories before 1700, about a quarter of the total, but during the first half of the 18th century they are listed on only 50, about 10 per cent. of the total. It would seem therefore that the practice of keeping salt meat through the winter was diminishing during the period, although there are numerous individual examples right up to the 1740s. John Smith (254) in 1731-32 had '2 sides of Bacon in ye Salt' worth sixteen shillings. John Steventon (58) had in his larder 'Two Salting Tubs with beefe & pork in salt' which were valued at three pounds. Thomas Smith (224) had 'one vessel to salt meat in', and there are many similar references. The value of beef and bacon was rarely more than £2, and most of the households where it was listed were concerned with farming. Very few tradesmen's inventories mention meat. Inventories usually describe meat as 'flitches' or 'flitchens' of bacon or beef. Only one inventory which mentions part of the brisket gives any further details about meat, although one innkeeper had 12 neats' (i.e. calves') tongues.

Many inventories give detailed pictures of the contents of kitchens, and from the contents of the most detailed it is possible to gain an impression of the rest. Kitchens which are described particularly well include Nos. *24, 36, 49, 73, 95, 103, 118, 119, 132, 148, 249,* and *264.*

At the centre of the kitchen was a *grate*, normally of iron, and often with racks called *niggards* forming a false bottom to catch unconsumed pieces of fuel. John Field's (119) weighed 39lbs., and was valued at 6s. 2d. In almost every household was a *fire shovel* or *slice* and a *pair of tongs* for stoking the fire. John Field's fire shovel was made of steel instead of the more usual wrought iron. Robert Peate (133) had a *coal hatchet* among the implements around his fireplace. More rarely there was a *poker* or *proker*. The area of the fire could be contracted by the use of *cheeks*. Often at the back of the grate was an iron *fire back* preventing the fireplace from being damaged by the continual heat. Such firebacks were some of the first objects to be made in cast-iron, and were often highly decorative. It is not surprising that in an ironmaking region they were relatively common. William Whitmore (26) had a 'plate behind the ffyer' worth 5s., and Margaret Dunton possessed a 'plate of cast metal' in one room, and a 'plate for ye back of ye fire' in another. A pair of *bellows* was often kept by the grate, and a *fender* or *defender* would prevent the unwary from falling in.

On either side of the grate might be *andirons*, large fire-dogs or trestles of iron on which revolved spits. *Cob-irons*, often called 'cobberts' or 'gobberts', long bars fitted with hooks, which rested against the back of a fireplace at an angle of about 45 degrees, were an alternative means of supporting a spit. *Creepers* were usually small fire-dogs placed between the andirons, although the word can refer to a small iron frying-pan with three legs. *Spits* were of different kinds to suit various sorts of meat. Richard Jones (111) and William Cheshire (249) had *bird spits* in their kitchens. A *broach* or *broche* was a long, tapering pin which was pushed through the meat. A joint might be further secured with skewers. William Cheshire (249) had a skewer frame with 12 skewers worth two shillings. A spit was turned by a machine called a jack, usually worked by a weight suspended on a chain and a system of gears. William Langley (110) had a *jack* and *weights*, and John Doddell in 1728 (24) a *'jack, chains and cords'.* The *clock* and *jack* owned by John Cherrington (195) may have been a clockwork device for turning the spit, and the dog-wheel among Andrew Sockett's (174) possessions may have been used for the same purpose. Beneath the spit there was usually a *dripping pan* of iron or tin plate, to catch the fat and juices exuded from the cooking flesh. A *basting spoon* or *basting ladle* of iron or brass would be employed to pour these liquids over the meat, and *flesh forks* were used to test it, or remove it when cooked.

Above a grate there were often *pot gales, geals* or *goals*, small swing cranes from which would be suspended *gale hooks* or *pot links*, to the end of which cooking utensils would be attached by *pot hooks, hangers* or *hanglesses*. The *cranes* owned by Ralph Leeks (199) and Thomas Calcott (264) and the 'sway pole and Links' in the house of William Langley (110) were probably larger versions of the usual gales. From the gales would be suspended a *kettle, boiler* or *furnace* which could be used for making soup, boiling vegetables or meat, or as a constant source of hot water. Pots of this kind were made either of brass or iron. The first Abraham Darby made cast-iron pots from the time he began to operate the Coalbrookdale ironworks in 1709, but the inventories make it clear that cast-iron pots were known in the district much earlier. Joshua Dunton (95) in 1680 had 'an iron furnace of cast metal', and iron kettles and frying-pans are mentioned in the 1660s. Cooking pots were often called *marmites* or *marmotts*, and smaller examples were known by various diminutive forms of the word, *marmaletts*, *marmalades* or *marmolotts*. Large metal pots could be of considerable value. Henry Stanworth (*103*) had a brass furnace worth £1 in 1685. Kettles are commonplace, but exactly what sort of utensil was the 'little Flanders Kettle' owned by Andrew Sockett (*174*) is uncertain. While cooking pots were in use, a *skimmer* or *scummer*, usually a perforated brass implement could be used to remove unwanted elements.

Other cooking utensils might stand in the grate itself. *Posnetts* were pots rather like modern saucepans, but with three feet, on which they could be stood among hot ashes. William Langley (*110*) had a utensil defined as 'a posnett with three feet'. Posnetts made of iron are listed as early as 1662, but they could also be made of brass, and in 1711 there is a reference to one made of maslin. *Skelletts* were similar long-handled cooking pots with feet, which enabled them to be stood in a shallow fire. *Frying-pans*, either of brass or iron are common, and Thomas Calcott (*264*) had one specifically for tossing. *Gridirons*, like that on the inventory of Joshua Dunton (*95*) are not uncommon. They would probably have had long handles like frying-pans. *Toasters* are commonly mentioned on the more detailed inventories, and must have been found in many households. John Duddell (*24*) had an iron toaster for bread, probably rather like a small gridiron, and Joyce Bradshaw (*106*), John Field (*119*), Benjamin Wright (*137*), Thomas Stanworth (*157*), and John Bromley (*181*) were among those who had *cheese toasters*.

*Chafing dishes* were used throughout the period for keeping food warm. Such a dish was placed on a *chafer* containing hot ashes or charcoal. Chafing dishes were sometimes made of brass and sometimes of iron. William Minshall (*109*) had examples of each. Richard Parwall (*4*) was among those who had *waffering* or *waffle irons*, used for baking waffles over a fire. Some cooking was done in ovens, probably in brick-built bread ovens. Inventories survive for only two bakers, and *mitts*, *turnells* and other receptacles for kneading are sufficiently common to suggest that bread was baked in many homes. Utensils for use in the oven are listed in most detailed inventories. Several include *pasty plates*, that of Thomas Cartwright (*32*) being described as a 'pewter pastry plate', that of Mary Shelton (*42*) a 'tin pastery plate', and that of William Langley (*110*) a 'tin pasty pan'. *Patty pans* for cooking small tarts or pies are mentioned on several inventories, among them that of John Eyton (*148*) who had 13 of them. William Howle (*84*) was among those who had *pudding plates*. Several inventories list plates for roasting apples, among them one of 1730 which itemises a *tin apple roaster*.

A great variety of other implements and receptacles were used in kitchens, although it is obvious that many of the smaller items were listed only by the most meticulous appraisers. *Mortars* and *pestles* were commonly used, usually of brass or cast iron, but Henry Stanworth (*103*) had a wooden mortar with iron hoops, and Peter Langley (*258*) possessed both marble and brass mortars. *Maslin kettles* occur fairly frequently in 18th-century inventories. Maslin was an alloy of copper and zinc alloyed in different proportions from brass, but the *maslin kettle* used in boiling fruit or brewing, as in the household of Francis Peat (*208*), was frequently of brass or tinned copper. *Cullinders,* often of tin, are common, but *pepper boxes* of brass or tin seem to have been confined to the wealthier households. In most kitchens there were *hacking knives,* and sometimes *cleavers* for cutting meat. Henry Stanworth (*103*) had a *hatchett* and a *chopping knife* in his kitchen. Perhaps the most esoteric items of kitchen equipment were the *syllabub cups* listed on the inventory of William Langley (*110*).

Brass and pewter were to be found in almost every household. Only 215 inventories, most of which do not detail household possessions fail to mention either brass or pewter; 615 include pewter, some 72.7 per cent. of the total. Brass was slightly less common, being listed on 463 or 54.7 per cent. of the inventories. Such items commonly made up a considerable proportion of the value of an estate, and the amount in the house of even a moderately wealthy farmer or town tradesman could often exceed in value the total possessions of many poorer people. Godfrey Williams in 1689 left brass and pewter worth £8, and John Binnell (*227*) had brass and pewter worth £8 10s. 0d. in 1688.

Pewter dishes, basins, plates, saucers, candlesticks, cups, spoons and chamber pots are all very common. *Porringers,* dishes suitable for porridge, are mentioned on many inventories. Pewter *gauns,* ladles for dispensing milk, are listed in many dairies, and are sometimes, confusingly, called guns. Some of the wealthier households had ornamental pewter; *salvers, tankards* (often called tancots), *flagons, salts* or salt cellars, and *mustard pots.* Measures were sometimes made of pewter. William Howle (*84*) had a gill, a half pint, a pint and a quart. Several inventories place a value on pewter. On that of Henry Stanworth in 1684 (*103*) it was assessed at 7d. or 8d. a pound. Thomas Jones's (*118*) 'old pewter' in 1692 was worth 6d. a pound, and the rest eightpence. Pewter dishes in the inventory of Richard Stainer (*154*) were valued at 10d. a pound, but most 18th-century inventories rate pewter at 7d. a pound.

Brass was similarly used for a variety of purposes. Mary Hunt (*100*) in 1682 had two great brass pots and a little one, one great brass kettle, one brass pan, a lesser brass kettle, two little bright brass kettles, and skillett, one other brass kettle, a brass chafing dish, two brass ladles, a brass skimmer, and a brass warming pan. Other inventories list brass candlesticks, posnets, basting spoons, caldrons, mortars and pepper boxes. On the inventory of Thomas Jones (*118*) in 1692 pans were assessed at 10d. a pound, but pots and candlesticks at as little as 4d. a

## INTRODUCTION

pound. The usual value in the 18th century was about 9d. a pound, slightly higher than pewter. In general the values of these materials in Shropshire seem to be marginally lower than those recorded by Mr. Steer in Essex.[102]

A few inventories, all of them made after 1700, include copper utensils, usually described as simply pots or cans. This may reflect the increasing availability of copper sheeting in England, but the amount of copper so used was insignificant when compared with that used alloyed with zinc in the form of brass.

The first tin plate mill in the West Midlands was set up at Bringewood near Ludlow in 1741–42.[103] The inventories show that tin plate utensils, as well as objects like candlesticks which were probably made of cast tin, were in common use in Shropshire well before that date. Tinware is mentioned in 17 inventories before 1700, and in 43 made in the 18th century. It was not confined to the homes of the wealthy, but can be found even in the houses of labourers. It was used for kitchen utensils and also for more elegant items. Richard Stanier (154) had two tin pudding pans worth a shilling. John Duddell (28) had patty pans, covers, pudding plates, a colander, a pastry pan, a baster, and a candlebox all of tin. Margaret Vickers in 1730 had a tin pudding plate, pudding pan and pudding cup, a skimmer, dripping pan, cover, candlestick, tuning dish, tobacco salver, egg slice, patty pans, quarts and pints, coffee pot, and dredger.

Wooden plates or trenchers were commonly used in Telford throughout the period under review. They were rarely considered to be worth more than a penny each, and sometimes, as on the inventory of Henry Stanworth (103) as little as a halfpenny. The most valuable were those of William Keen (30) who had a dozen worth 1s. 6d. They are probably not mentioned on the less detailed inventories as being of too little value. None of the Telford inventories reveal what sorts of wood were used for trenchers, but it is known from a Stottesdon inventory of 1723 that they were sometimes made of maple.[104]

The inventories suggest that food was normally transferred from the pewter plate or the trencher to the mouth by hand. Table cutlery is rarely mentioned, and most types were valued sufficiently highly to suggest that it was not often omitted when it was present. Only 19 17th-century inventories include cutlery, and most of them mention only spoons. Frequently they were of pewter and of low value, so they may often have been itemised with other pewter. Basil Richards (1) had silver spoons worth 8s. each, but his pewter spoons were valued at only 8d. a dozen. Mary Hunt (100) had 12 pewter spoons valued at a shilling. Margaret Justice (107) had spoons made of antimony. Forks occur on three 17th-century inventories, one of them as early as 1661, but the other two references are in the 1690s. One of them is in the inventory of

Joshua Johnson (*126*), the only one before 1700 to mention table knives. Between 1700 and 1750 table knives are mentioned on 10 inventories, and table forks on eleven. Rowland Goole (*147*) had six silver forks, while Peter Langley (*258*) had half a dozen silver-hafted knives and forks, worth, with their case, £3, as well as six old knives and forks, valued, with a sassafras knife, at four shillings. The presence on the inventories of William Cheshire (*249*) in 1725 of 11 knives and 11 forks worth 4s., and of Thomas Calcott (*264*) in 1744 of 14 knives and forks worth 3s., suggest that the price of table cutlery was falling, and that such items were becoming reasonably commonplace in the homes of the wealthy.

Wicker or twiggen was used in many kitchens for a variety of purposes, some of which are defined in the inventory of Francis Bayley (*130*) who had 'Sives and Ridles wiskits Baskets and other twigen wares'. It was used in particular for the storage of grain. Richard Hawkins (*59*) had 'Whiskets and other necessaries for keeping and holding corn'. John Smith (*254*) had a whisket of malt. William Langley (*11*) had two 'arkes' for corn, recalling the ark of bulrushes in which the infant Moses was placed. William Adney (*79*) had three straw bings with oats, but bings were as likely to have been made of solid wood as of basket-work. Similarly, not all household sieves or riddles were made of twigs since Andrew Socket (*174*) had a wire riddle.

### Water, Lighting and Heating

The inventories provide only a few insights into the supply of household water and its use in laundering or personal toilets. Buckets are mentioned frequently and occasionally there are references to stone or lead cisterns. Thomas Jones (*118*) had a leaden pump and cistern in his kitchen, and the inventory of the Rev. Henry Wood (*156*) mentions 'ye curb of ye well, bucket &c.), but these are the only direct references to sources of water. William Judgson (*171*) had a bathing tub, and Edward Harrington (*87*) a basin and ewer. Chamber pots, usually of pewter are quite common. Close stools, or commodes are also mentioned relatively frequently, as are the buckets, pails or pans which went into them. Some inventories include wash-tubs, and irons are mentioned on about twenty, the earliest in 1666. Usually they are described simply as smoothing irons. The inventory of John Cherrington (*195*) mentions box irons and flat irons, and that of Thomas Calcott (*264*) a 'box iron to heat smooth irons'. That of William Cheshire lists flat irons, a box iron, and heaters for them. The usual definition of a box iron is one in which there was a cavity to contain a heater.

The commonest form of household lighting of which there is evidence in the inventories is the candle, but few actual candles are mentioned, and the inventory of only one candlemaker's inventory is found in the

# INTRODUCTION

collection. Candlesticks feature very commonly, however, made of iron, tin, pewter, brass, or maslin. Candle-snuffers of brass, tin or iron are found in many inventories, and candle-boxes occur in some of those which are highly detailed. John Duddell (*28*) had a tin one. Lanterns are frequently listed, but not described in detail. Steel mills for providing fire are mentioned on several inventories (*144, 146, 242, 256*).

Stocks of coal are mentioned on only 12 inventories, of which two are of people engaged in mining and refer to heaps on the pit bank, and two others are of maltsters and probably refer to coking coal kept specially for that purpose. Otherwise coal is usually itemised in such a way as to suggest that it was not highly valued. In one case it is listed with undressed hemp, in another with muck, and in a third with old books. Coal is probably mentioned so rarely because it was cheap. The whole of the district was within easy reach of mines, even its outermost extremity, the township of Walcot being less than five miles from the busy pits of Ketley. In parts of Shropshire remote from collieries like the Bishop's Castle area, coal, with other fuels like faggots, furze and broom, appear on a relatively high proportion of inventories. In Telford, where transport had not added to its cost, it was obviously hardly worth noting.

## *The Dairy*

Dairy equipment is mentioned in 148 or 17.5 per cent. of the inventories. It ranges from the few pails and a churn to make butter to be found among the possessions of some of the very poor, to superbly-equipped dairies like that of Thomas Calcott (*264*), which, with its cheese vats and presses, its whey tub, scales and cheese ladders, was valued at £8 14s. 10d., more than the total possessions of many people. Some dairy equipment, particularly that of the 24 people who had equipment but no cows, was probably no longer in use. It is clear that some butter or cheese was made by people who were very poor. A Wellington man who died in 1679 had only two cows, and his total estate was valued at only £4 18s. 0d., but he had a churn to make butter. Michael Onions (*23*) left possessions worth only £16 12s. 9d., and his neighbour, Edward Darrall (*21*) had goods worth only £4 13s. 0d., but each left dairy equipment, the former 'one old churn with other necessaries belonging to the dairy' and the latter some 'milk vessels'.

The pails, vats, coolers, churns and other receptacles used in making butter and cheese could in most cases have also been used for brewing, but in practice they would not have been employed for both purposes, since both beer and dairy products would have been contaminated. It is usually clear from the context in the inventories for which purpose particular items were being used.

Dairy equipment was normally assumed to be made of wood, and in some inventories it is included under the heading of *wooden* or *treen* or, with the brewing equipment, as *coopery* ware. The inventory of William Leeke (*37*) uses coopery and trinen ware synonymously, and quotes barrels as an example. An inventory of 1685 mentions 'vessels of wood for milk and cheese', while one of 1702 refers to 'the wooden ware belonging to the dairy'. Some earthenware was also used in dairies. An inventory of 1719 itemises six earthen pan pots with a churn, a barrel turnell; one of 1714 includes Tickney milk pans, and one of 1725 mentions milk pans and stone pots. Milk was brought from the cow in a *can* or pail. The inventory of Phillip Howle (*223*) refers to 'pails to milk in'. Its temperature might then be reduced in a *cooler*. The inventory of Thomas Bryan (*188*) refers to 'a large oval cooler'. The milk might then be put into a shallow open container to allow the cream to rise. This might be a *mitt*, since one inventory of 1685 refers to 'five mitts for milk'. It might be ladled into the mitt from the cooler by a *piggin*, which was a small pail made like a barrel, but with one stave longer than the rest serving as a handle, or by a *gaun*, which was a cylindrical metal receptacle with a long handle, usually holding a measured quantity. An inventory of 1687 refers to a *milking gaun*, and one of 1707 to a *lading gaun*. Once the cream had risen to the surface it would be taken off with a *skimmer*, a utensil found in dairies as well as kitchens, and put aside for making butter. The skimmed milk would then be heated to about 68deg. F. in a *cheese vat,* sometimes corrupted to a *cheswit*, and rennet, extracted from calves' stomachs, would be added to bring about the separation of the curds and the whey. The curds would then be cut up and placed in a cloth, often called a *hair sieve* or *search*. It would then be placed under a *cheese press*, and would subsequently be placed upon a flight of shelves called a *ladder*, like that owned by Thomas Stanworth (*152*), or on 'a frame to bear cheeses upon' and the '7 shelves for that use' mentioned in the inventory of Phillip Howle (*223*). The whey might be poured through a funnel or *tundish*, sometimes called a *tuning dish* and then fed to pigs.

The cream would be stored in a *cream stean* like that owned by a Lilleshall farmer in 1711, and then worked in a *churn*. William Cheshire (*249*), Thomas Bryan (*188*), and John Harris (*31*) all had churns worked with staffs. After it had been in the churn for between 15 to 30 minutes it would be strained in a *sieve* or a *search*, and then kneaded in a *kneading mitt*, a utensil itemised with a churn in the inventory of Richard Bridgwood (*9*), or a *kneading turnell* of the sort mentioned in the inventories of Thomas Dunn in 1685, Catherine North in 1732, and John Smith (*54*). Salt would be worked in at this stage, and *salting mitts* are mentioned in inventories of 1732 and 1744, and an inventory of 1683 mentions a pail of salt butter. These implements were doused in boiling water before use, presumably in a *scalding turnell* of the type mentioned in the inventory of William Bill (*52*) or a scalding tub, listed in an inventory of 1713. When all the buttermilk was extracted, the butter would

## INTRODUCTION

be moulded and stored in a *stean*, an item mentioned in 1663 and 1664, or a tub, referred to in an inventory of 1702. It is impossible to assign a precise purpose to every receptacle listed among dairy equipment in the inventories. Occasionally *looms* are mentioned. They were open vessels like buckets and in the inventory of Ann Wright in 1681 were listed with barrels, pails, turnells, bowls and a gaun. William Leeke's (*37*) looms were itemised with his coopery ware. *Runlets* or *rindlets* or *rindling vessels* were small casks, listed in some dairies. *Kimnels* or *kummels* were small tubs, and one inventory refers specifically to milk kummels.

The importance of the pig to the dairy farmer is confirmed by the inventories. Of the 124 inventories listing dairy equipment, which also include cows, 85 also mention pigs. Thomas Smith (*224*) had, with his cheese press, an 'ould stound to keep wash' which was perhaps intended to feed whey or buttermilk to pigs.

*The Brewhouse*

Beer was the most commonly used beverage in Telford in the period under review, and while there is some evidence of large-scale brewing in public houses, and in at least one other establishment, most beer was brewed on a domestic basis. Two hundred and sixteen inventories, rather more than 25 per cent. of the total, record brewing equipment. Brewing was carried on particularly in the homes of the wealthy. One hundred and seventeen, or 54.6 per cent. of those who had brewing equipment had possessions whose total value exceeded fifty pounds.

The raw material of beer was malt made from barley which was commonly grown in the district. Barley was first steeped in water in a cistern for about sixty hours. Four inventories, among them that of Phillip Howle (*223*) make reference to *vessels 'to water barley in'*, while 18 mention a *weeting* or *wetting vat, fat, stund, vessel* or *tub,* John Brown (*255*) had a 'stone wheting fat'. The barley was then 'couched' in heaps on a malting floor, before being spread over the floor, which would encourage it to sprout and grow. William Banks in 1718 had 'barley on the couching floor'. It would be handled with a wooden *malt shovell*, a tool mentioned on the inventories of John Field (*119*), John Brown (*255*) and Thomas Calcott (*264*). Once it began to sprout the starch in the grain began to turn into sugar, and the process would then be stopped by placing the barley in a kiln. William Webb (*203*), who appears to have brewed on a considerable scale, had 160 bushels of dry malt on the floor, and 35 in the kiln. A smokeless fuel was necessary for the operation of a malt kiln. Mary Barrett (*27*) had both raw coal and charcoal listed on her inventory. The latter was probably coke, and intended for use in the kiln-house which adjoined her brewhouse. In the kiln the barley would be placed on a *hair cloth* placed over a *screen*. Such screens are mentioned in the inventories of Phillip Howle *(223)*, John Cherrington *(195)*, where it is itemised with a hair cloth, and Thomas Calcott *(264)*. Here are also occasional references to wire sieves or riddles used in malting. Malt was stored in bins or sometimes in whisketts or baskets, as in the inventory of Humphrey Mansell *(46)* or in bags as used by William Webb *(203)*.

The utensils used in brewing were generally assumed to be made of wood. An inventory of 1697 refers to 'Coopery ware in ye Malthouse'. One of 1689 itemises 'Wooden vessels of all sorts' in a brewhouse, while one of 1729 lists 'brewing vessels and other woodenware'. As in the dairies it is impossible to ascribe a precise function to every item of brewing equipment listed, and on many occasions different words were obviously used to signify similar items. Brewing stunds, tubs, turnells, furnaces, kummels, looms, vats, bouches, pales, boilers, and rindling tubs occur in many inventories, as do gauns for measuring and turning dishes or funnels. Some inventories list pecks, half pecks, strikes and half strikes, or other measures for malt. Before malt could be used in brewing it was ground in a *malt mill*. References to such mills occur on 63 inventories, sometimes itemised as *hand* malt mills, and on three occasions specified as being made of steel.

The ground malt would be put in a receptacle in which it would be boiled in water, usually about a peck of malt to 36 gallons, and then transferred to a vat where more malt would be added to it. In the inventory of William Webb *(203)* there is a reference to three *mash tuns*, exactly what these vessels would be called in a modern brewery, and also to a *guile tun*, a term which also occurs in an Essex inventory of 1691.[105] Mr. Steer defined a guile of liquor as a quantity brewed at one operation. After some hours in the mash tun, water was allowed to percolate through the malt, and the liquid, known as the wort, drawn off into a copper in which it was boiled with a quantity of hops. The latter are mentioned on numerous inventories in the collection. The receptacles used for this stage of brewing are not defined in the 17th century, but on the inventories after 1700 there are seven references to *coppers* or *copper furnaces* in brewhouses. On a small scale, it is likely that the 'old kettle to brew in', mentioned on an inventory of 1708 served the same purposes. After the boiling of the wort and hops, the liquid was put into another tub or vat, and yeast was added to bring about fermentation. The numerous *coolers* listed in brewhouses probably refer to receptacles used for cooling the wort after the boiling. An inventory of 1684 mentions a *cooling turnell*, and one of 1687 a *vessell to cool wort in*. Beer would be stored in barrels, hogsheads, kilderkins, and other receptacles in great variety, which would, in substantial households, be placed on a *rack* or *horse* in the cellar.

# INTRODUCTION

A curiosity revealed by the inventories is the considerable number of households before 1700 in which malt was kept, but where no brewing was done. Thirty-nine inventories which include malt in that period list no brewing equipment. In the following five decades there were only ten. It seems possible, therefore, that prior to 1700 malt was used for purposes other than brewing.

East Shropshire has never been celebrated for its cider, but several inventories show that cider was made in the area. *Crabs* worth a shilling are listed on an inventory of 1659, while one of 1661 includes a *crab mill stone*. A *crab mill* is included on an inventory of 1683, while Richard Bridgwood (*9*) had a *crab strainer*. The wealthy Richard Stanier (*154*) had a 'syder mill' in 1711. This is the latest reference to the making of cider, but William Webb (*203*) in 1741 had 18 bottles of it. Since he obviously made his living from the drink trade, it is possible that he had purchased it outside the district. The innkeeper William Judgson (*171*) also had some cider in 1725.

The inventories establish conclusively that the wealthier classes in the district began to drink tea and coffee in the early 18th century. The detailed mercers' inventories, the latest of which was taken in 1700, mention neither drink, from which it may reasonably be assumed that they were not then available locally. The first inventory to refer to tea is that of John Eyton (*148*) taken in 1708-9, which includes two tea-pots, one of them made of copper. The earliest reference to coffee is on the inventory of Thomas Newell (*77*) in 1731, which included both a coffee pot and a tea table. During the 1730s equipment for making both drinks became fairly commonplace in the homes of the wealthy. Margaret Vickers in 1735 had a tin coffee pot, while Peter Langley (*258*) in the same year had a coffee mill and a tea board. Thomas Calcott (*264*) in 1744 had a copper tea kettle, an iron tea kettle, a tin coffee pot, and a coffee mill. In all five inventories refer to tea, and six to coffee.

## *Conclusions*

The parishes of North Telford were still predominantly agricultural in the first half of the 18th century. Most farmers worked on a relatively small scale, but some holdings were obviously of considerable size. The pattern of farming varied between the smaller holdings on the coalfield, and the larger farms on the better soils on the edge of the Cheshire cheese region. On such farms innovations were gaining acceptance. The use of clover was spreading, as rye and draught oxen were slowly disappearing. The open fields were gradually being enclosed. After the depression of the early 18th century the size of dairy herds was growing, and the value of cattle increasing. The main centre of trade in the region was Wellington, where mercers offered for sale such goods as were not made in the district, and where there were many more craftsmen than in any of the other three parishes. As in other Shropshire market towns, the leather trades, at all stages from tanning to gloving, were of considerable importance, and the dyers carried on a considerable variety of cloth finishing processes. In the woodlands of Little Dawley, Wrockwardine Wood and Donnington, and on the commons of Lawley, Ketley and Dawley, mining was making a growing impact on the landscape.

It is possible to observe in the district many of the preconditions which made possible the rapid economic growth of the latter part of the 18th century. The inventory of Jane Hartshorne, with its steam engine and two comfortably furnished houses gives an impression of the scale on which her husband had invested in mining, and of the rewards which he had gained. The many debts upon bond and monies at use show that channels existed in the district which enabled savings to be profitably invested. There are many indications in the inventories of rising standards of comfort among the wealthier classes in the first half of the 18th century. Chests of drawers and looking-glasses were becoming commonplace. Tea and coffee were being drunk. Porcelain was appearing in the best rooms. Other social changes are also evident from the inventories. Illiteracy was decreasing, and it was less and less acceptable for a wealthy man to be unable to sign his name. Clocks were becoming cheaper and were more widely distributed and awareness of clock time must substantially have increased. The squatters on the commons and along the roadsides were almost certainly under-represented in this collection, but they, too, were one of the foundations of subsequent industrial growth. They gained their livings by mining, weaving, carpentry, shoemaking, or keeping horses, as well as by small-scale farming. They offered a range of skills, a reserve army of labour, and areas of housing which could easily and cheaply be expanded.

Yet to see the villages and hamlets of Telford and the market town which served them simply as industrial communities in embryo would be a gratuitous and unnecessary act of condescencion. Whatever the skills they practiced, whichever products they sold to pay their taxes or their shoemaker's bill, or to make money to spend on silk, sugar or soap at the mercer's, the majority of those whose inventories are included in this collection lived lives closely shaped by the seasons and the elements. The majority spent some part of each day tending to cows, pigs or horses. How well they ate depended in part on how well their wheat grew. Their main drink was often made in their own brewhouse, perhaps with malt made from their own barley. Their clothing and bed linen came in part from their own crops of hemp and flax, which might have to be stored as yarn for some years before enough was acquired to be taken to a weaver. The skills of butter- and cheese-making were widely practised, and flitches of beef and bacon from animals recently killed hung in many kitchens. This was a way of life which was to be entirely engulfed by the changes set in motion by men like Richard Hartshorne, the first Abraham Darby, and Edward Darrall, the collier. It is a way of life which, nevertheless, demands the utmost respect. The publication of this collection represents a sortie in strength into a territory which has hitherto only been hastily reconnoitred or dimly glimpsed from afar. The inventories will come to mean much more as more work is done on local estate records and parish documents, and when the inventories of the southern parts of Telford become available. There are few historical explorations which better aid our understanding of our whole past, and of our own society than attempts to perceive the rhythms of life of our pre-industrial ancestors, and to sense the first stirrings of the changes which were so dramatically to alter the nature of their existence.

### REFERENCES

1. Fernand Braudel, *Capitalism and Material Life, 1400–1800* (ed. 1974), xxii.
2. David G. Hey, 'The use of Probate Inventories for Industrial Archaeology' in *Industrial Archaeology*, X.2. (1973), pp. 201–213.
3. Barrie Trinder, *The Most Extraordinary District in the World* (1977), is an anthology of visitors' descriptions of the Ironbridge Gorge and surrounding area. Chapter V of Barrie Trinder, *The Industrial Revolution in Shropshire* (1973) describes the economic history of the lands of the Charlton family in North Telford during the 18th century.
4. G. F. Matthews, *Shropshire Probates in the Prerogative Court of Canterbury, 1700–49* (1928).
5. Publications which have been used for comparative purposes in this study include: Francis Steer, *Farm and Cottage Inventories of Mid-Essex, 1635–1749* (ed. 1969); D. G. Vaisey, *Probate Inventories of Lichfield and District, 1568–1680*, Collections for a History of Staffordshire, 4th series, X. Staffordshire Record Society (1969); John Moore, *The Goods and Chattels of our Ancestors* (1976); Robert Machin, *Probate Inventories and Manorial Excerpts of Chetnole, Leigh and Yetminster* (1976); unpublished collections of transcripts of inventories from Shrewsbury, Bishop's Castle, Bridgnorth, Ludlow, and Market Drayton have also been consulted.
6. *cf.* Francis Steer, *op. cit.*, p. 5.
7. The section on appraisers which follows is the work of Mrs. Nancy Cox.
8. D. G. Vaisey, *op. cit.*, p. 280.
9. Information from the 1672 Hearth Tax in the section which follows and elsewhere is taken from W. Watkins-Pitchford, *The Shropshire Hearth-Tax Roll of 1672* (1949).
   Figures from the Compton Census and other demographic material are from Silvi Sogner, 'Aspects of the demographic Situation in 17 Parishes in Shropshire, 1711–60' in *Population Studies*, Feb. 1964.
10. Shropshire Record Office (hereafter S.R.O.), Shrewsbury Borough Library MS 2481, Survey of the Shropshire Estates of the Earl of Craven; field name maps for Dawley Magna and Dawley Parva.
    Ironbridge Gorge Museum. Map of Little Dawley. 1825.

11. M. W. Hunt, 'Squatter Settlements in the Coalbrookdale area', a dissertation presented to the Royal Institute of British Architects as Subject F for Part 2 of the Examination in Architecture. 1975.
12. Peter Edwards, *The Farming Economy of North East Shropshire in the Seventeenth Century*, Oxford D.Phil.Thesis, 1976 (henceforth, Edwards, *Thesis*), p. 230.
13. An Account of John Charlton Esqr's Field Ground Before ye Fields was Inclosed and where it now Layd to him Again, 1702. S.R.O. 739/1.
14. Trevor Rowley, *The Shropshire Landscape* (1972), p. 144.
15. S.R.O. 999/M5/M6.
16. Florentia Herbert, 'The History of Wrockwardine', in the *Transactions of the Shropshire Archaeological Society*, 4th ser. V. 2 (1915), p. 279.
17. James Loch, *An Account of the Improvements on the Estates of the Marquis of Stafford* (1820), p. 171.
18. R. Machin, *op. cit.*, p.21.
19. D. G. Vaisey, *op. cit.*, pp. 6-7; David Lloyd, *Broad Street: its houses and residents through eight centuries* (1979), pp. 39-42, 49-52, 57-59, 65-68; Bridgnorth inventories in Lichfield Joint Record Office; Bishop's Castle inventories in Hereford Record Office,
20. The section on mercers is the work of Mrs. Nancy Cox. In addition to the inventories listed in Table VII, the following sources have been used and are referred to throughout the section: A mercer's account book (Tench). Cheshire record Office. DDX 326; Rev. R. G. Griffiths, 'Joyce Jeffreys of Ham Castle', in *Transactions of the Worcestershire Archaeology Society*, 1933, pp. 15-28, 1935, pp. 1-17; *The Household Book of the Lord William Howard*, Surtees Society, LXVIII (1878); Lord Beveridge and others, *Prices and Wages in England* (1939); E. B. Schumpeter, *English Overseas Trade Statistics, 1697-1808* (1960).
21. Will of John Justice, Lichfield Joint Record Office.
22. S.R.O. 739/1; Forester Rent Rolls, S.R.O. 1226/297.
23. R. S. Skinner, *Nonconformity in Shropshire, 1662-1816* (1964), pp. 5, 15; H. Owen and J. B. Blakeway, *A History of Shrewsbury* (1926), II, pp. 485-86.
24. S.R.O. 739/1. 1226/297.
25. The will of Thomas Wright of Wellington, uncle of Benjamin Wright, made on 25 February 1666-67, and proved on 4 May 1667. P.C.C. Wills, Public Record Office.
26. Will of William Phillips, the elder, of Wellington, gent., made on 18 September 1684, and proved on 12 December 1685. P.C.C. Wills, Public Record Office.
27. S.R.O. 1226/297.
28. Seaby's Numismatic Publications, *British Tokens and their values* (1970).
29. Letters of Administration of Margaret Wright, 13 October 1702, will of William Doughty of Wellington, proved 8 March 1716-17. Lichfield Joint Record Office.
30. Cheshire Record Office, DDX 326.
31. Seaby's Numismatic Publication, *British Tokens and their values* (1970).
32. Quoted by P. Corfield, 'A provincial capital in the late seventeenth century', in P. Clarke and P. Slack, *Crisis and order in English Towns, 1500-1700* (1972).
33. Daniel Defoe, *A Tour through England and Wales* (ed. G. D. H. Cole, 1959), i, p. 17.
34. Charles Wilson, *England's Apprenticeship, 1603-1736.* (1965), pp. 194-95.
35. See below, pp. 61-64.
36. The section on linen is drawn from Culpeper's *Complete Herbal* (n.d.) and Arthur Young, *The Farmer's Calendar* (6th ed. 1805), The assistance of Mrs.

## INTRODUCTION (REFERENCES)

Phillips and Mrs. Hilary Green who have legally grown flax and hemp is gratefully acknowledged.
37. T. C. Banfield, *Industry of the Rhine* (1846, rep. New York, 1969), I, p. 27.
38. The section on tobacco is based on W. A. Penn, *The Soverane Herb* (1901); C. H. MacInnes, *The Early English Tobacco Trade* (1926), and B. W. A. Alford W. D. and H. O. Wills and the development of the Tobacco Industry (1963).
39. The section on sugar and honey is based on D. Moore, *The Bee Book* (1976), R. Davis, *The rise of the British Shipping Industry in the 17th and 18th centuries* (1962), and N. Deere, *The History of Sugar* (1950).
40. D. G. Vaisey, *op. cit.*, pp. 93-94.
41. D. W. Jones, 'London Merchants and the crisis of the 1690s', in P. Clarke and P. Slack, *op. cit.*
42. Charlton Estate Rent Rolls, *passim*, S.R.O. 676.
43. S.R.O. 972/233/
44. The section on the leather trades is the work of Mr. V. Needham.
45. *The Book of Trades* (S.P.C.K., 1821), p. 332.
46. *Ibid*, p. 329/
47. *Ibid*, pp. 110, 331-32.
48. The section on dyers which follows is the work of Dr. J. J. Cox.
49. W. H. Beveridge, *op. cit.*; Rev. R. G. Griffiths, 'Joyce Jefferies of Ham Castle', *op. cit.*
50. S.R.O. 739/1.
51. William Partridge, *A Practical Treatise on Dyeing* (1823, rep. 1973).
52. *Ibid*.
53. The section on dyeing techniques is based on: J. B. Hurry, *The Woad Plant and its Dye* (1930); A. G. Perkins and A. E. Everest, *The Natural Organic Colouring Matters* (1918); Lewes Roberts, *The Merchant's Map of Commerce* (1638); F. Lauterbach, *Der Kampf des Waides mit dem Indigo* (1905); Anon. *The Whole Art of Dying* (London, 1705); J. J. Hummel, *The Dyeing of Textile Fabrics* (3rd ed. 1888); G. Martin, *Industrial and Manufacturing Chemistry (Organic)* (1918); K. N. Chandhuri, *The English East India Company 1600-1640* (1965). The practice of using woad and indigo together seems to have been introduced into England in 1577 by a Portuguese, Pero Vaz Devora. (Report to Lord Burghley: Lansdowne MSS., Vol. 24 [66]). We thank Mr. R. Broadhurst of the Colour Museum for this reference.
54. Arthur Young, *The Farmer's Calendar* (6th ed. 1805), p. 152.
55. S.R.O. 1226/296/7. We are indebted to Dr. Malcolm Wanklyn for this reference.
56. Joan Day, 'The Last of the Dyewood Mills', in *Industrial Archaeology*, III (1966), p. 119.
57. For a full account see the *Philosophical Transactions of the Royal Society* XXI (1678), p. 1056.
58. G. C. Carey, *Chemistry as it is compared with what it was* (1825).
59. The section on spinning and weaving which follows is principally the work of Mr. Tim Wastling. The assistance of Mrs. Hilary Green with specialist advice on the working of hemp and flax is gratefully acknowledged.
60. John Campbell, *A Political Survey of Britain* (1774), II, p. 88.
61. Edwards, *Thesis*, p. 196.
62. Arthur Young, *Tours in England and Wales* (L.S.E. Reprint, 1932), p. 162.
63. S.R.O. 972/271.
64. T. L. Wastling, 'Industrial Protest and Conflict in the West of England Woollen Industry in the Eighteenth Century'. Unpublished B.A. Thesis. University of Southampton. 1971.
65. Research for the section on millers was carried out by Mr. J. Lenton.
66. Grid refs. SJ 726149, 732145; S.R.O. 972/271.

67. Grid ref. SJ 612132; S.R.O. 999. D1, D2, D4, D10, D11.
68. Research for the section on blacksmiths was carried out by Miss J. Beddow. Information on the identification of tools was provided by Mr. E. Wood.
69. Barrie Trinder, *The Industrial Revolution in Shropshire* (1973), pp. 142-43.
70. Research on the Judgson family was carried out by the late Mr. F. Brown and Mrs. Brown.
71. S.R.O. 1226/297.
72. Research for the section on colliers was carried out by Mr. P. Dunn.
73. Barrie Trinder, *op. cit.*, pp. 49-50, 52-53.
74. *Ibid.*, pp. 196-97.
75. G. F. Matthews, *Shropshire Probates in the P.C.C. 1700-49* (1928).
76. Barrie Trinder, *op. cit.*, p. 160.
77. S.R.O., Shrewsbury Borough Library Collection MS. 328, ff. 5, 13.
78. J. Thirsk, ed. *The Agricultural History of England and Wales*, IV (1967), p. 400. (See Table XIV.)
79. Research for the section on agriculture was carried out by Dr. J. J. Cox, Mr. P. Dunn, Mr. J. Fowler, and Mr. J. Pagett.
80. Edwards, *Thesis*, p. 49.
81. Henry Tanner, 'The Agriculture of Shropshire' in *The Journal of the Royal Agricultural Society of England*, XIX. 1 (1858-59), p. 25.
82. D. Defoe, *A Tour through England and Wales* (ed. G. D. H. Cole, 1959), ii, p. 74; E. Kerridge, *The Agricultural Revolution* (1967), p. 129; Edwards, *Thesis*, pp. 46-47.
83. Edwards, *Thesis*, p. 179.
84. D. G. Vaisey, *op. cit.*, p. 22.
85. F. W. Steer, *op. cit.*, p. 52; Edwards, *Thesis*, p. 45.
86. Joseph Plymley, *A General View of the Agriculture of Shropshire* (1802), pp. 262-66.
87. F. W. Steer, *op. cit.*, p. 87.
88. *Ibid.*, p. 12.
89. See Plate Eight; D. G. Vaisey, *op. cit.*, p. 28.
90. F. W. Steer, *op. cit.*, pp. 13-14.
91. *Ibid.*, p. 15.
92. D. G. Vaisey, *op. cit.*, p. 30.
93. See above p. 25.
94. F. W. Steer, *op. cit.*, pp. 16-17.
95. See above, pp. 36-7.
96. D. G. Vaisey, *op. cit.*, p. 36; F. W. Steer, *op. cit.*, p. 20.
97. E. P. Thompson, 'Time, Work-Discipline and Industrial Capitalism' in *Past and Present*, XXXVII (1967), pp. 56-97. Research for the section on clocks was carried out by Mr. P. Dunn and Mr. J. Pagett.
98. Douglas Elliott, *Shropshire Clock and Watch Makers* (1979), pp. 14, 18-19, and *passim*.
99. The section on pottery is based on research carried out by Mr. P. Dunn.
100. *The Travels through England of the Rev. Dr. Richard Pococke*, ed. J. J. Cartwright (1888), i, p. 7.
101. The section on food is based on research carried out by Mr. P. Dunn and Mr. J. Pagett.
102. F. W. Steer, *op. cit.*, p. 65.
103. Kidderminster Public Library, Knight MSS., Stour Works Accounts, 1741-42.
104. The inventory of William Ible of Stottesdon, exhibited 18 June 1723. Herefordshire Record Office.
105. F. W. Steer, *op. cit.*, p. 34.

# A LIST OF PEOPLE

A list of people from the parishes of Dawley, Lilleshall, Wellington and Wrockwardine, whose wills or administration bonds are recorded in the Calendar of Wills, proved in the Bishop's Consistory Court of the Diocese of Lichfield and Coventry between 1651 and 1750.

## NOTES

The date in column five is that which appears on the inventory. That in column six is the date of exhibition. It is by this date that the document is located in the Record Office. In a very few cases the date of exhibition is earlier than the date of the inventory. All such examples have been carefully checked, on the inventory and in the Calendar, and found to be correctly transcribed.

The Calendar, which was compiled in the 19th century, lists the parish for each entry, but sometimes township or other places are named in error. 'Donnington', for example, sometimes indicates the Shropshire parish which lies between Albrighton and Tong (now spelt 'Donnington'), and sometimes the township in the ancient parish of Lilleshall. All references in the Calendar to Donnington have been checked, and are included in the list if they relate to Donnington in Lilleshall. Similarly all references to Horton have been examined, but most were found to relate to Haughton, near Stafford, and not to the small township of Wellington. It has not been possible to check every possible error of this kind. 'Aston' is a very common place-name, and there are several places so called in the Diocese, including a very small township in Wellington and an extremely populous parish on the edge of Birmingham. To have examined every entry for Aston to see if it related to the township in Wellington would not have been a profitable use of time. Nor has every reference to 'Willington' been examined to see whether it relates to Wellington, although one or two Calendar entries for Wellington actually refer to the parish of Willington in Derbyshire. Nevertheless, every reasonable effort has been made to ensure that every record of probate for the four parishes under review is included in this list.

While the Calendar theoretically begins in 1651, no probate records survive for the period of the Interregnum, and the earliest grants of probate or administration were actually made in 1660.

An asterisk (*) in column four indicates that the occupation of the person concerned has either been deduced from the contents of the inventory, or that it is known from the will or other sources.

## ABBREVIATIONS

nd = no date.                    no inv. = no inventory.

| Name | Parish | Township, etc. | Occupation | Inventory Date | Date exhibited | Value | Number (if published) |
|---|---|---|---|---|---|---|---|
| Aaron, Ann | Lill | Donnington | – | no. inv. | 25 Oct. 1738 | – | – |
| Acton, Joyce | Well | – | Widow | 17 Sept. 1658 | 12 Oct. 1660 | 06 19 02 | – |
| Adams, Allen | Well | Horton | Farmer* | 12 Jan. 1684–5 | 24 April 1685 | 31 01 00 | 102 |
| Adams, Andrew | Well | – | Yeoman | 12 Oct. 1713 | 7 Feb. 1713–4 | 228 14 02 | – |
| Adams, Elizabeth | Well | Horton | – | 29 Jan 1666–7 | 9 May 1667 | 01 17 06 | – |
| Adams, Henry | Well | – | Shoemaker | 9 Mar. 1728–9 | 8 April 1729 | 217 00 00 | 183 |
| Adams, John | Well | – | – | 19 Sept. 1676 | 20 Sept. 1676 | 13 04 00 | – |
| Adams, John | Well | – | – | no. inv. | 23 Oct. 1741 | – | – |
| Adams, Mary | Well | – | – | nd. | 24 April 1694 | 03 15 00 | – |
| Adams, Mary | Well | – | – | no. inv. | 28 April 1738 | – | – |
| Adams, Mary | Well | – | Tailor | no. inv. | 13 April 1748 | – | – |
| Adams, Richard | Well | – | – | 16 Jan. 1711–2 | 25 April 1712 | 15 19 02 | – |
| Adams, Roger | Wroc | – | – | 22 Mar. 1676 | 7 June 1676 | 131 11 00 | – |
| Adams, Sarah | Well | – | – | no. inv. | 15 April 1743 | – | – |
| Adams, Silvenus | Lill | – | Blacksmith | 24 April 1661 | 14 May 1661 | 63 11 00 | 33 |
| Adams, Thomas | Well | Leegomery | – | nd. | 23 Oct. 1741 | 04 07 00 | – |
| Adams, William | Well | – | – | 25 Sept. 1686 | 26 April 1687 | 04 05 06 | – |
| Adderley, Elizabeth | Well | – | – | no. inv. | 30 April 1736 | – | – |
| Adney, Elizabeth | Lill | Donnington | Widow, weaver* | 29 Mar. 1731 | 4 May 1731 | 19 00 06 | 76 |
| Adney, John | Lill | – | Webster | October 1729 | 31 Oct. 1729 | 13 15 00 | 75 |
| Adney, Richard | Lill | Donnington | Weaver* | 19 April 1738 | 26 April 1738 | 17 15 00 | 78 |
| Adney, William | Lill | – | Miller | 6 Dec. 1737 | 26 April 1738 | 49 05 00 | 79 |
| Alcock, Alice | Well | – | Widow | 12 Nov. 1708 | 13 Nov. 1707 | 01 08 00 | – |
| Allen, Daniel | Wroc | – | – | 27 April 1730 | 29 April 1730 | 17 15 00 | – |
| Allen, Robert | Wroc | Long Lane | Joiner | 2 Jan. 1737–8 | 28 April 1738 | 34 18 00 | 259 |
| Allen, Thomas | Wroc | Streetway | – | 17 April 1699 | 3 Oct. 1699 | 17 00 00 | – |
| Amies, Anne | Well | – | – | 15 Nov. 1740 | 3 April 1741 | 15 02 00 | – |
| Amies, Robert | Well | – | – | no. inv. | 15 April 1725 | – | – |
| Amiss, Robert | Lill | Donnington | Farmer* | 9 Jan. 1716–7 | 5 April 1717 | 71 10 06 | – |
| Amyes, Jane | Lill | – | Widow | 23 July 1735 | 31 Oct. 1735 | 18 11 10 | – |

… A LIST OF PEOPLE  121

| Name | Parish | Township, etc. | Occupation | Inventory Date | Date exhibited | Value | Number (if published) |
|---|---|---|---|---|---|---|---|
| Andrews, William | Daw | — | Husbandman | 24 Oct. 1737 | 2 Nov. 1737 | 16 06 09 | 29 |
| Ankers, Thomas | Lill | — | — | no inv. | 11 Mar. 1688 | — | — |
| Archer, Henry | Well | — | — | 25 June 1730 | 5 May 1731 | 04 16 00 | — |
| Arden, Ann | Daw | — | — | no inv. | 25 April 1739 | — | — |
| Assley, Richard | Well | — | — | 16 April 1729 | 31 Oct. 1729 | 09 01 00 | — |
| Aston, Edward | Lill | Muxton | Limeman | 18 Feb. 1708-9 | 4 May 1709 | 12 15 06 | 67 |
| Aston, Richard | Lill | Muxton | Cooper | 4 Jan. 1727-8 | 26 April 1728 | 07 19 11 | — |
| Atherley, William | Well | Lawley | Yeoman | 12 Oct. 1705 | 17 Oct. 1705 | 09 03 06 | — |
| Axon, Francis | Wroc | — | — | no inv. | 31 Oct. 1732 | — | — |
| Baker, Elizabeth | Daw | — | — | 9 June 1721 | 27 Mar. 1722 | 18 18 00 | — |
| Ball, Ann | Well | — | — | no inv. | 26 Oct. 1727 | — | — |
| Ball, Richard | Wroc | Quob Poole | Collier | 2 April 1735 | 16 April 1735 | 29 06 00 | 256 |
| Ball, Thomas | Wroc | The Moss | Farmer* | 13 April 1688 | 20 April 1688 | 56 02 06 | 225 |
| Ball, William | Wroc | Quobb Pool | Collier | 28 May 1717 | 1 June 1717 | 22 12 06 | 245 |
| Banes, Elizabeth | Daw | — | Farmer* | 3 Mar. 1668-9 | 29 April 1669 | 40 01 00 | — |
| Banger, Mary | Well | — | — | 7 July 1726 | 18 Oct. 1726 | 04 13 08 | 176 |
| Banks, William | Daw | — | Maltster* | Feb. 1718-9 | 7 April 1719 | 38 04 00 | — |
| Barker, Edward | Well | Leegomery | Farmer* | 5 July 1729 | 28 Oct. 1729 | 24 05 00 | — |
| Barker, John | Wroc | Pains Lane | Yeoman | 24 Dec. 1721 | 1 Jan 1721-2 | 16 19 06 | 247 |
| Barker, Mary | Wroc | — | Widow | 20 Oct. 1692 | 25 Nov. 1692 | 04 11 00 | — |
| Barker, Robert | Well | — | — | 21 April 1669 | 29 April 1669 | 60 05 02 | — |
| Barker, Sarah | Well | — | — | no inv. | 26 April 1721 | — | — |
| Barker, Thomas | Wroc | Pains Lane | Farmer* | nd. | 31 Mar. 1682 | 14 00 02 | 220 |
| Barker, William | Well | Hadley | Yeoman | 23 May 1690 | 17 Sept. 1690 | 306 15 06 | — |
| Barker, William | Well | Watling Street | Innholder | nd. | 19 Oct. 1725 | 74 18 05 | 172 |
| Barnes, Robert | Wroc | — | Weaver* | 31 Mar. 1701 | 21 Oct. 1701 | 06 15 00 | — |
| Barnes, Tryphosa | Well | — | Mercer* | 22 Oct. 1723 | 1 Nov. 1723 | 19 14 00 | 170 |
| Barnett, Sarah | Lill | — | Widow | 24 Dec. 1728 | 11 April 1729 | 196 00 00 | — |
| Barrett, John | Well | — | — | no inv. | 13 April 1748 | — | — |

| Name | Parish | Township, etc. | Occupation | Inventory Date | Date exhibited | Value | Number (if published) |
|---|---|---|---|---|---|---|---|
| Barrett, Mary | Daw | – | Widow | 23 Sept. 1730 | 27 Oct. 1730 | 14 04 00 | 27 |
| Barrett, Ralph | Lill | – | – | 10 Sept. 1683 | 26 Sept. 1683 | 46 03 10 | 49 |
| Barrett, Thomas | Daw | – | – | no inv. | 20 April 1726 | – | – |
| Basnett, Thomas | Lill | Donnington | Farmer* | 9 July 1705 | 19 Oct. 1705 | 85 15 00 | – |
| Bate, Catherine | See Pate | | | | | | |
| Bate, Tomasin | Lill | Muxton | – | 15 Oct. 1686 | 22 Oct. 1686 | 08 07 07 | – |
| Bate, William | Well | – | – | no inv. | 28 April 1721 | – | – |
| Bates, William | Lill | Muxton | Labourer | 28 Aug. 1684 | 1 April 1685 | 04 06 00 | 51 |
| Bates, Richard | Well | – | – | no inv. | 20 Nov. 1750 | – | – |
| Bathoe, David | Wroc | Admaston | Blacksmith | 16 Feb. 1657 | 3 April 1661 | 51 09 11 | – |
| Bathoe, Margery | Lill | – | Widow | 1 Oct. 1678 | 10 Oct. 1678 | 28 03 08 | – |
| Bayley, Edward | Daw | Dawley Green | Farmer* | 17 May 1666 | 18 May 1666 | 14 04 06 | – |
| Bayley, Francis | Well | Hadley | Yeoman | 15 July 1699 | 5 Oct. 1698 | 161 19 04 | 130 |
| Bayley, Margery | Daw | Dawley Green | Widow | 13 Aug. 1727 | 3 Oct. 1727 | 73 10 00 | – |
| Bayley, Michael | Daw | Dawley Green | Yeoman | Nov. 1716 | 4 April 1717 | 50 15 00 | – |
| Bayley, Sarah | Well | Hadley | Widow | 15 Oct. 1700 | 15 Oct. 1700 | 54 07 06 | – |
| Bayley, William | Well | Hadley | Yeoman | 29 Mar. 1700 | 9 April 1701 | 21 11 00 | – |
| Beamond, Richard | Well | Cluddley | Labourer | 3 Dec. 1714 | 15 April 1714 | 04 01 08 | 158 |
| Beard, Elizabeth | Lill | – | – | no inv. | 6 June 1712 | – | – |
| Beard, John | Well | – | Yeoman | 8 Mar. 1675–6 | 9 Mar. 1676–6 | 25 16 06 | – |
| Beard, Richard | Lill | – | Yeoman | 1 June 1704 | 19 Oct. 1704 | 413 04 00 | 62 |
| Beard, Richard | Lill | – | – | no inv. | 5 May 1727 | – | – |
| Beddow, Andrew | Well | – | – | no inv. | 22 Oct. 1714 | – | – |
| Beddow, John | Well | Wappenshall | Farmer* | 28 Aug. 1706 | 15 Oct. 1706 | 406 13 04 | – |
| Beddow, John | Well | Street Lane | – | 19 Jan. 1730–1 | 6 May 1731 | 18 12 00 | – |
| Beddow, John | Well | – | Cooper | 29 Jan. 1732–33 | 29 May 1733 | 244 16 00 | – |
| Beddow, John | Well | Street Lane | – | 27 Mar. 1738 | 28 April 1738 | 69 10 00 | – |
| Beddow, Thomas | Well | Wappenshall | Farmer* | 31 Dec. 1713 | 9 Feb. 1713–4 | 336 02 10 | – |
| Belcher, Anthony | Well | – | – | 24 May 1709 | 28 June 1709 | 13 12 06 | – |
| Belcher, Elizabeth | Well | – | – | no inv. | 26 April 1721 | – | – |

# A LIST OF PEOPLE

| Name | Parish | Township, etc. | Occupation | Inventory Date | Date exhibited | Value | Number (if published) |
|---|---|---|---|---|---|---|---|
| Belcher, John | Well | – | Farmer* | 30 Nov. 1731 | 20 Dec. 1731 | 79 06 08 | – |
| Bembo, Thomas | Wroc | Long Lane | Labourer | 11 Dec. 1729 | 29 April 1730 | 08 17 06 | – |
| Benison, Christopher | Daw | – | – | 12 Jan. 1701-2 | 7 May 1702 | 96 03 00 | 13 |
| Bennett, Henry | Daw | Malins Lee | Yeoman | 13 April 1669 | 29 April 1669 | 21 03 00 | – |
| Bennett, John | Well | Watling Street | Farmer* | 22 Feb. 1700-1 | 15 Mar. 1700-1 | 153 13 04 | – |
| Bennett, Francis | Well | Watling Street | – | 17 Aug. 1705 | 17 Oct. 1705 | 26 05 02 | – |
| Bennett, Thomas | Well | – | Blacksmith | 27 Mar. 1676 | 20 Sept. 1676 | 25 06 10 | 90 |
| Bennett, Thomas | Well | – | – | no inv. | 14 April 1748 | – | – |
| Besford, Edward | Daw | – | Farmer* | 7 Dec. 1692 | 21 April 1693 | 145 02 00 | – |
| Bickley, William | Well | Walcot | Milner | 2 April 1702 | 13 Oct. 1702 | 04 07 08 | 139 |
| Bill, Thomas | Lill | – | Yeoman | 12 June 1673 | 28 Nov. 1673 | 94 10 00 | – |
| Bill, William | Lill | Donnington | Yeoman | 6 April 1685 | 26 May 1685 | 65 08 04 | 52 |
| Binnell, Abigaill | Wroc | Clotley | Farmer* | 14 Oct. 1743 | 6 April 1744 | 186 15 00 | 263 |
| Binnell, Jane | Well | – | Spinster | 7 July 1702 | 12 Oct 1702 | 03 13 00 | – |
| Binnell, John | Wroc | Allscott | Yeoman | 18 Feb. 1688 | 17 April 1689 | 137 17 00 | 227 |
| Binnell, Richard | Wroc | – | – | no inv. | 3 April 1661 | – | – |
| Binnell, Thomas | Wroc | Allscott | Yeoman | 7 Oct. 1678 | 8 Oct 1678 | 15 12 04 | 215 |
| Binnell, Thomas | Wroc | Clotley | Yeoman | 24 Nov. 1700 | 9 April 1701 | 174 17 06 | 234 |
| Binnell, Thomas | Wroc | Allscott | Farmer | 11 Mar. 1727-8 | 25 April 1728 | 144 00 00 | 251 |
| Binnell, William | Wroc | Clotley | Farmer* | 7 July 1740 | 23 Oct. 1740 | 186 15 00 | 261 |
| Birch, William | Well | – | Apothecary & Chirurgeon | 16 April 1716 | 16 April 1716 | 308 19 06 | 160 |
| Bird, Mary | Well | – | – | no inv. | 19 Oct. 1725 | – | – |
| Bishop, Martha | Lill | – | Spinster | 12 May 1731 | 2 Nov. 1731 | 90 17 00 | – |
| Blackshaw, Elizabeth | Wroc | – | – | 29 Nov. 1727 | 25 April 1728 | 100 04 00 | 250 |
| Blakeman, Margaret | Well | Leaton | Weaver* | 1710 | 21 April 1710 | 09 04 00 | 151 |
| Blakeman, Roger | Well | Hadley | Webster | 5 Nov. 1685 | 10 Nov. 1685 | 10 09 00 | 105 |
| Blakeman, Thomas | Well | Hadley | Weaver* | 1 Sept. 1690 | 19 Sept. 1690 | 08 00 06 | 114 |
| Blest, Charles | Wroc | Bratton | Yeoman | 13 July 1730 | 29 Oct. 1730 | 181 10 00 | – |
| Blockley, Dorothy | Lill | – | – | no inv. | 31 Mar. 1710 | – | – |

| Name | Parish | Township, etc. | Occupation | Inventory Date | Date exhibited | Value | Number (if published) |
|---|---|---|---|---|---|---|---|
| Blockley, William | Lill | — | Carpenter | 2 Mar. 1676-7 | 4 May 1677 | 49 00 02 | — |
| Bolas, Robert | Well | Watling Street | — | no inv. | 26 Oct. 1738 | — | 45 |
| Bold, Thomas | Wroc | Trench Lane | — | 14 July 1722 | 2 Oct. 1722 | 19 18 08 | 248 |
| Bold, Edward | Wroc | Trench Lane | Yeoman | 2 July 1709 | 4 May 1709 | 04 17 04 | 241 |
| Botfield, Mary | Daw | — | — | no inv. | 27 Oct. 1736 | — | — |
| Boult, Thomas | Well | Wappenshall | Farmer* | 20 April 1669 | 29 April 1669 | 109 00 00 | — |
| Bowden, Nicholas | Well | — | Gentleman | 12 Jan. 1738-9 | 15 Jan. 1738-9 | 175 12 00 | — |
| Boycott, Richard | Lill | — | — | no inv. | 3 Oct. 1722 | — | — |
| Bradborne, George | Lill | — | — | no inv. | 6 Feb. 1694-5 | — | — |
| Bradborne, George | Lill | — | — | no inv. | 16 April 1714 | — | — |
| Bradborne, Jane | Lill | Muxton | Widow | 5 May 1707 | 22 Oct. 1707 | 07 19 06 | — |
| Bradborne, Mary | Lill | Muxton | Spinster | 9 Oct. 1710 | 1 Dec. 1710 | 09 18 03 | — |
| Bradborne, Mary | Lill | — | — | no inv. | 12 Oct. 1743 | — | — |
| Bradborne, Thomas | Lill | Donnington | Farmer* | 4 Oct. 1664 | 18 Nov. 1664 | 60 03 08 | — |
| Bradborne, Walter | Lill | — | — | no inv. | 24 April 1739 | — | — |
| Bradley, Elizabeth | Lill | Donnington | Farmer* | 18 Oct. 1687 | 19 Oct. 1688 | 43 10 00 | — |
| Bradley, Geoffrey | Lill | Donnington | — | no inv. | 30 Sept. 1697 | — | — |
| Bradshaw, Dorothy | Lill | Muxton | Widow | 26 Feb. 1676-7 | 4 May 1677 | 10 17 10 | — |
| Bradshaw, Joan | Lill | — | Servant | nd. | 15 Mar. 1671-2 | 63 06 06 | 39 |
| Bradshaw, John | Well | — | — | no inv. | 12 Oct. 1660 | — | — |
| Bradshaw, John | Well | — | — | no inv. | 24 Oct. 1740 | — | — |
| Bradshaw, Joyce | Well | — | Widow | nd. | 5 July 1687 | 32 04 03 | 106 |
| Bradshaw, Mary | Well | — | Widow | 2 April 1735 | 17 April 1735 | 16 07 00 | 190 |
| Bradshaw, Rowland | Well | — | — | nd. | 5 Oct. 1744 | — | — |
| Bradshaw, Thomas | Lill | Muxton | Farmer* | 13 Dec. 1720 | 17 May 1692 | 54 05 00 | 166 |
| Bradshaw, William | Well | — | Shoemaker | 13 Dec. 1720 | 27 April 1721 | 34 07 00 | 166 |
| Bradshaw, William | Well | — | — | no inv. | 24 Oct. 1740 | — | — |
| Bratton, William | Wroc | Long Lane | Farmer* | 22 May 1678 | 8 Oct. 1678 | 53 02 08 | — |
| Bridgin, Elizabeth | Lill | — | Widow | 10 May 1709 | 21 Oct. 1709 | 23 17 03 | — |
| Bridgin, Joseph | Lill | — | — | no inv. | 2 Nov. 1737 | — | — |

# A LIST OF PEOPLE

| Name | Parish | Township, etc. | Occupation | Inventory Date | Date exhibited | Value | Number (if published) |
|---|---|---|---|---|---|---|---|
| Bridgin, Robert | Lill | — | — | 2 Mar. 1703–4 | 28 April 1704 | 15 06 00 | — |
| Bridgin, Robert | Lill | — | — | 8 Feb. 1723–4 | 16 Oct. 1724 | 36 01 07 | — |
| Bridgwood, Richard | Daw | Little Dawley | Yeoman | 12 July 1679 | 12 Sept. 1679 | 21 01 05 | 9 |
| Bridgwood, Thomas | Well | — | — | 20 July 1676 | 22 Sept. 1676 | 16 07 00 | — |
| Briscoe, John | Well | — | — | 1725 | 21 Oct. 1725 | 50 16 00 | — |
| Briscoe, William | Well | Ketley Brook | Yeoman | 22 July 1745 | 10 April 1746 | 04 15 00 | 207 |
| Broadhurst, Walter | Lill | — | Gentleman | 16 Sept. 1707 | 22 Oct. 1707 | 187 08 06 | 65 |
| Broadhurst, William | Lill | — | — | no inv. | 5 Oct. 1727 | — | — |
| Bromhall, Robert | Well | — | — | 17 April 1716 | 19 April 1716 | 04 10 00 | — |
| Bromley, Adam | Well | — | Yeoman | 2 May 1705 | 17 Oct. 1705 | 44 07 08 | — |
| Bromley, Ann | Well | — | Widow | 22 July 1706 | 15 Oct. 1706 | 17 05 00 | — |
| Bromley, John | Well | Watling Street | Blacksmith | 27 June 1728 | 16 Oct. 1728 | 06 18 02 | 181 |
| Bromley, John | Well | Watling Street | Blacksmith | 10 June 1740 | 23 Oct. 1740 | 14 18 00 | 200 |
| Bromley, Thomas | Well | Watling Street | Labourer | 5 April 1707 | 23 April 1707 | 06 07 00 | — |
| Brooke, Richard | Wroc | — | Farmer* | 1 July 1689 | 1 Oct. 1689 | 111 04 04 | — |
| Brooke, Richard | Wroc | Charlton | Yeoman | 3 June 1664 | 31 May 1665 | 14 11 00 | — |
| Brooke, Richard | Wroc | — | — | no inv. | 28 Feb. 1714–5 | — | — |
| Brookes, Richard | Wroc | Pains Lane | — | no inv. | 21 April 1715 | — | — |
| Brookes, Robert | Lill | Muxton | Farmer* | 29 Nov. 1729 | 28 April 1730 | 127 04 00 | — |
| Brown, Benjamin | Well | — | — | no inv. | 9 Oct. 1747 | — | — |
| Brown, Edward | Wroc | Street Way, Charlton | Husbandman | 16 Mar. 1707–8 | 30 April 1708 | 19 10 06 | — |
| Brown, Elizabeth | Wroc | — | Widow | 23 April 1736 | 29 April 1736 | 11 00 00 | — |
| Brown, John | Well | — | — | no inv. | 28 Oct. 1729 | — | — |
| Brown, John | Well | — | Glover | 20 Dec. 1729 | 30 April 1730 | 129 01 00 | 184 |
| Brown, John | Wroc | Wrockwardine | Farmer* | 23 Sept. 1732 | 2 Nov. 1732 | 132 00 00 | 255 |
| Brown, Mary | Wroc | — | Widow | 22 Nov. 1737 | 28 April 1738 | 110 04 06 | — |
| Brown, Thomas | Wroc | Charlton | Farmer* | 23 Feb. 1693–4 | 24 April 1694 | 100 19 00 | — |
| Broxton, Nicholas | Well | — | Maltster | 23 Jan. 1705–6 | 24 April 1706 | 17 01 07 | — |
| Bryan, Robert | Well | — | — | 11 May 1683 | 26 May 1683 | 18 10 00 | — |

| Name | Parish | Township, etc. | Occupation | Inventory Date | Date exhibited | Value | Number (if published) |
|---|---|---|---|---|---|---|---|
| Bryan, Thomas | Well | — | Farrier | 19 Feb. 1731-32 | 28 April 1732 | 26 06 02 | 188 |
| Bryan, Thomas | Well | Hadley | — | 7 May 1667 | 10 May 1667 | 04 13 00 | — |
| Bryan, Thomas | Wroc | — | — | no inv. | 19 Oct. 1726 | — | — |
| Bulley, John | Well | Leegomery | — | 25 April 1699 | 27 April 1699 | 11 00 08 | — |
| Bullock, Elizabeth | Wroc | — | Schoolmistress | 10 June 1681 | 14 June 1681 | 64 13 04 | 218 |
| Burley, Mary | Wroc | — | — | no inv. | 17 Nov. 1712 | — | — |
| Busby, Richard | Well | — | — | no inv. | 26 April 1728 | — | — |
| Butler, Edward | Well | — | — | no inv. | 6 Oct. 1744 | — | — |
| Cade, Mary | Lill | Donnington | Widow | 12 Sept. 1664 | 18 Nov. 1664 | 24 13 10 | 35 |
| Calcott, Joshua | Wroc | — | Farmer* | 17 April 1714 | 3 May 1714 | 182 00 00 | 243 |
| Calcott, Thomas | Wroc | Allscott | Farmer* | 30 June 1744 | 6 Aug. 1744 | 772 19 10 | 264 |
| Cannadine, Thomas | Well | — | — | no inv. | 23 Oct. 1741 | — | — |
| Careswell, Sarah | Lill | — | — | 25 Feb. 1717 | 18 April 1718 | 30 07 00 | — |
| Carpenter, Henry | Well | — | — | 24 June 1679 | 16 Sept. 1679 | 04 18 00 | — |
| Carpenter, Robert | Well | — | — | 5 Oct. 1693 | 29 Nov. 1693 | 09 04 08 | — |
| Carter, Henry | Well | — | — | no inv. | 21 April 1693 | — | — |
| Cartwright, Elizabeth | Lill | — | Widow | 13 May 1661 | 14 May 1661 | 53 02 08 | 34 |
| Cartwright, Jane | Lill | Muxton | Spinster | 10 April 1705 | 30 April 1705 | 117 11 00 | — |
| Cartwright, Thomas | Lill | — | Farmer* | 9 April 1661 | 9 May 1661 | 618 00 06 | 32 |
| Cartwright, William | Lill | Muxton | Mathematician | 9 April 1718 | 18 April 1718 | 17 04 04 | 74 |
| Charles, Robert | Well | Street Lane | — | 20 April 1670 | 22 April 1670 | 51 00 10 | — |
| Charlton, Andrew | Well | — | — | no inv. | 3 May 1664 | — | — |
| Charlton, William | Wroc | Charlton | Farmer* | 19 Sept. 1704 | 28 April 1705 | 491 11 04 | 235 |
| Cheese, William | Well | — | Blacksmith | 28 Mar. 1695 | 28 April 1698 | 06 13 00 | 124 |
| Cherrington, John | Well | — | Malster/Dyer | 21 Feb. 1737-8 | 28 April 1738 | 230 03 10 | 195 |
| Cherrington, William | Well | — | — | no inv. | 9 Oct. 1747 | — | — |
| Cheshire, Mary | Wroc | — | — | no inv. | 16 Oct. 1728 | — | — |

… A LIST OF PEOPLE …

| Name | Parish | Township, etc. | Occupation | Inventory Date | Date exhibited | Value | Number (if published) |
|---|---|---|---|---|---|---|---|
| Cheshire, Rachel | Well | – | – | no inv. | 14 June 1679 | – | – |
| Cheshire, William | Wroc | Admaston | Gentleman | 14 Jan. 1725-6 | 21 April 1726 | 308 00 03 | 249 |
| Chilton, Thomas | Wroc | Admaston | Husbandman | 20 Aug. 1679 | 16 Sept. 1679 | 78 11 00 | – |
| Chirme, John | Well | – | Butcher | 24 May 1676 | 7 June 1676 | 47 00 00 | – |
| Chirme, John | Daw | – | – | no inv. | 17 Oct. 1721 | – | – |
| Chirme, Margaret | Well | Hadley | Spinster | 1 Mar. 1675-6 | 9 Mar. 1675-6 | 231 04 00 | – |
| Clare, Thomas | Daw | – | Collier | 4 June 1743 | 5 Oct. 1744 | 19 02 07 | – |
| Clark, Dorothy | Well | – | – | no inv. | 17 Nov. 1729 | – | – |
| Clark, Edward | Well | – | – | no inv. | 17 Sept. 1690 | – | – |
| Clark, Michael | Well | Leegomery | Farmer* | 14 Feb. 1715-6 | 18 April 1716 | 392 17 02 | – |
| Clark, Michael | Well | – | – | no inv. | 29 May 1733 | – | – |
| Clayton, William | Well | Ketley | – | 5 Oct. 1745 | 18 Oct. 1745 | 09 18 00 | – |
| Clayton, Edward | Lill | – | – | 23 Sept. 1721 | 20 Oct. 1721 | 06 17 06 | – |
| Cleaton, Elizabeth | Well | – | – | no inv. | 6 May 1709 | – | – |
| Cleaton, Francis | Well | Lawley | Farmer* | 26 Mar. 1686 | 4 May 1686 | 106 00 00 | – |
| Cleaton, Gabriel | Well | – | – | 16 May 1731 | 3 Nov. 1731 | 02 06 00 | – |
| Cleaton, George | Well | – | Labourer | 24 Mar. 1723 | 8 April 1724 | 03 05 07 | 168 |
| Cleaton, Jane | Lill | – | – | no inv. | 15 Oct. 1723 | – | – |
| Cleaton, John | Wroc | – | – | no inv. | 31 Oct. 1734 | – | – |
| Cleaton, Joseph | Well | – | Farmer* | 6 Sept. 1749 | 12 Oct. 1749 | 122 12 06 | – |
| Cleaton, Margaret | Well | – | – | 18 Oct. 1665 | 16 May 1666 | 19 01 04 | – |
| Cleaton, William | Well | Watling Street | Farmer* | nd. | 28 April 1738 | 265 05 00 | 196 |
| Clemson, Benjamin | Lill | – | – | no inv. | 21 July 1748 | – | – |
| Clewes, see Clowes | | | | | | | |
| Clibberrie, Thomas | Well | – | Blacksmith* | 31 Oct. 1673 | 26 Nov. 1673 | 03 18 00 | – |
| Clowes, Richard | Daw | – | Gentleman | 15 April 1679 | 17 April 1679 | 263 18 04 | 8 |
| Cooke, William | Well | – | Nailer | 10 Oct. 1705 | 26 April 1706 | 07 14 02 | 145 |
| Cooke, William | Wroc | – | Farmer* | 6 Aug. 1729 | 29 Oct. 1729 | 81 07 02 | – |
| Cookson, William | Well | – | – | no inv. | 3 April 1685 | – | – |
| Cookson, William | Well | Hadley | Weaver | 28 Mar. 1711 | 5 April 1711 | 18 12 07 | 152 |

# YEOMEN AND COLLIERS IN TELFORD

| Name | Parish | Township, etc. | Occupation | Inventory Date | Date exhibited | Value | Number (if published) |
|---|---|---|---|---|---|---|---|
| **Coomer, William** | Well | Arleston | Yeoman | 10 Mar. 1747-8 | 3 Nov. 1748 | 19 07 00 | — |
| **Cooper, Ebenezer** | Daw | Malins Lee | Yeoman | 6 Feb. 1720-1 | 27 April 1721 | 14 08 00 | — |
| **Cooper, James** | Well | — | Weaver* | 21 April 1698 | 28 April 1698 | 03 15 08 | — |
| **Cooper, Richard** | Wroc | — | — | nd. | 15 Oct. 1728 | 05 06 07 | — |
| **Cooper, Thomas** | Wroc | Hadley | Blacksmith | 29 Sept. 1684 | 10 Oct. 1684 | 15 06 06 | 222 |
| **Cooper, Thomas** | Well | — | — | 19 Sept. 1724 | 13 April 1725 | 19 11 00 | — |
| **Cooper, William** | Well | Allscot | Gentleman | 9 Sept. 1730 | 29 Oc. 1730 | 209 18 02 | 186 |
| **Cope, Joseph** | Wroc | — | Millner | 19 Feb. 1704-5 | 28 April 1705 | 33 13 00 | 238 |
| **Cope, Joseph** | Wroc | — | — | no inv. | 22 April 1737 | — | — |
| **Cope, Sarah** | Well | — | Widow | 27 Jan. 1712-3 | 27 Oct. 1713 | 04 11 00 | — |
| **Cope, Thomas** | Wroc | Allscot | Miller | 16 Jan. 1666-7 | 8 May 1667 | 34 07 08 | 211 |
| **Corbett, James** | Lill | Donnington | Yeoman | 30 April 1661 | 14 May 1661 | 61 07 00 | — |
| **Corbett, Robert** | Well | Lawley | — | 5 Jan. 1678-9 | 15 April 1679 | 05 16 06 | — |
| **Corbett, Robert** | Well | Lawley | Yeoman | 5 Feb. 1725-6 | 22 April 1726 | 41 05 00 | — |
| **Corbett, William** | Lill | Donnington | Yeoman | 29 Nov. 1689 | 20 Mar. 1689-90 | 41 04 06 | — |
| **Corbett, William** | Lill | Donnington | Farmer* | 11 Dec. 1732 | 31 Oct. 1732 | 39 06 11 | — |
| **Corfield, Richard** | Wroc | — | — | 29 Dec. 1683 | 8 Oct. 1684 | 05 00 00 | — |
| **Cornes, Sarah** | Lill | — | — | nd. | 15 Mar. 1691-2 | 04 09 03 | 228 |
| **Creswell, William** | Daw | Little Dawley | Labourer | no inv. | 13 Oct. 1742 | — | — |
| **Crippin, Thomas** | Daw | Ye fframe | Labourer | 28 July 1708 | 19 Aug. 1708 | 01 09 00 | — |
| **Crippin, William** | Well | — | — | 12 Oct. 1710 | 30 Nov. 1710 | 27 07 00 | 14 |
| **Croxton, Richard** | Wroc | — | — | no inv. | 14 Oct. 1742 | — | — |
| **Crump, Richard** | Well | — | Yeoman | 21 Nov. 1705 | 26 April 1706 | 15 11 06 | — |
| **Crump, Thomas** | Well | — | — | nd. | 30 April 1662 | 12 14 04 | — |
| **Crump, Thomas** | Wroc | — | — | no inv. | 5 Oct. 1727 | — | — |
| **Crumpton, Ann** | Well | — | — | no inv. | 15 April 1719 | — | — |
| **Currier, Samuel** | Wroc | — | Cordwainer | 21 Jan. 1739-40 | 23 Oct. 1740 | 51 18 06 | — |
| **Dabbs, John** | Wroc | Bratton | Husbandman | 20 Dec. 1665 | 16 May 1666 | 27 16 08 | 260 |
| **Dabbs, Jonathan** | Wroc | Long Lane | Yeoman | 4 Mar. 1737-8 | 26 April 1738 | 18 18 00 | — |

## A LIST OF PEOPLE

| Name | Parish | Township, etc. | Occupation | Inventory Date | Date exhibited | Value | Number (if published) |
|---|---|---|---|---|---|---|---|
| Dale, Humphrey | Lill | – | – | no inv. | 6 April 1731 | – | – |
| Dale, James | Lill | Lilleshall Lodge | Farmer* | 12 April 1706 | 26 April 1706 | 95 09 08 | 63 |
| Dale, Lewis | Lill | Lilleshall Lodge | Keeper | 12 Jan. 1676-7 | 4 May 1677 | 128 09 08 | 44 |
| Dale, Mary | Lill | Muxton | – | 11 April 1715 | 21 Oct. 1715 | 14 08 00 | – |
| Daniell, Hugh | Wroc | Bratton | Yeoman | nd. | 15 Sept. 1674 | 01 18 00 | – |
| Darbishire, Richard | Well | Preston | Farmer* | 7 Sept. 1727 | 3 Nov. 1727 | 37 19 00 | – |
| Darrall, Edward | Daw | Hollywell | Ground collier | 21 May 1726 | 21 Oct. 1726 | 04 13 00 | 21 |
| Darrall, Eliza | Daw | The Ridges | Widow | 25 June 1668 | 31 July 1668 | 11 04 07 | 6 |
| Darwall, Richard | Daw | – | Farmer* | 6 April 1666 | 18 May 1666 | 43 18 04 | 4 |
| Davis, Ann | Well | Hadley | Widow | 20 Dec. 1709 | 21 April 1710 | 03 02 08 | – |
| Davis, Basil | Wroc | Pains Lane | Yeoman | 29 Dec. 1680 | 16 April 1689 | 110 05 04 | – |
| Davis, Basil | Well | Lawley | Farmer* | 7 Oct. 1740 | 2 April 1741 | 98 06 00 | – |
| Davis Elizabeth | Wroc | – | – | no inv. | 15 Oct. 1728 | – | – |
| Davis, John | Wroc | – | – | no inv. | 24 June 1728 | – | – |
| Davis, Richard | Well | Ketley Brook | Weaver | 9 April 1701 | 9 April 1701 | 13 15 00 | – |
| Davis, Robert | Lill | – | – | 1 Aug 1670 | 16 Sept. 1670 | 36 02 00 | – |
| Davis, Silvanus | Well | – | – | 22 Sept. 1680 | 5 Oct. 1680 | 219 01 10 | – |
| Davis, Thomas | Well | Ketley Brook | – | 28 April 1676 | 20 Sept. 1676 | 38 00 00 | – |
| Davis, William | Daw | – | – | 26 Jan. 1727 | 21 Feb. 1727 | 19 13 02 | – |
| Davis, William | Well | Ketley Brook | Weaver | 20 July 1742 | 14 Oct. 1742 | 08 11 06 | 204 |
| Daw, Adam | Wroc | Admaston | Farmer* | 30 Dec. 1685 | 4 May 1686 | 21 02 06 | – |
| Daw, Edward | Wroc | Wroc. Wood | Yeoman | 7 Nov. 1683 | 13 Jan. 1683-4 | 48 18 02 | 221 |
| Daw, William | Wroc | Admaston | – | 2 April 1696 | 1 April 1696 | 01 18 10 | – |
| Dawes, Anne | Lill | Donnington | Widow | 13 Oct. 1676 | 20 Oct. 1676 | 83 06 04 | – |
| Dawes, Mary | Lill | Woodhouse | Widow | 4 Sept. 1715 | 21 Oct. 1715 | 14 00 00 | – |
| Dawes, Robert | Lill | Muxton | Husbandman | 7 Sept. 1725 | 19 Oct. 1725 | 62 19 06 | – |
| Dawes, Sarah | Lill | – | – | no inv. | 10 April 1740 | – | – |
| Dawes, William | Lill | Street Grange | Yeoman | 30 Nov. 1692 | 4 Jan. 1692-3 | 141 12 08 | 56 |

| Name | Parish | Township, etc. | Occupation | Inventory Date | Date exhibited | Value | Number (if published) |
|---|---|---|---|---|---|---|---|
| **Dawes, William** | Lill | Street Grange | – | 3 May 1720 | 7 Oct. 1720 | 39 10 00 | – |
| **Dawes, William** | Wroc | Admaston | Yeoman | 8 April 1729 | 28 Oct. 1729 | 56 12 08 | – |
| **Dawes, William** | Wroc | – | – | no inv. | 29 Jan. 1735-6 | – | – |
| **Dawes, William** | Lill | – | – | no inv. | 14 April 1743 | – | – |
| **Dawes, William** | Wroc | – | – | no inv. | 5 May 1747 | – | – |
| **Denston, Alice** | Well | – | Spinster | 23 Dec.1712 | – | – | – |
| **Dodd, Thomas** | Daw | – | – | 26 Feb. 1689–90 | 19 Sept. 1690 | 03 16 00 | – |
| **Dodd, Thomas** | Well | Aston | Farmer* | 30 June 1688 | 17 Oct. 1688 | 72 09 06 | – |
| **Doughty, William** | Well | – | Gentleman | 7 Dec. 1716 | 8 Mar 1716–7 | 433 05 10 | *161* |
| **Downes, Dorothy** | Well | – | – | no inv. | 6 April 1744 | – | – |
| **Downes, John** | Well | – | – | no inv. | 14 Nov. 1744 | – | – |
| **Downes, John** | Well | – | – | no inv. | 4 Nov. 1737 | – | – |
| **Downes, John** | Well | Walcott | Yeoman | 31 Mar. 1699 | 27 April 1699 | 185 18 00 | – |
| **Drurey, Matthew** | Well | Watling Street | – | nd. | 5 May 1731 | 09 07 06 | – |
| **Duddell, John** | Daw | Pool Hill | Carpenter | 22 Oct. 1724 | 13 April 1725 | 27 11 00 | *19* |
| **Duddell, John** | Daw | Pawn Hatch | Carpenter | 1 May 1728 | 15 Oct. 1728 | 59 11 04 | *24* |
| **Dunn, Thomas** | Lill | Donnington | Yeoman | 27 Mar. 1685 | 1 April 1685 | 28 01 04 | – |
| **Dunton, Joshua** | Well | – | Tanner* | 16 Oct. 1680 | 18 Jan. 1680–1 | 357 10 06 | *95* |
| **Dunton, Margret** | Well | – | Widow | 19 Feb. 1680–1 | 22 Mar. 1680–1 | 92 14 06 | – |
| **Eastop, Ann** | Well | – | Widow | 4 Nov. 1693 | 6 Mar 1693–4 | 04 10 06 | *120* |
| **Eastop, Jane** | Well | Ketley Wood | Widow | 15 Aug. 1720 | 17 Aug. 1720 | 10 17 06 | *165* |
| **Eastop, John** | Daw | Malins Lee | Yeoman | 11 Mar. 1722–3 | 15 Oct. 1723 | 137 05 00 | – |
| **Eastop, Joseph** | Well | Ketley Wood | – | 2 Mar. 1701–2 | 4 Mar. 1701–2 | 02 12 00 | *138* |
| **Eastop, Thomas** | Daw | Little Dawley | Blacksmith | 13 Jan. 1704–5 | 30 April 1705 | 19 10 00 | – |
| **Edge, Thomas** | Well | Hadley Park | – | 20 Sept. 1727 | 23 April 1728 | 05 06 06 | – |
| **Edwards, Mary** | Well | – | – | no inv. | 29 April 1735 | – | – |
| **Edwards, Samuel** | Wroc | Charlton | Yeoman | 28 July 1682 | 23 Aug. 1682 | 95 18 04 | – |
| **Edwards, Thomas** | Well | – | Farmer* | 12 Nov. 1695 | 1 April 1696 | 12 12 00 | – |
| **Edwards, William** | Daw | – | – | nd. | 2 Oct. 1722 | 15 12 00 | – |

# A LIST OF PEOPLE

| Name | Parish | Township, etc. | Occupation | Inventory Date | Date exhibited | Value | Number (if published) |
|---|---|---|---|---|---|---|---|
| Edwards, William | Well | Street Lane | — | 17 Oct. 1738 | 26 April 1738 | 11 03 00 | — |
| Elcock, Francis | Well | Aston | Yeoman | nd. | 20 April 1720 | 74 11 08 | — |
| Elcock, Thomas | Well | — | — | 10 Aug. 1677 | 4 Oct. 1677 | 41 06 02 | — |
| Embry, William | Well | — | — | 18 July 1689 | 1 Oct. 1689 | 04 01 10 | — |
| Evans, Ann | Well | — | Widow | 28 Nov. 1693 | 1 Dec. 1693 | 04 04 06 | — |
| Evans, Elizabeth | Well | — | — | no inv. | 28 Mar. 1683 | — | — |
| Evans, Evan | Lill | — | — | nd. | 17 Oct. 1672 | 22 07 04 | — |
| Evans, John | Wroc | Admaston | Farmer* | 17 June 1681 | 5 Oct. 1681 | 52 14 08 | — |
| Evans, John | Wroc | Leaton | Farmer* | 20 June 1702 | 13 Oct. 1702 | 112 15 00 | — |
| Evans, William | Well | — | Pipemaker | 12 Mar. 1693–4 | 13 Mar. 1693–4 | 12 04 00 | 122 |
| Evans, William | Daw | — | — | no inv. | 21 Oct. 1725 | — | — |
| Eykin, John | Lill | — | — | no inv. | 17 April 1679 | — | — |
| Eykin, Richard | Lill | Donnington | Farmer* | 21 Sept. 1659 | 12 Oct. 1660 | 94 19 04 | — |
| Eykin, Richard | Lill | — | — | no inv. | 16 Oct. 1724 | — | — |
| Eyton, John | Well | — | — | 7 Mar. 1708–9 | 6 May 1709 | 346 08 15 | 148 |
| Eyton, Charles | Daw | Malins Lee | Farmer* | 27 Aug. 1720 | 26 April 1721 | 64 12 06 | 17 |
| Farley, Richard | Daw | — | — | no inv. | 22 Sept. 1675 | — | — |
| Farley, Richard | Well | — | Shoemaker | 29 July 1741 | 23 Oct. 1741 | 19 10 00 | — |
| Farley, William | Daw | — | Webster | 25 April 1676 | 22 Sept. 1675 | 31 11 00 | 7 |
| Farrington, Robert | Well | — | — | no inv. | 21 April 1693 | — | — |
| Fearnalls, Ann | Daw | — | — | 9 April 1672 | 13 Mar. 1671–2 | 14 09 00 | — |
| Felton, Hercules | Wroc | Nash | Farmer* | 29 July 1668 | 29 July 1668 | 94 03 02 | 212 |
| Felton, Thomas | Well | Aston | Farmer* | 29 June 1697 | 1 Oct. 1697 | 86 03 02 | — |
| Felton, Thomas | Wroc | Leaton | Farmer* | 28 Mar. 1740 | 23 Oct. 1740 | 112 19 00 | — |
| Fenn, Richard | Wroc | Quom Pool | Collier | Mar. 1741–2 | 28 April 1742 | 38 12 00 | 262 |
| Fenn, Robert | Wroc | Wrock. Wood | — | 19 Jan. 1693–4 | 24 April 1694 | 16 14 00 | 229 |
| Fenton, William | Lill | Donnington Wood | — | 7 Feb, 1683 | 30 Mar. 1683 | 11 09 00 | — |
| Ferriday, John | Daw | — | — | 16 Sept. 1747 | 7 Oct. 1747 | 12 05 00 | — |

| Name | Parish | Township, etc. | Occupation | Inventory Date | Date exhibited | Value | Number (if published) |
|---|---|---|---|---|---|---|---|
| Ferriday, Robert | Daw | — | — | nd. | 19 Oct. 1725 | 09 14 00 | — |
| Ferriday, Robert | Daw | — | — | no inv. | 16 Oct. 1745 | — | — |
| Ferrington, Thomas | Wroc | Bratton | Farmer* | 17 July 1685 | 20 July 1865 | 44 13 04 | — |
| Fewtrell, Ann | Well | Watling Street | — | nd. | 19 May 1693 | 10 19 06 | — |
| Fewtrell, William | Well | Watling Street | — | nd. | 20 April 1693 | 09 09 06 | — |
| Field, John | Lill | — | — | no inv. | 19 May 1684 | — | — |
| Field, John | Well | — | Clerk | 29 July 1683 | 10 Sept. 1693 | 59 08 06 | 119 |
| Field, Miles | Well | — | Cordwainer | 28 Sept. 1680 | 5 Oct. 1680 | 53 13 00 | — |
| Field, Timothy | Well | — | Malster | 2 Dec. 1719 | 20 April 1720 | 48 16 04 | 94 |
| Fieldhouse, Mary | Well | Ketley | — | 9 Feb. 1725-6 | 19 Oct. 1726 | 02 15 00 | — |
| Fieldhouse, Thomas | Well | Ketley | — | 12 May 1688 | 17 Oct. 1688 | 04 02 04 | — |
| Fieldhouse, Thomas | Well | Ketley | Farmer* | 2 July 1705 | 18 Oct. 1705 | 77 08 02 | 143 |
| Flemming, Henry | Lill | Donnington | — | 12 Sept. 1738 | 25 Sept. 1738 | 23 05 08 | — |
| Fletcher, Thomas | Well | Street Way | Ropemaker | 21 Dec. 1680 | 19 April 1681 | 11 12 08 | 96 |
| Fletcher, Thomas | Well | — | — | nd. | 29 Oct. 1730 | 04 08 06 | — |
| Followfield, Dorothy | Well | — | Widow | 23 Aug. 1700 | 16 Oct. 1700 | 100 04 02 | — |
| Forester, Dorothy | Well | Dothill | Spinster | 25 Mar. 1674 | 1 April 1674 | 35 00 00 | — |
| Forester, Edward | Well | Leegomery | Husbandman | 16 May 1675 | 22 Nov. 1675 | 63 13 02 | — |
| Forester, Francis | Well | Watling Street | — | no inv. | 2 Oct. 1677 | — | — |
| Forester, Jane | Well | Leegomery | Spinster | 16 May 1675 | 24 Sept. 1675 | 63 13 02 | — |
| Forester, Mary | Well | — | — | no inv. | 21 Sept. 1663 | — | — |
| Forgam, Ann | Well | — | — | nd. | 20 July 1704 | 20 00 00 | — |
| Fosbrook, Abraham | Well | — | — | 14 Sept. 1715 | 20 Oct. 1715 | 19 15 07 | — |
| Foulke, Ann | Well | — | — | no inv. | 18 April 1688 | — | — |
| Fowler, John | Well | — | Gentleman | 4 Nov. 1737 | 4 Nov. 1737 | 04 19 00 | — |
| Fox, John | Wroc | — | Farmer | 4 Nov. 1669 | 14 Sept. 1670 | 22 19 08 | — |
| Fox, Thomas | Well | — | — | no inv. | 19 April 1750 | — | — |
| Francis, John | Well | — | Yeoman | 12 Oct. 1675 | 7 Mar. 1675-6 | 40 15 06 | — |
| Francis, John | Well | — | — | no inv. | 11 April 1729 | — | — |
| Francis, Mary | Well | — | — | no inv. | 19 Oct. 1687 | — | — |

# A LIST OF PEOPLE

| Name | Parish | Township, etc. | Occupation | Inventory Date | Date exhibited | Value | Number (if published) |
|---|---|---|---|---|---|---|---|
| Freeman, Alan | Well | Hadley | Farmer* | 22 Sept. 1723 | 19 Oct. 1725 | 151 05 00 | — |
| Freeman, James | Well | Ketley | — | 22 Feb. 1683-4 | 19 Mar. 1683-4 | 23 09 04 | *101* |
| Freeman, Jane | Well | Hadley | Widow | 27 June 1722 | 8 Aug. 1722 | 173 00 00 | — |
| Freeman, Thomas | Well | Ketley | — | 7 Aug. 1717 | 20 Dec. 1717 | 09 17 06 | — |
| Freeman, Thomas | Well | — | — | no inv. | 27 June 1707 | — | — |
| Fryer, Thomas | Wroc | — | — | no inv. | 21 June 1707 | — | — |
| Fryer, Thomas | Wroc | Admaston | — | 27 Jan. 1665-6 | 16 May 1666 | 17 10 02 | — |
| Garbett, Francis | Well | — | — | no inv. | 22 April 1737 | — | — |
| Gears, Abraham | Well | — | Baker | 16 Mar. 1691-2 | 17 Mar. 1691-2 | 04 08 09 | — |
| Gerrard, Thomas | Well | — | — | 10 April 1744 | 5 April 1745 | 04 17 06 | — |
| Gibbons, John | Daw | Little Dawley | — | 5 Aug. ........ | 25 April 1739 | 10 02 06 | — |
| Gittins, John | Daw | — | — | no inv. | 28 April 1730 | — | — |
| Gittins, Richard | Daw | Little Dawley | — | 7 Mar. 1661-2 | 2 May 1662 | 50 09 04 | *2* |
| Gittins, Richard | Daw | — | — | no inv. | 13 April 1722 | — | — |
| Glover, Richard | Well | Ketley | Collier | 18 Aug. 1721 | 31 July 1722 | 08 17 08 | *167* |
| Golbourn, George | Well | Hadley | Farmer* | 20 Feb. 1684 | 1 April 1685 | 82 00 00 | *104* |
| Golbourn, George | Wroc | Wrockwardine | Farmer* | 6 Jan 1727-8 | 24 April 1728 | 124 06 06 | — |
| Golbourn, John | Well | Ketley Brook | Yeoman | 16 Feb. 1671-2 | 17 Feb. 1671-2 | 24 17 04 | — |
| Golbourn, John | Well | Wellington | Yeoman | 14 April 1699 | 27 April 1699 | 31 18 06 | — |
| Golbourn, Roger | Well | Hadley | Farmer* | 30 Jan. ...... | 13 Sept. 1661 | 38 05 00 | — |
| Gollings, Richard | Well | — | Taylor | nd. | 6 May 1747 | 27 00 00 | — |
| Goodales, Richard | Well | Wrekin | Farmer* | 7 May 1692 | 6 June 1692 | 20 17 10 | *117* |
| Goodwin, Susanna | Lill | — | Widow | 22 Jan. 1711-2 | 26 April 1712 | 18 17 08 | — |
| Goole, Ann | Well | — | — | no inv. | 12 April 1716 | — | — |
| Goole, Rowland | Well | Watling Street | Innholder | 18 April 1708 | 30 April 1708 | 721 16 00 | *147* |
| Gough, Francis | Wroc | Bratton | Farmer* | 7 July 1696 | 30 Sept. 1696 | 35 16 00 | — |
| Gould, Margaret | Well | — | — | no inv. | 29 Nov. 1693 | — | — |
| Grice, Elizabeth | Well | Hadley | Farmer* | 20 June 1667 | 4 Oct. 1667 | 124 00 00 | — |
| Grice, Jane | Well | — | — | no inv. | 26 Oct. 1750 | — | — |

| Name | Parish | Township, etc. | Occupation | Inventory Date | Date exhibited | Value | Number (if published) |
|---|---|---|---|---|---|---|---|
| Grice, John | Well | Horton | – | 13 June 1672 | 30 Aug. 1672 | 23 14 08 | – |
| Grice, Joseph | Well | Hadley | Farmer* | 20 Sept. 1665 | 2 Nov. 1665 | 157 13 00 | – |
| Grice, Joseph | Well | – | – | no inv. | 14 April 1748 | – | – |
| Grice, Thomas | Well | Hadley | – | no. inv. | 15 Oct. 1685 | – | – |
| Griffiths, Rowland | Well | Walcot | Farmer* | 27 Mar. 1665 | 31 May 1665 | 33 11 04 | 85 |
| Griffiths, Thomas | Well | Ketley | Day labourer | 26 April 1708 | 30 April 1708 | 14 11 06 | – |
| Groome, John | Wombridge | Oakengates | – | 18 Mar. 1662-3 | 6 April 1663 | 34 11 00 | – |
| Groome, John | Well | – | Farmer* | 20 Feb. 1677-8 | 12 April 1678 | 28 10 10 | – |
| Groome, Margaret | Well | – | Farmer* | 10 Dec. 1683 | 15 Jan. 1683-4 | 25 06 08 | – |
| Guy, Elizabeth | Lill | Donnington Wood | – | 17 April 1716 | 20 April 1716 | 05 13 00 | – |
| Guy, Thomas | Lill | Donnington Wood | – | 27 Mar 1705 | 30 April 1705 | 14 17 00 | – |
| Haines, John | Wroc | Pains Lane | – | no inv. | 10 April 1733 | – | – |
| Haines, Robert | Well | Lawley | Ground collier | 1 June 1719 | 9 Oct. 1719 | 04 11 06 | – |
| Hall, Alice | Lill | Muxton | – | 18 April 1704 | 28 April 1704 | 03 04 06 | – |
| Hall, Anne | Well | – | Spinster | nd. | 17 April 1723 | 115 10 00 | – |
| Hall, Elizabeth | Well | – | – | no inv. | 19 April 1693 | – | – |
| Hall, John | Well | Aston | Farmer* | 19 Sept. 1675 | 22 Sept. 1675 | 260 13 04 | – |
| Hall, John | Wel | – | – | no inv. | 17 April 1718 | – | – |
| Hall, Katherine | Lill | Donnington | Farmer* | nd. | 6 April 1710 | 138 06 10 | 69 |
| Hall, William | Lill | Donnington | Farmer* | 13 Nov. 1696 | 9 April 1697 | 145 02 04 | – |
| Hall, William | Lill | Muxton | Yeoman | 14 Nov. 1702 | 29 April 1703 | 154 16 04 | 60 |
| Hall, William | Well | Lawley | – | 30 Aug. 1736 | 29 Oct. 1736 | 72 00 00 | – |
| Hall, William | Lill | Donnington | – | no inv. | 19 April 1750 | – | – |
| Hammersley, Elizabeth | Lill | – | Farmer* | 5 Mar. 1676-7 | 4 May 1677 | 93 15 00 | – |
| Hammersley, Richard | Lill | – | – | no inv. | 16 Oct. 1724 | – | – |
| Hammersley, William | Lill | – | Farmer* | 6 June 1707 | 22 Oct. 1707 | 45 00 10 | – |
| Hampton, John | Well | Horton | Yeoman | 11 July 1723 | 5 Oct. 1723 | 117 17 06 | 169 |

# A LIST OF PEOPLE

| Name | Parish | Township, etc. | Occupation | Inventory Date | Date exhibited | value | Number (if published) |
|---|---|---|---|---|---|---|---|
| Hancox, Richard | Well | — | Surgeon | 14 April 1728 | 25 April 1728 | 09 03 03 | *180* |
| Hancox, Thomas | Wroc | — | — | no inv. | 29 April 1730 | — | — |
| Hand, Richard | Wroc | — | — | 25 Jan. 1698-9 | 26 April 1699 | 09 15 00 | — |
| Handson, William | Well | — | — | 19 Nov. 1737 | 28 April 1738 | 04 15 00 | — |
| Handy, John | Well | — | Labourer | 5 Oct. 1711 | 18 Oct. 1711 | 01 16 11 | *153* |
| Harper, Jeremiah | Well | Eyton | Farmer* | 10 June 1680 | 5 Oct. 1680 | 48 18 06 | — |
| Harper, Robert | Lill | Donnington | Yeoman | 15 April 1708 | 28 April 1708 | 46 06 06 | — |
| Harper, Robert | Well | — | Shoemaker | 8 Oct. 1742 | 14 Oct. 1742 | 18 15 03 | *205* |
| Harper, Susannah | Lill | Donnington | Widow | 30 Aug. 1709 | 21 Oct. 1709 | 38 00 00 | — |
| Harper, Thomas | Well | — | Gentleman | 17 June 1669 | 24 Sept. 1669 | 58 03 04 | — |
| Harrington, Andrew | Well | — | — | 20 Mar. 1727-8 | 23 April 1728 | 19 07 07 | — |
| Harrington, Edward | Well | — | Yeoman | 27 May 1670 | 31 May 1670 | 128 05 08 | *87* |
| Harrington, Richard | Well | — | Farmer* | 20 Sept. 1684 | 6 Oct. 1684 | 32 01 00 | — |
| Harris, John | Daw | — | Farmer* | 29 Mar. 1729 | 11 April 1729 | 185 10 04 | *25* |
| Harris, John | Daw | — | Farmer* | 6 Mar. 1746-7 | 5 May 1747 | 132 05 01 | *31* |
| Harris, Joyce | Daw | — | — | no inv. | 20 April 1749 | — | — |
| Hartshorne, Edward | Well | — | — | no inv. | 25 April 1739 | — | — |
| Hartshorne, Jane | Well | — | Widow of coalmaster | 10 April 1737 | 4 Nov. 1737 | 546 14 00 | *194* |
| Hartshorne, Walter | Daw | Malins Lee | Master collier | 24 Aug. 1696 | 6 Aug. 1696 | 120 03 04 | *12* |
| Harvey, Sarah | Well | — | Widow | 21 Aug. 1723 | 15 Oct. 1723 | 09 09 06 | — |
| Harvey, William | Well | — | Glover | 2 Oct. 1722 | 4 Oct. 1722 | 11 15 11 | — |
| Hatchett, Catherine | Lill | — | Widow | 31 Dec. 1708 | 4 May 1709 | 38 07 06 | — |
| Hatchett, Mary | Wroc | — | — | no inv. | 6 May 1731 | — | — |
| Hatchett, Richard | Lill | — | Yeoman | 9 Dec. 1703 | 28 April 1704 | 34 01 02 | — |
| Hatchett, Thomas | Wroc | — | Farmer* | 29 April 1724 | 14 Oct. 1724 | 33 14 00 | — |
| Hatchett, Thomas | Wroc | Wrockwardine | Farmer* | 30 April 1741 | 23 Oct. 1741 | 73 08 00 | — |
| Haughton, Francis | Well | — | Gunsmith | 14 April 1679 | 17 April 1679 | 25 01 10 | *93* |
| Haughton, Henry | Lill | — | Vicar | 30 Oct. 1710 | 1 Dec. 1710 | 59 15 02 | *70* |
| Haughton, Margaret | Lill | — | Widow | 5 Aug. 1718 | 3 Oct. 1718 | 23 05 00 | — |

| Name | Parish | Township, etc. | Occupation | Inventory Date | Date exhibited | Value | Number (if published) |
|---|---|---|---|---|---|---|---|
| Haughton, Richard | Well | – | Gunsmith | 5 Oct. 1678 | 8 Oct. 1678 | 29 05 08 | 92 |
| Hawkins, Francis | Wroc | Charlton | Farmer* | 16 Dec. 1679 | 16 Jan 1679–80 | 454 18 04 | 217 |
| Hawkins, Jonathan | Wroc | Charlton | Farmer* | 7 April 1747 | 9 Oct. 1747 | 191 09 06 | 265 |
| Hawkins, Mary | Wroc | Charlton | – | 4 Oct. 1686 | 5 Oct. 1686 | 75 00 00 | – |
| Hawkins, Mary | Lill | – | – | no inv. | 2 April 1716 | – | – |
| Hawkins, Martha | Lill | – | – | 2 Mar. 1727–8 | 26 April 1728 | 15 11 00 | – |
| Hawkins, Richard | Lill | Muxton | Farmer* | 27 June 1702 | 15 Oct. 1702 | 54 04 01 | 59 |
| Hawkins, Robert | Wroc | Charlton | Yeoman | 14 April 1675 | 15 April 1675 | 143 10 00 | 252 |
| Hawkins, Robert | Wroc | Charlton | Farmer* | 10 Nov. 1729 | 30 April 1730 | 190 18 00 | – |
| Hawkins, Thomas | Well | – | – | no inv. | 19 Oct. 1739 | – | – |
| Hawkins, Thomasin | Lill | Muxton | Farmer* | 3 Dec. 1713 | 16 April 1714 | 238 01 10 | 71 |
| Hawkins, William | Lill | Muxton | Husbandman | 3 Oct. 1705 | 19 Oct. 1705 | 15 06 00 | – |
| Hawkes, Joseph | Lill | Donnington | – | 25 Oct. 1721 | 13 April 1722 | 01 18 06 | – |
| Hayward, John | Wroc | Charlton | Yeoman | 9 Feb. 1735–6 | 29 April 1736 | 138 08 00 | – |
| Hayward, Joseph | Wroc | – | – | no inv. | 29 April 1730 | – | – |
| Hayward, Richard | Wroc | – | – | no inv. | 2 Nov. 1732 | – | – |
| Healing, William | Well | – | Carpenter | 17 April 1710 | 21 April 1710 | 01 18 06 | – |
| Hewlett, George | Daw | – | Collier | 5 Mar. 1724–5 | 13 April 1725 | 369 05 00 | 20 |
| Hewlett, Mary | Daw | – | – | 5 Sept. 1727 | 3 Oct. 1727 | 15 05 00 | – |
| Hicks, John | Well | – | Baker | 31 July 1738 | 26 Oct. 1738 | 49 15 00 | 197 |
| Hicks, see also Icke | | | | | | | |
| Higgins, Alice | Well | – | – | no inv. | 22 Aug. 1750 | – | – |
| Higgins, Elizabeth | Well | – | – | 8 Mar. 1707–8 | 30 April 1708 | 15 06 06 | – |
| Higgins, Richard | Well | Ketley | Clothier | 28 Dec. 1676 | 4 May 1677 | 45 06 02 | – |
| Higgins, Richard | Lill | Donnington | Yeoman | 19 May 1684 | 20 May 1684 | 164 11 08 | – |
| Higgins, Richard | Lill | Donnington | – | 21 June 1710 | 1 Dec. 1710 | 128 14 00 | – |
| Higgins, Thomas | Daw | – | Weaver | 30 Sept. 1684 | 6 Oct. 1685 | 20 10 00 | 10 |
| Higgins, Thomas | Lill | – | – | no inv. | 27 May 1714 | – | – |
| Hill, Elizabeth | Well | – | – | no inv. | 4 May 1731 | – | – |
| Hill, Elizabeth | Well | – | – | nd. | 26 June 1734 | 04 10 00 | – |

# A LIST OF PEOPLE

| Name | Parish | Township, etc. | Occupation | Inventory Date | Date exhibited | Value | Number (if published) |
|---|---|---|---|---|---|---|---|
| Hill, John | Well | – | – | 17 Nov. 1666 | 19 Dec. 1666 | 142 04 00 | – |
| Hill, John | Well | – | – | no inv. | 27 Nov. 1691 | – | – |
| Hill, John | Well | – | – | 15 May 1712 | 13 Oct. 1712 | 07 18 06 | 155 |
| Hill, John and Ann | Well | – | – | nd. | 5 Oct. 1683 | 01 05 09 | – |
| Hill, Mary | Well | Watling Street | Widow | 29 April 1730 | 30 April 1730 | 10 13 02 | – |
| Hill, Ann | Well | Arleston | Widow | nd. | 5 Oct. 1683 | 17 10 00 | – |
| Hind, Thomas | Well | – | – | 17 Oct. 1688 | 19 April 1689 | 05 00 10 | – |
| Hitchcocks, Thomas | Lill | Cheshill Grange | Farmer* | 4 Mar. 1668–9 | 29 April 1669 | 70 00 00 | – |
| Hitchen, Thomas | Well | Preston on WMs | Farmer* | 7 July 1682 | 6 Aug. 1682 | 88 11 04 | 99 |
| Holland, George | Well | – | – | no inv. | 27 April 1704 | – | – |
| Holmes, John | Lill | – | – | no inv. | 24 Jan. 1703–4 | – | – |
| Holmes, Robert | Lill | – | – | no inv. | 19 Oct. 1711 | – | – |
| Hooper, John | Well | – | Husbandman | 24 Jan. 1680–1 | 24 Feb. 1680–1 | 12 05 00 | – |
| Horner, Edward | Well | – | – | no inv. | 14 April 1725 | – | – |
| Horton, William | Well | – | – | 2 Oct. 1680 | 7 Oct. 1680 | 52 00 00 | – |
| Hotchkiss, William | Well | Walcot | Farmer* | 23 April 1680 | 7 Oct. 1680 | 39 12 00 | – |
| Howle, Elizabeth | Wroc | – | Farmer* | 24 Feb. 1683–4 | 4 May 1686 | 68 07 08 | – |
| Howle, John | Well | Ketley | – | 24 May 1739 | 25 May 1739 | 14 13 06 | – |
| Howle, Mary | Well | Lawley | Widow | 16 Mar. 1696 | 1 April 1696 | 02 15 00 | – |
| Howle, Phillip | Wroc | – | Farmer* | 17 July 1685 | 10 Nov. 1685 | 66 05 10 | 223 |
| Howle, Susanna | Well | Dothill | Spinster | 17 Sept. 1677 | 2 Oct. 1677 | 161 11 01 | – |
| Howle, Thomas | Well | – | Skinner | 20 Mar. 1675–6 | 18 April 1676 | 52 00 08 | 89 |
| Howle, Thomas | Lill | – | – | nd. | 18 Sept. 1685 | 03 10 10 | – |
| Howle, William | Well | – | Glover | 14 Nov. 1664 | 2 June 1665 | 25 10 02 | 84 |
| Howlett, William | Well | Lawley | Yeoman | 3 Mar. 1726–7 | 18 April 1727 | 137 18 06 | – |
| Hughes, Edward | Wroc | – | – | 29 Dec. 1737 | 27 April 1738 | 04 10 00 | – |
| Hughes, John | Wroc | – | – | 7 Mar. 1674–5 | 26 Mar. 1675 | 50 13 04 | – |
| Hughes, John | Lill | Donnington | – | 24 Aug. 1711 | 19 Oct. 1711 | 15 18 04 | – |

| Name | Parish | Township, etc. | Occupation | Inven-Tory Date | Date exhibited | Value | Number (if published) |
|---|---|---|---|---|---|---|---|
| **Hughes, Margaret** | Lill | Donnington | Widow | 17 April 1720 | 22 April 1720 | 09 19 00 | — |
| **Hughes, William** | Wroc | Charlton | — | 3 April 1661 | 3 April 1661 | 09 12 08 | — |
| **Humphreys, Edward** | Wroc | Bullocks Brook | — | 16 Feb. 1667-8 | 26 Feb. 1667-8 | 47 07 09 | — |
| **Hunt, Mary** | Well | — | Widow | 20 June 1682 | 31 Oct. 1682 | 92 17 04 | *100* |
| **Hunt, Richard** | Well | — | Yeoman | 1 April 1679 | 15 April 1679 | 50 16 18 | — |
| **Husband, Catherine** | Lill | — | Widow | 17 Mar. 1696-7 | 29 Aug. 1696 | 13 02 03 | — |
| **Husband, John** | Lill | — | Yeoman | 20 May 1682 | 1 June 1682 | 277 00 10 | — |
| **Icks**, *see also* **Hicks** | | | | | | | |
| **Icks, Elizabeth** | Well | — | — | nd. | 19 Oct. 1725 | 02 01 00 | — |
| **Icke, Joseph** | Well | Hadley Park | Yeoman | 3 Dec. 1706 | 23 April 1707 | 104 05 04 | — |
| **Icke, Roger** | Well | — | — | 4 Feb. 1734-5 | 17 April 1735 | 14 11 00 | — |
| **Icke, Samuel** | Wroc | — | — | 22 Feb. 1741-2 | 29 April 1742 | 08 01 02 | — |
| **Icke, Thomas** | Wroc | Trench Lane | Labourer | 30 April 1708 | 30 April 1708 | 05 10 02 | *240* |
| **Icke, William** | Well | Leegomery | Farmer* | 9 Sept. 1726 | 21 Oct. 1726 | 270 07 00 | *177* |
| **Icke, William-** | Wroc | Tench Lane | — | 17 April 1731 | 4 May 1731 | 14 11 06 | *253* |
| **Inson, Thomas** | Well | Hadley | Yeoman | 9 Oct. 1714 | 19 Oct. 1714 | 15 10 00 | — |
| **Ison, James** | Well | Ketley | Weaver | 13 Aug 1702 | 15 Oct. 1702 | 03 18 11 | — |
| **Jackson, Margaret** | Well | — | — | no inv. | 2 April 1734 | — | — |
| **Jackson, Richard** | Well | — | Tailor | 26 April 1699 | 3 Oct. 1699 | 30 06 00 | *129* |
| **Jackson, Richard** | Well | — | Tailor | 14 April 1708 | 30 April 1708 | 07 11 06 | — |
| **Jackson, Roland** | Well | — | — | no inv. | 17 Oct. 1738 | — | — |
| **Jackson, William** | Well | — | Tailor | 12 Oct. 1702 | 13 Oct. 1702 | 08 13 00 | *140* |
| **James, John** | Lill | — | — | no inv. | 1 June 1733 | — | — |
| **James, Sarah** | Lill | — | — | no inv. | 6 April 1744 | — | — |
| **Jebb, Thomas** | Wroc | Allscott | Farmer* | 22 Nov. 1726 | 19 April 1727 | 160 14 06 | — |
| **Jennings, Edward** | Well | — | — | no inv. | 17 Oct. 1739 | — | — |
| **Jennings, William** | Well | — | — | 21 July 1740 | 23 Oct. 1740 | 13 15 06 | — |

# A LIST OF PEOPLE 139

| Name | Parish | Township, etc. | Occupation | Inventory Date | Date exhibited | Value | Number (if published) |
|---|---|---|---|---|---|---|---|
| Johns, Thomas | Lill | – | – | 21 Dec. 1668 | 29 April 1669 | 09 16 00 | – |
| Johnson, Edward | Well | – | Malster* | 21 April 1703 | 26 April 1703 | 16 08 02 | – |
| Johnson, Jane | Well | – | – | no inv. | 3 June 1689 | – | – |
| Johnson, John | Wroc | Bratton | Farmer* | 2 July 1742 | 14 Oct. 1743 | 26 08 00 | 126 |
| Johnson, Joshua | Well | – | Mercer | 5 Mar. 1695-6 | 1 April 1696 | 768 06 04 | 115 |
| Johnson, Richard | Well | – | – | 15 Feb. 1691-2 | 17 Mar. 1691-2 | 49 17 00 | 112 |
| Johnson, Robert | Well | – | Mercer | 28 April 1690 | 20 June 1690 | 144 00 00 | – |
| Johnson, Robert | Well | – | Mercer | no inv. | 13 Aug. 1725 | – | – |
| Johnson, Sarah | Well | – | Spinster | 20 July 1726 | 18 Oct. 1726 | 19 04 00 | – |
| Johnson, Thomas | Well | – | – | no inv. | 25 Oct. 1728 | – | – |
| Johnson, Thomas | Wroc | – | – | no inv. | 23 Oct. 1741 | – | – |
| Jones, Alice | Well | – | – | no inv. | 26 April 1721 | – | – |
| Jones, Edward | Well | – | Hatter | 7 Feb. 1662-3 | 25 Feb. 1662-3 | 11 19 08 | – |
| Jones, Edward | Well | – | Yeoman | 2 July 1678 | 8 Oct. 1678 | 102 05 00 | – |
| Jones, Edward | Well | – | Husbandman | 15 April 1681 | 5 Oct. 1681 | 22 18 10 | 97 |
| Jones, Eleanor | Well | – | – | no inv. | 12 April 1678 | – | – |
| Jones, Elizabeth | Well | – | – | no inv. | 29 May 1733 | – | – |
| Jones, Francis | Well | Arleston | – | 23 Aug. 1670 | 16 Sept. 1670 | 37 06 08 | – |
| Jones, Frances | Daw | Little Dawley | Widow | 30 June 1735 | 30 Oct. 1735 | 175 06 06 | – |
| Jones, Jane | Well | – | Widow | 27 April 1703 | 28 April 1703 | 04 00 00 | – |
| Jones, John | Well | – | – | no inv. | 28 Sept. 1689 | – | – |
| Jones, John | Wroc | Bratton | Yeoman | 21 Dec. 1729 | 29 April 1730 | 33 10 00 | – |
| Jones, John | Well | – | – | 8 Mar. 1744 | 17 Oct. 1745 | 16 03 06 | – |
| Jones, Lewis | Well | – | Day labourer | 17 Mar. 1685-6 | 4 May 1685 | 16 06 08 | – |
| Jones, Mary | Well | – | Widow | 9 April 1719 | 14 April 1719 | 15 06 06 | – |
| Jones, Owen | Well | – | Yeoman | 10 Mar. 1672-3 | 19 Mar. 1672-3 | 77 17 00 | – |
| Jones, Richard | Well | Arleston | Tanner | 5 Oct. 1683 | 5 Oct. 1683 | 04 10 00 | – |
| Jones, Richard | Daw | – | – | 18 Sept. 1689 | 28 Sept. 1689 | 323 19 04 | 111 |
| Jones, Richard | Daw | The Frame | – | 16 May 1695 | 28 May 1695 | 12 10 06 | – |
| Jones, Thomas | Daw | – | Husbandman | 13 May 1681 | 16 May 1681 | 09 13 04 | – |

| Name | Parish | Township, etc. | Occupation | Inventory Date | Date exhibited | Value | Number (if published) |
|---|---|---|---|---|---|---|---|
| Jones, Thomas | Well | — | Gentleman | 22 July 1692 | 25 Nov. 1692 | 09 13 04 | 118 |
| Jones, Thomas | Well | Hadley | Tailor | 27 Sept. 1698 | 5 Oct. 1698 | 03 08 11 | — |
| Jones, Thomas | Well | Arleston | — | 14 April 1747 | 9 Oct. 1747 | 19 10 00 | — |
| Jones, William | Well | — | — | nd. | 17 Oct. 1723 | 110 14 06 | — |
| Jordan, Margaret | Daw | — | — | 24 June 1691 | 2 Oct. 1691 | 45 02 06 | — |
| Judgson, Elizabeth | Well | — | Innholder | 6 Jan. 1715-6 | 16 April 1716 | 79 13 04 | 159 |
| Judgson, Elizabeth | Well | — | — | no inv. | 26 April 1726 | — | — |
| Judgson, John | Well | — | Innholder | 9 April 1708 | 30 April 1708 | 65 10 08 | 146 |
| Judgson, Richard | Well | — | Glover | 13 May 1729 | 29 April 1730 | 35 00 00 | — |
| Judgson, William | Well | — | Innholder | 12 July 1725 | 19 Oct. 1725 | 109 18 06 | 171 |
| Justice, Margaret | Well | — | Mercer | 3 Oct. 1687 | 12 Feb. 1687-8 | 21 04 06 | 107 |
| Juson, see Inson | | | | | | | |
| Juxon, Thomas | Well | — | — | no inv. | 19 Oct. 1687 | — | — |
| Keen, William | Daw | — | Yeoman | 20 Mar. 1744 | 4 April 1745 | 34 16 00 | 30 |
| Key, Joan | Lill | Lilleshall Heath | Widow | 20 April 1716 | 5 Oct. 1716 | 19 18 00 | — |
| Key, John | Lill | Cheswell Grange | Tailor | 11 Nov. 1698 | 28 April 1699 | 96 00 00 | — |
| Key, Richard | Lill | Muxton | Yeoman | 15 Sept. 1667 | 4 Oct. 1667 | 101 08 09 | — |
| Key, William | Lill | — | — | no inv. | 22 April 1715 | — | — |
| Kilvert, Richard | Lill | Muxton | Yeoman | 11 Aug 1669 | 24 Sept. 1669 | 30 11 10 | — |
| Lacon, John | Daw | Malins Lee | Yeoman | 20 Mar. 1725 | 13 April 1725 | 35 08 06 | — |
| Lanckyshire, Robert | Well | — | Draper | 18 Mar. 1662-3 | 2 July 1666 | 36 06 08 | — |
| Lane, Martha | Well | — | — | no inv. | 8 Dec. 1742 | — | — |
| Lane, Mary | Well | Eyton | Farmer* | 3 Sept. 1683 | 2 Oct. 1683 | 36 16 00 | — |
| Lane, Phillip | Well | Ye Lodge | — | 23 May 1696 | 25 May 1695 | 14 14 06 | — |
| Langham, Nicholas | Well | — | — | nd. | 1 Sept. 1662 | 22 05 08 | — |
| Langley, Benjamin | Well | — | — | 12 Mar. 1735-6 | 22 Mar. 1735-6 | 09 13 06 | 191 |

# A LIST OF PEOPLE

| Name | Parish | Township, etc. | Occupation | Inventory Date | Date exhibited | Value | Number (if published) |
|---|---|---|---|---|---|---|---|
| Langley, Eleanor | Wroc | — | — | no inv. | 5 May 1731 | — | — |
| Langley, Henry | Wroc | — | — | no inv. | 4 April 1692 | — | — |
| Langley, Peter | Wroc | — | — | no inv. | 17 Oct. 1711 | — | — |
| Langley, Peter | Wroc | Leaton | Gentleman | 21 July 1735 | 15 Nov. 1735 | 223 04 09 | 258 |
| Langley, Roland | Lill | Donnington | — | 6 Jan. 1663–4 | 9 April 1664 | 22 10 00 | — |
| Langley, Thomas | Wroc | — | Farmer* | 5 Dec. 1709 | 21 April 1710 | 58 19 00 | 110 |
| Langley, William | Well | Allscott | Clerk | 24 May 1689 | 18 June 1689 | 161 16 02 | — |
| Latham, Thomas | Wroc | Donnington | Yeoman | 8 June 1698 | 7 Oct. 1698 | 103 05 00 | 232 |
| Lathe, Henry | Lill | — | — | 6 Jan. 1668–9 | 16 Nov. 1669 | 189 13 06 | — |
| Lathe, Joan | Wroc | — | Farmer* | 7 Mar. 1668–9 | 29 April 1669 | 29 15 00 | — |
| Lawrence, Hugh | Lill | — | — | nd. | 2 Oct. 1696 | 22 00 00 | — |
| Lawrence, John | Wroc | Clotley | — | 17 April 1676 | 2 Oct. 1677 | 102 06 00 | — |
| Lawrence, John | Wroc | — | — | no inv. | 24 Oct. 1740 | — | — |
| Lawrence, Samuel | Well | — | — | no inv. | 14 Oct. 1742 | — | — |
| Lawrence, Thomas | Wroc | Clotley | Farmer* | 27 April 1688 | 17 Oct. 1688 | 342 13 04 | 226 |
| Lea, Andrew | Wroc | Leaton | Farmer* | 10 Aug. 1749 | 21 April 1749 | 131 19 00 | — |
| Lea, Mary | Wroc | Charlton | Farmer* | 30 May 1685 | 10 Nov. 1685 | 345 13 04 | — |
| Lea, Rowland | Wroc | Charlton | Gentleman | 10 Mar. 1673–4 | 8 April 1674 | 515 10 00 | — |
| Leeke, Ann | Lill | — | Widow | 24 Nov. 1675 | 9 Mar. 1675–6 | 31 16 08 | 41 |
| Leeke, Catherine | Lill | — | — | no inv. | 30 Mar. 1730 | — | — |
| Leeke, John | Lill | — | — | no inv. | 5 April 1717 | — | — |
| Leeke, Ralph B. | Well | — | — | nd. | 25 April 1739 | — | 199 |
| Leeke, Richard | Wroc | Pains Lane | Collier | 23 June 1690 | 1 July 1690 | 110 14 00 | — |
| Leeke, Thomas | Lill | — | Miller | 8 June 1711 | 19 Oct. 1711 | 57 03 04 | — |
| Leeke, William | Lill | — | Miller | 12 Oct. 1668 | 11 Nov. 1668 | 38 13 09 | — |
| Leighton, Sarah | Wroc | Charlton | Widow | 3 May 1698 | 5 Oct. 1698 | 31 00 00 | 37 |
| Leplain, Ann | Wroc | — | — | no inv. | 11 April 1746 | 156 11 03 | — |
| Lewis, Katherine | Well | — | Spinster | 13 April 1725 | 13 April 1725 | 16 08 00 | — |
| Lewis, Morgan | Well | Hadley | — | nd. | 28 Jan. 1660–1 | 40 03 10 | — |
| Light, Francis | Lill | — | Carpenter | 21 Mar. 1683–4 | 20 Mar. 1683–4 | 09 01 02 | 50 |

| Name | Parish | Township, etc. | Occupation | Inventory Date | Date exhibited | Value | Number (if published) |
|---|---|---|---|---|---|---|---|
| Light, Francis | Lill | Donnington | Labourer | 24 Mar. 1708–9 | 4 May 1709 | 18 12 06 | — |
| Light, Richard | Lill | — | Husbandman | 13 Oct. 1671 | 10 Oct. 1671 | 64 05 00 | — |
| Light, Thomas | Lill | — | Yeoman | 2 April 1687 | 28 April 1687 | 43 10 00 | — |
| Littlehales, Richard | Daw | — | Farmer* | nd. | 18 May 1666 | 28 10 08 | — |
| Littleton, Richard | Well | — | — | no inv. | 29 Oct. 1730 | — | — |
| Lloyd, Barbara | Well | — | — | nd. | 6 Oct. 1719 | 06 02 00 | — |
| Lloyd, Joseph | Well | — | — | no inv. | 3 Nov. 1731 | — | — |
| Lloyd, Thomas | Well | — | Currier | 12 Oct. 1703 | 21 Oct. 1703 | 16 12 06 | — |
| Lloyd, William | Well | — | — | nd. Oct. 1738 | 27 Oct. 1738 | 06 17 00 | 198 |
| Locke, Ann | Wroc | Pains Lane | — | 16 Nov. 1685 | 14 Feb. 1687–8 | 08 15 03 | — |
| Lockley, Edward | Well | Watling Street | Glover | 11 Nov. 1681 | 6 April 1682 | 54 02 04 | — |
| Lockley, Thomas | Well | Aston | Farmer* | 4 Sept. 1659 | 3 April 1661 | 30 12 00 | 81 |
| Lodge, John | Well | — | Feltmaker | 18 Nov. 1700 | 22 Nov. 1700 | 87 18 00 | 134 |
| Lodge, Thomas | Well | — | Feltmaker | 5 April 1701 | 9 April 1701 | 09 18 00 | 136 |
| Lomas, see Lummas | | | | | | | |
| Longdon, Robert | Wroc | — | — | no inv. | 4 Oct. 1716 | — | — |
| Lowe, John | Well | — | Yeoman | 5 Nov. 1729 | 9 April 1729 | 05 08 06 | — |
| Lowe, Thomas | Wroc | Bratton | Yeoman | 3 Nov. 1727 | 9 April 1728 | 470 10 00 | — |
| Lummas, Eleanor | Wroc | — | — | 7 Sept. 1739 | 19 Oct. 1739 | 164 00 00 | — |
| Lummas, John | Wroc | — | Farmer* | 9 April 1740 | 11 April 1740 | 33 15 00 | — |
| Lummas, Richard | Wroc | Pains Lane | Master collier | 4 Sept. 1711 | 16 Oct. 1711 | 93 14 02 | 242 |
| Lummas, Richard | Well | — | — | no inv. | 15 April 1743 | — | — |
| Lummas, Richard | Well | — | - | no inv. | 19 April 1750 | — | — |
| Lyth, John | Well | Walcot | Farmer* | 10 June 1714 | 20 Oct. 1714 | 108 06 06 | — |
| Manlove, William | Well | — | Yeoman | 16 Mar. 1721–2 | 11 April 1722 | 02 19 02 | — |
| Mannering, Roger | Wroc | Charlton | Farmer* | 25 Nov. 1676 | 1 Dec, 1676 | 52 13 04 | — |
| Manning, Anne | Well | — | Widow | 5 Feb. 1678–9 | 11 Feb. 1678–9 | 11 05 10 | — |
| Mansell, Alice | Lill | — | — | no inv. | 21 Oct. 1709 | — | — |
| Mansell, Benjamin | Well | — | — | 23 Nov. 1734 | 1 April 1735 | 59 16 06 | — |

A LIST OF PEOPLE 143

| Name | Parish | Township, etc. | Occupation | Inventory Date | Date exhibited | Value | Number (if published) |
|---|---|---|---|---|---|---|---|
| Mansell, Humphrey | Lill | – | Labourer | 15 April 1679 | 7 April 1679 | 19 02 02 | 46 |
| Mansell, John | Lill | Muxton | Farmer* | 7 Dec. 1715 | 20 April 1716 | 28 16 00 | – |
| Mansell, John | Lill | – | – | 21 Mar. 1719–20 | 22 April 1720 | 08 02 06 | – |
| Mansell, John | Well | – | – | no inv. | 3 Sept. 1742 | – | – |
| Mansell, John | Well | – | Glover | 11 Mar. 1743 | 15 April 1743 | 14 02 7½ | 206 |
| Mansell, Mary | Lill | – | Widow | 21 Sept. 1686 | 7 Oct. 1686 | 19 02 00 | – |
| Mansell, Richard | Lill | Cheshill Grange | – | 4 Aug. 1684 | 10 Oct. 1684 | 124 03 03 | – |
| Mansell, Richard | Lill | – | – | no inv. | 5 May 1747 | – | – |
| Mansell, Thomas | Well | – | – | 1 Oct. 1719 | 7 Oct. 1719 | 12 12 11 | – |
| Mansell, Walter | Well | – | Tanner | 30 Nov. 1710 | 30 Nov. 1710 | 10 16 00 | – |
| Manwaring, George | Well | – | – | no inv. | 15 Oct. 1728 | – | – |
| Manwaring, John | Well | – | – | no inv. | 30 April 1662 | – | – |
| Marigold, John | Well | Leegomery | Farmer* | 10 May 1681 | 5 Oct. 1681 | 82 13 06 | – |
| Marigold, Margaret | Well | – | – | no inv. | 17 April 1689 | – | – |
| Marigold, Mary | Well | – | – | no inv. | 12 Nov. 1685 | – | – |
| Marigold, Roger | Well | – | – | no inv. | 12 Nov. 1685 | – | – |
| Marigold, Walter | Well | Arleston | Yeoman | 29 Jan. 1700–1 | 9 April 1701 | 192 09 00 | – |
| Marigold, Walter | Well | Leegomery | – | no inv. | 30 Oct. 1735 | – | – |
| Marigold, William | Well | Leegomery | Yeoman | 28 Feb. 1676–7 | 2 May 1677 | 515 10 04 | 91 |
| Marigold, William | Well | Leegomery | – | no inv. | 2 Nov. 1737 | – | – |
| Massey, James | Well | Watling Street | Innholder | 29 Sept. 1740 | 23 Oct 1741 | 93 19 00 | 201 |
| Massey, Margaret | Wroc | – | Farmer* | 10 Sept. 1693 | 29 Nov. 1693 | 39 01 00 | – |
| Matthews, Ann | Lill | – | – | no inv. | 21 Oct. 1676 | – | – |
| Matthews, Edward | Lill | Donnington | Yeoman | 5 July 1731 | 2 Nov. 1731 | 120 15 00 | – |
| Matthews, Elizabeth | Lill | – | – | no inv. | 20 May 1726 | – | – |
| Matthews, John | Wroc | – | – | no inv. | 22 Mar. 1675 | – | – |
| Matthews, Samuel | Well | – | – | no inv. | 27 Feb. 1723–4 | – | – |
| Matthews, Thomas | Lill | Donnington | Yeoman | 24 June 1708 | 21 Oct. 1708 | 13 09 06 | – |
| Matthews, Thomas | Lill | Donnington | Carpenter* | 29 Mar. 1734 | 22 May 1734 | 22 10 00 | – |

| Name | Parish | Township, etc. | Occupation | Inventory Date | Date exhibited | Value | Number (if published) |
|---|---|---|---|---|---|---|---|
| Matthews, William | Wroc | — | — | no inv. | 16 July 1723 | — | — |
| Maydon, Thomas | Well | Ketley | Glover | 23 June 1703 | 20 Oct. 1703 | 28 11 00 | — |
| Millington, John | Well | — | Yeoman | 25 April 1709 | 6 May 1709 | 12 08 03 | — |
| Millington, Margaret | Well | — | Widow | 29 Sept. 1711 | 18 Oct. 1711 | 09 00 08 | — |
| Minnion, Ann | Lill | Muxton | Farmer* | 7 Dec. 1716 | 18 April 1718 | 200 07 00 | — |
| Minnion, John | Lill | Muxton | Gentleman | 7 Aug. 1716 | 5 Oct. 1716 | 200 07 00 | — |
| Minshall, William | Well | — | — | 8 Aug. 1683 | 2 Oct. 1683 | 39 03 10 | — |
| Minshall, William | Well | Leegomery | Farmer* | 29 Oct. 1687 | 27 Mar. 1688 | 360 14 00 | 109 |
| Minton, John | Wroc | Admaston | — | no inv. | 17 April 1723 | — | — |
| Mitton, Edward | Well | Aston | Gentleman | 25 Mar. 1704 | 30 Mar. 1704 | 365 08 03 | — |
| Mitton, Jane | Well | — | Spinster | 9 Nov. 1720 | 20 April 1721 | 19 03 06 | — |
| Moore, Edward | Well | — | — | 2 June 1713 | 7 Oct. 1713 | 18 09 08 | — |
| Morgan, Mary | Well | — | — | no inv. | 28 April 1687 | — | — |
| Morley, Anne | Wroc | Allscott | Widow | 10 Jan. 1690–1 | 30 April 1691 | 09 10 06 | — |
| Morris, Elizabeth | Well | Watling Street | — | no inv. | 24 April 1667 | — | — |
| Morris, James | Well | — | Whitesmith | 20 Dec. 1699 | 12 Jan. 1699–1700 | 18 13 00 | 131 |
| Morris, John | Well | — | Weaver* | nd. | 4 Oct. 1716 | 02 16 06 | — |
| Morris, Robert | Well | — | — | 12 Jan. 1746–7 | 16 Jan. 1746–7 | 72 15 00 | — |
| Moss, John | Well | — | Shoemaker | 20 July 1728 | 16 Oct. 1728 | 06 19 06 | 182 |
| Moulton, Anne | Lill | Donnington | — | 25 Nov. 1710 | 4 Dec. 1710 | 06 13 00 | — |
| Moulton, Thomas | Lill | Donnington | Yeoman | 25 Feb. 1684–5 | 1 April 1685 | 20 13 03 | — |
| Moulton, Thomas | Lill | — | Farmer* | 12 Mar. 1735–6 | 28 April 1736 | 75 00 00 | — |
| Mountford, Alice | Wroc | Bratton | Farmer* | 7 Feb. 1698–9 | 27 April 1698 | 155 16 06 | 233 |
| Mountford, Richard | Wroc | Bratton | Yeoman | 13 July 1694 | 2 Oct. 1694 | 184 16 06 | 231 |
| Mountford, Richard | Wroc | Bratton | Yeoman | 13 Mar. 1704–5 | 28 April 1705 | 94 15 04 | — |
| Nevall, Thomas | Well | Horton | Carpenter | 26 April 1692 | 24 May 1692 | 39 01 02 | — |
| Newe, Elinor | Wroc | — | Farmer* | 6 Oct. 1681 | 5 Oct. 1681 | 55 03 08 | 219 |
| Newe, George | Wroc | — | — | 4 Jan 1680–1 | 29 Mar. 1681 | 32 14 07 | — |

# A LIST OF PEOPLE

| Name | Parish | Township, etc. | Occupation | Inventory Date | Date exhibited | Value | Number (if published) |
|---|---|---|---|---|---|---|---|
| Newell, Thomas | Lill | – | Farmer* | 3 Jan. 1676-7 | 4 May 1677 | 91 12 00 | 43 |
| Newell, Thomas | Lill | Donnington | – | no inv. | 5 Oct. 1716 | – | – |
| Newell, Thomas | Lill | Donnington | Gentleman | 18 May 1731 | 26 May 1731 | 219 09 08 | 77 |
| Newnes, John | Well | – | Yeoman | nd. | 26 April 1728 | 116 02 00 | – |
| Newnes, Samuel | Well | Eyton | Yeoman | 28 Dec. 1717 | 16 April 1716 | 148 00 00 | – |
| Newton, Bazel | Well | Walcot Waste | Farmer* | 23 Sept. 1729 | 29 Oct. 1729 | 63 12 00 | – |
| Newton, Jane | Well | – | Widow | 30 Mar. 1705 | 28 April 1705 | 07 09 02 | – |
| Newton, John | Daw | Malins Lee | Yeoman | 29 Dec. 1691 | 26 Jan. 1691-2 | 39 04 00 | – |
| Newton, Thomas | Daw | – | – | 11 Mar. 1668-9 | 29 April 1669 | 57 10 00 | – |
| Newton, William | Daw | – | Farmer* | 17 Mar. 1661-2 | 2 May 1662 | 58 16 00 | – |
| Newton, William | Well | – | – | no inv. | 24 April 1712 | – | – |
| North, Catherine | Well | Ketley | Widow | 28 Feb. 1732-3 | 13 May 1734 | 46 19 00 | – |
| North, John | Well | – | – | nd. | 26 April 1721 | 03 03 00 | – |
| North, John | Well | Ketley | Farmer* | 2 Nov. 1726 | 18 April 1727 | 49 04 09 | 178 |
| Norton, Roger | Well | Ketley | Yeoman | 26 Mar. 1694 | 24 April 1694 | 03 05 08 | – |
| Oakley, William | Well | Ruckley | Yeoman | 17 Mar. 1704-5 | 28 April 1705 | 95 17 10 | 141 |
| Onions, Michael | Daw | Stoney Hill | – | 18 Nov. 1727 | 15 Oct. 1728 | 16 02 09 | 23 |
| Onions, Robert | Well | – | – | 5 Nov. 1701 | 25 Nov. 1701 | 10 16 00 | – |
| Onions, Thomas | Well | Ketley Wood | Collier | 14 April 1702 | 4 May 1702 | 25 00 00 | – |
| Ore, Francis | Well | – | Blacksmith | 29 April 1692 | 15 May 1692 | 01 06 4½ | 116 |
| Ore, Francis | Well | – | Clerk | 15 Aug. 1704 | 18 Sept. 1704 | 15 03 04 | – |
| Owen, Edward | Lill | – | Webster | 9 April 1714 | 16 April 1714 | 76 01 04 | 72 |
| Owen, Elizabeth | Well | Ketley | – | 6 Mar. 1700-1 | 9 April 1701 | 07 08 06 | – |
| Owen, Henry | Lill | Donnington | – | 21 May 1664 | 18 Nov. 1664 | 13 12 04 | – |
| Owen, Joanna | Lill | – | – | no inv. | 2 April 1741 | – | – |
| Pace, John | Well | Aston | Yeoman | 30 April 1681 | 27 June 1681 | 103 10 00 | – |
| Paddey, Robert | Well | – | Gentleman | 5 Feb. 1716-7 | 5 April 1717 | 63 03 00 | – |
| Padmore, see Podmore | | | | | | | |

| Name | Parish | Township, etc. | Occupation | Inventory Date | Date exhibited | Value | Number (if published) |
|---|---|---|---|---|---|---|---|
| Pain, John | Well | Shawbirch | — | 1724 | 13 April 1725 | 06 08 00 | — |
| Pain, Thomas | Daw | — | — | no inv. | 22 Mar. 1680-1 | — | — |
| Palmer, Joseph | Well | — | — | 18 Nov. 1687 | 8 Nov. 1687 | 05 13 08 | — |
| Palmer, Thomas | Lill | — | — | nd. | 2 Mar. 1721-22 | 02 15 04 | — |
| Parkes, Charles | Well | — | — | 14 Mar. 1678 | 8 Oct. 1678 | 11 10 04 | — |
| Parker, William | Wroc | — | — | Missing | 7 Nov. 1690 | — | — |
| Parrock, John | Lill | — | Labourer | nd. | 10 April 1724 | 06 10 00 | — |
| Pate, see Peate | | | | | | | |
| Pawley, Thomas | Daw | — | — | 9 Nov. 1688 | 18 April 1689 | 33 05 00 | — |
| Pearce, Margaret | Well | Watling Street | Widow | nd. | 3 Oct. 1699 | 03 17 02 | — |
| Pearce, Ralph | Wroc | Long Lane | Farmer* | 1 June 1671 | 17 Oct. 1671 | 19 06 02 | 214 |
| Pearce, Robert | Well | Walcot | Webster | 17 April 1704 | 26 April 1704 | 02 03 10 | — |
| Pearce, William | Well | Watling Street | Wheelwright | 15 Oct. 1726 | 6 Dec. 1726 | 88 17 06 | — |
| Peate, Catherine | Daw | — | Widow | 31 July 1719 | — | 26 06 00 | — |
| Peate, Francis | Well | Seven Stars | Blacksmith | 12 Dec. 1746 | 16 Feb. 1756-7 | 65 19 03 | 208 |
| Peate, George | Well | The Lane | Blacksmith | 12 Feb. 1686-7 | 15 Feb. 1686-7 | 27 00 00 | — |
| Peate, George | Well | — | — | nd. | 18 June 1744 | 49 18 06 | — |
| Peate, John | Well | Street Lane | Blacksmith | 7 Oct. 1687 | 19 Oct. 1687 | 54 05 00 | 108 |
| Peate, John | Well | — | Feltmaker | 22 April 1698 | 28 April 1698 | 03 05 06 | — |
| Peate, John | Daw | Little Dawley | Farmer* | 19 Sept. 1715 | 21 Oct. 1715 | 43 17 04 | — |
| Peate, Margaret | Well | — | — | no inv. | 11 April 1711 | — | — |
| Peate, Mary | Daw | — | Widow | 5 July 1697 | 30 April 1697 | 09 03 00 | — |
| Peate, Paul | Daw | — | — | nd. | 7 June 1664 | 05 09 06 | — |
| Peate, Richard | Well | Streetway, Hadley | Blacksmith | 7 Jan 1709-10 | 21 April 1710 | 13 04 06 | 150 |
| Peate, Robert | Well | — | Blacksmith | 9 Oct. 1700 | 15 Oct. 1700 | 05 06 08 | 133 |
| Pemberton, Edward | Wroc | — | — | no inv. | 5 Oct. 1744 | — | — |
| Pemberton, Jane | Wroc | — | — | no inv. | 17 Sept. 1690 | — | — |
| Pemberton, Jane | Wroc | — | — | no inv. | 14 April 1748 | — | — |
| Pemberton, John | Wroc | — | — | 21 July 1735 | 30 Oct. 1735 | 13 10 06 | 257 |

# A LIST OF PEOPLE

| Name | Parish | Township, etc. | Occupation | Inventory Date | Date exhibited | Value | Number (if published) |
|---|---|---|---|---|---|---|---|
| Pemberton, Mary | Wroc | Leaton | Farmer* | 3 Aug. 1739 | 19 Oct. 1739 | 71 05 06 | — |
| Pemberton, Roger | Wroc | Leaton | Yeoman | 10 June 1661 | 30 April 1662 | 1,112 00 00 | 210 |
| Pemberton, William | Wroc | Leaton | Gentleman | 24 Mar. 1693–4 | 28 Mar. 1693–4 | 33 15 00 | 230 |
| Pemberton, William | Wroc | Leaton | Yeoman | 20 Nov. 1729 | 20 Mar. 1729–30 | 55 12 03 | — |
| Penson, Andrew | Lill | — | — | no inv. | 5 Aug. 1707 | — | — |
| Penson, Joseph | Lill | — | — | no inv. | 8 Nov. 1743 | — | — |
| Penson, Margaret | Lill | — | — | no inv. | 12 Oct. 1727 | — | — |
| Penson, Robert | Lill | Lilleshall Manor | — | 20 Feb. 1737 | 20 April 1737 | 27 01 00 | — |
| Penson, Thomas | Lill | Lilleshall Manor | — | 2 Mar. 1677 | 12 April 1678 | 29 19 00 | — |
| Penson, Thomas | Lill | Lilleshall Manor | Farmer* | 16 Nov. 1686 | 28 April 1687 | 38 09 06 | — |
| Penson, William | Lill | — | — | no inv. | 4 Oct. 1667 | — | — |
| Peploe, Humphrey | Daw | Middle Leasow, Little Dawley | Farmer* | 8 May 1665 | 2 June 1665 | 78 08 10 | 3 |
| Peploe, Nathan | Daw | Little Dawley | — | 15 Mar. 1732–3 | 29 May 1733 | 28 01 00 | 28 |
| Peploe, Podmore | Daw | Little Dawley | — | 20 April 1715 | 22 April 1715 | 14 13 06 | 15 |
| Perkins, William | Daw | — | Shoemaker | 6 May 1702 | 22 May 1702 | 13 07 00 | — |
| Perry, John | Daw | — | Farmer* | nd. | 25 April 1739 | 37 13 00 | — |
| Perry, Roger | Well | — | — | 18 Sept. 1691 | 18 Sept. 1691 | 00 19 04 | — |
| Phillips, Eleanor | Well | — | Widow | 11 Nov. 1692 | 29 Nov. 1692 | 90 04 00 | — |
| Phillips, Joseph | Well | — | — | no inv. | 21 Mar. 1717–8 | — | — |
| Phillips, Mary | Daw | — | — | no inv. | 19 April 1689 | — | — |
| Phillips, Rebecca | Well | — | — | no inv. | 15 Oct. 1672 | — | — |
| Phillips, Richard | Well | — | Gentleman | 14 Aug. 1705 | 17 Sept. 1705 | 277 19 09 | 144 |
| Phillips, Thomas | Wroc | — | — | no inv. | 29 April 1730 | — | — |
| Picken, Mary | Wroc | Bratton | Farmer* | 8 Jan 1693–4 | 24 April 1694 | 38 03 02 | — |
| Picken, Thomas | Wroc | Bratton | Yeoman | 14 Nov. 1683 | 10 Mar. 1683–4 | 38 05 00 | — |
| Picken, Thomas | Well | — | — | no inv. | 17 Oct. 1705 | — | — |

| Name | Parish | Township, etc. | Occupation | Inventory Date | Date exhibited | Value | Number (if published) |
|---|---|---|---|---|---|---|---|
| Picken, Thomas | Wric | Admaston | Husbandman | 28 Feb. 1709-10 | 21 April 1710 | 38 10 00 | — |
| Picken, William | Lill | Donnington | Farmer* | 22 June 1749 | 12 Oct. 1749 | 189 00 00 | — |
| Pickerell, Christopher | Wroc | — | — | 30 Jan. 1730-1 | 29 Jan. 1730-1 | 03 17 06 | — |
| Pickerell, Margaret | Well | — | Widow | 23 Sept. 1738 | 19 Oct. 1739 | 26 09 06 | 244 |
| Pickering, Allen | Wroc | Pains Lane | Yeoman | nd. | 4 Mar. 1714-5 | 19 10 00 | — |
| Pickering, Allen | Wroc | Bratton | Yeoman | 25 Feb. 1715-6 | 16 April 1716 | 157 05 00 | — |
| Pickering, Eleanor | Well | Horton | Farmer* | 11 Sept. 1670 | 14 Sept. 1670 | 33 18 04 | — |
| Pickering, Mary | Wroc | — | — | no inv. | 30 Oct. 1746 | — | — |
| Pickering, Richard | Well | — | — | 21 Jan. 1736 | 4 Nov. 1737 | 11 09 00 | — |
| Pickering, Robert | Well | Shawbirch | — | 24 Mar. 1733-4 | 17 April 1735 | 18 15 02 | — |
| Pitchford, George | Well | Street Lane | Husbandman | 26 Dec. 1671 | 13 Mar. 1671-2 | 09 01 07 | — |
| Pitchford, Thomas | Wroc | — | — | 12 Mar. 1693-4 | 24 April 1694 | 05 00 00 | — |
| Plymley, John | Well | — | — | no inv. | 26 May 1671 | — | — |
| Plymley, Richard | Well | — | Gentleman | 3 Jan. 1700-1 | 17 Mar. 1700-1 | 10 10 00 | 135 |
| Podmore, Elizabeth | Well | — | — | no inv. | 20 April 1750 | — | — |
| Podmore, Samuel | Well | — | Yeoman | nd. | 10 April 1740 | 16 19 00 | — |
| Podmore, Sarah | Well | Arleston | Widow | nd. | 10 April 1740 | 09 18 00 | — |
| Podmore, William | Well | Arleston | Farmer* | 18 April 1734 | 31 Oct. 1734 | 222 11 06 | — |
| Poole, Francis | Well | — | Farmer* | 22 Jan. 1674-5 | 26 Mar. 1675-6 | 64 15 00 | — |
| Poole, George | Well | — | Labourer | 19 Sept. 1672 | 9 Oct. 1672 | 28 00 00 | — |
| Poole, George | Daw | — | — | no inv. | 17 April 1679 | — | — |
| Poole, Humphrey | Well | Ketley | Farmer* | 9 Oct. 1744 | 5 April 1745 | 62 15 00 | — |
| Poole, John | Well | Arleston | — | 31 July 1677 | 2 Oct. 1677 | 19 06 06 | — |
| Poole, John | Well | Aston | Yeoman | 23 May 1706 | 25 May 1706 | 156 01 03 | — |
| Poole, Mary | Daw | — | — | no inv. | 16 Oct. 1735 | — | — |
| Poole, William | Well | Arleston | Farmer* | 30 Nov. 1675 | 7 Mar. 1675-6 | 54 06 04 | — |
| Poulford, William | Well | Wappenshall | Yeoman | 4 Jan. 1721-2 | 15 Jan. 1721-2 | 38 02 00 | — |
| Powell, Samuel | Well | — | — | no inv. | 20 April 1737 | — | — |
| Poyner, Roger | Daw | — | — | 6 June 1687 | 20 April 1688 | 114 04 06 | — |
| Poyner, William | Daw | — | Yeoman | 20 Feb. 1715-6 | 25 Feb. 1715-6 | 03 05 06 | 16 |

# A LIST OF PEOPLE

| Name | Parish | Township, etc. | Occupation | Inventory Date | Date exhibited | Value | Number (if published) |
|---|---|---|---|---|---|---|---|
| Prestwood, Francis | Well | — | — | no inv. | 26 Oct. 1738 | — | — |
| Price, Eleanor | Well | — | — | no inv. | 10 April 1740 | — | — |
| Price, Elizabeth | Well | — | — | no inv. | 15 April 1714 | — | — |
| Price, Richard | Wroc | Admaston | Husbandman | 27 June 1663 | 31 May 1665 | 14 07 06 | — |
| Price, Robert | Well | Aston | Farmer* | 21 May 1740 | 3 April 1741 | 45 00 00 | — |
| Pritchard, John | Well | — | — | 13 Jan. 1692-3 | 20 April 1693 | 35 19 00 | — |
| Pritchard, Mary | Lill | — | — | no inv. | 26 April 1728 | — | — |
| Pritchard, Thomas | Well | Hadley | Farmer* | 12 Nov. 1728 | 8 April 1729 | 34 15 06 | — |
| Pritchett, Eleanor | Well | — | — | 12 April 1700 | 5 Feb. 1699-00 | 93 11 00 | — |
| Pucksley, Daniel | Wroc | Wrockwardine Wood | Webster | 6 Jan. 1704-5 | 23 Jan. 1704-5 | 09 06 04 | 236 |
| Puller, Francis | Well | — | Saddler* | 25 Jan. 1721-2 | 10 April 1722 | 17 12 06 | — |
| Pursell, Thomas | Well | Aston | — | 21 Nov. 1701 | 21 Nov. 1701 | 03 18 03 | — |
| Randle, Richard | Well | Street Lane | Yeoman | 17 Mar. 1701-2 | 5 May 1702 | 23 16 06 | 137 |
| Reynolds, Eleanor | Wroc | — | — | no inv. | 10 Nov. 1685 | — | — |
| Reynolds, Jeffrey | Wroc | — | — | 26 Aug. 1672 | 27 April 1669 | 10 10 00 | — |
| Reynolds, Thomas | Well | — | Butcher* | 2 June 1690 | 17 Sept. 1690 | 27 00 10 | 113 |
| Reynolds, William | Well | Street Lane | Carpenter | 14 Oct. 1700 | 15 Oct. 1700 | 02 06 00 | — |
| Rhodes, Mary | Daw | — | Widow | 9 April 1729 | 11 April 1729 | 07 05 01 | — |
| Rhodes, Richard | Daw | — | — | 14 Feb. 1735 | 29 April 1736 | 04 12 00 | — |
| Rhodes, Thomas | Daw | — | — | 8 Nov. 1731 | 28 April 1732 | 10 05 00 | — |
| Richards, Basil | Daw | Little Dawley | Yeoman | 27 May 1659 | 20 Sept. 1661 | 121 07 08 | 1 |
| Richards, Daniel | Daw | Malins Lee | Husbandman | 27 April 1669 | 29 April 1669 | 10 13 02 | — |
| Richards, Frances | Daw | Little Dawley | Widow | 13 Nov. 1666 | 26 Nov. 1666 | 32 02 10 | 5 |
| Richards, John | Daw | Little Dawley | Gentleman | 8 Oct. 1707 | 22 Oct. 1707 | 38 06 08 | — |
| Richards, Robert | Wroc | Bratton | Yeoman | 7 Dec. 1709 | 21 April 1710 | 199 04 04 | — |
| Richards, Robert | Wroc | Bratton | Yeoman | 20 Sept. 1728 | 15 Oct. 1728 | 113 10 00 | — |
| Richards, William | Daw | Little Dawley | Gentleman | 26 Mar. 1716 | 27 Mar. 1716 | 195 10 00 | — |
| Richardson, Daniel | Daw | — | — | no inv. | 14 Nov. 1733 | — | — |

149

| Name | Parish | Township, etc. | Occupation | Inventory Date | Date exhibited | Value | Number (if published) |
|---|---|---|---|---|---|---|---|
| Richardson, John | Wroc | — | Husbandman | 12 Oct. 1728 | 8 April 1729 | 27 04 00 | — |
| Riddings, Jane | Well | — | — | no inv., 1720 | 22 April 1720 | — | — |
| Rider, Robert | Well | — | — | no inv. | 30 April 1736 | — | — |
| Roberts, Dorothy | Wroc | — | — | no inv. | 2 Nov. 1732 | — | — |
| Roberts, Lucy | Well | — | Widow | 15 Mar. 1663-4 | 28 Mar. 1664 | 07 15 00 | — |
| Roe, Alice | Daw | — | — | no inv. | 29 April 1698 | — | — |
| Roe, Alice | Wroc | Wrockwardine | Farmer* | 14 Aug. 1713 | 9 Oct. 1713 | 93 03 06 | — |
| Roe, Ann | Daw | Little Dawley | Widow | 1 Nov. 1731 | 2 Nov. 1731 | 03 05 06 | — |
| Roe, Benjamin | Daw | — | Yeoman | no inv. | 2 Nov. 1748 | — | — |
| Roe, Elizabeth | Well | — | — | no inv. | 17 Mar. 1691-2 | — | — |
| Roe, Jonathan | Wroc | — | — | no inv. | 17 June 1701 | — | — |
| Roe, Richard | Well | Wappenshall | Farmer* | 27 May 1676 | 4 July 1676 | 64 00 00 | — |
| Roe, Richard | Well | — | Tailor | 17 Feb. 1727-8 | 23 April 1728 | 100 17 4¼ | 179 |
| Roe, Robert | Well | Hadley | Clerk | 5 Aug 1717 | 20 Dec. 1717 | 19 02 04 | 162 |
| Roe, Thomas | Wroc | — | Yeoman | 27 April 1669 | 27 April 1669 | 21 10 00 | — |
| Roe, Thomas | Wroc | — | Farmer* | 6 Dec. 1679 | 21 April 1680 | 203 08 00 | 216 |
| Roe, Thomas | Daw | Little Dawley | Yeoman | 8 June 1730 | 27 Oct. 1730 | 126 08 00 | 26 |
| Roe, William | Well | Arleston | Farmer* | 29 Jan. 1669 | 7 July 1670 | 79 17 06 | — |
| Roe, William | Well | Arleston | Gentleman | 19 Sept. 1679 | 21 April 1680 | 170 14 00 | — |
| Rowley, Elizabeth | Lill | Donnington | Farmer* | 6 Sept. 1704 | 7 Sept. 1706 | 81 04 02 | — |
| Rowley, George | Well | — | Blacksmith | 5 April 1731 | 4 May 1731 | 11 00 10 | — |
| Rowley, John | Well | — | Apothecary* | 12 Jan. 1729-30 | 29 April 1730 | 53 06 06 | 185 |
| Rowley, Richard | Lill | Donnington | Yeoman | 7 Mar. 1687 | 11 Oct. 1687 | 78 18 06 | — |
| Royston, Eleanor | Lill | Donnington | Widow | 18 Jan. 1716 | 11 Aug. 1716 | 26 19 00 | — |
| Royston, John | Lill | — | — | no inv. | 26 April 1738 | — | — |
| Royston, Thomas | Lill | Donnington | Yeoman | 2 May 1702 | 7 May 1702 | 18 00 00 | — |
| Royston, William | Lill | Donnington | — | 21 April 1715 | 27 Mar. 1716 | 15 13 06 | — |
| Rushton, Ann | Daw | — | — | no inv. | 22 April 1737 | — | — |
| Russell, Edward | Wroc | — | — | no inv. | 19 Oct. 1703 | — | — |

# A LIST OF PEOPLE

| Name | Parish | Township, etc. | Occupation | Inventory Date | Date exhibited | Value | Number (if published) |
|---|---|---|---|---|---|---|---|
| Salter, Richard | Wroc | — | — | 23 Oct. 1685 | 10 Nov. 1685 | 03 15 04 | — |
| Sambrook, John | Well | — | Maltster | 10 Aug. 1748 | 3 Nov. 1748 | 25 18 06 | — |
| Sandys, Eleanor | Well | — | Widow | 1 Nov. 1698 | 9 Feb. 1698-9 | 02 16 10 | 128 |
| Savin, Humphrey | Well | Hadley | Farmer* | 3 Oct. 1728 | 8 April 1729 | 39 12 00 | — |
| Scaltock Peter | Wroc | — | — | 8 April 1724 | 8 April 1724 | 03 17 01 | — |
| Schofield, Jane | Wroc | Wrockwardine | Schoolmistress | 31 Jan. 1704-5 | Feb. 1704-5 | 64 18 8½ | 237 |
| Shakesaft, Edward | Well | — | Cordwainer | 19 April 1709 | 21 April 1709 | 18 14 06 | 149 |
| Shaw, Richard | Well | — | — | no inv. | 17 Oct. 1711 | — | — |
| Shelton, Andrew | Lill | — | Farmer* | 30 May 1690 | 2 June 1690 | 453 11 04 | — |
| Shelton, Jane | Lill | — | Widow | 18 April 1707 | 28 April 1707 | 82 05 00 | — |
| Shelton, John | Lill | Muxton | Yeoman | 22 Sept. 1680 | 7 Oct. 1680 | 291 09 06 | 47 |
| Shelton, John | Lill | Muxton | Farmer* | 16 May 1707 | 27 June 1707 | 431 01 00 | 64 |
| Shelton, John | Lill | Donnington | — | 1 June 1733 | 1 June 1733 | 21 15 06 | — |
| Shelton, Mary | Lill | Muxton | — | 24 May 1676 | 20 Sept. 1676 | 129 01 07 | 42 |
| Shelton, Mary | Lill | — | — | no inv. | 4 Oct. 1744 | — | — |
| Shelton, Phillipia | Lill | Muxton | Farmer* | 3 Jan. 1708-9 | 9 Mar. 1708-9 | 211 13 06 | 66 |
| Shelton, Richard | Lill | — | — | 19 Sept. 1677 | 4 Oct. 1677 | 397 00 00 | — |
| Shelton, Richard | Lill | — | Farmer* | 2 Aug. 1683 | 5 Oct. 1683 | 246 01 08 | 48 |
| Shelton, Richard | Lill | Muxton | Yeoman | 6 May 1701 | 27 Nov. 1701 | 237 01 06 | — |
| Shelton, Robert | Lill | — | Yeoman | 13 Nov. 1671 | 31 Jan. 1671-2 | 175 13 04 | 38 |
| Shelton, Robert | Lill | — | Farmer* | 12 Nov. 1717 | 20 Dec. 1717 | 276 09 02 | 73 |
| Shelton, William | Lill | — | — | no inv. | 26 Nov. 1660 | — | — |
| Shelton, William | Lill | Muxton | Farmer* | 8 Dec. 1727 | 17 June 1728 | 183 18 00 | — |
| Shelton, William | Lill | Muxton | Yeoman | 11 July 1720 | 26 April 1721 | 09 04 06 | — |
| Sherrard, John | Well | — | — | no inv. | 3 Sept. 1717 | — | — |
| Sherrington, Frances | Well | — | — | no inv. | 17 Oct. 1723 | — | — |
| Shipman, John | Well | — | Blacksmith | 14 June 1718 | 3 Oct. 1718 | 26 16 06 | 163 |
| Sillitoe, John | Well | — | — | 23 July 1714 | 10 Aug. 1714 | 59 08 06 | — |
| Simmonds, Francis | Daw | — | — | nd, | 16 Feb. 1674-5 | 22 08 02 | — |

| Name | Parish | Township, etc. | Occupation | Inventory Date | Date exhibited | Value | Number (if published) |
|---|---|---|---|---|---|---|---|
| **Simmonds, John** | Lill | The Hinks | Farmer* | 19 April 1690 | 5 May 1690 | 156 13 08 | 55 |
| Simmonds, Thomas | Well | Watling Street | — | 12 Sept. 1660 | 5 Dec. 1660 | 20 13 08 | — |
| Skett, Thomas | Lill | — | Farmer* | 19 April 1707 | 23 April 1707 | 57 00 00 | 121 |
| **Smart, Alice** | Well | — | Dyer | 9 Mar. 1693 | 24 April 1694 | 25 01 00 | 98 |
| **Smart, John** | Well | — | Dyer | 25 April 1683 | 12 July 1682 | 172 03 08 | — |
| Smith, Dorothy | Wroc | — | — | no inv. | 15 Jan. 1683–4 | — | — |
| Smith, Edward | Wroc | — | Labourer | 1 May 1684 | 8 Oct. 1684 | 04 18 00 | 164 |
| Smith, George | Well | Admaston | Weaver | 12 June 1720 | 7 Oct. 1720 | 04 16 04 | 209 |
| Smith, John | Wroc | The Hinks | Yeoman | 25 May 1654 | 18 Sept. 1661 | 19 09 10 | 54 |
| Smith, John | Lill | Allscott | Yeoman | 3 Dec. 1686 | 13 Dec. 1686 | 190 06 04 | 254 |
| Smith, John | Wroc | Admaston | Yeoman | 3 Mar 1731–2 | 28 April 1732 | 160 11 01 | — |
| Smith, John | Wroc | Little Dawley | Yeoman | 26 Feb. 1693–4 | 24 April 1694 | 149 10 06 | — |
| Smith, John | Daw | — | — | nd. | 14 April 1743 | 12 05 07 | — |
| Smith, Richard | Well | — | — | no inv. | 23 April 1728 | — | — |
| Smith, Thomas | Wroc | Admaston | Yeoman | 19 May 1670 | 30 May 1670 | 519 00 00 | 213 |
| Smith, Thomas | Wroc | — | — | no inv. | 15 Jan. 1683–4 | — | — |
| Smith, Thomas | Wroc | — | Webster | 29 June 1687 | 19 Oct. 1687 | 70 11 04 | 224 |
| Smith, Thomas | Well | — | — | no inv. | 12 Oct. 1749 | — | — |
| Smith, Walter | Wroc | Allscott | Yeoman | 16 April 1667 | 8 May 1667 | 141 16 08 | — |
| Smith, William | Well | Watling Street | Farmer* | 4 Oct. 1659 | 12 Oct. 1660 | 63 00 08 | 82 |
| Smith, William | Well | — | Carrier | 21 Feb. 1680–1 | 1 June 1681 | 72 14 07 | — |
| Smith, William | Well | Ketley Brook | Apparitor | 18 April 1699 | 27 April 1699 | 18 05 00 | 174 |
| Sockett, Andrew | Well | — | Mercer | 21 Nov. 1725 | 21 April 1726 | 51 01 04 | — |
| Sockett, John | Well | — | — | 5 April 1725 | 13 April 1725 | 39 06 6½ | 142 |
| Sockett, Mary | Well | — | Widow | 26 April 1705 | 28 April 1705 | 01 13 00 | — |
| Sockett, Mary | Well | — | Widow | 11 April 1743 | 11 Aug. 1743 | 03 17 04 | — |
| Sockett, Mary | Well | — | — | no inv. | 11 April 1746 | — | — |
| Sockett, Roger | Well | — | — | no inv. | 4 Oct. 1722 | — | — |
| Sockett, Roger | Well | — | — | no inv. | 24 Oct. 1727 | — | — |
| Sockett, William | Well | — | Clergyman | nd. | 2 Nov. 1732 | 34 06 01 | 189 |

# A LIST OF PEOPLE

| Name | Parish | Township, etc. | Occupation | Inventory Date | Date exhibited | Value | Number (if published) |
|---|---|---|---|---|---|---|---|
| Spearman, Ann | Lill | — | — | no inv. | 17 Oct. 1721 | — | — |
| Spearman, Ann | Lill | — | — | no inv. | 16 Oct. 1670 | — | — |
| Spearman, John | Lill | Donnington | Yeoman | 18 April 1684 | 20 May 1684 | 247 10 02 | — |
| Spearman, John | Lill | — | — | no inv. | 31 Oct. 1729 | — | — |
| Spearman, Richard | Lill | — | — | no inv. | 31 Oct. 1729 | — | — |
| Spearman, Richard | Lill | — | — | no inv. | 20 April 1737 | — | — |
| Spender, James | Lill | — | Yeoman | 21 July 1748 | 25 July 1748 | 31 15 10 | 80 |
| Stanier, Rachel | Well | — | — | no inv. | 19 Oct. 1726 | — | — |
| Stanier, Richard | Well | Aston | Gentleman | 16 Oct. 1711 | 17 Oct. 1711 | 1,327 15 09 | 154 |
| Stanley, Robert | Well | — | Stone cutter | 21 Mar. 1740-1 | 23 Oct. 1741 | 06 09 06 | 202 |
| Stanworth, Henry | Well | — | Cordwainer | 13 Feb. 1684-5 | 4 April 1685 | 23 06 02 | 103 |
| Stanworth, Margaret | Well | — | — | nd. | 24 May 1734 | 10 18 00 | — |
| Stanworth, Thomas | Well | — | Shoemaker | 2 Feb. 1713-4 | 23 Feb. 1713-4 | 28 08 05 | 157 |
| Stanworth, William | Well | — | Shoemaker | 21 April 1694 | 24 April 1695 | 09 14 02 | 123 |
| Stanworth, William | Well | — | — | nd. | 5 Oct. 1727 | 29 04 00 | — |
| Stevens, John | Lill | — | Farmer* | nd. | 19 Oct. 1725 | 48 08 06 | — |
| Stevens, Thomas | Lill | — | Widow | 1 Aug. 1671 | 15 Aug. 1671 | 22 05 10 | — |
| Steventon, Elizabeth | Daw | Cheshill | Widow | nd. | 6 April 1744 | 38 10 00 | — |
| Steventon, John | Lill | Grange | Yeoman | 2 Jan. 1701-2 | 1 May 1702 | 274 07 06 | 58 |
| Steventon, John | Well | — | Butcher | 12 Jan. 1746-7 | 24 Feb. 1746-7 | 116 15 06 | — |
| Steventon, Margaret | Well | — | — | no inv. | 13 April 1748 | — | — |
| Steventon, Richard | Well | Lawley | Yeoman | 26 Mar. 1683 | 28 Mar. 1683 | 59 03 00 | — |
| Steventon, Richard | Daw | Malins Lee | Farmer* | 1 June 1702 | 15 Oct. 1702 | 40 12 00 | — |
| Steventon, Richard | Daw | Malins Lee | Yeoman | 5 May 1722 | 2 Oct 1722 | 33 03 06 | — |
| Steventon, Richard | Daw | — | — | nd. | 4 April 1745 | 17 10 04 | — |
| Steventon, Richard | Well | — | — | no inv. | 11 April 1746 | — | — |
| Steventon, Roger | Well | Watling Street | Farmer* | 21 Jan. 1666-7 | 4 Oct. 1667 | 121 00 11 | — |
| Stilgoe, Charles | Wroc | Clotley | Farmer* | 4 Sept. 1685 | 18 Sept. 1685 | 160 07 06 | — |
| Stilgoe, Charles | Well | — | Yeoman | 10 Aug. 1697 | 26 Oct. 1697 | 17 13 00 | — |

| Name | Parish | Township, etc. | Occupation | Inventory Date | Date exhibited | Value | Number (if published) |
|---|---|---|---|---|---|---|---|
| Stilgoe, Edward | Well | – | Farmer | 10 Aug. 1697 | 26 Oct. 1697 | 122 07 05 | – |
| Stilgoe, Thomas | Well | – | Corviser | 29 April 1695 | 10 June 1695 | 18 15 06 | 125 |
| Stockings, William | Well | Aston | Yeoman | 15 Jan. 1741-2 | 29 April 1742 | 07 18 00 | – |
| Stowers, Charles | Well | – | Gardener | 7 Feb. 1736-7 | 22 April 1737 | 04 06 10 | 192 |
| Stringer, Joseph | Lill | – | – | no inv. | 2 Nov. 1731 | – | – |
| Stringer, William | Lill | Lubstree Park | Farmer* | 2 Nov. 1705 | 26 April 1706 | 450 03 00 | – |
| Swift, Eleanor | Well | – | – | no inv. | 11 Mar. 1708-9 | – | – |
| Swift, Elizabeth | Well | Legomery | – | 13 April 1672 | 29 May 1672 | 102 13 06 | – |
| Swift, Elizabeth | Lill | Donnington | Farmer* | 25 July 1729 | 31 Oct. 1729 | 126 13 00 | – |
| Swift, Jane | Lill | Donnington | – | no inv. | 9 Oct. 1725 | – | – |
| Swift, John | Well | Legomery | Farmer* | 10 April 1718 | 18 April 1718 | 41 19 00 | – |
| Swift, Thomas | Well | Legomery | – | 6 Aug. 1703 | 20 Oct. 1702 | 112 05 10 | – |
| Swift, Thomas | Lill | Donnington | Farmer* | 11 Sept. 1727 | 26 April 1728 | 100 01 00 | – |
| Swift, Thomas | Lill | Donnington | Farmer* | 30 Oct. 1740 | 2 April 1741 | 114 12 00 | – |
| Sylvester, Paul | Lill | – | Farmer* | 8 April 1681 | 21 April 1681 | 56 06 02 | – |
| Talbot, Gabriel | Well | – | – | no inv. | 4 April 1675 | – | – |
| Taylor, James | Well | – | Carrier* | 7 Aug. 1717 | 17 April 1718 | 04 10 02 | – |
| Taylor, John | Well | – | Corviser | 13 Sept. 1661 | 18 Sept. 1661 | 78 14 10 | – |
| Taylor, John | Well | – | Tailor | 5 Aug. 1673 | 24 June 1673 | 29 02 04 | – |
| Taylor, John | Wroc | Wrockwardine Wood | Husbandman | 20 Oct. 1705 | 26 April 1706 | 01 10 00 | – |
| Taylor, Joshua | Well | – | Dyer | 10 Nov. 1725 | 21 April 1726 | 29 00 00 | 173 |
| Taylor, Mary | Wroc | Wrockwardine Wood | Widow | 16 May 1740 | 2 April 1741 | 09 17 10 | – |
| Taylor, Mary | Wroc | – | – | no inv. | 29 April 1742 | – | – |
| Taylor, Phillip | Wroc | Allscott | Farmer* | 2 Nov. 1733 | 24 May 1734 | 82 15 06 | – |
| Taylor, Robert | Daw | Dawley Green | Collier | 9 June 1685 | 18 Sept. 1685 | 48 00 00 | 11 |
| Taylor, Sarah | Well | – | Widow | 15 Nov. 1727 | 25 April 1728 | 44 17 00 | – |
| Taylor, Thomas | Wroc | Wrockwardine Wood | Farmer* | 21 Aug. 1735 | 30 Oct. 1735 | 08 17 00 | – |

# A LIST OF PEOPLE

| Name | Parish | Township, etc. | Occupation | Inventory Date | Date exhibited | Value | Number (if published) |
|---|---|---|---|---|---|---|---|
| Thomas, David | Wroc | – | Tailor | 10 Oct. 1727 | 24 April 1728 | 39 15 00 | – |
| Thomas, Richard | Well | – | – | no inv. | 21 Jan. 1691-2 | – | – |
| Thomas, Richard | Well | – | – | no inv. | 27 June 1693 | – | – |
| Tipton, Edward | Well | Lawley | – | 15 Feb. 1723 | 17 Feb. 1723-4 | 02 12 00 | – |
| Tomkis, Thomas | Well | – | Yeoman | nd. | 30 Oct. 1746 | 60 00 10 | – |
| Tunis, Mary | Well | – | – | no inv. | 26 Oct. 1750 | – | – |
| Turner, Francis | Well | – | Currier | 11 Feb. 1742 | 15 April 1743 | 10 00 00 | – |
| Turner, John | Well | Arleston | Farmer* | 30 May 1726 | 18 Oct. 1726 | 312 00 00 | 175 |
| Turner, Margaret | Well | – | – | no inv. | 17 Oct. 1711 | – | – |
| Turner, Thomas | Lill | – | – | no inv. | 25 Oct. 1735 | – | – |
| Turner, William | Well | – | – | no inv. | 24 April 1707 | – | – |
| Turner, William | Well | Arleston | Farmer* | 9 Nov. 1685 | 10 Nov. 1685 | 415 15 02 | – |
| Upton, Frances | Lill | Muxton | – | 9 Dec. 1675 | 11 Dec. 1675 | 10 05 00 | – |
| Upton, Francis | Wroc | Charlton | – | nd | 18 April 1671 | 26 01 06 | – |
| Upton, Robert | Lill | Muxton | Weaver | 9 Dec. 1675 | 11 Dec. 1675 | 09 08 04 | – |
| Upton, Robert | Lill | – | – | no inv. | 27 Sept. 1676 | – | – |
| Venables, Sarah | Wroc | Allscott | Widow | 13 April 1726 | 22 April 1726 | 06 06 00 | – |
| Vernon, Elizabeth | Lill | – | Spinster | 27 Jan. 1710 | 19 April 1710 | 03 01 10 | – |
| Vernon, Humphrey | Lill | – | Wheelwright | 16 Oct. 1700 | 17 Oct. 1700 | 10 13 00 | 57 |
| Vickers, Ann | Well | – | – | no inv. | 29 April 1730 | – | – |
| Vickers, Elizabeth | Wroc | – | – | no inv. | 26 April 1728 | – | – |
| Vickers, Francis | Lill | – | – | no inv. | 16 April 1714 | – | – |
| Vickers, John | Wroc | Wrockwardine Wood | Yeoman | 19 Mar. 1723-4 | 10 April 1724 | 18 13 06 | – |
| Vickers, John | Wroc | Wrockwardine Wood | Yeoman | 8 Nov. 1728 | 11 April 1729 | 47 13 00 | – |
| Vickers, John | Wroc | – | – | no inv. | 5 May 1731 | – | – |
| Vickers, Margaret | Well | – | Spinster | 22 Feb. 1730-1 | 4 April 1731 | 30 07 02 | – |

| Name | Parish | Township, etc. | Occupation | Inventory Date | Date exhibited | Value | Number (if published) |
|---|---|---|---|---|---|---|---|
| Vickers, Richard | Wroc | Wrockwardine Wood | Yeoman | 23 Feb. 1704-5 | 30 April 1705 | 32 08 08 | 239 |
| Vickers, Thomas | Well | – | – | no inv. | 3 Oct. 1727 | – | – |
| Vickers, Thomas | Well | – | – | no inv. | 15 Jan. 1727-8 | – | – |
| Vickers, Thomas | Wroc | Wrockwardine | – | 1 July 1729 | 29 Oct. 1729 | 06 02 00 | – |
| Wade, John | Wroc | – | – | 2 Feb. 1718-9 | 13 April 1719 | 12 08 00 | – |
| Wade, Richard | Wroc | Allscott | Yeoman | 20 July 1690 | 17 Sept. 1690 | 120 08 00 | – |
| Walford, Esther | Well | – | – | no inv. | 4 Nov. 1737 | – | – |
| Walford, John | Well | – | Apothecary and Surgeon | 9 Mar. 1730-1 | 6 May 1731 | 59 08 07 | 187 |
| Walker, Elizabeth | Well | – | – | 18 May 1670 | 14 April 1671 | 216 18 10 | 86 |
| Walker, John | Well | – | – | 20 Aug. 1669 | 22 Sept. 1669 | 211 01 04 | – |
| Walker, John | Well | – | Butcher | 20 June 1692 | 25 Nov. 1692 | 97 10 00 | – |
| Walker, John | Well | – | – | no inv. | 18 Oct. 1726 | – | – |
| Walker, Martha | Well | Wellington | Widow | 27 May 1718 | 31 May 1718 | 15 17 02 | – |
| Walker, Roger | Well | – | Butcher | 19 Nov. 1703 | 27 April 1704 | 51 19 10 | – |
| Walkington, Jane | Well | – | – | no inv. | 17 Oct. 1704 | – | – |
| Ward, Mary | Well | – | – | no. inv. | 30 Oct. 1746 | – | – |
| Ward, Robert | Daw | Little Dawley | Yeoman | 8 May 1676 | 22 Sept. 1676 | 124 09 00 | – |
| Ward, Thomas | Well | Aston | – | 23 Jan. 1741-2 | 29 April 1742 | 43 14 06 | – |
| Warter, John | Wroc | – | – | 20 Sept. 1687 | 19 Oct. 1687 | 09 03 08 | – |
| Warter, Thomas | Well | – | Shoemaker | 12 May 1665-6 | 16 May 1666 | 38 00 00 | – |
| Watkiss, Francis | Wroc | Walcot | – | no inv. | 24 April 1728 | – | – |
| Watkiss, George | Well | – | – | no inv. | 11 April 1722 | – | – |
| Watkins, William | Daw | Malins Lee | Blacksmith | 1 July 1724 | 19 Oct. 1725 | 16 07 06 | 18 |
| Webb, William | Well | – | Maltster* | 17 Dec. 1741 | 29 April 1742 | 276 13 06 | 203 |
| Wedge, Bartholomew | Well | – | – | 27 April 1727 | 4 Nov. 1737 | 10 17 02 | – |
| Wedge, Edward | Well | – | – | 4 Jan. 1734-5 | 17 May 1735 | 20 15 00 | – |
| Wedgewood, William | Wroc | – | – | nd. | 3 Feb. 1684-5 | 22 17 04 | – |

# A LIST OF PEOPLE

| Name | Parish | Township, etc. | Occupation | Inventory Date | Date exhibited | Value | Number (if published) |
|---|---|---|---|---|---|---|---|
| Wellington, Lawrence | Daw | The Ridges | Gentleman | 26 Nov. 1726 | 18 April 1727 | 87 05 00 | 22 |
| Wheeler, Elizabeth | Well | Street Lane | Widow | 11 Mar. 1713-4 | 15 April 1715 | 28 14 00 | — |
| Wheeler, George | Well | Street Lane | Farmer* | 2 Oct. 1677 | 4 Oct. 1677 | 11 10 04 | — |
| Wheeler, George | Well | — | — | 23 Mar. 1712-3 | 18 April 1713 | 29 05 00 | — |
| Wheeler, William | Well | — | — | no inv. | 26 Dec. 1727 | — | — |
| Whillocks, see Willett | | | | | | | |
| White, Thomas | Lill | Muxton | Yeoman | 27 July 1734 | 29 Oct. 1735 | 75 15 00 | — |
| Whitehead, John | Well | — | — | no inv. | 24 May 1734 | — | — |
| Whitehead, William | Daw | Little Dawley | — | 14 Oct. 1725 | 21 Oct. 1726 | 03 09 03 | — |
| Whitfield, John | Well | — | — | no inv. | 2 Oct. 1691 | — | — |
| Whitefield, Robert | Well | Hadley | Farmer* | 13 May 1747 | 7 Oct. 1747 | 30 14 06 | — |
| Whitmore, William | Lill | Lilleshall Lodge | Yeoman | 16 Sept. 1667 | 4 Oct. 1667 | 134 11 04 | 36 |
| Whittel, William | Lill | — | — | no inv. | 5 May 1747 | — | — |
| Whittingham, George | Well | — | — | no inv. | 10 Sept. 1750 | — | — |
| Whittingham, James | Well | — | Glover | 14 Aug. 1736 | 29 Oct. 1736 | 10 16 00 | — |
| Whittingham, Thomas | Well | Hadley | — | 3 Oct. 1711 | 18 Oct. 1711 | 18 04 08 | — |
| Wicksteed, Thomas | Lill | Muxton | Gentleman | 16 Nov. 1711 | 26 April 1712 | 164 04 08 | 88 |
| Wilkes, George | Well | Wheat Leasows | Husbandman | 2 Feb. 1671-2 | 15 Mar. 1671-2 | 127 08 06 | — |
| Willett, George | Well | — | — | 26 Dec. 1721 | 3 Jan. 1721-2 | 90 13 04 | — |
| Willett, George | Well | Hadley Park | Farmer* | 25 Feb. 1728-9 | 9 April 1729 | 55 16 06 | — |
| Williams, Ann | Lill | Donnington | Farmer* | 1 Oct. 1714 | 22 Oct. 1714 | 113 14 06 | — |
| Williams, Elizabeth | Lill | — | Farmer* | 7 Aug. 1730 | 27 Oct. 1730 | 18 13 02 | — |
| Williams, Godfrey | Lill | — | Farmer* | 1 Oct. 1689 | 5 Oct. 1689 | 252 00 06 | — |
| Williams, Godfrey | Lill | — | Farmer* | 25 Mar. 1720 | 22 April 1720 | 80 04 04 | — |
| Williams, John | Lill | — | — | 27 Jan. 1701-2 | 30 April 1702 | 09 13 00 | — |
| Williams, John | Wroc | — | — | no inv. | 16 Oct. 1728 | — | — |
| Williams, John | Lill | Donnington | — | nd., April 1730 | 27 April 1730 | 17 18 06 | — |
| Williams, Richard | Well | — | — | no inv. | 8 April 1729 | — | — |
| Windsor, Diana | Lill | Lawley | — | 20 Oct. 1711 | 31 Oct. 1711 | 14 10 8½ | — |

| Name | Parish | Township, etc. | Occupation | Inventory Date | Date exhibited | Value | Number (if published) |
|---|---|---|---|---|---|---|---|
| Windsor, Margaret | Lill | – | – | no inv. | 2 May 1662 | – | – |
| Windsor, Richard | Lill | – | – | no inv. | 15 May 1661 | – | – |
| Windsor, Thomas | Lill | – | Yeoman | 2 Dec. 1675 | 23 Dec. 1675 | 440 00 00 | 40 |
| Windsor, Thomas | Lill | – | – | no inv. | 11 Mar. 1745–6 | – | – |
| Winshurst, Joan | Lill | Donnington | Spinster | 12 April 1694 | 14 April 1694 | 06 15 00 | – |
| Winshurst, Ralph | Lill | Honnington | Yeoman | 7 July 1685 | 20 July 1685 | 209 10 08 | 53 |
| Wood, Elizabeth | Well | – | – | no inv. | 7 June 1687 | – | – |
| Wood, Henry | Well | – | Clergyman | 8 Jan. 1712–3 | 9 Oct. 1713 | 189 14 02 | 156 |
| Wood, Robert | Well | – | – | no inv. | 1 Dec. 1710 | – | – |
| Woodhouse, Thomas | Well | – | Surveyor | 2 April 1666 | 18 May 1666 | 52 02 06 | – |
| Woolley, Joseph | Lill | Muxton | Farmer* | 5 July 1709 | 25 Jan. 1709-10 | 89 14 00 | 68 |
| Woolley, John | Lill | Muxton | Yeoman | 2 Aug. 1716 | 5 Oct. 1716 | 04 14 06 | – |
| Woolley, Margaret | Lill | – | Widow | nd. | 28 April 1736 | 13 15 06 | – |
| Woolley, Mary | Lill | Wilmore Grange | Widow | 24 Aug. 1676 | 22 Sept. 1676 | 18 05 04 | – |
| Woolley, Thomas | Lill | Wilmore Grange | Labourer | 20 Oct. 1715 | 21 Oct. 1715 | 03 10 00 | – |
| Woolley, Walter | Lill | Wilmore Grange | – | 1 Mar. 1738–9 | 2 Mar. 1738–0 | 41 00 00 | – |
| Woolley, William | Lill | Muxton | – | 14 Nov. 1712 | 17 Nov. 1712 | 154 00 00 | – |
| Woolley, William | Well | – | – | no inv. | 28 Oct. 1729 | – | – |
| Worrall, William | Lill | – | Yeoman | 16 Sept. 1709 | 21 Oct. 1709 | 07 01 02 | – |
| Wright, Adam | Well | – | – | 12 Oct. 1705 | 17 Oct. 1705 | 14 07 06 | – |
| Wright, Ann | Lill | – | – | 17 Mar. 1680–1 | 22 Mar. 1680–1 | 22 11 06 | – |
| Wright, Benjamin | Well | – | Mercer | 21 Sept. 1700 | 25 Sept. 1700 | 246 13 00 | 132 |
| Wright, Charles | Well | – | Labourer | 27 Sept. 1697 | 1 Oct. 1697 | 04 10 08 | – |
| Wright, Elizabeth | Well | – | – | 21 Nov. 1701 | 25 Nov. 1701 | 03 13 06 | – |
| Wright, Francis | Well | Leegomery | Dyer* | 21 April 1698 | 28 April 1698 | 288 11 07 | 127 |
| Wright, Joan | Lill | – | – | 5 April 1703 | 9 April 1703 | 58 16 08 | 61 |
| Wright, John | Wroc | – | Yeoman | 2 Sept. 1698 | 5 Oct. 1698 | 14 06 03 | – |

# A LIST OF PEOPLE

| Name | Parish | Township, etc. | Occupation | Inventory Date | Date exhibited | Value | Number (if published) |
|---|---|---|---|---|---|---|---|
| **Wright, John** | Daw | – | – | 16 Sept. 1715 | 17 Sept. 1715 | -8 17 00 | – |
| **Wright, John** | Lill | – | – | 2 Mar. 1732-3 | 8 Mar. 1732-3 | 19 18 00 | – |
| **Wright, John** | Well | – | Dyer | 4 April 1737 | 4 Nov. 1737 | 09 18 06 | 193 |
| **Wright, Margaret** | Well | – | – | nd. | 13 Oct. 1702 | 09 10 06 | – |
| **Wright, Mary** | Well | Leegomery | – | 16 Oct. 1718 | 6 Oct. 1719 | 112 18 10 | – |
| **Wright, Priscilla** | Daw | – | – | nd. | 4 May 1731 | 13 00 06 | – |
| **Wright, Richard** | Lill | – | – | no inv. | 15 Oct. 1728 | – | – |
| **Wright, Sarah** | Well | – | – | no inv. | 2 June 1665 | – | – |
| **Wright, Thomas** | Well | – | Dyer | 30 Dec. 1662 | 21 Jan. 1662 | 270 15 07 | 83 |
| **Wright, Thomas** | Well | – | – | no inv. | 20 April 1726 | – | – |
| **Wynne, John** | Daw | – | – | 24 April 1706 | 26 April 1706 | 03 01 00 | – |
| **Wyke, Humphrey** | Well | – | – | no inv. | 30 Oct. 1746 | – | – |
| **Yardley, John** | Lill | – | – | nd. | 28 May 1686 | 04 11 08 | – |
| **Yarsley, John** | – | Oakengates | Collier | 3 July 1719 | 7 Oct. 1719 | 19 16 08 | 246 |
| **Yates, Edward** | Wroc | – | – | no inv. | 13 Oct. 1743 | – | – |
| **Yates, Richard** | Well | – | – | no inv. | 11 April 1729 | – | – |

# THE INVENTORIES, 1660-1750

## The Inventories of Dawley, Lilleshall, Wellington and Wrockwardine: 1660-1750

*(The transcripts of the probate inventories in the Lichfield Joint Record Office [B/C/11] appear by courtesy of the Staffordshire County Archivist.)*

THE INVENTORIES are printed parish by parish in alphabetical order, and within each parish chronologically according to date of appraisal. Each inventory has a heading which gives the name of the deceased, his parish or place of residence, his occupation (which may be taken from other sources than the inventory), the date of the inventory, the date of exhibition, and the names of the appraisers. In some cases additional information from the will or the parish register has been added, but no attempt has been made to explore exhaustively all the possible sources of genealogical information concerning the deceased.

For alternative versions of surnames the List commencing on p. 119 should be consulted. Where two names are given in the headings of an inventory they are both quoted on the original, and are wholly different names by both of which, it may be presumed, the deceased was known.

The inventories have been transcribed exactly as written, but all amounts of money have been copied in a standardised six-digit form, which is used on many of the originals. The names of rooms are used as sub-titles even if they appear in the texts of the originals. All Roman numerals have been converted to Arabic. Sub-totals on the originals have been omitted. Dashes indicate gaps on the originals caused by tears, folds, or similar causes, but the inventories have been well-kept by their various custodians, and such damage is rare. The totals of the inventories are those calculated by the appraisers, but the values of untotalled inventories have been calculated and inserted.

An asterisk (*) by the name of an appraiser indicates that he gave his assent to the inventory with a mark and not with a signature.

# THE INVENTORIES OF DAWLEY

## 1. Bassall Richards

Of Little Dawley, yeoman, taken by Richared Clowes, Thomas Newton and Richard Darrell, on 27 May 1659, and exhibited on 20 September 1661.

*Hall. Imprs.*

one table, one form 4 stooles one chier one plate of irone two pare of pott geales fier shovels and tonge  15 ten: pewter dishes great and small one brase kover one chaffing dish of brase two brase candlesticks two pewter candlesticke three pewter saltes three poringeres of pewter one flagen too tankards one bole of pewter  .  03 03 08

*Parlor. Ittem.*

one longe table with too formes one chier one twigen chier one little cabert one carpett of Kiddermuster stuffe one bed stid on doune bed a feather bed one matteress one boulstores too blakcnetes one coverlid: faie|courtanes and valens of linen and woolen one waring pane 4 cushenes one coueing baskett  .  .  .  06 10 00

*the new Chamber*

one ioyne bed one low bed one ffeather bed on flocke bed one (one) old case three boulsteres 4 blanckette too coverlides one chist too cofferes one side box one Cubbord one chier one firshoule and tonge one litle grate a plate of Iron one close stoole  .  .  04 16 00

*Chamber over the Hall*

Itteim. too bead stede one couved beade one feather bed one coverlet and one blankett three cases for flockes three boulster cases too other coverlids too Blankettes two twilsheets too curtaines of wollen and linnen too smale chests one salt box and too parcells of Hops  .  .  .  .  .  .  .  03 10 00

*Chamber over the parlor*

too ioyned beds one feather bed too cases too boulsters foure blanketts three coverlitts seaven pillowes three greene curtaines four paire of Hempten sheets one dozen of flaxen napkens one dozen and halfe of hempten napkens one dozen of hurden napkens four flaxes pilloe beares one flaxen table cloth
one flaxen Cubbert cloath, foore paire of Hempten sheetes fourteene paire of Hurden sheets one hempten table cloath and five hurden table cloaths too hempten toweles one twiggen biskett one coffer and four hurden hand towels  .  .  .  .  10 10 00

*Kitchin Chamber*

one flock bed and boulster one blankett and one coverlid one twilsheete flax and hempe in the house spune and in yarne and unspune too basketts and one wiskett foure brasen weights with a wooden beame and scales too wooden coffers  .  .  .  .  02 05 00

foore brasen pots foore brasen kettles three brasen panns twelve
pewter dishes, one cast morter and an iron pestle foure Iron spitts
too paire of cobberts three iron dripping pans one brasen skimmer          09 03 00

One dozen of silver spoons .         .         .         .         .         .         04 16 00
one dozen of pewter spoones         .         .         .         .         .         00 00 08
Coopery ware of all sorts, trinen ware of all sorts     .         .         .         04 02 06
ten bags         .         .         .         .         .         .         .         01 00 00
one marmalet, one cast brasse pan and a chafer .        .         .         .         01 05 00
one laund Iron and one Iron cleaver and an Iron Crow .      .         .         00 03 06

Corne and malt in the House         .         .         .         .         .         09 00 00
Corne of all sorts in the barne         .         .         .         .         .         07 00 00
Corne of all sorts growing on the grownd.         .         .         .         22 00 00
Ten kine and one bull         .         .         .         .         .         .         30 00 00
ffoore yeerelings and three too yeare old beastes     .         .         .         10 00 00
ffore reareing calves .         .         .         .         .         .         .         01 06 08
one horse         .         .         .         .         .         .         .         04 00 00
five swine         .         .         .         .         .         .         .         02 10 00
fifty seaven old sheepe & eleven lambs     .         .         .         .         09 18 00
beefe and bacon ready in the house         .         .         .         .         07 00 00
Butter and cheese and all other provision.         .         .         .         05 10 00
wearing apparell         .         .         .         .         .         .         10 00 00
Item. all other things left unappprised in this Inventary .         .         00 05 00
                                        Some totall .         .         121 07 08


## 2. Richard Gittins

Of Little Dawley, taken by Richard Clowes, John Podmore and John Richards on 7 March 1661-62, and exhibited on 2 May 1662.

*Imprs. in the house*
One table board too chieres and litle table: one form one grat: one
firshovle one pare of tongs: five pewter dishes. one salt one brasen
candlesticke: one flagen: one tancket: tow posnetts: one strainer:
two kettles three Yrone potts: two pales: one stunde and buckett
prised all at one pound sixten shillings         .         .         .         .         01 16 00

*In the milkhouse*
boules stunds and trinen ware at         .         .         .         .         .         01 00 00
two planckes one benche: one stoole one frineinge pane: one
Salteinge boole too steen potts         .         .         .         .         .         00 03 00
One old Coberte: and one prese one wheele all prised at         .         .         00 06 00

*In the Chamber over the milkhouse*
One Chaff bed too boulster one pillow two coverlides at         .         .         00 14 00
One wich too coffers one box         .         .         .         .         .         00 02 06
yorne 10 li at.         .         .         .         .         .         .         .         00 05 00
Cheese 9 at         .         .         .         .         .         .         .         00 04 06
Corne and woole         .         .         .         .         .         .         00 06 00

# THE INVENTORIES OF DAWLEY 165

*Ittm over the house*

| | |
|---|---|
| bed coveres 6: and pillowes 6: and one pillow: one coffer all at | 02 00 00 |
| Fouer Fliches of bacon at . . . . . . . | 02 00 00 |
| Ittm. sheetts eight pare two tabe clothes six napkines & two pillow beares at . . . . . . . . . | 03 00 00 |
| Ittm. wearing apparel at . . . . . . . | 03 00 00 |
| Corne one the grounde . . . . . . . | 06 13 04 |
| Otes in the house . . . . . . . . | 00 16 00 |
| Ittm. Seven kyne and hayfores at . . . . . . | 22 00 00 |
| two swine . . . . . . . . . | 00 01 00 |
| five sheepe one lam . . . . . . . . | 01 00 00 |
| Item hay and strawe at . . . . . . . | 03 00 00 |
| husbandrey stuffe . . . . . . . . | 00 05 00 |
| More sheep seven . . . . . . . . | 01 08 00 |
| Sum total . . | 50 09 04 |

## 3. Humphrey Peploe

Of the Middle Leasow, Little Dawley, husbandman, taken by John Richards, Richard Bridgwood and Richard Darrell junior, on 8 May 1665, and exhibited on 2 June 1665. In his will Humphrey Peploe left legacies to his son John, to Nathan son of Podmore Peploe, to his brothers William, John and Thomas, with the residue of the esate going to his wife Jane.

| | |
|---|---|
| Imprimis his wearing apparrell prisd at . . . . . | 03 10 00 |
| Item ffive kine And one twintar heyfar . . . . . | 15 13 04 |
| It ffowre yearling Calves prised . . . . . . | 04 00 00 |
| It too weanling Calves . . . . . . . | 01 00 00 |
| It. One Nag . . . . . . . . . | 02 00 00 |
| It. Thirtee 7 Sheepe yong & ould . . . . . . | 07 00 00 |
| It. Too Swine prisd att . . . . . . . | 01 00 00 |
| It. Corne And Mawlte wth othar graine in the howse and Barne thresht And unthresht at . . . . . . . | 03 00 00 |
| It. Corne Otes & Barlee growing upon the ground . . | 12 10 00 |
| It. one Cart wth barefoot wheeles One plow one harrow togeathe wth All othar Implements of husbandry prised at . . | 02 10 00 |

*It. In the Chamber ovar the howse*

| | |
|---|---|
| three ffethar beds sixe ffethar boulsters with covarletts And blankitts belonging to that bedding . . . . . . | 10 00 00 |
| It Too bed Steedes . . . . . . . . | 00 07 00 |
| It One big Chest and fower little Coffars wth one Smaule Trunke . | 01 00 00 |
| It Linginges of All sortes 16 table Cloahes Napkins Sheetes and such like . . . . . . . . . . | 03 00 00 |
| It: Too silvar spoones And A Maslin Cup ovar guilte prisd Att | 01 00 00 |
| It. Too Bible bookes . . . . . . . . | 00 10 00 |
| It. Too brass pans one warming pan One brass pot three brass kettles too brason Candlestockes And All othar brasen ware . . . | 02 15 00 |
| It. Pewtar of All Sortes . . . . . . . | 01 10 00 |
| It. Iron belonging to the fire grate Awndiarns fire shouell Tonges And othar thinges thereunto belonging . . . . | 00 10 00 |

| | | | |
|---|---|---|---|
| It. Howshold pvission as beeffe bacon buttar and cheese | 01 | 10 | 00 |
| It. Goodes in the howse one short table A little falling table wth cheeres joyne stooles Othar Stooles Cushines benches And Shielves beelongeing to the howse | 00 | 18 | 00 |
| It. Bouches And Shelves in the butteree | 00 | 05 | 00 |
| It. Cowparie ware and trinin ware As barrils stunds payles And All other ware of the like sort | 00 | 13 | 04 |
| It. One Cheese press | 00 | 02 | 06 |
| It. One hakne saddle one bridle one pad And girthes | 00 | 08 | 00 |
| It. Powltry As geese and hennes | 00 | 06 | 08 |
| It. One Strawne whiskitt one fflaskitt wth All othar thinges unpraised | 00 | 10 | 00 |
| | 78 | 08 | 10 |

## 4. Richard Darwall

Of Dawley, taken by Richard Clowes, John Newton* and John Steed* on 6 April 1666, and exhibited on 18 May 1666.

*Imprs. in the hall*

| | | | |
|---|---|---|---|
| two chires one brase pan one kettle two brase potts three one yron pott one warmeing pan at | 02 | 03 | 04 |
| Itm. three drping panes two broches one pare of Cobborts one plat for the fyer too grats one pare of oundyrons too pare of tonges one fyer slice at | 01 | 08 | 00 |
| Itm. one friing pan one smouthing yron one brase candlestick at | 00 | 04 | 00 |
| Itm. Eleven pewter dishes three porringers nyne sawseres one pewter Candlestick two flagenes one pewter salt one tankert prised at | 01 | 11 | 00 |
| Itm. one pare of wafere yrons one heckell at | 00 | 04 | 00 |

*Itm. in the parlor*

| | | | |
|---|---|---|---|
| too feather beds three boulstrs too pillowes four blacketts one green Rudg six gren courtaines one Cobbart one Cheest two boxes too bedsteedes at | 05 | 16 | 00 |
| Itm. too chaffe bedes in the chamber too boulstrs 4 bedhillings too bedsteds prised at | 00 | 08 | 00 |

*Itm in the little Chamber*

| | | | |
|---|---|---|---|
| one Chaffe bed too canveses one boulstor one bedsteed att | 00 | 06 | 00 |
| itm. trine ware of all sortes and foor pare steenes all att | 01 | 02 | 00 |
| Itm. Corne in the house of all sortes at twentye six strickes at | 02 | 10 | 00 |
| Corne one the ground at | 01 | 06 | 08 |
| Itm. beefe and bacone butter and Cheese att | 04 | 10 | 00 |
| Itm. Linenes 29 pare of sheets and a halfe too douzen of napkines Six pillow beres six toweles table six at | 05 | 08 | 00 |
| Itm. his wearing apparill | 02 | 00 | 00 |
| Itm. all implements for husbandrey and yron ware at | 00 | 13 | 04 |
| Itm. five kine three horses and too yonge beese too swine | 13 | 00 | 00 |
| Itm. yarne in house | 01 | 00 | 00 |
| Itm. poulterrey of all sorts | 00 | 05 | 00 |
| Itm. three whiches | 00 | 03 | 00 |
| Sum totalis | 43 | 18 | 04 |

## 5. Frances Richards

Of Little Dawley, widow, who died on 12 November 1666, taken by Richard Bridgwood, Podmore Peploe and William Easthope on 13 November 1666. The inventory was exhibited and her will proved on 26 November 1666.

| | |
|---|---|
| Imprimis | |
| her wearing apparrill . . . . . . . | 02 10 00 |
| Item one standing bed one bedstead And one Trickelebed . . | 01 01 00 |
| Ite. one cheare one forme 2 yine Stooles . . . . | 00 03 00 |
| Ite. one ffetherbed & bowlstar & pillow . . . . | 01 10 00 |
| Ite. too kiverlids too blanquits & too fflocke beds too bowlstares And five payre of Sheetes . . . . . . | 04 00 00 |
| Ite. one table Cloth towells And Napkins . . . . | 00 10 00 |
| Ite. one truncke wth more linines table Clothes and Sheetes . . | 05 00 00 |
| Ite. one ould quoffar . . . . . . . | 00 01 06 |
| Ite. one cast backe one grate one fire Shovell one payre of tonges & pot linkes one Chafar & Chafin dish . . . . | 00 04 00 |
| Ite. five pewter dishes one candle Stick one Sault one tancot and cup . . . . . . . . . | 00 02 00 |
| Ite. one brass pan one brass kettle one brass pott one dreeping pan And one broche . . . . . . . . | 01 05 00 |
| Ite. one Barrill one Stund one payle And one Gawne . . | 00 09 00 |
| Ite. Buttar & Cheese and other puission . . . . | 02 00 00 |
| Ite. one payre of Curtines And A Carpitt for A Table . . | 00 09 00 |
| Ite. All trinin Ware not as yet presed . . . . | 00 03 00 |
| Ite. too Stone And A hawlfe of wooll . . . . | 01 10 00 |
| Ite. too kind And other Cattle . . . . . | 07 10 00 |
| Ite. too And twentie Sheepe . . . . . | 04 00 00 |
| Ite. three Swine big And little . . . . . | 01 15 00 |
| Ite. for geese hens and Duckes . . . . . | 00 04 00 |
| Ite. for All mannor of graine in the howse and barne . . | 04 16 00 |
| | 32 02 10 |

## 6. Eliza Darrall

Of The Ridges, Little Dawley, widow, taken by John Richards, Richard Bridgwood and William Darrall on 25 June 1668, and proved on 31 July 1668.

*In her Chamber.*

| | |
|---|---|
| Imprs. one paire of Joined beddsteeds with the Curtains and valens . | 00 10 00 |
| one ffeather bedd and a Canuas bedd-sticke . . . | 01 10 00 |
| 2 feather boulsters . . . . . . . | 00 08 00 |
| 2 pillows & 2 pillow beares . . . . . . | 00 02 00 |

*Item*

| | |
|---|---|
| One green Rugg & 2 blankets . . . . . | 00 10 00 |
| one pillion & Saddle cloath . . . . . . | 00 03 06 |
| one Little box . . . . . . . | 00 01 00 |
| Wearing apparell . . . . . . . | 06 13 07 |

*Item. Above Staires in ye Closet*

| | |
|---|---|
| one Coffer . . . . . . . . . | 00 02 06 |
| one dozen of hempne Napkins . . . . . | 00 03 00 |
| four paire of sheetes and an odd sheete . . . . | 01 00 00 |

*Item*

| | |
|---|---|
| all the rest of the small & great linnens not named . . . | 00 00 06 |
| | 11 04 07 |

## 7. William Farley

Of Dawley, webster, taken by Richard Jones, Richard Rycroft, Richard Jordan, Thomas Swift* and Thomas Churme* on 25 April 1676. The register records the grant of probate or administration as 22 September 1675. Farley's death is unrecorded in the Dawley Parish Register.

| | |
|---|---|
| Imp. 2 Cowes and 2 Calfes . . . . . . . | 05 10 00 |
| 3 yearlings . . . . . . . . . | 02 10 00 |
| one nag one mare . . . . . . . . | 04 00 00 |
| 3 Stales of bees . . . . . . . . | 00 10 00 |
| Corne growing of the growne . . . . . . | 02 00 00 |
| one Iron bounde Cart . . . . . . . | 01 00 00 |
| 2 Weavers Loomes wth ye appurtenances . . . . | 02 00 00 |
| one mault mill . . . . . . . . | 01 00 00 |
| 12 Pewter dishes & brasse of all Sortes . . . . | 01 10 00 |
| 2 Iron Pots . . . . . . . . . | 00 10 00 |
| one truckell bed one feather bed and 2 blankets In the parlor . | 02 00 00 |
| 4 Coffers and one Cheir ov ye howse . . . . | 00 10 00 |
| 2 beeds ov the parlor . . . . . . . | 00 05 00 |
| Linninge of all Sorts. . . . . . . . | 02 10 00 |
| Plowes Harrow and all manner of husbandry . . . | 00 06 00 |
| one table board wth all sorts of wooden ware . . . | 01 05 00 |
| Wearing Apparrel . . . . . . . . | 03 00 00 |
| things unseine & forgotten . . . . . . . | 00 05 00 |
| Debts owing to the deceased . . . . . . | 01 00 00 |
| The totall is . . . | 31 11 00 |

## 8. Richard Clowes

Of Great Dawley, gent, taken by William Ashwood of Madeley and Podmore Peploe of Little Dawley on 15 April 1679 and exhibited on 17 April 1679.

*Itm in ye Hall*

| | |
|---|---|
| Two Tables two fformes three chaires three stooles one Halbeard one ffire Shovell & paire of Tonges & one paire of Bellows at . . | 01 00 00 |

*Itm in the Parler*

| | |
|---|---|
| Two Tables Eight Chaires one Couch seaven Cushions one Joyned Stoole two Desks A Chest of Drawers a Livery Table three Carpets a Fire shovell & Tonges one paire of Virginalls one Map two pictures & Coates of Armes A Chess board & three Brushes at . . . | 02 00 00 |

# THE INVENTORIES OF DAWLEY

*Item in ye Buttery*
One Table one press one Joyne stoole foure Cushons Glass Bottell
Glasses & Earthen ware at . . . . . . . 00 13 04

*Item in ye Seller*
One Hogshed & six Barrells at . . . . . . 01 00 00

*Itm in ye first Roome over ye parler*
Two Beds & Bedstids one press one Chaire one Trunke one Chest
three Boxes & ye ffurniture for ye Beds . . . . . 04 00 00

*Item in ye next Roome over ye Parler*
One Bed wth ye furniture two stooles a Llivery Table & A Llooke-
ing glass and two ould Trunkes & two ould Boxes . . . 02 05 00

*Itm in ye first Roome over ye Buttery*
One Bed wth ye furniture two Chaires three stooles a Llivery Table
A Llokeing Glass one Cushions one paire of And Irons A paire of
Tonges A paire of Bellows . . . . . . . 03 00 00

*Item in ye next roome over ye Buttery*
one Bed wth ye furinture one Chaire one stoole one Table two
Cushions & two ould Carpetts at . . . . . . 02 00 00

*Itm in ye Chamber over ye hall*
one Bed wth ye furinture two Bedsteeds one Chest & one Coffer . 02 00 00

*Item in ye Roomes over kitchin*
Two Bedds & Bedstids wth ye furinture one press one Chest two
Trunks one stoole & one paire of Bellows at . . . . 02 00 00

*Itm in ye Kichin Dayhouse & Llittle Roome beyand ye kichin*
One dresser one forme wth all sorts of Wooden ware at . . 00 10 00

Itm Brass & Pewter of all sorts at . . . . . . 04 10 00
Itm Iron ware of all sorts at . . . . . . 02 00 00

*Itm in ye Brewhouse & Milkhouse adioyning & ye Roomes overhead*
Brewing vessells A Weeting fatt one Mault Mill one Cheese press &
other Wooden Llumbe . . . . . . . 02 10 00

Itm. Corne in ye Barne & in ye house of all sorts & Haye . . 07 00 00
Itm. All sorts of Husbandry Ware & Impliments thereunto belonging . 02 10 00
Itm. ffoure oxen five Cowes two Hayfers & one Ould Mare at . . 37 10 00
Itm. three store Swine at . . . . . . . 01 00 00
Itm. Poultrey at . . . . . . . . 00 05 00
Itm. Provision for house keeping of all sorts . . . . 05 10 00
Itm. Silver Plate of all sorts . . . . . . . 10 00 00
Itm. Ready Money in ye house . . . . . . 40 00 00
Itm. Debts owing upon Bond & otherwise . . . . 160 00 00
Itm. Corne upon growing ye Ground . . . . . 05 00 00
Itm. his wearing Apparrel & Money in his purse . . . . 10 00 00
Itm. for things omitted . . . . . . . 00 05 00
Itm. Llinens of all sorts . . . . . . . 05 10 00

       Sum totall is . . . 263 18 04

## 9. Richard Bridgwood

Of Little Dawley, yeoman, taken by Francis Boycott of Uppington, gent, William Tipton of Dawley, gent and Andrew Darrall of the Croppings, Little Dawley, physician on 29 April 1679, and exhibited on 12 September 1679.

| | |
|---|---|
| Imprs. for ffunerall charges. | 01 00 00 |
| Item the Decedent his wearing Apparell. | 01 00 00 |

### In the Chambr over the Parlor

| | |
|---|---|
| Four paire of Bedsteeds wth Testers & one Truckle bed | 01 02 00 |
| Twoo feather beds wth two feather boulsters | 01 15 00 |
| Three fflock boulsters | 00 01 06 |
| Two feather pillows. | 00 02 06 |
| Two fflock beds | 00 04 00 |
| Two Chaff beds & two boulsters | 00 04 00 |
| One Thrum Coverlett & Two Matts | 00 02 00 |
| Two Blanketts | 00 02 00 |
| Two Twill sheets | 02 02 00 |
| One great Joined Chest | 00 13 04 |
| Two Coffers. | 00 03 00 |
| One Turning Table. | 00 02 06 |
| One Leafe for a Table & a fframe in the house | 00 04 00 |
| One ould Brass Pott. | 00 08 00 |
| One Warming pann. | 00 01 06 |
| ffive Slipings of yarne—hurden | 00 02 06 |
| Two Chaires and Two Cushins | 00 02 00 |
| Two pick forks | 00 00 06 |

### In the Hall Chamber

| | |
|---|---|
| Two paire of Joint Bedsteeds wth Testers | 00 16 00 |
| One flock bed | 00 01 08 |
| One Chaff bed | 00 01 00 |
| Two Chaff boulsters. | 00 01 00 |
| One Coverlett and a Blankett | 00 01 10 |
| One Long Table and a fframe | 00 15 00 |
| Two Joint Benches. | 00 01 06 |
| Two fformes. | 00 02 06 |
| Three Joint Stooles. | 00 02 00 |
| One old Cup-board. | 00 04 00 |
| One Wood beam and Scales | 00 00 02 |
| Two doz: of Trenchers | 00 00 04 |
| One Tuning Dish & a Sie boli & two pottlids | 00 00 06 |
| One Garden Rake with Iron teeth. | 00 00 06 |
| One Churn and a Kneading Mitt | 00 02 06 |
| Two Brewing Stoonds | 00 03 00 |
| One Cooler and a Pillion | 00 01 00 |
| One Brass pann | 00 04 00 |
| One Bottle and two Rakes. | 00 00 03 |
| Three Sickles. | 00 00 03 |
| One Pecke and halfe of barley | 00 00 08 |

## THE INVENTORIES OF DAWLEY

*In the Chamber over the house*

| | |
|---|---|
| Two Chaff beds one Coverlett two Twill sheets One Blankett two feather boulsters one fflock boulster . . . . . | 00 15 00 |
| One Chest and two Coffers . . . . . . | 00 07 00 |
| One Barrell one old Churne & two Strickes . . . . | 00 03 04 |
| One Saddle and two Hors Colers . . . . . . | 00 01 04 |
| Tooles for husbandry and old Iron . . . . | 00 05 00 |
| In Coopery Ware . . . . . . . | 00 03 04 |
| Three paire of Homes & one paire of Traces And a Tartree and one Pack saddle Tree . . . . . . . | 00 05 00 |
| In hewed Timber for husbandry . . . . . | 00 05 00 |
| ffour Sheetes . . . . . . . . | 00 01 04 |
| In two Straw Whisketts to keep corne . . . . | 00 01 06 |

*At the Staire head*

| | |
|---|---|
| Two Bedsteeds and one Kneading Mitt . . . . | 00 04 00 |
| One Straw baskett & a haire Sive & a Rying sive . . . | 00 00 06 |

*In the Dwelling house*

| | |
|---|---|
| One Press Cup-board . . . . . . . | 00 06 08 |
| One paire of Sheets & three hurden Napkins & a Table . . | 00 02 06 |
| One Chaire and a Leafe for a Table . . . . | 00 01 06 |
| One Grate a fire shovell & a paire of Tonges . . . | 00 01 08 |
| One Iron pott and a Marmitt . . . . . | 00 03 00 |
| Two Little Brass Kettles . . . . . . | 00 00 08 |
| Three Iron broaches & a Pestell an Andiron & pottlinks . . | 00 03 00 |

*In the Buttry*

| | |
|---|---|
| In Cooperyware . . . . . . . | 00 10 00 |
| Two Dressers and five Shilves . . . . . . | 00 03 08 |

*At the Staire fotte*

| | |
|---|---|
| One Little Barrell one Stoond & one Bottle . . . | 00 02 00 |
| One Little paile one piggen one peck one Cann . . . | 00 01 04 |

*In the Chambr over the Bakehouse*

| | |
|---|---|
| Three Railes two boards & a paire of Tutores . . . | 00 04 00 |

*In the Bakehouse*

| | |
|---|---|
| One Cheese press one Wetting fatt one Crabb Strainer . . | 00 07 00 |

*In the Cole house*

| | |
|---|---|
| One old Bedsteed a pack saddle and a paire of Panniers and some old Timber . . . . . . . . | 00 03 04 |

*In the Cart house*

| | |
|---|---|
| One Paire of Cartsides and other old Timber . . . | 00 02 00 |

*In the Barne*

| | |
|---|---|
| One great Corne Hutch . . . . . . | 00 08 00 |
| ffour Ewe Nares and an Ash Nare . . . . . | 00 05 00 |

*In the ffould*
One Tumbrell wth Iron bound Wheeles . . . . . 01 00 00
One old Cart body one Oxe Harrow . . . . . 00 05 00

*In the Stable*
One old Trough . . . . . . . . 00 01 03

*In the Cart house or Coate*
one broaken paire of Cart Wheels two plowes One Tumbrell body
one paire of Riples one Stead . . . . . . 00 03 00

In poultry four hens & a Cocke three Ducks & a Drake . . . 00 03 00

One poore yeare old Colt . . . . . . . 00 06 08
Three yearling beastes . . . . . . . . 03 10 00

At Podmore Peploe's a Joint bedsteed . . . . . 00 06 08

In things omitted and unseene . . . . . . 00 02 06

The totall Sume is . . . . . . . . 22 01 05

The ffunerall charges being deduced . . . . . 01 00 00

There remains . . . . . . . . 21 01 05


## 10. Thomas Higgins

Of Dawley Magna, weaver, taken on 30 September 1684 and exhibited on 6 October 1685. The appraisers are not named.

Imprmis his wearinge Clothes and Money in purse . . . 02 10 00
Item his weaveinge loomes with all materials . . . . 03 00 00
Item 1 Cow Beast . . . . . . . . 04 00 00
Item 1 fether bed 2 fether boulsters 1 pillow 3 Ruggs and 2 Blanc-
ketts 1 coverlid 3 and one flooke bed . . . . . 03 00 00
Item eight pairs of Sheets 1 doz and halfe of napkins foure pillow
bers 2 towells 2 table clothes . . . . . . 02 10 00
Item one Brasse Pott 3 Brasse Kettles and two Iron Potts 1 Iron
Possnett . . . . . . . . . 01 00 00
Item six pewter dishes 1 candlestick 1 porenger 1 doz and halfe of
spoones 1 pewter cupp . . . . . . . 00 12 00
Item money due to be paide . . . . . . 02 08 00
Item one Barrell 1 Stund 1 Turnell 1 Churne 1 Bouke one gaune and
1 kneadeinge vessell Six boules 2 doz and 6 Trenchers one wood
morter . . . . . . . . . 00 12 00
Item one Broache and one pair of Racks one Iron vessill one fryinge
pan . . . . . . . . . . 00 05 00
Item one Chestt & one Cuffer . . . . . . 00 05 00
one Boarde one Joyne Stoole . . . . . . 00 02 06
Item Hempe dressed and not dressed . . . . . 00 18 06
Item One axe one Bill one Broome hooke . . . . 00 02 00

all comes to . . . 20 10 00

# THE INVENTORIES OF DAWLEY

## 11. Robert Taylor

Of Dawley Green, collier, taken by Thomas Higgins senior,* Richard Higgins and Thomas Higgins junior, on 9 June 1685 and exhibited on 18 September 1685.

Imprs.
| | | |
|---|---|---|
| five cowes and a heifer | 12 | 00 00 |
| Sheep yong and old | 01 | 10 00 |
| Corne on the ground And in the house | 02 | 10 00 |
| one Joyned bedsteed And too other bedsteeds | 00 | 12 04 |
| one fether bed and boulster | 01 | 00 00 |
| one flocke bed and boulster And one Chafe bed and boulster | 00 | 05 00 |
| bed hillings and blankitts | 01 | 00 00 |
| Linigs of all Sorts | 02 | 00 00 |
| one gilt and piggs | 00 | 16 00 |
| brass and pewter | 01 | 00 00 |
| Irone potts and pans | 00 | 13 04 |
| Iron ware of all sorts | 00 | 04 00 |
| Wooden Vessells of all Sorts | 00 | 06 08 |
| Cobbort thre Coffers And a box and one table board | 00 | 07 00 |
| Cheares and Stooles | 00 | 01 06 |
| Whitmeat and backon | 00 | 13 04 |
| his wareing apparell | 01 | 00 00 |
| money in the house & And in his purse | 02 | 00 00 |
| bonds bills and other dessperate Depts | 20 | 00 00 |
| Earthenware and things omitted and forgotten | 00 | 01 06 |
| The totall sum: | 48 | 00 00 |

## 12. Walter Hartshorne

Of Malins Lee, master collier, taken by John Gough, Roger Roe* and Roget Sockett on 24 August 1696 and exhibited on 6 August 1696.

*Imprs In the kitchen*
One Iron Jack one Grate ffire shovell & Tonges One long wheele one Segg Chaire & three stooles . . . . . . 00 13 04

*In the parlor*
Two Joyned Small Tables one joyned forme two chaires one ioyned presse one Clocke one small grate ffire shovell & Tonges . . 01 10 00

*In the Cellar*
Three Hogsheads & ffoure Barrells Brewing Vessells & other wooden ware . . . . . . . . . 01 06 08

*In the dineing Roome*
One ffeather bed ffeather bolster bedsteds & appurtences one joyned Chest One joyned Screen one joyned table & one side table three joyned Chaires & two Segg Chaires one ioyed fforme one small iron grate & one small wheele . . . . . 02 00 00

*In the Little Roome*
One fflock bed and one Segg Chaire . . . . 00 05 00

*In the Cockloft*
One fflock bed & one paire of bedsteds . . . . . 00 05 00

*In the Cheese Chamber*
one ffeather bed two Chaffs beds & one fflocke bed two old paire of bedsteds one Salt box & Twenty Small Cheese & Nine Cheese Shelves . . . . . . . . 01 13 04

*In the parlor Chamber*
One ffeather bed bedsteds & appurtenaces one joyned hanging presse Three joyned Chests with the Linnens one joyned Table one Trunk one Deske Two Chaires . . . . . 02 00 00

Brasse & pewter . . . . . . . 02 00 00
Three Bullocks Six Cows Two Bulls & one heyfor Three yearlins & ffoure Calves . . . . . . . 36 00 00
Three Mares One Mare & Colt & one Twinter Colt . . . 09 00 00
Implemts. of husbandry . . . . . . 06 00 00
hay & Corne upon ye ground and Compost . . . 06 00 00
Coles upon ye Banke . . . . . . 20 00 00
Tooles & working geare belonging to ye Colliery . . . 05 00 00
Weareing Apparrell & moneye in pockett. . . . 01 00 00
Creditts & desperate debts . . . . . . 20 00 00
Trumpery & other thinges unseene . . . . 01 00 00
Sixteene Sheepe . . . . . . . 02 10 00
ffoure Small Swine . . . . . . . 01 10 00
Iron ware & Tinne ware . . . . . . 00 10 00

120 03 04

## 13. Christopher Benison

Of Dawley, taken by Richard Jordan and John Holmes on 12 January 1701–2 and exhibited on 7 May 1702.

*Impris*
ffour Cowes . . . . . . . . 12 00 00
one Mare & one horse . . . . . . 05 00 00
Nine sheep . . . . . . . . 02 10 00
one Mixson of Muck . . . . . . 00 15 00
Corne in the Barne of all sortes . . . . . 05 00 00
hay in the Barne . . . . . . . 03 10 00
one Rick or stack of hay & straw . . . . . 01 00 00
Two shotes & one ffatt Swine . . . . . 03 10 00
Implemts. of husbandry . . . . . . 00 15 00

*In the Hall*
Pewter of All sorts . . . . . . . 01 10 00

# THE INVENTORIES OF DAWLEY

| | |
|---|---|
| Two table Boards one fforme two Low stooles five Chaires two Cupboards two shelves . . . . . . | 01 05 00 |
| two ffurnaces two potts & four kettles . . . . | 02 10 00 |
| two drepping pans 2 frying panns . . . . . | 00 10 00 |
| Two warming pans 3 broaches 1 grate . . . | 00 15 00 |
| One pair of Cobberts fire shovell & tongs . . | 00 06 00 |
| two pair of pott Linkes one fflesh forke & one Skymmer . . | 00 04 00 |
| One Cleaver one Cast Iron [sic] 2 pair of poot hookes . . . | 00 02 06 |

*In the parlour*

| | |
|---|---|
| One feather bed 2 boulsters 2 pillows 3 blanketts one Chaff bed one pair of Curtaines and one bedstead one Low bedstead one fflock bed & boulster & two blanketts . . . . . | 05 00 00 |
| One Ovell Table 3 chaires 1 Coffer . . . . | 00 12 06 |
| One standing presse . . . . . . . | 00 13 00 |

*In the best chamber*

| | |
|---|---|
| 2 ffeather beds 3 feather boulsters one pillow two Ruggs four blanketts two setts of Curtaines two Bedsteads . . . . | 08 00 00 |
| Two Chests one Trunke one box two chaires . . . . | 01 00 00 |
| Linnens of all sorts . . . . . . . . | 07 00 00 |

*In the Chamber over the parlour*

| | |
|---|---|
| Two bedsteads two fflock beds 4 blankets one Rugg . . . | 01 10 00 |
| One Coffer 5 straw Whisketts . . . . . | 00 10 00 |
| household pvision of all sorts . . . . . | 05 00 00 |
| 60 stone of hemp . . . . . . . | 12 00 00 |
| 12 stone of yarne . . . . . . . . | 03 00 00 |
| One Rope one bagg of ffeathers 3 wheeles . . . | 01 00 00 |
| Wooden ware of all sorts . . . . . . | 01 00 00 |
| Pack cloaths & baggs . . . . . . . | 00 10 00 |
| The tooles belonging to the trade . . . . . | 02 10 00 |
| his wareing apparrell & money in his purse . . . | 02 10 00 |
| things omitted & not seen . . . . . . | 00 05 00 |
| Two barrells of Tarr & one brasse pann . . . . | 03 00 00 |
| Sum total . . | 96 03 00 |

## 14. William Crippin

Of The Frame, Dawley, labourer, taken by Podmore Peploe and Arthur Ankret on 12 October 1710 and exhibited on 30 November 1710. In his will Crippin left to his wife Ann and his son John the possession of the rented cottage he lived in and the lands belonging to the Phiny (i.e., Finney) Barn. He was buried on 17 Aug. 1710.

| | |
|---|---|
| Imprs. 4 Cowes . . . . . . . | 10 00 00 |
| 1 Little horse . . . . . . . . | 01 00 00 |
| 1 mare at . . . . . . . . . | 03 00 00 |
| 1 hog at . . . . . . . . . | 00 10 00 |
| 2 Bed and Blanketts & Coverlid Boulsters & Pillows . . . | 03 00 00 |

| | |
|---|---|
| Linings for table & Beding . . . . . . . | 01 00 00 |
| Brass Pewtere tinware & other Lumbers . . . . . | 01 00 00 |
| his warring Aparrell 2 shillings in his pockett . . . . | 01 00 00 |
| 1 Grate fire shovell & 1 pr tonges . . . . . . | 00 10 00 |
| 1 Broach & Gobburns 1 Table Board & 1 Forme . . | 00 05 00 |
| Things omitted & not seene . . . . . . | 00 02 00 |
| debts . . . . . . . . . . . | 06 00 00 |
| Tottall . . | 27 07 00 |

## 15. Podmore Peploe

Of Little Dawley, taken by Richard Hall and John Churn on 20 April 1715 and exhibited on 22 April 1715. Podmore Peploe was buried on 10 November 1714. He was the father of Samuel Peploe (1667–1752), who was educated at Penkridge School and Jesus College, Oxford, and became Bishop of Chester in 1726.

| | |
|---|---|
| Imprs | |
| his wareing Apparell. . . . . . . . . | 03 02 06 |
| Itm . . . . . . . . . . . | 01 01 00 |
| moneys in pockett . . . . . . . . . | 01 01 00 |
| Itm | |
| debts due to him . . . . . . . . | 10 05 00 |
| things not seen & omitted . . . . . . . | 00 05 00 |
| | 14 13 06 |

## 16. William Poyner

Of Great Dawley, taken by William Kerby and Ralph Littlehales on 20 February 1715–16 and exhibited on 25 February 1715–16.

| | |
|---|---|
| Impris. an old Second hand string watch [sic] . . . . | 00 15 00 |
| A gray Sagathy Coat . . . . . . . | 00 10 00 |
| a Black Druggett Coat . . . . . . . | 00 05 00 |
| an old black Serge wastcoat . . . . . . | 00 02 00 |
| an old black cloath pair of Breeches . . . . . | 00 01 06 |
| an old fustian frock . . . . . . . . | 00 01 00 |
| an old dark cloath coat & Breeches & an old black cloath Wastcoat . | 00 07 06 |
| four pair of old white sleeves . . . . . . | 00 01 00 |
| three old necks . . . . . . . . | 00 01 06 |
| an old pair of black stockings . . . . . . | 00 00 04 |
| an old pair of wooden heeld Shoes . . . . . | 00 01 06 |
| a pair of old Boots & Spurrs . . . . . . | 00 05 00 |
| three old penknives & ye Case . . . . . . | 00 01 00 |
| three old flaxen shirts . . . . . . . | 00 04 06 |
| an old hatt . . . . . . . . . | 00 00 06 |
| three pairs of old Gloves . . . . . . . | 00 00 09 |

## THE INVENTORIES OF DAWLEY

| | | |
|---|---|---|
| five old second hand Bookes | 00 05 00 |
| two old Small copy Bookes | 00 00 04 |
| an old Box & a writeing stool | 00 02 00 |
| an old powder Box | 00 00 01 |
| Tot | 03 05 06 |

### 17. Charles Eyton

Of Malins Lee, Dawley, gent, taken by Pelham Reynolds and Richard Bellis on 27 August 1720 and exhibited on 26 April 1721.

| | |
|---|---|
| Imprs. Three oxen | 09 15 00 |
| Item. Two Heyfers | 05 15 00 |
| Item. Three Twinters | 04 10 00 |
| Item. Two Yearelings | 01 10 00 |
| Item. Three Calves | 01 00 00 |
| Item. Eighteen Sheep | 04 10 00 |
| Item. One Gray mare & Colt | 03 17 06 |
| Item. One other Colt | 01 19 00 |
| Item. one Black horse | 07 17 06 |
| Item. Two Tumbrells & one pare of Thripples | 02 06 00 |
| Item. one ox harrow | 00 10 00 |
| Item. Three plows | 00 02 00 |
| Item. One Rolle ffan & Cartrope | 00 06 06 |
| Item. Three Ladders | 00 02 00 |
| Item. one ox waine | 02 03 06 |
| Item. Two Sleades & Two harrows | 00 12 00 |
| Item. Yoakes & other Implemts. of husbandry & Ironware | 01 04 00 |
| Item. hay | 05 00 00 |
| Item. hardcorne | 02 02 00 |
| Item. muck | 00 10 00 |
| Item. Two chest whitches | 00 12 00 |
| Item. one Copper ffurnis | 01 15 00 |
| Item. one malt mill | 00 08 00 |
| Item. plow Timber & other Timber | 01 00 00 |
| Item. Brass | 00 10 02 |
| Item. Pewter | 00 09 04 |
| Item. one fflowleing peece | 00 10 00 |
| Item. Iron ware | 00 01 00 |
| Item. Twenty old Bookes one deske & Trumpryware | 01 00 00 |
| Item. one sword & one paire of pistolls | 00 10 00 |
| Item. Two old watches | 02 00 00 |
| Things omitted & not seen | 00 05 00 |
| | 64 12 06 |

### 18. William Watkiss

Of Malins Lee, Dawley, blacksmith, taken by Jacob Smith and William Keen on 1 July 1724 and exhibited on 19 October 1725.

It. *In the Housplass*
It. one Tabell Bord and one form . . . . . . 00 08 00
It. one Brass pan one Brass Keettell and a Brass pot . . . 00 12 00
It. one old Cobort . . . . . . . . 00 05 00
It. Eight Small Poutter Disshess . . . . . . 00 05 00
It. one Iarn pot and a Keettell . . . . . . 00 04 00
It. one Geen [sic] Cheers and other Lumber Goods . . . 00 05 00

It. *In the Parler*
It. one fether Beed Bedstids and Hingings . . . . 01 00 00
It. one Cheest one Coffer one Box one press . . . . 01 12 00

It. *In the Buttery*
It. Wooden Vessells of all sorts . . . . . . 00 10 00

It. *In the Chamber over the Hous*
It. two old Coffers and an old pare of Beedsteads . . . 00 02 06

It. *In an old Rome*
It. two Pare of Lowms and an old Wooden Molt Mill . . . 04 00 00

It. *In the Shop*
It. one pare of Ballos and Envell and other Working Twoolls . . 01 10 00
It. three Milking Cowss . . . . . . . 05 10 00
It. two yeare olds . . . . . . . . 02 00 00
It. one Shep . . . . . . . . . 00 04 00
It. Hiss Waring aparell . . . . . . . 00 15 00
Things omitted and Not seen . . . . . . 00 05 00

                                                totel . . 16 07 06

## 19. John Duddell

Of Pool Hill, Dawley, carpenter, taken by Thomas Barrett and John Holbrooke on 22 October 1724 and exhibited on 13 April 1725. He was buried on 20 October 1724. He was probably the father of John Duddell, who died in 1728 (*24*).

Item
*In ye Chop* ye Tooles Belonging to his Trade . . . . 01 00 00

*Item In ye Ciching*
one Table and Gine Chear and Chrach . . . . . 00 14 00
and Iornware of all Sorts . . . . . . . 02 02 06
and Brass of all Sorts . . . . . . . 00 16 00

*Item In ye Bruhouse and Coler*
Tumbes and Barrels and other wooden ware . . . . 01 16 00

THE INVENTORIES OF DAWLEY

*Item In ye Parler*
one Cobbort and pare of Bedstids . . . . . . 00 15 00

*Item In ye Rume over ye Chiching*
one Bed and other forniture . . . . . . 04 10 00

*Item In ye Rume att ye Stare head*
one pare of Beadstids and two Blanckets . . . . . 00 10 00

*Item In ye Rume over ye Parler*
Beding and other forniture . . . . . . . 03 05 00

Three Corves . . . . . . . . . 07 00 00

Implements of Husbandry . . . . . . . 01 02 06

His Waring Appariell and Monney in Pockett . . . 03 00 00

and Linings of all Seorts . . . . . . . 01 00 00

          Totall . . . 27 11 00

## 20. George Hewlett

Of Great Dawley, collier, taken by Thomas Barrett and Jonas Slaney on 5 March 1724-25 and exhibited on 13 April 1725.

*Imprimis. In the Dwelling house*
one Table, one fform & Joyn'd stool . . . . . 00 05 00
one boyler . . . . . . . . . 00 02 00
one Grate Tongues & Ironware . . . . . . 00 10 00
Brass & pewter . . . . . . . . 02 00 00
Brass bench & two Chaires . . . . . . . 00 03 06

*In the Chambre over the house*
three beds & furniture . . . . . . . 05 00 00
one Chest two little Tables, Two boxes one Trunck and two Chaires . 00 10 00
one Chest one Coffer & five Chaires . . . . . 00 06 00
hops . . . . . . . . . . 03 00 00
one long Wheel & Table Linning . . . . . . 00 05 00
one Looking glass . . . . . . . . 00 00 06
weareing Apparrell & money in his pockett . . . . 04 00 00

*In the Buttery*
one Cupboard, one Table & forme . . . . . 00 05 00
Hogsheads Barrells & brewing vessells . . . . 01 05 00
Trumpery Ware & things unseen . . . . . . 00 10 00
Hay—one Cow & one Swine . . . . . . 04 13 00
Implemts. belonging to ye Colepitt . . . . . 00 10 00
Money due & oweing upon bills bonds and other securitys . . 350 00 00

          Totum . . . 369 05 00

## 21. Edward Darrall

Of Holywell, Dawley, ground collier, taken by George Arden and Daniel Darrall on 21 May 1726 and exhibited on 21 October 1726.

*Imprs. In the Kitchen*
One Round Table Three old Chairs, one Boyler two Iron Ketles one Little Brass Kettle two old pails one Iron Pot Milk Vessells one frying pan four pewter dishes one warming pan other pewter things one smal Grate one fier shovel two pair of Tongues one Cradle & pewter shelves . . . . . . . . 00 15 00

*In ye Little Room*
One Kneading Trough one smal Brewing stund one old Cuppard one Little Wheele one Churn Working Tools . . . . . 00 04 06

*In the Buttry*
Two smal Barrels & one Tun dish . . . . . . 00 02 06

*In ye Chamber over the Kitchen*
One pair of Bedsteads one old ffeather Bed sheets coverings &c. One Join Chest & two old Chairs . . . . . . 00 15 00

*In ye Chamber over ye Little Room*
Two old pair of Bedsteads two old Chaff Beds covering &c. two old Coffers & Linen Yarn . . . . . . . 00 05 00

| | |
|---|---|
| Wearing Apparel & Wearing linen of all sorts . . . . | 00 10 00 |
| Household provision . . . . . . . | 00 10 00 |
| one old Cow . . . . . . . . . | 01 10 00 |
| Things Omited and unseen . . . . . . . | 00 01 00 |
| Toto . . . | 04 13 00 |

## 22. Lawrence Wellington

Of The Ridges, Dawley, gent, taken by John Smith and John Woolley on 26 November 1726 and exhibited on 18 April 1727. Wellington left the Ridges Farm to his son Lawrence, the Ridges Mill and the New Pool let to the Coalbrookdale Company, to his daughter Susannah, a farm called Hazlewood's Living to his daughter Martha, and the Croppings Farm to his wife Grace, and his sons John, Richard and Thomas, Michael Onions (23) was an under-tenant occuping a cottage on the farm.

| | |
|---|---|
| Imprimis In the Kitchen goods at . . . . . . | 03 00 00 |
| Item Goods in the parlor . . . . . . . | 02 10 00 |
| Item In the Dining Roome . . . . . . . | 01 10 00 |
| Item In the Roome over the House . . . . . | 02 10 00 |
| Item In the Roome over the Parlor . . . . . | 01 10 00 |
| Item In the Little Roome . . . . . . . | 00 10 00 |

# THE INVENTORIES OF DAWLEY

| | | |
|---|---|---|
| Item In the Seller and Buttrey | | 02 00 00 |
| Item In the Malthouse | | 03 00 00 |
| Item Implements of Husbandry | | 07 00 00 |
| Item Swine | | 02 00 00 |
| Item ffour Cowes and seven Calves | | 14 00 00 |
| Item Hay | | 07 00 00 |
| Item The Corne in the Barne | | 07 15 00 |
| Item Horses and Mares | | 16 00 00 |
| | Totall | 67 05 00 |
| | A Lease for one Life | 20 00 00 |
| | Totall | 87 05 00 |

## 23. Michael Onions

Of Stoney Hill, Dawley, taken by E. Hill and John Duddell on 18 November 1727 and exhibited on 15 October 1728. He was buried on 25 October 1727.

Imprs.

| | |
|---|---|
| *In the Dwelling house* Pewter and Brass Bench | 00 10 00 |
| Iron Ware and Brass of all sorts | 00 09 00 |
| One Table and Chair | 00 11 00 |
| other furniture | 00 04 00 |

*In the Buttery*

| | |
|---|---|
| Two Hogsheads and six Barrells | 01 05 00 |
| Two old Horses ad the Vessells stand on | 00 01 00 |
| One old Cupboard | 00 02 06 |

*In the Brewhouse*

| | |
|---|---|
| Two Boylers and Three Brewing Vessells | 00 18 00 |
| Two Pails | 00 01 06 |
| One old Churn with other necessaryes belonging to Dairey | 00 02 06 |
| Tools belonging to Husbandry | 00 02 00 |

*In the Room over the Brewhouse*

One old Bed and Steads Two old Tables and form Two Chests 2 Boxes One coffer and three chairs . . . . . . . 01 03 09

*In the Room over the House*

Two old beds and Steads Three old Coffer and three old Boxes . 00 10 00

*In the Room over the Buttery*

| | |
|---|---|
| Two old Beds and Steds and one Chest | 00 07 06 |
| Two Cows and Hay 3 littl Pigs 1 Calfe | 06 05 00 |
| Linnen of all Sorts and Wearing Apparrell | 01 10 00 |
| | 14 02 09 |
| Desparate Debts | 02 00 00 |
| | 16 02 09 |

## 24. John Duddell

Of the Pawn Hatch, Dawley, carpenter, taken on 1 May 1728 and exhibited on 15 October 1728. The appraisers are not named on the inventory, In his will made on 18 April 1728 he left his whole estate to his wife Dorothy. He was buried on 23 April 1728. It was probably this John Duddell who was baptised on 26 December 1687, and was the son of the John Duddell who died in 1724 (*19*).

*In ye Kitchen*

| | | |
|---|---|---|
| Twelve pewter dishes 35s Two Dozen of pewter plate 12s one pewter salver 1s | 02 | 08 | 00 |
| Three pewter porringers | 00 | 00 | 06 |
| Two Dozen of Tin patty pans three tin Covers Three tin Pudding pans one Aple plate A Tin Cullinder A tin baster A Cheese Toaster and a tin pasty plate. | 00 | 05 | 00 |
| One Round Tables & one Clock and Case 35s | 02 | 03 | 00 |
| one old broaken Warming pan | 00 | 00 | 06 |
| one Brass Bonch | 00 | 15 | 00 |
| one Grate Niggards, two pairs of tonges and two fier shovels 20s one Cleever 1s 6d | 01 | 01 | 06 |
| One flesh forck 3d one Bras Basting spoon 3d | 00 | 00 | 06 |
| Two pair of pott Goales 1s one Brass skimer 3d | 00 | 01 | 03 |
| Two pairs of potthooks and a Mead | 00 | 01 | 00 |
| One Jack Chain and Cord 20s Three Iorn spitts 3s | 01 | 03 | 00 |
| Two Iorn Drooping pans 30d two brass Candlesticks 6d. | 00 | 03 | 00 |
| Three Iorn Candlesticks & one Iorn pudding plates | 00 | 01 | 06 |
| One tin Candlebox 6d one Join Chair 3s | 00 | 03 | 06 |
| Six Seg Chairs 1s two Join stooles 1s | 00 | 02 | 00 |
| Two ffrying pans 2s A Small Table 1s | 00 | 03 | 00 |
| An Iorn Toaster for bread 4d | 00 | 00 | 04 |
| A pair of Cobbards 1s one bacon Chratch 4s | 00 | 05 | 00 |

*In ye Parler*

| | | |
|---|---|---|
| One Join Copboard 30d one Round Table 11s | 00 | 13 | 06 |
| twelve Seg Chairs 8s one warming pan 1s | 00 | 09 | 00 |
| one Join bed and tester with Hangings | 00 | 15 | 00 |
| one fether bed and boulster a chaf bed | 01 | 10 | 00 |
| Two Blankets and Rogg 12s | 00 | 12 | 00 |
| A little fether bed and Bolster one Coverlid and Smal Blanket & a pair of Bedsteads | 01 | 00 | 00 |

*In ye Chamber over ye Parler*

| | | |
|---|---|---|
| One trunk 3s two Join Chestes 13s one box 1s 6d | 00 | 17 | 06 |
| one Cupboard 4s two pair of bedsteds 8s | 00 | 12 | 00 |
| one flock bed 30d and one featherbed & two bolsters 20s A long wheel and A little Wheel 5s. | 01 | 07 | 06 |
| thirteen slippens of Hempen yarn | 00 | 04 | 04 |
| A Close Stoole and Pan | 00 | 02 | 00 |

# THE INVENTORIES OF DAWLEY

*Att ye Stair head*
One Join Chest 8s an old Coffer and four shelves 30d one bran Tub 6d .    00 11 00

*In the best Room*
| | |
|---|---|
| one pair of Bedsteads hanging and Counterpane . | 00 15 00 |
| one feather bed and two bolsters . | 02 00 00 |
| two blanketts A Chaff bed . | 00 08 00 |
| one Join Hanging Pross . | 01 05 00 |
| one Chest pf Drawers . | 00 12 00 |
| one Round Table 6s one Join Chest 6s . | 00 02 00 |
| A larg Twig basket 10d A smal Trunk 6d . | 00 01 04 |
| two old Seg Chairs . | 00 00 06 |

*Linen of all Sorts*
| | |
|---|---|
| Two pair of flaxensheets . | 01 05 00 |
| four pair of hempen sheets . | 01 05 00 |
| Twelve pair of Hurdeon sheets . | 02 00 00 |
| one flaxen Table Cloth A Dozen and halfe of fflaxen napkins . | 00 15 00 |
| Two Dozen of Hordon Napkins . | 00 10 00 |
| four Cours Table Cloths . | 00 02 00 |
| Six Course hand Towels . | 00 02 06 |

| | |
|---|---|
| Wearing Apparrel and linen of all sorts . | 03 00 00 |
| Money in Purse . | 01 02 06 |

*In ye Brewhouse*
| | |
|---|---|
| A kneading Tub 1s a Dresser 1s . | 00 02 00 |
| A large Brass Kettle 10s Two Iorn pots 12s . | 01 02 00 |
| Two Iron kettles 18d A mastin kettle 2s . | 00 03 06 |
| A puter Chamber pot 6d a Churn 30d . | 00 03 00 |
| Three brewing vessels . | — |
| A large Cooller 30d A smal Table 1s . | 00 03 06 |
| An Iron furnace and boyler . | 00 15 00 |
| about a Dozen of Trenchers . | 00 01 00 |
| three pails and a Gawn . | 00 01 06 |
| five old twil Baggs . | 00 02 06 |

Household provision of al sorts   .       02 10 00

*In ye Celler*
| | |
|---|---|
| Two qt vessells . | 00 05 00 |
| Three half hogsheads . | 00 09 00 |
| A fferken . | 00 01 00 |
| A Dresser 1s A Cheespress 5s A Bench 6d . | 00 06 06 |
| A Horse for Barrels . | 00 02 00 |
| Two Little shelves 6d A Tundish 6d . | 00 01 00 |
| An old Chees Tub 1s Milk Vessells 1s . | 00 02 00 |

*In ye Stable*
| | |
|---|---|
| Three pairs of Traces 5s three pairs of Homes 1s6d . | 00 06 06 |
| A new Coller . | 00 01 06 |
| A Tumbrill . | 01 00 00 |

| | | |
|---|---|---|
| four milking Cowes and one Heifer | | 15 00 00 |
| four horses 12£12s two piggs 20s | | 13 12 00 |
| His Shop of Tools | | 06 00 00 |
| A Smal parcel of boards | | 00 10 00 |
| Things Omited and unseen | | 00 10 00 |
| | Toto | 59 11 04 |

## 25. John Harris

Of Dawley, taken by John Woolley and Richard Swinnterton* on 29 March 1729 and exhibited on 11 April 1729.

*In the Kitchen*

| | |
|---|---|
| Two Join Chairs one Brass bench | 00 08 00 |
| one Warming pan one Join skreen | 00 05 08 |
| one Little square Table two brass Kettles ten pewter dishes A dozen of plates one Iron grate & niggards | 02 02 06 |
| one fier shovel one pair of tongues | 00 02 06 |
| two Iron spits one Iron pan | 00 06 06 |
| one Iron potslid A flesh fork | 00 00 09 |
| A brass spoon A Cleaver | 00 00 04 |
| A hanging plates one Iron pot and pothooks one pair of pot links | 00 04 08 |
| A wood Mortar and pestell | 00 01 06 |
| A tin Cover A tin Cullinder | 00 01 00 |
| A tin pan A pudding plate | 00 00 11 |
| Seventeen trenchers A pewter Candlestick four Seg chairs | 00 00 09 |
| two wood chairs one Join stool | 00 00 10 |
| one Maslin Kettle one Iron Candlestick four Iron pots and a boyler | 01 00 05 |

*In the Parler*

| | |
|---|---|
| one Join bedstead one feather bed and bolster one Chaff bed and bolster two blankets | 01 12 00 |
| one Coverlid one side table | 00 06 00 |
| one desk one box one table & form | 00 11 00 |

*In the Chamber over the Parler*

| | |
|---|---|
| one pair of bedsteads & hangings | 00 10 00 |
| one feather bed one Rugg two old Coffers one table & form | 01 11 06 |
| A straw whisket about 20 strike of barley one flasket A smal parcel of linen yarn two dozen of napkins twelve pair of sheets two table Cloths A pillow bord two smal parcells of Woolen Cloth | 01 12 00 |

*In the Chamber over the Kitchen*

| | |
|---|---|
| Three pair of bedsteads & four Chaff beds one feather bed | 01 12 00 |
| one Join Chest one form one coffer | 00 09 06 |
| Nine sliggions of Noggon yarn | 00 02 06 |
| A feather bolster and pillow | 00 01 00 |
| two Chaff bolsters about 2 strikes of Massorn two pair of sheets blankets and Coverlid | 00 18 08 |

## THE INVENTORIES OF DAWLEY

*In the Room over the Entry*

| | | |
|---|---|---|
| A spining wheel a long wheel | 00 | 04 | 00 |
| A Tewter a long plank | 00 | 05 | 00 |
| Three wood bottels About two strike of wheat four siths and sneadds | 00 | 19 | 06 |
| A little Tub About four strike of Vetches A straw whish | 00 | 09 | 06 |
| an Auger and gouge | 00 | 00 | 08 |
| other Lumber | 00 | 02 | 06 |

*In the Room over the buttry*

| | | |
|---|---|---|
| A long Table and form two cofers about 15 strike of oats | 02 | 02 | 06 |

*In the Entry*

| | | |
|---|---|---|
| Two Barrell two Tubbs | 00 | 15 | 00 |
| Two pailes and 2 Gaunes | 00 | 01 | 00 |
| A turnel A basket two Mathooks | 00 | 02 | 07 |
| A Wagon Rope A Seeth | 00 | 01 | 02 |

*In the Buttry*

| | | |
|---|---|---|
| one Churn three Barrells | 00 | 12 | 06 |
| one brewing Tub A search | 00 | 04 | 06 |
| Milk Vessels of All sorts | 00 | 03 | 00 |

*In the fold*

| | | |
|---|---|---|
| one wagon one Tumbrill | 09 | 00 | 00 |
| one Basket and Rop one cratch | 00 | 06 | 00 |
| three stoor Pigs 14 Cowes | 51 | 00 | 00 |
| one bull seven yearlings | 11 | 00 | 00 |
| Nine Young Cattel | 20 | 00 | 00 |
| Implements of husbandry | 02 | 00 | 00 |
| six sucking Calves a parcel of muck | 02 | 14 | 00 |

*In the barn*

| | | |
|---|---|---|
| A smal parcel of unthresht Corn unthresht oats | 07 | 00 | 00 |
| About 6 strike of Vetches | 00 | 02 | 00 |

*on the backside of the barn*

| | | |
|---|---|---|
| one Rick of Clover part of A Rick of hay | 08 | 00 | 00 |

*In Highwayes barn*

| | | |
|---|---|---|
| Clover and Hay | 03 | 00 | 00 |

*In the fold*

| | | |
|---|---|---|
| A parcel of muck | 01 | 00 | 00 |

*In the stable*

| | | |
|---|---|---|
| plow and art Gears of all sorts | 02 | 10 | 00 |
| Ten Horses and Colts | 30 | 00 | 00 |

*over the stone house*

| | | |
|---|---|---|
| A parcel of undresst hemp | 00 | 04 | 00 |

*In Mr. Barrets Cart house*

| | |
|---|---|
| About 20 battels of undresst flax . . . . . . | 00 04 00 |
| Wearing Apparel and Money in purse . . . . | 05 00 00 |
| Household provision of all sorts . . . . . | 05 10 00 |
| Things omitted and unseen . . . . . . . | 00 05 00 |
| | 185 10 04 |

## 26. Thomas Roe

Of Little Dawley, yeoman, taken by George Arden and Edward Whittingham on 8 June 1730 and exhibited on 27 October 1730. In his will made on 1 February 1725-26 he is described as being of Malins Lee. He left leasehold property at The Hem to his wife, Ann. He was buried on 6 June 1730.

*In the Kitchen*

| | |
|---|---|
| one Clock and Case . . . . . . . . | 02 10 00 |
| one Tabel form and Joine bench . . . . . | 00 10 00 |
| A warming pan 4s a Skreen 4s . . . . . | 00 08 00 |
| Two Seg Chairs 18d one Iron pan 2s . . . . | 00 03 06 |
| Two Iron Spits 30d one Iron Mortar 5s A Puding plat Chafing dish and Gridiron 4s a Brass Skimer 1s . . . . . | 00 12 06 |
| A Lanthorn 18d a Little Table 18d . . . . | 00 03 00 |
| A fflesh fork 6d two Iron Candlesticks 6d a Salt box 6d A hacking knife 1s . . . . . . . . . | 00 02 06 |
| one Gun 5s pewter of All sorts 30s . . . . | 01 15 00 |
| one Iron Grate fier shovel & Tongs 10s A brass pot 5s. . . | 00 15 00 |
| three pair of pot geals . . . . . . . | 00 01 00 |

*In the Scullery*

| | |
|---|---|
| Milk Vesels of all sorts . . . . . . . | 01 05 00 |
| two water pails 3s an Iron Kettle pot hoods &c. 30d three brass Kettles 20s two barrells 5s A wood bottle 18d . . . | 01 12 00 |

*In the Pantry*

| | |
|---|---|
| one Little Table and old forme . . . . . | 00 01 06 |

*In the Cellar*

| | |
|---|---|
| two Barrells . . . . . . . . . | 00 08 00 |

*In the Parlor*

| | |
|---|---|
| one Round Table . . . . . . . . | 00 10 00 |
| three Seg Chiars 3s 6d, A Close Stool and pan 10s A looking Glass 10d . | 00 14 04 |

*In the boack Chamber*

| | |
|---|---|
| one Truckle bedstead a fether bed Bolsterrs Covings &c . . | 02 00 00 |
| one hanging press . . . . . . . . | 01 01 00 |
| one Long Table Board . . . . . . . | 00 02 06 |

# THE INVENTORIES OF DAWLEY

*In the Little Chamber*

| | | |
|---|---|---|
| one Joine beadstead one feather bed two bolsters two pillows a Chaff Bed Blankets Rug &c . . . . . . | 04 | 00 00 |
| one Desk 3s on Chest 5s . . . . . . | 00 | 08 00 |

*Linen of All Sorts*

| | | |
|---|---|---|
| Six flaxen Napkins 9s. one Duson of Course Napkins 6s two Table Clothes 7s . . . . . . . | 01 | 02 00 |
| four paire of Course Sheets . . . . . | 01 | 05 00 |
| one pare of hempen Sheets . . . . . | 00 | 10 06 |
| one pare of flaxen sheets . . . . . . | 00 | 14 00 |
| two hand towels . . . . . . . | 00 | 01 06 |
| Waring Linen of all sorts . . . . . | 01 | 10 00 |
| Wearing Apparrol and Linen of all sorts . . . | 05 | 00 00 |

*In the Servants Room*

| | | |
|---|---|---|
| A Long Wheel 18d a Little Wheel 18d . . . . | 00 | 03 00 |
| A pair of Bedsteads A Chaf Bed A fether Bolster Coverings &c | 00 | 12 00 |

*In ye back Kitchen*

| | | |
|---|---|---|
| A Cheese press 18s a Large brewing Vessel 10s A furnace 15s a half strike 30d . . . . . . . | 02 | 02 06 |
| 20 Slippons of hempen Yarn . . . . . | 01 | 05 00 |
| Household provision of all sorts . . . . | 05 | 00 00 |
| Things omited and unseene . . . . . | 00 | 10 00 |

*In ye Milkhouse*

| | | |
|---|---|---|
| one Long Cooler . . . . . . . . | 00 | 07 00 |

*In ye Malt house*

| | | |
|---|---|---|
| twelve strikes of Corne . . . . . . | 01 | 10 00 |
| About 40 strike of Malt . . . . . . | 06 | 00 00 |
| A har Cloth 5s A Traine and a halfe of felleys 10s . . | 00 | 15 00 |

*In the Groundes*

| | | |
|---|---|---|
| ffife Milking Cowes . . . . . . . | 15 | 10 00 |
| two two yeare old heifers . . . . . . | 04 | 10 00 |
| three yearlings . . . . . . . . | 04 | 10 00 |
| one pair of working oxon . . . . . . | 09 | 00 00 |
| two sucking Calves . . . . . . . | 00 | 13 00 |
| two horses £11 a mare and colt £8 . . . . | 19 | 00 00 |
| four ews and one Lamb . . . . . . | 01 | 00 00 |
| one barren Heifer . . . . . . . | 03 | 10 00 |

*Implements of husbandry*

| | | |
|---|---|---|
| one Slead 5s one Tumbril 3£ . . . . . | 03 | 05 00 |
| one old Waine 20s three plowes two pare of harrows 40s . | 03 | 00 00 |
| A Role 30d A Grindlestone 30d . . . . . | 00 | 05 00 |
| Toe Chaines 2s hors Gears of All Sort 25s hackney sadle & bridles &c 10s | 01 | 19 00 |
| Draught Yoaks . . . . . . . | 00 | 07 06 |
| Crank Cart Sadle &c. . . . . . . | 00 | 03 06 |

*In the fold*
| | | |
|---|---|---|
| About 50 Load of Muck . . . . . . . | 02 10 00 |
| two Pigs . . . . . . . . | 02 10 00 |

*In the Barne*
| | | |
|---|---|---|
| about 26 strike of corn to Thrash . . . . . . | 03 05 00 |
| a ffan to winnow with . . . . . . . | 00 10 00 |
| a Rick of old Clover . . . . . . . . | 03 00 00 |
| aBout two stacks of Coles . . . . . . . | 00 10 00 |
| Tot . . | 126 08 00 |

## 27. Mary Barrett

Of Great Dawley, widow, taken by John Woolley and Charles Lawrence on 23 September 1730 and exhibited on 27 October 1730.

*The Room over the Kitchin*
| | | |
|---|---|---|
| ffive Rings . . . . . . . . . | 02 00 00 |
| The wearing apparell Wollen & Linnen . . . . . | 05 00 00 |
| The household Linnen . . . . . . . | 01 00 00 |
| a Coffer in the kitchin . . . . . . . | 00 03 06 |

*In ye Passage*
| | | |
|---|---|---|
| The Clock & case . . . . . . . . | 01 10 00 |

*In ye Parlour*
| | | |
|---|---|---|
| one smal oval Table . . . . . . . . | 00 05 00 |
| ffour Books . . . . . . . . . | 00 10 00 |

*In the Cellar*
| | | |
|---|---|---|
| one milk Bench . . . . . . . . | 00 00 06 |

*In ye Brewhouse*
| | | |
|---|---|---|
| Two smal Tubs . . . . . . . . | 00 02 06 |
| a hair Cloth on ye kiln . . . . . . . | 00 08 00 |

*In the Kiln house*
| | | |
|---|---|---|
| Charcoale . . . . . . . . . | 00 01 06 |

*In the Colehouse*
| | | |
|---|---|---|
| Raw Coale , , , , , , , , | 00 12 00 |
| money in Pockett . . . . . . . . | 02 10 00 |
| | 14 03 00 |

THE INVENTORIES OF DAWLEY

## 28. Nathan Peploe

Of Little Dawley, taken by George Arden and Edward Whittingham on 15 March 1732-33 and exhibited on 29 May 1733. He was the son of Podmore Peploe (*15*), and brother of Samuel Peploe, Bishop of Chester. He married Ann Hall on 9 June 1694, and was buried on 17 February 1732-33.

*In the Parlor*
| | |
|---|---|
| one pair of Bedsteads one ffeather Bed one Chaf Bed one Rugg two Blankets one Bolster two pillows and hangings with three Seg chairs | 05 00 00 |
| one Table | 00 05 00 |

*In the Chamber over the Parlor*
| | |
|---|---|
| one Chest four pair of flaxen sheets & one pair of hempen sheets | 02 16 00 |
| Wearing apparel and money in purse | 20 00 00 |
| | 28 01 00 |

## 29. William Andrews

Of Dawley, husbandman, taken by Francis Ruckson and Thomas Bridgin on 24 October 1737 and exhibited on 2 November 1737.

| | |
|---|---|
| Impres. three cowes and two heifars | 08 00 00 |
| Item hemp in the Roof | 01 05 00 |
| Item hard Corn and Lent Tillin | 01 07 09 |
| Item hay and muck in the mickton | 01 08 00 |
| one pig | 00 05 00 |
| *Item In the Dwelling house* | |
| ffore puter dishes fore chears one little Table | 00 11 00 |
| brass and Iorn | 00 04 00 |
| *Item In the Parlar* | |
| One bed on Table one Chest one Chire | 00 18 06 |
| *Item In the Chambar over the parlar* | |
| one cofor, two pare of bedstids two Chaff beds | 00 15 00 |
| *Item In the Buttery* | |
| two barrles one church two tubs | 00 08 06 |
| for Lubar and things not seen | 00 06 06 |
| for his waring apparrill and money in his purs | 00 17 06 |
| | 16 06 09 |

## 30. William Keen

Of Dawley, yeoman, taken by Thomas Childs of Sidbury, gentleman, and Thomas Edwards of Madeley, yeoman, on 29 March 1744 and exhibited on 4 April 1745.

*Within Doors & first in the House Place*

| | | | |
|---|---|---|---|
| a Dozn of Pewter Dishes & 2 Dozn Plates | 01 | 06 | 00 |
| The Dresser & Shelves | 00 | 06 | 00 |
| A Dozn of Wooden Trenchers | 00 | 01 | 06 |
| Ten pewter Candlesticks two Salts a Tin Over & Tunning dish. | 00 | 01 | 02 |
| Two Seggen'd Bottomed Chairs | 00 | 00 | 08 |
| A wooden screen | 00 | 01 | 06 |
| A table & form | 00 | 04 | 06 |
| An old Clock & Worm eaten Case. | 00 | 08 | 00 |
| A Wooden stool, wooden Bench & other Trifling Wooden ware | 00 | 02 | 00 |
| An old warming pan & frying Pan. | 00 | 03 | 06 |
| A Grate, Tongs fireshovele & Pot gails &c. | 00 | 05 | 00 |
| Two old Pails & Some Earthen Ware | 00 | 01 | 00 |
| Two Iron Potts & a marment | 00 | 05 | 00 |
| Books & the Linen of all sorts | 00 | 12 | 00 |

*In the Buttery*

| | | | |
|---|---|---|---|
| a little Milking Gawn & Little Table | 00 | 01 | 06 |

*In the Parlour*

| | | | |
|---|---|---|---|
| a Little Table & two Seggen Chairs | 00 | 02 | 00 |

*In the further Buttery*

| | | | |
|---|---|---|---|
| a Long Tubb & Wooden Benches. | 00 | 08 | 00 |
| a Milking Pail. | 00 | 01 | 06 |

*In the Brewhouse*

| | | | |
|---|---|---|---|
| a Little Iron furnace or Boyler | 00 | 06 | 00 |
| Three little Tubbs. | 00 | 04 | 06 |
| a cheese Press | 00 | 02 | 00 |
| Two Hair sieves & a Tunning Dish. | 00 | 02 | 00 |

*In the Cellar*

| | | | |
|---|---|---|---|
| five Barrells Three Wooden Bottles Benches & some old good for nothing things | 00 | 11 | 00 |

*Upstairs*

| | | | |
|---|---|---|---|
| A Bedsted & Hangings | 00 | 05 | 06 |
| Another Bedsted & Bed without Hangings | 00 | 10 | 00 |
| Two little old Churns | 00 | 03 | 06 |
| Fifteen Slippings of Linnen Yarn | 00 | 07 | 00 |
| Another Bed Bedsteds Hangings & furniture | 00 | 15 | 00 |
| a Chest & some old chairs. | 00 | 04 | 00 |
| Another Truckle Bed & steds without Hangings. | 00 | 10 | 00 |
| Half a score small cheeses. | 00 | 10 | 00 |

*In the Barn*

| | | | |
|---|---|---|---|
| Corn threshed & unthreshed | 02 | 00 | 00 |
| A Small parcell of Hay | 00 | 15 | 00 |

*Without Doors*

| | |
|---|---|
| Implements of Husbandry of all sorts & Geering for three Horses | 03 10 00 |
| Two Milking Cows & two young Cattle | 10 00 00 |
| Three old Mares & a Young one | 09 10 00 |
| | 34 16 00 |

## 31. John Harris

Of Great Dawley, yeoman, taken by John Meeson and Joseph Hussey on 6 March 1746–47 and exhibited on 5 May 1747. He was buried on 27 February 1746–47.

*Goods in the House*

| | |
|---|---|
| One Iron Grate & Cheeks, Fire Shovel Tongues & hanging plate | 00 10 00 |
| One Cast Iron Purgatory plate | 00 04 00 |
| Two Iron Spitts and One Iron Dripping Pan | 00 05 00 |
| One Iron Furnace | 00 07 00 |
| One long Table & Frame & two Forms | 00 06 00 |
| One Old Wood Chair and Screen | 00 01 06 |
| One Pewter Frame and Drawers | 00 05 00 |
| One Old Glass Cage | 00 00 06 |
| Ten Pewter Dishes, & One Dozen of plates and Salver | 01 06 06 |
| Three pewter porringers, & 23 Wood Trenchers | 00 02 11 |
| One Old side Table & do square Table | 00 01 06 |
| One Old Brass Kettle, two Small Maslin Kettles and Suace pan | 00 07 06 |
| A Tin Plate & Cullinder, A pair of Bellows, & two Old pewter Candlesticks | 00 03 06 |

*Goods in the Parlour*

| | |
|---|---|
| One Old Feather Bed, Bedsteads & Hangings | 01 10 00 |
| One Coverlid and One Blankitt | 00 04 00 |
| One Old Table and Form, & One Joint Stool | 00 03 00 |
| One Small Chest, and One small Cupboard | 00 05 00 |
| One Old Clock and Case, & One Small looking Glass | 01 02 00 |

*Goods in the Deary*

| | |
|---|---|
| Two Churns and Churnstafs, and One Mitt | 00 08 00 |
| One Cheese tub, and two pails, Six Barrels and One Cooler | 01 14 06 |
| A Milk Bench and plank | 00 03 06 |
| Two Wood Bowls, five Milk pans & two Steans | 00 02 00 |

*Goods in the Entry*

| | |
|---|---|
| Two Small Tubs One Kneading Tub, & Three Gauns | 00 06 00 |
| One Cheese press and One little Wheel | 00 05 00 |

*Goods in the Room over the Parlour*

| | |
|---|---|
| One Feather Bed and Bedsteads One Coverlid and Blanket | 02 00 00 |
| One Hanging Press two small Coffers & One Chest | 01 00 00 |
| One Table, One chair & One Old Box | 00 02 06 |

Two pair of fine Hemp sheets, & two Do table cloths two Doz of
Napkins two pillows Bears & Eleven pair of Hurden Sheets . . 04 03 00

*Goods in the Room Over Dairy*
One Chaff Bed and Steads One Old Quilt and Blanket . . . 00 05 00
28 Slippins of Hurden Yarn 15 of Hemp do . . . . 00 19 06

*Goods in the Room over the House*
One Chaff Bed and Steads two Blankits and Coverlid . . . 00 08 00
Five Stone of Hemp and two of Flax . . . . . 00 15 06
Seven Fleeces of Wool in the Room over the entry . . . 00 04 08

*Outward Stock*
Nine Cows . . . . . . . . . 27 00 00
Seven two year olds . . . . . . . . 10 10 00
Nine Year Old Calfs . . . . . . . . 09 00 00
Thirteen Sheep . . . . . . . . 03 00 00
Six Horses & One Year old Colt . . . . . . 31 10 00
Three Pigs . . . . . . . . . 02 14 00
Gearing for the Horses . . . . . . . 00 18 00
One Old Waggon One Old Tumbril and One other pair of Wheels . 06 06 00
two ploughs, two old pair of Harrows . . . . . 01 00 00
Four Tun of Hea and Clover . . . . . . 05 00 00
40 Strikes of Smutted Corn & 30 Strikes of Barley . . . 06 05 00
100 Strikes of Oates . . . . . . . . 06 05 00

Wearing Apparrel and Money in purse . . . . . 02 10 00
Things Omitted and unseen . . . . . . 00 05 00

          Total . . . . 132 05 01

## THE INVENTORIES OF LILLESHALL

### 32. Thomas Cartwright

Of Lilleshall, taken by Joseph Fisher, Thomas Windsor and Thomas Harper on 9 April 1661, and exhibited on 9 May 1661. He was buried on 6 April 1661.

*Imprimis in the Hall*
1 litle Table 1 screen 1 table and frame 1 joyned fforme 3 Cheires 1 jack Toow spitt 1 grate 1 Iron back behynd the Fyre 2 payr of potgeales 2 Broches 2 payer of tongues 1 Fyre Shovell 1 payre of Chack 1 grid iron 1 dreeping pan appraised to . . . . 05 00 00

*Item in the Parlor belowe the Hall*
one joyned Bed with vallence & Curteynes 2 Fether Bedd 2 bowlsters 1 Truckle Bedd 6 Blancketts & coverings 1 pillow apprayshed to . . . . . . . . . 12 00 00
*Item* 2 joyned Presses one joyned chest 9 stooles 1 cheyre 1 grate 1 little table 1 litle Cupbord apprayshed to . . . .

*Item in ye New parlor*
1 Joyned Table & Frame 6 stooles coved with cloth 3 lether cheyers 6 cushins 1 joyned Bed with curteynes & vallenes 1 fether Bed wth 2 blanketts & 1 Rugg & one Pillow & 1 livrye Table apprayshed to . 10 00 00

*In the Chamber over ye Hall*
2 Joyned Bedstedds 2 Fether Bedds, 2 boulsters 1 Shinr of Curtaines 4 Blanketts 2 Coverings & 2 Truncks 1 joyned Presse Appraised to . . . . . . . . . 06 13 04

*Item in the Chamber over ye Parlor*
one Bedsteed 1 Bed & 3 blanketts 1 Bowlster apprayshed to . . 02 00 00

*Item in the store Chamber*
70 Cheeses 8 fflitches of Bacon 6 fflitches of Beefe 2 Pott of Butter Appraised to . . . . . . . . 14 08 00

*Item in the Kitchin*
3 Brasse Potts, 1 Iron Pott 1 Iron kettle 1 Chaffer 2 Possernetts 5 brass kettles 1 warming pann 1 Furnace 1 Frying pan aprayshed to . 05 00 00

*Item* 31 dishes of Pewter 1 Bason & Cvr 3 Saults 3 Tankerts 2 Flaggons 1 Pewter Pastye plate 1 Bason 3 Candlestickes appraysed to . . . . . . . . . . 04 00 00

*Item in Naperye Ware*
3 Dozen of Diap napkins 6 dozen of fflaxen Napkins 2 dyap Tableclothes 10 other Tableclothes 3 Towells 7 Pillow Beers 3 payre of Holland sheetes 38 payre of other sheets apraised to . . . 23 07 07

*Item in Trindle & Cooprie Ware*
8 Barrells 3 stonds 1 close bowke 1 ffirking 4 dozen of Trenchers
1 Pwdring Tubb 5 Payles 2 Gawnes appraysed to . . . 02 10 00
Item 4 Oxen praysed to . . . . . . 26 00 00
Item 6 Calves & 5 yonge Beasts . . . . . 21 06 08
Item 10 Cowes praysed to . . . . . . 42 00 00
Item 1 Nagge appraysed to . . . . . . 05 00 00
Item 4 store swyne appraysed to . . . . . 02 00 00
Item waynes Tumbrills plowes Harrowes yokes chaynes & all other
Implemtts of Husbandrye appraysed to . . . . 10 05 00

Item debts oweing to the Testator by Speralltye . . . 330 00 00
Item the Testors weareing Apparrell apprysed to . . . 06 13 04
Item 18 silver boles & 12 silver spoones appraysed to . . . 10 00 00
Item too and Fiftye sheepe apprised to . . . . 10 00 00
Item Corne in the House & Barne . . . . . 12 00 00
Item Corne upon ye Grownd appraised to . . . . 05 06 08
Item 2 Carpetts & one Cupbord Clothe with Silke Fringe appraysed
to . . . . . . . . . 01 00 00
Item 1 Lease granted by the Right Worshipfull Sr Richard Leveson
Btt of the Honable order of the Bath to the Testator for 1 lief yet
in being appraysed to . . . . . . . 50 00 00
Item ould Lomber & all other thinges that may happen to be For-
gotten . . . . . . . . . . 01 10 00

Somme . . . 618 00 06

## 33. Silvanus Adams

Of Lilleshall, blacksmith, taken by Thomas Winshurst*, William Penson and Richard Shelton on 24 April 1661 and exhibited on 14 May 1661. He was buried on 2 May 1659.

Impris his Wearinge Apparell . . . . . 05 00 00
It ffoure Mares . . . . . . . 11 10 00
It three Cows & two yeare ould heyfors . . . . 11 00 00
It six sheepe . . . . . . . . . 01 10 00
It one Joyned bed and three paire of plaine bedstids . . 01 10 00
It one greate Cheste one Truncke one Cubboarde one Coffer three
Tables two Chaires and one fforme . . . . . 01 10 00
It one greate Turnell foure stoundes five Barrells three Closboukes
one Ringlinge tub and three pailes . . . . . 01 10 00
It one Carte one Tumbrell one paire of Iron bounde Wheles and
one plowe . . . . . . . . . 01 10 00
It two paire of horse geares & one harrowe . . . . 00 10 00
It seaven pewter dishes one pewter fflaggon and other small pewter . 00 16 00
It foure brasse kettles two Iron pots . . . . . 01 10 00
It one ffetterbed three bowsters two Chafbeds one pillowe and
two pillowbeers . . . . . . . . 02 00 00
It ffoure bed hillinges & foure blankets . . . . 02 00 00
It two paire of fflaxen sheetes two paire of hempton sheetes six
paire of hurden sheets . . . . . . . 03 00 00

## THE INVENTORIES OF LILLESHALL

| | |
|---|---|
| It two Table Clothes two Towels and one douszen of Napkins | 01 00 00 |
| It foure quishins | 00 02 00 |
| It two ffire grates one fire shoovell one paire of tonges three spits one paire of Racks one dreepinge pan & other small Irons | 02 00 00 |
| Ite Corne and Malte in ye house | 01 00 00 |
| Ite Beefe and Bacone | 01 00 00 |
| Ite Butter and Cheese | 00 10 00 |
| It one swine | 00 04 00 |
| It two little birdinge Guns | 00 10 00 |
| Ite two Grindlestones | 00 04 00 |
| Ite in his shop two Anvels two paire of Bellows, three Dizlees one beckhorne three greate hammers three other hamers besides other tools as ffiles, seats bousters tongues punchees & other small tooles & Iron. | 09 00 00 |
| It the Reversion of a lease, of a small pcell of ground which was belonginge to the deceased. | 03 00 00 |
| Ite all other thinges that mighte be forgotton & lefte out | 00 05 00 |
| Some totall | 63 11 00 |

### 34. Elizabeth Cartwright

Of Lilleshall, widow, taken by Joseph Fisher, Thomas Winshurst* and John Worrall* on 13 May 1661 and exhibited on 14 May 1661. She was buried on 12 June 1658.

| | |
|---|---|
| Imprimis Two Mares | 06 00 00 |
| Item Two Bullocks | 06 08 04 |
| Item ffoure cowes | 09 06 08 |
| Item Two heifers and a calfe | 04 06 08 |
| Item Two brasse pots, three brasse pans, three Kettles, Two posnetts, one warming pan, one brasse mortar, one brasse candlesticke; and one brass skimer | 04 00 00 |
| Item ffourteen pewter dishes, Two candelsticks Two Saltcellars, and one chamber pott | 01 00 00 |
| Item Two old ffeatherbeds, Two old chaff beds, ffoure Bolsters Two Pillowes one Coverlet & two blankets | 02 00 00 |
| Item one old ioyned bedsted one trundlebed, one cubbord, Two Coffers, one table and two Chaires | 01 10 00 |
| Item one fflaxen sheet, three paire of hempen sheets, two tablecloths, one towel | 01 03 04 |
| Item Two Silver Spoones | 00 08 00 |
| Item One Iron Back, one grate, one paire of Tongs, two Spits & one Iron pot | 01 00 00 |
| Item one waine wth Iron bound wheeles two yokes wth Chaines, one Tumbrol, one Plough & all other Implements of husbandry | 02 00 00 |
| Item Two Barrells, one paile; one wetting fat, Two little looms, wth other old lumber | 00 10 00 |
| Item the deceased wearing appel | 03 00 00 |
| Item one frying pan and whatever old that belonged to ye deceased as old Lomber | 00 10 00 |
| Some total is | 53 02 08 |

## 35. Mary Cade

Of Donnington, Lilleshall, widow, taken by Thomas Moulton and Richard Rowley, with others, on 12 September 1664, and exhibited on 18 November 1664. She was buried on 1 March 1662-63.

| | | |
|---|---|---|
| Impris. one Cowe | 03 | 00 | 00 |
| Itm one Cowe let out to hire wth the interest | 03 | 10 | 00 |
| Itme brasse and pewter | 01 | 06 | 08 |
| Item one iron ketle one iron morter two spitts & two Dreepinge pans | 01 | 10 | 00 |
| Itm one feather bed and bed steads two coverletts two blanketts two paire of hempton sheets one flaxen sheet one flaxen table cloathe and one Diaper table cloath | 05 | 00 | 00 |
| Itm halfe a duz of flaxen napkins two diaper napkins and two towells | 00 | 14 | 08 |
| Itm wooll | 00 | 08 | 00 |
| Itm barrells stunds coolers and peales | 01 | 00 | 00 |
| Itm two sofes two formes stooles & chaires | 00 | 08 | 00 |
| Itm one fryinge pan | 00 | 01 | 06 |
| Itm one paire of iron bound wheels and all other implements of husbandry | 03 | 00 | 00 |
| Itm her wareinge apparell | 03 | 00 | 00 |
| Itm two ioyned chestes one trunke and three coffers | 01 | 10 | 00 |
| Itm any left out or forgotten unprized | 00 | 05 | 00 |
| Sume is | 24 | 13 | 10 |

## 36. William Whitmore

Of Lilleshall Lodge, yeoman and apparently keeper, taken by Thomas Windsor and John Whitmore on 16 September 1667 and exhibited on 4 October 1667. William Whitmore, 'ye keeper' was buried on 15 September 1667. In his will made on 4 June 1667 he left to his wife, Margaret, his leasehold property at The Hammers in Donnington township.

Imprs.

| | | | |
|---|---|---|---|
| Three Cowes | 05 | 00 | 00 |
| one Mare | 02 | 00 | 00 |
| one Bull | 02 | 00 | 00 |
| one Bullcalfe | 01 | 00 | 00 |
| two Heyfors | 05 | 00 | 00 |
| two Swine | 01 | 00 | 00 |
| Geese and Henns | 00 | 07 | 00 |
| two ffether beds | 02 | 00 | 00 |
| ffouer Boulsters and three Pillowes | 01 | 00 | 00 |
| Seaven Blacketts and three Covrlids | 02 | 06 | 08 |
| one little Longe Bed | 00 | 06 | 00 |
| Two Coffers | 00 | 05 | 00 |

## THE INVENTORIES OF LILLESHALL

| | |
|---|---|
| two Trunckes | 00 13 04 |
| one Deske | 00 03 00 |
| one Presse and Cubbard | 00 15 00 |
| one Box with Drawers in | 00 02 06 |
| two Tables with Cubbards in | 00 10 00 |
| one little Table | 04 00 00 |
| one Joyned Chare | 00 05 00 |
| two other Chares | 00 02 00 |
| one Chestt | 00 02 00 |
| ffouer Basketts | 00 02 06 |
| Twelve Pewter Dishes Eight Plates ffouer Saucers nine pewter Candlesticks three Pewter Chamber potts two fflaggons one Tankards and one Dozen of Spoones | 03 00 00 |
| ffourteene Glass Bottles fouer stone bottles and Six glasses | 00 02 00 |
| Three Brasse Pottes one Big brasse Kettle three other Kettles one Litte Pann two Skellets and a Skimmer | 04 00 00 |
| one Dreepeing Pann and Two Spitts | 00 05 00 |
| ffyer Shovell and Tonges | 00 02 00 |
| one plate behind the ffyer | 00 05 00 |
| one small Pare of Racks | 00 04 00 |
| one Large Grate | 00 04 00 |
| one Pare of fflaxen Sheetes Nine Pare of hempen Sheetes Twelve pare of Canvis Sheetes fouer Towells fouer Table Cloathes three dozen of Napkins ffouer pillowe Beeres | 05 13 00 |
| Six dozen of Trenchers | 00 05 00 |
| Woodden Ware as Boles Dishes Ladles &c | 01 00 00 |
| Cooperey Ware a Churne a Cheesetub a bouke a Piggin a Gaune a little turnell and a bigg Scaldinge Turnell | 00 12 00 |
| two halfe hoggsheads & two other Barrells | 00 16 03 |
| Butter and Cheese in the house | 02 10 00 |
| Bacon in the house | 01 05 00 |
| Hopps in the house | 00 06 08 |
| Bowes Gunns and all Manner of Keepers Implements and engins | 01 10 00 |
| Implements of Husbandry two Plowes two Pare of Iron traces a Cart Sadle & other Small thinges | 00 10 00 |
| Corne in the house one hundred Strike of Maultt three Strike of Wheate Sixtey strike of Maslin tenn strike of Pease and tenn Strike of Oates | 17 14 00 |
| a Stagg Skin and fouer buckskins | 00 15 00 |
| Money in the house at the time of his Death | 79 00 00 |
| Thinges omitted and not Appraysed | 00 05 00 |
| Sume totall | 134 11 04 |

## 37. William Leeke

Of Lilleshall, miller, taken by Thomas Windsor and Robert Shelton on 12 October 1668 and exhibited on 11 November 1668. He was buried on 23 September 1668.

| | |
|---|---|
| Im. One Cow and two heifors prizd | 06 10 00 |
| Item one little mare prizd | 02 10 00 |

| | | |
|---|---|---|
| Item Brass and Pewter of all sorts . . . . . | 02 00 00 |

*Item Goods in the dwelling house*
viz one little cubbord one table board, Chires, Stooles fourmes, one dreeping pan one Iorne potte, two broashes one paire of Coberts Grate for the fyre fireshovell and Tongues Pott goales and Bellows . 01 10 00

*Item In ye Chamber ovr ye house*
| | |
|---|---|
| beding and other Small Implements of household goods . . | 06 10 00 |
| Item Linnens of all sorts . . . . . . . | 01 10 00 |
| Item Butter & Cheese in the house . . . . . | 01 00 00 |

*Item in the Chitchin or backhouse and in the Seller*
Coopery ware as barrells Loomes and other small traineryware . 01 05 00

*Item In the Barne*
| | |
|---|---|
| Corne & hay . . . . . . . . . | 04 00 00 |
| Item the Swine as prised . . . . . . . | 02 00 00 |
| Item the deceased wareing Apparell . . . . . | 02 10 00 |
| Item Ready mony in his Cooffer . . . . . . | 00 10 00 |
| Item things omitted and not seens. . . . . . | 00 05 00 |
| Sume is . | 31 00 00 |

## 38. Robert Shelton

Of Lilleshall, yeoman, taken by Thomas Winshurst,* Richard Shelton, Lewis Dale* and Richard Crowder on 13 November 1671, and exhibited on 31 January 1671-71. He was buried on 25 October 1671.

| | |
|---|---|
| Imprm. one oxe praysed at . . . . . . . | 06 00 00 |
| one bull & one bullocke at . . . . . . . | 06 00 00 |
| seven younge beasts praysed at . . . . . | 16 06 08 |
| seven cowes at . . . . . . . . | 22 03 04 |
| five horses and Mares at . . . . . . . | 20 00 00 |
| three ould swine & five shoates at . . . . . | 04 05 00 |
| Twenty three sheepe at . . . . . . . | 06 00 00 |
| Waines Cartes plowes yokes Chaines and all Implements of husbandry whatsoever wee prayse at . . . . . | 12 00 00 |
| Sawed boards about ye house at . . . . . | 06 00 00 |
| Hay about ye house and barne at . . . . . | 10 00 00 |
| Hard Corne in ye barne at . . . . . . | 09 13 00 |
| Barley in the barne . . . . . . . | 16 13 04 |
| Oates wee prayse at . . . . . . . . | 14 00 00 |
| peease wee prayse at . . . . . . . | 04 00 00 |
| Brasse wee prayse at. . . . . . . . | 04 10 00 |
| Three Masslin Candlesticks at . . . . . . | 00 10 00 |
| pewter at . . . . . . . . . | 01 02 00 |
| Tinn ware at . . . . . . . . . | 00 04 00 |
| one Jacke and one Iron pott at . . . . . . | 01 00 00 |

## THE INVENTORIES OF LILLESHALL

| | | |
|---|---|---|
| Twoo broken plates at ye fire | 00 10 00 | |
| one Iron dreeping pan & twoo broaches | 00 07 06 | |
| Two grates twoo fire shovels twoo pare of tonges & one grid Iron and one pare of Cobberts and one Mortter and pot geales at | 01 00 00 | |
| The table board and stooles and chaires & shelves in the house at | 01 10 00 | |
| one gun and three pistolls at | 01 10 00 | |
| The bed in the ould parler & all yt belonges to it at | 03 00 00 | |
| one presse one coffer one Chaire in ye same Roome at | 01 03 04 | |
| Holland ware in ye same Roome at | 00 05 00 | |
| two kneading turnells two cheespreses and one wheele and all the Lumber in the kitchin at | 02 00 00 | |
| The Barrells and Cheesfatts and milke pans and all thinges in ye buttery at | 01 10 00 | |
| one Little bed and one barrell and Chestub and three bottels at | 01 06 08 | |
| twoo little beds and one forme at | 01 10 00 | |
| one other bed & all ye belonges to it at | 02 00 00 | |
| Linnens in ye house ready made at | 03 00 00 | |
| Cheese at | 01 12 00 | |
| yarne in ye house at | 00 03 04 | |
| fflax in ye house at | 00 05 00 | |
| one bed in ye best Chamber at | 05 00 00 | |
| one table one coffer one truncke & one box | 01 00 00 | |
| two Chayres & twoo stooles at | 00 07 00 | |
| Eight strike of Malt at | 01 00 00 | |
| one straw basket & an ould Hodgshead | 00 02 00 | |
| twoo little tables in ye parler & one forme at | 01 10 00 | |
| one press bed at | 01 00 00 | |
| wearing Apparell at | 06 03 04 | |
| two desks twoo boxes one truncke and ye . . . in ye parler at | 01 00 00 | |
| Hempe & flax at | 01 00 00 | |
| bookes at | 01 00 00 | |
| If anythinge bee forgotten wee prayse it at | 00 02 06 | |
| money in his purse | 01 00 00 | |
| The whole sum is | 175 06 00 | |
| There is due Uppon bills & bonds as wee suppose certayne | 150 00 00 | |
| There is due Uppon bills & bonds as wee suppose desperate | 107 13 04 | |
| Money yt was in ye house | 12 00 00 | |

### 39. Joan Bradshaw

Of Lilleshall, servant to Thomas Windsor, taken by William Worrall and Thomas Bradburne* and exhibited on 15 March 1671-72. The Inventory is undated. Joan Bradshaw was buried on 8 March 1671-72.

| | | |
|---|---|---|
| Imprimis. In Reddy Mony | 00 05 00 | |
| Item. Her wearing apparell, of stuff or woollen | 03 00 00 | |
| Item. Her Linnen of all Kinds; both small or great whether Holland, Scotch cloth, fflaxen, hempen or hurden | 03 00 00 | |
| Item. In bondes | 57 00 00 | |
| Item. for whatsoever we have omitted any way | 00 01 06 | |
| The whole amounting to | 63 06 06 | |

## 40. Thomas Windsor

Of Lilleshall, yeoman, taken by Henry Haughton, vicar, Ralph Barrett, Andrew Shelton, Thomas Bradbourne* and John Holmes on 22 December 1673 and exhibited on 23 December 1672. He was buried on 15 December 1673.

| | |
|---|---|
| Imprimis. Readey moneys in the house And his Apparrell prized at | 60 00 00 |
| It. a Lease in beinge for Two Lives prized at | 100 00 00 |

*It. in his Bedchamber*

| | |
|---|---|
| Two Standinge Beds wth a Testore. Two ffether Beds Bousters pillowes Coverlids Blankets Curtaines Vallons & other ffurniture thereunto belongeinge prized at | 10 00 00 |
| It. in the said roome one Cupboarde Two Chests one Truncke one Table Booarde one Joyned forme Chaires quishins and other ffurniture in the said Roome prized at | 02 00 00 |

*It. in the Chamber over the said roome*

| | |
|---|---|
| one Joyned Bed with Curtaines Vallons & other furniture thereunto Belongeinge prized at | 05 00 00 |
| It. in the said roome on Table Two Chests one Truncke Two Coffers one Joyned forme Chaires quishins & other furniture therein prized at | 03 00 00 |

*It. in the Hall*

| | |
|---|---|
| one Table Booard Two Joyned formes Chaires Stooles quishins & other things theireunto Belongeinge prized at | 01 10 00 |

*It. in the Chamber over the said Hall*

| | |
|---|---|
| one Bed one Table one Coffer & other furniture Theire in prized at | 01 00 00 |

*It. in the next roome theireunto Adioyninge*

| | |
|---|---|
| Two Beds with Beddinge & all other furniture in the said roome prized at | 02 00 00 |
| It. Linnens of all sorts in the severall roomes prized at | 05 00 00 |
| It. Brass & peuter of all sorts in the severall roomes prized at | 10 00 00 |
| It. Iron Ware of all sorts in the said House prized at | 01 10 00 |
| It. Barrells Tubs peales and other Wooden Ware of all sorts in the said House prized at | 02 10 00 |
| It. Butter Cheese Beefe Bacon and other pvition in the said house prized at | 05 00 00 |
| It. five Draught horses prized at | 20 00 00 |
| It. Eight Cowes prized at | 24 00 00 |
| It. Corne in the house and Barnes prized at | 20 00 00 |
| It. Corne sowed or Growinge on the ground prized at | 03 00 00 |
| It. Heay prized at | 05 00 00 |
| It. Two Carts one Tumbrell and all other Implements of Husbandrey theireunto belonging prized at | 08 00 00 |

## THE INVENTORIES OF LILLESHALL

| | |
|---|---|
| It. Three Hives of Bees prized at | 00 10 00 |
| It. pullen of all sorts prized at | 00 05 00 |
| It. Debts oweinge unto the deceased | 100 00 00 |
| It. more Desprate Debts oweinge | 50 00 00 |
| It. all other things that might not come to our knowledge or fforgotten prized at | 00 15 00 |
| Summ Totall is | 440 00 00 |

### 41. Ann Leeke

Of Lilleshall, widow, taken by Lewis Dale,* Andrew Shelton, John Holmes and William Cartwright on 24 November 1675, and exhibited on 9 March 1675–76. She was buried on 3 November 1675.

*Imprimis*

| | |
|---|---|
| her weareinge Apparrell | 02 00 00 |
| It moneys in her purse | 03 00 00 |

*It in the dwellinge house*

| | |
|---|---|
| one Table Board, one press Cubboard fformes & Chaires prized at | 01 05 00 |

*It In the parlor*

| | |
|---|---|
| one Joyned Bed one Chest one Coffer one Chaire prized at | 01 00 00 |

*It. In the Chamber ovr the plore*

| | |
|---|---|
| Two paire of bedstids & Beddinge & Bedclothes theire unto belonginge prizd at | 04 00 00 |
| 2 Coffers prized at | 00 03 04 |

*It. in a little room Adioyninge to the plore*

| | |
|---|---|
| one little Table Board & one fforme prizd | 00 05 00 |

*It. in the Kitchin*

| | |
|---|---|
| one ffurnace & Brewinge vessels therein prizd at | 02 00 00 |

*It in the sellar*

| | |
|---|---|
| Barrells and other Wooden vessels prizd at | 00 13 04 |

| | |
|---|---|
| It. Butter & Cheese in the house & Bacon | 01 00 00 |
| It. Store swine & pullen prizd at | 01 10 00 |
| It. Lynnens of all sorts | 04 00 00 |
| It Brass & pewter of all sorts prizd at | 03 00 00 |
| It Iron Ware of all sorts prized at | 01 00 00 |
| It Two Cowes & one Twinter heifer prizd at | 07 00 00 |
| It all other things that mighte not Come to our knowledge prized at | 00 02 00 |
| The totall summ is | 31 16 08 |

## 42. Mary Shelton

Of Muxton, taken by Richard Shelton and Richard Crowther on 24 May 1676 and exhibited on 20 September 1676. She was buried on 5 May 1676.

| | | | |
|---|---|---|---|
| 16 pare of Sheetes and one Singell sheete | 05 | 18 | 00 |
| 1 dusen and 4 napkines | 00 | 10 | 00 |
| 2 Tabell Cloathes and 4 towells | 01 | 07 | 00 |
| 2 Sillver boules | 05 | 00 | 00 |
| 4 Silver spownes 1 silver Birdcall and one silver seale | 01 | 06 | 08 |
| 9 peesces of gould | 09 | 16 | 00 |
| one bond | 27 | 00 | 00 |
| another bond | 06 | 00 | 00 |
| the Remainder of A bond | 14 | 00 | 00 |
| the Remainder of another bond | 10 | 00 | 00 |
| A bill of debtes | 02 | 10 | 00 |
| A bond of | 20 | 00 | 00 |
| 3 ffether bedes 4 fether boulsters & 3 fether pillowse 3 blanketts 3 Coverledes and one Chafe bed | 06 | 06 | 00 |
| 5 pillowe bieares | 00 | 10 | 00 |
| 2 Joyne bedstides one Joyne pres and one peece of weanescote | 01 | 12 | 08 |
| 4 Cuschines | 00 | 04 | 00 |
| 2 Chearse | 00 | 02 | 06 |
| one Cheste & 2 Cofirse | 00 | 15 | 00 |
| one Tabell boarde | 00 | 04 | 00 |
| 2 Whiches and A Straw bascet | 01 | 02 | 00 |
| one Joyne forme | 00 | 01 | 00 |
| 8 pewter dischis one bason 2 sawsers 6 spownes one tankarde one fladgin 2 salltes 2 Chamberpotes | 01 | 09 | 02 |
| 3 bras panes 2 brasse cettelse 2 bras potes one bras morter one pestel on bras candellsticke | 02 | 09 | 04 |
| one Lowkeing glas | 00 | 02 | 06 |
| one warming pan | 00 | 02 | 00 |
| one grate 1 pare of tonges 1 spit | 00 | 05 | 00 |
| one Chafforne | 00 | 05 | 00 |
| one small wheele | 00 | 02 | 06 |
| one beame & scales with 5 leade waites wayinge 20 li | 00 | 03 | 02 |
| one tin pastery plate | 00 | 01 | 00 |
| 10 strikes of mallte | 01 | 07 | 00 |
| of dreg mallt 2 strike & A hallfe | 00 | 05 | 00 |
| pte of A briscote of beefe | 00 | 02 | 00 |
| 2 sides of backen | 01 | 10 | 00 |
| 1 chese pes | 00 | 01 | 00 |
| 3 stundes one hallfe strike 1 hallfe peck 1 search 1 sive & 1 riddell | 00 | 10 | 06 |
| A stone of Rough hempe | 00 | 03 | 00 |
| Teare of hempe and yarne | 01 | 03 | 00 |
| one Close Stoule & Pan | 00 | 07 | 00 |
| one Iron pot one brass cettell | 00 | 02 | 06 |
| 5 Chesfets 4 millke boles 2 dosen of trencherse one Clansinge sive one butter printe A Baskett wth hops in it | 00 | 12 | 00 |
| one brasce scumer | 00 | 01 | 00 |

| | | | |
|---|---|---|---|
| 3 steanse & one milke pan . . . . . . . | 00 | 00 | 08 |
| one bascet for linen Clothes 1 Churne 2 Steanes 1 Reele one pare of earwingels . . . . . . . . . | 00 | 02 | 06 |
| 3 peales 1 pidgin . . . . . . . . | 00 | 02 | 00 |
| 2 Small barrellse . . . . . . . . | 00 | 05 | 00 |
| one Callfe . . . . . . . . . | 00 | 12 | 00 |
| wearinge Apparrel . . . . . . . . | 07 | 00 | 00 |
| In hir pocket . . . . . . . . . | 04 | 00 | 00 |
| one bed ticke . . . . . . . . . | 01 | 10 | 00 |
| | 129 | 01 | 07 |

## 43. Thomas Newell

Of Lilleshall, taken by John Husband, Richard Shelton, Richard Crowther and Richard Eykin on 3 January 1676–77 and proved on 4 May 1677. He was buried on 11 December 1676.

| | | | |
|---|---|---|---|
| Inpr. Two Geldings & one Mare prised at . . . . | 10 | 00 | 00 |
| It five Cowes prised at . . . . . . . | 17 | 00 | 00 |
| it fowre twinter Bease prised at . . . . . . | 08 | 00 | 00 |
| It Three Earlings prised at . . . . . . . | 03 | 00 | 00 |
| It two weaninge Calves prised at . . . . . . | 01 | 00 | 00 |
| It one fat swine & two store swine prised at . . . | 02 | 04 | 00 |
| It corne of all sorts prised at (in the house) . . . | 07 | 00 | 00 |
| It hay prised at . . . . . . . . | 03 | 00 | 00 |
| It corne growinge prised at . . . . . . . | 04 | 00 | 00 |
| It one cart one tumbrell and all other Implemts of husbandry prised at . . . . . . . . . . | 05 | 00 | 00 |
| It ducks Gease & hens prised at . . . . . | 00 | 10 | 00 |

*It in the Backhouse*

| | | | |
|---|---|---|---|
| one weeting fat one big turnell & other things therein prised at . | 01 | 10 | 00 |

*It in the dwellinge howse*

| | | | |
|---|---|---|---|
| one longe table 6 joyned stooles one Cubbord 3 Chaires one little table one fire grate fire showell & tonges one jack three spits prised at . . . . . . . . . . | 03 | 00 | 00 |
| It Brass & pewter of all sorts prised at . . . . | 05 | 00 | 00 |
| It two Iron pots one drepinge pan 2 frying pans & other Ware prised at . . . . . . . . . . | 00 | 15 | 00 |
| It Butter & Cheese hemp & flax prised . . . . | 02 | 00 | 00 |

*It in the Chamber over the dwelling howse*

| | | | |
|---|---|---|---|
| goods of all sorts prised at . . . . . . . | 01 | 00 | 00 |
| It 12 paire of sheetes one dussen of napkins three towells three table clothes too plillows Beares & all other lynnens prised at . . | 04 | 10 | 00 |

*It in the Chamber over the plor*

| | | | |
|---|---|---|---|
| two paire of plaine bedsteds 4 Coffers 3 straw wiskets prised at | 02 | 10 | 00 |

*It in the said Chamber*
One fetherbed one Chaffbed Bedclothes thereon, & other things in
the said Chamber prised at . . . . . . .    02 00 00

*It in the plor*
one fether Bed and bedclothes & boulster prised at . . .    01 10 00
*It in the sd roome*
one chest & one table Boord & other things therein prised at .    00 10 00

*It in the little Butterie adioyning to the sd roome*
two Fligges of Bacon & one Turnell & other things therein prised .    01 00 00

*It in the Bigger plot*
two Beds & beddinge & bedclothes theron prised at . . .    02 00 00

*It in the Butterie adioyinge to the dwellinge howse*
one Brewing Stond One little Barrell one chourne & other wooden
vessels therein prised at . . . . . . .    00 10 00

It his weareinge Apparrel prised . . . . . .    03 00 00

It all other things that might not come to our knowledge prised at .    00 03 00

In toto .    91 12 00

## 44. Lewis Dale

Of Lilleshall Lodge, keeper, taken by Andrew Shelton and Richard Lockley on 12 January 1676-77 and exhibited on 4 May 1677. He was buried on 1 December 1676.

Impr. Nine Cowes and a bull . . . . . . .    40 06 08
fore too yere ould hefers . . . . . . . .    09 06 08
fore yere oulds . . . . . . . . .    04 10 00
too Coults . . . . . . . . . .    07 10 00
too Ould horses . . . . . . . . .    06 00 00
One fat Swine and fore young Swine . . . . .    03 15 00
Six fliches of Bacon . . . . . . . . .    03 12 00
for Chese and Butter . . . . . . . .    04 00 00
In Bras and pewter and Ironware . . . . . .    06 00 00
All maner of wooden ware . . . . . . .    02 10 00
All manner of poultrey . . . . . . . .    00 05 00
halph a Befe . . . . . . . . . .    01 10 00
Corne in the Barne and Upon the Ground . . . .    05 00 00
his wareing Aparill and money in his purs . . . .    10 00 00
All mannr of Beding and Linens . . . . . .    20 00 00
All mannr of Husbandry ware . . . . . . .    02 00 00
for three Gunnes . . . . . . . . .    02 00 00
All manner of trumpere or Anything forgoten . . . .    00 05 00

128 09 08

## THE INVENTORIES OF LILLESHALL

### 45. William Blockley

Of Lilleshall, carpenter, taken by Hugh Laurence* and William Hammersley on 2 March 1676-77 and exhibited on 4 May 1677. He was buried on 25 February 1676-77.

| | |
|---|---|
| Imprimis: In Ready Mony . . . . . . . | 01 10 00 |
| Item: Wearing apparrell . . . . . . . | 03 00 00 |

*Item: In his bed Chamber*
One Joyn bed with all its furniture one Press one Chest one coffer one table board one fforme . . . . . . 04 00 00

*Item: In ye chamber over his bed Chamber*
one Joyn bed one Truckell bed with all their Furniture together . 03 00 00

*Item: In ye little bed chamber*

| | |
|---|---|
| 2 beds well furnished . . . . . . . | 01 10 00 |
| Item: Linen of all sorts whatsoever . . . . . | 03 00 00 |

*Item: In ye house*
one Press one Table board with fformes chairs stooles & all things thereunto belonging . . . . . . . . 01 00 00

*Item: In ye Chamber over ye house*

| | |
|---|---|
| for all Bacon Butter Cheese straw baskets &c. . . . . | 04 00 00 |
| Item: Brass Pewter & Iron ware of all sorts anywhere belonging to ye house . . . . . . . . . | 02 06 08 |
| item: Barrells, boucks, turnells, tubs and all sorts of Trindell ware . | 01 10 00 |
| Item: Three Cowes . . . . . . . . | 11 00 00 |
| Item: Too store piggs . . . . . . . | 01 00 00 |
| Item: Poultry of all sorts . . . . . . . | 00 05 00 |
| Item: Implements of husbandry of all sorts made or unmade . . | 03 00 00 |
| Item: Tooles in The Shop of all sorts bigg or little . . . | 07 00 00 |
| Item: Corne on ye ground . . . . . . | 01 10 00 |
| Item: ffor things forgotten . . . . . . . | 00 08 06 |
| The whole sume amounts to . | 49 00 02 |

### 46. Humphrey Mansell

Of Lilleshall, labourer, taken by Walter Brodhurst and John Husband on 15 April 1679 and exhibited on 7 April 1678. He was buried on 13 March 1678-79.

| | |
|---|---|
| Impris. The deceds wearing apparrell & money in his purse . . | 02 00 00 |
| Three Cowes & one calfe . . . . . . . | 07 00 00 |
| One horse . . . . . . . . . | 01 10 00 |
| 2 Sowes & ten pigs . . . . . . . . | 01 00 00 |

*In the parlour*
1 Table & frame joynd forme 5 turned chairs & 1 chest & 6 cushions   00 10 00

9 pair of Course sheets 3 hempen sheets 1 hempen table cloth 11 napkins 1 pillow beer . . . . . . . 00 12 00

*In the Chamber over it*

1 halfe headed bedsted 1 Chaffe bed 1 feather boulster 1 pair blanketts 1 coverlid & 1 pillow . . . . . 00 10 00
1 Truckle bedsted 1 Chaffe bed & boulster & 1 blankett & 1 coverlid . . . . . . . . . 00 02 06
1 chest 1 coffer & 1 deske . . . . . . 00 02 06
1 old ffirken wth some verinice in it . . . . 00 00 06
2 mault whisketts 2 strikes 1 pecke 1 hair sieve & 1 search . . 00 01 00
mault . . . . . . . . . 00 02 06

*In the Chamber over ye house*

2 Truckle bedsteds 1 featherbed 1 flocke bed 2 chaffe boulsters 2 blanketts & 2 coverlids . . . . . . 01 00 06
beefe & bacon . . . . . . . 00 10 00

*In the house*

9 pewter dishes 3 porrengers 6 spoones 2 pewter candlestickes 3 brass candlesticks 2 sawcers 1 pewter chamberpott 1 strongwater bottle 1 flagon 3 pewter guns & 1 tankard . . . 00 13 04
1 brasse furnace 1 brasse pott 3 kettles 1 skellet 1 ladle & 1 skimmer 01 00 00
1 Iron pott 1 dripping pan 1 frying pan 1 grate 1 fireshovel & 1 pair of tongs 1 chafing dish 1 pair of pott gales 1 pair of pott hookes & 1 hacking knife 1 Spitt 1 Smoothing Iron & 1 pair of cobbarts . . . . . . . . 00 06 08
1 table 3 stooles 1 chair 1 spinning wheele . . . 00 01 06

*In the Buttery*

4 barrells 1 chiere 1 bottle 2 peals 5 brewing vessells & 1 Cooller 1 piggin & 1 milking stund . . . . . . 00 00 06

*In the Barne*

hay, saw'd boards 2 pitch forkes 1 spade 2 rakes 2 broome hookes 1 hay hooke . . . . . . . . 00 03 04
Corne on ye ground . . . . . . . 00 06 08
debts oweing to the dec'd whereof some are desperte . . 01 00 00
Things omitted forgotten & not seen . . . . 00 02 06

Totall . . . . 19 02 02

## 47. John Shelton

Of ye Walnut Tree, Muxton, Yeoman, taken by Henry Haughton, Andrew Shelton, John Spearman and William Roston on 22 September 1680 and exhibited on 7 October 1680. He was buried on 7 July 1680.

Item in Ready Money . . . . . . . 05 00 00
Item Wearinge Apparrell . . . . . . 10 00 00
Item Six four year old Bullocks . . . . . 18 00 00
Item Nine 3 year ould beasts . . . . . 13 10 00

| | |
|---|---|
| Item ffive yearlings | 04 00 00 |
| Item Ten Cowes | 21 05 00 |
| Item Six Calves | 04 00 00 |
| Item Three Mares & Two Colts | 15 00 00 |
| Item one Score of Sheep | 02 10 00 |
| Item Three Swine a Sow & piggs | 02 10 00 |
| Item Poultrey of all sorts | 00 05 00 |
| Item Corne in the house & Barne of all sorts Threst & Unthrest wth Malte | 27 00 00 |
| Item Beef Bacon Butter & Cheese | 01 10 00 |
| Item Brass & pewter of all sorts | 02 00 00 |
| Item Beds & Beddinge of all Sorts with their furniture & Appurtenances thereto belonginge | 15 00 00 |
| Item Linnen of all Sorts | 06 00 00 |
| Item Trunke Chests Coffres Tabl boards Chairs & Stooles of all sorts | 02 00 00 |
| All Implements of Husbandry | 05 00 00 |
| Item Trindell ware of all sorts | 01 02 00 |
| Item Dripping pans grates Broaches & Ironware of all Sorts within ye house | 00 10 00 |
| Item Hemp and fflax | 00 05 00 |
| Item due upon Bond | 120 00 00 |
| Item despreate debts | 15 00 00 |
| Item for all things Omitted or forgotten of what Nature Soever within doors and without | 00 02 06 |
| Summa totalis | 291 09 06 |

## 48. Richard Shelton

Of Lilleshall, taken by Thomas Wicksteed, Thomas Howell, Walter Brodhurst, William Blakemore, Thomas Proolock* and Edward Fleming on 2 August 1683 and exhibited on 5 October 1683. He was buried on 22 July 1683.

*Imprs. the Chamber next ye Streete*

| | |
|---|---|
| 4 pares of hempen sheetes | 02 00 00 |
| two pare of fflaxen Sheetes | 01 00 00 |
| one Dozen of fine napkines | 00 08 00 |
| two Dozen of Coorse Napkines | 00 08 00 |
| three fine Tabell Clothes | 00 10 00 |
| two pare of hurden Sheetes | 00 06 00 |
| two hurden Tabell Clothes | 00 01 00 |
| one Cofer | 00 06 00 |
| one Joyne Chest | 00 08 00 |
| 18 poundes of fflax | 00 06 08 |
| 30 poundes of hempe | 00 10 00 |
| one fetherbed wth bed stides on Rudge and 3 blankets 1 pare of Sheetes wth boulster pillow | 02 10 00 |
| 29 ould cheeses | 01 10 00 |
| for a pshall of woll & yorne | 00 07 00 |
| 1 Stoole | 00 01 06 |
| 2 halfe Strikes | 00 01 06 |

| | |
|---|---|
| 3 Strikes of wheate . . . . . . . . | 00 10 00 |
| 2 Cushines . . . . . . . . . | 00 00 08 |

*in ye Chanber over ye house*

| | |
|---|---|
| one cofir wth oulde linenes in it . . . . . | 00 07 00 |
| one pare of flaxen sheetes . . . . . . . | 00 10 00 |
| 10 pillow beares . . . . . . . . | 00 10 00 |
| one Cofir . . . . . . . . . . | 00 05 00 |
| one bidge chest . . . . . . . . | 00 05 00 |
| one Joyne bed wth ye furnetuer there to . . . . | 02 00 00 |
| one halfe teasterbed & furnetier there to belonginge . . | 01 10 00 |
| 12 Strikes of muncorne . . . . . . . | 01 16 00 |
| one Straw bascet . . . . . . . . | 00 01 00 |
| one littell Cofir . . . . . . . . | 00 01 00 |
| for beefe & baken . . . . . . . . | 00 13 00 |

*in ye Chamber over the new parler*

| | |
|---|---|
| 48 Cheeses . . . . . . . . . | 02 00 00 |
| 20 poundes of fflax . . . . . . . . | 00 06 08 |
| one Joyne bed wth ye furneture there to belong . . | 02 10 00 |
| one large press . . . . . . . . | 01 00 00 |
| 4 Cushines . . . . . . . . . | 00 02 00 |
| 6 Shilfes . . . . . . . . . . | 00 02 00 |
| one Chest . . . . . . . . . | 00 10 00 |
| 4 pare of hempen Sheetes . . . . . . . | 01 16 00 |
| 3 pare of flaxen Sheetes . . . . . . . | 01 10 00 |
| 3 Tabell clothes one being Diaper . . . . . | 01 00 00 |
| 4 pillow beares . . . . . . . . | 00 04 00 |
| 15 napkines fine . . . . . . . . | 00 07 06 |
| 13 more napkins . . . . . . . . | 00 06 06 |
| 2 Diaper napkins . . . . . . . . | 00 02 00 |
| 12 Slipinges of flaxen yorne . . . . . . | 00 06 00 |
| one bed in ye littel Chamber . . . . . . | 01 00 00 |

*In the Parler next ye Streete*

| | |
|---|---|
| one bibel & other small Bookes . . . . . . | 00 10 00 |
| one Joyne Bed wth ye furneteur thereto belonginge . . | 03 00 00 |
| one Large Chest . . . . . . . . | 00 06 00 |
| one Tabell & Carpett . . . . . . . | 00 07 00 |
| one large Press . . . . . . . . | 01 00 00 |
| 2 Stooles . . . . . . . . . | 00 01 00 |
| one box . . . . . . . . . | 00 01 00 |
| one Closse Stoole & pan . . . . . . . | 00 02 00 |
| one burdinge Gun . . . . . . . . | 00 05 00 |
| 3 Chene dishes . . . . . . . . | 00 01 00 |
| one lookinge Glass . . . . . . . . | 00 00 06 |
| one Reele . . . . . . . . . | 00 00 06 |

*In the Comon Roume callde ye house*

| | |
|---|---|
| one Tabell wth 2 formes . . . . . . . | 01 00 00 |
| 2 cheares . . . . . . . . . | 00 06 08 |
| 3 Stooles wth A Liverey Tabell . . . . . | 00 10 00 |
| 2 Salt Cofiers . . . . . . . . . | 00 02 00 |
| one pare of gardin Sheares . . . . . . . | 00 01 00 |

# THE INVENTORIES OF LILLESHALL 209

| | |
|---|---|
| 2 fire Shovells 1 pare of Tongues | 00 02 00 |
| one grate wth 2 pare of potkeales & 3 pare of pot hookes | 00 10 00 |
| 2 drpinge panes | 00 05 00 |
| 3 broaches | 00 02 00 |
| one Warminge pan | 00 03 04 |
| one Cuttinge iron | 00 00 06 |
| 2 Chusshines | 00 01 00 |
| in ye Sarvantes Chamber one bed | 00 10 00 |

*In ye new parler*

| | |
|---|---|
| 7 Cheares | 00 17 06 |
| 1 Stoole | 00 00 06 |
| one Casce of boxes | 00 02 00 |
| one deske | 00 01 06 |
| one puter Still | 00 01 06 |
| one littell grate | 00 01 06 |
| Glasse bottelles & Earthen plates | 00 02 00 |
| one lookeinge glas | 00 02 06 |
| one littell Tabell & Carpet | 00 02 06 |

*In ye Butterey*

| | |
|---|---|
| fore brass potes | 01 00 00 |
| five brasse panes | 03 00 00 |
| 17 puter dishes | 01 10 00 |
| 3 puter ffladgynes | 00 04 06 |
| 6 porringers | 00 02 00 |
| 3 puter Chamber potes | 00 01 06 |
| 3 puter Salltes | 00 01 00 |
| 1 pot posnit | 00 02 06 |
| 4 kettells | 00 06 08 |

*In ye kitchin*

| | |
|---|---|
| 2 Iron pottes | 00 10 00 |
| 3 Skellets | 00 02 00 |
| 2 ffleshe forkes | 00 00 06 |
| 2 bastinge Spoones | 00 00 06 |
| one brasse Skimer | 00 04 00 |
| one brass furnes | 00 05 00 |
| 2 fryinge panes | 00 01 06 |
| Cowperey ware of all Sortes | 01 00 00 |
| one mallte mill | 01 00 00 |
| one Cheese pres | 00 02 00 |
| one hare suiech & sarch | 00 00 06 |
| one wich | 00 14 00 |
| 4 wheeles | 00 02 00 |
| one pare of bellie | 00 00 06 |
| one pare of pot keales | 00 00 06 |
| one Iron forke | 00 00 06 |
| one littell Tabell & 2 formes | 00 03 00 |
| 3 Stooles | 00 00 06 |
| 133 Cheeses | 04 10 00 |

|  |  |
|---|---|
| Earthenware . . . . . . . | 00 00 06 |
| Shilfes in ye kitchin Chamber . . . . | 00 05 00 |
| one hare Cloth . . . . . . | 00 02 06 |
| one Strike . . . . . . . | 00 00 08 |
| 12 Strikes of mallte . . . . . . | 01 05 00 |

*The Cattell of all Sorts*

|  |  |
|---|---|
| fferst 13 Cowes . . . . . . | 32 10 00 |
| 3 Twinter Heaifors . . . . . . | 06 00 00 |
| 4 yerling Heaifors . . . . . . | 06 00 00 |
| 4 Caalves . . . . . . . | 02 00 00 |
| 4 horses and mares . . . . . . | 15 00 00 |
| 3 Coultes . . . . . . . | 10 00 00 |
| 2 Sucking Coultes . . . . . . | 04 00 00 |
| 5 bidge swine & 4 pidges . . . . . | 04 00 00 |
| poultrey of all Sortes . . . . . | 00 06 08 |
| 30 Tun of hay . . . . . . | 15 00 00 |
| 30 Strikes lode of muncorne & wheate . . | 20 00 00 |
| 09 [*sic*] Strikes lode of dreg 25 Strikes lode of Barley . | 12 00 00 |
| pease and fiches 5 str . . . . . | 01 13 04 |
| in ye Seller 12 small barrilles . . . . | 01 00 00 |

*Implyments of husbandrey*

|  |  |
|---|---|
| 3 pare of Bound wheeles 2 Tumbrelles 1 Cartes boddey . . | 09 00 00 |
| plow timber & wainte Timber . . . . | 01 00 00 |
| 3 axes 2 mattox 2 brume hookes . . . . | 00 08 00 |
| 2 spades 1 drawinge hooke 1 buck hooke . . | 00 02 00 |
| collers holmes & treases . . . . . | 00 11 00 |
| 3 harrowes 2 plowes wth Irones . . . | 01 00 00 |
| 2 Waintes Ropes . . . . . . | 00 04 00 |
| 2 bille wth pikilles . . . . . . | 00 04 00 |
| 2 tuters . . . . . . . | 00 02 00 |
| Sawde Timber . . . . . . | 01 00 00 |
| Due upon bond . . . . . . | 20 00 00 |
| Waringe Apparill & monie in his purse . . | 03 00 00 |
| munes out upon mortegadge . . . . | 20 00 00 |
| thinges omitted or Came not to our View . . | 00 00 12 |
|  | 246 01 08 |

## 49. Ralph Barrett

Of Lilleshall, taken by Ralph Windsor,* Hugh Lawrence,* John Holmes and Thomas Leeke on 10 September 1683 and exhibited on 26 September 1683. He was buried on 8 September 1683.

|  |  |
|---|---|
| Imps.one Bay Mare . . . . . . | 03 00 00 |
| It one Cow . . . . . . . | 02 00 00 |

# THE INVENTORIES OF LILLESHALL

| | |
|---|---|
| It 3 Swine & 5 piggs . | 03 05 00 |
| It Geese & other Poultre . | 00 12 00 |

*In the parlour*

| | |
|---|---|
| One Paire of Bedstids with a Fetherbid a Chaff bed 2 Bolsters 2 Blanketts one green Rugg, one Coulitt Curtins & vallens & one paire of sheets . | 03 00 00 |
| It one Truckle Bed with a ffetherbed 2 Bolsters 2 Blanketts one green Rugg & a pair of sheets . | 02 00 00 |
| It one Table & fforme one great Press one Livery Table one Greene Chaire one Chest & a Deske & 3 Joynd Stools 2 Cubbord Cloths one Cushin and a warminge Pann . | 02 15 00 |
| It 3 Large Pewter dishes 2 Lesser dishes Tenn pewter plates 2 Candlesticks one salt & one Mustard Pott . | 01 05 00 |
| It 2 Halbeards one halfepike & a sword . | 00 10 00 |

*In the house place*

| | |
|---|---|
| Imprs one Table & 3 fformes . | 01 00 00 |
| it one screene one Chair . | 00 10 00 |
| Cushins . | 00 03 00 |
| It 4 Pewter Gauns 2 fflagons & 2 Pewter Potts . | 00 14 00 |
| It 10 dishes of Pewter 3 small plates 3 Porringers one Salt one Tinn Puddinge pann & other small Tinn ware . | 00 13 04 |
| It one Large Drippinge Pann & 2 Lesser . | 00 05 00 |
| It one paire of Andirons one ffire grate 2 ffire Shovells 2 paire of Tongs one Cleaver 2 paire of Pot geales & a rostinge plate one Smoothinge Iron a basting spoone one Iron Pott & potthookes one ffryinge Pann 2 Spitts Creepers & some white earthenware . | 01 00 00 |

*In the Kithin*

| | |
|---|---|
| One brasse ffurnace . | 00 06 00 |
| One Pudding plate a little ffire grate one paire of pothookes & a paire of potgeales one Small Brass Pott one Small Brass kettle & 2 skelletts 2 Little Iron Potts a Pirchpann & a Markinge Iron . | 00 10 00 |
| One old Cupbord one Big Turnell 4 Tubbs 5 pales one Churne one Lesser Tubb a soping Tubb one Kimnell 2 ffirkins one Barrell one litle Table one Bottell one Tunninge dish one cheese press one Little Forme one hair sive & a halfe strike . | 02 06 00 |

*In the Roome ovr ye Kitchin*

| | |
|---|---|
| It 4 barrells one Tubb one Small Turnell . | 00 10 06 |
| It 2 other old Tubbs & other old woodware . | 00 02 00 |
| It one Bed & Beddinge . | 00 08 00 |

*In the Seller*

| | |
|---|---|
| Two Barrells one Dresser one bolltell & some earthen ware . | 00 05 00 |

*In ye Chambr ovr ye plor*

| | |
|---|---|
| Imprs 2 pairs of plain Bedstids one ffether bed 3 old ffether Bolsters 2 Chaff beds 3 pillowes 2 Blanketts & 2 Coverlitts . | 01 13 04 |

| | | |
|---|---|---|
| It one little Table Board 2 Chairs one Close stoole 4 Coffers & 2 old Truncks . . . . . . . . | 00 18 00 | |
| fforty pounds of drest hempe . . . . . | 10 00 00 | |

*In the Chambr ovr ye house*

| | | |
|---|---|---|
| It one plan paire of Bedstids one ffether bed 2 ffether Bolsters one Blankett 2 Couvlitts one pillow & an old Curten . . . | 01 15 00 | |
| 5 pillow Coates 2 Dozen of ffine nabkins one dozen & 4 Courser Nabkins 3 course Towills 4 paire of ffine sheetes & one odd sheete 4 paire of Hempen sheetes 3 paire of Hurden Sheetes 3 fine Table Cloths 4 Courser table Cloths one wallett 3 ffine Towells & 2 Courser . . . . . . . . . | 06 02 00 | |
| one old Bedstid 5 Coffers 2 straw wisketts a parcell of Hoopes one dozen & a halfe of Bottells . . . . . . . | 00 19 06 | |
| One stone of ffleece wooll . . . . . . | 00 13 04 | |
| One fforme & shelfe . . . . . . . | 00 02 00 | |
| One paire of skates . . . . . . . | 00 00 06 | |
| One Iron Morter & pestell . . . . . . | 00 01 06 | |
| his Wearinge apparrell . . . . . . . | 02 00 00 | |
| Winter Corne in the Barne . . . . . . | 01 00 00 | |
| Barley in the Barne . . . . . . . | 00 11 00 | |
| Hay in the Barne . . . . . . . | 00 13 04 | |
| Hempe & fflax undrest . . . . . . | 00 13 04 | |
| One peece of an Iron Crow one Mattock one Spade & an old Axe one Iron Rake & pick forks & a Muckhooke . . . | 00 02 00 | |
| Manuare & other things that might not come to our knowledge . | 00 06 08 | |
| Sum totall is . . | 46 03 10 | |

## 50. Francis Light

Of Lilleshall, carpenter, taken by Andrew Shelton, Richard Ekyin, Thomas Light and William Penson on 21 March 1683-84, and exhibited on 20 March 1683-84. He was buried on 29 July 1683.

*Imp. in the house*

| | | |
|---|---|---|
| one Table board A stoole and Cheeres . . . . | 00 10 00 | |
| Brass & Pewter of all sorts . . . . . . | 00 13 04 | |
| Iron of all sorts . . . . . . . | 00 02 06 | |
| his workeing Tooles . . . . . . . | 00 06 08 | |
| Beding of all sorts . . . . . . . | 01 06 08 | |
| one Barrell & some other wooden ware . . . . | 00 10 00 | |
| Bacon Butter & Cheese . . . . . . | 00 13 04 | |
| 2 poor old cows . . . . . . . | 04 00 00 | |
| Corne sowd on the Ground . . . . . . | 00 03 04 | |
| for his wareing Cloathe and mony in his pocket . . . | 00 13 04 | |
| for much . . . . . . . . | 00 02 00 | |
| | 09 01 02 | |

THE INVENTORIES OF LILLESHALL 213

## 51. William Bate

Of Muxton, labourer and thatcher, taken by Ralph Winshurst, John Mansell and John Greenall on 28 August 1683 and exhibited on 1 April 1685. He was buried on 19 August 1684.

*In the Howse*

| | | |
|---|---|---|
| Item His wareing Apparell wee value at | 00 10 00 | |
| Item: One Table board one Joint forme a Chair a dresser a bouch and spining wheele | 00 10 00 | |
| Item a plate a Iron grate a fire shouell and Tongues a p of Bellows and some other odd things we value at | 00 03 00 | |
| Item One Iron pott wee value at | 00 03 00 | |
| Item: some little ould brass and pewter wee value at | 00 02 06 | |

*In the little parlour*

| | |
|---|---|
| Item: One Joint old beddstead with a feather bedd and two Chaff boulsters and two Blanketts | 01 05 00 |
| Item An old Chest and a barrell | 00 05 00 |

*In the Chamber*

| | |
|---|---|
| Item: One Chaff Bedd with bolster and one Couvring a barrell and old chears some other odd things wee value at | 00 09 06 |
| Item: 4 pair of Course sheetes wee value at | 00 08 00 |
| Item In another Roome some Old things | 00 02 06 |

*In the Buttree*

| | |
|---|---|
| Item 2 Tubbs and some odd things wee value at | 00 05 00 |
| Item: all other things omitted in this Inventory wee value at | 00 02 06 |
| The sume is | 04 06 00 |

## 52. William Bill

Of Donnington, yeoman, taken by Richard Lockley, George Bradborne and William Shelton on 6 April 1685 and exhibited on 26 May 1685. He was buried on 30 March 1685.

| | |
|---|---|
| Impris. four Cowes | 10 00 00 |
| Itm one bullock | 02 10 00 |
| Itm two yearlings & one twinter | 03 00 00 |
| Itm one Mare one nagg & two yearling colte | 10 00 00 |
| Itm two store piggs | 00 10 00 |
| Itm two ioyned beddsteeds two feather bedds four bolsters & all things thereunto belonging | 06 00 00 |
| Itm one Course beddsteed & a flock bedd | 00 10 00 |
| Itm one table board two ioyned formes & one Cubbard | 02 10 00 |
| Itm brass & pewter | 01 15 00 |

| | | |
|---|---|---|
| Itm one iron pott one iron possnett one dreeping pan & a fire plate . | 01 00 00 |
| Itm fire shovell & tonges pott feales one spitt one frying pan & a paire of Cobbetts . | 00 05 00 |
| Itm three barrells two lowmes a scalding turnell one Churne & all other trinnen wares . | 02 00 00 |
| Itm linnens of all sorts . | 03 10 00 |
| Itm two Chests & three Coffers one old press . | 01 15 00 |
| Itme Corne & mault in the house & corne growing on the ground . | 10 00 00 |
| Itm Chaires stooles & spinning wheeles . | 00 10 00 |
| Itm hempe & flax . | 00 10 00 |
| Itm three flitches of bacon . | 01 00 00 |
| Itm two paire of Cart wheeles one Cart body two tumbrells plowes irons & all other husbandry wares . | 04 00 00 |
| Itm one weavers loome & other weavers geares . | 01 10 00 |
| Itm Butter & Cheese . | 00 10 00 |
| Itm his weareing apparrell & money in his purse . | 02 00 00 |
| Itm any thing left out or forgotten unpraised . | 00 03 04 |
| Totall sume . | 65 08 04 |

## 53. Ralph Winshurst

Of Honnington, Lilleshall, yeoman, taken by James Colley* and George Colley on 17 July 1685 and exhibited on 20 July 1685. He was buried on 10 July 1685.

| | |
|---|---|
| Imprimis 9 Cowes . | 24 15 00 |
| Itam 3 three year oulds . | 07 10 00 |
| It 10 two year oulds . | 17 10 00 |
| It 7 year oulds . | 10 00 00 |
| It 7 Weanlins . | 05 05 00 |
| It 2 Horses 3 Mares & one Sucking Coult . | 17 10 00 |
| It 6 Sheep . | 00 18 00 |
| It 5 Swine . | 03 06 08 |
| It Rey in ye house . | 04 00 00 |
| It Mallt . | 06 00 00 |
| It Wheat & Ry Groing . | 15 00 00 |
| It Barley Groing . | 15 00 00 |
| It Pease Groing . | 09 00 00 |
| It Oates Groing . | 04 00 00 |
| It Cartes Plowes & Harrows with all Sorts of impliments of husbandrey . | 10 00 00 |

*It In ye Parler*
| | |
|---|---|
| 2 beds & all other furniture in ye Same Roome . | 10 00 00 |

*It In ye Parlor Chamber*
| | |
|---|---|
| One Bed & all other furniture in ye Same Roome . | 10 00 00 |

*It In ye Little Chamber*
one Bed & all other furniture in ye Same Roome . . . 03 00 00

*It In ye Roome over ye kitchin*
one bed & all other furniture in ye Same Roome , , , 01 10 00
It Hopps in ye Same Roome . . . . . . 01 10 00

*It In ye kitchin*
one table & all other furniture in ye Same Roome . . 02 00 00
It One Clock . . . . . . . . . 01 10 00

It Brasse of all Sortes . . . . . . . 02 10 00
It Pewtor of all Sortes . . . . . . . 03 00 00
It One furnis & all other Iron Ware . . . . 04 00 00
It One Jack . . . . . . . . . 00 06 00
It one Mallt Mill . . . . . . . . 01 00 00
It One weeting fatt & all other trinin Ware . . . 02 10 00
It All Sortes of Lining . . . . . . . 04 00 00
It Lining yorne . . . . . . . . 01 00 00
It. Beefe & bacon . . . . . . . . 01 10 00
It Cheese . . . . . . . . . 03 10 00
It the testators waring Reparrel . . . . . 05 00 00
It All things forgott . . . . . . . . 02 00 00

        toto . . . 209 10 08

## 54. John Smith, *alias* Steward

 Of The Hinks, Lilleshall, yeoman, taken by Thomas Lowe, Richard Bassett,[*] John Mansell, John Steventon and Robert Key on 3 December 1686 and exhibited on 13 December 1686.

Imprs. Tweelve cow beasts vallued att . . . . 36 00 00
Item. Nine yearling Calves att . . . . . 08 00 00
Item. One Mare and Coulte att . . . . . 08 10 00
Item. an other mare and Coult att . . . . . 15 00 00
Item. one Sow and three pigs att . . . . . 02 00 00
Item. Corne in the barne and corne & malte in the house . . 08 00 00
Item. A lease grant of a tenement called the Hincks heald of Miles fild for eighty yeares depending on two lives . . . 40 00 00
Item. Another lease of pte of a tenement cottage called Cheshall grange hoald of Mr. Richard Binton for aleaven yeares depending on two lives. . . . . . . . . . 20 00 00

*Item. In the hall*
foure tables, five Chares five stoules one Coubart, seven pewtar dishes eight small peaces of pewtar, fire shovell tungs & frying pan, pott gailes, and a warming pan . . . . . 03 12 00

*Item. In the little Chamber*
one paire of bedsteds one feather bed one boulstar two pillows a Coverlid two blanckits & a sheete . . . . . . 02 00 00

*Item. In the parlar*
one bed furnished wth Curtains & vallants, two feather beds, two feather boulstars, one pillow, two blankits, one Rug, one Table, one forme, one Chest, one Chire, one glass Cage, one flaskitt, two pewtar dishes, & ŏne pewtar sawsar . . . . 05 15 00

*Item. In the dayhouse*
one large table, on forme one greate Couffor, two barrells, three loumes, foure turnels, two brass Cettles, one iron marmott, two Churnes, two gauns, two bottles, three Cheesfats, one kneading turnell & a Cheese press . . . . . . 03 04 04

*Item. In the buttery*
three barrels foure bouches & some other small goods of little vallue . . . . . . . . . . 01 00 00

*Item. In the Cheese Chambar*
three Couffars, nine pair of sheets, three table Clothes, and other small linin . . . . . . . . . 02 10 00
It. bookes . . . . . . . . . 00 10 00
Item. Cheese in the house . . . . . . 05 00 00

*Item. In the Chambar over the day house*
two paire of bed steads one boulstar one covering & two blankits, two strawe wiskits & a woole [sic] . . . . 01 05 00
Item. hemp and hemp seed . . . . . . 01 10 00
Item. hay in the barne & in Stacks . . . . 20 00 00
Item. Cooler Cheese press and other things nott fitt to be removed ; 00 10 00
Item. Implements belonging to husbandry . . . 03 10 00
Item. wearing appel & money in his keeping . . . 02 10 00
          Total sum is . . 190 06 04

Monies lett out butt desparate . . . . . 16 00 00

## 55. John Simons

 Of The Hinks, Lilleshall, taken by William Simons, Jonathan Charlton, Richard Simons and William Charlton on 19 April 1690, and exhibited on 5 May 1690.

Imprs. Thirteene Cows & a bull . . . . . 30 00 00
Ittm Nine Twinters . . . . . . . 10 10 00
Ittm Seaven yearlings . . . . . . 05 10 00
Ittm Three Bulloks . . . . . . . 05 10 00
Ittm. Nine rearings . . . . . . . 03 00 00

THE INVENTORIES OF LILLESHALL

| | |
|---|---|
| Ittm three Mares & fower Coults . . . . . . | 15 00 00 |
| Ittm a Sow & piggs . . . . . . . . | 01 06 08 |
| Ittm Corne & hay . . . . . . . . | 07 00 00 |

*Ittm. in the parlor*

| | |
|---|---|
| one bed furnished three chears one chest one litle table one cubord & three boxes . . . . . . . . | 03 10 00 |

*Ittm in the hall*

| | |
|---|---|
| 3 tables 5 Chears one form one cupod 15 peeces of small pewter a warming pan a bottell a pot and three stooles . . . . | 02 00 00 |

*Ittm in the litle Chamber*

| | |
|---|---|
| one bed furnished and one cofor . . . . . . | 03 00 00 |

*Ittm in the butre*

| | |
|---|---|
| 4 barils & a hogshead . . . . . . . | 00 11 00 |

*Ittm in the darie*

| | |
|---|---|
| 2 cettls a forme a cofor 2 dressors with other woden ware . | 02 05 00 |

*Ittm over the hall*

| | |
|---|---|
| 2 fliches of bacon 9 cheese 2 cofors & a cart rope . . . | 01 15 00 |

*Ittm over the derie*

| | |
|---|---|
| 2 paire of bed steds a cradle a spining wheele & a sadle . . . | 00 15 00 |

| | |
|---|---|
| Ittm a cart & other instruments of husbandre . . . . | 04 15 00 |
| Ittm a lease of the Hinks for 76 years depending on 2 lives . . | 40 00 00 |
| Ittm Monie oweing without sperialtie . . . . . | 01 16 00 |
| Ittm Wearing aparill & Monie in his keepeing . . . . | 02 10 00 |
| The some is . . | 156 13 08 |

## 56. William Dawes

Of the Street Grange, Lilleshall, yeoman, taken by James Dale, Robert Holmes and Richard Poole on 30 November 1692 and exhibited on 4 January 1692-93.

| | |
|---|---|
| Imp. nineteen Coews at . . . . . . . | 40 00 00 |
| 2 oxzen and 2 bullocks . . . . . . . | 10 10 00 |
| Ten younge Cattell . . . . . . . . | 14 15 00 |
| Eight year old Cavles . . . . . . . | 16 07 00 |
| 2 horses and 2 mares . . . . . . . | 13 05 00 |
| 2 Colts at . . . . . . . . . | 02 15 00 |
| Corne in the barne and growing on the ground and in the house . | 14 06 00 |

| | | |
|---|---|---|
| ffoure store piggs | 01 00 00 |
| three ffeather beds blankets and bolsters belonging to them | 10 00 00 |
| Linnes of all sort | 04 02 06 |
| Brass and pewter | 02 01 04 |
| 2 table boards and 4 forms belonging to them and 1 chest | 02 01 08 |
| one Cupored one Screene one Table and 9 Chaires | 01 02 06 |
| Iron Ware of all sorts | 01 06 08 |
| wooden ware of all sorts | 00 13 04 |
| Impellments of Husbandry | 05 00 00 |
| wearing Apparell and money in his purse | 03 00 00 |
| other small things fforgot and out of sight | 00 06 08 |
| The totall Sume | 141 12 08 |

## 57. Humphrey Vernon

Of Lilleshall, wheelwright, taken by Thomas Turner and Robert Shelton on 16 October 1700 and exhibited on 17 October 1700. According to the inventory he died on 13 May 1700, but the parish register records his burial on 10 May.

| | | |
|---|---|---|
| Imprimis | | |
| for his wearing Apparell | 00 05 00 |
| Two Little Cowes | 04 00 00 |
| one Pigg | 00 16 00 |

*In ye house*

| | | |
|---|---|---|
| puter of all sorts | 00 06 00 |
| One Little Iron pott one Brass Skellett and one Brass Basting Ladle | 00 05 00 |
| one Iron Grate one pare of Tongs one ffire Shovel and one pare of pot geals | 00 02 00 |
| 4 old Cheairs | — — — |

*In ye Chamber below*

| | | |
|---|---|---|
| one Bed and Bedstids | 01 00 00 |
| one old Cubbard and a little Table | 00 05 00 |

*In ye Buttery Small things*

| | | |
|---|---|---|
| that is to severall small things of wooden weare | 00 13 04 |

*Above stares*

| | | |
|---|---|---|
| one old bed and stids | 00 10 00 |
| one Chest | 00 05 04 |
| one Long wheel | 00 03 00 |
| one Little wheel | 00 02 00 |
| ffor Hay in the Barne | 01 00 00 |
| ffor a few Little Cheeses | 00 06 00 |
| for his working Tooles | 00 10 00 |
| for things seen and not seen | 00 02 06 |
| Totall | 10 13 02 |

## 58. John Steventon

Of Cheshill Grange, Lilleshall, yeoman, taken by Thomas Oliver, Henry Whitmore and Richard Apley on 2 January 1701–02 and exhibited on 1 May 1702. He died on 16 December 1701 and was buried on 18 December 1701. In his will dated 12 December 1701 he left his entire property to his wife Mary.

*In the Parlour Chamber*

Imprs. Two pair of bedsteds wth feather beds Boulster blanketts Curtains Vallens & all things thereunto belonging two Trunks two Coffers one box & one Table vall'ed at . . . . . 14 00 00
Itm. Linen of all Sorts valle'd at . . . . . 22 00 00
Itm Three dozen & a half of Flax valled at . . . 00 17 06

*In the Parlour*

Itm One pair of bedsteds wth feather beds bolsters Blanketts Curtains vallons & all things thereunto belonging, One Chest one table and form, one Hanging press, one Chair books of all sorts 2 pieces of stuff valled at . . . . . . . 12 00 00

*In the Passage Chamber*

Itm Three pre of bedsteds wth 2 feather bed & 1 flock bed boulsters blanketts & all things thereunto belonging One Coffer one box wth other Small things vall'ed at . . . . . 10 00 00

*In the Hall Chamber*

Itm Cheese vall'ed at . . . . . . 04 00 00
Itm Beef butter Lard & other provision for the house use vallued at . 01 10 00
Itm Malt valued at . . . . . . . 00 12 06
Itm Wooll valu'd at . . . . . . . 00 12 00
Itm Two tables, one Wiskett one Cradle hops Yarn & two in the Same room valu'd at . . . . . . 02 06 08

*In the Kitchin Chamber*

Itm One trunk wth beans & pease Corn two Wheels timber for husbandry use valu'd at . . . . . . 01 15 00

*In the Kitchen*

Itm One Churn 2 Cheesetubs 2 brewing tubs 1 turnell 1 bag of Pease wth benches tressells Roaps Sieves Mall, Wedges Wheels wth sev.all other thing's too tedious to name valu'd at . . . 04 00 00

*In the Passage*

Itm One Barrell of drink wth Peals benches & sev'all other things of Small value valu'd at . . . . . . 01 00 00

*Itm. In the Larder*

Two Salting tubs wth beefe & pork in Salt valu'd at . . . 03 00 00
Itm. Three Barrells of Drink valu'd at . . . . 01 10 00

Itm Cheese fats Mits Stands bottles of Wood & Glass wth sev'all
other things valu'd at . . . . . . . 02 00 00

*In the Hall*

Itm Twenty eight pewter dishes beside plates porringers flaggons
candlesticks & other small things of pewter valu'd at . . . 05 00 00
Itm Five brass kettles 1 pot 1 warming pan wth other small things
of brass valu'd at . . . . . . . . 05 00 00
Itm Two Iron pots one dripping pan one broch cobbards Grate fire
shovell tongs Pestill Mortar & sev'all other things of Iron valu'd at . 01 00 00
Itm Two tables & forms 1 Skreen 1 press 1 cupboard 7 Chairs
Stools, Shelves, with sev'all other small things valued at . . 04 00 00
Itm One Cart 2 tumbrells 1 pr of Harrows 1 plow valu'd at . 08 10 00
Itm Four pr of traces Collars holmes Saddles bridles & other
Materialls for gearing four horses valu'd at . . . . 02 00 00
Itm Three Swine valu'd at . . . . . . . 04 10 00

*In the Barn*

Itm The Barley in the Straw valu'd at . . . . . 14 00 00
Itm Wheat in the Straw valu'd at . . . . . . 02 00 00
Itm Two Ricks of Hay & one of Straw valu'd at . . . 14 00 00
Itm One Stack of Wheat valu'd at . . . . . . 10 00 00
Itm One stack of barley & 1 of Fitches valu'd at . . . 10 00 00
Itm One stack of Oates valu'd at . . . . . . 04 00 00
Itm Two pieces of Corn on the Ground valud . . . 20 00 00
Itm Hemp in watering valu'd at . . . . . . 02 00 00
Itm Ten Cows valu'd at . . . . . . . 33 06 08
Itm Eight two Year olds valu'd at . . . . . . 18 00 00
Itm Eight Year olds valu'd at . . . . . . 10 00 00
Itm Three Mares valu'd at . . . . . . . 16 00 00
Itm Two Year old Colts valu'd at . . . . . . 05 00 00
Itm One Cheese press 2 Chuters one wheel barrow wth pig troughs
wth Lathers Souls for tying of Cattle on chaine 'Cop one Grindle
stone Coals Pickwells Sharewells & other small instruments belong-
ing to the barn house valu'd at . . . . . . 02 10 00
Itm Poultry of all sorts valu'd at . . . . . . 00 15 00
Itm Pocket money & waring valued at . . . . . 01 01 06

274 07 06

## 59. Richard Hawkins

Of Muxton, yeoman, taken by William Rostons and Thomas Basnet on 27 June 1702 and exhibited on 15 October 1702. He was buried on 21 June 1702.

Imps. The Decedents wareing apparrell valued and appraised at
twenty shillings . . . . . . . . 01 00 00
Item Books valued and appraised to two shillings and sixpence . 00 02 06
Item In ready money held to five shillings . . . . 00 05 00
Item Five milking Cows valued and appraised to ten pounds . . 10 00 00

## THE INVENTORIES OF LILLESHALL

| | |
|---|---|
| Item Four twinter heifers valued and appraised to five pounds six shillings and eightpence . . . . . . . | 05 06 08 |
| Item Three yearlings or young Beasts one year old appraised and valued to two pounds . . . . . . . | 02 00 00 |
| Item Three weaning calves appraised and valued to twenty shillings . | 01 00 00 |
| Item Two Mares and one cold appraised and valued to seven pounds . | 07 00 00 |
| Item One sow and six small pigs valued and appraised to fifteen shillings . . . . . . . . . | 00 15 00 |
| Item All the Poultrey appraised and valued to five shillings . . | 00 05 00 |
| Item Fiften pair of sheets course and fine valued to forty shillings . | 02 00 00 |
| Item All other table Linnens valued and appraised to twenty shillings . . . . . . . . . | 01 00 00 |
| Item The Brass and pewter valued and appraised to three pounds . | 03 00 00 |
| Item The Iron ware valued and appraised to twenty shillings . . | 01 00 00 |
| Item four Joined tables and three Joine formes with the appurts. praised an valued to thirty shillings . . . . . | 01 10 00 |
| Item Four Joine Chests one press three stools two boxes to chairs appraised to forty shillings . . . . . . | 02 00 00 |
| Item Ten joined Chairs valued and appraised to ten shillings . . | 00 10 00 |
| Item Five feather beds with the appurts. appraised & valued to five pounds . . . . . . . . . | 05 00 00 |
| Item Four Coffers one dish board two Dressers four Benches one Glass cage appraised and valued to twenty shillings . . | 01 00 00 |
| Item The hogsheads and barrells and all other vessels for brewing and making Mault valued and appraised . . . . | 01 19 11 |
| Item The Wooden Ware belonging to the Dairy appraised to thirteen shillings and four pence . . . . . . | 00 13 04 |
| Item The Corn and the Granary straw and wiskets and other necessarys for keeping and holding Corn valued and appraised to ten shillings . . . . . . . . . | 00 10 00 |
| Item The Whitmeat with the other prissions valued and appraised to twenty shillings . . . . . . . . | 01 00 00 |
| Item One Gear cloth with four sacks and bags valued and appraised to six shillings and eightpence . . . . . | 00 06 08 |
| Item Corne in the ground of all sorts valued and appraised to fifty shillings . . . . . . . . . | 02 10 00 |
| Item The implements belonging to ye Husbandry of all sorts appraised valued to forty three shillings and four pence . . | 02 03 04 |
| Item The Dung in the Midden for manuring the Land valued and appraised to six shillings and eight pence . . . . | 00 06 08 |
| Total of the whole appraisement is fifty four pounds four shillings and one penny appraised and valued by us . . . | 54 04 01 |
| Debts Due by ye Dec.d at ye time of his Death . . . . | 40 00 00 |

## 60. William Hall

Of Muxton, yeoman, taken by Thomas Wright, Edward Wootton and John Wooton on 14 November 1702 and exhibited on 29 April 1703. He was buried on 13 November 1702.

| | |
|---|---|
| Foure oxen | 22 00 00 |
| five Cowes and a bull | 15 00 00 |
| A Coult | 04 00 00 |
| And a mare | 03 00 00 |
| three young Bease & a Cow and Calfe | 08 10 00 |
| three yearlings | 03 00 00 |
| Three score and Seaven Sheep | 12 00 00 |
| a pich pann And Mauke | 00 02 06 |
| one bull | 02 10 00 |
| two bigg swine and two stores | 04 10 00 |
| The Corne In ye barne in the house & one ye ground | 25 00 00 |
| the hay In the barne | 10 00 00 |
| one Wane two tombrills & two paire of wheels | 02 15 00 |
| All the rest of the Implymts of husbandrey | 02 05 00 |
| one sestern 3 stone troughs & a grindstone | 00 11 00 |
| the powtrey | 00 05 00 |

*In the parler*

| | |
|---|---|
| one fithr bed & all belongeing to it | 03 00 00 |
| one press one table and three Chears | 01 05 00 |
| one box and a Lantern | 00 02 00 |
| White yearne wares and a brush | 00 02 06 |
| Six barrells one table & two formes | 02 05 00 |

*In the house*

| | |
|---|---|
| A furness And all ye pewter | 03 00 00 |
| All ye brass a broch and two dreeping panns | 01 00 00 |
| two Iron potts a fire shovell and tongs | 00 12 00 |
| A kneading trough 2 sarches a hare siv tub | 00 06 00 |
| And old strike & old churn and Semplier | 00 02 06 |
| And Ax a spade mattok broomhooke | 00 06 00 |
| A Sadle And pilling the bridle | 00 03 08 |
| A Long Wheel And three Litle ones | 00 10 00 |
| Sive and Ridle A half Strick & A peck | 00 03 04 |
| one Screen one Cheare 3 stooles a pair of balles | 00 04 00 |
| one shilf 3 dozen of trenchers six noggins | 00 04 06 |
| A frying pann brandr & potracks | 00 03 00 |
| Iron pottlid & a hacking knife smoothing Irons & heaters | 00 05 00 |
| 4 mugs and a twiggen can | 00 00 08 |
| A Churne Stoone and tubs | 01 00 00 |
| Two Chees lathrs A mortr and pestell | 00 02 02 |
| 2 bowls a gaune & a piggen 2 vessls two old barrels | 00 04 06 |
| three woden bottels & little table a dressr and a shilf | 00 07 00 |
| two kimnels 3 bottels 4 milk pans three woden plattrs | 00 07 00 |
| the stoons & yerthen ware In the buttrey | 00 05 00 |
| five chesspitts and two siths | 00 06 00 |

*In the Chambr ovr the house*

| | |
|---|---|
| buttr & Chees & baken | 03 00 00 |
| ye Shilfs a weel And pannel And some Woole | 00 10 00 |
| hempseed & the hemp and flaxe | 03 01 00 |
| some baskitts | 00 04 02 |

*Roome ovr the parlr*

| | |
|---|---|
| 2 fithr beds & all things belonging to yem | 04 10 00 |
| two Cheares and two Coffers | 00 08 00 |

*the Chamber ovr the buttry*

| | |
|---|---|
| two beds and all belonging to them | 02 02 00 |
| Sheets table Cloths And Napkins & all mannr of napery ware | 05 03 04 |
| A trey—A cvrinne sheet | 00 10 00 |
| his Wareing Apparell And Money In his purse | 05 10 00 |
| All things forgotten And out of Sight | 00 02 06 |
| The totall is | 154 16 04 |

## 61. Joan Wright

Of Lilleshall, widow, taken by Thomas Salt and Thomas Leeke on 5 April 1703, and exhibited on 9 April 1703. She died on 24 March 1703.

| | |
|---|---|
| Imprs. ffour Small chaires 3s one Table Board 10s | 00 14 00 |
| One Glass Cage 2s two paire of Cubbords 3s 6d | 00 05 06 |
| One Screene 6s Wooden vessells of all sorts 10s | 00 16 00 |
| One Malt Mill 15s. One ffeather bed two blanckitts Bedsteads 2li | 02 15 00 |
| Iron Ware of all sorts | 00 02 00 |
| One Brass kettle and one Brass pott | 01 03 04 |
| Three Chaires Two wheels one Glass Cage | 00 08 04 |
| One pewter fflagon Six pewter plates One Chamber pott one Brandy bottle A pewter Candlestick seaven pewter dishes | 00 18 06 |
| A small brass chaffinge dish | 00 01 08 |
| A new peece of Cloath | 01 00 00 |
| Waringe Linnens | 01 10 00 |
| hemp and Yarne | 00 10 00 |
| One Chest & one Coffer | 00 08 00 |
| One Small paile One Iron pott & one cheare | 00 13 06 |
| One Bed & Bedsteds 2 Boulsters 2 pillowes 3 blanckitts with hangings and Curtains & Rodds | 03 00 00 |
| A Caster hat and Wearinge Apparel | 02 15 00 |
| One Iron Dreepinge pann and one Iron pott | 00 06 00 |
| A Camblet Hood and Saddle Cloath | 00 05 06 |
| Bees | 00 12 00 |
| One Tubb and A strawe whiskitt | 00 02 06 |
| An old Cheese press and 3 old plancks | 00 05 00 |
| An old Cubbard 5s money in her purse 40 li | 40 05 00 |
| Sum totalis | 58 16 08 |

## 62. Richard Beard

Of Lilleshall, Yeoman, taken by Walter Brodhurst, Thomas Leeke and Henry Whitmore on 1 June 1704 and exhibited on 19 October 1704.

He died on 21 May 1704 and was buried on 24 May. In his will dated 19 May 1704 he left land at Woodseaves, Market Drayton, to his son Richard after the death of his widow.

| | |
|---|---|
| Imps. | |
| his wearing apparrell and money in his purse | 10 00 00 |

*In the new parlour*

| | |
|---|---|
| one hanging press | 01 10 00 |
| one ovall table | 00 10 00 |
| one Lookeing Glass | 00 10 00 |
| one Long Table and one joyned Forme | 00 15 00 |
| one Large Couch: Chair and Cushion | 00 10 00 |
| one dozen of joynd Chairs covered with Cloth | 01 10 00 |
| fifteen pictures in Frames | 10 15 00 |

*In the old parlour:*

| | |
|---|---|
| Two joynd Bedsteads with 4 ffeather Beds & Boulsters Blanketts and hangings thereunto belonging | 14 00 00 |
| one Joynd press | 01 10 00 |
| one Chest, one Little Box: 3 Chairs: one Little Table; one Close Stoole 4 pictures: one old Looking Glass | 01 10 00 |

*The Chamber over the New Parlour:*

| | |
|---|---|
| one pair of Bedsteads, and 2 ffeather Beds with Boulsters: Blanketts and all things belonging it | 05 05 00 |
| 3 Chests, one Little Table: 3 Chairs, 3 stools Covered with Cloth and seven small pictures and a Looking Glass | 02 00 00 |
| 30 pair of sheets, 6 dozen of napkins and other Linnens | 16 06 08 |

*The Chamber over the old Parlour:*

| | |
|---|---|
| one joynd Bedstead with 2 ffeather Beds Boulsters, Blanketts and hangings | 05 00 00 |
| one other Bedstead with 2 ffeather Beds Blanketts Boulsters and hangings | 04 00 00 |
| one truckle Bed and 2 ffeather Beds thereupon with all things belonging to it | 03 03 04 |
| one Chest, 4 Coffers and 2 Chairs | 00 16 00 |

*In the house place:*

| | |
|---|---|
| one Long Table one Little Table; 2 Joynd Forms one joynd Chair, one joynd Stoole, 3 Leathern Chairs, one other Chair and Stoole | 01 13 04 |
| one joyned press | 00 10 00 |
| 3 Brass pans 6 Brass potts. 4 Brass kettles. 2 skillets. 2 brass Candlesticks one pair of Brass snuffors and one Copper Can | 04 07 00 |
| 30 Pewter Dishes: 3 dozen of plates: 4 pewter Candlesticks 2 fflaggons and 2 Pewter Cans one dozen of pottengers 6 salts and 2 Mustard pots | 05 06 08 |
| one Jack: Cubbards; dripping pans; fire shovells; Tongues potgoals; and skewers and other materials | 02 00 00 |
| one Birding Gunne | 00 05 00 |

## THE INVENTORIES OF LILLESHALL

*The Chamber over the house:*

| | |
|---|---|
| 18 strike of Muncorne | 02 05 00 |
| 20 strike of pease | 02 00 00 |
| 60 strike of Maulte | 07 10 00 |
| 10 sacks and Baggs | 00 02 00 |
| 6 spining wheels bigg and Little | 00 13 04 |
| one Mault Mill | 00 13 04 |
| 20 slippings of yarne | 01 10 00 |
| Beef and Bacon | 02 00 00 |
| one Truckle ffeather Bed with all things belong to it | 01 10 00 |
| one side saddle | 00 10 00 |

*The Kitchen Buttery and Buttery Chamber*

| | |
|---|---|
| one Joynd Press one old Table, and 2 Little Tables, one old fform and Dish calhe | 01 03 04 |
| Brewing Vessels and wooden ware of all sorts | 02 00 00 |
| one feather Bed: 2 Coffers: and 2 old Covered Chairs | 01 15 00 |
| one old ffurnace | 00 16 00 |

*In the Seller:*

| | |
|---|---|
| 11 Barrells | 02 04 00 |

*The Chamber over the Kitchen*

| | |
|---|---|
| for Butter and Cheese | 04 00 00 |
| 3 old Coffers and 3 old Shelves | 00 12 00 |
| 5 dozen of Trenchers | 00 05 00 |
| for Wooll | 04 04 00 |
| for 7 sacks of Hops | 26 05 00 |
| Tow dressed and undressed. | 03 18 00 |

| | |
|---|---|
| one new Cart, and new wheels | 04 00 00 |
| 2 Tumbrells and 3 pair of wheels | 03 16 00 |
| 2 pair of Harrows. 3 plows and other Implements of husbandry | 01 02 06 |
| Corne in the Barne unthreshd | 01 15 00 |

*In the Cowhouse Binge:*

| | |
|---|---|
| 2 Chees presses one Provender Coffer spades & pikells one Crow of Iron and other small materials | 01 10 00 |

*In the Stable:*

| | |
|---|---|
| one Mare and Coult | 07 00 00 |
| 3 Geldings: one yearling Coult. and 2 old Mares. | 19 00 00 |
| for Gears for 4 horses | 00 12 00 |

| | |
|---|---|
| one stack of Corne in the Ground. | 10 00 00 |

| | |
|---|---|
| 14 Cows and a Bull | 39 10 00 |
| 14 yong Cattell | 30 15 00 |
| 6 weaning Calves | 03 00 00 |
| 4 swine | 04 00 00 |
| for Poultry | 00 05 00 |

| | | |
|---|---|---|
| Winter Corne in ye Ground. | | 14 00 00 |
| Lent Tillage . | | 10 00 00 |
| 40 Weathers. 12 Ews and Lambs and 8 Hogg sheep | | 13 17 06 |
| A Chattell Lease at Whistons in Stoke psh for 7 years to come & unexpired . | | 100 10 00 |
| for things omitted . | | 01 00 00 |
| | sum tot is . . | 413 04 00 |

## 63. James Dale

Of Lilleshall Lodge, keeper, taken by John Spearman and Thomas Hughes on 12 April 1706 and exhibited on 26 April 1706. He was buried on 20 March 1705–06.

| | | |
|---|---|---|
| Impris. | | |
| Household Goods of all sorts | | 12 05 00 |
| Item | | |
| Horses Cattells and sheep . | | 25 07 06 |
| Item | | |
| Implements of Husbandry . | | 14 06 08 |
| Item | | |
| Corn upon the ground | | 25 00 00 |
| Item | | |
| The Deceaseds wearing Clothes | | 01 00 06 |
| Item | | |
| A Chatell Lease | | 28 00 00 |
| | In toto . . | 95 09 08 |

## 64. John Shelton

Of Muxton, taken by Francis Wright, William Woolley, William Royston and Thomas Haywood on 16 May 1707 and exhibited on 27 June 1707. He was buried on 14 May 1707. In his will dated 9 February 1706–07; In his will dated 9 February 1706–7 he left property to his wife Philippa (66) which after her death was to go to other relations. It included a house in Newport called Hoar Withy let to John Old which went to his nephew Richard, son of William Shelton; three days work in the Norbroom Field at Newport which went to William, another son of WIlliam Shelton; Cherrington house in Newport which went to Mary, his niece, daughter of his brother Robert; and Bradborn's Tenement in Donnington which went to his sister Elinor as long as the lease continued.

| | |
|---|---|
| Imprs. | |
| four mares and seaven Colts at | 50 00 00 |
| Nineteen Cows & calfes and two bulls at . | 50 00 00 |

# THE INVENTORIES OF LILLESHALL 227

| | | |
|---|---|---|
| four Oxen at . . . . . . . . . | 16 00 00 |
| One and twenty young Beasts at . . . . . . | 30 00 00 |
| three and twenty of sheep at . . . . . . | 04 00 00 |
| 46 store sheep . . . . . . . . | 06 00 00 |
| 3 store Piggs at . . . . . . . . | 02 00 00 |

*Item In the over house place*

| | |
|---|---|
| 24 dishes at . . . . . . . . . | 04 00 00 |
| two dozen and a halfe of Plates . . . . . . | 00 15 00 |
| ten pewter Porringers 4 pewtr candlsticks & 2 pewtr cans . . | 00 10 00 |
| two brass kettles 2 brass potts a brass candlstick and a Skimer and bason . . . . . . . . . . . | 01 10 00 |
| 4 Iron spitts 2 driping Pans & Jack & Racks . . . | 02 05 00 |
| 3 Iron Potts Morter and 2 pestells . . . . . | 00 15 00 |
| 2 Pair of fire shovells and tongs grate & pot gales . . . | 00 12 00 |
| 2 flesh forks 2 candlesticks a hacking knife and two smoothing Irons . . . . . . . . . . . | 00 03 00 |
| one old table 1 form 3 chairs & 2 stools . . . . . | 00 05 00 |

*Item In the Parlor*

| | |
|---|---|
| 3 tables & 1 dozen of chairs . . . . . | 02 16 00 |

*Item in the Room over it*

| | |
|---|---|
| 2 beds and all thereunto belonging & 2 little tables & a trunk . . | 08 00 00 |

*Item in the lowr Parlor*

| | |
|---|---|
| 1 bed 2 chest 2 trunks 1 Coffer 1 box 1 table a little cabinet 1 chair 1 warming pan & 2 Joine stools . . . . . . | 07 00 00 |

*Item In the Room over*

| | |
|---|---|
| 2 beds 1 table saddle & pillin . . . . . . | 03 00 00 |

*Item in the store chamber*

| | |
|---|---|
| 6 flitches of bacon & 2 flitches of Beefe . . . . . | 04 00 00 |
| In the sam Room 6 dozen Napkins & 30 pair of sheets . . . | 14 00 00 |
| One Chest . . . . . . . . . | 00 05 00 |

*Item In the Buttry*

| | |
|---|---|
| 12 barrells . . . . . . . . . | 01 05 00 |

*Item In the Lower room*

| | |
|---|---|
| one bed . . . . . . . . . | 01 10 00 |

*It In the brew house*

| | |
|---|---|
| 1 brass kettle 3 forms 2 peels lading gaun a large wheel and a little one . . . . . . . . . . | 01 10 00 |

*It in the Lower House*

| | |
|---|---|
| one table 1 Cubbard 1 skreen . . . . . . | 01 05 00 |

*in the Store chamber*

| | |
|---|---|
| malt and Corn | 15 00 00 |
| a Malt Mill | 00 10 00 |
| a hair cloath wetting vessell 1 strike & halfe strike | 01 00 00 |
| Hemp | 03 10 00 |
| Wains Carts and Husbandry ware | 10 00 00 |
| Corn growing upon the Land | 07 10 00 |
| Lumber and things omitted | 01 00 00 |
| His Waring Apparrell and money in his Pockett | 100 00 00 |
| Debts due upon sperialty | 60 00 00 |
| Debts desperate | 20 00 00 |
| | 431 01 00 |

### 65. Walter Brodhurst

Of Lilleshall, gentleman, taken by Thomas Tildesley and Thomas Turner on 16 September 1707 and exhibited on 22 October 1707. He was buried on 4 August 1707.

| | |
|---|---|
| Imprs. Nyne Cows | 18 00 00 |
| Three Heifers | 04 10 00 |
| Two Bullocks one Bull and one other Heifer | 09 00 00 |
| Two other Bullocks and four Calves | 04 00 00 |
| Three Mares and a Colt | 07 00 00 |
| Two year old Colts and two Sucking Colts | 05 00 00 |
| ffour Swine | 03 00 00 |
| Twelve Sheep | 01 10 00 |
| Barley in the Barne | 05 00 00 |
| A parcell of Pease and Oats | 05 00 00 |
| A parcell of Wheat unthresht | 02 10 00 |
| Hay and Straw in the Barnes | 05 00 00 |
| Implements of Husbandry and Plow timber | 05 00 00 |

*In the lower Parlour*

| | |
|---|---|
| Three Tables and one Couch | 01 00 00 |
| Twelve Chairs and a reading Desk | 01 00 00 |
| ffour Cushions | 00 02 06 |

*In the house place*

| | |
|---|---|
| Brass and Pewter | 03 00 00 |
| Two little Tables Six Chairs one Skreen and a form | 01 00 00 |
| A Cupboard | 00 06 08 |
| One Iron Jack one Grate four spits one ffire Shovell and Tongs & other Iron Ware | 01 05 00 |

## THE INVENTORIES OF LILLESHALL

*In the Brewhouse*

| | |
|---|---|
| One old brasse ffurnace and one old Iron Boyler | 00 13 04 |
| ffour brewing Tubs and two Coolers | 01 00 00 |

*In the Larder*

| | |
|---|---|
| Two Tables and a Press & other Small things | 00 15 00 |
| One Table in the Buttery | 00 03 00 |

*In the upper Parlour*

| | |
|---|---|
| Two Tables and Twelve Chairs | 02 00 00 |

*In the little Parlour*

| | |
|---|---|
| Two ffeather beds Bedsteds Blankets & other ffurniture | 03 00 00 |
| One Chest of Drawers & one Trunk & two boxes | 00 15 00 |

*In the two little lower Rooms*

| | |
|---|---|
| Two Bedds Blankets and ffurniture | 01 10 00 |

*In the Milkhouse*

| | |
|---|---|
| Three Barrells and two little Turnills | 01 00 00 |

*In the Cellar*

| | |
|---|---|
| Eleaven Barrells and three horses | 02 00 00 |

*In the Parlour Chamber*

| | |
|---|---|
| A ffeather bed Bedsted Quilt Blanketts Curtains and ffurniture | 05 00 00 |
| A Chest of Drawers a little Chest a Table two Chairs and three stools | 02 00 00 |
| A looking glass | 00 05 00 |

*In the Chamber over the house place*

| | |
|---|---|
| One ffeather bed and Bedsted Curtains Blanketts and ffurniture | 02 00 00 |
| A little Table a box of Drawers two Chairs and three Stools & a little looking glass | 00 10 00 |

*In the little red Chamber*

| | |
|---|---|
| Two Beds Bedsteds and ffurniture | 02 00 00 |
| One hanging Presse one Chest and one stool | 00 12 00 |

*In the Maids Chamber*

| | |
|---|---|
| One little Bed and Bedsted | 00 06 08 |

*In the Cheese Chamber*

| | |
|---|---|
| One tub one coffer and Cheese shelves | 00 15 00 |
| A small parcell of Cheese and Wooll | 01 10 00 |

*In the Servant mens Chamber*

| | |
|---|---|
| One Chaffe bed and Coffer | 00 06 08 |

*In the Back house*

| | | |
|---|---|---|
| One old steel Malt Mill one old tub and Hair Cloath | . . . | 00 06 08 |
| Nappery Wares . . . . . . . | . | 02 00 00 |
| one pair of Iron Skrews . . . . . | . | 00 16 00 |
| A parcell of Books . . . . . . | . | 00 10 00 |
| His wearing Apparrell & money in his Purse | . . | 02 10 00 |
| Lumber . . . . . . . . | . | 00 10 00 |
| Things omitted and out of sight . . . . | . | 00 10 00 |

A Lease of a Messuage or Tenemt Cottage and Lands thereto belonging held by onely one Infant life supposed to be worth . . 40 00 00

            Totalis . . 187 08 06

## 66. Philippa Shelton

  Of Muxton, widow of John Shelton (*64*), taken by Thomas Turner, William Woolley, William Royston and William Shelton on 3 January 1708–09 and exhibited on 9 March 1708–09. She was buried on 31 December 1708.

*Goods in the House*

| | | |
|---|---|---|
| Impris Pewter of all sorts . . . . . | . | 03 10 00 |
| Brass of all sorts . . . . . . | . | 01 10 00 |
| Iron ware of all sorts . . . . . | . | 02 00 00 |
| Tables stooles and a form and two old Chaires . | . | 00 05 00 |

*Goods in the Parlour*

| | | |
|---|---|---|
| Item Three Tables and Elaven Chaires . . . | . | 02 00 00 |

*Goods in the Chamber over the Parlour*

| | | |
|---|---|---|
| Item Two beds and bedsteads Blanketts & all things belonging to them . . . . . . . . | . | 03 10 00 |
| Two little tables one Trunck and three Chaires . . | . | 00 10 00 |

*Goods in the Lower Chamber*

| | | |
|---|---|---|
| Item one Bed and Bedsteads Blanketts and Curtaines and all things belonging . . . . . . . | . | 03 00 00 |
| Two Chests one little Table one Coffor and one Trunk and one Cabenett att . . . . . . . | . | 01 15 00 |
| Six Barrells . . . . . . . | . | 01 00 00 |

*Goods in the Servts Chamber*

| | | |
|---|---|---|
| Item one Bed and Bedsteds and one Table att . | . | 00 15 00 |

*Goods in the Chees Chamber*

| | | |
|---|---|---|
| Item Chees at . . . . . . . | . | 07 00 00 |
| Old Bacon at . . . . . . . | . | 00 07 00 |

one Chest one Trunk two Coffers . . . . . 00 15 00
three vergine barrels one Trunk and two old Coffers . . . 00 15 00

*Goods in the Maids Chamber*
Item one Bed and bedsteds . . . . . . . 00 10 00
two small beer Barrells & 2 Churns . . . . . 00 06 00
trind Ware in the Dairy . . . . . . . 00 08 00

*Goods in the Brewhouse*
Item One Copper . . . . . . . . 00 10 00
Two Brewing Tubs one cooler and Two Turnells . . . 00 15 00
one Joynd fform and one Kneading Turnell and two peals . . 00 02 06

*in the Lower House*
Item Mault . . . . . . . . . 02 10 00
all sorts of Graine . . . . . . . . 01 00 00
Item one Table one Screen on Press Cubbard . . . . 02 00 00

*In the Mault House*
Item one Weeteing fatt Hair Cloath and two Tubs . . . 00 10 00

ffifteen Cows one Bull four Bullocks . . . . . 50 00 00
47 Sheep at . . . . . . . . . 05 00 00
Seaventeen young beasts . . . . . . . 25 10 00
Tenn year old Calves . . . . . . . 05 00 00
7 Horses and Colts of all sorts . . . . . . 21 00 00
five Hoggs att . . . . . . . . 02 00 00
one Chesnutt Horse . . . . . . . . 04 00 00
Corn on the Ground . . . . . . . . 05 00 00
Hard Corne in the Barne . . . . . . . 10 00 00
Barley in the Barne . . . . . . . . 08 00 00
Oates and Pease in the Barne . . . . . . 02 00 00

Item Hay att . . . . . . . . . 15 00 00

Implements of Husbandry . . . . . . . 08 00 00
Hemp and fflax drest & undrest . . . . . . 03 00 00
Linnens of all sorts . . . . . . . . 08 00 00
Money in the House weareing apparrell and Money in Pockett . 05 00 00
Things Omitted and forgotten . . . . . . 02 10 00

                                                              211 13 06

## 67. Edward Aston

Of Muxton, lime man, taken by Thomas Newell and John James of Lilleshall on 18 February 1708-90 and exhibited on 4 May 1709. He was buried on 8 February 1708-09.

Imprs. Waring Apparrell and Money in his purse . . . . 00 15 00

*In the Chambar over the house*

| | | |
|---|---|---|
| Itm one paire of Bedsteds A Chaff bed Blankets and Coverlids | . | 00 06 00 |
| A Chest an Box . . . . . . . | | 00 07 00 |

*In the Chambar*

| | | |
|---|---|---|
| Itm one Bed A paire of Bedsteeds with all things belonging to them | . | 01 00 00 |
| A Coffer . . . . . . . . | | 00 01 00 |

*In the House*

| | | |
|---|---|---|
| Itm A Little Table an ould Cubboard . . . . | | 00 05 00 |
| Ironware of all Sorts . . . . . . | | 00 07 00 |
| Butter and Cheese . . . . . . . | | 00 04 00 |
| Three Cowes Two Twinters Two Calves . . . . | | 09 09 00 |
| Things omitted . . . . . . . | | 00 01 06 |
| | | 12 15 06 |

## 68. Joseph Woolley

Of Muxton, taken by William Corbett, John James* and John Spearman on 5 July 1709 and exhibited on 25 January 1709-10.

| | | |
|---|---|---|
| Imps. | | |
| A wagon and one mare two geldens and one stone hors | . . | 41 01 06 |
| one other mare . . . . . . . . | | 03 10 00 |
| three cowes . . . . . . . . | | 07 10 00 |
| one yeare ould calfe . . . . . . . | | 01 00 00 |
| one yeare ould coult . . . . . . . | | 02 00 00 |
| two waineing calves . . . . . . . | | 01 00 00 |
| one swine . . . . . . . . | | 00 10 00 |

*goods in ye house*

one long table two forms a screen a bigg pres one Littill table pewter dishes four pewter plates and four pewter poliengers two pewter candelsticks and one pewter cann. . . . . 02 00 00
two bras cetills an Iorn pot and a warming pan . . . . 00 04 00
one small grate wth fire shovell and tonges and frying pan . . 00 08 06

*goods in ye parlor*

| | | |
|---|---|---|
| one fether bed and all yt belongs thereto . . . . . | | 01 05 00 |
| one table and one forme . . . . . . | | 00 06 00 |
| one chest . . . . . . . . | | 00 05 00 |
| one cobert . . . . . . . . | | 00 01 00 |

*ye chamber over ye parlor*

| | | |
|---|---|---|
| one small bed and two cofors . . . . . | | 00 15 00 |
| Hay in ye barn and gras un cut down . . . . | | 05 00 00 |
| Corn growing on ye grownd . . . . . | | 10 00 00 |
| manure in ye fould . . . . . . . | | 01 00 00 |

THE INVENTORIES OF LILLESHALL            233

| | | |
|---|---|---|
| flax towed in ye house | 00 | 18 | 00 |
| Chese in ye house | 02 | 00 | 00 |
| two other mares | 05 | 15 | 00 |
| Linings of all sorts | 02 | 00 | 00 |
| ould Lumber | 01 | 00 | 00 |
| waring Aparill | 00 | 10 | 00 |
| Things not seen omited or forgotten | 00 | 05 | 00 |
| | 89 | 14 | 00 |

## 69. Katherine Hall

Of Donnington, widow, taken by Thomas Wright, Richard Robotham, William Cartwright and Robert Reynolds and exhibited on 6 April 1710. There is no date on the inventory.

*Imprs.*

| | | | |
|---|---|---|---|
| Two Oxen | 11 | 00 | 00 |
| Five Cows | 15 | 00 | 00 |
| Four year olds | 06 | 10 | 00 |
| Two Swine | 02 | 05 | 00 |
| An old Tumbril | 01 | 00 | 00 |
| And old Cart & A wains body and plow | 01 | 00 | 00 |
| A Pair of Harrows | 00 | 13 | 04 |
| Three Tewtors | 00 | 13 | 04 |
| A Cheese press | 00 | 02 | 00 |
| Three Mares and A fole | 18 | 00 | 00 |
| Implyments of Husbandry of all Sorts | 00 | 05 | 00 |
| Winter Corn growing on the Ground Twelve Strike and ½ | 10 | 00 | 06 |
| Barley Growing 30 Strike and Pease | 20 | 00 | 00 |
| French Wheat | 00 | 01 | 06 |
| Muxton Living one years value | 20 | 00 | 00 |

*Goods in the Parlour*

| | | | |
|---|---|---|---|
| one feather bed A Coverlid and one blanket two boulsters & all thereto belonging | 05 | 10 | 00 |
| A Long Table two forms & A Chest & A Chair | 01 | 00 | 00 |
| A warming pan | 00 | 03 | 00 |

*Goods in the house*

| | | | |
|---|---|---|---|
| A long Table two forms | 00 | 15 | 00 |
| five big pewter dishes | 01 | 05 | 00 |
| Three little pewter dishes six plates two pewter Candlesticks & A pewter Cup & all the rest of the pewter | 00 | 12 | 00 |
| Iron ware two spits one Iron grate with two Nigots with fire Shovel & tongs & a pair of Racks | 00 | 14 | 00 |

*goods in the buttery*

| | | | |
|---|---|---|---|
| An Iron Pestel & frying pan | 00 | 01 | 06 |
| One Iron pot & two brass Kettles & A brass pan | 00 | 13 | 00 |

| | | |
|---|---|---|
| Six barrels & a Hogsheaed | | 01 00 00 |
| A dresser A screen & three Chees fats & two Cheesplates | | 00 15 00 |
| A Chees tub A Churn two Pales and A Gone | | 00 13 00 |

*In the Kitchen*

| | | |
|---|---|---|
| A Suck & two Colters A Shovel & evil A Hopper and Kneading Turnel A Tub A hand Saw wth old iron | | 00 19 00 |
| A wheelbarrow | | 00 03 00 |

*In the Chambr over the parlour*

| | | |
|---|---|---|
| Two Stone Cisterns & A Stone Trough | | 00 13 00 |
| One feather bed two boulsters two Chaff beds one Rug one Blanket with all things thereto belonging | | 03 00 00 |
| One Joynt press | | 00 15 00 |
| A round Table | | 00 10 00 |
| Linnens of all sorts two pair of fine sheets three pair of round Sheets two table Cloths one dozen and half of Napkins with the rest | | 02 01 00 |

*The Chamber over ye house*

| | | |
|---|---|---|
| Two pair of bedstids one feather bed two boulsters one bed of feathers & flocks together one Chaff bed five blankets | | 04 00 00 |
| One Chest and two Coffers | | 00 10 00 |
| Wearing Apparel & money in her pocket | | 03 00 00 |
| Five Stone of hemp | | 00 15 00 |
| Nine Stone of flax | | 01 07 00 |
| A Which | | 00 10 00 |
| Things forgotten and out of sight | | 00 05 00 |
| Sume total is | | 138 06 10 |

## 70. The Revd. Henry Haughton

Vicar of Lilleshall, taken by Thomas Willett and Godfrey Williams on 30 October 1710 and exhibited on 1 December 1710. He died on 10 October and was buried on 12 October 1710.

*Imprs. In ye House place*

| | | |
|---|---|---|
| Iron ware of all sorts | | 01 05 00 |
| one Long Table and too Joynd fformes | | 01 00 00 |
| ffive Chairs and 3 Joynd stools | | 00 15 00 |
| one square table | | 00 06 08 |

*In ye Kitchen*

| | | |
|---|---|---|
| one ffurnace and one Little Boyler one Brass pott and 3 Little Kettles and one Little Iron pott and 3 pails | | 02 03 04 |

*In ye parlour*

| | | |
|---|---|---|
| one Bed and all belonging to it | | 02 00 00 |
| one Little Round Table | | 00 03 04 |

THE INVENTORIES OF LILLESHALL                235

| | |
|---|---|
| 3 Chairs | 00 03 00 |
| 2 hanging presses | 00 10 00 |

*In ye pantry*

| | |
|---|---|
| Brass and pewter of all sorts | 01 15 00 |
| Trindle wear of all sorts | 01 00 00 |

*In ye sellar*

| | |
|---|---|
| 6 half Hogsheads and 2 Barrells | 01 05 00 |

*The Room over ye Kitchin*

| | |
|---|---|
| two Beds and all belonging to them | 04 00 00 |
| 6 Chairs and 6 Cushions | 00 15 00 |
| one Couch Chair and a Little old Table | 00 03 04 |

*The Roome over ye House*

| | |
|---|---|
| one Bed and all belonging to it | 01 05 00 |
| three Tables | 01 00 00 |
| one Chest 3 Chairs one Little Desk and one Coffer and one Livery Cubbard | 01 00 00 |
| one Looking Glass | 00 04 00 |

*The Roome over ye parlour*

| | |
|---|---|
| one Little Bed and one hanging press | 00 10 00 |
| Linnins of all sorts | 05 00 00 |
| Hay and Corne in the Barne | 05 00 00 |
| two Swine | 02 00 00 |
| 3 Cows 3 yearlings and one year old Calfe | 11 10 00 |
| one Silver Can | 06 10 00 |
| his wearing apparel and mony in his pocket | 07 00 00 |
| for things omitted and out of sight | 00 02 06 |
| Som old Boocks | 01 10 00 |
| Sum | 59 15 02 |

## 71. Thomasin Hawkins

Of Muxton, taken by George Benbow, William Shelton and William Corbett on 3 December 1713 and exhibited on 6 April 1714.

| | |
|---|---|
| Corne & Hay | 57 12 00 |
| Horses | 30 00 00 |
| Chattle | 53 05 00 |
| Swine | 05 00 00 |
| Cartes plowes & Husbandrey Materialls | 05 10 00 |
| Turkeys Hens & poultery | 00 15 00 |

*goods in ye house*

| | |
|---|---|
| one Warmeing pan | 00 04 00 |

pewter 16 dishes and 2 Dozen of plates . . . . . 02 17 00
4 Brass Kettles, one Boyler one pan 2 sause pans & a Skellett . . 02 00 00
3 Iron pots . . . . . . . . . 00 15 00
one Jacke . . . . . . . . . 00 06 00
one Grate a paire of Tongues a fire shivll & creper & frogg . . 00 15 00
dreeping pan & grid Iron . . . . . . . 00 16 00
6 chires . . . . . . . . . 00 12 00
a cuffer & table . . . . . . . . 00 05 00
5 Candle stickes . . . . . . . . 00 03 00

### Goods in the Dining Roome

one table & forme & Cuffer & Joyne stoole . . . . 00 06 00
6 pewter poringers . . . . . . . . 00 03 00
one Chamber pott . . . . . . . . 00 00 06

### Goods in the Milke house

3 Wooden 3 Chespotts 2 seethes 2 sives 10 Tickney Milkpans 7
steanes one pan . . . . . . . . 00 06 00

### In Mr. Hawkins Chambr

2 Beads . . . . . . . . , . 03 10 00
a hanging press Cubbart & Deske . . . . . . 00 15 00

### In ye parlor

a Chest of Drawers a Cubbet & Deske . . . . . 00 15 00
3 Chires a Table & Close stoole . . . . . . 00 12 00
a Clocke . . . . . . . . . 03 00 00
2 Tables . . . . . . . . . 00 16 00
6 Joyne Chires & 6 Segg Chires . . . . . . 01 04 00
one grate . . . . . . . . . 00 02 00
3 picktures . . . . . . . . . 04 00 00
Glasses & Bottles . . . . . . . . 00 05 00
Window Hangings . . . . . . . . 00 03 00
Small picktures . . . . . . . . 00 05 00

### In ye pantery

a Table a forme & a stoole & a glass case . . . . 00 08 00
5 Tickney dishes . . . . . . . . 00 02 06

### In ye green Chamber

one Bead & 2 Chests . . . . . . . 03 10 00
one Chire & 2 Baskets . . . . . . . 00 04 00

### In ye parlor Chamber

one Bead . . . . . . . . . 05 00 00
one Table & Chire a stand & Trunk . . . . . 01 00 00
one Lookeing Glass . . . . . . . . 00 05 00
Window Hangings . . . . . . . . 00 03 06

### In the Kitching Chamber

one Bead . . . . . . . . . 05 00 00

THE INVENTORIES OF LILLESHALL 237

| | |
|---|---|
| 3 Cane Chires & cushing a Table & a Cubbort a box & Stand | 01 05 00 |
| one glass | 00 05 00 |
| window Hangings | 00 03 06 |
| a bead 2 Cuffers & a Chire | 01 15 00 |
| 8 paire of fine sheets | 04 16 00 |
| 8 paire of sheets att | 04 00 00 |
| 5 paire of sheets | 01 05 00 |
| 8 paire of sheets | 01 00 00 |
| 13 Table Clothes | 01 06 00 |
| 3 Dozon of ffine Napkins | 01 10 00 |
| one Huckoback side Cloth a Dozen of Napkins & Table Cloths | 00 18 00 |
| 2 Dozon of Corse Napkins 9 pillow beares & 8 pillow beares | 01 03 00 |
| 6 Diaper Towels a dozen of corse Towells 5 Table Cloths | 00 13 00 |
| 6 small pillow beares | 00 03 00 |
| Cheese | 04 00 00 |
| 10 Barrells & ffirkins | 03 14 00 |
| 5 Tubs a weeting full & Churne | 01 13 00 |
| a Cheese press | 00 10 00 |
| a baskett & Chaine at ye well | 00 07 06 |
| 2 stone Ewers & 2 Laders | 00 13 00 |
| 3 Wheeles & 3 Chamber pots | 00 10 06 |

*In ye Milkhouse*

| | |
|---|---|
| a Cheese tub & kneading tub, 2 Barrells & 2 Bushels a haire Cloth | |
| 2 turnels & a Cuffor | 01 00 00 |
| 6 Bagges | 00 08 00 |
| a halve peck & a malt shivll | 00 02 00 |
| 2 spades | 00 02 00 |
| Horse geeres & sadles | 01 10 00 |
| a Carte Rope & Hopper | 00 03 00 |
| a Shivell & a Bill | 00 01 09 |
| s spits & a paire of Cobbots | 00 07 00 |
| a dozen of Silver Spoones | 04 04 00 |
| a silver Tankett | 05 00 00 |
| Things forgott and unseene | 01 00 00 |
| Tottall | 238 01 01 |

## 72. Edward Owen

Of Lilleshall, webster, taken by Walter Bradbourne and John Evans on 9 April 1714 and exhibited on 16 April 1714. He died on 1 April and was buried on 3 April 1714.

*Imps. In ye House place*

| | |
|---|---|
| one Little Table and fforme and Chair | 00 06 00 |
| Woodenware of all sorts | 00 02 06 |
| Trindlewear of all sorts | 00 04 06 |
| one ffeather bed and all appertaining to it | 01 10 00 |
| Linnins of all sorts | 00 02 00 |

*Over ye house place*

| | |
|---|---|
| two paire of Bedsteads and 3 old Coffers. | 00 13 04 |
| fflax dressd and undressd . | 00 17 00 |
| Brass and Pewter of all sorts | 01 05 00 |
| Iron ware of all sorts | 00 09 00 |
| Three Cows . | 07 10 00 |
| one working loome and Gears and materialls belonging to his trade . | 01 10 00 |
| Bonds & Bills and desperate debts . | 60 00 00 |
| for his wearing Apparell and mony in his pockett | 01 00 00 |
| for things omitted . | 00 02 00 |
| Sum | 76 01 04 |

## 73. Robert Shelton

Of Lilleshall, yeoman, taken by Thomas Turner and John Shelton on 12 November 1717 and exhibited on 20 December 1717. In his will made on 6 August 1716 he left his moveable property to his wife Joan and his tenement in Lilleshall to his son Richard.

*Imprs. goods in ye house place*

| | |
|---|---|
| Iron ware of all sorts | 03 00 00 |
| one Skreen . | 00 15 00 |
| 4 Chairs and 2 joynd stooles: | 00 07 00 |
| one Long Table and 2 joynd fformes | 01 05 00 |
| one dresser and pewter shelves | 01 05 00 |
| 2 Bacon Cratches | 00 10 00 |
| Brass and pewter of all sorts | 00 08 00 |
| one Glass cage | 00 02 00 |

*In ye over parlour*

| | |
|---|---|
| one hanging press . | 01 02 06 |
| one Chest of drawers | 01 00 00 |
| one press and Cubbard | 01 00 00 |
| one Table | 00 09 00 |
| 6 chairs one stand 2 stools and a Little Coffer | 01 01 06 |
| one Little Looking Glass | 00 01 06 |

*In the Lower parlour*

| | |
|---|---|
| one Bed and all belonging to it | 05 00 00 |
| one round table . | 00 08 00 |
| one Chest . | 00 10 00 |
| 3 Chairs and a Close Stoole. | 00 18 00 |

*the Servants Chamber*

| | |
|---|---|
| one Bed and all belonging to it | 02 00 00 |

# THE INVENTORIES OF LILLESHALL

*the Chamber over ye over parlour*

| | |
|---|---|
| one Bed and all belonging to it | 05 00 00 |
| one Chest of drawers | 01 05 00 |
| one Chest one desk and one Box | 00 15 00 |
| 5 Chairs | 00 15 00 |

*In the Chamber over the House*

| | |
|---|---|
| 2 Joynd Beds and a truckle bed | 08 00 00 |
| 5 Chairs one Coffer and a Box | 00 13 00 |
| one pair of Bedsteads one Coffer and a box | 00 14 00 |
| Hemp and flax 7 stone | 01 18 00 |
| 2 stone of wooll | 01 05 00 |
| Cheese | 10 00 00 |
| Linnen of all sorts | 10 00 00 |
| white ware of all sorts | 00 10 00 |

*In the Sellar*

| | |
|---|---|
| 8 Barrells and a big Turnell | 02 15 00 |

*In the Kitchen*

| | |
|---|---|
| one stone Cisstern | 01 05 00 |
| one mault Mill and a Chees press | 01 10 00 |
| one furnace | 02 00 00 |
| one Little table and Joynd forme | 00 06 00 |
| Wooden ware of all sorts | 03 10 00 |
| one hair cloth | 00 15 00 |
| old Mault | 01 15 00 |

| | |
|---|---|
| 9 Cowes and a Bull | 33 00 00 |
| 6 three year old Cattle | 18 00 00 |
| 6 two year olds | 11 10 00 |
| 8 year olds | 08 00 00 |
| 8 horses and Mares | 30 00 00 |
| 12: sheep | 03 12 00 |
| Implements of husbandry of all sorts | 22 00 00 |
| 3 swine | 09 00 00 |

| | |
|---|---|
| hard corne of all sorts | 10 00 00 |
| Barley | 18 15 00 |
| pease | 10 00 00 |
| oats | 06 05 00 |
| Hay | 15 00 00 |

| | |
|---|---|
| poultry of all sorts | 01 00 00 |
| one strike and halfe of hemp seed | 00 06 00 |
| 5 spining wheels and 3 Reels | 01 00 00 |

| | |
|---|---|
| for pictures in all the Roomes | 00 06 08 |
| one Close Bassket 2 butter Basskets and two voider Basskets | 00 05 00 |

| | | | |
|---|---|---|---|
| Corne on the ground . . . . . . | 02 | 10 | 00 |
| Coales . . . . . . . . | 00 | 12 | 00 |
| his wareing Apparrell and mony in his pockett . . . . | 05 | 10 | 00 |
| for things omitted and not seen . . . . . . | 01 | 10 | 00 |
| | 276 | 09 | 02 |

## 74. William Cartwright

Of Muxton, mathematician, taken by Charles Wickstead and Thomas Ward on 9 April 1718 and exhibited on 18 April 1718.

*In the Kitchen*

| | | | |
|---|---|---|---|
| Imp. Pewter dishes, 5 pewter porringers 2 pewter tankards 2 pewter candlesticks 1 pewter chamber pot & one close stool pan & six pewter quarts . . . . . . . . . | 01 | 00 | 00 |
| One Brass warmeing pan one skellett one basteing spoon one Candlestick & one brass kettle . . . . . . | 00 | 04 | 00 |
| Two spits one Large Dreeping pan 1 cleever 1 hacking knive one Iron basteing spoon one flesh forke one pair of Tongues one case mettle frog one grate with nigards two smoothing Irons 3 fier shovells & one Kettle Two Iron candlesticks one Iron pott 1 Tin driping pan one egg slice one Tin cancle Backe Six Iron skeres & one Iron maid . . . . . . . . | 00 | 15 | 02 |
| One skreen chair one forme one table one dresser one turning table . | 00 | 10 | 00 |

*In the Old Parlor*

| | | | |
|---|---|---|---|
| One pair of Join bed steads one Cubbard one feather bed one chaff bed on feather bolster one chaff bolster three blanketts . . | 02 | 00 | 00 |

*In ye New Parlor*

| | | | |
|---|---|---|---|
| One Long table one form 3 join stools four Join chairs and four Turkey quishions . . . . . . . . | 01 | 00 | 00 |

*In the Buttrey*

| | | | |
|---|---|---|---|
| One Barrell and a turnell . . . . . . . | 00 | 05 | 00 |

*In the Brewhouse*

| | | | |
|---|---|---|---|
| One Guileing tub three Narrow tubs One cooler One Neading turnell one half strike & one Little round Turnell . . . | 00 | 07 | 00 |

*In the Sellar*

| | | | |
|---|---|---|---|
| One hogshead and two Barrells . . . . . . | 00 | 12 | 00 |

*In the Parlour Chamber*

| | | | |
|---|---|---|---|
| One arm Joyn chair and two Tables . . . . . | 00 | 10 | 00 |

# THE INVENTORIES OF LILLESHALL

*In the old Parlour Chamber*
One pair of bedstids one table & two old coffers . . . 00 04 02

*In the Chamber over the house*
One flock bed Two pillows Two old Blanketts one piece of Kiderminster stuff one chaff bed one flock boulster one White rugg one pair of bedstids one Little Square table one close stoole one feather bed & feather boulsters Two old Blanketts one other Feather bed & chaff bed . . . . . . . . . 01 12 00

*In the closett*
One hundred books, three leg staffe one plaine table one wood Quadrant one small Brass Quadrant one brass seal one Brass sights one pair of Brass Compasses One pensell one slate one spectacle Glass . . . . . . . . . . 01 12 00
One pair of Globes and box . . . . . . 00 10 00
Wareing apparell & moneys in Pockett . . . . . 02 00 00
Things omitted and not seen . . . . . . 00 10 00

17 04 04

## 75. John Adney

Of Lilleshall, webster, taken by Thomas Turner and William Corbett on 30 October 1729 and proved on 31 October 1729; He was buried on 25 October 1729.

Goods of all sorts . . . . . . . . 01 10 00

*In Chamber* 1 bed & 2 Chairs . . . . . . 01 10 00

*In the room above* 2 little beds & 4 Chairs . . . . 02 00 00

one old Cow, 1 Year old Heifer & two Calves . . . 04 00 00
one little swine . . . . . . . . 01 00 00

2 old Looms & Implements belonging to his Trade . . 02 10 00
Wearing Apparrell & Money in his Pockett . . . . 01 00 00
Things omitted & out of sight . . . . . . 00 03 00

13 15 00

## 76. Elizabeth Adney

Of Donnington, widow, taken by William Hammersley and Richard Shelton on 29 March 1731 and exhibited on 4 May 1731. She was buried on 25 March 1731.

*In ye House place*
15 pewter dishes . . . . . . . . 01 00 00

| | |
|---|---|
| 14 od pewter plates | 00 06 00 |
| 2 od Can 2 Candlesticks porringers salt & mustard Cup | 00 03 00 |
| one od warming pan a Candlestick & dredger | 00 04 00 |
| 2 brass kettles | 00 06 00 |
| 3 od Iron potts | 00 05 00 |
| 1 Mortar & pestle | 00 02 00 |
| A dresser of drawers | 00 06 00 |
| a dripping pan 2 basting Ladles Skymer flesh form Candlestick Hacking knife bellows Salt box Iron Candlestick | 00 05 00 |
| A Grate kreepers fire shovell & Tonges frying pan | 00 04 00 |
| one od round table a square table & form | 00 02 00 |
| 4 old Chairs a sawce pan | 00 01 00 |
| a parsell of old trenchers & od Lantern | 00 01 00 |

*In ye parlour*

| | |
|---|---|
| one old bed & steads | 01 00 00 |
| one Chest & Linnen | 01 00 00 |
| 4 od Chairs | 00 01 06 |
| one Lookeing Glass | 00 04 00 |
| 2 small square tables | 00 01 06 |
| one small Lookeing Glass | 00 01 00 |

*Chamber over ye Parlour*

| | |
|---|---|
| 2 od Beds & Steads & hangings | 01 10 00 |
| 4 od Chairs | 00 02 00 |
| one od trunk one Coffer Small Lookeing Glass 2 Small Chests | 00 06 00 |
| 3 od prints 2 Glasses | 00 01 00 |

*Chamber over ye House*

| | |
|---|---|
| one od Chaff bed | 00 05 00 |
| a table a Chest 2 weels & form some other Lumber 2 od Tubbs | 00 14 00 |
| some wheat In ye Chest malt & Bacon | 00 18 00 |

*In ye Shop* 6 Looms & Gairs . . . . . 02 00 00

*In ye Butterry*

a Cooler 2 barrills & Churn . . . . . 00 05 00

*Barn*

a Thrave of Corn . . . . . 00 03 00

*In ye yard*

| | |
|---|---|
| a Stone Cistern | 00 02 06 |
| 2 od Cows & Calves | 04 00 00 |
| 2 Sterkes | 02 00 00 |
| Wearing apparrell & money In pockett | 00 05 00 |
| things Omitted & out of sight | 00 05 00 |
| Totall | 19 00 06 |

# THE INVENTORIES OF LILLESHALL

## 77. Thomas Newell

Of Donnington, gentleman, taken by Thomas Higgins and John Sillitoe* on 18 May 1731 and exhibited on 26 May 1731. He was buried on 5 May 1731.

| | |
|---|---|
| Therteen milk Cows at £3.10 a peice | 45 10 00 |
| Too Bulls At | 04 10 00 |
| Six too year old Heifers & one Bullock at £2.15 a peice | 19 05 00 |
| Ten year old Calfes at £1.15 a peice | 17 10 00 |
| Nine Rearing Calves at 16s a peice | 07 04 00 |
| One Black Mare and Colt | 07 00 00 |
| One old Chestnett mare | 03 00 00 |
| One young Chesnet mare | 07 00 00 |
| Two old Black mares at £3.15 a peice | 07 10 00 |
| One young Black mare | 06 00 00 |
| Too Too years old Black Colts | 08 00 00 |
| One Too year old hoarse Colt | 01 10 00 |
| ffour yearling Colts at £1.10 a peice | 10 00 00 |
| ffour store Hogs at £1.7.6 a peice | 05 10 00 |
| Corne in the Barne | 08 00 00 |
| Corne in the ground | 15 00 00 |
| Hay on Stacks | 07 10 00 |
| Corne and mault in the House | 01 10 00 |
| Wagons Carts and all other Implems of Husbandry | 11 10 00 |

*In the Chamber over the parler*

| | |
|---|---|
| one suit of Bed hangins and one Quilt | 02 10 00 |
| one Looking Glass | 00 04 00 |
| Six Chiars | 00 09 00 |

*In the Roome over the Litle parlour*

| | |
|---|---|
| One suite of Curtaines and one old counterpen | 01 00 00 |
| A Dozen pair of Sheets | 02 10 00 |
| Three ffine Table Cloaths | 00 12 00 |

*In the Dairy*

| | |
|---|---|
| Six small Brass milk pans and too Treas | — — — |

*In the Pantrey*

| | |
|---|---|
| nineteen pewter Dishes and ffour Dozen of plates One salver one passett cup one Chamber pot | 03 10 00 |
| One Napkin press | 00 03 06 |
| A Tea Talle and all belonging to it | 01 00 00 |
| One silver Tankard | 06 00 00 |

*In the parlour*

| | |
|---|---|
| One writing Desk | 00 15 00 |
| Six Cane Chairs | 00 09 00 |
| One looking Glass | 00 03 00 |
| one weather Glass | 01 00 00 |
| One Grate | 00 05 00 |

### In the Kitchin
| | |
|---|---|
| one ffender | 00 01 06 |
| One Grate | 00 10 00 |
| One purgatory | 00 04 00 |
| one plate frame and a ffrog. | 00 02 00 |
| One Coffee Pot | 00 01 02 |
| One Cubert | 00 02 10 |
| Too Guns | 00 15 00 |
| One Looking Glass | 00 01 02 |

### In the Chamber over the Brewhouse
| | |
|---|---|
| One Mault mill | 00 10 00 |
| Wearing Aparill and Money in pockett | 02 05 00 |
| Things omitted and not seen | 00 07 06 |
| totall | 219 09 08 |

## 78. William Adney

Of Lilleshall, miller, taken by William Adney and William Hammersley on 6 December 1737, and exhibited on 26 April 1738. He was buried on 21 November 1737.

### House Place
| | |
|---|---|
| one Clock & Case | 02 00 00 |
| one Long Table & form | 00 07 06 |
| 2 Small Square tables one small round table | 00 04 00 |
| a Small Dresser wth 2 Drawers wth Shelves | 00 05 00 |
| 6 pewter Dishes 4 old plates | 00 17 00 |
| 5 pewter pollingers 2 pewter Candlesticks | 00 02 00 |
| 2 pewter Quorts 2 pewter pints 5 spoons one Cup | 00 04 06 |
| one Iron morter & pestle one pot | 00 05 00 |
| one Brass Kettle on maslin & 2 Brass Candlesticks | 00 10 00 |
| Ye Grate one frog one pair of Tonges & fir Shovele | 00 06 00 |
| pott Links pan holder flesh fork | 00 01 06 |
| one pair of racks one spitt one Iron broiler | 00 03 00 |
| one box Iron old Iron Candlestick a Cast fireplate | 00 05 00 |
| one Brass frog a pair of Belloes a Salt Box | 00 02 06 |
| 6 old Chairs 3 pails a Gaun & Cheese Tub a Bottle Wood Dish Seive Badstaff | 00 07 00 |
| old Skreen old Cupboard Lanteen Little Wheele. | 00 03 06 |
| a Chest wth Linnen | 02 00 00 |
| a feather Bed two Bolsters one pillow one rug 3 blanketts Bedsteads &c. | 02 00 00 |
| an old Chest & Close Stoul | 03 06 00 |

### Farther parlour
| | |
|---|---|
| one old Cupboard | 00 02 06 |

### Celler
| | |
|---|---|
| 5 Barrells | 00 15 00 |

### Buttery
A Barrell a Churn 2 kimnells 2 Cheese mitts 2 Seives 5 old Trenchers    00 07 00

### Farther Buttery
a Square Table    .    .    .    .    .    .    .    .    00 02 00

### Chamber over ye Parlour
one Chaff Bed Bedsteads & rug    .    .    .    .    .    .    00 08 00

### Chamber over ye house
3 Straw Bings wth some oats Cheese & Bacon    .    .    .    .    01 00 00

### Brewhouse
one small Brass Boiler 2 Brewing Tubs 3 Benches 2 Coolers    .    .    01 15 00
one old pail    .    .    .    .    .    .    .    .    .    00 01 00

### In ye Yard
| | |
|---|---|
|3 Cows    .    .    .    .    .    .    .    .    .|06 00 00|
|5 horces    .    .    .    .    .    .    .    .|15 00 00|
|one Cart & Tumbrell other Implements of husbandry   .    .    .|04 00 00|
|Geering for 5 horses .    .    .    .    .    .    .    .|01 00 00|
|two Store swine    .    .    .    .    .    .    .|01 00 00|
|Corn in ye Barn    .    .    .    .    .    .    .|05 00 00|
|Wearing Apparrell money In pockett    .    .    .    .    .|02 00 00|
|a Grinding Stone other old lumber Earthenware .    .    .    .|00 05 00|

                                                                        49 05 00

## 79. Richard Adney

Of Donnington, taken by John Taylor* and Thomas Southern on 19 April 1738 and exhibited on 26 April 1738.

### In the house and Buttery
a Cupboard one Barrell A Cheese Tub a pail a Chaffing dish 2
Candlesticks and other things    .    .    .    .    .    .    00 15 00

### In ye Chambr
one Bed & furniture a Chest and other Linnen    .    .    .    .    02 10 00

### In ye Shop
Two Looms and Geering    .    .    .    .    .    .    .    04 00 00

Money In house and wareing apparrell    .    .    .    .    .    10 10 00

                                                                        17 15 00

## 80. James Spender

Of Lilleshall, yeoman, taken by James Brookes and Robert Light on 21 July 1748 and exhibited on 25 July 1748.

*In the House place*

| | |
|---|---|
| An old Table and fform | 00 05 06 |
| a Cupboard and Chair | 00 06 00 |
| a Dresser of Drawers a Little Table and Close stool | 00 08 06 |
| a Little old Cupboard and an old Chair | 00 04 00 |
| ffire Shovell & Tongs an Iron Jack Two Spitts Mortar & Pestle ffrying Pan & Marmant | 00 13 06 |
| Pewter containing Eight old Dishes and fifteen Plates | 01 08 00 |
| The Iron Grate and fender | 00 07 00 |

*In the Parlour*

| | |
|---|---|
| a Feather Bed, Bedsteds, Bolsters, sheets, Blanketts hangings & furniture | 01 10 00 |
| a Chest of drawers, one Ovall Table and Eight join'd Chairs | 01 02 00 |
| a Clock and Hanging Press | 01 19 00 |

*In the Brewhouse*

| | |
|---|---|
| One Brass ffurnace and one Iron ffurnace | 01 08 00 |
| all the Brewing Bessells | 01 00 00 |
| a Pealing Iron a Little Table one Saddle, one long Wheele | 00 09 00 |
| Half a strike and Two old Benches | 00 01 04 |

*In the Scullery*

| | |
|---|---|
| Two Pailes a Churn, one Cheese Tub & a wooden Bottle | 00 03 06 |

*In the Cellar*

| | |
|---|---|
| Three Barrells and a horse | 00 13 00 |

*In the Chamber over the Brewhouse*

| | |
|---|---|
| one ffeather Bed & another Chaff Bed & furniture | 01 10 00 |
| a Chest with Linnen and a Tray | 00 16 06 |

*In the Chamber over the Parlour*

| | |
|---|---|
| one ffeather Bed Bedsteds hangings and furniture | 01 10 00 |
| a Chest of Drawers, a Chest and four chairs | 01 02 00 |

*In the Chamber over the House place*

| | |
|---|---|
| Two ffeather Beds, Bedsteds & furniture (one of them half Testr. with hangings) | 02 10 00 |
| one Chest one long Table & form | 00 09 06 |

*In the Garrett*

| | |
|---|---|
| a Small parcell of Cheese, a Wheel and an old Coffer | 01 12 00 |
| The Hay in the Carthouse Tallant | 02 00 00 |

| | £ | s | d |
|---|---|---|---|
| one old Cart & Wheels, a Pair of Harrows and Plow | 01 | 10 | 00 |
| The Clover over the Horse Tallant | 02 | 00 | 00 |
| Horse Gearing | 00 | 12 | 00 |
| a Rick of Clover in the Hill Leasow | 03 | 00 | 00 |
| a Tumbrell Body and old wheels | 00 | 04 | 00 |
| Wearing Apparell | 01 | 00 | 00 |
| Lumber and things omitted | 00 | 02 | 06 |
| Total | 31 | 15 | 10 |

## THE INVENTORIES OF WELLINGTON

### 81. Thomas Lockley

Of Aston under the Wrekin, taken by Edward Pemberton, Thomas Lawrence and Edward Clarke* on 4 September 1659 and exhibited on 3 April 1661.

| | |
|---|---|
| ffirst. Sheepe in the Wreakin of all sorts . . . . . | 10 00 00 |
| one ould Cow & a heafer & his part of ye wild beasts . . . | 07 00 00 |
| Hay & Corne of all sorts in the barne . . . . . | 03 00 00 |

*In the parlour*
| | |
|---|---|
| one Joyned bed with all things thereto belonging One Joyned Presse one Table board one coffer. . . . . . . | 02 13 04 |

*In the Chamber over the parlour*
| | |
|---|---|
| one little bedstead with all things thereto belonging two coffers . | 00 06 08 |

| | |
|---|---|
| Corne in the house . . . . . . . . | 01 10 00 |
| Wooll . . . . . . . . . . | 02 10 00 |

*In the house*
| | |
|---|---|
| One little Cupboard one Table one bench three chaires . . . | 00 06 08 |
| Brasse & Pewter of all sorts. . . . . . . | 01 00 00 |
| Woodden ware of all sorts . . . . . . . | 00 06 08 |
| Two little Iron Potts . . . . . . . | 00 04 00 |
| Husbandry implements . . . . . . . | 00 02 00 |
| His wearing apparell . . . . . . . . | 01 00 00 |
| Crabbs . . . . . . . . . | 00 01 00 |
| Beefe bacon & Butter . . . . . . . | 00 05 00 |
| All things forgott . . . . . . . . | 00 05 00 |
| Toto . . . | 30 12 00 |

### 82. William Smith

Of Watling Street, Wellington, apparently a carrier, taken by Samuel Thrapp, Thomas Bennett, John Bennett and Thomas Harper on 4 October 1659, and exhibited on 12 October 1660.

*Imprimis in the house or hall*
| | |
|---|---|
| one table and frame, one forme, one joyned Cheare, two chaires with seats of flaggs and two stooles praised to . . . . | 01 00 00 |
| Item. one Cupboard and Presse . . . . . . | 00 14 00 |
| Item. one pewter Gonn, two flagons six pewter dishes 4 candlesticks one salt, one Tankert one Botle . . . . . | 01 00 00 |
| Item about four yards of wainscott . . . . . | 00 06 00 |

*In the Kitchin*

It. 2 skimers, bastinge spoone 2 brasse kettles, 3 Brass potts, 1 warminge pan 1 posnett, 1 Chafer, 2 skelletts . . . .  01 12 00

It. one Iron Morter and pestelle, 2 grates 3 smoothing Irons. 1 jack iorne spitt 2 paire of pot gaoles, 2 paire of Cobbarts, 1 Iron crow, 1 picke, 1 fryinge pan, one Drippinge pan, 2 spitts, 1 Iron pott, 1 paire of Tongs & fireshovell . . . . .  01 00 00

It. 1 Cupbord and Presse, 8 horshewes 1 table and frame 2 turnd Chears, 1 disbord, 3 shilves and 1 dresser . . . .  01 06 08

*In the Butterie*

Item. 6 Barrells, 1 hoghead, 2 payles, 2 stonds, 2 dosen of Trenchers and other Trynenwares . . . . . . .  00 15 00

*In the Chamber by the butterie*

It. 1 bedstead, 1 Featherbed & bolster 2 pillowes 1 flockbed, 2 blancketts, 1 Coveringe . . . . . . .  01 05 00

*In the Chamber over the house*

It. 1 bedstead with yellowe Curtaines, 1 fetherbed 2 bolsters, 1 pillow, 1 blankett, 1 greene Rugg, 1 paire of sheets . .  01 00 00

It. one bedstead with halfe a Teaster, 1 Truckle bed, 1 fether bed, 1 bolster, 1 coveringe, 2 coffers . . . . .  00 10 00

It. 2 small Chests . . . . . . . .  00 15 00
It. 9 Fleces of wooll . . . . . . . .  00 10 00
It. 1 old carbine & 1 old sword . . . . . .  00 02 06
It. lynnen & Napperie ware . . . . . . .  00 05 00
It. his wearinge apparrell . . . . . . .  00 05 00

*In the Chamber over the kitchin*

It. 2 bedsteads with beddinge & bedcloathes 3 packsadles 2 hackney sadles, 2 waine Ropes, 6 maling cords, 4 mountin boards 2 Baggs, pte. of a white hide . . . . . . .  01 00 00

It. 1 waine & 1 Tumbrill with Iron bound wheeles, wheelborough 2 lathes 2 plowes, 1 harrowe 1 other harrow without kymes . .  04 00 00

It. ould Timber & poles in ye backside . . . .  01 00 00
It. 1 pomp and stone trough . . . . . .  00 06 08
It. Manure . . . . . . . . .  01 00 00
It. i Chest of horsegeares . . . . . . .  00 10 00
It. a parcell of haye . . . . . . . .  00 10 00
It. a pcell of Barley and fetches . . . . . .  04 00 00
It. 28 sheepe . . . . . . . . .  04 00 00
It. 4 cowes and one heyfer . . . . . . .  11 00 00
It. 15 colts 3 year ould . . . . . . .  02 00 00
It. 2 swine and foure piggs . . . . . . .  01 06 08
It. 1 malt handmill . . . . . . . .  00 06 08
It. For anie other thig whatsoever that may chaunce to be forgotten  00 02 06
It. Nine Naggs and Mares wth packsadles packcloathes girths wontyes and cords . . . . . . . .  27 00 00

63 00 08

## 84. Thomas Wright

Of Wellington, dyer, taken by Richard Browne, Joshua Dunton and Phillip Howle* on 30 December 1662 and exhibited on 21 January 1662-63.

| | |
|---|---|
| Imprimis | |
| Six two year old Beasts | 12 00 00 |
| Two mares and two two yeare old Colts | 08 00 00 |
| Two Cowes | 06 00 00 |
| Hay and straw | 02 00 00 |
| A Grindle stone | 00 10 00 |
| Two ffatts in the dye-house | 01 10 00 |
| Two furnaces | 08 00 00 |
| One Leade ffatt | 02 10 00 |
| Six hundred of Woade | 04 00 00 |
| Two troughes and a kindyr | 00 05 00 |
| In ffusticke and Logwood | 00 05 00 |
| Two quarters of Red-wood | 00 10 00 |
| Shumack and Galls | 00 11 06 |
| Three hundred of mather | 04 00 00 |
| Indico 10 ho.weight | 01 00 00 |
| Allom 1c 2q | 02 00 00 |
| Copperis 3c weight | 01 10 00 |
| Red-wood | 00 01 00 |
| A ffurnace in the presse-house | 01 00 00 |
| A Leaden ffatt | 02 00 00 |
| A Hott presse and a Crow | 02 10 00 |
| In woodenware in the presse house | 01 00 00 |
| Twenty dishes of pewter and two fflagons | 01 00 00 |
| ffoure Brasse pans, 4 Brass potts, a warming pan, a Brasse-Candle sticke a Chafing dish, a morter, and a Chafer | 05 00 00 |
| One Jack, 2 Dreeping pans, a Grate, a fire-shovell, a payre of Tongs, 2 payre of Cobberts, 3 broaches, an Iron morter and pott hookes | 02 00 00 |
| A presse Cupboard, 2 Chaires, a table and dish-bench | 01 00 00 |
| One shooting Gun | 00 06 00 |
| | |
| *In the Hall* | |
| one Table board 6 Joyne stooles, a skreene, waine-scott, 2 cushions and a waine-scott portall | 02 10 00 |
| one hundred weight of Galls | 02 16 00 |
| | |
| *In the shop* | |
| 6 payre of sheers | 02 00 00 |
| In ffusticke | 00 05 06 |
| The Collering of 140 yards of Glanion | 01 03 04 |
| The Collering of 50 yards of Cloath | 01 00 00 |
| | |
| *In the chamber over the Kitchen* | |
| one bed-stead, one presse, one safe, 2 Coffers and a Keauing table | 01 10 00 |
| One ffeather-Bed, one fflock Bed, a couerlett, boulster, and curtaines | 01 00 00 |

*In the Cock-lofts,*
shelves & Coffers, Corne and Graine, butter and Cheese. . . 02 00 00

*In the Chamber over the Hall;*
one bed stead, one Tricle Bed, one waine scott portall, one presse,
& 2 coffers . . . . . . . . . 02 00 00
The Beding and bed cloaths curtaines and valianes; beeing 4 flock
beds and a feather bed . . . . . . 03 00 00

*In the Cock-loft*
One Bed stead a Tricle Bed Bed and bed cloathes . . 00 15 00

*In the best chamber*
one bed stead one great Table board, one little Table, 2 fforms
2 Chests, 2 chaires one Trunk, wainescott & a glasse cupboard . 03 10 00
One ffeather Bed and one fflock Bed a boulster and other ffurniture
belonging to that Bed . . . . . . 01 10 00
One silver Bole . . . . . . . 01 10 00
In napery ware and linnens of all sorts . . . . 05 00 00

*In the House that Richard Johnson lives in:*
2 Tables, one Cupboard, 2 Joyne stooles, a Jack, a Broach, a weting
vessell & other goods in that House . . . . 02 10 00
Debts owing by Bond to the Testator . . . . 32 00 00
debts owing without bond to ye Testator . . . 38 00 07
One standing Taintrey and one ffier Tantrey . . . 01 00 00
One Lease from ffrancis Charlton esq. for three lives . . 50 00 00
One Lease from Sr John Corbett Baronet for three lives . . 120 00 00
In Timber lying in the new street and in the woods . . 07 00 00
In money in the House . . . . . . 08 00 00
The Testatr wearing apparrell . . . . . 05 00 00
and for all other things not herein mencioned . . . 01 00 00

270 15 07

## 84. William Howle

Of Wellington, glover, taken by Robert Birthood* and Humphrey Bennett* on 14 November 1664 and exhibited on 2 June 1665.

Impr.
3 brass kettles 1 skellett 3 brass Potts 1 Iron Pott . . 02 01 00
13 pewter dishes 1 pewter cupp 2 pewter Salts 1 pewter Candlesticke 1 pewter Gill 1 Flaggon 1 pewter pinte 1 pewter quart 1
pewter Sawser . . . . . . . 01 09 10
1 Iron morter & pestell 1 Fryinge panne 2 Iron Spitts 2 payre of
Cobberts 1 Chafinge dish 2 Smoothinge Irons . . . 00 06 08
1 payre bellows 2 Chayres 2 Joyned Stooles 1 Table 1 Foorme
1 press 2 Wood Stunds 1 puddinge plate . . . . 00 16 00

*In ye little Chamber*

| | | |
|---|---|---|
| 1 bible 1 Longe spininge Wheele 1 Large brass spoone 1 Joyned bed & furniture 1 Table board 1 Twigge basket . . . . | 01 14 04 |
| 9 payre & one sheete 2 napkins 1 Table Cloth 1 pillowe beere. . | 01 08 02 |
| 1 Coffer 4 beere barrells 1 stund 1 wood Turnel 1 box . . . | 00 07 00 |
| 6 Steanes of butter 1 Little brewing Stund . . . . | 01 08 00 |
| A pewter Salt 2 dozen of Trenchers 3 milk bowles 1 Churne 3 Winnow Sheetes 1 Iron pirle 1 Coffer 2 porringr dishes 1 pewter measure 6 noggins 2 Water payles 2 bucketts: 1 Can 2 piggins . . | 00 10 00 |
| 1 pr brass Scales 3 Sives & one Search 1 Large Turnell 1 Strike & one Hoope 1 halfe hoope 1 Little wheele 1 Table board 1 Foorme . | 00 06 08 |
| 1 Truckle bed 1 Standinge bed 1 Coffer 1 Straw whiskett . . | 00 18 00 |
| 2 bowlsters 1 pillow 2 beds 1 Coverlidd 1 blanckett . . . | — |
| 6 bundles of Hempe 1 Trunke . . . . . . | — |
| 1 Cow 1 horse . . . . . . . . | 02 15 00 |
| 1 Hay Reeke . . . . . . . . . | 01 10 00 |
| 1 Bay of hay . . . . . . . . . | 00 19 06 |
| 35 quarts of Turnipp Seeds A peece of new woollin Cloth . . | 01 00 00 |
| Left his wife in money & goods . . . . . . | 08 00 00 |
| The Tottall Summe of the above Inventory is . . . . | 25 10 02 |

## 85. Rowland Griffiths

Of Walcot, taken by George Brooke, Edward Russell, Samuel Brooke and Robert Meton on 27 March 1665 and exhibited on 31 May 1665.

| | | |
|---|---|---|
| Imprim. Two Black Cowes . . . . . . . | 06 10 00 |
| Item. Two eare ould Bullocks . . . . . . | 03 00 00 |
| It. One barrin Hifer . . . . . . . . | 01 10 00 |
| It. Two eare ould Hiefors . . . . . . . | 02 10 00 |
| It. ffoure earling bease . . . . . . . | 02 17 04 |
| It. one dune mare . . . . . . . . | 02 06 08 |
| It. Corne & Hay in ye barne . . . . . . | 01 00 00 |
| It. Corne growing on the ground . . . . . . | 02 10 00 |
| It. One Seine . . . . . . . . . | 00 12 00 |
| It. Brasse & Pewter . . . . . . . . | 01 10 00 |
| It. Trinen Ware . . . . . . . . | 00 13 04 |
| It. Three flichens & a quarter of Bakon . . . . . | 01 10 00 |

*It. in the Roome ovr the entrey*

| | | |
|---|---|---|
| one ffither Bed Boulster a Pillow & two Blanckets . . . | 02 05 00 |

*It. in the little Chamber*

| | | |
|---|---|---|
| one chaff bed one Boulster & one Blanket . . . . | 00 10 00 |

*It. in the Seller ovr the little Chamber*

| | | |
|---|---|---|
| one fither Bed one flock bed one boulster & one coverlid . . | 01 06 08 |
| It. All the Linens in the saide Howse . . . . . | 02 06 00 |
| It. An ould dixnary & other Bookes . . . . . | 00 10 00 |
| It. whitemeate . . . . . . . . | 00 10 00 |
| It. Taw . . . . . . . . . | 00 03 04 |

| | | |
|---|---|---|
| It. a grate | | 00 03 04 |
| It. Implemts of Husbandry | | 00 06 08 |
| It. An all things forgotten | | 00 01 00 |
| | The whole | 33 11 04 |

## 86. Elizabeth Walker

Of Wellington, taken by Richard Browne, Joshua Dunton and William Turner on 18 May 1670 and exhibited on 14 April 1671.

*Impr. In the hall*
| | |
|---|---|
| 2 Tables one Joyned Cubbard 3 Stooles & 2 chaires | 00 14 00 |
| Itt one Iron grate & one Iron plate | 00 06 00 |

*Itt in the parlore*
| | |
|---|---|
| one Tableboard 2 formes and 2 Joynt Stooles | 00 12 00 |
| one Joyned Beddsted one ffeatherbed one flockbed on Boulster one Carpett wth other ffurniture to the Bedd. | 02 00 00 |

*Itt in the Chamber over the Shopp*
| | |
|---|---|
| one Tableboard 2 formes 6 Joyned Stooles & Chaeres 2 Stooles Covered with Cloth, one little square table one Screene & a glass-case | 00 17 04 |
| one Jonte Bedsteed one fflockbed one ffeather Bed one Boulster 2 pillows Curtains & Vallends and other ffurniture | 02 01 00 |
| a Carpett & 14 quishins | 00 09 00 |

*Itt in the Longe Chamber*
| | |
|---|---|
| 2 Tableboards 2 benches one Joyned Presse one Cheste & one Coffer | 02 00 00 |
| eight Twigen baskets | 00 05 00 |
| Loose Boards over head | 00 10 00 |
| one Carpett & a Curtaine | 00 05 00 |

*Itt in the little Chamber*
| | |
|---|---|
| 2 ould Joyned bedds one fetherbed one fflock bed with other furniture | 02 11 08 |
| one Chest one Coffer one Trunke one Square Table & 2 stooles | 00 13 04 |

*Itt in the Chamber over the house*
| | |
|---|---|
| 3 ould Bedsteds 2 flockbed & Some other furniture 3 strawen whisketts | 01 00 00 |
| 19 paire of sheets 6 dozen & Half of napkins 7 table Clothes, 5 Pillow beeres with all other napperye ware | 16 00 00 |

*Itt in the kitchen*
| | |
|---|---|
| 4 Brasse potts, 5 kettles, one Brasse pann, one ffurnace, 3 brass Candle stickes, one Chafing dish, one small mortor one warming pan & a Skimmer | 06 00 00 |

one Iron grate, 4 Spitts one Iron dreeping pann and some other
Iron ware . . . . . . . . . . 01 02 06
one Jack . . . . . . . . . 00 05 00
24 Pewter Dishes 2 pewter gauns, 7 fflaggons, 7 porringers, 6
Candlesticks, And some other Small Pewter . . . 04 02 06

*Itt in the Buttery Chamber*
one ffeather Bedd one fflock Bed, with other ffurniture, 2 ould
Coffers one boxe . . . . . . . . 01 10 00

Itt the Tooles in ye Shopp . . . . . . . 00 06 08
Itt Coopere ware . . . . . . . . 03 00 00
Itt Treene ware . . . . . . . . 00 10 00
Itt Corne growing . . . . . . . . 04 00 00
Itt Corne & other pruissions in the house . . . . 01 06 08
Itt money & Plate . . . . . . . . 05 10 00
Itt one mare . . . . . . . . . 02 06 08
Itt 2 kyne one Twinter heifer 2 yearlings and 2 sheepe . . . 07 11 00
Itt 3 swine . . . . . . . . . 02 00 00
Itt. Debts sperate . . . . . . . . 74 00 07
Itt Debts desperate . . . . . . . . 78 02 00

Some totall . . 216 18 10

## 87. Edward Harrington

Of Wellington, yeoman, taken by William Phillips of Wellington, gent., William Bate of High Ercall, yeoman, Edward Pemberton of Admaston, yeoman, and William Minshall the elder of Leegomery, yeoman, on 27 May 1670 and exhibited on 31 May 1670.

Imp. ffoure oxen . . . . . . . . 21 00 00
Itm. foure kine . . . . . . . . 12 10 00
Itm. Two mares, A young mare & an ould one . . . . 05 00 00
Itm. Three young swine . . . . . . . 01 10 00

*Itm. In the barn*
A cop for a waine A paire of Traces & three ladders . . . 01 00 00
Itm. One waine & ripples the wheeles thereto belonging beeing
bound with iron . . . . . . . . 03 10 00
Itm. Two Tumbrells Two paire of draughts, and one other ould
paire of iron bound wheeles . . . . . . 01 10 00
Itm. Three draught yokes & a cop yoke one iron chaine one chubb
chaine, Two harrowes & a copsole & all other implemts of husbandry . . . . . . . . . 01 05 00
Itm. A barre of iron ffive wedges Two spades & a waine rope . . 00 15 00

*Itm. In the parlour*
one paire of joyned bedsteades a feather bed with hangings & other necessaries thereto belonging with two carpetts one for a long table & the other for a short one . . . . . . . 03 10 00

Itm. In the parlour
One large table with two joyned formes two ioyned chaires one short folding table one high cupboard & two paire of handirons viz one large paire with brasse heades the other a little pair . . 03 10 00

*Itm. In the loft over the parlour*
one paire of ioyned bedsteads with the feather bed & the furniture thereto belonging . . . . . . . 03 00 00
Itm. In the same chamber
One long table one bench one chest one nursing stoole Two livery cupboards one desk A bason & ewer A looking glasse & a warming panne . . . . . . . . . . 02 10 00
Itm. In the same chamber
two low ioyned stooles with coverings, a Carpett for the long table & a short Grate . . . . . . . . 00 10 00

*Itm. In the Chamber over the hall*
two ioyned bedsteads with the furniture thereto belonging . . 02 10 00
Itm. In the same Chamber
one long coffer one chest a little square table one other little coffer & a little boxe . . . . . . . . 01 00 00

*Itm. In the Chamber over the porch*
In ye greate truncke & other places all sorts of linnens with some of his wives cloathes . . . . . . . 05 00 00
Itm. In the same chamber
Three ould trunckes one boxe with drawers two tables & one chest . 00 10 00
Itm. In the same chamber
foure fleeces of wooll . . . . . . . 00 03 00

*Itm. In the Chamber over the Buttrey*
a paire of Joyned bedsteads with the furniture thereto belonging . 00 10 00

Itm. Pewter of all sortes . . . . . . . 02 00 00
Itm. Brasse of all sortes . . . . . . . 04 00 00

*Itm. In the hall*
Two table boardes three formes two of them being ioyned ones one skreene, one ioyned presse one cupboard one chaire two stooles one Jacke to turne the spitt three spitts Two dreeping panns one grate one iron pott a paire of cobirons two paire of tounges & two fire shovells an iron morter & pestell a paire of pott hangles and the pott Geales . . . . . . . . . 04 00 00

*Itm. In the Buttrey*
two barrells and a hogsheade . . . . . . 00 15 00
Itm. Trinnen ware of all sortes with an ould haire cloath . . 01 00 00

Itm. Corne Growing upon the ground & in the house with other provisions . . . . . . . . . 26 00 00
Itm. Money in the house . . . . . . . 01 10 00

THE INVENTORIES OF WELLINGTON 257

| | | |
|---|---|---|
| Itm. Two ould silver spoones & a little silver cup . . . | 01 10 00 |
| Itm. his wearing apparell bookes saddle & bridle . . . | 05 00 00 |
| Itm. In a note drawne by his appointmt in debts supposed to be desperate . . . . . . . . . . | 09 07 00 |
| Itm. Yarne hempe dressed & undressed and growing upon the ground | 01 00 00 |
| Itm. Mucke or Compost . . . . . . . | 01 00 00 |
| Itm. All things forgotten . . . . . . . | 00 10 00 |
| sum tot . . | 128 05 08 |

## 88. George Wilkes

Of the Wheat Leasows, Wellington, husbandman, taken by John Manwaring, Francis Bayley and Robert Whittingham on 2 February 1671-72 and exhibited on 15 March 1671-72.

| | |
|---|---|
| Imprimis. Sixteene Cowes supposed to be worth three pounds a cowe . . . . . . . . . . . | 48 00 00 |
| Itm. Seven tooe Eares old Bease prised at forty shilling a Beaste . | 14 00 00 |
| Itm. One yeare old Caulfe prised at one pound . . . . | 01 00 00 |
| Itm. One Horse and a Mare prised at tenne pounds . . . | 10 00 00 |
| Item. Tow Swine prised at one pound tenne shillings . . . | 01 10 00 |
| Item. Poultrie prised at foure shillings . . . . . | 00 04 00 |
| Itm. Foure stalles of Beese prised at twenty Shillings . . . | 01 00 00 |
| Itm. Rye and Barley in the Barne prised at Six pounds . . . | 06 00 00 |
| Itm. Oats and pease prised at one pound three shillings and fourpence . . . . . . . . . . . | 01 03 04 |
| Itm. Haye supposed to be worth nine pounds tenne shillings . | 09 10 00 |
| Itm. Corne sowed one pound six shillings eight pence . . . | 01 06 08 |
| Itm. Bacon and Beefe prised at tow pound sixteene shilling eight pence . . . . . . . . . . . | 02 16 08 |
| Itm. Cheese and Butter prised at Eight pounds tenne shillings . | 08 10 00 |
| Itm. Brasse and Pewter prised at tow pounds tow shillings six pence . | 02 02 06 |
| Itm. One Presse 2 table-Boards 2 Formes one pound eighteen shillings | 01 18 00 |
| Itm. Chayers and Stooles prised at tenne Shillings . . . | 00 10 00 |
| Item. Three joynd Beddsteds prised at one pounde tenne shillings . | 01 10 00 |
| Itm. Bedding and Boulsters and Caddows & coverings prised at 5 pounds 3 shilling . . . . . . . . | 05 03 00 |
| Itm. Grate Fire-Shovel tongs and other Iron ware prised at tenne shillings . . . . . . . . . . | 00 10 00 |
| Itm. All the Linnions and Napery Ware prised at 2 pounds . | 02 00 00 |
| Itm. All the Barrills Stonds pailes & other manner of woodden ware prised at 1 pound tenn shillings . . . . . | 00 10 00 |
| Itm. One Carte and Wheels with other Implements of Husbandry Prised at 2 pounds . . . . . . . . | 02 00 00 |
| Itm. His wearing Apparill prised at 5 pounds . . . | 05 00 00 |
| Itm. Things forgotte and unprised 5 shillings . . . | 00 05 00 |
| Summa Totall . | 127 08 06 |

## 89. Thomas Howle

Of Wellington, skinner, taken by Thomas Laurence, Charles Stilgoe, William Dawe,* Humphrey Howle* and R. Jones on 20 March 1675-76 and exhibited on 18 April 1676.

*In the house*

| | |
|---|---|
| Impris. one Table Board and frame, one forme and twoo Joyned stooles | 00 10 00 |
| Item One Joyned cubort and Little Cubort | 00 04 00 |
| Item one Joyned screene | 00 05 00 |
| Item Iron ware of all sortes. | 00 06 00 |
| Item Brass and pewter of all sortes | 03 15 00 |

*In the parlor*

| | |
|---|---|
| Item one Joyned paire of Bedsteeds one feather Bedd Boulsters & furniture thereunto belonginge | 03 00 00 |
| Item one Little Square Table board | 00 01 00 |

*In the Chamber over ye house*

| | |
|---|---|
| Item one Joyned Table board & frame three Coffers, one Joyned press & one Turn'd chayre | 01 00 00 |
| Item on Joyned paire of Bedstedds, half Tester'd, one ffeather Bedd, Boulsters & Blanckketts | 01 00 00 |

*In the Chamber over ye parlor*

| | |
|---|---|
| Item twoo paire of Bed stedds twoo fflocke or Chaff Bedds and ffurniture thereunto belonginge | 01 00 00 |
| Item one coffer, Joyn'd stooles & chayres | 00 03 06 |
| Item lynnen of all sortes | 03 15 04 |

*In the Buttery & kitchen*

| | |
|---|---|
| Item wooden ware of all sorts | 02 10 00 |
| Item one steele Mault mill | 02 00 00 |
| Item Lether & Gloves of all sorts | 05 00 00 |
| Item wooll | 01 00 00 |
| Item Boards | 00 10 00 |
| Item Swyne | 02 05 00 |
| Item Beefe and Bacon | 02 00 00 |
| Item Cheese & Butter | 00 12 00 |
| Item his wareinge Apparrell | 05 00 00 |
| Item debts sperate | 10 00 10 |
| Item debts desperate | 06 00 00 |
| Item thinges forgotten & not seene | 00 05 00 |
| Sume | 52 00 08 |

## 90. Thomas Bennett

Of Wellington, blacksmith, taken by John Bennett, Thomas Bennett, Thomas Lloyd, Samuel Bennett and Thomas Bennett on 27 March 1676 and exhibited on 20 September 1676.

## In the Chamber over the Shopp

Impris.

| | | |
|---|---|---|
| One Standinge Bedd, and furniture thereunto belonginge | 02 00 00 |
| Item one Trunk Bedd & furniture . | 00 05 00 |
| Item one Table Board; one Joyned forme, five Joyned Stooles, on Joyned Cupbord & halfe a duzen Boxes . | 01 00 00 |
| Item two Joyned Chests . | 00 10 00 |
| Item one Lookinge Glass . | 00 03 06 |

### In the Little Chamber

| | |
|---|---|
| Item one Bedd and furniture | 00 05 00 |

### In the house

| | |
|---|---|
| Item Brass and pewter | 01 00 00 |
| Item one Table Board | 00 02 00 |
| Item stooles & Chayres | 00 03 00 |
| Item Iron ware of all sortes. | 00 16 08 |
| Item one Joyned Cupboard | 00 02 06 |

### In the Little Parlor

| | |
|---|---|
| Item one Joyned Table Board | 00 02 06 |
| Item Lynnin of all sortes | 03 00 00 |
| Item wooden ware of all sortes | 01 10 00 |
| Item one bible booke | 00 06 08 |

### In the Shopp

| | |
|---|---|
| Item workinge Tooles of all sortes. | 10 00 00 |
| Item Wareinge Apparell | 02 10 00 |
| Item the Revention of the Lease during the life of John Bennett of Watling Street | 01 00 00 |
| The Sume | 25 06 10 |

## 91. William Marigold

Of Leegomery, yeoman, taken by Michael Clarke, Thomas Swift and John Griffiths on 28 February 1676-77 and exhibited on 2 May 1677.

| | |
|---|---|
| Imps. his weareing apparrell | 02 00 00 |
| It. Money in his purse | 06 00 00 |
| It. Bedsteads Beds & Bedding | 11 00 00 |
| It. Brasse & pewter | 03 10 00 |
| It. Grates Spitts dreepeing pans & other iron ware | 01 00 00 |
| It. Chests & Coffers | 00 17 06 |
| It. Two presses | 01 10 00 |
| It. Tables & fourmes | 02 10 00 |
| It. Chaires stooles & Cushions | 00 13 04 |
| It. Linnens | 05 00 00 |
| It. Towe & yarne | 01 00 00 |
| It. Beefe Bacon & Cheese | 04 00 00 |

| | | |
|---|---|---|
| It. Cowes & Oxen & some other young cattell . . . . | 50 06 08 |
| It. Horses & colts . . . . . . . . | 10 00 00 |
| It. Sheepe . . . . . . . . . | 13 06 08 |
| It. Swine . . . . . . . . . | 01 12 06 |
| It. Poultry & Bees . . . . . . . . | 00 10 00 |
| It. Corne on the ground . . . . . . . | 08 00 00 |
| It. Corne & Hay in ye barne & Corne & mault in ye house . . | 08 10 00 |
| It. Dunge . . . . . . . . . | 00 10 00 |
| It. Plowes waines & other implements of husbandry . . . | 03 06 08 |
| It. Two Chattall Leases . . . . . . . | 380 00 00 |
| It. Things unnominated & forgotten . . . . . | 00 07 00 |
| Sum of . | 515 10 04 |

## 92. Richard Haughton

Of Wellington, gunsmith, taken by Samuel Bennett and Thomas Orrel on 5 October 1678 and exhibited on 8 October 1678.

*In the House*

| | |
|---|---|
| Imprimis. One Table Board and forme . . . . . | 00 02 00 |
| Item. one Joyne forme . . . . . . . | 00 01 00 |
| Item. one Joyne Screene . . . . . . . | 00 02 00 |
| Item. one Glass case . . . . . . . . | 00 01 00 |
| Item. one dishboard . . . . . . . . | 00 00 06 |
| Item. twoe Cheires, and one stoole . . . . . | 00 01 00 |
| Item. one paile or Boulke . . . . . . . | 00 00 06 |

*Iron ware*

Item. One Grate, one fiershovell, and tongues, one frying panne, one morter, and one Spitt. A pair of Gobberds, one Iron Cettle, and dreping panne together with other small nesessaries in Iron . .   00 06 08
Item. ffor Brasse Ware likewise in the house . . . .   00 06 00

*In the Parler*

Item. one Table Board, and frame, one forme, A Joyne presse, twoe Joyne Stooles, twoe chiers . . . . . . .   01 00 00
Item for Pewter of all sorts . . . . . . .   00 08 00

*In the Citchin*

Item one Table Board, and a little forme, and wooden vessells .   00 07 00

*In the Chamber over the House*

Item one Table Board and frame, one forme, A Joyne Chest and Coffer, one Joine Bedd with the Appurtenences thereunto belonginge . . . . . . . . . .   02 00 00

*In the Chamber over the Parlor*

Item. One Joyne Bed with th' appurtenences one Truckle bed one Chest . . . . . . . . . .   02 02 00

## In the Chamber over the Shop

| | | |
|---|---|---|
| Item. one Standinge Bed with thappurtenances thereunto belonginge One Table bord and forme and one Coffer . . . . | 00 | 18 00 |
| Item ffor linnings of all sortes . . . . . | 01 | 00 00 |
| Item. fform decedents wareing Apparrell . . . . | 01 | 00 00 |
| Item for twoe Swine and twoe piggs . . . . | 01 | 00 00 |
| Item. for his workings tooles and Implements concerninge his Trade . | 16 | 00 00 |
| Item. for things unseene . . . . . . | 01 | 10 00 |
| Item. for debts due to the Decedent . . . . | 01 | 00 00 |
| Sume Totall . | 29 | 05 08 |

## 93. Francis Haughton

Of Wellington, gunsmith, taken by Samuel Bennett and Thomas Orrell on 14 April 1679 and exhibited on 17 April 1679.

### In the House

| | | |
|---|---|---|
| Impr. one Table Board & frame . . . . . | 00 | 02 00 |
| Item: One Joyne forme . . . . . . | 00 | 10 00 |
| Itme One Joyned screene . . . . . . | 00 | 02 00 |
| Item one Glass Case . . . . . . . | 00 | 01 00 |
| Item one dishbord twoe Chieres & one Stoole . . . | 00 | 01 00 |
| Item one Paile or Boulk . . . . . . | 00 | 00 06 |

### Ironware

| | | |
|---|---|---|
| Item One Grate, one fier shoovell & tongues one Barre fier slice, one frying Panne, one Morter, one spitt, one pair of Gobberds, one Iton Cettle, one Dreepinge panne together with other necessaries in Iron . . . . . . . . . | 00 | 06 00 |
| Item. ffor Brass ware likewise in the howse . . . | 00 | 06 00 |

### In the Parlour

| | | |
|---|---|---|
| Item One Table Board and frame one forme one Joyne Press twoe Joyne stooles. . . . . . . . | 01 | 00 00 |
| Item ffor Pewter of all sorts . . . . . | 00 | 07 00 |

### In the Cittchen

| | | |
|---|---|---|
| Item One Table Bord and frame & wooden vessells . . | 00 | 07 00 |

### In the Chamber over the Parlour

| | | |
|---|---|---|
| Item One Joyne Chest one Truckell Bed one Planke or table & forme | 00 | 16 00 |

### In the Chamber over the Shopp

| | | |
|---|---|---|
| Item One Standing Bed with the Appurtenences thereunto belonginge Item One table Bord & frame and forme one Coffer . . | 00 | 18 00 |
| Item for Linninges of all sortes . . . . | 00 | 10 00 |
| Item ffor the Deceds wareing Apparell . . . . | 01 | 00 00 |
| Item ffor twoe Piggs or swine . . . . . | 01 | 06 08 |

| | | | |
|---|---|---|---|
| Item ffor his working tooles & Implements Concerning his trade | 16 | 00 | 00 |
| Item ffor one Mare | 01 | 10 | 00 |
| Item ffor things unseene | 00 | 10 | 00 |
| Item ffor debts due to the deced | 00 | 05 | 00 |
| Totall | 25 | 01 | 10 |

## 94. Miles Field

Of Wellington, cordwainer, taken by Richard Jones, Snr., William Turner and John Hodgkiss* on 28 September 1680, and exhibited on 5 October 1680. He died on 25 September 1680. The addition was appraised by Richard Jones, Thomas Tart and William Turner.

*The household Goods as ffollows*
*In the house*

| | | | |
|---|---|---|---|
| Imp. Brass & Pewter of all sorts | 02 | 06 | 08 |
| It. Iron wares of all sorts | 01 | 00 | 00 |
| one Table one Skreen one Brass bench & other wood ware | 00 | 13 | 04 |

*In the Room over ye house*

| | | | |
|---|---|---|---|
| One Standing Bedsteeds feather bed furniture thereunto belonging one Table board one Joyned forme one Carpett & one Coffer | 02 | 10 | 00 |

*In the Chamber over the Buttrey*

| | | | |
|---|---|---|---|
| one Truckle bedsteds & flock bed wth the furniture one little Table one Trunke One Joyned Stoole One Chaire & one flaskett | 01 | 00 | 00 |

*In the little Chamber over ye shop*

| | | | |
|---|---|---|---|
| One Standing bedsteed flockbed & furniture & one coffer | 00 | 15 | 00 |

*In the other Chamber over ye shop*

| | | | |
|---|---|---|---|
| one Standing Bedsted with ye furniture & one desk Trunk & one desk & one Table | 01 | 13 | 04 |

*In the Cock loft*

| | | | |
|---|---|---|---|
| One Truckle Bedsteed flock bed wth furniture wth other things | 00 | 05 | 00 |

*In the Buttrey*

| | | | |
|---|---|---|---|
| Barrells Stounds & other wood wares & vessells of all sorts | 00 | 10 | 00 |
| 2 Silver Spoones | 00 | 06 | 08 |
| Linnens of all sorts | 02 | 00 | 00 |
| his waring apparrell | 02 | 10 | 00 |
| Things Omitted | 00 | 05 | 00 |

*The Cattelll, Stock for his Trade & otherwise wth money &c.*

| | | | |
|---|---|---|---|
| It. Mault Mill | 01 | 00 | 00 |
| Leather dressed in the Cutting Room | 00 | 13 | 04 |
| Leather undressed six cips | 00 | 16 | 00 |

| | |
|---|---|
| Eight payre of Offalls & part of four butts wth some Smaller pieces . | 02 00 00 |
| Hemp for his Trade . . . . . . . . | 00 03 00 |
| Boots shoes & lasts &c. . . . . . . . | 02 00 00 |
| One Swine . . . . . . . . . | 00 13 04 |
| hay . . . . . . . . . . | 00 12 00 |
| hard Corne Threshed & unthreshed . . . . | 02 10 00 |
| Barley . . . . . . . . . . | 01 00 00 |
| One Cow . . . . . . . . . | 01 10 00 |
| Debts . . . . . . . . . . | 20 00 00 |
| Leather at ye Curryers . . . . . . . | 01 10 00 |
| Money in the house . . . . . . . . | 02 13 04 |
| Things Omitted . . . . . . . . | 00 05 00 |
| Suma total . . | 53 13 00 |

An Addition to an Inventory of ye Goods Cattells & Chattells of Miles ffield of Wellington in the County of Salop Cordwayner. decd. taken Sept. 28th & exhibited at Salop. Octob. 5th 1680 now made & compleated Ap. 12th 1681.

| | |
|---|---|
| One Assignment of one Chattell Lease of a living called the hinks & keinton meadows in the pish of Lillishall & County of Salop . . | 250 00 00 |

## 95. Joshua Dunton

Of Wellington, apparently a tanner, taken by Roger Icke, Andrew Shelton, William Turner and Ralph Barrett on 16 October 1680 and exhibited on 18 January 1680–81.

*In ye Hall*

| | |
|---|---|
| one Joyned press and glass Cage . . . . . . | 01 00 00 |
| one Table borde and frame, foure Joyne Stooles, two chayres, one forme, one screene, one plate of cast mettle, one grate, one fier shuvell one paire of Tongs and creeper, one Jack and pot geales . | 01 10 00 |
| one pewter Still . . . . . . . . | 00 06 08 |
| one dozen and a halfe of bottles . . . . . . | 00 03 00 |

*In ye Chitchen*

| | |
|---|---|
| Twenty pewter dishes twenty plates Two basons four Candlesticks three Chamber pots three fflaggons one bed pan one mustard pot one Salte one porrenger . . . . . . . | 04 00 00 |
| one furnace of cast mettall, one pot, one plate for ye fier one mortor one chafer . . . . . . . . | 03 00 00 |
| one grate foure Spits one paire of Racks one paire of Cobberts three dreeping pans one grid Iron one frying pan one chafing dish one hacking Knife . . . . . . . . . | 01 10 00 |
| one dresser one Coffer one bench Two trayes one boule one dozen of Trenchers two payles, one gaune, one grater . . . . | 00 05 00 |
| one brass pot . . . . . . . . . . | 00 06 08 |

*In ye buttery*

foure brass pots foure brass kettles, two brass pans, one warming pan, one brass morter and pestle, two brass basting spoones, one paire of Snuffers . . . . . . . . 03 16 05

*In ye ground Seller*

foure hogsheads, three barrells, Two Runlets, four brewing loomes, three Collers, four wood bottles, two stone bottles, one little table And frame one kneading trough one Churne one Coffer . . 05 00 00

*In ye best Chamber*

one drawing table and forme, one livery table three greene Chayres one Joyned forme one hanging press . . . . . 02 08 04

*In ye Long Chamber*

| two tables and frames, one Chest, foure Chayres, one forme, five stooles, one livery table . . . . . . . | 02 10 00 |
|---|---|
| one paire of bedstids, two fither beds, two blancketts and a Coverlet, one boulster, with Vallants and Curtines appertayning . . . | 03 13 04 |
| one Rugge foure Carpets . . . . . . . | 01 00 00 |
| nyne paire of fflaxen Sheetes . . . . . . | 06 00 00 |
| Eyghteene paire of Sheetes more . . . . . . | 04 10 00 |
| one peece of Dyaper . . . . . . . | 02 05 00 |
| one peece of new fflaxen . . . . . . . | 01 15 00 |
| Eyght table Clothes of Dyaper and fflaxen . . . . | 03 00 00 |
| Six Course table Clothes . . . . . . . | 00 15 00 |
| Six dozen of fflaxen Napkins . . . . . . | 03 15 00 |
| four dozen of other Napkins . . . . . . | 01 04 00 |
| one Dozen of pillowes beares . . . . . . | 00 18 00 |
| one dozen of towells . . . . . . . | 00 06 08 |
| one paire of Aund Irons . . . . . . . | 00 05 00 |
| Holland Ware. . . . . . . . . | 00 10 00 |

*In the Hall Chamber*

| Two paire of bedstids wth theire furniture . . . . | 02 10 00 |
|---|---|
| Six pillowes . . . . . . . . . | 00 12 00 |
| Eyght Chaires covered with leather . . . . . | 01 00 00 |
| Six Cushens . . . . . . . . . | 00 12 00 |
| one Livery Cubbert one Chest . . . . . . | 00 10 00 |
| one fierpan and tongs and Savor . . . . . . | 00 01 00 |
| one looking glass . . . . . . . . | 00 06 08 |

*In ye Cock loft*

| one Table and frame one Joyne forme one Coffer one Joyne stoole . | 00 10 00 |
|---|---|
| new frayle . . . . . . . . . | 00 05 00 |
| Two fither Beds foure fither boulsters Two flock Beds wth theire furniture . . . . . . . . . | 03 10 00 |

*In ye Chamber over ye Buttery*

one bed and furniture one Chest, one Livery table one Joyne stoole . 02 13 04

## At ye Starehead

| | | |
|---|---|---|
| one chest | 00 06 08 |
| one peece of drest leather, Red & White leather . | 00 19 00 |

## Silver Plate

| | |
|---|---|
| one Silver Can Seven Silver Spoones | 10 00 00 |

## In ye granery and Sowed

| | |
|---|---|
| Twenty eyght strickes of Wheate And Sowed on the land | 04 04 00 |
| Six strickes of Maulte | 00 15 00 |
| Two tubbs, a stricke and halfe stricke | 00 04 00 |

## In ye Barne

| | |
|---|---|
| Corn unthrashed there Wheate & Barley . | 15 00 00 |
| A Stricke of pease | 02 00 00 |

## In ye Mault house

| | |
|---|---|
| Six and Twenty Bull hydes es tanned strucken Leather two hydes & six Bull hydes more . | 38 12 00 |

## In ye Tanne house

| | |
|---|---|
| Six dicker & five hydes of Rype leather . | 42 05 00 |
| thirteene Kips tanned | 02 05 00 |
| Twenty one horse hydes | 03 13 06 |
| Sixty eyght dozen of Caulfe Skins . | 57 00 00 |
| ffifty seven hydes untanned | 26 02 06 |
| Sixteen kips . | 02 10 06 |
| one horse hyde more | 00 04 00 |
| Barke . | 30 00 00 |

## In ye other Barne

| | |
|---|---|
| Haye . | 06 00 00 |

## Implements of husbandrye

| | |
|---|---|
| Two paire of Iron bound wheeles one Carte body two tumbrell bodyes And all other Implements of husbandry . | 08 00 00 |

## Cattle

| | |
|---|---|
| Two Mares one Colt nag | 04 00 00 |
| Two Cowes | 04 12 00 |
| Two Swine | 01 10 00 |
| Wearing Apparrell with monyes in his pocket And Bookes | 10 00 00 |
| A Cast of Pistolls and houlsters | 01 00 00 |
| Manure for the grounde | 01 10 00 |
| The Mill Stone and other tooles belonging to the Tan house | 02 00 00 |
| Boardes over ye Tanhouse and Stable | 01 00 00 |
| one little Sistorne and trough | 00 05 00 |
| Desperate Debts | 10 00 00 |
| things not seene omitted or forgotten | 00 10 00 |
| | 357 10 06 |

## 96. Thomas Fletcher

Of the Street Lane, alias Watling Street Way, Wellington, ropemaker, taken by Thomas Binnell and Thomas Laurence on 21 December 1680 and exhibited on 19 April 1681.

*Imp. In the house*

| | |
|---|---|
| one Table boord without a frame, one other little low side table, one Joyned chaire one Turned chaire, Two stooles one paile to carry water in one iron pot one Grate one paire of Niggards, a paire of Tounges a paire of pot hookes & a paire of pot Goales . . . | 01 00 00 |
| In the same Roome | |
| foure small peices of pewter & six pewter spoones . . . | 00 08 00 |

*Itm In the chamber at the upper end of the house*

| | |
|---|---|
| one other ould Table boord with a ioyned frame, a ioyned forme one Joyned bedstead, a flockebed a bolster filled with feather, one blanket & a Couering . . . . . . . | 02 06 08 |
| Itm In the same Chamber | |
| one flaxen sheete & Two paire of hempen . . . | 00 13 04 |
| Itm Two fflitches of Bacon & foure small cheeses . . . | 00 14 00 |

*Item in the lower Chamber*

| | |
|---|---|
| one barrell & a little wooddon vessell . . . . . | 00 01 06 |
| Itm one ould horse & a little Two year ould heifor . . . | 01 13 04 |

*Itm in the shop*

| | |
|---|---|
| Three stone weight of hempe & a halfe . . . . . | 00 07 06 |
| Itm his working Tooles . . . . . . . | 00 05 00 |
| Debts sperate . . . . . . . . . | 03 00 00 |
| Item desperate Debts . . . . . . . | 02 00 00 |
| Item All things forgotten . . . . . . . | 00 03 04 |
| | 11 12 08 |

## 97. Edward Jones

Of Wellington, husbandman, taken by Adam Wright, Richard Harrington,* William Corbett,* John Hill, John Ravenall* and Francis Ore, junior, on 15 April 1681 and exhibited on 5 October 1681.

*Impr. in the house*

| | |
|---|---|
| one table board one old Joyned Press one old screene bentches and stooles praised at . . . . . . . . | 00 13 04 |
| It one fire grate a paire of tonges A fire shovell and pot gailes praised att . . . . . . . . . | 00 02 06 |

## It in the Parlor

one standing bed wth testor and beding thereunto belonging, one little chest a little ceauing board A trickle bed a joyned forme one desk and other old trainen ware . . . . . . 01 10 00

## It In ye chamber ov ye house

some old trumpery of ye value of . . . . . . 00 02 06

## It In ye Chamber over ye parlor

one standing bed with testor one bedsted wth halfe head and beding thereunto belonging . . . . . . . . 00 16 00
It one old Joyned press one old trunk and old coffer prised at . 00 08 00
It Linnens and naperey ware praised at . . . . . 00 05 00
It brass and pewter of all sorts praised at . . . . . 00 07 06
It trainen weare and other utensells of ye house . . . . 00 02 06
It Corne in ye bearne . . . . . . . . —
It Corne on the ground . . . . . . . . 01 04 00
It the decesed Persons wareing Apparrell . . . . . 01 00 00
It Six horses (viz) nag and mares being all poore and old wth theire geeares prised at . . . . . . . . . 10 00 00
It One Cow on twinter beast and two yeare old beasts praised att . . 04 05 00
It two young swine prised . . . . . . . . 00 01 00
It one old Cart wth a paire of wheeles Iorne bound one plow and other implements for husbandrey . . . . . . 01 10 00
It things not seen or forgott . . . . . . 00 02 06

Sume tot . . 22 18 10

## 98. John Smart

Of Wellington, dyer, taken by William Phillips, jnr., William Podmore and Richard Palin on 25 April 1682 and exhibited on 12 July 1682.

| | |
|---|---|
| Three Kyne . . . . . . . . . | 10 00 00 |
| One Sow and Six Piggs . . . . . . . | 02 00 00 |
| One Cubbard and one Pressed in the House . . . | 03 00 00 |
| Brasse and Pewter in the House . . . . . | 06 00 00 |
| Iron Ware and other Goods in the House . . . . | 03 00 00 |
| One Bed with the ffurniture, one Press, Two Table Boards & other Goods in the Parlor . . . . . . . | 05 00 00 |
| Eight Barrells of Ale, Beere and Syder and other Goods in the Two Buttreys . . . . . . . . . | 06 00 00 |
| Two Beds with the ffurniture One Table Board, and two Chests and other Goods in the Upper Chamber over the House . . | 11 14 00 |
| Three Beds and Two Chests and other goods in the Cockloft . . | 05 00 00 |
| One Bed and One Table Board and other Goods in the Upper Chamber over the Parlor . . . . . . . | 03 00 00 |
| ffifty Measures of Malt and other Graine with other Goods in the other Cockloft . . . . . . . . . | 08 00 00 |
| Lynnens and New Lynnen Cloth & Yearne . . . . | 13 07 06 |
| ffour ends of Lynsee and Woollen Cloth . . . . | 02 02 06 |

| | | | |
|---|---|---|---|
| ffoure paire of Sheeres and other things in the Shopp . . . | 04 | 00 | 00 |
| Two ffurnaces and one Wadfat in the dyehouse . . . . | 08 | 10 | 04 |
| Allam, Coprice, Mather and other Colouring stuffe . . . | 03 | 05 | 00 |
| Brewing Vessells . . . . . . . . . | 01 | 09 | 00 |
| His Tainters . . . . . . . . . | 02 | 00 | 00 |
| Money oewing to him by Bond . . . . . . | 56 | 00 | 00 |
| Money oweing to him without Sperialtie . . . . . | 11 | 00 | 10 |
| His Wearing Apparrell and Bookes. . . . . . | 06 | 10 | 00 |
| All things forgotten and unseene . . . . . . | 01 | 04 | 06 |
| The Totall Sume . | 172 | 03 | 08 |

## 99. Thomas Hitchen

Of Preston-upon-the-Weald Moors, Wellington, taken by Thomas Rowley, Richard Lathe, John Wade,* Allen Pickering* and Samuel Bennett on 7 July 1682 and exhibited on 6 August 1682.

*Impris. The goods in the dwelling house*

| | | | |
|---|---|---|---|
| One Table borde & frame Two Joyne formes Six Chayres & a little table . . . . . . . . . . | 00 | 15 | 04 |
| Pewter | | | |
| Tenne pewter dishes. . . . . . . . | 01 | 00 | 00 |
| one flagon one Tankert one Candlestick . . . . . | 00 | 02 | 06 |
| one dozen of spoones one Salt . . . . . . | 00 | 00 | 06 |
| Two Chamber potts . . . . . . . . | 00 | 01 | 00 |
| Brass | | | |
| five kettles one little panne two potts one skellet one Candlesticke . | 01 | 05 | 00 |
| Iron ware | | | |
| One grate one fier shuevell one paire of tonges one paire of potgeales one paire of pot hookes one spit one paire of gobberts one dreepinge pan one Chaffinge dish one pestle . . . . | 00 | 04 | 06 |
| one Iron Pote . . . . . . . . . | 00 | 02 | 00 |

*In the Parlor*

| | | | |
|---|---|---|---|
| One Joyned bedstide wth a fither bed & the appurtinances thereunto belonginge . . . . . . . . . | 02 | 10 | 00 |
| One Joyned press two quoffers one Chest one box . . . | 01 | 00 | 00 |
| one warminge pan . . . . . . . . | 00 | 01 | 00 |
| Two paire of fflaxen sheetes five paire of hempen sheetes one paire of hurden sheetes . . . . . . . . | 01 | 02 | 00 |
| Two dozen of napkins . . . . . . . | 00 | 08 | 00 |
| Two Table clothes Two pillowsbeares . . . . . | 00 | 06 | 00 |
| five chshens . . . . . . . . . | 00 | 02 | 00 |
| flax three pounds & hempe two pounds . . . . . | 00 | 03 | 00 |

*In the Chamber over ye parlor*

| | | | |
|---|---|---|---|
| One fither Bed one boulster one Coverlet one blanket . . . | 01 | 00 | 00 |
| Two flock beds two boulsters two coverlets . . . . | 00 | 10 | 00 |
| two quoffers . . . . . . . . . | 00 | 02 | 00 |
| five strikes of pease . . . . . . . . | 00 | 10 | 00 |

# THE INVENTORIES OF WELLINGTON

### In the Store Chamber

| | | |
|---|---|---|
| Eyghteene ould cheeses forty new cheeses Small ones | 03 | 00 00 |
| Two ffletches of Backon one fflitch of Beefe | 01 | 00 00 |
| Three strikes of Rye | 00 | 10 00 |
| Tenne strikes of Maulte | 01 | 10 00 |
| Twenty Slippings of noggen yaurne | 00 | 10 00 |

### In the Buttery

| | | |
|---|---|---|
| Six Barrells | 00 | 10 00 |
| One Churne | 00 | 01 00 |
| Three payles one wooden bottle | 00 | 02 00 |
| Two Turnells three bowles | 00 | 02 00 |
| ffoure Cheese fitts | 00 | 02 00 |
| one frying pan | 00 | 01 00 |
| one Tynne pan | 00 | 00 06 |

### In the kitchen

| | | |
|---|---|---|
| ffoure Loomes or Stoondes one kneading turnell one Cheese press two Spininge wheeles | 00 | 15 00 |

### Implements of husbandrye

| | | |
|---|---|---|
| One cart one pare of Iron bound wheeles one Tumbrell body one pair of ould wheeles And all of the Implemts of husbandry of what kind soever | 05 | 00 00 |
| One Maulte Mill | 01 | 06 00 |
| Hay gotten In ye barne | 00 | 13 04 |

### Corne growinge

| | | |
|---|---|---|
| five strikes soweing of harde corne | 02 | 00 00 |
| Eyght Strickes Soewinge of Barlye | 02 | 13 04 |
| Two Strickes Soewinge of Pease | 00 | 10 00 |
| Two Strickes Soewinge of Oates | 00 | 10 00 |
| Cattle | | |
| Eyght Cowes | 16 | 00 00 |
| foure heyffers | 06 | 00 00 |
| Two Yerlings two waynings | 03 | 00 00 |
| Two mares one coulte | 07 | 10 00 |
| Two stoore Swine | 01 | 00 00 |
| Wearinge Apparrell | 02 | 10 00 |
| debts sparet et desperate | 20 | 00 00 |
| Things omitted & not Seene | 00 | 10 00 |
| The totall Sum is | 88 | 11 04 |

## 100. Mary Hunt

Of Wellington, widow, taken by John Bradshaw of Wellington, George Buttery of Huntington and John Smitheman of Little Wenlock on 20 June 1682 and exhibited on 31 October 1682.

## In the Hall

| | | |
|---|---|---|
| Twenty pewter dishes | . . . . . . . | 02 10 00 |
| Three Guns & eight Flaggons | . . . . . | 01 00 00 |
| Elleaven Pewter Plates | . . . . . . | 00 11 00 |
| seven pewter Candlesticks . | . . . . . | 00 10 06 |
| nyne Pewter porringers | . . . . . . | 00 04 00 |
| two Pewter Cans | . . . . . . . | 00 03 00 |
| three Chambr Potts & a quart Pott | . . . | 00 04 00 |
| foure salts & a mustard Pott a Little Cupp & a Toster & a Bason | . | 00 07 06 |
| Two great Brasse Potts & one Little one . | . . . | 01 08 06 |
| one Iron Pott. | . . . . . . . . | 01 00 00 |
| one greate Brasse Kettle | . . . . . . | 00 16 00 |
| one Brasse Pann | . . . . . . . | 00 02 00 |
| one other Lesse Brasse Kettle | . . . . . | 00 16 00 |
| two Little Bright Brasse Kettles & skillett | . . . | 00 06 00 |
| one other Brasse Kettle a Brasse Chafeing dish two Brasse Ladles & a Brasse skimmer . . . . . . . . . | | 00 09 00 |
| one Brasse warming Pann . | . . . . . | 00 04 00 |
| one doz. of Pewter spoones | . . . . . | 00 01 00 |
| foure Iron spitts & 2 Iron pans | . . . . | 00 10 00 |
| one Iron Grate, 2 Iron Niggards one Iron Creep & paire of Tongues one fire shovell one Iron frying Pann one Iron Plate one Paire of Bellows Pott hanglisses & Pott hookes . . . . | | 00 14 00 |
| smoothing Iron Pestle & mortar . | . . . . | 00 02 00 |
| one Iron flesh forke . | . . . . . . | 00 00 06 |
| Two table Boards two skreens one joynd Cheair one turnd Cheare one joynd forme two joynd stooles one Joynd Cubbard one Dish bench & one other bench . . . . . . | | 01 12 10 |

### In the Parler

| | | |
|---|---|---|
| one feather Bed Boulster & Pillow one Blanckett & Rugg one Joynd Bedsted with Curtains & Valletts . . . . . | | 06 00 00 |
| two table Boards one joyned forme foure joynd stooles one joynd Chaire & three turnd Chaires . . . . . . | | 02 01 02 |
| one Joynd Chest . | . . . . . . . | 00 12 00 |
| six cushions . | . . . . . . . . | 00 06 00 |
| two doz of Hurden Napkins three paire of Hempten sheets nyne paire of hurden sheets two hempton Table Cloths & two hurden Table Cloths eight Course towells . . . . . | | 04 06 00 |

### In the Roome over the Parlor

| | | |
|---|---|---|
| one Joynd Bedsted two feathr Beds two ffeather Boulsters one Blankett one Counterpan with Curtain & vallett with other things thereunto Belonging. . . . . . . . | | 08 00 00 |
| one Table board foure joynd stooles one joynd forme . . . | | 02 05 00 |
| Six Cusshions one Carpett one Ticken for a Bed & boulstr & one Little Carpett . . . . . . . . | | 02 00 00 |
| one Joynd Chest one Livery Table . . . . | | 01 08 00 |
| one Twigen Cheare two turnd chairs one Twigen Baskett foure China dishes & one lookeing Glasse . . . . . | | 00 15 00 |
| eight pairs of Flaxen sheets. . . . . . . | | 05 06 08 |
| three large flaxen Table Clothes . . . . . . | | 01 10 00 |
| three lesser flaxen Table Clothes . . . . . . | | 00 13 04 |

THE INVENTORIES OF WELLINGTON 271

five silver spoones 3 silver bodkins & a little silver dish . . . 02 03 06
one diaper Table Cloth & one flaxon Cubbard Cloth with fring . 00 15 00

*In the Roome over the house*
two Joynd Bedsteds one Tuckle Bed one feathr Bed two fflock Beds three feathr Boulsters two Coverlids three Blanketts & a Rugg . . . . . . . . . . . 06 00 00
one Table with a Joynd frame one Joynd forme one Qoffer one Cheare one Twiggen Flaskett & one Twigge Baskett . . . 00 14 00
30 pound of drest hemp . . . . . . . 01 02 06
foure slippen of yorne . . . . . . . 00 06 08

one sow in Pigg & a hogg . . . . . . . 01 14 00
foure Kine . . . . . . . . . 12 00 00
all sorts of Graine upon ye Land . . . . . . 04 06 08
two hogsheads 4 Barrells . . . . . . . 02 00 00

in the Maulthouse . . . . . . . .
one weeting vessell two Brewing stunds & two Kimnels . . 01 05 00
two Payles & a Churne . . . . . . . 00 05 00

Things omitted & not exprest . . . . . . 01 00 00

The deceadnts wearing Apparrell . . . . . . 10 00 00

        Totall in all . . . 92 17 04


## 101. James Freeman

Of Ketley and Shifnal, taken by George Holland, Thomas Smith,* Eleanor Davids* and Francis Ore on 22 February 1683-84 and exhibited on 19 March 1683-84. The property at Shifnal was appraised by Thomas Smith,* William Evans,* Edward Jones and Ralph Langley. The administrator's account, with its evidence of the copying of the inventory is also included

*Imprs. in the house*
two old table boards wth frames two old Chires and old Jack praised at . . . . . . . . . . . 01 10 00
It. two brass panns one brass pott & one Iorne pott . . . 03 10 00

*It in the parlor*
one Joynd bedsteed wth a fither bed one paire of Sheets and blankett praised at . . . . . . . . 03 00 00
It. one Joyned press one old Cubbort two old Chires one old Chest and one old table board praised at. . . . . . 02 00 00
It. one pewter Chamberpott four Candlesticks one looking glass and a beaver brush praised at . . . . . . . 00 04 00

*It. In ye butterey*
four small drink vessells viz firkins or kinderkins & one old Cheese
tubb praised at . . . . . . . . 00 09 06

*It. In the backhouse*
one old kneading tubb one old strike one old Cuffer two old steends
three old ioyned stooles one old Churne A payle a piggin & a bole
dish at. . . . . . . . . 00 10 00
It. foure pewter dishes praised at . . . . . 00 06 00
It. one dreeping pan two broaches a fire shovell & a paire of tongues
praised at . . . . . . . . 00 05 06

*It. In the Chamber ovr ye house*
one bed & bedsteeds . . . . . . 03 02 06

*It. In ye Chamber ovr ye butterey*
two old Cuffers one Box one old paire of bedsteeds & one old
forme . . . . . . . . . 00 06 06

*It. In ye Chamber ovr ye parlor*
one bed wth ye furniture . . . . . . 02 00 00
It. two old Spining wheeles three old Cuffors & one old Table board . 00 09 00
It. of Napery 13 napkins & one old table cloth praised at . . 00 12 00
It. five duzen of trenchers & 9 pewter spoons at. . . . 00 03 06
It for things forgott and not seene. . . . . 00 04 06
It his wearing Apparell twenty shillings . . . . 01 00 00
totl . . 19 12 06

It. his funerall expenses seven pounds

A true and perfect Inventory of ye Goods of James ffreeman in his house in Shifnal.

*Imps. over the Kitching*
1 ould fflock Bed and Bedsttes and tester 1 ould table frame . . 00 13 00
*over ye house*
1 ould Bedsteed and tester and 1 Bedsteeds and ½ tester 1 ould
table Bord and fframe . . . . . . 01 00 00
*it. over ye hall*
1 ould Bedsteeds and tester . . . . . . 00 08 00

It. 1 ould Coberst and Grate in ye house . . . . 01 00 00

*It. in ye hall*
1 ould table bord and fframe . . . . . . 00 15 00

03 16 00

It in ye house more 1 ould fframe and 3 plankes . . . 00 00 08

The true and perfect Accompt of Thomas Freeman sonn & Administrator of all and singular the goods rights and Credits Cattle & Chattells of James Freeman late of Ketley in the pish of Wellington deced. made as well of his receipts and of his payments and disbursements forth of the said deceaseds estate as ffolloweth vizt.

# THE INVENTORIES OF WELLINGTON

**The Charge**
    This Accompatant chargeteth himself with the prices and value of all and singular the goods rights and credits Cattle and Chattles of the said deced comprized in two Invys thereof made & exted into the Regestry of the Court wch being put togeather amount in toto to the sum of £23.00..06

Whereof this Accompant craveth allowand and dischargeth himself as followeth

| | |
|---|---|
| Impris. for funeral expenses of the said deced. . . . . | 07 00 00 |
| Item paid for Ltres of Action . . . . . | 00 07 00 |
| Item paid for drawing this Accompt and engrossing it Coppying the Invy, Proctors Reteyning fee and fee of three Court days . . | 00 15 00 |
| Item for expences in coming to Lich to give ye Rect . . . | 00 07 06 |
| | 08 09 06 |
| Et sui dedulis dedaiendis et allocatis de jure in hae pte allocandis restat in manibus hui Compatantis Suma . . . . . | 14 10 00 |

    And this Accomptant doth offer to the pties interested in the residue of this estate that they shall take their respective propritions thereof in goods as they remain in their kind and are set down in the two Invys now exted.

## 102. Allen Adams

    Of Horton, Wellington, taken by Thomas Dawes, William Adans and Robert Key on 12 January 1684-85 and exhibited on 24 April 1685|.

*Imps: in the mantion house*

| | |
|---|---|
| one long table, one Joyne forme one Joyne Skreen, one Joyne presse, one little table, and two twigen cheires vallued at . . | 01 15 00 |
| It four large pewtar dishes, aleaven lesser dishes, two plates four sawsars, eight pewter porringers vallued at . . . . | 02 00 00 |
| It foure brasse pans: foure brasse cettles; two brass candlestics, one chafeing dish, one warming pan, a pewtre candlestick . . . | 03 10 00 |
| It Two Iron pots; one dreeping pan; some broches, one pare of cobarts, three fir shuvels, & two pare of toungs vallued att . . | 01 10 00 |
| It one cast plate, one iron grate, one iron mortar & pestell, one hand cleaver; three tin pans, one frying pan; pott gailes, a flesh forke, a skimer; & two shilfes vallued at . . . . . | 01 10 00 |

*Item In the plar*

| | |
|---|---|
| one Joyne table, one Joyne forme, two Joyne stowles, one little table, two Joyne cheires, two green cheires, two cushins, one Joyne presse, & a close stowll vallued at . . . . . . | 03 00 00 |
| It one sett of Curtaines, one green Rug, one blankit, a featherbed and boulstr, a flock bed & matt; one iron crow, an halfe hundredwaight being cast mettle, & a looking glass vallued att . . | 02 00 00 |

*It In the Chambar over the house,*

| | |
|---|---|
| one Joyne bed; a feather bed & boulster, one Red Rug; & blankitt, sett of red curtains & Vallants vallued . . . . . | 03 00 00 |

| | | | |
|---|---|---|---|
| It one little Cubbart, one levery Cubbart, one little table, a cheire & chest . . . . . . . . . . | 01 | 10 | 00 |
| It Linin and napparie, a large byble, wth some other small books, vald . . . . . . . . . . | 01 | 10 | 00 |

*It In the roome over the plar*

| | | | |
|---|---|---|---|
| two Joyne beds; a featherbed & boulstar one blankitt, one Coverlid, and a Red Rug vallued at . . . . . . . | 02 | 00 | 00 |
| It Three Cuffors, one Cradle, two pillins, a halfe strike and a peck . | 01 | 00 | 00 |

*It In the buttery*

| | | | |
|---|---|---|---|
| four barrels; some little turnels, four shilfes one churne, foure coolers, two dusson of trenchars, six meat piynns and a dusson of pewter sponnes vallud at . . . . . . . . | 01 | 05 | 00 |

*It In the bakehouse*

| | | | |
|---|---|---|---|
| one large wich, a ovull weeting fatt a haire cloath, malt showell & a iron peale valud att . . . . . . . . . | 01 | 10 | 00 |

*It In the lower building*

| | | | |
|---|---|---|---|
| one Cheese press, one tutor, a knead turnell, five other tubs & turnels; one peale a saddle & pan . . . . . . | 01 | 00 | 00 |
| It Implements of husbandry; of all sorts being butt few . . | 01 | 05 | 00 |
| It. Corne on the ground, and hay in the barne, vallud at . . | 00 | 15 | 00 |
| It weareing aparrell, all sorte of Lumbar & things unseene . . | 01 | 10 | 00 |
| the whole is . . . | 31 | 10 | 00 |

funarall expenses and other debts att least li 80 00 00

## 103. Henry Stanworth

Of Wellington, cordwainer, taken by William Phillips, Junr., Robert Johnson, Benjamin Wright and Thomas Dicken on 13 February 1684–85 and exhibited on 4 April 1685.

| | | | |
|---|---|---|---|
| Imprs. One ffeather bedd 56 pound weight at 6d ye pound . . | 01 | 10 | 04 |
| one bolster & 2 pillowes 29 lb weight at 6d ye pound . . . | 00 | 14 | 06 |
| one Coverled one blackett & one block bed at . . . . | 00 | 14 | 00 |
| one Joynd bedd & a Matt & ye Curtains belonging to ye same. . | 01 | 12 | 00 |
| One cidderminst Carpett . . . . . . . . | 00 | 05 | 00 |
| one Table one forme & 4 ioyned Stooles . . . . . | 01 | 00 | 00 |
| One Chest . . . . . . . . . . | 00 | 15 | 00 |
| One Cushion 1s 3 Shelves 1s. 6d . . . . . . | 00 | 02 | 06 |

*In ye roome ovr ye house*

| | | | |
|---|---|---|---|
| One othr ioyned bedd 15s one Trundle bedd 5s . . . . | 01 | 00 | 00 |
| the curtaines & valance to ye last named ioyned bedd . . . | 00 | 05 | 00 |
| One ffeather bedd & bolster 62 lbs weight at 6d ye pound . . | 01 | 11 | 00 |
| One Rugg 4s two blanketts 2s 8d . . . . . . | 00 | 06 | 08 |

| | |
|---|---|
| One fflock bolster 2s ond chaffe bed 1s 6d . . . . | 00 02 06 |
| One ffeathr bolstr 2s one othr feathr bolster 5s . . . . | 00 07 00 |
| One Couled & 2 old blanketts . . . . . | 00 04 00 |
| One Fflock bedd . . . . . . . | 00 05 00 |
| One Table 8s one forme 2s . . . . . . | 00 10 00 |
| 2 Shelves 2s One Chest 10s One Cheare Table 4s . . | 00 16 00 |
| One large bible 7s & other books 3s . . . . . | 00 10 00 |

*In a Little roome*

| | |
|---|---|
| One Table 3s 6d One caire 1s . . . . . . | 00 04 06 |
| 22 glass bottles . . . . . . . . | 00 02 09 |

*In an upper Garrett*

| | |
|---|---|
| One bedd wth th apptusces 12 a Coffer 2s a plancke & a Lather 2s 6d . . . . . . . . . . | 00 16 06 |

*In an othr little roome*

| | |
|---|---|
| A coffer 2s 2 Shelves 3s . . . . . . . | 00 05 00 |
| 6 Pewter dishes 14 lbs weight at 7d ye pound . . . | 00 08 02 |
| fflagons & othr hollow pewter 14 lb at 8d ye pound . . | 00 09 04 |
| one Dreeping pan 2s 4d one Iron plate & Niggetts 3s . . | 00 05 04 |
| other Iron Ware 8s 6d A frying pan 1s 6d a Warming pan 2s 6d | 00 12 06 |
| A Ladle & Skimmer 1s 6d Tin Ware 9d a pair of Wooden Stakes 6d . | 00 02 09 |
| A Hatchett & a Chopping knife 10d. . . . . . | 00 00 10 |

*In the House place*

| | |
|---|---|
| one Cubbort at 12s . . . . . . . . | 00 12 00 |
| Dressers Shelves 2 ioyned Stooles 2s 1 Chaire & othr wooden ware in the house . . . . . . . . . | 00 09 00 |
| A brasse furnace £1 a brasse pott 10s a brasse Kettle 2s. 6d . . | 01 12 06 |
| A hogshead 4s 2 barrels 5s 6d one firkine 1s . . . | 00 10 06 |
| A large Turnell 3s A large Stund 4s one othr Stund 1s 6d one othr Stund 1s one Turnell 1s 6d one othr Stund 1s Two pales a large wooden Tundish & a lading Gaune 3s A Wood Mortr wth Iron hoopes 1s 2 doz of Trenchers 1s othr Small Wooden ware 1s 2 pecks & a Strike 2s 2 old tubs 1s 6d 2 searches & a sive 1s 6d 2 cooling Turnells 3s 6d . . . . . . . . . | 01 06 06 |
| one Joynd box . . . . . . . . | 00 03 06 |
| Two old Turkey work Cushions . . . . . . | 00 01 06 |
| All the Linnen . . . . . . . . . | 01 10 00 |
| All Wareing Apparrell . . . . . . . | 01 00 00 |
| Itm things unseene & forgott . . . . . . | 00 02 06 |
| Sum tot . . | 23 06 03 |

## 104. George Golbourne

Of Hadley, taken by John Dale, Allen Freeman and Thomas Whittingham of Hadley on 20 February 1684–85 and exhibited on 1 April 1685.

| | |
|---|---|
| Imprimis ffor his ship | 08 00 00 |
| ffor younge Cattell | 12 00 00 |
| ffor ffive Cows | 10 00 00 |
| ffor ffive Horses | 15 00 00 |
| ffor Implymts of Husbandry | 04 00 00 |
| ffor Howshould Goods | 03 00 00 |
| ffor two store piggs | 00 10 00 |
| | 52 00 00 |

A Note of what he was Indebted viz

| | |
|---|---|
| To Mr. Walter Marygould | 35 00 00 |
| To Mr. John Owld | 17 00 00 |
| To Mr. Francis Baxster | 08 00 00 |
| To Mr. Thomas Powell | 08 00 00 |
| To Thomas Jones by Bond | 10 00 00 |
| To John Simons | 04 00 00 |
| Some | 82 00 00 |

So that his debts are 30 li moore than all his goods come too, and therefore desireth to aquitted and discharged ffrom any ffurther trouble.

## 105. Roger Blakeman

Of Hadley, webster, taken by William Cuxson, Thomas Whittingham and John Dale on 5 November 1685 and exhibited on 10 November 1685.

| | |
|---|---|
| Imprimis: One Cowe | 01 10 00 |
| Item: One heifer | 01 00 00 |
| Item Two Sheep | 00 05 00 |
| Item: Two Beds and furneture | 02 00 00 |
| Item: Brass and pewter | 01 00 00 |
| Item: Two Lloomes and Geares | 02 00 00 |
| Item: One Cubbert | 00 02 06 |
| Item: One chest two couffers | 00 06 06 |
| Item: One Table | 00 02 06 |
| Item: Linnins | 01 10 00 |
| Item: Things not seen | 00 05 00 |
| Item: his weareing Apparreill | 00 15 00 |
| Item: in Ready Money | 00 02 06 |
| The Sume is | 10 09 00 |

## 106. Joyce Bradshaw

Of Wellington, widow, taken by Adam Wright and Andrew Sockett and exhibited on 5 July 1687. The inventory is undated.

# THE INVENTORIES OF WELLINGTON

*Imprimis in the parlore*

| | | | |
|---|---|---|---|
| one Table & Joyne stooles one forme and one Little Table | 01 | 02 | 06 |
| Item one Skreeene 3 Cheirs with Turned staves one nursing stoole | 00 | 14 | 00 |
| Item one Chest | 00 | 06 | 08 |
| Item one p of Cobberts one Grate 3 little skellets | 00 | 08 | 00 |
| Item 2 skimers and a warming pan | 00 | 04 | 06 |
| Item one Jack & three Spitts | 00 | 15 | 00 |
| Allso a frying pan | 00 | 00 | 09 |
| Item one morter & Pestell | 00 | 04 | 06 |
| Item one Iron plate | 00 | 01 | 00 |
| Item one grid Iron & a Cheese Toaster | 00 | 01 | 06 |
| Item one grate one paire of Tonges a Fire shovell & niggorts | 00 | 07 | 00 |
| Item one Iron Dreeping pan | 00 | 06 | 00 |
| Item one Tinn Cover | 00 | 00 | 06 |
| Item one Press | 01 | 00 | 00 |
| Item Pewter 56 lb | 01 | 17 | 04 |
| Item Qne Iron plate | 00 | 00 | 04 |
| Item one p of Links | 00 | 09 | 00 |
| Item a Little Brass Candlestik | — | — | — |
| Item a nother Candlestik | 00 | 00 | 09 |
| Item 1 p of Bedsteads a Sett of Green Curtains one Cover lett one Rugg 1 Blankett 1 under Bed one Fither Bed 3 pillows 1 fither Bolster | 05 | 10 | 00 |
| Item 1 Brewing Stund | 00 | 02 | 06 |

*In the Parlour Chamber*

| | | | |
|---|---|---|---|
| Imprimis one Table Board and a fourme | 00 | 16 | 00 |
| Item a Livry table | 00 | 05 | 00 |
| 1 Joyne Chiare | 00 | 05 | 00 |
| Item 1 Twiggon Chire | 00 | 01 | 06 |
| Item a Little Table | 00 | 01 | 06 |
| Item a Little Table | 00 | 01 | 06 |
| Item a halfe headed bedsted | 00 | 10 | 00 |
| Item 2 Blankets 1 Coverlett | 00 | 06 | 08 |
| Item 1 fither Bedd, 1 fither Bolster & 1 fither Pillow | 02 | 09 | 06 |
| Item 6 Coushing Covers | 00 | 03 | 00 |
| 9 doz of Trenchers | 00 | 03 | 00 |
| Item one Chest | 00 | 10 | 00 |
| Item 3 Coffers | 00 | 06 | 08 |
| Item 1 Wheele | 00 | 02 | 06 |
| Item 1 Carpett 6 coushines | 01 | 00 | 00 |
| Item a Truckle bedsteeds 1 under Bed | 00 | 04 | 00 |

*In ye Closett*

| | | | |
|---|---|---|---|
| Imprimis 6 napkins flaxed 5 Course napkin 11 more of the same sort | 00 | 11 | 00 |
| Item 6 Course Towles | 00 | 01 | 06 |
| Item 1 paire of flax sheetes | 00 | 13 | 04 |
| Item 3 paire of hemp sheetes | 01 | 06 | 00 |
| Item 1 daper Table Cloth | 00 | 13 | 04 |
| Item 5 yard of flaxen in a Table Cloth | 00 | 10 | 00 |

| | |
|---|---|
| Item 1 p of sheets | 00 12 00 |
| 1 diaper towell | 00 02 06 |
| 1 Course Table Cloth | 00 02 06 |
| Item 4 Course short Table Clothes | 00 03 00 |
| Item a single napken & Pillows Beare | 00 01 00 |
| 1 paire of horden sheets | 00 05 00 |
| Item 1 table cloth and a wallett | (sic)00 00 00 |
| 1 doz of flax napkins | 00 10 00 |
| Item 11 fine flax napkins | 00 13 06 |
| 5 odd ones | 00 02 06 |
| 7 Lased pillows Bears | 00 13 04 |
| Item 2 playne ones | 00 03 00 |
| 1 paire of Lased Sheets | 00 18 00 |
| 1 fine flax table Cloth fringd | 00 08 00 |
| 1 fine flax table cloth | 00 11 00 |
| Item 2 paire of fine Laced sheets | 00 06 08 |
| 3 odd flax sheets | 00 06 00 |
| Item more Pewter 12 lb weight | 00 08 00 |
| Item 1 Silver Boule 6 ounces | 01 08 00 |
| 1 course sheete a rough Table Cloth and a napken | 00 03 09 |
| Item a silver Bodken | 00 02 06 |
| Tot | 32 04 03 |

## 107. Margaret Justice

Of Wellington, mercer and widow, taken by Andrew Sockett and Timothy Icke on 3 October 1687 and exhibited on 12 February 1687-88.

Imprs.
| | |
|---|---|
| 11 yards 3 qrters white holland at 10d | 00 09 09 |
| 8 yards white holland at 12d | 00 08 00 |
| 8 yards & halfe white holland at 18d | 00 12 09 |
| 9 yards and halfe more at 15d | 00 11 10 |
| 8 yards & halfe kenting at 10d | 00 07 01 |
| 13 yards white musling at 16 | 00 17 04 |
| 7 yards 3 qrters stript musling at 18 | 00 11 07 |
| 17 yards and a halfe muslin at 17d | 01 03 04 |
| 4 yards white dimothy | 00 02 00 |
| 7 yards and halfe white Callico | 00 07 06 |
| 7 yards bla Callico | 00 04 00 |
| 12 yards Glazed Callico | 00 08 00 |
| 18 yards blew Linin | 00 12 00 |
| 3 Remnants blew Lin | 00 02 00 |
| 4 Remnants Cullerd Callico | 00 02 00 |
| 12 yards halfe Course blew Callico | 00 06 00 |
| 2 Remnants white Callico | 00 03 00 |
| 1 Remnant Callico muslin | 00 03 00 |
| 4 yards dammaged Callico | 00 02 00 |
| 12 yards halfe Lutesring at 2/4 | 01 09 02 |

# THE INVENTORIES OF WELLINGTON

| | | |
|---|---|---|
| 5 yards ducape Sattin at 6/8 | 01 13 00 |
| 10 yards & halfe Brode allamode | 01 04 06 |
| 24 yards narrow allamode | 02 09 00 |
| 1 Remnant Perssian silke | 00 06 00 |
| 1 Remnant Sarsnett | 00 08 00 |
| 1 Remnant Spotted Silke | 00 05 00 |
| 3 Dozen ffringe for whiskes | 00 02 03 |
| 1 Dozen and halfe silk ffring | 00 01 00 |
| A parcell of Taffety ribins | 07 09 00 |
| A parcell fferrit ribins | 02 02 00 |
| A pcell of galloones | 01 18 00 |
| Caddeax & Cottons | 00 15 00 |
| 12 yards ½d ribin | 00 00 04 |
| 6 neck whisks | 00 12 00 |
| 12 neck whiskes | 00 14 00 |
| 2 neck whiskes Twind | 00 03 00 |
| 3 more neck whiskes | 00 03 00 |
| 2 small Plaine ones | 00 01 06 |
| 2 laced whisks | 00 03 00 |
| 3 Fanns at 8d | 00 02 00 |
| 2 wiskes at 15d | 00 02 06 |
| 3 set hoods | 00 09 00 |
| 2 Crowne hoods | 00 07 00 |
| 2 Allamode Hoods | 00 04 06 |
| 2 Lute sring hoods | 00 08 00 |
| A pcell Silke & Gause hoods | 01 00 00 |
| A parcell Gause quines Rufflells Children caps Sattin Caps Silke Sleeves and stommechers | 01 06 07 |
| A pcell of fine threds | 07 04 07 |
| A pcell of Tapes & Inkles White and Cullerd | 01 10 07 |
| 14 onces Coventry blew | 00 03 00 |
| A pcell ffine thred | 00 01 02 |
| A pcell of worsted hose | 01 00 08 |
| 1 Pound of od pcells of silke | 00 10 00 |
| A pcell Laces Loopd lace & necklaces | 00 06 05 |
| Psalters p-mers & other bookes | 00 05 11 |
| Comb cases writeing pap waxe buttons & thred bone lace | 00 09 01 |
| 2 Crape stommechers bugle Cuffes made Cravatt & other made Lin | 01 18 04 |
| A pcell white thred bone laces | 03 01 01 |
| open Tapes filling lace footeing & other fine thred | 04 14 11 |
| buttons Pins Packthred Side peeces head roles quilted caps needle worke patternes Comes Claspes needles Temple wires Thimbles Leadeing Strings Tobacco boxes & needle bookes | 03 01 00 |
| In Resings Currans Sug Spices & grocerry in several pcells | 09 07 00 |
| Counter shilves scales & weights in the shopp | 00 16 00 |

*household goods*

| | | |
|---|---|---|
| 78 lbs Pewter at 7ds | 02 09 00 |
| 1 Tin dredger a Cover & Tun dish | 00 00 06 |
| 1 warmg Pan 18d | 00 01 06 |
| 1 Caster hat | 00 12 00 |
| 6 Alcuine Spoones 1 flint Glass | 00 00 06 |
| 2 Lookeing Glasses | 00 03 10 |

| | | | |
|---|---|---|---|
| 1 Jack 1 pr of Tongs & fire shovle | 00 | 11 | 08 |
| 1 dish bord fframe | 00 | 01 | 06 |
| 3 little Tubs 1 Cubbard | 00 | 07 | 00 |
| 1 Spit 10d 1 paire of Gobbarts 2/-. | 00 | 02 | 10 |
| 1 flesh hook 1 Iron Creeper | 00 | 00 | 09 |
| 1 Dozen Trenchers 1 grate 1/6 | 00 | 02 | 03 |
| 1 other grate 2/6 1 smoothing Iron | 00 | 03 | 04 |
| 1 byble 12d 1 ffrying pan 2/- | 00 | 03 | 00 |
| 4 Pillows 12 Pound at 5d | 00 | 05 | 00 |
| 1 ffeather bed 2 boulsters 70 Pound | 01 | 15 | 00 |
| | | | |
| 1 bed 1 boulster 80 Pound at 6d | 02 | 00 | 00 |
| 1 bed & Boulster 58 Pound at 6 | 01 | 09 | 00 |
| 1 kettle 2 little kettles 2 scellitts | 01 | 01 | 00 |
| 1 small brass Pot | 00 | 02 | 08 |
| 1 paire of bedsteads | 00 | 05 | 00 |
| 1 Small stund & 1 water Paill | 00 | 01 | 08 |
| 1 bed Tick unmade | 00 | 05 | 00 |
| 1 old Trucle bedsteds 3 Curtains 1 set of vallients | 00 | 06 | 00 |
| 1 under Chaff bed | 00 | 01 | 06 |
| 3 Curtins 1 paire vallients | 00 | 03 | 06 |
| 4 old Cloth Chaires | 00 | 06 | 00 |
| 3 old blankett. 1 Counter Paine | 00 | 10 | 00 |
| 4 paire Coarse sheetes | 00 | 10 | 00 |
| 1 Cobbart Cloth 5 flax napkins | 00 | 07 | 00 |
| 2 Pillows beares 5 Table Clothes | 00 | 09 | 04 |
| 2 halfe hogsheds | 00 | 06 | 08 |
| 1 Barrell 2 Bottles 2 fferkins 2 Coolers 1 small mitt 1 stund | 00 | 09 | 11 |
| 1 old Carpett | 00 | 01 | 00 |
| debts due | 03 | 09 | 00 |
| things omited & not seen | 00 | 02 | 06 |
| | | | |
| | 83 | 07 | 08 |
| | | | |
| debts do be Paide by the exetrix | | | |
| to Mr Ambler | 17 | 15 | 00 |
| To Mr dalley | 15 | 14 | 06 |
| To Mr scot | 12 | 15 | 06 |
| To Mr Watkis | 05 | 08 | 10 |
| To Mr Seamoore | 06 | 14 | 00 |
| To Mr Smith | 01 | 07 | 00 |
| To James morris | 00 | 05 | 10 |
| To Mrs Richardson | 00 | 04 | 06 |
| To Andrew Sockett | 01 | 18 | 06 |
| | | | |
| Totall of ye debts | 62 | 03 | 08 |
| | | | |
| The Personall Estate is | 21 | 04 | 00 |

## 108. John Peate

Of the Street Lane in the parish of Wellington, blacksmith, taken by Timothy Field, Gabriell Cleaton* and John Golbourne* on 7 October 1687, and exhibited on 19 October 1687.

*Imprs. The goods in ye Parlour*
one Joyned bed one table board one Cubbard one Cofer . . 04 10 00

*Item ye goods in ye house*
one table board for brasse & pewter & for Iron of all sorts & for wooden vessells of all sorts . . . . . . . 04 00 00

*for goods in ye Chamber over ye Parlour*
one table board 2 beds one Cofer . . . . . . 03 00 00

*ffor goods in ye Chamber over ye house*
one table board one Joyned bed . . . . . . 02 10 00

| | |
|---|---|
| ffor goods & Tools in ye Shop . . . . | 03 00 00 |
| ffor Cattle of all sorts . . . . . . | 25 00 00 |
| ffor 2 horses & there geares . . . . . | 05 00 00 |
| ffor two Swine . . . . . . . | 01 10 00 |
| ffor one Cart & ye Implements of husbandry . . . | 02 10 00 |
| ffor things forgotten & omitted . . . . . | 00 05 00 |
| ffor his weareing apparrell . . . . . . | 03 00 00 |
| | 54 05 00 |

## 109. William Minshall

Of Leegomery, taken by Roger Bennett, Andrew Sockett and William Icke on 29 October 1687 and exhibited on 27 March 1688. In his will dated 2 June 1686 he left the lease of his property in Leegomery to Mary and Margaret, daughters of his son-in-law Francis Wright. He had property in Wellington leased by William Turner which he left to Francis and Mary Wright, and a leasehold estate in Little Wenlock sub-let to Andrew Wright, the profits from which were bequeathed to John and Margaret Wright.

| | |
|---|---|
| Imprs. 4 oxen . . . . . . . | 19 00 00 |
| 2 Bullocks . . . . . . . . | 07 00 00 |
| 10 Cows 1 heifer £3.3s.4. . . . . . . | 34 16 08 |
| 4 two yeare old Bullock 2 two yeare old heifers . . . | 12 00 00 |
| 6 yeare old Calves at 20/0 . . . . . . | 06 00 00 |
| 1 3 yeare old Colt 1 two year old 1 one yeare old . . | 07 10 00 |
| 1 Mare . . . . . . . . | 04 10 00 |
| 3 Swine . . . . . . . . | 04 00 00 |
| 2 Stoore Piggs . . . . . . . | 01 00 00 |
| 1 waine Bod 1 pr Iron Bound wheeles & 1 pr of Ripples . | 04 00 00 |
| 1 waine Bod Bare foote wheeles & Ripples . . . | 02 00 00 |
| 2 Tumbrill Bodys 2 pr draught & 2 pr Iron Bound wheeles . | 07 00 00 |
| 4 Plows 3 paire of Irons 2 Ploe Copsalls . . . . | 00 15 00 |
| 4 waine Caps 3 pr Rathes . . . . . . | 01 05 00 |
| 2 Harrows . . . . . . . . | 00 10 00 |
| 1 pcell of Clift intended for Implements of husbandry . . | 00 15 00 |

| | |
|---|---|
| 1 hand Barrow 1 wheel Barrow . . . . . | 00 02 00 |
| 3 draught yokes 1 Cop yoke 3 oxe Chaines 1 foote Chaine & 2 Copsalls . . . . . . . . | 01 00 00 |
| 3 paire homes 3 Collers 3 pr Iron horse Chaines . . . | 00 10 00 |
| 2 Cart Ropes . . . . . . . . | 00 05 00 |
| 2 mattockes 1 Pick 1 Docking Iron . . . . | 00 05 00 |
| 3 axes 2 Bills 1 hatchett . . . . . . | 00 06 08 |
| 3 hand saws & 1 Trowell . . . . . . | 00 03 00 |
| 2 Broome hookes . . . . . . . | 00 01 00 |
| 4 old Augers . . . . . . . . | 00 02 06 |
| 1 pair Compasses . . . . . . . | 00 00 04 |
| 1 Gouge 3 Chissles . . . . . . . | 00 01 06 |
| 1 Spoke Shafe 1 Drawing knife . . . . . | 00 00 06 |
| 1 Iron Crow . . . . . . . . | 00 02 06 |
| 1 whimble Brace & bits . . . . . . | 00 00 06 |
| 3 Spades 3/6 2 paire pinsors & 3 hammers 2/6 . . . | 00 05 06 |
| 1 maule 2 Iron wedges . . . . . . | 00 01 06 |
| 2 Hoppers 18 2 pair weedeing Toungs 12 1 Saw 4/6 . . | 00 06 06 |
| 2 Drawing hookes 1 muck hooke ........tting Iron . . | 00 04 00 |
| 3 hey Rakes 12d 4 Muck forkes 4/0 . . . . | 00 05 00 |
| 12 Rik forks 7/0 . . . . . . . | 00 07 00 |
| old rackes & Chaines and other old iron . . . . | 00 06 08 |
| 2 grindlestones 4 Ladders . . . . . . | 00 12 00 |
| 2 sithes 2/6 2 stalls Bees 5/0 . . . . , | 00 07 06 |
| 6 Ducks 1 mallard 1 Cock & 6 henns . . . . | 00 05 00 |
| 68 Sheepe at 4li ye Score . . . . . . | 13 12 00 |

*Goods In ye house*

| | |
|---|---|
| 1 Table Boord 2 Joyne benchs . . . . . | 00 18 00 |
| 1 fframe of Joyne Cubbarts . . . . . | 00 06 08 |
| 1 Low Skreene 3 Chaires . . . . . . | 00 05 00 |
| 3 Brass Ponns 1 dish bord fframe . . . . . | 01 03 04 |
| 12 Pewter dishes . . . . . . . | 01 00 00 |
| 2 Pewter Candlesticks . . . . . . | 00 01 06 |
| 3 Brass Candlesticks . . . . . . . | 00 05 00 |
| 1 Pewter Gun 1 flaggon 1 qrt Pot . . . . . | 00 06 08 |
| 3 Iron dreepeing Panns . . . . . . | 00 08 00 |
| 2 Brass Potts 2 Brass kettles . . . . . | 01 03 04 |
| 1 Iron morter & pestell . . . . . . | 00 02 06 |
| 2 Small Brass Potts . . . . . . . | 00 05 00 |
| 1 Brass morter 1 Brass Chafeing dish . . . . | 00 03 00 |
| 1 Iron Chafeing dish . . . . . . . | 00 01 00 |
| 1 Pudding Plate 2 ffrying Pans . . . . . | 00 04 04 |
| 2 fire Shovells 2 pr Toungs . . . . . . | 00 03 00 |
| 2 fouling Guns . . . . . . . | 01 00 00 |
| 1 flesh hooke 2 basteing Spoons . . . . . | 00 01 00 |
| 1 Iron Grate 1 Iron Creeper . . . . . | 00 10 00 |
| 1 Cast plate 3 Spitts 1 Pot in ye wall . . . . | 00 06 00 |
| 2 Bills 1 Pike Staff . . . . . . . | 00 02 06 |
| 1 Bagg Salt 1 Salt Box . . . . . . | 00 05 00 |
| 1 pr Bellys & 1 Lanthorne . . . . . . | 00 01 00 |
| 1 pr Cobbarts 1 hanging Spit . . . . . | 00 01 06 |
| 1 Brass Skimmer . . . . . . . | 00 00 06 |
| 2 pr Pot Hanglesses & pott hookes . . . . | 00 02 00 |

### Goods in ye Parlor

| | |
|---|---|
| 1 Joyne Bed Curtins Valliants feather bed & other furniture | 03 10 00 |
| 1 Joyne hanging Press | 00 15 00 |
| 1 Table Board & Carpett 6 Joyne Stooles & one Chaire | 00 13 04 |
| 1 Chest 1 Coffer | 00 10 00 |
| 1 hanging Curtaine undr ye stairs | 00 00 06 |
| 2 ffine & 3 Course Table Clothes | 00 13 04 |
| 5 Pillows beares | 00 04 00 |
| 10 pr Sheets 2 Dozn napkins | 03 13 04 |
| 1 old warming Pan 1 Lookeing Glass | 00 01 06 |

### Goods in ye Inner Butterry

| | |
|---|---|
| 2 Lrg hogsheds | 00 16 00 |
| 2 Large Barrells 1 Smaler under ye staires in ye Parlor | 00 12 00 |
| 5 other Smaler Vessells | 00 09 00 |
| 1 Lrg wooden Bottle & 2 Smaler | 00 02 06 |
| 1 Tun dish 1 Small mitt 4 milk Pans 1 Cheese Ladder | 00 02 00 |

### Goods in ye outward Butterry

| | |
|---|---|
| 1 little Table one Churne with Cheese ffatts | 00 06 00 |

### Goods in ye Cock loft

| | |
|---|---|
| 98 Cheeses 77 more in ye store Chamber & 2 Steanes butter | 10 00 00 |

### Goods in the Best Chamber

| | |
|---|---|
| 2 pair of Joyne bedsteads 1 set of Curtins & Valliants 2 ffeather beds & other furniture | 04 10 00 |
| 1 little Table 1 Joyne Chaire 1 old Coffer 1 old Trunck | 00 07 00 |

### Goods in ye Chamber at ye Stairehead

| | |
|---|---|
| 1 Plaine bedstead 1 ffeather bed | 01 13 04 |
| 1 Coffer 1 Cast Plate | 00 07 08 |
| 30 Pound drest hempe | 00 12 06 |
| 40 Pound drest flax | 00 06 08 |

### Goods in yt Cald ye maides Chamber

| | |
|---|---|
| 2 low beds 2 ffeather beds and other furniture | 02 00 00 |
| 1 old Coffer & Joyne forme | 00 02 00 |

### Goods in Ye Stoore Chamber

| | |
|---|---|
| 2 Straw whisketts | 00 04 00 |
| 2 old Cuffers & 1 Table boord | 00 06 08 |
| 1 Saddle 1 Packnell | 00 10 00 |
| 1 Spining wheell | 00 04 00 |
| Corne & malt Beife & Bacon | 04 00 00 |
| loose Bords & Joyce over ye maides Chamber & Stoore Chamber | 02 00 00 |

### Goods In ye Kitchin

| | |
|---|---|
| 1 mault mill | 01 06 08 |
| 2 Stunds 1 kneading mitt | 00 07 06 |

| | | |
|---|---|---|
| 2 Coolers 2 Rindlin Rubs 1 Brass furnace | 01 00 00 |
| 1 Cheese press 1 moulding board | 00 03 10 |
| 1 wall Cestern 5 old Pailes | 00 10 00 |
| | |
| hey Corne unthrashd and Corne Sowd | 27 10 00 |
| 1 Lease of a liveing in Leegommerry for one life | 66 00 00 |
| 1 Lease of a liveing in little Wenlock for one old life | 42 00 00 |
| moneys in ye house | 10 19 00 |
| 1 waine Rope | 00 04 00 |
| 2 Tutors & Coles in Stocke & hemp undrest | 01 00 00 |
| | |
| his weareing Apparrell | 06 00 00 |
| | |
| due for Rent at last micaellmas for ye liveing in wenlock | 10 10 00 |
| due ffrom John ffrancis of wellington | 00 15 00 |
| William Turners Rent in ffrancis Wrights hands | 01 05 00 |
| due ffrom Andrew wright of little wenlock | 09 00 00 |
| | |
| Things unseen & forgotten | 00 10 00 |
| | |
| The totall sum of this Inventory is | 360 14 00 |

## 110. William Langley

Of Wellington, clerk, taken by John Bradshaw, Thomas Bickley, and John Grosvenor on 24 May 1689 and exhibited on 18 June 1689.

| | | |
|---|---|---|
| Imp. The Deceased signett Ring | 01 00 00 |
| his watch | 01 15 00 |
| silver Plate | 18 17 00 |
| A peece of Gold | 00 06 08 |

*Corn Growing on ye ground*

| | | |
|---|---|---|
| Muncorn & wheat | 07 12 00 |
| Barley growing | 04 10 00 |
| Corne in ye barne | 03 07 06 |

*In ye pantrey*

| | | |
|---|---|---|
| 6 Turkey worke chairs | 01 07 00 |
| 6 Turkey worke stooles | 00 12 00 |
| a Little table & A forme | 00 07 00 |
| A glascease & 5 china basons 2 sillibub cups one Jugg & bottle | 00 05 00 |
| A boxe of drawers with A stand | 00 04 00 |

*In ye Kitching*

| | | |
|---|---|---|
| one table and forme | 00 07 00 |
| 4 Joyned chairs | 00 12 00 |
| one screen | 00 06 00 |
| one press | 00 16 00 |
| one Jack & weights | 00 04 00 |
| one Grate & creeper | 00 05 00 |

# THE INVENTORIES OF WELLINGTON 285

| | | |
|---|---|---|
| 4 broatches | | 00 02 06 |
| A pair of racks | | 00 04 00 |
| fire shovel & tonges | | 00 02 00 |
| one Iron barr being A sway pole & Links | | 00 03 00 |
| A warming pan | | 00 01 00 |

*In ye great Chambr*

| | | |
|---|---|---|
| 5 pictures in 2 frames | | 00 10 00 |
| A pair of bedsteads | | 00 16 00 |
| A sett of red curtains & valletts | | 01 10 00 |
| one bed and boulster & Quilt | | 02 00 00 |
| A pair of bedsteads | | 00 13 04 |
| blew curtains one bed & one boulster | | 02 00 00 |
| A Counterpane | | 00 03 04 |
| 4 blew chairs & A blew couch | | 00 12 00 |
| 4 blew stooles | | 00 06 00 |
| It. 6 red Cloath chairs | | 01 04 00 |
| 6 red cloath stooles | | 00 12 00 |
| one Chest | | 00 10 00 |
| 2 Livery cupboards | | 00 06 08 |
| 2 Turkey Worke carpetts | | 02 10 00 |
| 3 silke Cusheons | | 00 05 00 |
| A blew Cupboard cloath | | 00 01 00 |
| 2 Cabbinetts | | 00 02 06 |
| one table | | 00 06 00 |
| A small Coate of arms | | 00 00 06 |
| A Feather bed 4 bolsters & 4 pillows | | 02 00 00 |
| 11 blanketts | | 00 15 00 |
| 3 Ruggs | | 01 03 00 |
| 2 setts of curtains & A carpett | | 00 05 00 |
| bookes in ye study that were not disposed of in his lifetime to his sons | | 20 00 00 |

*In ye Chamber over the kitchin*

| | | |
|---|---|---|
| A pair of bedsteads | | 01 10 00 |
| A pair of curtains of Kederminster stuff | | 00 03 00 |
| A pair of curtains & bedsteads | | 00 08 00 |
| One bed 2 bolsters & a coverlid | | 01 13 04 |
| A hanging press | | 00 14 00 |
| A Round table | | 00 05 00 |
| A Joyned chair | | 00 06 00 |
| one Truckle bed | | 00 03 00 |
| one bed one bolster & one blankett | | 01 00 00 |
| A Coverlett | | 00 02 06 |
| 9 cusheons of Gilt Leather & 7 paper pictures in frames | | 00 05 06 |

*In ye Room over ye pantry*

| | | |
|---|---|---|
| A pair of Joyned bedsteads | | 00 10 00 |
| A sett of green curtains & valletts | | 00 05 00 |
| A feather bed one bolster & 2 pillows | | 02 00 00 |
| 2 blanketts & A rugg | | 00 10 00 |
| one Little Table | | 00 01 06 |

*In ye Cock loft*

| | | | |
|---|---|---|---|
| one old bedstead | 00 | 06 | 00 |
| A Large chest | 00 | 06 | 00 |
| 3 Matts | 00 | 01 | 06 |
| an Iron bound trunke | 00 | 00 | 06 |
| A Coffer | 00 | 03 | 00 |
| A hopper | 00 | 00 | 06 |
| A coffer | 00 | 00 | 06 |
| It. A wain Rope | 00 | 01 | 06 |
| A little old trunke | 00 | 01 | 06 |
| 2 fflock beds & 3 bolsters | 00 | 01 | 00 |

*In ye hall*

| | | | |
|---|---|---|---|
| 4 long tables | 01 | 00 | 00 |
| 3 long formes | 00 | 02 | 06 |
| 5 shorte tables | 00 | 10 | 06 |
| 2 Livery tables | 00 | 05 | 00 |
| 2 Arkes for corne | 01 | 00 | 00 |
| 2 Joyned chaires | 00 | 03 | 00 |
| 2 Joyned bedsteads | 00 | 16 | 00 |
| 2 truckle bedsteads | 00 | 06 | 00 |
| Linnens of all sortes | 02 | 10 | 00 |

*In ye seller*

| | | | |
|---|---|---|---|
| 7 barrells | 01 | 10 | 00 |
| 2 horses for barrells to stand on | 00 | 02 | 00 |
| 2 shelves | 00 | 01 | 00 |
| A dropper | 00 | 01 | 00 |
| 2 closeboukes | 00 | 02 | 00 |
| A little Coffer | 00 | 01 | 06 |

*In ye buttery*

| | | | |
|---|---|---|---|
| one Cupboard | 00 | 06 | 00 |
| one Frying pann | 00 | 01 | 06 |

*In ye brewhouse*

| | | | |
|---|---|---|---|
| 2 turnells | 00 | 03 | 06 |
| 3 brewing stunds | 00 | 10 | 00 |
| 2 tunning dishes | 00 | 01 | 00 |
| A steel malte mill | 01 | 00 | 00 |
| 20 wooden bottles | 00 | 01 | 00 |
| boards & timber | 01 | 05 | 00 |
| 4 brass potts | 01 | 00 | 00 |
| 3 Kettles | 01 | 02 | 06 |
| one kettle one skillett & a sawspan | 00 | 04 | 00 |
| A posnett with 3 feet | 00 | 01 | 06 |
| A skimmer & A basting Ladle | 00 | 01 | 00 |
| pewter of all sorts | 04 | 02 | 08 |
| A bed pann | 00 | 03 | 04 |
| A brass pan | 00 | 18 | 00 |

## THE INVENTORIES OF WELLINGTON

| | |
|---|---|
| A Chamber pott . . . . . . . | 00 01 00 |
| A tinn pasty pann . . . . . . . | 00 00 08 |
| Brick & tyle crests & Gutters . . . . . | 10 00 00 |
| A pair of old carte wheels A harrow & carte body & a pair of tumbrell draughts . . . . . . . . | 00 10 00 |
| Corne & Malte in ye house . . . . . . | 00 15 08 |
| Hemp & fflax undressed . . . . . . | 00 12 00 |
| A Cow . . . . . . . . | 03 12 06 |
| The Deceased his waring apparell . . . . . | 05 00 00 |
| Money in his pockett . . . . . . | 02 15 07 |
| Booke debts Received . . . . . . | 05 14 11 |
| Debts desperate . . . . . . . | 17 17 06 |
| things out of sight & fotgotten . . . . . | 00 05 00 |
| Summa totalis . | 159 01 02 |
| Two store swine & bacon omitted when the apprisers subscribed this Inventory afterwards apprised to ye value of . . . . | 02 00 00 |
| Item for hay . . . . . . . . | 00 10 00 |
| Item for Compost . . . . . . . | 00 05 00 |
| | 02 15 00 |
| The whole amount is . . | 161 16 02 |

## 111. Richard Jones

Of Wellington, taken by Francis Ore, Thomas Griffiths and William Salter on 18 September 1689 and exhibited on 28 September 1689.

*Imprimis in ye Best Chamber*

| | |
|---|---|
| one feather Bed one Bolster on Blanket one Coverlid a Set of Curtains & Valins and a Bedsted fore Chaires one table one Stand and a Couch . . . . . . . . . | 04 16 08 |

*Item in ye middle Chamb.*

| | |
|---|---|
| one feather Bed one flock Bed one Bolster 2 blankets one Coverlid one Bedsted and a Set Curtains a Great Trunk a Coffer a Desk 2 Chaires and a Clos Stoole . . . . . . . | 03 13 06 |

*Item in ye Parlor Chamb*

| | |
|---|---|
| One feather Bed one Bolster one pillow one Bedsted and Curtains on Desk one Chair one Coffer 15 books 2 trunks 6 peices of fring one Blaket and a Rug . . . . . . . | 05 01 00 |

*Item in the Store Chamb.*

| | |
|---|---|
| 32 Cheeses a Spining wheel and a little table . . . . | 01 03 00 |

*Item in the room behind the Parlor*
23 bonds of leather one Bed one Bolster and one coffer . . 02 08 00

*Item in the Parlor*
8 chairs one Couch 2 tables 2 Jont Stooles 2 Glass Cases 2 Carpets one fire Shovel and Tongs one fenders and hooks . . . 02 16 00

*Item in the Citchen*
Puter of Brass of all sorts one Jack one Grate one fire Shovel and Tongs 2 Spits one Bird Spit 1 pair of Racks a fender 2 Pot gails a fouleing Gun 2 Smothing Irons 1 frying pan one driping pan 1 table 3 Joint Stools a Screen 1 Chaire a puter frame . . . 06 13 08

*Item in the little Parlor*
one Table 2 Stooles on Livery Table 2 chairs and wainscot . 01 02 00

*Item in 2 little Roomes*
two Beds 2 bolsters 2 Blankets one Coverlid 2 Bedsteds a Desk and one Trunk . . . . . . . . 03 00 00

*Item in the Buttery*
2 Barrels 5 Kinderkins 2 Ferkins one Dropper and a Turnell Trenchers . . . . . . . . . 02 00 00

*Item in the Brewhouse*
Wooden vessels of all sorts . . . . . . 01 02 00
a furnace a boiler an Iron Pott . . . . . . 02 00 00

*Item in ye malt house*
A Jug a hare Cloth a Malt mill a Strike a half Strike a Straw whisk a pack saddle and flax and 30 Strike of Oates . . . 05 17 00

*Item for horned Beas*
fore Cowes one Boollock three heifers . . . . . 17 10 00
Item for five Swine . . . . . . . . 03 00 00
Item for one Colt and fore horses . . . . . . 08 00 00
Item for twenty six sheep . . . . . . . 04 10 00
Item for Hard Corn in the Barne . . . . . . 15 10 00
Item for Barly in the Barne . . . . . . . 08 00 00
Item for Beanses in the Barne . . . . . . 05 00 00
Item for pease in the Barne . . . . . . . 03 00 00
Item for Hey in the Barne . . . . . . . 12 00 00
Item for Muck about the howse . . . . . . 03 00 00
Item for All the leather in the tanhowse . . . . . 100 00 00
Item for all the barke about the tan howse . . . . 20 00 00
Item for the mill and Instruments of trade . . . . 03 00 00
Item for the Revarsion of the leas . . . . . . 50 00 00
Item for dubious or Doubtfull Debts . . . . . 10 00 00
Item for Nappery ware . . . . . . . 06 01 00

THE INVENTORIES OF WELLINGTON 289

| | | |
|---|---|---|
| Item for wareing Aparel and Mony in his purs . . . . | 12 05 06 |
| Item for Lumber about the house thing things not valued and out of sight . . . . . . . . . | 00 10 00 |
| sum tot . . | 323 19 04 |

## 112. Robert Johnson

Of Wellington, mercer, taken by John Bradshaw, Adam Wright and William Newton on 28 April 1690 and exhibited on 20 June 1690.

| | |
|---|---|
| Imp. | |
| Three hundred Strikes of Malt at . . . . . . | 35 00 00 |
| one hundred Measures of Barley . . . . . . | 10 00 00 |
| Silver plate . . . . . . . . . | 09 00 00 |
| Ready Money . . . . . . . . | 30 00 00 |
| For debts Sperate and desperate . . . . . . | 40 00 00 |
| Weareing Apparrell . . . . . . . . | 10 00 00 |
| Things omitted or forgotten . . . . . . | 10 00 00 |
| | 144 00 00 |

## 113. Thomas Reynolds

Of Wellington, butcher, taken by Roger Walker, Richard Betton and Samuel Bennett on 2 June 1690 and exhibited on 17 September 1690. The pence column for the first five items is obliterated on the original.

*Imprimis in ye house*

| | |
|---|---|
| One table borde & a Joyne forme one cubbert or press one Joyne Chayre one Joyne stoole . . . . . . . . | 00 10 — |
| one big brass Kettle two little brass kettles one brass pot one skellet one basting spoone . . . . . . . . . | 01 06 — |
| Six pewter dishes three plates two saultes one candle stick one chamber pot . . . . . . . . . . | 00 08 — |
| one Iron pot one dripping pan on pudding plate two Iron Candlesticks one flesh forke one toaster . . . . . . | 00 04 — |
| one grate & niggards one paire of tongs two spitts one paire of gayle hookes one paire of pothookes one frying pan . . . | 00 05 — |
| two Turnells one payle two halfe barrells & one ferkin . . . | 00 06 00 |
| In monyes . . . . . . . . . | 14 05 00 |

*In ye Chamber or Store*

| | |
|---|---|
| one Bed & stids wth its furniture . . . . . . | 02 00 00 |
| one Joyne Chest one Coffer five paire & a halfe of Sheetes . . | 02 00 00 |

*In ye Chamber over ye house*

| | |
|---|---|
| one table borde two formes three coffers one Joyne Chaire one safe one little Table . . . . . . . . . | 00 15 04 |

|  |  |
|---|---|
| one bedstide & bed & coverlet one trundle bed stids & an ould paire of bedstids | 00 16 00 |
| one table cloth one Napkin. | 00 03 00 |
| three shifts | 00 06 00 |

*In ye Cole house*

|  |  |
|---|---|
| one little table & a small stund | 00 01 06 |
| Wearing Apparrell | 00 15 00 |
| Things omitted or not seen. | 00 03 04 |

*In ye Shop*

|  |  |
|---|---|
| his tooles or working gambrells setlesses & knives | 00 03 00 |
| debts in ye booke sparet & desparet | 02 13 00 |
|  | 27 00 10 |

### 114. Thomas Blakeman

Of Hadley, taken by Thomas Smitheman, George Crudgington and William Cuxson* on 1 September 1690 and exhibited on 19 September 1690.

|  |  |
|---|---|
| Impr. Two Loomes and geares | 04 00 00 |
| Item. One Bedd and furniture | 01 00 00 |
| Itm. Brass and pewter | 00 05 00 |
| Item. two trebles | 01 00 00 |
| Item. his weareinge Cloathes and aparrell. | 01 00 00 |
| Item. money in his pockett. | 00 02 06 |
| Item. two boxes and a deske | 00 08 00 |
| for things unapraised and not seene | 00 05 00 |
| Sume. | 08 00 06 |

### 115. Richard Johnson

Of Wellington, taken by Roger Walker and Adam Wright on 15 February 1691-92 and exhibited on 17 March 1691-92.

*In ye Chamber over ye parellor*

|  |  |
|---|---|
| And the furniture belong thereto two feather beds | 04 06 00 |
| Three Leathern Cheirs & two Cloth Cheirs | 00 07 00 |
| Three forms one short Table & Little Table | 00 10 00 |
| one short Cubbard 1 Trunck 1 Close Stoole And A pan 1 Chest | 00 15 00 |
| one Looking glass & Chenny wares | 00 06 00 |

*In The Chambr over ye house*

|  |  |
|---|---|
| two feather beds & Truckle flock bed & ye furniture belonging to them | 04 02 06 |
| Two old Trunckes 1 Coffer 1 Deske 2 boxes And a Little Table | 00 10 04 |

## THE INVENTORIES OF WELLINGTON

*In The Garratt*

| | |
|---|---|
| And furniture belonging to it 1 flock bed 2 bed stites 5 pillows one boulster & 1 Coffer . . . . . . | 00 16 06 |

*In the Parelor*

| | |
|---|---|
| And the furniture there one Table 1 form 1 Chest 3 Leathern Cheirs And 2 other Cheirs . . . . . . . | 01 01 06 |

*In the Chambr over ye Sellor & what belongs to it*

| | |
|---|---|
| 1 Table 1 Coffer . . . . . . . | 00 07 00 |

*In ye Sellor & what therein is*

| | |
|---|---|
| two Hogsheads 2 barrels & one halfe barrell . . . . | 01 03 10 |

*In ye Kiching & what therein is*

| | |
|---|---|
| for brueing Vessels . . . . . . . | 01 03 04 |

*In the house & what therein Is belonging to it*

| | |
|---|---|
| 1 hangeing Cubbard 1 press 1 Round Table 1 dishboard 1 Skrine 1 Dresser 3 Cheirs And one Joyn Stoole . . . . | 01 05 06 |
| Three Little brass potts 2 brass pans 2 Kettles 1 Skellet 1 warming pan and A Little brass Morter 2 brass Candle stocks & one Skimmer . | 02 03 10 |
| Two Alkemy dishes . . . . . . . . | 00 02 03 |
| 15 Peawter dishes 2 gunes 3 flaggons two Chamber Pots 3 Sawsers 6 plats 4 poringers 2 peawter Candlesticks 2 salt sellers & 2 pewter Canes . . . . . . . . . | 02 19 09 |
| Two Iron Potes three Iron Driping pans Three Iron Candle sticks 1 Iron Grate A Crper & a plate, a fire shovell 3 pare of Tonges 1 flesh fork 1 Jacke 1 Cafeing dish and A frying pane . . . | 02 08 01 |
| Three Spits 2 gobbards 2 pare of pottgales Two pare of pott houckes | 00 11 00 |
| Lineing of All Sorts . . . . . . . | 08 17 00 |
| Tallow & Candles . . . . . . . . | 02 01 00 |
| Trinerey wares . . . . . . . . | 00 13 04 |
| A Little wheele & A great wheele . . . . . . | 00 03 06 |
| one Cow . . . . . . . . . | 02 00 00 |
| one Swine . . . . . . . . . | 00 11 06 |
| Corn And hey . . . . . . . . | 02 03 04 |
| Beaufe And Baccon . . . . . . . . | 01 00 04 |
| ffor wareing Apparel & Sheifts . . . . . . | 05 10 00 |
| Things forgotten and omitted . . . . . . | 00 07 03 |
| debts sperate & desperate . . . . . . . | 01 00 00 |
| | 49 17 00 |

### 116. Francis Ore

Of Wellington, blacksmith, taken by William Cheese and William Cooke* on 29 April 1692 and exhibited on 15 May 1692.

| | |
|---|---|
| Imprimis 2 hamers 9 li wite . . . . . . | 00 02 04 |
| a ruber file . . . . . . . . . | 00 00 08 |

| | |
|---|---|
| 2 p of Tonges | 00 01 00 |
| an Axtree for a grind stone | 00 00 06 |
| 3 punches and a sette | 00 00 04 |
| A hamber. Like a naylers hamber | 00 00 06 |
| a p of old Sheirs | 00 00 06 |
| 12 old ovr worne files broken & whole | 00 01 06 |
| A Shoo Box | 00 00 03 |
| 2 naile persors & a Jack windles | 00 00 03 |
| an old screw plate an p of plyers | 00 00 06 |
| a Syth Cog a horn and 2 blood stikes | 00 00 04 |
| 4 rolars & a hardey | 00 00 04 |
| A Logg of Timber | 00 02 06 |
| a Bench 2 grind stones | 00 04 00 |
| a grate 43 and a halfe | 00 10 10½ |
| Sum is | 01 06 04½ |

## 117. Richard Goodales

Of the Wrekin, Wellington, taken by Edward Clark and Charles Stilgo on 7 May 1692 and exhibited on 6 June 1692.

| | |
|---|---|
| Imprimis. Seaven Cows | 16 10 00 |
| Itim. too Twinters & too yearlings | 03 10 00 |
| Itim. A mare & too Colts | 05 15 00 |
| Itim. fourty sheepe | 05 06 08 |

*Itim. In ye house*

one Joynd table on brass bench with brass & pewter too paire of pot gailes one hand Iron . . . . . . . . . 02 12 00

*Itim. In ye parlour*

one Joyned table on brass bench with brass & pewter too paire of Chaires & one Cubert . . . . . . . . 05 00 00

*Itim In ye buttrey*

foure barrells two brewing stunds one Cooler with some other vessells of wood for ye deary . . . . . . 06 16 06

*Itim. In ye Chamber over ye parlor*

one lowe paire of bedsteds for a servant to lay in with its furniture one Chest too old Coffers . . . . . . . 00 13 04

*Itim. In ye Chamber over ye house*

one old bed too whiskitts to hold corne one Cheese Shilfe . . 00 18 00

*Itim. In ye Little Chamber*

one old bed one Cuffer a kneading Turnell and a Cheese press. . 00 13 04

| | |
|---|---|
| Item. his Waring Aparell | 01 00 00 |
| Itim. Corne upon ye Ground | 05 01 06 |

| | | | |
|---|---|---|---|
| Itim. one old Cart with Ironbound wheeles one Tumbrell with naked wheels one plow one harrow with other Implements of husbandry . . . . . . . . . | 01 | 02 | 00 |
| Itim. Muck and Compost . . . . . . . | 00 | 10 | 00 |
| Itim. Geese and other poultry . . . . . . | 00 | 04 | 06 |
| All things forgot . . . . . . . . | 00 | 05 | 00 |
| | 49 | 17 | 10 |
| Debts and arreers of Rents . . . . . . . | 30 | 00 | 00 |
| Rests . . . . . . . . . . | 20 | 17 | 10 |

## 118. Thomas Jones

Of Wellington, gent., taken by Richard Lewis, John Bradshaw and Timothy Ffield on 22 July 1692 and exhibited on 25 November 1692.

*In the Kitchen*

| | | | |
|---|---|---|---|
| Six pewtr Dishes Six porrengrs & Tenne plates wt. 57 lb. at 8d p pound . . . . . . . . . | 01 | 18 | 00 |
| Ould pewtr 68 lb. at 6d p p . . . . . . | 01 | 14 | 00 |
| ffowre brasse pans wt. 36 lb. at 10d p pd. . . . . | 01 | 10 | 00 |
| One square brass hand Candlestick . . . . . | 00 | 01 | 06 |
| One warmeing panne . . . . . . . | 00 | 03 | 06 |
| One brasse pott one pott posnett twoo Candlesticks wt. 51 lb. at 4d p lib. . . . . . . . . . | 00 | 17 | 00 |
| Twoo old Kettles twoo old Skelletts wt. 10 lb. at 5d. . . | 00 | 04 | 02 |
| One brasse Morter wt. 28 lb. at 7d. p lib.. . . . | 00 | 16 | 04 |
| Twoo ffireshovells One Barre ffireshovell One Little ffireshovell & Tongs with brasse knobbs One Grid Iron One Creeper ffowre broaches One paire of Gob Irons One Iron pestell wt. 104 lb. at 2d p lib. . . . . . . . . . | 00 | 17 | 04 |
| Two Iron Dripping panns one Skymmer wt. 24 lb. at 4d p lib . | 00 | 08 | 00 |
| One Jack 10s. One Grate & Niggerts 10s. tot. . . . | 01 | 00 | 00 |
| One Iron back . . . . . . . . | 00 | 12 | 00 |
| Twoo Skreenes . . . . . . . . | 00 | 16 | 00 |
| One little Table and Joynt Stoole . . . . . . | 00 | 04 | 00 |
| One Leaden pump and Cesterne . . . . . . | 01 | 00 | 00 |
| One old Salt Coffer . . . . . . . . | 00 | 00 | 06 |

*In the Brewhouse*

| | | | |
|---|---|---|---|
| One Iron Marmalett . . . . . . . . | 00 | 05 | 00 |
| One brasse ffurnace . . . . . . . . | 01 | 00 | 00 |
| Twoo brewing Stunds 2 barrells one Kneading Tubb Twoo little Gaunes twoo spinning Wheeles . . . . . . | 00 | 16 | 00 |
| One Stone Cesterne . . . . . . . . | 00 | 04 | 00 |

*In the Milkhouse*

| | | | |
|---|---|---|---|
| Twoo Small Rundletts One Little Table One Churne Twoo bottles . | 00 | 06 | 00 |

*In the Malt Roome*
One Skreene for Malt One large Wooden Whitch . . . 00 09 00

*In the Buttrey*
A Livery Cupoard & One old Table . . . . 00 06 00

*In the Celler*
ffowre barrells & one hogshead . . . . . 00 12 00
horses for the barrells to stand on . . . . . 00 04 00

*In the Dineing Roome*
Twoo little Tables one fform One Chaire One Joynt Stoole . . 00 12 06
One Meate Cubboard . . . . . . . 00 06 00

*In the Hall*
ffowre Chaires One Table & ffourme & old Carpett . . . 00 18 06
One halfe hundred Lead Wayte & 2 brasse waytes . . . 00 07 00
One Clock . . . . . . . . . 00 10 00

*In the Parlor*
Six Chaires . . . . . . . . . 00 18 00
One Couch . . . . . . . . . 00 04 00
One Round Table . . . . . . . . 00 08 00
One Long Table and framme & Carpett . . . . 01 00 00
One Grate . . . . . . . . . 00 04 00
One Lookeing Glasse . . . . . . . 00 04 00

*In the parlor Clossett*
One Little Table One Desk . . . . . . 00 07 00

*In the Hall Clossett*
One Close bouch . . . . . . . . 00 00 06

*In the Chamber over the Kitchen*
Three Shopp bookes . . . . . . . 00 02 00
Twoo Little Tables One Nurseing Stoole Twoo Chaires One old
Trunck . . . . . . . . . 00 07 06
One ffeather bedd & boulster One Redd Rugg blancketts One Joynt
bedstead and other ffurniture . . . . . 01 10 00
Twoo paire of Trundle bedsteeds One ffeather bedd & boulster &
blancketts . . . . . . . . 01 00 00

*In the Chamber Over the Dineing Roome*
One Chest of drawers . . . . . . . 00 10 00
One hanging presse . . . . . . . . 01 00 00
ffowre Chaires and twoo Stooles . . . . . 00 06 00
One Cupboard with Drawers . . . . . . 00 10 00
Twoo blancketts & a Redd Rugg One bedsteed One old Coverlett
and Redd Curtaines & Vallins . . . . . 01 00 00

*In the Chamber over the hall*

| | | | |
|---|---|---|---|
| One Cupboard with drawers & Cubboard Cloth . . . . | 00 | 10 | 00 |
| One old Bedd Bedsteed & other ffurniture belonging to it . . | 01 | 00 | 00 |
| One Chest and Linnens in itt . . . . . . . | 06 | 00 | 00 |
| One Trunck Three Chaires One small Iron Grate Twoo Cushions . | 00 | 05 | 00 |

*In the Chamber over the parlor*

| | | | |
|---|---|---|---|
| Three Cloth Chaires Three Cloth Stooles . . . . . | 00 | 11 | 00 |
| One Side Table with drawers . . . . . . . | 00 | 04 | 00 |
| Twoo Stands . . . . . . . . . . | 00 | 01 | 00 |
| One large old Trunck One Chest . . . . . . | 00 | 12 | 00 |
| One Close baskett . . . . . . . . . | 00 | 01 | 00 |
| One bedd & bedsteed with Cloth Coloured Serge Curtaines and Vallens & other ffurniture . . . . . . . . | 03 | 00 | 00 |
| One Silver Cupp & Three Silver Spoones . . . . . | 03 | 10 | 00 |
| One Silver Tankard . . . . . . . . . | 06 | 00 | 00 |

*In the Closett*

| | | | |
|---|---|---|---|
| Twoo old Shopp bookes . . . . . . . . | 00 | 03 | 00 |

*In the Garrett*

| | | | |
|---|---|---|---|
| One Rindle Tubb & lather Three Cheswitts One old Churne Two old Stunds Twoo paire of Scales & beams One old paire of Bedsteeds One Straw Whiskett . . . . . . . . . | 00 | 11 | 00 |
| One Still and ffote . . . . . . . . . | 00 | 05 | 00 |
| Wareing Apparrel . . . . . . . . . | 02 | 00 | 00 |
| Bookes of all Sorts . . . . . . . . . | 00 | 10 | 00 |
| One yeare old heyfer . . . . . . . . | 01 | 00 | 00 |

*In the Stable*

| | | | |
|---|---|---|---|
| One Coffer and Some ffew Implemts of husbandry . . . | 00 | 07 | 00 |
| Item for odd thinges omitted . . . . . . | 00 | 05 | 00 |
| Totall Sume is . . | 55 | 04 | 04 |

## 119. John Field

Of Wellington, clerk, taken on 29 July 1693 and exhibited on 19 September 1693. The appraisers are not named.

*In ye Roome over the Hall*

| | | | |
|---|---|---|---|
| one ffeather & boulster wt 84 lb at 7d . . . . . | 02 | 09 | 00 |
| one coverlett, twoe Blanketts, four paire of bedsteeds, Cover and Matt and Beddcord, Three Curtaines . . . . . | 00 | 13 | 04 |
| one other old ffeather bedd and boulster wt 49 at 5d lb. with a small flockbedd under it, 3s. . . . . . . . | 01 | 03 | 05 |
| one old Kiverlett and blankett, one paire of bedsteeds, Cover and Matt and Cord . . . . . . . . | 00 | 09 | 00 |

| | |
|---|---|
| Three Curtaines and Vallence and 3 Curtaine Rodds | 00 04 00 |
| one side Table one old Carpett | 00 03 00 |
| ffoure Segg Chaires | 00 02 00 |
| one broken lookeing Glass and Dale Box | 00 00 08 |

*In the Chamber over ye Shop*

| | |
|---|---|
| one ffeather bed and boulster wt 105 lb at 7d | 03 01 03 |
| one Coverlett and one blankett | 00 05 06 |
| Three Greene Curtaines and Vallence 2 Iron Curtaine Rodds | 00 01 06 |
| ffive Segg Chaires | 00 03 04 |
| one Joyned Chayre and Cushion | 00 02 06 |
| one small side table and Carpett | 00 04 06 |
| one Desk upon a fframe | 00 06 00 |
| one pair of boules | 00 04 00 |
| one hundred thirty one Books bound of all sorts 14 bookes unbound | — — — |

*In ye Chamber over ye Kitchen*

| | |
|---|---|
| one ffeather bedd and boulster and 2 Pillowes wt 56 lb at 3½ d lb | 00 16 09 |
| one blankett | 00 01 06 |
| one paire of bedsteeds Matt Cover and bed cord one linnen Curtaine | 00 06 08 |
| one old Truncke | 00 00 08 |

*In ye Little Chamber over ye house*

| | |
|---|---|
| one small Trundle bedstead matt and cord | 00 02 00 |
| one chest, Six paire and one of Course hurden sheetes | 01 12 00 |
| halfe a Douzen of fine flaxen Napkins | 00 04 08 |
| one Douzen and halfe of hempen Napkins | 00 06 00 |
| Three Table Cloathes and 1 Cupboard Cloth | 00 03 00 |
| one baskett | 00 00 03 |
| one bridle Rayne and headstall and Coller | 00 01 04 |

*Over ye Buttery*

| | |
|---|---|
| one Trundle bedsteed one matt and Cord | 00 03 00 |
| one box | 00 00 08 |

*In ye Cockloft*

| | |
|---|---|
| 4 old straw whisketts one Cart Rope | 00 02 00 |
| one Table box | 00 01 00 |
| one Saddle | 00 03 00 |
| one old padd | 00 00 06 |

*In ye Malt Chamber*

| | |
|---|---|
| one long wheele | 00 00 08 |
| 2 vergs. barrells | 00 02 00 |
| one straw whiskett | 00 01 00 |
| one Malt Shovell one old strike | 00 00 10 |
| one pickerill | 00 00 04 |
| 3 Baggs | 00 03 00 |

## THE INVENTORIES OF WELLINGTON

*In ye kitchen*

| | | |
|---|---|---|
| Six pewter dishes and one Kandlesticke of ye best pewter wt. 22 lbs at 8d lb. | 00 14 08 |
| ffowre old pewter dishes, one bason and other old pewter wt. 16 lb. at 6d ye lb. | 00 08 00 |
| Eleaven pewter plates wt. 10lb. at 8d ye lb. | 00 06 08 |
| one Pewter Tankerd. | 00 01 00 |
| one warmeing Panne | 00 01 10 |
| Two brass Kettles and a posnett, one brasse pott 19 lbs. at 4d. | 00 06 04 |
| one brasse basting spoone and Skimmer | 00 01 00 |
| Two brasse drincking potts Two muggs | 00 01 00 |
| one Tynne Cover | 00 00 04 |
| one Iron Dripping panne | 00 02 00 |
| one chafeing Dish | 00 00 08 |
| Twoe Iron broaches 14 lb at 2d. | 00 02 11 |
| one paire of Iron Racks wt. 25 lb. at 3d lb | 00 06 03 |
| one Iron plate | 00 01 00 |
| one Iron grate and Niggarts wt. 39 lbs. at 2d lb. | 00 06 02 |
| one ffire shovell and Tongs. | 00 01 06 |
| one old ffire shovell Steale. | 00 00 03 |
| one Jack | 00 08 00 |
| one Iron Marmalett. | 00 01 00 |
| one Bill | 00 00 08 |
| one iron pott. | 00 02 06 |
| one pudding plate 2 fflesh forkes & a Cheese Toster | 00 00 06 |
| one Skreene. | 00 07 00 |
| Three Joynt Stooles. | 00 03 00 |
| one Glass Case wth some white ware in it | 00 01 06 |
| 3 Three footed Stooles and a Chaire | 00 00 03 |
| one dish bench and dresser. | 00 06 06 |

*The brew howse*

| | |
|---|---|
| fowre Turnells | 00 03 00 |
| Twoe brewing Stunds | 00 04 00 |
| one Cooler | 00 01 06 |
| Twoe Churnes | 00 01 06 |
| Three Cheswitts | 00 00 08 |
| twoe barrells and a bench wch they stand on | 00 03 06 |
| one little spinning wheele | 00 00 09 |
| one board | 00 00 02 |
| Twoe pailes | 00 01 00 |
| one Wash Tubb and another old Tubb | 00 02 00 |
| one Shealfe | 00 00 06 |
| one bench | 00 00 09 |
| one hacking block | 00 00 02 |
| one steele Malt Mill | 01 00 00 |
| one brasse ffurnace | 01 18 00 |
| one Table board and fframe | 00 10 00 |

*In the buttery*

| | |
|---|---|
| Twoe hogsheads | 00 08 00 |
| Two barrells and a little fferken | 00 04 00 |

*In the Hall*
| | | |
|---|---|---|
| one little Table | | 00 02 06 |
| Twoe Store piggs | | 01 04 00 |
| one Cow | | 03 00 00 |

*In ye Barne*
| | | |
|---|---|---|
| one wheelbarrow | | 00 03 00 |
| one Tewter | | 00 00 09 |
| A parcell of hay | | 01 13 04 |
| one Little Cartbody & bare foote Wheeles | | — — — |

| | | |
|---|---|---|
| Item his wearing apparell and money in his purse | | 01 00 00 |
| A Library of books appraised to | | 07 07 07 |
| Tot | | 37 19 09 |

| | | |
|---|---|---|
| Mr. Middleton | | 05 00 00 |
| Byrd | | 10 00 00 |
| Roger Walker | | 05 00 00 |
| Preist | | 06 00 00 |
| Mr. Phillipps | | 10 00 00 |
| Pemberton | | 10 00 00 |
| ffrancis Wright | | 07 10 00 |
| | | 53 00 00 |

| | | |
|---|---|---|
| Servts. Wages | | 00 07 00 |
| ffunerall Expenses | | 02 02 06 |
| Mr. Turner for ye keeping ye Cow | | 01 09 00 |
| Charges of taking lrs of Adminstrason and other Expences about it | | 02 00 00 |
| | | 59 08 06 |

## 120. Ann Eastop

Of Wellington, widow, taken by Gabriel Cleaton* and Thomas Freeman* on 4 November 1683 and exhibited on 6 March 1693-94.

*Imprs. in Birchen Meadow*
| | | |
|---|---|---|
| One Cow | | 03 00 00 |
| one Ewe and a lame | | 00 06 08 |
| one ricke of hay | | 00 06 08 |

*In ye Carte house*
| | | |
|---|---|---|
| The barly | | 00 05 00 |

*In the Dwelling house*
| | | |
|---|---|---|
| one Cubbort | | 00 09 00 |
| one Table board & frame | | 00 01 06 |
| Pot gailes | | 00 00 08 |
| A pestile | | 00 00 04 |

*In ye old womans Chamber*

| | |
|---|---|
| One Cheast . . . . . . . . | 00 01 00 |
| An old Coffer . . . . . . . | 00 04 00 |
| one table board . . . . . . . | 00 06 00 |
| A dresser and planke . . . . . . | 00 02 06 |
| Two Barrells . . . . . . . . | 00 02 06 |
| one pair of Bedsteads one flockbed and Blanket. . . . | 00 06 08 |
| one coffer . . . . . . . . | 00 01 06 |
| A strawe whiskett . . . . . . . | 00 01 00 |
| one Pikel and board . . . . . . . | 00 00 06 |
| A brass Kettale . . . . . . . | 00 03 00 |
| one piegen and Cheswitt & svall other od things . . . | 00 02 00 |
| Two nogen sheets & one hempn sheet . . . . | 00 04 00 |
| The waring Apparel . . . . . . . | 00 02 06 |
| things omited and unseene . . . . . . | 00 00 06 |
| The totall . . | 06 12 00 |
| for funeral charges and all other charges in the time of sickness . | 04 10 06 |

### 121. Alice Smart

Of Wellington, widow of dyer, taken by John Laurence and Roger Sockett on 9 March 1693-94 and exhibited on 24 April 1694.

*Imprs. In the Garrett*

one old paire of Bedsteds one Bed & Bolster being pte ffeather & pte fflox: One Table Board fraime & fforme & Two old Coffers One Truckle bedsted . . . . . . . . 01 05 00

*It In the Garrett over the house*

One old ffeather bed & bedstead & two blanketts & one Rug & one Bolster One long Coffer & one Chaire . . . . . 00 16 00

*It In the Roome over the Shopp*

One Chest of Drawers One ioyned Chest two cloth Chaires ffoure old Turkey worked Cushions One lookeing glasse One Grate & hand Irons Two Silver spoones One Taster & one Tumbler One Twiggin voider . . . . . . . . . . 03 05 00

*It. In the Chamber over the house*

One Trunk with Linnen Vizt. Eight paire of Sheetes Two Dozen of Napkins ffoure pillow beers Three Table Cloathes One deske Three seales . . . . . . . . . . 03 10 00

*It In the house*

One little box of drawers one Seate with a drawer One Screene One Table Three ioyned Stooles One Iron pott Two Shovel fires & two

paire of Tonges One Iron dreepeing pan one pasty plate two broaches
One Jack Three Iron Candlesticks One Iron grate one flesh forke . 02 00 00
Brasse and pewter of all sortes . . . . . 05 00 00

*It In the Shopp*
One hanging presse Six ioyned Chaires one ioyned fforme . . 03 00 00

*It In the dye house & Dye house Chamber*
All Sorte of Wooden Ware & Brewing vessells & three wheeles. . 01 00 00

Wareing apparrel . . . . . . . 05 00 00
Thinges forgotten & unseene . . . . . 00 05 00

                                                    Totall . . . 25 01 00

### 122. William Evans

Of Wellington, pipemaker, taken by Robert Peate* and Nathaniel Spruce* on 12 March 1693-94 and exhibited on 13 March 1693-94.

Impr. one old Bed Bedsted and Rugg . . . . . 00 15 00
Linnens . . . . . . . . 01 00 00
one old pott wth other old Brass and pewter . . . 01 00 00
one Chest and one Quoffer . . . . . . 00 10 00
one old table and press . . . . . . 00 05 00
one little Table and one old Chaire . . . . 00 04 00
one grate ffireshovell and Tongs . . . . . 00 05 00
Two Beds wth ye furniture thereto belonging . . . 02 00 00
weareing Apparrell . . . . . . . 01 10 00
his wife's weareing Apparrell . . . . . 01 10 00
his workeing Tools and Clay . . . . . 01 00 00
Debts Sperate and desperate . . . . . 02 00 00
Things not seene omitted or forgotten . . . . 00 05 00

                                                                                       12 04 00

### 123. William Stanworth

Of Wellington, shoemaker, taken by Michael Clarke, Charles Payne and William Jones on 21 April 1694 and exhibited on 24 April 1694.

*Imprs. In ye house or Lower Roomes*
9 Pewter dishes . . . . . . . 00 12 00
5 Pewter Guns . . . . . . . 00 05 00
5 old flaggons . . . . . . . 00 02 06
ii old Plates . . . . . . . . 00 03 00
2 old Chamber potts . . . . . . 00 02 00
2 Small Pewter Candlesticks . . . . . 00 01 00
1 Small Skellit 1 warming Pann & 1 pot . . . . 00 07 00

# THE INVENTORIES OF WELLINGTON

| | |
|---|---|
| 2 old Porringers | 00 01 00 |
| 1 old table & form | 00 02 06 |
| 1 old Chair & 2 Stooles | 00 01 06 |
| 1 Grate 1 fire Shovell 1 Spitt | 00 02 10 |
| 1 old Bed & furniture | 00 13 04 |

*In ye Buttery*

| | |
|---|---|
| 3 Barrells | 00 06 00 |

*In ye over Roomes*

| | |
|---|---|
| 1 old table & form | 00 05 00 |
| 1 box & old desk | 00 02 00 |
| 1 Joyn Bed & furniture | 01 10 00 |
| 1 Chest | 00 04 00 |
| 1 truckle bed & furniture | 00 06 00 |
| 6 paire Sheetes | 00 17 00 |
| 2 table Clothes | 00 03 06 |
| 6 napkins | 00 01 06 |
| 2 old Pillow beeres | 00 01 00 |
| 1 old Cow | 02 00 00 |

*In ye Shop*

| | |
|---|---|
| 5 paire of Shooes | 00 10 06 |
| his old lasts & Stock of Leather | 00 05 00 |
| 2 Barrells 2 turnells & 1 old Batterd ffurnace | 00 12 00 |
| 1 old steele mill | 00 10 00 |
| things omitted & not seene | 00 02 06 |
| | 10 09 02 |
| funeral expenses | 01 16 00 |
| totall | 09 14 02 |

## 124. William Cheese

Of Wellington, blacksmith, taken by John Taylor and William Jones on 28 March 1695 and exhibited on 28 April 1698.

*Imprs. in the house*

| | |
|---|---|
| pewter | 01 00 00 |
| Brass | 00 15 00 |
| one Iron Jack & other Iron ware | 00 10 00 |
| One joyned Screene dishboard Table and Chairs small tables & one fforme | 01 10 00 |
| Bacon and Beefe | 00 15 00 |

*Item In the Chamber over the house*

| | |
|---|---|
| One ffeather bed joyned Bedsted & apptences with one Truckle bed | 02 00 00 |
| Two joyned chests and one Deske with Linnens | 02 00 00 |

*Item In the chamber over ye Shopp*
Two ffeather beds bedsteads & Appences One hanging press one Chest one Coffer & ffoure small boxes & one ffowling peece . . 04 00 00

*Item In the Garrett*
one Bed & Bedsteads & Apptences . . . . . 00 10 00

*In the Buttry*
ffoure Barrells two full & two Empty & Brewing vessells . . 01 00 00
one malt mill . . . . . . . . . 00 10 00
Malt & other graine . . . . . . . . 04 00 00

*In the Shopp*
One Anvell Bellowes & Implemts of Trade . . . . 04 00 00
Two Shoate Swine . . . . . . . . 00 13 00
Wareing Apparrell . . . . . . . . 01 00 00
woodden ware & things unappraised & unseene . . . . 01 00 00

           Totall . . 24 13 00

due from William Cheese to Mr. Boycot for Iron . . 18 00 00

ye totall oof ye Estate . . . . . . . 06 13 00

## 125. Thomas Stillgoe

  Of Wellington, corviser, taken by William Bradshaw, Rowland Bradshaw and William Jackson on 29 April 1695 and exhibited on 10 June 1695.

Impris
Shoes made up in the Shop . . . . . . 02 14 10
Item instruments belonging to the trade . . . . . 00 06 00
Leather drest and undrest . . . . . . . 01 17 00
Wearing apparell . . . . . . . . 02 10 00
his beds and furniture . . . . . . . 03 00 00
pewter . . . . . . . . . 00 04 00
two Barrells, one paile, one basting spoone, six trenchers . . 00 06 06
two chaires . . . . . . . . . 00 01 00
his Shop booke . . . . . . . . 07 06 03

               18 15 06

Whereof Sixteen Shillings lyes despate

## 126. Joshua Johnson

  Of Wellington, mercer, taken by William Birch, William Phillips and John Grice on 5 March 1695-96 and exhibited on 1 April 1696

## Imps.

| | | |
|---|---|---|
| 28 yards of Cloth | 01 | 11 06 |
| 12 yds of Cloth | 00 | 13 00 |
| 25 yds of Cloth | 01 | 13 04 |
| 16 yards of Cloth | 00 | 16 00 |
| 44 yards of Cloth | — | 15 00 |
| 5 yards of Cloth | 00 | 04 07 |
| 6 yards of Cloth | 00 | 09 06 |
| 19½ yds of Cloth | 01 | 04 04½ |
| 15 yds of blac Cloth. | 00 | 15 00 |
| 8 yards ½ of Cloth | 00 | 09 02½ |
| 15 yards of Cloth | 01 | 02 06 |
| 4 yds of Cloth | 00 | 04 04 |
| 11 yds of Lincy | 00 | 08 08½ |
| 14 yds of Cloth | 01 | 08 00 |
| 10 yds of ffrize | 01 | 06 08 |
| 10½ yds of kersey | 01 | 03 07½ |
| 16 yds of Kersey | 02 | 06 09 |
| 14½ yds of kersey | 02 | 01 01 |
| 1 piece of mixt kersey | 03 | 05 00 |
| 1 piece of mixt kersey | 02 | 15 00 |
| 5 yards of stript Cloth | 00 | 12 06 |
| 17½ yds of kersey | 02 | 12 06 |
| 8 yds of Broad cloth | 02 | 16 00 |
| 5 yds ½ of mixt kersey | 00 | 14 08 |
| 5 yds of ffrize | 00 | 09 02 |
| 1 yd ½ of kersey | 00 | 03 00 |
| 2 yds ¼ of Broadcloth | 00 | 06 09 |
| 1 Remnant of Broadcloth | 00 | 04 00 |
| 2 yds of mixt kersey | 00 | 05 00 |
| 6 yds ¾ of mixed kersey in 3 remnants | 00 | 13 06 |
| 4 small remnants of cloth | 00 | 04 00 |
| 2 piece of mixt serges | 03 | 16 00 |
| 4 pieces of mixt Serges | 06 | 14 00 |
| 2 pieces of mixt serges | 03 | 16 00 |
| 1 piece of Stript Serge | 02 | 03 00 |
| 30 yds of mixt serge. | 02 | 15 00 |
| 30 yds ½ of Stript serge | 02 | 10 10 |
| 14 yds of serge | 01 | 10 04 |
| 18 yds of mixt serge. | 02 | 02 00 |
| 6 yds ½ of serge | 00 | 13 00 |
| 19 yds ½ of Shalloon | 01 | 09 03 |
| 23 yds of Tammey | 01 | 14 06 |
| 8 yds ½ of mixt serge in 6 remnants | 00 | 14 00 |
| 22 yds ½ of Stript Linin | 01 | 06 03 |
| 26 yds of Stript Stuff | 01 | 06 00 |
| 8 yds ½ of Druggitt | 00 | 07 01 |
| 7 yds ½ of Cantaloon | 00 | 06 03 |
| 4 yds of Gray serge att | 00 | 08 08 |
| 5 yds of purple Tammey | 00 | 04 02 |
| 7 yds of fflowerd linin | 00 | 07 07 |
| 10 ¾ of fflowerd linin | 00 | 10 09 |
| 3 yds of Linin | 00 | 02 03 |

| | |
|---|---|
| 8½ yds of glazed linin | 00 08 06 |
| 3 yds ½ of blew stript cloth | 00 04 01 |
| 5 yds ½ of Shalloone | 00 07 04 |
| 6 yds of Stript prunella | 00 10 00 |
| 9 yds of grey serge | 00 05 00 |
| 9 yards of stuff | 00 04 06 |
| 1½ yd of Cloth | 00 01 07½ |
| 8 yds of blew linin | 00 06 00 |
| 1 remnant of Buccoram | 00 01 04 |
| 5 yds of white holland | 00 05 10 |
| 1 piece of wt ffustion | 00 15 00 |
| 11 yds of ffustion | 00 12 10 |
| 17 yds of fflowerd ffustion | 00 14 02 |
| 11 yds of Vermillion | 00 11 00 |
| 19 yds of colerd ffust at 10: 11 of fflowerd | 01 06 02 |
| 19 yds of Stript Camlett | 00 19 00 |
| 9 yds of calemanca | 01 04 09 |
| 3 yds of mild serge | 00 07 00 |
| 7 yds of wt Lanill | 00 04 08 |
| 35 yds of Lincy | 01 06 03 |
| 4½ yds of Lincy | 00 03 04½ |
| 20 yards of narrow Linin Cloth | 00 17 09 |
| 11 yds of Linin Cloth | 00 09 02 |
| 14 of White Linin | 00 09 04 |
| 3 yds ½ of Hempton | 00 02 02¾ |
| 3 yds of Hempton | 00 02 00 |
| 7½ yds of yellow canvace | 00 11 03 |
| 32 doz of ffine thrid | 04 00 00 |
| 17 lb of black & browne thrid | 01 09 09 |
| 8 of Cullerd thrid | 00 14 00 |
| 10 papers of wt & cullerd tapie | 01 00 00 |
| 1 doz of blew Inckles | 00 08 06 |
| 1 doz of Stript tapie | 00 07 00 |
| 3 doz and 3 pieces of Colerd Inkle | 01 02 09 |
| 1 doz of Holland taip | 00 08 06 |
| 1 lb of Coventry blew thrid | 00 03 00 |
| A parcell of Loose thrid | 00 04 00 |
| 3 pieces of twist and 2 of Inkle | 00 02 00 |
| 5 doz of Stetapie | 00 00 10 |
| 4 pap[e] clasps | 00 04 06 |
| a pcell of hard wax | 00 02 00 |
| 8 old pieces of old Ribans | 00 08 00 |
| A parcell of other Ribans | 00 12 00 |
| 4 doz of pace boards | 00 05 04 |
| A parcell of Cotton taipe & Cadoure | 00 07 00 |
| 5 pieces of galoomes | 01 02 06 |
| 2 pieces of Statute galoomes | 00 05 00 |
| 3 pieces of Pgin galloomes | 00 15 00 |
| 27 yds of Coppe galloome | 00 05 07½ |
| 8 pieces of fferitt | 02 12 00 |
| 2 remnants of Taby | 00 04 00 |
| 48 of Silver thrid | 00 16 00 |
| 1 groce of silver buttons | 00 09 00 |

## THE INVENTORIES OF WELLINGTON 305

| | |
|---|---|
| 6 doz white thrid buttons . . . . . . | 00 00 06 |
| 8 groce of buttons . . . . . . . | 01 04 00 |
| 4 groce of buttons . . . . . . . | 01 00 00 |
| 2 groce of buttons . . . . . . . | 00 03 00 |
| 6 groce of brest buttons . . . . . . | 00 10 00 |
| 12 groce of gympe buttons . . . . . . | 01 00 00 |
| 4 parcells of odd buttons . . . . . . | 00 06 00 |
| 7 *lb* of silke buttons . . . . . . . | 06 06 00 |
| 5 groce of haire buttons . . . . . . | 00 17 06 |
| 8 groce of small gympe buttons . . . . . | 00 06 00 |
| 9 glasses . . . . . . . . | 00 09 00 |
| 2 dozen of Packthrid . . . . . . | 01 00 00 |
| 4 paper bookes . . . . . . . | 00 02 00 |
| 9 reames of apound paper . . . . . . | 00 15 00 |
| 1 Reame of white Capp paper . . . . . | 00 03 04 |
| 1 Reame of paper at . . . . . . . | 00 02 04 |
| 1 Reame of Large paper . . . . . . | 00 04 00 |
| Clock lines and curtaine Rings . . . . . | 00 02 00 |
| Inke horne & powder hornes . . . . . | 00 04 00 |
| 1 Reame of writeing paper . . . . . . | 00 07 00 |
| 2 doz of Cards . . . . . . . | 00 02 04 |
| 1 doz of Cards at . . . . . . . | 00 03 00 |
| ½ of Cards at . . . . . . . . | 00 01 00 |
| 3 Bibles at . . . . . . . . | 00 08 06 |
| 1½ doz of construeing bookes . . . . . | 00 04 00 |
| 4 Psalters at . . . . . . . . | 00 02 04 |
| 2 doz of horning bookes . . . . . . | 00 01 08 |
| ½ doz of primers . . . . . . . | 00 01 00 |
| ½ of Testaments . . . . . . . | 00 04 00 |
| 1 Bible at . . . . . . . . | 00 02 04 |
| 6 *lb* of Bee wax . . . . . . . | 00 05 00 |
| 18 *lb* of Browne Sugar . . . . . . | 00 10 06 |
| ¾ of a hund of Reasens of the Sun . . . . | 01 10 00 |
| 14 *lb* of currens . . . . . . . | 00 05 10 |
| 6 of black Ginger . . . . . . . | 00 02 06 |
| 6 of white Ginger . . . . . . . | 00 04 00 |
| 1 *lb* of Cloves & mace . . . . . . | 00 14 00 |
| 3 oz of white pepper . . . . . . | 00 01 06 |
| 6 *lb* of black pepper . . . . . . . | 00 14 00 |
| 4 *lb* of Gemece pepper . . . . . . | 00 06 00 |
| 3 *lb* of seedes . . . . . . . . | 00 01 06 |
| 16 pair of woollen stockins . . . . . . | 00 03 09 |
| 3 paire of Mens stockins . . . . . . | 00 06 06 |
| 10 paire of Grey Stockins . . . . . . | 00 18 04 |
| 6 paire of Colored Stockins . . . . . | 00 06 00 |
| 6 other paire of stockins . . . . . . | 00 09 00 |
| 17 paire of Stockins . . . . . . . | 00 04 03 |
| 1½ doz of Stockins . . . . . . . | 00 02 06 |
| 2 barrells of Herrings . . . . . . | 02 00 00 |
| 1 fferkin of Soap . . . . . . . | 01 05 00 |
| 2 doz of Candles . . . . . . . | 00 10 00 |
| 47 *lb* of Tobacco . . . . . . . | 03 10 06 |

| | | | | |
|---|---|---|---|---|
| 1 doz ½ of the best bone | 05 | 05 | 06 |
| 16 *lb* of Tobacco | 01 | 01 | 04 |
| 30 *lb* of Tobacco | 02 | 05 | 00 |
| 6 of Tobacco | 00 | 06 | 00 |
| 1 Gallon of Brandy | 00 | 06 | 00 |
| 1 Large Glass | 00 | 02 | 06 |
| 1 Counter wth 3 boards on ye side | 00 | 13 | 00 |
| under ye Counter 6 drawers | 00 | 06 | 00 |
| 1 Joint Box | 00 | 03 | 06 |
| 5 drawers at | 00 | 05 | 00 |
| 2 lettices for ye Shop windows | 00 | 12 | 00 |
| 1 old morter at | 01 | 04 | 06 |
| 1 Iron beame and Scales | 00 | 06 | 08 |
| 6 paire of Scales at | 00 | 08 | 06 |
| 1 paire of hop Scales and beame | 00 | 03 | 00 |
| 1 counter in ye Shopp | 00 | 06 | 08 |
| 1 more | 00 | 01 | 00 |
| 1 nest of drawers | 00 | 03 | 04 |
| 1 nest of drawers | 00 | 05 | 00 |
| 1 press in the Shopp | 00 | 09 | 00 |
| 1 cwt of Lead waights | 00 | 12 | 00 |
| 4 lb of brass waights | 00 | 03 | 00 |
| pewter measures in the Shopp | 00 | 02 | 04 |
| 3 weanscotts for the Shopp | 00 | 04 | 00 |
| 11 Dale and oake boxes | 00 | 08 | 00 |

*The house Goods*

Impr.
| | | | | |
|---|---|---|---|---|
| 1 ffeather bedd & bolster | 02 | 00 | 06 |
| 1 ffether bedd att | 01 | 11 | 03 |
| 1 ffeather bedd and bolster | 03 | 14 | 08 |
| 1 ffeather bedd and bolster | 01 | 11 | 03 |
| 1 ffeather bedd and bolster | 02 | 13 | 00 |
| 1 Bolster & 5 pillows | 00 | 12 | 03 |
| 1 Bolster | 00 | 06 | 08 |
| 1 Bedsted matt & curtaines in ye washhouse | 00 | 16 | 00 |
| 1 under bed bolster and stedds in ye house | 00 | 14 | 00 |
| 1 Bedsted under Bedd & curtaines in ye best Chamber | 02 | 00 | 00 |
| 1 Press Bed | 01 | 06 | 08 |
| 2 Bedsteds 1 under bed & curtaines in the garrett | 01 | 05 | 00 |
| 1 Chest in ye garrett | 00 | 05 | 00 |
| 1 bedsted & curtaine & counterpane yt was in ye Talbot | 01 | 05 | 00 |
| 1 Small Table | 00 | 03 | 00 |
| 3 window Curtaines | 00 | 05 | 00 |
| 1 Joine box & small Trunc | 00 | 05 | 00 |
| 5 Curtaine rodds | 00 | 02 | 06 |
| 1 Large Chest in ye garrett | 00 | 10 | 00 |
| 1 Small Chest and a trunc in ye garrett | 00 | 09 | 00 |

*The goodes in ye house*
| | | | | |
|---|---|---|---|---|
| 4 white blankitts and a counterpane in the garritt | 01 | 00 | 00 |
| 95 pounds of Flax | 03 | 03 | 04 |
| 1 Large Bible and Dictionary and other small bookes | 01 | 00 | 00 |

| | |
|---|---|
| 1 Large Chest in ye best chamber | 01 06 08 |
| 9 pounds of fflaxen yarn | 00 13 06 |
| 1 Small Chest | 00 02 06 |
| 2 Trunks & a box in the best chamber | 00 09 00 |
| 4 window calico curtains | 00 02 06 |
| 1 Chest of drawers | 01 00 00 |
| 6 Leather Chaires in ye best Chamber | 01 10 00 |
| 4 old Leather chairs | 00 12 00 |
| 1 Couch & dressing Table in ye best chamber | ·00 15 00 |
| 1 Lookeing glass in the best Chamber | 00 10 00 |
| 6 Blankitts | 00 15 00 |
| 1 Iron plate in the best Chamber | 00 01 00 |
| A parcell of pictures & white weare | 00 10 00 |
| 1 small Trunc & Close stool and ye pan | 00 10 00 |
| one Round Table in ye house | 00 01 00 |
| 1 Looking glass in the house | 00 05 00 |
| 1 old screene 1 glass cage and glasses | 00 08 00 |
| 3 pictures | 00 02 06 |
| 5 Segg Chaires | 00 02 06 |
| 1 Iron Jack | 00 13 04 |
| 3 Iron dreepeing pans | 01 00 00 |
| 2 gunns | 00 13 04 |
| 3 old swords & one Hanger | 00 08 00 |
| 1 tipt hanger | 01 00 00 |
| 2 pistolls | 00 02 00 |
| 2 smoothing Irons | 00 04 00 |
| 2 Fire pans and two pair of tongs | 00 09 00 |
| the drawers in ye dresser | 00 12 00 |
| 1 Iron fflesh Fork 1 duz of Iron Skewres and frame & other small Iron candlesticks | 00 04 00 |
| 1 Warming pan | 00 02 06 |
| 1 Cradle | 00 04 00 |
| 11 Knives and 6 Forkes | 00 06 08 |
| 3 Iron Spitts | 00 04 00 |
| 2 Lanthorns | 00 01 06 |
| 1 paire of bellows | 00 00 06 |
| 1 paire of gobberts | 00 01 00 |
| 1 Table in the Buttery one Cobbert and 4 Join Stooles | 00 13 04 |
| 1 Iron grate In gail & creeper | 00 06 08 |
| 2 traies | 00 01 00 |
| 3 paire of sheetes | 01 10 00 |
| 3 paire of sheetes | 01 00 00 |
| 1 paire of sheetes | 00 12 00 |
| 1 Table Cloth and 12 napkins | 00 15 00 |
| 5 pillow Cloths | 00 08 00 |
| 1 Fine Table Cloth | 00 10 00 |
| 3 doz of napkins | 01 04 00 |
| 24 ells of fflaxen | 02 05 00 |
| 42 yds of diaper | 02 10 00 |
| 1 doz and 10 napkins | 00 08 00 |
| 9 old Table Cloths | 00 09 00 |
| 1 Bedticque and Bolster | 01 03 00 |
| 10 paire of Sheets | 03 10 00 |

| | | |
|---|---|---|
| 1 doz of napkins | 00 | 08 | 00 |
| 20 Slippins of Hurden yarne | 00 | 08 | 00 |
| 8 ells of fflaxen Cloth | 00 | 16 | 00 |
| 4 paire of Sheetes more | 01 | 10 | 00 |
| 2 Table Cloths | 00 | 05 | 00 |
| 55 *lb* of old pewter | 01 | 12 | 01 |
| 120 *lb* of Pewter at | 04 | 10 | 00 |
| 140 *lb* of Pewter | 04 | 13 | 04 |
| 2 pewter Salsers | 00 | 06 | 00 |
| 79 *lb* of pott Brass | 01 | 03 | 00 |
| 26 of Kettle Brass | 00 | 15 | 02 |
| 1 posnett | 00 | 03 | 00 |
| 1 Scimmer at | 00 | 00 | 06 |
| 1 Small Skellett | 00 | 01 | 06 |
| 1 paire of Hand Irons | 00 | 04 | 00 |
| 10 Strike of Rye | 01 | 10 | 00 |
| 1 Strike Seedness of Corne upon ye ground | 01 | 00 | 00 |

*Goodes in the Malthouse*

| | | |
|---|---|---|
| 1 Skreene for dressing of Malt | 00 | 05 | 00 |
| 1 wheele barrow | 00 | 02 | 00 |
| 200 strike of malt | 26 | 13 | 04 |
| 130 strike of Barley | 15 | 03 | 04 |

*In ye Stable*

| | | |
|---|---|---|
| 1 grey mare | 04 | 00 | 00 |
| 1 Sadle | 00 | 02 | 06 |
| 1 Sadle & howsing | 00 | 03 | 06 |

*In ye Brew house*

| | | |
|---|---|---|
| 1 Iron mill wth ye hopper | 00 | 18 | 00 |
| 1 old Small Table | 00 | 01 | 06 |
| 1 Iron grate & Racks | 00 | 10 | 00 |
| 1 ffurnace | 01 | 00 | 00 |
| 1 Iron pott | 00 | 05 | 00 |

*In ye Buttery*

| | | |
|---|---|---|
| 3 barrells | 00 | 14 | 06 |
| 2 Coolers | 00 | 07 | 00 |
| 2 Stunds | 00 | 04 | 06 |
| 1 Stunde | 00 | 10 | 00 |
| 5 Barrells | 01 | 05 | 00 |
| 4 Barrells | 00 | 11 | 00 |
| 3 ffirkins | 00 | 04 | 06 |
| 8 doz of glass Bottles | 00 | 16 | 00 |
| Book depts | 48 | 11 | 08 |
| Debts due upon Bond | 410 | 00 | 00 |
| Due from Richard Rodnurst | 09 | 05 | 00 |
| Weareing apparrell and money in purse | 15 | 00 | 00 |
| Things omitted | 03 | 10 | 00 |
| | 768 | 06 | 04 |

## 127. Francis Wright

Of Leegomery, dyer, taken on 21 April 1698 and exhibited on 28 April 1698. The appraisers are not named.

| | | |
|---|---|---|
| Impp. Six oxen . . . . . . . | 27 | 00 00 |
| Seven Cowes . . . . . . . . | 23 | 06 08 |
| ffourteen young bease . . . . . . | 23 | 00 00 |
| Two Mares & Two Colts . . . . . | 12 | 00 00 |
| Three Swine . . . . . . . . | 02 | 03 04 |
| one hundred fforty Two lambs & Sheepe . . . | 25 | 00 00 |
| Corne in the Barn . . . . . . . | 04 | 10 00 |
| Corn on the Ground . . . . . . . | 26 | 10 00 |
| Impleyments of husbandry . . . . . . | 10 | 15 00 |

*Goods in the house*

A grate ffireshovell & Toungs Clock Iron Jack Spitt Dreeping pan & Brass & Pewter . . . . . . . . 05 10 00

A Table & fformes Screen Cupboard ffore sides of Bacon & other small things . . . . . . . . . 05 00 00

*In the Parlor*

one Joyned Bed & one Truckle bed & bedding Curtains & Vallins . 05 00 00
one chest with a few Linnens 2 small Tables 3 Chaires 2 warming panns & some old things in the new Roome Dyes Press & papers . 03 00 00

*In the best Chamber*

2 Joynd beds & Bed Cloathes feather beds Curtains & Vallins . 05 00 05
Two Chaires 1 Coffer 1 Deske 1 Chest and some linnens . . 02 10 00

*In the Side Chamber*

2 beds 1 Chest 1 Coffer with a few linnens . . . 04 06 08

*In the new Chamber*

Corn Malt Cheese linnen Cloath linnen & woolen yarn and other small things . . . . . . . . . 06 05 00

*In the Chamber over the house*

1 Joynd bed feather bed 1 Coofer with some Wheate 2 Coofers one Tub with Oates 1 Sadle 1 pillin & pillin Cloath . . . 03 03 04

*In the Cock loaft over the house*
3 old Basketts & 4 fliches of beef

*In The Chamber att the Staire Head*
one old bed and 2 Cooffers

} . . . . 00 16 08

*Over the Same Roome*
3 Spinning wheels 1 Reele with some other Trumpery . . . 00 06 08

*In the Brew house*
1 ffurnace 1 Malt Mill Two Cheese presses Kneading & Brewing Vessells . . . . . . . . . 02 15 00

*In the Dye house*
2 old ffurnaces on wings 3 Doz handles old Iron & other old things . 05 15 00

*in the Shop*
ffive paire of Sheares with some collouring Stuffe and a Sheare board 03 05 00

Teanters Hookes . . . . . . . . 01 00 00

*In the Cellars*
13 Hogsheads 4 Barrells 2 small Tables a Brass pan & some small things . . . . . . . . . . 02 02 06

Poultrey of all sorts . . . . . . . . 00 05 00

*In Roger Cleatons house in Wellington*
2 tables Three formes 2 joynd presses 1 lead cistern 2 paire Two paire of Bed steads . . . . . . . . 07 10 00

*In Joyn Haynes his house att Wellington*
one Table 2 presses 6 Joynd Stooles . . . . . 01 13 04

Desperate Debts by Shop Booke . . . . . . 02 10 00

The Reversion of a lease in Leegomery . . . . . 60 00 00

Bookes of all Sorts . . . . . . . . 00 06 00

Wearing Apparrell & money in his pockett . . . . 06 00 00

288 11 07

## 128. Eleanor Sandys

Of Wellington, widow, taken by Andrew Socket Senr. and Roger Socket on 1 November 1698 and exhibited on 9 February 1698-99.

*Imprs. In ye house place*
1 old table 1 old standing Press . . . . . . 00 04 00
1 old Broken Skreene 2 old Chaires 1 little table like a Joyn Stoole
1 water Paile . . . . . . . . . 00 06 00
1 Iron grate 1 paire of tounges . . . . . . 00 02 06
2 Little old flagins 1 old Peuter Gun 1 Salt . . . . 00 02 00
14 Small Peutr dishes about 1 pound & half A peece . . . 00 08 00

## THE INVENTORIES OF WELLINGTON

*In ye Parlor*

| | | | |
|---|---|---|---|
| 1 Little old table 1 old kneding turnell 2 little Bruing Stunds 2 old turnell & 1 old strike 1 Ann dish . . . . . . | 00 | 08 | 00 |
| 1 pr old bed steads with a old bed 1 pr old sheetes & 2 old Blanketts | 00 | 13 | 04 |

*In ye Roome over the house*

| | | | |
|---|---|---|---|
| 1 halfe headed bed 1 old Chest 1 old Coverlid 1 old Blankett . . | 00 | 08 | 00 |

*In ye Roome over ye Parlor*

| | | | |
|---|---|---|---|
| 1 halfe headed old Bedstead & one Chaff old Bed . . . | 00 | 04 | 00 |
| 16 loose Boards over ye Parler 1 old warming Pan 4 old Baggs 1 old Pudding Plate 2 Iron peels A pcell turnip seede . . . . | 00 | 14 | 00 |
| things omitted & not seene. . . . . . . | 00 | 05 | 00 |
| wearing Apparrell most tooke away before she was Burryed . . | 00 | 06 | 00 |
| total is . . | 03 | 19 | 10 |
| Furnerall Charges & kings duty . . . . . . | 01 | 03 | 00 |
| totall . . . | 02 | 16 | 10 |

## 129. Richard Jackson the Elder

Of Wellington, tailor, taken by Edward Webb and George Harrington on 26 April 1699 and exhibited on 3 October 1699.

*In the house*

| | | | |
|---|---|---|---|
| 1 old Table 1 old press 2 old Chaires & three Stools . . . | 00 | 05 | 00 |
| 2 little brass ketles & other small Brass . . . . | 00 | 06 | 08 |
| Pewter dishes & other small pewter things . . . . | 00 | 08 | 00 |
| an old Glass cage wth tickney ware belonging to it . . . | 00 | 02 | 06 |
| 2 litle Iron potts 2 dreeping pans 1 Spitt 1 pr bellows . . . | 01 | 03 | 00 |
| 1 Grate fire shovell tongs pott racks & Chafeing dish . . . | 00 | 01 | 02 |
| A paile & other wooden things in the house . . . . | 00 | 00 | 10 |
| 2 litle flitches of pig bacon . . . . . . . | 00 | 07 | 00 |

*In the Chamber*

| | | | |
|---|---|---|---|
| 1 old ffether bed wth furniture . . . . . . | 00 | 10 | 00 |
| 1 old Coffer 1 pare of truckle bedsteds & one old table & forme wth 2 old bookes . . . . . . . . | 00 | 03 | 00 |

*In the next Roome*

| | | | |
|---|---|---|---|
| 1 old Coffer 1 press 1 doz: of botles . . . . . | 00 | 05 | 06 |

*In the Roome over the house*

| | | | |
|---|---|---|---|
| 1 old Coffer with Linnens 1 old Chest 1 old flock bed . . . | 00 | 13 | 06 |
| hemp . . . . . . . . . | 00 | 04 | 00 |
| 1 strike of wheate . . . . . . . . | 00 | 06 | 00 |
| 7 strike of Barly . . . . . . . . | 01 | 02 | 00 |
| 2 old whisketts 1 old wheele . . . . . . | 00 | 01 | 00 |

*In the Milkhouse*
| | |
|---|---|
| Earthen & wooden ware . . . . . . . | 00 02 06 |

*Catle*
| | |
|---|---|
| 1 litle old Mare . . . . . . . . | 00 12 00 |
| 1 Cow & heifer & weaneing calfe . . . . . . | 04 10 00 |
| 5 strikes soweing of winter Corne upon ground . . . . | 02 05 00 |
| 2 dayworke of Lent Tilling Sowed . . . . . | 00 12 00 |
| Car wheeles & Implemts of husbandry . . . . | 00 05 00 |
| The reversion of a Lease of the house wherein ye sd deced did live being for a very old Life . . . . . . . | 01 16 00 |
| for the Revcon of a Lease of a cottage in Mary Palmers possion being for Lives . . . . . . . . | 05 00 00 |
| ffor the Revercon of a Lease of a house & lands in Richd Jackson's possion son of ye deced . . . . . . . | 05 00 00 |
| debts sperate & desperate . . . . . . . | 03 00 00 |
| wearing Apparell & money in purse . . . . . | 02 00 00 |
| things omitted & forgotten . . . . . . . | 00 05 00 |
| | 30 06 00 |

## 130. Francis Bayley

Of Hadley, yeoman, taken by William Turner, Thomas Judgeson and Henry Harrington on 15 July 1699 and exhibited on 5 October 1699.

*Imprimis*
| | |
|---|---|
| in Readye money in the house . . . . . . | 07 00 00 |
| It goods in ye house & in other Roomes in ye Said house Brass and pewter . . . . . . . . . | 05 16 08 |
| It Two Joynd Cubbards & presses . . . . . . | 01 14 04 |
| It Two llonge Tables & one Square on . . . . | 01 10 00 |
| It Two formes & Three Joynd stools & shilfs . . . . | 00 06 00 |
| It one Joynd cheere & six other cheers . . . . . | 00 06 08 |
| in Lumber weare belonginge to the House as peals Barels Stonds other vessels . . . . . . . . . | 01 15 00 |
| It ffoure Cofferts & one Chest at . . . . . . | 01 10 00 |
| It one screen and two Little Dressers at . . . . | 00 13 04 |
| It Two Joynd Bedds with Beding And ffurnyture belonging to it . | 10 00 00 |
| It Three other Standing Beds &c with ye Beddinge belonge to it at . | 07 10 00 |
| It One Truckell Bed with Bedding and ffurnyture belonginge to it . | 02 06 08 |
| It Two payer of fflaxen Sheets at . . . . . . | 01 10 00 |
| It ffoure payre of hemten sheets . . . . . . | 01 10 00 |
| It tenn payer of canvise sheets at . . . . . . | 02 15 00 |
| It ffoure fflaxen Pillowes beers at . . . . . . | 00 09 00 |
| It Two llonge Towells at . . . . . . . | 00 08 00 |
| It Two fflaxen Tablecloaths two hemton Tablecloths & two course Tablecloaths at . . . . . . . . . | 01 00 00 |
| It Two dozin of fflaxen naptkins and one dozin of Course naptkins at . . . . . . . . . . | 01 10 00 |
| It Twenty Ells of hempten cloth . . . . . . | 01 10 00 |
| It in woole A Stone and halfe . . . . . . | 01 10 00 |

THE INVENTORIES OF WELLINGTON                313

| | | |
|---|---|---|
| It in Sives and Ridles wiskits Baskets and other Twigon wares . . | 00 06 08 |
| It Six Baggs at . . . . . . . . | 00 06 00 |
| It one Longe Spinning Wheel and Two Little wheeles at . . | 00 06 00 |
| It ffive Silver Spoones at . . . . . . . | 01 05 00 |
| It Six Oalkinie Spoones . . . . . . . | 00 01 00 |
| It Two Broaches & Cobbards . . . . . . | 00 06 08 |
| It Two payre of pottlings One grate one ffire Shovel And one payre of Tongs at . . . . . . . . . | 00 13 04 |
| It one ffrine pan at . . . . . . . . | 00 02 00 |
| It one wayne one Tumbril one payre of wheels at . . . | 04 00 00 |
| It in Chaines plowes Irones and yockes harrows Axes bills & vills And other Implements belonging to husbantry at . . . | 01 00 00 |
| It one scostowne one harcloth one ffurnice . . . . | 02 10 00 |
| It ffoure oxen at . . . . . . . . | 15 00 00 |
| It Seven kyne at . . . . . . . . | 17 10 00 |
| Item ffive yonge Beasts at . . . . . . . | 08 00 00 |
| Item Three yearlings at . . . . . . . | 03 15 00 |
| It ffoure caulfes at . . . . . . . . | 03 00 00 |
| It Two mares and one colt . . . . . . . | 08 00 00 |
| It Twenty Eyght Sheep & Lambs . . . . . . | 05 00 00 |
| It Three Swine at . . . . . . . . | 02 10 00 |
| It in poultrye at . . . . . . . . | 00 03 00 |
| It in Cheese butter Beefe & Bacon . . . . . . | 05 00 00 |
| It Corne and mault in ye house . . . . . . | 02 10 00 |
| It Corne of all Sorts growing on ye ground . . . . | 20 00 00 |
| It his wearing Apparrill at . . . . . . . | 01 06 08 |
| It Things fforgott . . . . . . . . | 00 03 04 |
| Some toto is . . . . | 161 19 04 |

## 131. James Morris

Of Wellington, whitesmith, taken by Timothy Field and Andrew Harrington on 20 December 1699 and exhibited on 12 January 1699–1700.

*Imprs. Goods in ye House*

| | |
|---|---|
| one grate fire shovele & Tongs . . . . . . | 00 03 06 |
| one Jacke one Morter & pestel & other Smal Iron Thinges . . | 00 05 06 |
| Brass & Pewter one broach & a payre of Cubirons . . . | 01 02 00 |
| Two Joyne Cheyres & one Joyne Stoule & two other Cheyres . . | 01 03 00 |

*Item Goods in ye Chamber*

| | |
|---|---|
| one press & one Table & Two Cheyres . . . . . | 00 07 00 |

*Item Goods in ye Chamber over ye house*

| | |
|---|---|
| one Joyne bedsted A fether bed thereunto belonging . . . | 01 00 00 |
| one Chest & five Small boxes . . . . . . | 00 06 00 |

*Item Goods in ye Rome over ye Litle Chamber*

| | | |
|---|---|---|
| one bedsted And A flockbed thereunto belonging | | 00 10 00 |
| one Chest & Coffer & desck Linens of all sorts | | 01 06 00 |

*Item Goods in ye Shop*

| | | |
|---|---|---|
| Sale Goods | | 01 10 00 |
| Towles in ye Shop & Iron & Steele | | 06 00 00 |
| Trinnon Ware of all sorts & things omited | | 00 10 00 |
| depts desprat & otherways | | 01 10 00 |
| Weareing Apparell | | 04 00 00 |
| | | 18 13 00 |

## 132. Benjamin Wright

Of Wellington, mercer, taken by J. Pemberton, William Doughty and John Judgson on 21 September 1700 and exhibited on 25 September 1700.

*Imprs. In the shop*

| | |
|---|---|
| 1 piece of mild serge | 02 01 00 |
| 1 piece of mixt ditto | 01 12 00 |
| 2 pieces mixt sagathy | 02 14 00 |
| 19 yds spotted ditto at 18d | 01 07 06 |
| 1 piece dyed serge | 02 05 00 |
| 15 yds blk serge at 2/1 | 01 13 03 |
| 15 yds mild serge at 2/2 | 01 12 06 |
| 13½ yds mixt serge at 2/d | 01 02 06 |
| 9 yds Ditto at 22d | 00 16 06 |
| 10 yds ditto at 20d | 00 16 08 |
| 9 yds Spotted at 18d | 00 13 06 |
| 8 yds ½ mixt serge at 19d | 00 13 05 |
| 10½ yds ditto at 21d | 00 18 04 |
| 1½ yds ditto at 18d | 00 02 03 |
| 11 yds Shaloom at 19d | 00 17 05 |
| 18 yds ditto at 18d | 01 07 00 |
| 8 yds Red Ramy at 17d | 00 11 04 |
| 2 remnants blk ditto | 00 01 00 |
| 2 ps Stript & flowerd 24 yds & 23 Cantaloons at 8½ | 01 14 00 |
| 22 yds & ½ Stuffs at 7d | 00 13 01 |
| 17 yds Lineing plaine at 11d | 00 15 07 |
| 6 yds & ½ blew Lincey at 13d | 00 07 06 |
| 7 yds mixt Kersey at 2/6 | 00 17 06 |
| 7 yds ditto at 2/11 | 01 00 05 |
| 6 yds ditto at 3/6 | 01 01 00 |
| 5 yds & ½ ditto at 3/ | 00 16 06 |
| 16 yds & ½ at 2/4 | 01 18 06 |
| 7 yds ditto at 2/6 | 00 17 06 |
| 7 yds ditto at 20d | 00 11 08 |
| 3½ yds ditto at 2/4 | 00 08 02 |

# THE INVENTORIES OF WELLINGTON

| | |
|---|---|
| 4 yds ditto at 2/ | 00 08 00 |
| 2 yds ¾ ditto 2 Remnants at 2/4 | 00 06 05 |
| 7 yds ½ Frize at 2/- | 00 15 00 |
| 4 yds ½ mixt Kersey at 2/6 | 00 06 03 |
| 18 yds dyed Kersey at 22d | 01 13 00 |
| 8 yds dyed plain at 22d | 00 15 08 |
| 4 yds & ½ ditto at 18d | 00 06 08 |
| 4¼ yds ditto at 16d | 00 05 08 |
| 17 yds mild plain at 13d | 00 18 05 |
| 29 yds ditto at 13d | 01 11 05 |
| 5 yds Flanen at 11d | 00 04 07 |
| 20 yds Ditto at 8 | 00 13 04 |
| 5 yds Flanen at 8d¼ | 00 03 05 |
| 2 yds ditto broad at 11d | 00 01 10 |
| 11 yds white Crape at 11d | 00 10 01 |
| 2 Rugs at 5/6 | 00 11 00 |
| 1 Cradle Rug | 00 02 04 |
| 1 piece wte Fustion | 01 01 00 |
| 15 yds Ditto at 15d | 00 18 09 |
| 28 yds ditto at 10d | 01 03 04 |
| 1 ps: Coloured Ditto | 00 14 00 |
| 12 yds ditto at 10d | 00 10 00 |
| 11 yds ditto at 8d | 00 07 04 |
| 4 yds & ½ blew Linen at 13d | 00 04 10½ |
| 5½ yds ditto at 12d | 00 05 06 |
| 15 yds glazed Linen at 13d½ | 00 16 10 |
| 8 yds Coloured Linen at 8½ | 00 05 08 |
| 12 yds wh- Buckrom at 14d | 00 14 00 |
| 8 yds colord: Ditto at 13 | 00 08 08 |
| 3 yds ditto at 11d | 00 02 09 |
| 4½ yds Canvas at 17d | 00 06 04 |
| 12 Ells & ½ white Ozembrigs | 00 12 06 |
| 23 Ells & ½ brown ditto at 10d | 01 00 01 |
| 3 Chamy Skins at 9d | 00 02 03 |
| 5 pair of woolen stockings | 00 06 03 |
| 3 pre ditto at 14d | 00 02 04 |
| 3 pe blew ditto at 10d | 00 02 06 |
| 3 pe ditto at 8d | 00 02 00 |
| 2 pe Childrens ditto at 4d | 00 00 08 |
| 10 paire ditto at 2½ | 00 02 01 |
| 3 pe Stirups ditto at 9d | 00 02 03 |
| 1 pair socks & 1 Cap | 00 00 08 |
| 5 pe dyed woosted at 2/1 | 00 10 05 |
| 2 pe ditto at 2/2 | 00 04 04 |
| 1 pe mixt | 00 02 04 |
| 1 pe boys ditto | 00 01 06 |
| 1 pe ditto | 00 01 10 |
| 2 pe blew Girles at 20d | 00 03 04 |
| 1 pe red | 00 02 00 |
| 5 li 8oz silk at 17/- | 04 03 06 |
| 6 ps: 7 yds 4d Taffity at 3/6 | 01 01 07 |
| 2 ps: 6d & 8d at 7/- | 00 14 00 |
| 8 ps: 21 yds Callome at 4/3 | 01 16 00 |

| | |
|---|---|
| 46 yds Loope Lace at 2d½ | 00 09 07 |
| footings statute Galloom Cadias & of Ribbons | 01 00 00 |
| 6 oz: of silver galloom & Twist | 01 00 00 |
| 3 oz & ½ silver thred at 4/- | 00 14 00 |
| 1 gs: 3 doz: silver buttons at 7/ | 00 08 09 |
| 28 yds Copper Lace at 2d½ | 00 05 10 |
| 18 yds silver Galloom at 10d½ | 00 16 07 |
| | |
| 6 gross buttons at 3/6 | 01 01 00 |
| Gimp & thrid mow hair Coats & breasts | 01 02 00 |
| 7 doz: mens & womans Thimbles | 00 03 06 |
| 2 li of Packthred at 10d | 00 01 08 |
| 4 li blk thred at 2/1 | 00 18 04 |
| 13 doz; 2 Rolls No Thred at 2/10 | 01 16 03 |
| 2 li whited bro: at 3/3 | 00 06 06 |
| 11 oz: Coventry Blew at 2d | 00 02 03½ |
| 4 ps: holland Inckle at 9½d | 00 03 02 |
| ½ ps: holland Broad Tape | 00 00 06 |
| 7 li Colored & whe thred at 18d | 00 10 06 |
| 2 ps: Inckles at 12 | 00 02 00 |
| 1 paper blew Tapes | 00 01 10 |
| 1 paper Colord Ditto | 00 01 09 |
| 1 ps: Cornation Tape | 00 00 08 |
| 9 pss. Colored Inckle at 7½ | 00 05 07½ |
| 2 ps: board string twist at 3d | 00 00 06 |
| 8 ps: blew Inckle at 7d½ | 00 05 00 |
| [ gs: Laces at 6/- | 00 03 00 |
| 2 gs: & 2 doz: ditto at 3/ | 00 01 09 |
| Staytape | 00 00 05 |
| 3 doz: Leather Laces at 2/- | 00 00 06 |
| 1¼ li nans Thred at 6/ | 00 07 06 |
| A parcell outnall Thred | 00 05 00 |
| 3 doz: pins at 10/6 | 00 05 03 |
| ½ doz: at 7/6 | 00 03 09 |
| | |
| ½ doz: Guilt primers | 00 01 06 |
| 13 plain Primmers at 2/6 | 00 02 08½ |
| 9 Guilt hornbooks 18 plain dito | 00 02 06 |
| 3 doz: washballs at | 00 01 00 |
| 2 doz: ditto | 00 00 06 |
| hooks & Eyes | 00 03 00 |
| 5 barrells lam black | 00 00 10 |
| 10 packs of Cards at 2d | 00 01 08 |
| 4 pound suge Candy at 8d | 00 02 08 |
| 9½ Rems whe paper at 2/- | 00 19 00 |
| 2 Rem bro ditto at 18d | 00 03 00 |
| white Cap | 00 02 06 |
| 5 R writing paper at 5d | 00 02 01 |
| 7 li Jama: peper at 16d | 00 09 04 |
| 4½ li white ditto at 2/4 | 00 03 06 |
| 3½ li Lace Ditto at 15d | 00 03 10½ |
| 1½ li White Ginge at 9d | 00 01 10½ |
| 2 li Long pepper at 6d | 00 01 00 |

## THE INVENTORIES OF WELLINGTON

| | |
|---|---|
| li 1½ Annelseeds at 7d | 00 00 10½ |
| 3 li stone blew at 10d | 00 02 06 |
| 2 pd gum: at 6d | 00 01 06 |
| 2 li fflos: sull: at 8d | 00 01 04 |
| li 1½ Rice at 03d | 00 00 04½ |
| ½ Smelt at 8d | 00 00 04 |
| ½ grains | — — — |
| 4 li Carrow Seeds at 5d | 00 01 08 |
| ½ c starch at 24/- | 00 12 00 |
| 1 doz 10 li hemp at 9d | 00 16 06 |
| 12 li Rosen at 2d | 00 02 00 |
| ½ c Pitch at 12/- | 00 06 00 |
| ¼ c & 24 li of hops at 5d | 02 06 00 |
| Corks | 00 06 00 |
| 3/4 c 7li Rea: S: at 32/- | 01 06 00 |
| 4 li Currons at 7d | 00 02 04 |
| 25 li ffine Bastard Suger 6½d | 00 15 06½ |
| 41 li ffine In: Ditto at 4½d | 00 16 02½ |
| 36 li ditto at 4½d | 00 13 06 |
| lc malassus at. | 01 03 00 |
| 50 li Sope at 5d | 01 00 06 |
| 3 gs: of pipes at 8d | 00 02 00 |
| 11 pd Cutt Tobacco at 9d | 00 08 03 |
| Needles | 00 02 00 |
| 10½ doz: Candles at 3/6 | 01 15 00 |
| 26 li Cutt Tobacco at 14d | 01 10 04 |
| lc - 2 q - 7li Tobacco uncutt | 04 18 00 |
| 1 - 1 - 0 Stems at 3d | 01 15 00 |
| weights scales & Beams | 02 00 00 |
| Ingen & Flatter Trofe to dress tobacco in tobacco kifes & boxes & 2 hamers | 05 00 00 |
| 7 Ell Linen Cloth at 11d. | 00 06 05 |
| 1 Quoffer in ye workhouse 1 Cubbord 2 Tubs | 00 05 00 |

### In the Kitchin

| | |
|---|---|
| Pewter Dishes 152 li at 7d | 04 08 08 |
| Hollow pewter 24 li at 6d | 00 17 00 |
| 3 doz: 10 plates at 8s. | 01 10 08 |
| 1 brass Candlestick | 00 00 06 |
| 6 Iron dito | 00 01 00 |
| 1 Iron Chafing Dish | 00 01 00 |
| 1 Lock smoothing Iron | 00 01 00 |
| 2 flat dito | 00 01 00 |
| 3 spitts | 00 02 00 |
| 1 Jack. | 00 08 00 |
| 1 Iron Plate wth 26 scures | 00 01 00 |
| 2 Iron Plates to warm drink | 00 00 08 |
| 1 pr Bellows | 00 00 06 |
| 1 brass Ladle | 00 00 06 |
| 1 basting spoon | 00 00 03 |
| 1 pe of tin snuffers & pan | 00 00 02 |
| 1 Flesh fork | 00 00 02 |
| grate Fender etc | 00 06 00 |

| | |
|---|---|
| 1 pe of Iron Racks | 00 02 06 |
| Fire Shovel & Tongs | 00 01 00 |
| Choping knife | 00 00 03 |
| Links & pothooks | 00 00 06 |
| 1 Frying pan | 00 01 06 |
| 1 dresser with Drawers | 00 10 00 |
| Skreen | 00 06 08 |
| Cloth brush | 00 00 04 |
| Salt box | 00 00 08 |
| Sedg Bottom & Chairs | 00 01 00 |
| 1 Oval Table | 00 03 06 |
| 8 knives & 7 forks | 00 02 06 |

*In the Buttery*

| | |
|---|---|
| — brass potts | 00 08 00 |
| 1 brass skellet & 2 ketles | 00 06 00 |
| 1 Copper sauce pan | 00 00 04 |
| 1 doz Trenchers | 00 01 00 |
| 4 wooden Bowls | 00 00 06 |
| 2 tyn Cullenders | 00 00 04 |
| 1 ffish plate 2 Tin Covers | 00 00 04 |
| 1 Cheese Toaster | 00 00 02 |
| 1 Drudger & 1 pepper box | 00 00 02 |
| 1 Brass Skimer | 00 00 04 |
| 2 Grates for Smoothing Irons | 00 00 02 |
| 3 Rowling pins | 00 00 03 |
| 2 wood Ladles & Cheese boards | 00 00 03 |
| 1 Iron Chafing Dish | 00 00 06 |
| 1 Pudding plate | 00 00 02 |
| 22 oz: of plate at 4/6 | 04 19 06 |
| An old watch | 00 06 08 |

*In the Parlour*

| | |
|---|---|
| 1 Table Carpett & form | 00 03 06 |
| 5 Leather Chairs | 00 15 00 |
| 1 Sedg Bottom | 00 00 06 |
| 3 cushions | 00 00 06 |
| 1 skreen | 00 00 06 |
| 1 shelf & books | 00 10 00 |
| 1 Cubbord | 00 04 00 |
| 1 grate ffire shovel & Tongs | 00 03 00 |

*In the Little Back Kichen*

| | |
|---|---|
| 1 ffurnace & Boyler | 01 00 00 |
| 4 payles & 2 gaunes | 00 02 00 |
| 1 old ffrying pan & La back | 00 00 06 |
| 1 water bouch | 00 00 04 |
| 1 hanging Table | 00 00 06 |
| 2 Iron & 1 Tin Dreeping pans | 00 04 00 |
| 1 Tyn Pastry Pan | 00 00 06 |
| 1 Baster | 00 00 02 |
| 2 water dishes | 00 00 02 |
| 1 Wood Cover for ye ffurnace & Badstaff | 00 00 03 |

## THE INVENTORIES OF WELLINGTON

*In the Hall*

| | |
|---|---|
| 1 Table & Carpett | 00 08 00 |
| 6 Leather Chairs | 00 09 00 |
| 2 wood Elbow chairs | 00 02 06 |
| 1 small Table | 00 01 06 |
| 1 ffolding Skreen | 00 02 00 |

*In the Cellar*

| | |
|---|---|
| 7 large Barrells | 00 14 06 |
| 3 Small Barrels | 00 04 00 |
| 1 Brewing Stund | 00 05 00 |
| 2 Tuning Dishes 1 Turnell | 00 04 00 |
| 2 Wood Bottles | 00 01 00 |

*At the Stair head*

| | |
|---|---|
| 1 hanging press | 00 10 00 |
| 1 Chest | 00 04 06 |
| 1 Lade | 00 00 06 |
| Linen | 08 09 00 |

*In the Garrott*

| | |
|---|---|
| 1 Spitt 4 Barrells 1 Turnel | 00 02 00 |

*In the Parlor Chamber*

| | |
|---|---|
| 1 Bed Bedsted & Curtains | 03 00 00 |
| 1 Blankett & Rugg | 00 12 00 |
| 1 Table | 00 02 00 |
| 6 Chairs | 00 06 00 |
| 1 grate ffire shovel & Tongs | 00 03 00 |
| hangings for the Roome & 2 window Curtains (old) | 00 05 00 |

*In the Passage Chamber*

| | |
|---|---|
| 1 Table | 00 01 06 |
| 1 Childs Chair | 00 01 00 |
| 1 Quoffer & Blanket in it | 00 01 00 |
| 1 Iron Pitch pan | 00 00 06 |
| 1 pe hand irons | 00 02 00 |
| 5 wisks | 00 00 03 |
| 1 Hedge Bill | 00 00 04 |

*In the Chamber o're the old Kitchin*

| | |
|---|---|
| 1 Bedsted 2 Blanketts & one old Counterpan | 00 02 06 |

*In the Hall Chamber*

| | |
|---|---|
| 1 Bedsted Boulster & Counter pan 2 Blanketts Curtains & hangings for ye Room | 01 00 00 |
| 5 Chairs & 1 Stoole | 00 04 00 |
| 1 Couch | 00 02 06 |
| 1 Table Glass & Stand | 00 08 00 |
| 1 grate | 00 02 00 |
| 6 Turkie Cushions | 00 06 00 |

### In the White Chamber

| | |
|---|---|
| 1 Bedd Bedsted Boulster Pillow 2 Blanketts 1 Rug & Curtains. | 01 10 00 |
| 2 Chairs | 00 00 06 |
| 2 Stools | 00 00 06 |
| 1 Table & old Carpett | 00 02 00 |
| 4 window Curtains | 00 02 00 |
| 1 Desk & 1 glass | 00 01 00 |

### In the Chamber o're the Shop

| | |
|---|---|
| 1 Bed Bedsted Bolster 1 Pillow 2 Blanketts 1 Coverlett. | 01 10 00 |
| 2 Seg Chairs & 1 Stoole | 00 00 06 |
| 1 Trunk 1 Table 1 Glass & 1 Carpett | 00 06 00 |
| 1 Window Curtain | 00 00 06 |

### In the Chamber ore the warehouse

| | |
|---|---|
| 1 Bedd Bedsteds Boulster and Pillow 2 Blanketts & Rug | 01 00 00 |
| 1 coffer | 00 01 06 |
| 1 warming pan | 00 01 06 |
| 3 old Chairs | 00 00 06 |
| 1 Bell | 00 00 06 |

### In the Tobacco Room

| | |
|---|---|
| 1 old Bedd & Bedsted 3 old Blanketts Rug & Bolster 2 Chairs & 1 coffer | 00 05 06 |

### In the house o're the way

| | |
|---|---|
| 1 ffurnace | 00 10 00 |
| 3 brewing stunds | 00 03 00 |
| 1 water stund | 00 01 00 |
| 4 Large Turnells | 00 06 00 |
| One Small Turnel | 00 00 06 |
| 2 Searches & 1 fine | 00 01 00 |
| 1 Table | 00 03 00 |
| 1 other table & form | 00 04 00 |
| 2 Bedsteds | 00 04 00 |
| 1 dish Bench | 00 01 00 |

### In the malt house Barn & Stable

| | |
|---|---|
| 2 Steel malt mills | 01 05 00 |
| 5 pickerils & a pair of weeding Tongs | 00 02 00 |
| empty Casks | 00 10 00 |
| A straw whisket | 00 00 04 |
| 4 Rakes & 1 Long board | 00 01 06 |
| 1 Skreen | 00 05 00 |
| 2 Twig whiskets | 00 00 04 |
| a double whych | 00 08 00 |
| 1 strik 1 half strike 1 peck 1 half peck & 1 Quarter Peck & 1 half Quarter peck | 00 04 00 |
| 1½ Strike of Oats | 00 01 06 |
| 2 Bundels of Laths | 00 00 09 |
| 3 Ridles & 2 Sieves | 00 01 00 |

# THE INVENTORIES OF WELLINGTON

| | | |
|---|---|---|
| 83 new & old Boards | 02 | 10 | 00 |
| A harrow | 00 | 02 | 06 |
| 3 Ladders | 00 | 02 | 06 |
| A dung hook | 00 | 00 | 04 |
| 2 Spades | 00 | 02 | 00 |
| a pack sadle | 00 | 02 | 06 |
| 2 Hackney sadles | 00 | 04 | 00 |
| 1 pad | 00 | 00 | 06 |
| Corn & Hay | 25 | 00 | 00 |
| A Mare & Colt | 08 | 00 | 00 |
| A Cow & Calfe | 03 | 10 | 00 |
| 1 Hogg | 01 | 00 | 00 |
| wearing apparel & mony in purse | 05 | 00 | 00 |
| Odd things not named | 01 | 00 | 00 |
| debtts due to him | 46 | 00 | 00 |
| | 246 | 13 | 00 |

## 133. Robert Peate

Of Wellington, blacksmith, taken on 9 October 1700 and exhibited on 15 October 1700. The appraisers are not named.

| | | |
|---|---|---|
| Imprs. 3 Cowes 1 Calfe 2 old horses or mares | 07 | 00 | 00 |
| Item Som Corn & Hay | 02 | 00 | 00 |
| Item workeing tooles and Implements of Husbanderey | 02 | 00 | 00 |
| *Item In ye house* | | | |
| 1 table Board | 00 | 02 | 06 |
| 1 old Cubart | 00 | 02 | 00 |
| 1 Cole Hatchett 1 Small Grate nigards Tounges & fire Shovell | 00 | 02 | 06 |
| 1 kettle 1 Iron Pot 1 Small marmalade | 00 | 06 | 08 |
| 1 Lanthorn 2 Pailes 2 Pailes other smal wooden ware 6 Glass Bottles | 00 | 05 | 00 |
| 9 Small Peuter dishes | 00 | 10 | 00 |
| Small Brass & Pewter things more | 00 | 04 | 00 |
| *In ye Buttery* | | | |
| 4 Barrells 2 turnells 1 Cheese Press 2 Stunds 1 Rundlett | 00 | 13 | 04 |
| *In ye Roome over he house* | | | |
| Item 1 feather bed steads & furniture | 01 | 00 | 00 |
| 1 flock bed & furniture | 00 | 08 | 00 |
| 3 Coffers 3 pr Sheetes 2 Pillow beares 6 napkins and other small Linings | 00 | 18 | 00 |
| Hemp & yarn | 00 | 05 | 06 |
| weareing Aparrell | 01 | 00 | 00 |
| things omitted & not seene | 00 | 02 | 06 |
| | 16 | 18 | 06 |

The Relict of Robart Peate is a Poore widow, owes her landlord for Rent eleven Pounds 12 shillings and Ten Pence to be Paide out of this psonall estate . . . . . . . . . 11 12 10

Totall is . . 05 06 08

## 134. John Lodge

Of Wellington, feltmaker, taken by Vincent Southall and Timothy Field on 18 November 1700 and exhibited on 22 November 1700.

*Imprs. In ye Parlor*
| | |
|---|---|
| 1 Bedstead . . . . . . . . . | 00 10 00 |
| one Table Bord 2 Joyn formes and 1 Cupboard . . . . | 01 05 00 |
| 1 lookeing Glass and 1 Chaire . . . . . . | 00 02 00 |
| one Table Board 2 formes one Coffer and 1 Truckle Bed . . | 00 15 00 |

*In ye Chamber over ye house*
| | |
|---|---|
| one Bed 1 Truckle Bed Two Coffers . . . . . | 00 13 06 |

*In ye house*
| | |
|---|---|
| Two Tables 1 Cupboard 1 forme 3 Stooles . . . . | 00 08 06 |
| one Dishboard 1 Salt Box and 2 Chaires . . . . . | 00 04 00 |
| 2 Brass Pans 6 Pewter dishes 2 Brass potts 1 warmg pan . | 01 10 00 |
| 3 Porringer dishes 1 Chamber Pott 4 flagins . . . | 00 06 00 |
| 1 Brass Kettle 2 Pewter Cans 1 Iron Dreeping Pan 2 Broaches . . | 00 18 00 |
| 2 Paire Cobboons 1 mortar 1 mortar pestle and 2 Candlesticks . | 00 06 00 |
| Tin ware of All Sorts . . . . . . . | 00 10 00 |
| Linens of All Sorts . . . . . . . . | 01 00 00 |
| Wareing Apparell . . . . . . . . | 04 00 00 |
| 1 Chest Bed and Bedstead and furniture thereunto belonging . . | 03 00 00 |
| 7 Pewter dishes . . . . . . . . . | 00 10 00 |
| 1 horse and hey . . . . . . . . . | 04 00 00 |
| 1 Cow . . . . . . . . . . . | 02 10 00 |
| debts due By Speriallty . . . . . . . | 40 00 00 |
| desperat debts . . . . . . . . . | 25 00 00 |
| things omitted and not seene . . . . . . | 00 10 00 |
| | 87 18 00 |

## 135. Richard Plymley

Of Wellington, gent., taken on 3 January 1700–01 and exhibited on 17 March 1700–01. The appraisers are not named.

| | |
|---|---|
| The Deceds Wareing apparrell valued at . . . . | 03 00 00 |
| A trunck . . . . . . . . . . | 00 01 06 |
| Money in his Pockett . . . . . . . | 00 05 00 |
| Eleaven bookes . . . . . . . . | 01 00 00 |
| Two Razers . . . . . . . . . | 00 01 06 |
| one hors . . . . . . . . . . | 06 00 00 |
| One brass Candlestick and other Small things . . . | 00 02 00 |
| Tot . . . | 10 10 00 |

## 136. Thomas Lodge

Of Wellington, feltmaker, taken by John Francis and Andrew Sockett Senr. on 5 April 1701 and exhibited on 9 April 1701.

Imprs.
| | | | |
|---|---|---|---|
| 1 fflock bed 1 Rugg sheetes & other furniture for ye Bed | 01 | 00 | 00 |
| A parcell of woole made Hatts | 04 | 00 | 00 |
| workeing Tooles | 00 | 14 | 00 |
| 1 old horse Blinde of one Eye & his Geares | 02 | 10 | 00 |
| 1 old Trunk 1 old Chest | 00 | 06 | 00 |
| A Parcell of old Boards & other wooden Trumpery | 00 | 06 | 00 |
| 1 Little old Brass Pott | 00 | 05 | 00 |
| his wareing Aparrell | 00 | 15 | 00 |
| things omitted & not seene | 00 | 02 | 00 |
| | 09 | 18 | 00 |

## 137. Richard Randle

Of the Street Lane, Wellington, yeoman, taken by George Wheeler,* John Randle* and Samuel Bennett on 17 March 1701–02 and exhibited on 5 May 1702.

*Impris. In ye house*

| | | | |
|---|---|---|---|
| One Cubbert | 00 | 03 | 00 |
| two ould Seg Chares | 00 | 00 | 06 |
| two Stunds | 00 | 01 | 06 |
| one Churne | 00 | 00 | 08 |
| one Butter bowle or tub | 00 | 00 | 09 |
| one Water payle one gaune & A piggen & milke mitt | 00 | 01 | 00 |
| two small Milke Bowles | 00 | 00 | 03 |
| two ould Barrells | 00 | 01 | 06 |
| three little stooles | 00 | 00 | 03 |
| one kneadinge Mitt | 00 | 00 | 09 |
| one dozen of Trenchers & halfe A dozen of Noggens | 00 | 00 | 06 |
| Pewter of all sorts | 00 | 05 | 00 |
| Brass of all sorts | 00 | 10 | 00 |
| one Small grate, fier shuvell & tongs one smoothing Iron & pott gayles & pot hookes | 00 | 01 | 02 |
| one spitt & Cobberts | 00 | 01 | 00 |
| one fryinge pan | 00 | 00 | 04 |

*In ye Soller or Chamber over the house*

| | | | |
|---|---|---|---|
| one little ould Table borde | 00 | 01 | 06 |
| one small Chest | 00 | 01 | 04 |
| two Beds & bedstids wth ye furniture thereunto belonginge | 01 | 00 | 00 |
| two spinninge wheeles | 00 | 02 | 00 |
| one paire of Flaxen sheetes | 00 | 03 | 00 |
| one paire of Hempen sheetes | 00 | 02 | 00 |
| two paire of Hurden sheetes | 00 | 02 | 06 |
| Six Napkins | 00 | 01 | 06 |
| Six hand towells & Cheese clothes | 00 | 00 | 09 |
| one paire of wooll Cards & one paire of **Nogge** Cards | 00 | 00 | 04 |
| one Reele | 00 | 00 | 01 |

*Implemts of husbandrye*

| | | |
|---|---|---|
| One ould Cart & wheeles . . . . . . . | 00 09 00 |
| One plow & 1 Harrow . . . . . . . | 00 04 00 |
| Three paire of ould horse geares or treases, Hoames & Collors thereunto belonginge . . . . . . . . | 00 04 00 |
| One Ax one bill & broome hooke . . . . . . | 00 01 04 |
| two Reaping hookes. . . . . . . . . | 00 00 03 |
| two ould pack sadles wth wountges & girths to them belonginge | 00 01 06 |
| One Mathooke . . . . . . . . . | 00 00 09 |
| one ould hacking Sadle & bridle . . . . . . | 00 01 00 |
| One horse & 2 Mares . . . . . . . . | 04 10 00 |
| three Cowes . . . . . . . . . . | 06 00 00 |
| five Twinters . . . . . . . . . . | 05 10 00 |
| two yearlings . . . . . . . . . . | 01 10 00 |
| Corne Sowed upon ye ground . . . . . . | 00 18 00 |
| Hard Corne & Oates in ye barne . . . . . . | 00 10 06 |
| Haye & Strawe . . . . . . . . . | 00 10 00 |
| The totall sum is . | 23 16 06 |

## 138. Joseph Eastrop

Of Ketley Wood, Wellington, taken by Richard Jordan and William Watkiss* on 2 March 1701–02 and exhibited on 4 March 1701–02.

| | | |
|---|---|---|
| Impr. Two old pillows, two Bolsters and one Chaffe bed . . | 00 08 00 |
| one Rugg, One Blankett, & one paire of Bedsteds . . . | 00 08 00 |
| Two Coffers and one Truncke . . . . . . | 00 05 00 |
| one Spade, one mattock, Three Sithes, Two Axes One Broomhooke, One paire of Traces, two pick-evells, Two Augers . . . | 00 06 00 |
| one Kneding Tubb . . . . . . . . | 00 02 06 |
| One Lanthorne; One Kettle; One plate . . . . . | 00 01 00 |
| Linnen & Wareing Apparell . . . . . . . | 01 00 00 |
| Thinges Omitted & Unseen . . . . . . . | 00 02 00 |
| | 02 12 00 |

## 139. William Bickley

Of Walcot, Wellington, milner, servant to Thomas Mills, taken by Francis Garbet, Thomas Norton and John Grice on 2 April 1702 and exhibited on 13 October 1702.

| | | |
|---|---|---|
| Two beds and Bedding belonging to them . . . . | 01 00 00 |
| Eight pare of sheets better and worse . . . . . | 01 04 00 |
| One Table Cloth and one pillowe beer . . . . . | 00 02 00 |
| One Dusen of Napkins . . . . . . . | 00 03 00 |
| Brass and Pewter . . . . . . . . | 00 07 00 |
| Iron ware of all sorts . . . . . . . . | 00 02 06 |

### In ye Parler
| | | |
|---|---|---|
| One chest one Box and two Quofers . . . . . | 00 04 00 |

### In ye House
| | | |
|---|---|---|
| Two boxes and two Quofers . . . . . . | 00 03 00 |
| Two barrels . . . . . . . . . | 00 02 06 |
| One Stund one Turnel and two Gauns . . . . | 00 02 04 |
| One table Board and two Cheers . . . . . | 00 03 00 |
| Bookes and Waring Apparel . . . . . | 00 13 04 |
| All things unseen unthought of and forgotten . . . | 00 01 00 |
| The Totall . . | 04 07 08 |

## 140. William Jackson

Of Wellington, tailor, taken by John Judgson and Thomas Kanadine on 12 October 1702 and exhibited on 13 October 1702.

| | | |
|---|---|---|
| Imprs. 2 pressing Irons . . . . . . . | 00 03 00 |
| It. 2 pair of sheeres . . . . . . . . | 00 03 00 |
| It. 1 Bible & other Books . . . . . . . | 00 07 00 |
| Book debts good & bad . . . . . . . | 07 00 00 |
| It. wareing Cloathes . . . . . . . . | 01 00 00 |
| The summe is . | 08 13 00 |

## 141. William Oakely

Of Ruckley, Wellington, yeoman, taken by John Watkiss,* Samuel Oare* and John Grice on 17 March 1704-05 and exhibited on 28 April 1705.

### Impr. In ye Chamber
| | | |
|---|---|---|
| one joyne Bed with ye furniture there belonging . . . | 01 00 00 |
| too chests one coffer & one trunke one Box , , , , | 00 15 00 |
| Foure Cheires & one spining Wheele . . . . | 00 02 00 |

### It in ye Buttery
| | | |
|---|---|---|
| too Little Barrells with small milking vessells . . . | 00 05 00 |

### It. in ye Sallor
| | | |
|---|---|---|
| one standing Bed with ye furniture thereto belonging too little Coffers one Box . . . . . . . . | 00 10 00 |

### It. in ye House
| | | |
|---|---|---|
| five pewter Dishes too plates one pewter cann foure pollingers . | 00 13 04 |
| One presse one cheire one table one fforme one cradle one stoole three Benches . . . . . . . . | 00 06 08 |
| too Brasse Kettells . . . . . . . . | 01 00 00 |

| | | |
|---|---|---|
| too Eyorn pots one marmot | . . . . . | 00 13 04 |
| one Grate one paire of tongs two paire of pott Linkes one plate | . | 00 02 00 |
| Trinnen ware of All sorts . . . . . . . | | 00 02 06 |
| Foure Strawe wiskets . . . . . . . | | 00 04 00 |

*It in ye weavers Roome*

| | | |
|---|---|---|
| one standing Bed with All thereto Belonging | . . . . | 00 05 00 |
| Linnen & naperie ware of All sorts | . . . . | 01 05 00 |
| one Large spining Wheele too small mitts one cheese press | . . | 00 05 00 |
| Corne of All sorts in House & Barne | . . . . | 01 10 00 |
| Beefe & Baken . . . . . . . . | | 00 13 04 |
| Five Cows . . . . . . . . . | | 11 13 04 |
| too three yeare ould Heiffers | . . . . . | 03 05 00 |
| two twinter Heiffers . . . . . . . . | | 02 15 00 |
| foure Cavles . . . . . . . . . | | 02 13 04 |
| foure Horses . . . . . . . . . | | 07 00 00 |
| too pigges . . . . . . . . . | | 00 14 00 |
| one cartt with one paire of Eyorne Bound Weeles one Harrow one plowe with other Impliments of Husbandry | . . . . | 02 00 00 |
| Debts without sptiallty . . . . . . | | 55 00 00 |
| Bookes & waring Apparrell . . . . . . . | | 01 00 00 |
| of All things unseen unthought & forgotten | . . . . | 00 05 00 |
| totall . . . | | 95 17 10 |

## 142. Mary Sockett

Of Wellington, widow, taken by Richard Yeates and Thomas Kanadine on 26 April 1705 and exhibited on 28 April 1705. A second inventory, taken and exhibited on the same dates by the same appraisers, and of the same value, describes the deceased as 'of Preston Brockhurst'.

| | | |
|---|---|---|
| Imprs. | | |
| Ten shillings due for Rent from William Maddox | . . . | 00 10 00 |
| Item. 1 old Byble . . . . . . . . | | 00 02 00 |
| Item. 1 old history Booke . . . . . . . | | 00 02 00 |
| She had noe Clothes fit to ware she came to me with in 9 Dayes I was forced to By her A mant & Peticott ye Rest of her clths wear not worth sixteen Shillings but were Vallued them Soe. . . . . . . . . | | 00 16 00 |
| Totall . . | | 01 10 00 |
| Things omitted & not seene . . . . . . | | 00 03 00 |
| | | 01 13 00 |

There was Layd out upon her funerall weare six pounds

## 143. Thomas Fieldhouse

Of Ketley, Wellington, taken by John Symmons Senr., John Symmons Junr. and Thomas Freeman* on 2 July 1705 and exhibited on 18 October 1705.

| | |
|---|---|
| Imp. his wearing Apparell & Money in his purse . | 02 10 00 |
| It fifteen geldings & mares sadles & other gears belonging to ye sd horses & Mares . . . . . . . . | 35 00 00 |
| It five backbands . . . . . . . . | 00 03 00 |
| It three ould Kine . . . . . . . . | 06 00 00 |
| It foure earling calves . . . . . . . | 03 00 00 |
| It three young calves . . . . . . . | 01 00 00 |
| It Nineteen sheepe & seven lambs . . . . . | 01 18 00 |
| It one swine . . . . . . . . . | 00 15 00 |
| It corne & straw in ye barne . . . . . . | 02 10 00 |
| It A payre of wheeles . . . . . . . | 02 10 00 |
| It poultry . . . . . . . . . | 00 02 00 |
| It goods in ye house place . . . . . . | 05 00 00 |
| It goods &c in ye brew house . . . . . . | 01 10 00 |
| It goods in ye parlour . . . . . . . | 06 00 00 |
| It goods in ye roome over ye brewhouse . . . . | 02 00 00 |
| It goods in ye chambor over ye house . . . . | 01 10 00 |
| It goods in ye chamber over ye parlour . . . . | 04 00 00 |
| It goods in ye cellar . . . . . . . . | 00 10 00 |
| It dunge . . . . . . . . . | 01 00 00 |
| It An ould coffer . . . . . . . . | 00 03 06 |
| It things unnominated & forgotten . . . . . | 00 06 08 |
| | 77 08 02 |

## 144. Richard Phillips

Of Wellington, gent., taken by William Harper and Thomas Ward on 14 August 1705 and exhibited on 17 September 1705.

*In the Closett Room*

| | |
|---|---|
| One Small Chest marked EW with several Small Remnants of Lynnen Cloth . . . . . . . . | 01 00 00 |
| One small box Carved with severall parcells of Lynnen in . . | 00 10 00 |
| One other plain broad box at . . . . . . | 00 10 02 |
| One other great box with several sorts of Lynnen in . . | 00 13 04 |
| Three vyolins vallued at . . . . . . . | 01 02 06 |
| Three floats . . . . . . . . . | 00 02 09 |
| One warming pan . . . . . . . . | 00 02 03 |
| Five Sett of Chims . . . . . . . . | 00 10 04 |
| One pair of boots . . . . . . . . | 00 01 10 |
| One Steal bow . . . . . . . . | 00 00 09 |

### In the Closett
One Silver Cup with ears one Small guilt silver boal one Silver Whistle & 2 botkins . . . . . . . . . 03 02 10

### In the Kitchen
One Jack, grate, ffendor, pott racks 2 pair of Tong's & one fire Shovell . . . . . . . . . . 00 18 00
One Iron drippen pan, one Tin drepen pan & Tin Cover one fryan pan & one pudding plate . . . . . . . 00 06 00
Two brass potts one Iron pott 2 brass Ketles one hacking knife 2 flesh fforks one brass baister, one Chafeing dish one spitt & one paire of bellyes . . . . . . . . . 01 04 00
One skreen, one Large ovall table one little ovall table, one Shrot fform 2 Joynt Stooles 3 old Chairs 2 pailes one milking gaun & one hacking block . . . . . . . . . 01 06 03
Two Large pewter dishes . . . . . . . 01 00 00
Seaven Small pewter dishes. . . . . . . 00 03 03
One douzen of old fashion plates . . . . . 00 09 00
Two pewter Flaggons . . . . . . . 00 05 00
Two Little brass Ketles 2 brass Chafeing dishes . . 00 07 00

### In the Room Adjoyning to the Kitchen
Two Small peices of Flaxen Cloth 12 Ells . . . . 00 18 00
Two Small peices of Whitten'd hemp 16 Ells . . . 00 16 00
hempen Cloth 60 Ells . . . . . . . 03 05 00
One Trunk marked 1661 of old Cloths . . . . 00 03 00
One Chest of new Lynnen Cloth Containing 14 peices with other wearing Lynnen . . . . . . . . . 15 10 00
One bed stead, side table & one desk . . . . 00 05 00
A Clock & Chims . . . . . . . . 02 10 00
A Lookeing glass . . . . . . . . 00 02 06
A Closet . . . . . . . . . . 00 02 06
One old Sett of Red Curtains & vallance

### In Mr. Richds. Own Chambr.
One Trunk with Lynnens in as follows
One douzen of ffine hempen napkins . . . . 00 05 00
One douzen of Course hempen napkins . . . . 00 02 06
7 table Cloths & one Sheet . . . . . . 01 00 06
5 hempen pair of Sheets unmaid . . . . . 02 02 00
3 paire of Course hempen Sheets . . . . . 01 00 00
One dyaper table Cloth & 1 pair of Sheets . . . 01 00 00
2 pair of Flaxen sheets & 1 pair of hempen . . . 01 12 00
5 douzen of hempen napkins . . . . . . 01 05 06
One douzen & halfe of holland napkins . . . . 00 15 00
14 dyaper napkins . . . . . . . . 00 10 00
1 peices of Cloth to make 8 napkins . . . . 00 06 00
Two dale boxes with some Remnts. of Callicoe & Severall old wearing Lynen in . . . . . . . . 00 11 00
One broad oak box with a Silk body of a gown & hood & skarf & several other peices of Silk remnants & Lynnens . . 04 01 05

# THE INVENTORIES OF WELLINGTON

| | |
|---|---|
| One bed Stead with Curtains and Vallans one ffeather bed & 2 boulsters 3 blanketts & one Red Rugg . . . . . | 02 03 03 |
| A Sadle . . . . . . . . . | 00 03 00 |
| One truckle bed stead & feather bed upon it 2 boulsters & 1 pillow 2 blanketts & Coverlid . . . . . . . | 01 05 11 |
| One Large Chest with his wearing Apparrell in . . . | 04 00 00 |
| One Close Stoole and Stand . . . . . . | 00 05 00 |

*In the Garrott*

| | |
|---|---|
| One Large Chest with 2 Course handtowells 2 pair of Course sheets with several shifts and sheets and other wearing Lynnens . . | 02 05 00 |
| Do. A Fur mantle with 3 old pettycoats . . . . | 00 10 00 |
| An old Truckle bed stead with feather bed upon it & 2 blankitts and Coverlid . . . . . . . . | 00 15 00 |
| One dale box & 4 Ells of new flaxen Cloth 2 pair of hempen sheets 5 yds of flaxen Cloth 2 holland pillowbees 3 other pillow bees besides other wearing Shifts . . . . . . | 02 01 10 |

*In the Parlor*

| | |
|---|---|
| One sett of Curtains for a bed with vallance with silk ffringe about ye vallance . . . . . . . . . | 01 10 00 |

*In the Brewhouse*

| | |
|---|---|
| One Furnace & one boyler . . . . . . . | 02 10 00 |

*In the Malthouse*

| | |
|---|---|
| One Rinling Tub . . . . . . . . | 00 07 00 |
| A Steal mill . . . . . . . . . | 00 10 00 |
| A weeting Tubb . . . . . . . . | 00 07 00 |
| Two harrows . . . . . . . . . | 00 07 09 |
| One Fire Shovell . . . . . . . . | 00 00 03 |
| A malt Skreen . . . . . . . . | 00 09 00 |

*In the barn Corn unthrast*

| | |
|---|---|
| Wheat, peas, fitches &c. . . . . . . . | 05 10 00 |
| hey . . . . . . . . . . | 04 05 00 |

*In the Celler and brew house*

| | |
|---|---|
| Seven old barrells . . . . . . . . | 00 08 09 |

*In the ground*

| | |
|---|---|
| Two Cows . . . . . . . . . | 04 05 00 |
| Two Twinter heafers . . . . . . . | 04 10 00 |
| Two Lesser twinters heafers . . . . . . | 03 00 00 |
| Three Earlings . . . . . . . . | 03 00 00 |
| Muck in ye barn Fold . . . . . . . | 00 10 00 |
| Corn in ye grannery . . . . . . . . | 35 00 00 |
| Money's found in Cash . . . . . . . | 143 07 10 |
| Summe . . . . . . . . . | 275 19 09 |
| by a Note . . . . . . . . . | 02 00 00 |
| Tottall Summe . . . . . . . . | 277 19 09 |

## 145. William Cooke

Of Wellington, nailer, taken by Thomas Kanadine and Roger Sockett on 10 October 1705 and exhibited on 26 April 1706.

Imps.
| | |
|---|---|
| One ffeather bed bedsteads & apptences | 00 15 00 |
| Two other beds & apptences | 00 15 00 |
| Two Chests & one Table Board | 00 06 08 |
| Linnens | 01 00 00 |
| pewter & Brasse | 01 05 00 |
| One Joyned Cubboard one Screene & one Table | 00 13 04 |
| One other Screene ffire Shovell & Tongues, One Grate & other Iron Ware & One paire of Bellows | 00 06 08 |
| One Barrell & other Woodden ware | 00 06 08 |
| Implemts of Trade & workeing Iron & Stocke of Trade | 01 10 00 |
| Weareing apparrell | 00 13 04 |
| Thinges Omitted & unseene | 00 02 06 |
| | 07 14 02 |

## 146. John Judgson

Of Wellington, innholder, taken by James Rushbury and John Hall, gent., on 9 April 1708 and exhibited on 30 April 1708.

| | |
|---|---|
| Imprs. one Bullock and one Cow in Calfe | 07 10 00 |
| Three old Horses | 03 02 06 |
| Six Swine | 02 08 00 |
| hay in the Barne | 07 00 00 |
| hemp and fflax | 01 00 00 |

*In ye Little parlor*

One Bed and all furniture one Screene Eight Stooles and one little table . . . . . . . . . . 02 00 00

*In the parlor Chamber*

one Bed & ffurniture one Screene one table and Six Stooles . . 01 10 00

*In the Kitching Chamber*

three Beds & ffurniture one press two Chests one Table 8 stooles & one trunk . . . . . . . . . 03 05 00

*In the Crowne Chamber*

two Beds & ffurniture two Tables one Chest two fforms tenn Stooles and one Lookeing Glass . . . . . 08 03 06

*In the Top Lofts*

3 Beds and ffurniture . . . . . . . 02 10 00

*In the Roome over the Cellar*
two Beds and other ffurniture . . . . . . 01 10 00

*In the Kitching*
two Tables one Screene one fforme and three stooles . . . 00 13 04
Brass and pewter . . . . . . . . 02 00 00
Ironware of all sorts . . . . . . . . 01 03 04
wooden ware of all sorts one ffurnace Brewing vessells and Steele Mill 04 10 00
drinke in the Cellar . . . . . . . . 08 00 00
Malt unbrewed . . . . . . . . 02 00 00
Linnen of all sorts . . . . . . . . 05 00 00
wareing Apparell and ready Money . . . . 02 00 00
Things not seen omitted or forgotten . . . . 00 05 00

                                                                                                                                               65 10 08

## 147. Rowland Goole

    Of Watling Street, Wellington, innholder, taken by Richard Poole and William Cleaton* on 18 April 1708 and exhibited on 30 April 1708.

Imp.
Three Cowes one Little Bullock Vallued at . . . . 09 00 00
2 Horses and one mare . . . . . . 09 00 00
8 Swine att . . . . . . . . . 05 10 00
14 Truss of hay . . . . . . . . 14 00 00
Sixty strike of Oats . . . . . . . . 03 00 00
12 strike sowing of Wheat . . . . . . 05 00 00
16 strike sowing of Oates . . . . . . 01 00 00
20 strike of Beanes & Pease . . . . . . 01 10 00
12 strike of Corne in the house . . . . . 01 00 00

*In the Parlor*
6: Chaires one Little Table one skreene one Lookeing Glass . . 01 15 00

*In the hall*
6: Chaires 2 Little Tables . . . . . . 00 08 00

*In the Pantry*
one Bedd one Table one Chaire . . . . . 02 00 00

*In the New Roome*
one Table and 3 Chaires . . . . . . 00 05 00

*In the Swan Chambre*
one Bed 3 Tables 12: chaires one looking Glass & 2 pr of Curttens
for windows . . . . . . . . . 06 00 00

*In the Bottle Chambre*
one Bed 2 pr of Curtaines for the Windows . . . . 02 00 00

*In the Chambr ovr ye New Roome*
one Bed one Table 4: chaires . . . . . 02 00 00

*In the hall Chambre*
2 Beds one Little Table 9 Chaires & one Lookeing Glass . . 09 00 00

*In the Post Chambre*
one bed 2 Tables Six Chaires & one Lookeing Glass . . . 04 00 00

*In the Closett*
2 Runletts 3 Dozn of Glasses . . . . 00 10 00

*In the Chambr ovr ye Kitchen*
2 beds 2: Chests one Table one hangin Press one Clock. . . 07 00 00

*In the maids Chambre*
one bed 2: Benches one Lookeing Glass . . . . 02 00 00

*In the Garretts*
5 beds . . . . . . . . 04 00 00

*In the Kitchin*
6 Sides of Bacon 5 fflitches of Beefe twelve Neats tongs . . 03 10 00
2 Tables one Skreen 6 Chaires . . . . . 00 16 00
1 Jack 1: Grate 1: Iron | Purgatory a ffire shovle & tongs spitts drooping pans together wth all other Iron ware . . . 02 18 06
7 Dozn of Pewter Plates 24 Pewter Dishes 11 Pewter Quarts 11 Pewt. Pintes 10 Pewter Chamber potts togeather wth all other Pewtr.. . . . . . . . . 09 10 00
ffive Brass Kettles 1 brass pott togeather wth all Brass . . 02 00 00

*In the Brewhouse*
3 Brewing Tubbs: Cooler . . . . . . 01 00 00

*In the Celler*
16 hogshead full of Beere . . . . . . 35 00 00
Nine Barrells some full and some empty . . . . 02 10 00

*Linens*
Some holland some fflaxon some hempton & some hurden in all 40 pr of Sheets . . . . . . . 20 00 00
12 Doz of Napkins 20 Pillow's Beares 20 Table Clothes . . 06 04 00

*Silver*
2 Silver Tankards fower Silver Salts one Silver Cupp 1 Doz of silver spoones half Doz. Silvr. fforkes 3 Sillver Tumblers . . . 20 00 00

# THE INVENTORIES OF WELLINGTON

| | |
|---|---|
| Warring Apparrell and money in his Pocketts . . . . | 03 00 00 |
| 2 old Watches vallued at . . . . . . | 03 00 00 |
| Debts oweing by Sperialltys . . . . . | 350 00 00 |
| Desperate Debts . . . . . . . | 172 00 00 |
| Tot . . . | 721 16 06 |

## 148. John Eyton

Of Wellington, esquire, taken by William Icke, William Reynolds and Thomas Newell on 7 March 1708–09 and exhibited on 6 May 1709. The original is badly faded and certain sections are illegible.

*In ye Parler*

| | |
|---|---|
| One ovell table & one Little Table . . . . . | 00 06 00 |
| six Segg Chaires & one with armes . . . . . | 00 05 00 |
| A grate & ffireshovell and Tongues . . . . | 00 05 00 |
| A Looking Glass a mapp & pare of Bellows . . . | 00 02 06 |
| The hangings of ye roome . . . . . . | 00 03 04 |

*In ye Hall*

| | |
|---|---|
| One Large Ovell table & one Long Table . . . . | 00 15 00 |
| A couch Two old maps & ffourteen Segg Chaires . . | 00 14 08 |
| A clock & one pare of Brass scales & Weights . . . | 01 13 10 |
| Two small pictures . . . . . . . | 00 00 08 |

*In ye Kitchin*

| | |
|---|---|
| Eighteen Pewter Dishes & ffive dozen & tenn plates with other small pewter . . . . . . . . | 05 05 00 |
| Three large Brass potts 2 Little ones & 2 masslen Kettles . . | 02 00 00 |
| One Warming pan & two brass Candlesticks . . . | 00 10 08 |
| Two brass Chaffing Dishes & one brass Snuffer pott . . | 00 03 00 |
| One Copper Tea pott & Two copper Canns . . . | 00 04 06 |
| Three sase panns . . . . . . . | 00 02 00 |
| One Jack & Apurtenances & three Broches . . . | 01 04 00 |
| Two racks & a pare of Gobbotts . . . . . | 00 08 00 |
| A grate two ffireshovels & a pare of toungs . . . | 00 06 00 |
| ffive ....ings for plates . . . . . . | 00 02 00 |
| One driping pann & 2 rings for ye stone harth . . . | 00 03 03 |
| ........... a chopping knife a pare of Iron Candlesticks . . | 00 03 00 |
| ................ . . . . . . . . | 00 01 00 |
| ........... Iron spoons three fflesh fforks a skimer . . . | 00 02 00 |
| Eight Iron Skeepe & fframes . . . . . | 00 00 03 |
| One iron morter & pesttell . . . . . . | 00 03 00 |
| ffour Smoothing Irons & two heaters . . . . | 00 04 00 |
| ffour Iron Candlesticks . . . . . . | 00 00 06 |
| Three ffouleing peeces . . . . . . | 02 00 00 |
| One ffrying pan & one pare of potthooks . . . | 00 01 08 |

| | |
|---|---|
| Three tin culliners ffour covers & 3 pasty pans . . . . | 00 05 06 |
| Two tynn candlesticks a tea pott a cheese dish and a tynn can and 13 patty panns . . . . . . . . | 00 01 06 |
| A tynn Dripin pan . . . . . . . . | 00 00 04 |
| a Joyn Dishbench wth Drawers . . . . . | 00 06 08 |
| A screen & a table . . . . . . . . | 00 12 00 |
| A Bacon Rack Three Chairs & a stoole . . . . | 00 03 00 |
| One dale box and a Cubbord . . . . . | 00 02 06 |
| two wooden boxes & a hacking block . . . . | 00 01 00 |
| one Iron marment . . . . . . . . | 00 02 06 |
| ffour nogens five trenchers & a pare of bellows . . . | 00 00 06 |

*In ye Brewhouse*

| | |
|---|---|
| One ffurnise & one Boyler . . . . . . . | 00 16 00 |
| Three Brewing Stunds & ffoure Coolers . . . . | 01 07 00 |
| A malt mill . . . . . . . . | 00 08 00 |
| Two Bouks & two gaunes . . . . . . | 00 02 06 |
| A Wash Stund & a mitt to soape in . . . . | 00 02 08 |
| A churn & cleansing sift . . . . . . | 00 02 04 |
| Two Benches a horse & Three Wooden Bottles . . . | 00 04 00 |

*In ye Sellar*

| | |
|---|---|
| ffoure halfe hogsheads & 16 barrells . . . . | 03 05 00 |
| Two Drap & a tundish . . . . . . | 00 02 00 |
| Two tables three Joyne stooles 2 shelves & 2 heads . . | 00 07 02 |

*Over ye Brewhouse*

| | |
|---|---|
| Boards & railles a pare of beadsteads and a Twigen baskett wth ffeathers . . . . . . . . | 03 08 02 |

*In ye Garrett*

| | |
|---|---|
| Wheat and malt . . . . . . . . | 04 05 00 |
| A ffoulding Skreen & two spining wheels . . . . | 00 04 06 |
| Two strawn Whisketts five boxes an old Coffer . . . | 00 04 00 |
| A Sidesaddle 2 footestooles a bridle bill 2 Girths and an old Tubb . | 00 10 06 |

*In ye farther Chamber*

| | |
|---|---|
| Two sadlecloths a pilloon an old coffer . . . . | 00 06 00 |
| one pare of Bedsteads & a pare of Kervings . . . | 00 02 06 |

*In ye fellows Chamber*

| | |
|---|---|
| One fflock bead wth steads & ffurniture . . . . | 00 06 08 |
| Two Dale boxes & a roll strap . . . . . | 00 01 08 |

*In Masters Chamber*

| | |
|---|---|
| A Joyne pare of beadsteads ffeather bead and ffurniture . . | 02 15 00 |
| Two more small beads & ffurniture . . . . | 02 05 00 |
| One Chest with coarse lining . . . . . | 01 15 00 |
| Two hanging presses . . . . . . . | 00 15 00 |
| The napkin press . . . . . . . | 00 15 00 |

| | |
|---|---|
| Two chests of Draws | 00 14 00 |
| Two Lookeing glasses | 00 06 08 |
| A ffire shovell & toungs & two chaires | 00 03 04 |
| Two mantles | 04 00 00 |
| A velvet peticoate & velvett scarfe. | 05 00 00 |

*In ye Dineing Roome*

| | |
|---|---|
| One Large bead & ffurniture | 05 00 00 |
| Gapan tables one black & ye other white | 02 00 00 |
| A scriptoire | 01 10 00 |
| the Cheny with Glasses | 00 06 00 |
| A large trunk with ffine linging | 14 10 00 |
| A Glass Case with toys | 00 10 00 |
| A small ovell table & a square table | 00 07 00 |
| Two turky work chaires & five cloth Chaires | 01 01 06 |
| ffour Clothe Stools & a close stoole | 00 05 00 |
| One ffire shovell toungs Creeper & Bellows | 00 04 00 |
| A Twigen Skreen a Chimney peece & old hangins | 00 02 00 |
| Two chests of Drawes | 01 00 00 |

*In ye ffarther Little roome*

| | |
|---|---|
| Tenn stone of Woole | 05 00 00 |

*In ye Parlor Chamber*

| | |
|---|---|
| One Bead & ffurniture | 03 10 00 |
| A Chest with old Hangins | 00 18 00 |
| A Couch a Chaire & a Square Table | 00 04 00 |
| Twenty four Ells of new Tickin | 01 16 00 |
| Nine yards of Blankettin | 00 05 00 |
| Grate ffire shovell & toungs | 00 05 00 |
| Hangings of ye roome & Looking glass | 00 10 00 |
| Netts and Lines | 01 01 10 |
| A small parcell of fflax & yarn | 00 04 00 |

*In ye milk house*

| | |
|---|---|
| ffoure shilves one short Bench steans & milk pans | 00 01 06 |

*In ye place next ye kichin*

| | |
|---|---|
| Three shelves & an old frame of a table | 00 01 00 |
| A parcell of Glass Bottles | 00 06 00 |

*In ye Walker street Barn*

| | |
|---|---|
| Rye straw & corn unthreshd | 04 15 00 |
| One Cart Tumbrill & Draught plow & irons, A Dragg and all other Implements of Husbandry | 05 02 08 |
| Part of a Bay of Hay | 02 10 00 |

*In Rabisons Roomes*

| | |
|---|---|
| Munnkorn Oates & Pease threshed & Six Baggs | 15 13 06 |

*In Mr. Binnells Barn*
Part of a Bay of Pease & two ladders . . . . . 02 00 00

*In Timo: ffields Malthouse*
Malt and Barley . . . . . . . . 14 03 00
Sheep Cows and two swine . . . . . . . 13 00 00

*In ye stable*
Three mares and two Geldings . . . . . . 21 10 00
Three sadles and ffive Bridles . . . . . . 01 07 06

*In Mistriss Closett*
A German clock a silver cup & other plate and a small nesst of Drawes 09 15 10
Knifes & forkes & Irons to keep ye children of ye ffire . . . 00 08 00
moneys in ye house . . . . . . . . 18 19 09

Corn upon ye Ground att Wellington & Eyton . . . 22 10 00
Much a roleing stone a swine troh . . . . . . 01 04 00

Wareing aparrell . . . . . . . . 05 00 00
Books in ye Studdy . . . . . . . . 38 12 06

Things omitted and fforgotten . . . . . 00 10 00

346 08 15

## 149. Edward Shakeshaft

Of Wellington, corviser, taken by Timothy Field, Andrew Beddow and William Floyd on 19 April 1709 and exhibited on 21 April 1709. He died on 16 April 1709.

Imprimis. The Shooes in the Shop and Boots and Leather . . 04 00 00

*Item. The goods in the House*
ye peuter of all Sorts The Brass of all sorts and the Iron ware of all sorts . . . . . . . . . . 02 01 08

*Item. The goods in the Roome over the Shop*
one feather bed and bedstids and the furniture belonging to it . 01 13 04
6 Chires and one little Table Board . . . . . 00 10 06

*Item. The Goods in the Rome over the house*
one Feither bed & bedstids and the furniture belonging to it . 01 05 00
One little Table and one little Chest & four Chires . . . 00 12 00

Item. Nappring ware of all sorts . . . . . . 01 13 04
Item. Trinnen ware of all sorts . . . . . . 00 13 02
Item. Booke debts due desporall & other wayes . . . . 02 00 00
Item. His wareing Aparrell . . . . . . . 03 10 00
Item. Things omitted and forgotten . . . . . 00 15 06

18 14 06

## 150. Richard Peate the elder

Of the Streetway, Hadley, Wellington, blacksmith, taken by John Sicall and Nicolas Broxton on 7 January 1709-10 and exhibited on 21 April 1710.

Imprs.

*In ye Chamber*

| | |
|---|---|
| 1 Bedd 1 Bolster 1 Blankett & 1 Coverlid & hangings wth one pr of sheets & Bedsteeds . . . . . . . . | 01 01 06 |
| 2 pr of Sheets more . . . . . . . . | 00 07 00 |
| 1 : Chest . . . . . . . . | 00 06 00 |
| 1 hive of Bees . . . . . . . . | 00 01 06 |
| 1 Trunke & 1 Box . . . . . . . . | 00 07 00 |
| 1 Bedd wch wee are Informd is in Ed: Barkhams hands wee valued to . . . . . . . . | 00 10 00 |
| And alsoe in Jon Cleatons hands . . . . . . | 05 10 06 |
| Rent due at Madeley . . . . . . . | 00 12 00 |
| due from Geo: Peate . . . . . . . | 01 10 00 |
| 2 Flichings of Bacon . . . . . . . | 01 00 00 |
| hemp . . . . . . . . . | 00 10 00 |
| Wareing Apparell of All sorts . . . . . . | 01 00 00 |
| Things omited & forgoten . . . . . . . | 00 02 06 |
| Tot . . . | 13 04 06 |

## 151. Margaret Blakeman

Of Hadley, taken by Thomas Owen, Thomas Whittingham and William Cookson* and exhibited on 21 April 1710. The inventory is undated.

| | |
|---|---|
| fortey Shillings that was oweing . . . . . . | 02 00 00 |
| Impr | |
| Two looms and gears . . . . . . . | 03 00 00 |
| two Beads and furniture . . . . . . . | 01 10 00 |
| Item Bras and pewter . . . . . . . | 00 08 00 |
| Item cofers and boxes . . . . . . . | 00 05 00 |
| Item her waring cloathes and aparill . . . . . | 01 00 00 |
| Item for Lumber goods . . . . . . . | 00 06 00 |
| Item two pots and iron things . . . . . . | 00 06 00 |
| Item for Linens . . . . . . . . | 00 02 00 |
| Item money in her pocket . . . . . . . | 00 01 06 |
| Items things unpraised and not seen . . . . . | 00 05 00 |
| Sum . . . | 09 04 00 |

## 152. William Cookson

Of Hadley, weaver, taken by William Icke and Thomas Freeman on 28 March 1711 and exhibited on 5 April 1711.

*Imprs. In the Kitchen*
one ovall Table; one Short Skreene; one Grate, ffire Shovell & Tongues & other Iron ware; one old dishing bench & 3 pewter dishes & other old pewter & 3 old Segg Chaires; ffoure Stooles & one warmeing pan & Six Candlesticks . . . . .     01 00 00

*Item In ye parlor*
Two Tables & three fformes; ffive old Chaires & a Cubboard and one old Grate . . . . . . . . .     00 12 00

*Item In ye Shopp*
Implemts of Trade . . . . . . . .     01 06 08

*Item In the Little parlor*
one old Bedd & ffoure Chaires . . . . . .     00 14 08

*Item In ye Buttery*
Two Barrells; one hogshead; Brewing Vessells Two Kinderkins & other wooden ware . . . . . . . .     00 15 06

*Item In the Chamber over ye parler*
One old Bed & Bedsteads; one Livery Table; one old Chest; 3 old Coffers & Seaven Small Boxes . . . . .     01 00 06

*Item In ye Chamber over ye house*
One old Bed; Table & Coffer; one old forme & one Segg Chaire; one horse and one old Truckle Bed . . . . .     00 08 00

*Item In the Chamber over ye Shoppe*
Three old paire of Bedsteads & two Chaffe bedds & one Whiskett .     00 05 06

Item: Cattle of all sorts . . . . . . .     02 00 00
Item: Corne growing & in & abot. the house . . . .     02 00 00
Item: hay & ffodder. . . . . . . .     00 10 00
Item: Weareing apparrell & thinges omitted & unseene . . .     00 19 00

    18 12 07

## 153. John Handy

Of Wellington, labourer, taken by William Bradshaw and James Cole on 5 October 1711 and exhibited on 18 October 1711.

*First in the Houseplace*
an old Table two Plates four Tikney Dishes one little Pot one little
Grate and two old Chairs . . . . . . . 00 10 00

*In a litte Roome adjoyning to the Houseplace*
One Bed and ffurniture being old and outworn . . . . 00 13 04
ffive old Sheetes . . . . . . . . 00 05 00
Three old Chairs . . . . . . . . 00 01 00

*In the Roome over the House place*
one old fflock Bed with an old Hilling and one old Chest . . 00 07 00

                                                        01 16 11

## 154. Richard Stanier

Of Aston, Wellington, gent., taken by Thomas Bache, John Reynolds, Richard Lee and Francis Hotchkiss on 16 October 1711 and exhibited on 17 October 1711.

Imprs.
Seaven Cowes & One Bull . . . . . . . 36 00 00
ffoure other Cowes . . . . . . . . 20 00 00
ffour Twinter Bullocks & One Twinter heyfer . . . 17 10 00
ffive yearlings . . . . . . . . 11 00 00
Six Calves . . . . . . . . . 07 00 00
Twelve Oxen . . . . . . . . . 78 00 00
one hundred fforty & Three Sheep . . . . 35 15 00
Thirty ffive Lambs . . . . . . . . 06 02 06
One Black mare, one schewed mare, one Little Bay mare, Two
Colts & Seaven Cart horses . . . . . . 63 00 00
ffive Swine . . . . . . . . . 07 10 00
Thirty Eight Strikes Seednesse of Oates . . . . 06 00 00
One Stack of Hardcorne . . . . . . . 20 00 00
One Stack of peas . . . . . . . . 09 00 00
Eight Strike of hardcorne in the Barne . . . . 01 12 00

*In the Granary*
Twenty Strikes of Mault . . . . . . . 04 10 00
ffoure Strikes of muncorne . . . . . . . 01 00 00
Six Strikes of Wheat . . . . . . . . 01 16 00
Timber of all sorts . . . . . . . . 05 00 00
Cowpery Ware of all Sorts . . . . . . . 01 00 00

*Linnens*
Two dozen & ffour paire of hempen & fflaxen Sheets . . 25 04 00
Two paire of holland Sheetes . . . . . . 05 00 00
Two dozen & two paire of hurden Sheetes . . . 07 16 00
Seaven dozen of diaper Napkins & Seaven table cloths of ye same . 09 00 00
A Suite of fflaxen . . . . . . . . 01 04 00

| | |
|---|---|
| Three Suites of hookaback . . . . . . . | 02 08 00 |
| One Suite of hurden & other odd Linnens . . . . | 02 00 00 |

## In the Kitchen

| | |
|---|---|
| One hundred & Nineteene pounds of pewter dishes &c. . . | 04 19 02 |
| ffive dozen of pewter plates . . . . . . | 02 10 00 |
| Nine Brasse Candlesticks . . . . . . . | 00 09 00 |
| Two paire of Iron Snuffers & Tinn Candlesticks . . . | 00 01 06 |
| ffour ffowling Guns . . . . . . . . | 02 00 00 |
| Six Iron Candlesticks . . . . . . . | 00 02 00 |
| A Jack & Cord & Seaven Iron Spitts, one paire of Racks . . | 03 00 00 |
| One Iron Grate, ffire Slice & Tongues & One paire of hand Irons & Iron Proker . . . . . . . . . | 01 05 00 |
| A Screene & ffoure old Chaires . . . . . . | 00 05 00 |
| Three dreepeing pans & two pudding pans . . . | 00 15 00 |
| An Iron Mortar & pestell . . . . . . . | 00 06 00 |
| Six Iron potts . . . . . . . . . | 02 10 00 |
| Three Brasse Kettles, Two Skelletts, One brasse pott . . | 00 15 00 |
| A Salt Box . . . . . . . . . | 00 05 00 |
| An hearth Grate & ffender . . . . . . . | 01 00 00 |
| two paire of potthookes . . . . . . . | 00 02 00 |
| A warmeing pan . . . . . . . . | 00 06 00 |
| two Tyn pudding pans . . . . . . . | 00 01 00 |
| Tobacco Tongues & Stiller . . . . . . . | 00 08 00 |

## In the hall

| | |
|---|---|
| A large Cheese presse . . . . . . . | 01 10 00 |
| One long Table & Two fformes . . . . . . | 01 00 00 |
| One large Ovall Table Leafe without a fframe . . . | 00 05 00 |
| One little Ovall Table . . . . . . . | 00 05 00 |
| One Square Table . . . . . . . . | 00 05 00 |
| ffour Leather Chaires . . . . . . . | 00 10 00 |
| Six Joyned Chaires . . . . . . . . | 00 12 00 |
| Sixteen Small pictures & Map . . . . . . | 00 05 00 |
| Three Saddles & Bridles . . . . . . . | 01 00 00 |
| An Elbowe Chaire & a Little Table . . . . . | 00 02 00 |

## In the parlour

| | |
|---|---|
| One large Couch; Ten Tapestry Chaires & two more of ye Same that are in the Little Chamber that's over ye parlour Clossett. Eight Leather Chaires; Two Elbowe Segg Chaires; one Inlaid Table under the mapp; and one oake ovall Table; one Clock and weather Glass one Mapp & other pictures . . . . . . . | 22 10 00 |

## In the Buttery

| | |
|---|---|
| One Table and Two Joyned Stooles . . . . . | 00 07 00 |
| One dish Bench . . . . . . . . | 00 05 00 |
| One napkin presse . . . . . . . . | 00 10 00 |
| One Safe & Livery Table . . . . . . . | 00 08 00 |
| One Glasse Case . . . . . . . . | 00 05 00 |
| **Weights Scales & Beame** . . . . . . . | 01 05 00 |

# THE INVENTORIES OF WELLINGTON 341

*In the Cellar*

| | |
|---|---|
| Six Barrells; Two hogsheads; Two Kinderkins & one ffirkin | 02 05 00 |

*In the Milke house*

| | |
|---|---|
| Three Leads for Milke; one Lead for Salting of Beefe | 05 00 00 |
| Two Barrells & one Kinderkin | 00 15 00 |
| Two Churns | 00 04 00 |

*In the Small Beer Buttery*

| | |
|---|---|
| Two hogsheads; Two Barrells & One ffirkin | 01 03 00 |

*In the Brewhouse*

| | |
|---|---|
| A Malt Mill | 01 10 00 |
| Two Bucking Stunds; Two Brewing Stunds Three Coolers; a kneading Tubb, a wetting vessel & severall small thinges | 03 14 00 |

*In the parlour Chamber*

| | |
|---|---|
| One ffeather Bed, Bolster, Bedsteads, Curtains & vallens belonging to the same; a Chest of 4 drawers, A large Lookeing Glass; Two Elbowe Caine Chaires, Ten other Cane Chaires, A Close Stoole, ffire Shovell & Tongues | 14 00 00 |

*In the hall Chamber*

| | |
|---|---|
| One ffeather Bedd; Bedsteads & ffurniture belonging to ye Same | 05 00 00 |
| One Little dressing Table | 00 04 00 |
| Six Segg Chaires | 00 06 00 |
| One Close Stoole Box | 00 02 00 |
| Two Small Stunds | 00 02 06 |

*In the Little Chamber*

| | |
|---|---|
| One hainging presse | 01 00 00 |
| One chest | 00 07 00 |
| One Square Table | 00 02 06 |
| Two Chaires | 00 02 00 |
| One Bed; Bedstead, Boulster & ffurniture belonging to the same | 03 00 00 |
| Two Small Lookeing Glasses | 00 03 00 |

*In the Kitchen Chamber*

| | |
|---|---|
| One Bed & ffurniture belonging to the Same | 03 00 00 |
| One Chest of drawers | 00 10 00 |
| One Chest & Coffer | 00 11 00 |
| A Close Stoole Box | 00 01 06 |
| One Large Box & Livery Table | 00 06 00 |
| One Little Trunk & ffive Chaires | 00 08 00 |
| Doctor Sacheverells picture | 00 02 00 |
| A ffire shovell & Tongues | 00 02 00 |

*In the Little Roome over the parlour Clossett*

| | |
|---|---|
| One Bed & ffurniture belonging to the same | 02 10 00 |
| A Little Table & Three Chaires | 00 05 00 |

| | | |
|---|---|---|
| A Cupboard . . . . . . . . . | 00 02 00 | |
| A writeing presse . . . . . . . . | 00 10 00 | |

*In the Buttery Chamber*

| | | |
|---|---|---|
| A Bed & ffurniture belonging to the same . . . . | 02 10 00 | |
| A Little Table . . . . . . . . | 00 04 00 | |
| two large Boxes . . . . . . . . | 00 05 00 | |
| A portmantua Truncke . . . . . . . | 00 04 00 | |

*Servants. Chamber*

| | | |
|---|---|---|
| Two Bedsteads & Beds . . . . . . . | 02 00 00 | |
| a Little Cupboard . . . . . . . . | 00 02 00 | |
| Wool . . . . . . . . . . | 40 00 00 | |

*In the 1st Garrott on the Top of ye Staires*

| | | |
|---|---|---|
| Two old Beds & Bedsteads & ffurniture belonging to ym & a paire of Bedsteads . . . . . . . . . | 02 10 00 | |

*In the 2d Garrott*

| | | |
|---|---|---|
| Two Beds & Bedsteads . . . . . . . | 05 00 00 | |
| Two Square Tables, Two Small Stooles, an old small presse, a stone of Course locks of wool . . . . . . . | 00 11 00 | |

*In the Verjuire Chamber*

| | | |
|---|---|---|
| Two hogsheads, One Barrell, One Kinderkin . . . | 00 12 00 | |
| one Cradle, One Long Wheele . . . . . . | 00 06 03 | |
| Two Chests, Two Coffers . . . . . . . | 00 15 00 | |
| Seaven Stone of hemp . . . . . . . | 01 03 04 | |

*In the Store Chamber*

| | | |
|---|---|---|
| ffive hundred weight of Cheese . . . . . . | 05 00 00 | |
| One Grosse of Bottles & other thinges . . . . | 01 10 00 | |

*On ye Staire Case*

| | | |
|---|---|---|
| One Clocke . . . . . . . . . | 02 10 00 | |

*Roome over the Ox house*

| | | |
|---|---|---|
| One Bed & Two Bedsteads . . . . . . . | 01 03 00 | |

*In the Backe Court*

| | | |
|---|---|---|
| One Cheese presse, Two Stone Cisterns and Two Barrells . . | 00 18 00 | |

*In the Great Workehouse*

| | | |
|---|---|---|
| Working Tooles and Implemts. of husbandry of all Sorts . . | 07 00 00 | |

*In the Little workehouse and Comon Stable*

| | | |
|---|---|---|
| homes, Geers, Collars, Traces for Seaven horses . . . . | 01 15 00 | |
| Yoakes & Chaines for twelve oxen . . . . . | 01 10 00 | |

THE INVENTORIES OF WELLINGTON 343

| | |
|---|---|
| Two waggons, One waine, Three Tumbrells, One Cart, One Cart Body, One old waine Body, One Tumbrell Body & all other Implemts. of husbandry . . . . . . . | 30 00 00 |

*In the Barne*

| | |
|---|---|
| Hay . . . . . . . . . . | 25 10 00 |
| A Syder Mill & Materialls belonging to it . . . . | 01 00 00 |
| Debts Sperate and desperate and moneys by him or in his pockett plate weareing apparrell and thinges omitted and unseen . . | 710 00 00 |
| Totall . . . | 1,327 15 09 |

## 155. John Hill

Of Wellington, taken by William Pearce and John Hill on 15 May 1712 and exhibited on 13 October 1712.

*Imprs. In the house Place*

| | |
|---|---|
| 4 Small old Brass Kettles . . . . . . . | 00 10 00 |
| 2 old Iron Pots 1 Small marmalade . . . . | 00 04 00 |
| 7 small Pewter dishes 2 plates & som spoones . . . | 00 06 00 |
| 1 old Skreene 1 old Chair & other wooden ware . . . | 00 05 06 |

*Item in the Buttery*

| | |
|---|---|
| one old flock bed & Bedsteads 2 little Barrells & other woodenware . | 00 08 00 |

*Item In the Chamber*

| | |
|---|---|
| 1 old Bed & Bedsteads & 1 old table . . . . . | 00 10 00 |

*Item above Staires*

| | |
|---|---|
| one Chaff bed & old Coffer . . . . . . | 00 04 00 |
| Item one white Cow left to my daughter mary . . . | 03 00 00 |
| one Poore Barren Cow . . . . . . . | 02 00 00 |
| one small Pigg . . . . . . . . | 00 04 00 |
| Waring Clothes . . . . . . . | 00 05 00 |
| things omitted & not seene . . . . . . . | 00 02 06 |
| | 07 18 06 |

## 156. Henry Wood

Vicar of Wellington, taken by William Icke and John Skitt on 8 January 1712–13 and exhibited on 9 October 1713.

| | |
|---|---|
| An Ovill Table & another Little Table | 00 06 06 |
| a Sett of Window Curtins in ye Parlor | 00 06 00 |
| a Couch 6s 8d, Three Cloth chaires & 2 Stooles 8s all | 00 14 08 |
| 1 Bed & furniture | 04 10 00 |
| i paire of Bedsteads | 00 03 00 |
| a Sett of Hangings & Window Curtins | 00 05 06 |
| a Quilt 3s 4d, a Close Stoole 2s, a Trunk 5s all | 00 10 04 |
| 2 paire of Sheets &; a duzen of Napkins | 00 12 00 |
| a Grate 3 fireshovells & 4 pair of Tongs & plates | 00 07 06 |
| a warming Pann 4s Eight Plates 4s all | 00 08 00 |
| 5 knifes & a forke | 00 02 00 |
| The Racks In the Kitchen | 00 08 00 |
| The Dishboard & Skreen | 00 14 08 |
| The Bacon Cratch 1s 6d, ye Curb of ye Well Buckett &c. 9s. all | 00 10 06 |
| 2 Barrells 6s 2 Saddles 2 bridles 13s 4d all | 00 19 04 |
| 1 Horse | 12 00 00 |
| The Studdy of Bookes | 45 00 00 |
| 2 Stone & a half of Flax | 00 07 06 |
| Coles | 00 07 00 |
| Hay & Flax over the Stable & to be gathered | 00 15 00 |
| Wareing Apparell & Money In Pockett | 20 00 00 |
| Reversion of a Lease | 100 00 00 |
| Things forgotten | 00 06 08 |
| | 189 14 02 |

## 157. Thomas Stanworth

Of Wellington, taken by Andrew Sockett Junr. and Thurston Sandys on 2 February 1713-14 and exhibited on 23 February 1713-14. One line is illegible on account of a fold on the original. Thomas Sockett and Robert Turner are named at the foot of the inventory as the principal creditors of the deceased.

| | |
|---|---|
| Item Imprs. | |
| 74 lbs of Pewter att 7d a pound | 02 03 02 |
| 1 Warming Pan | 00 04 00 |
| 1 Dreping Pan | 00 01 06 |
| 5 Stools | 00 01 06 |
| 1 Creen | 00 05 00 |
| 1 Dish Bench | 00 06 00 |
| 1 Cheese Tooster | 00 00 03 |
| 1 Puding Plat | 00 01 00 |
| 1 Spitt | 00 00 08 |
| 1 Ovell table | 00 04 00 |
| 1 Frying Pan | 00 01 00 |
| 2 Brass Spoons | 00 01 00 |
| 5 Iron Candlesticks | 00 00 10 |
| A Morter & Pestell | 00 01 03 |
| 1 Flesh fork & Chafin Dish | 00 01 02 |
| 1 Bar fiar sclice | 00 01 04 |
| 1 fiar sclice & Toungues | 00 01 00 |

## THE INVENTORIES OF WELLINGTON

| | |
|---|---|
| 1 pr of Brod Cobarts | 00 05 00 |
| 1 Larg Iron Plate | 00 02 00 |
| 1 Hanging Plate | 00 00 10 |
| 1 Long Plate | 00 00 08 |
| The grat & Nigarts | 00 03 00 |
| The Pot links & hucks | 00 01 06 |

*The Buttery & Seller*

| | |
|---|---|
| 3 old Barrells & 1 Tunn dish | 00 05 00 |
| 3 old Bools & Chees ladder | 00 00 08 |
| 8 Glass Bottles & 1 old funnell | 00 00 09 |
| 2 Horses | 00 02 00 |
| 2 old Peals | 00 01 00 |
| 1 Washing Tub | 00 01 00 |
| 1 small Brass kettle | 00 01 00 |
| 2 old Iron Potts | 00 02 00 |
| 1 Juge | 00 00 06 |
| 11 Trenchers | 00 01 00 |
| 4 Spoons 3 Small Steans & 2 Nogins | 00 00 08 |
| 1 Old Box | 00 00 06 |
| 1 Plank & Bord | 00 03 00 |
| 2 Pigg Trough | 00 00 06 |

*In ye Brew house*

| | |
|---|---|
| 1 Copper | 02 00 00 |
| 12 Brewing Tubs | 00 06 00 |
| 2 Small Coolers | 00 03 06 |
| 1 Strik | 00 01 06 |
| 2 Reals & 1 Plank | 00 01 06 |
| Wooden heels | 00 01 00 |
| 12 duz of Lasts old | 00 16 00 |
| for Leather & peces of leather | 01 16 00 |
| 2 old Barrells | 00 01 06 |
| 1 Old ffrying Pan | 00 00 06 |

*The Bed Over ye house*

| | |
|---|---|
| 1 Boulster & 3 Pillowes Waight 85 lbs att 6d a pound | 01 15 04 |
| 1 Coverlett & 1 Blankett & 1 Matt | 00 03 06 |
| The Bed stides & Curtens & Bed Cord | 00 06 08 |
| 1 Chest | 00 06 00 |
| 1 Trunk | 00 02 00 |
| 1 old Trunk | 00 01 00 |
| 1 Old Stoole | 00 00 04 |

*In ye Room Over ye Shop*

| | |
|---|---|
| 1 Bed & 1 Bowlster & 1 Pillow Waight 102 lbs att 6 | 02 10 00 |
| The Bed Stides & Curtens & Vallins Cord & Matt 2 Blanketts & 1 old Rugg | 01 05 00 |
| 1 pr of old hempteon sheets | 00 03 00 |
| 1 pr Pewter Pott | 00 01 00 |
| 1 Table & foorm | 00 07 00 |
| 1 Chest | 00 09 00 |

| | | |
|---|---|---|
| 1 Said Table . . . . . . . . | 00 05 00 |
| 3 Earthen Dishs & 2 Basons & 1 Mugg & Salts . . . | 00 01 00 |
| 6 Joyn Cheers . . . . . . . . | 00 12 00 |
| 1 pr of flaxen sheets & 1 Pillows beer . . . . | 00 09 00 |
| 1 Old Trunk . . . . . . . . . | 00 02 06 |
| 1 old high Crown hall . . . . . . . | 00 02 00 |
| The Looking Glass & Pickters . . . . . . | 00 06 00 |
| 1 Old Covfer & 1 old Table. . . . . . . | 00 02 06 |
| The Linens in ye Chest Over ye house . . . . | 01 00 00 |
| 3 spoons . . . . . . . . . | 00 00 06 |
| 1 Larg Press . . . . . . . . . | 00 05 00 |
| 1 Grat & Niggarts . . . . . . . . | 00 02 00 |
| 1 old Floock Bed & 2 Old Blanketts . . . . | 00 04 00 |
| 3 Olc Covfers & 1 Plank . . . . . . . | 00 03 00 |
| 5 bottles & old Warming Pan Steal & 1 Old hatchett . . | 00 01 00 |
| Peggs . . . . . . . . . . | 00 00 06 |
| Feathers . . . . . . . . . | 00 00 08 |
| ............................ . . . . . . | 00 01 04 |
| 2 Bottles . . . . . . . . . | 00 00 02 |
| 1 old Trunk & 1 old Tub . . . . . . . | 00 01 00 |
| 1 Old Blew Apporn . . . . . . . . | 00 00 09 |
| 2 Hambers & 1 Cuting knife & 1 Punchen head 1 Seise Strike . | 02 00 06 |
| 3 Seals & 1 Old Shop Tub . . . . . . . | 00 02 06 |
| 6 Ducks . . . . . . . . . | 00 02 00 |
| All Waring Aparrell . . . . . . . . | 01 10 00 |
| Som desparrage debts to the value of four pounds six shillings . | 04 06 00 |
| So         The totall of the Estate & debts . . | 28 08 05 |

The debts of the said Thomas Stanworth as apraised by us and Avowed by his creditors ar

| | | |
|---|---|---|
| Due to Mr. Leeke half a years rent . . . . | 01 18 06 |
| funeral expenses . . . . . . . . | 01 00 00 |
| The totall of his debts . . . . . . . | 55 16 05 |
| his personall Estat & debts . . . . . . . | 28 06 05 |
| | 27 10 00 |

His debts amount to more than his Estate and debts by 27.10.00

### 158. Richard Beamond

Of Cluddley, Wellington, day labourer, taken by James Izon and Samuel Deacon on 3 December 1714 and exhibited on 15 April 1714.

Imprs.
| | | |
|---|---|---|
| Five Coffers . . . . . . . . . | 00 05 00 |
| An old bed & fforms . . . . . . . | 00 05 00 |
| a Barrell & Churne . . . . . . . . | 00 02 06 |
| 1 Gaun & stund . . . . . . . . | 00 02 00 |
| 2 paire Polraikes Bounges & Grate. . . . . . | 00 01 06 |
| 4 old Pewter dishes . . . . . . . . | 00 04 00 |
| 1 Cow & Som Hay . . . . . . . . | 02 15 00 |
| wearing Aparrell . . . . . . . . | 00 06 08 |
| Total . . . | 04 01 08 |

## 159. Elizabeth Judgson

Of Wellington, innkeeper and widow, taken by James Rushbury and Nathan Peploe on 6 January 1715–16 and exhibited on 16 April 1716.

*Imprs. In the Kitchen*

| | |
|---|---|
| One Iron Jack one Grate ffire shovell & Tongues one Dreeping pan and other Iron ware . . . . . . . . | 01 00 00 |
| Item ffourteen pewter dishes nine & Twenty pewter plates Seaven Chamber potts Six pewter Quarts & Six pewter pints Seaven porrengers & Two Salts . . . . . . . . | 01 10 00 |
| Two Tables one Warmeing pan & two ffrying pans one Little Table one fforme & Three Segg Chairs . . . . . . | 00 10 00 |

*In the Butterry and the Brewhouse and Sellar*

| | |
|---|---|
| Two Brewing Stunds Three Turnells Ten Hogsheads ffive Barrells one Copper ffurnace and one Iron boyler and one Table and other wooden ware . . . . . . . . . | 06 00 00 |

*In the parlour*

| | |
|---|---|
| one ffeather Bed and Appurtences one Table Skreen one Joyned Chaire ffire Shovell and Tongues . . . . . . | 01 13 04 |

*In the New Roome*

| | |
|---|---|
| One Bed & Appurtences; one Table & one fforme . . . | 01 00 00 |

*In the Crown Chamber*

| | |
|---|---|
| Two ffeather Beds and Appurtences one Lookeing Glass Two Tables; Two fformes six Green Cloth Chaires and one Joyned Chair & one Chest . . . . . . . . . . . | 10 00 00 |

*In the parlour Chamber*

| | |
|---|---|
| One ffeather bed & appurtences one Table & one Chaire . . | 01 10 00 |

*In the Kitchen Chamber*

| | |
|---|---|
| Two ffeather beds and one fflock bed and Appurtences; one Chair two Chests & Three Boxes . . . . . . . | 05 00 00 |

*In the Garrotts*

| | |
|---|---|
| Three fflock beds and Appurtences & other Beds . . . | 01 00 00 |
| Linnens of all sorts . . . . . . . . | 15 00 00 |
| Corne & Grayne of all sorts . . . . . . | 05 00 00 |
| One Cow one Calfe; One Horse; one Mare . . . . | 09 10 00 |
| Hay in the Barnes and ffeilds . . . . . . | 20 00 00 |
| Weareing Apparell & Money in pockett & things unseen & unappraised . . . . . . . . . . | 01 00 00 |
| | 79 13 04 |

## 160. William Birch

Of Wellington, apothecary and surgeon, taken by William Sockett and John Leake on 16 April 1716 and exhibited on the same day. In his will made on 15 May 1715 he left his own house in Wellington and that occupied by Richard Richards to trustees so that the income could be paid to his niece Elizabeth Rogers and his nephew John Rogers. His kinsman Robert Johnson, mercer, received £100 and his servant maid Catherine Lewis £5.

*Imprims. In ye house*
| | |
|---|---|
| It. pewter | 02 00 00 |
| 1 Grate Candlesticks Fenders Iack & other Iron things | 01 00 00 |
| 1 Table Chairs & other wooden things 1 warming pann brass pott & other brass & Tin things | 01 00 00 |
| Bookes | 00 10 00 |

*In ye Parlour*
| | |
|---|---|
| It. 2 Tables 2 Glasses Clocke & Chines 8 cane chairs & a Chimney peice | 03 00 00 |

*In ye Little upper roome*
| | |
|---|---|
| It. 1 Bed & Furniture | 05 00 00 |
| 1 Glass. 1. paire Chest of Drawers | 02 00 00 |
| 5 Chairs & Pictures | 00 10 00 |
| 1 Little Table | 00 02 00 |

*In ye Chambr ovr ye Parlour*
| | |
|---|---|
| It. 1 bed & Furniture | 02 00 00 |
| 1 couch 2 Chests | 01 00 00 |
| boxes & chaires | 00 05 00 |

*In ye Chambr ovr ye house*
| | |
|---|---|
| It. 1 bed & Furniture | 03 00 00 |
| 1 Couch. 1. Chest. 1 Table | 02 00 00 |
| 6 Chairs – 1. Glass | 02 10 00 |

*In ye Green Roome*
| | |
|---|---|
| It. 1 Bed & Furniture | 01 00 00 |
| 1 couch. 1. Chest of Drawers | 02 00 00 |
| 4 chairs. 1. Table. 1 Spinnett | 01 00 00 |

*In ye Garrett.*
| | |
|---|---|
| It. 1. Bed & Furniture | 01 00 00 |
| 1 Chair | 00 01 00 |
| Cheeses. IL Hops 10s | 01 10 00 |

*In ye Dark Parlour*
| | |
|---|---|
| It. 1 Bed & furniture & 1. Chair | 01 10 00 |

| | | |
|---|---|---|
| 2 Barrells with some drink in . . . . . | 00 | 05 00 |
| 1 Little table & other small things . . . . . | 00 | 02 00 |

*In ye Shop*

| | | |
|---|---|---|
| It. Druggs medicine potts chests bottles morters &c. . . . | 20 | 00 00 |

*In ye cellar*

| | | |
|---|---|---|
| It. 13. vessells wth ye Drink . . . . . | 02 | 00 00 |
| 2 Tables & Glass Bottles . . . . . . | 00 | 08 00 |
| 1. Cubboard Stunds & other od things . . . . | 00 | 05 00 |

*In ye Brewhouse*

| | | |
|---|---|---|
| It. Brewing vessells & pales . . . . . . | 00 | 02 00 |
| 1. Sadle &c. . . . . . . . . | 01 | 00 00 |
| Linnens in ye house . . . . . . . | 07 | 00 00 |

*In ye Malthouse*

| | | |
|---|---|---|
| It. Malt & Barley . . . . . . . | 20 | 00 00 |
| Utensills . . . . . . . . | 00 | 15 00 |

*In ye Stable*

| | | |
|---|---|---|
| It. 1 Chest & boards . . . . . . . | 02 | 16 00 |
| 2 piggs . . . . . . . . . | 01 | 00 00 |
| Wareing Apparell . . . . . . . | 05 | 00 00 |
| moneys in ye house . . . . . . . | 200 | 00 00 |
| Plate . . . . . . . . . | 10 | 00 00 |
| Debts . . . . . . . . . | 05 | 00 00 |
| Tot . . . | 308 | 19 06 |

## 161. William Doughty

Of Wellington, gent., taken by Richard Littleton and Thurston Sandys on 7 December 1716 and exhibited on 8 March 1716–17.

*Impris. In ye House place*

| | | |
|---|---|---|
| A large Wainscott Skreen at . . . . . | 00 | 05 00 |
| A Lesser Wainscott Skreen . . . . . . | 00 | 02 00 |
| An Oval Table & Square Table . . . . . | 00 | 06 06 |
| A Dresser with Drawers . . . . . . | 00 | 06 00 |
| pewter of all sorts . . . . . . . | 03 | 10 00 |
| 3 Buffett stooles . . . . . . . | 00 | 00 06 |
| Six old Chaires . . . . . . . | 00 | 02 06 |
| Tin ware of all Sorts . . . . . . . | 00 | 02 06 |
| A warming pan . . . . . . . | 00 | 02 06 |
| An old Coffer . . . . . . . . | 00 | 02 00 |
| A Grate Niggards ffender fire shovle And Tongs links and potthooks . | 00 | 13 00 |

| | | |
|---|---|---|
| Small Iron things hanging in ye Chimney. | 00 02 06 | |
| A Chafeing Dish | 00 01 00 | |
| A Jack two Spitts Copparts & frying pan. | 00 10 00 | |
| Two Smoothing Irons a hamer a horse lock three Iron Candlesticks. | 00 04 00 | |
| Books | | |
| A Old Large Bible & six other Books | 00 10 00 | |
| And twenty other Books | 00 10 00 | |
| a bacon Cratch | 00 01 06 | |
| a Looking Glass | 00 00 06 | |
| Six knives & forkes. | 00 03 00 | |
| Six little fforks | 00 00 06 | |
| a Window Curtain & Brush. | 00 01 00 | |
| Brass Candlesticks & other Small Brass things | 00 07 00 | |

*In ye parler*

| | |
|---|---|
| a bed with all its ffurniture and window Curtains | 02 10 00 |
| 7 Chaires and eight Cushions | 00 15 00 |
| a Chest of Drawers and Glass | 00 12 06 |

*In ye Buttery*

| | |
|---|---|
| a Joynd fforme a Dresser Wooden ware & earthenware. | 00 04 00 |

*In ye Brewhouse*

| | |
|---|---|
| A Malt Mill | 01 00 00 |
| a small Spinning wheele | 00 02 00 |
| A Joyn Stoole | 00 00 04 |
| Three Tubs & two turnells a Curne Two paire of skels a Water piggin 2 peals 2 gawns | 00 15 00 |
| A brass churne four brass cettles & a saucepan a brass pott & iron pott. | 01 00 00 |

*In ye Seller*

| | |
|---|---|
| Two Barrells two firkins & two horses | 00 06 00 |

*In ye parler Chamber*

| | |
|---|---|
| Two beds with ffurniture for one. | 01 15 00 |
| an oval Table & 3 Chaires. | 00 05 00 |

*In ye Room over ye brewhouse*

| | |
|---|---|
| a bed with its furniture | 01 00 00 |
| one Chest & Coffer & old Trunk 2 old Boxes | 00 08 00 |
| 2 Corn Tubs & wisscate | 00 03 06 |
| The Close Stoole & pan a old Chaire & Table a Small box & Deske a pillon & Cloth old said sadle & 2 bridles a paile & sursogle & halter &c. | 00 05 06 |
| Two Twigon basketts | 00 01 06 |
| A hanging Shelf & furnell | 00 02 00 |

*In ye Chamber over ye house place*

| | |
|---|---|
| a bed & its ffurniture | 02 00 00 |
| Tirteen slipons of yarn 27 pound of flax. | 01 06 06 |

THE INVENTORIES OF WELLINGTON                                             351

| | |
|---|---|
| 3 Trunks & 5 Boxes . . . . . . . | 00 07 00 |
| fire shufle Tongs & fender . . . . . . | 00 04 00 |
| 5 Segg Chaires . . . . . . . . | 00 02 06 |
| A Dressing Box & Glass . . . . . . | 01 10 00 |
| a Table & Drawer & Small Glass . . . . . | 00 04 00 |
| Linnen of all sorts fifteen pounds . . . . . | 15 00 00 |
| Silver Plate . . . . . . . . . | 03 00 00 |

*Implements of husbandry* . . . . . . . 00 14 00

| | |
|---|---|
| A pigg and Cow . . . . . . . . | 05 05 00 |
| Hay in ye Stable . . . . . . . . | 03 00 00 |
| three Tubs there . . . . . . . . | 00 04 00 |
| Muck in ye Dunghill . . . . . . . | 00 05 00 |
| Wareing Apparell & money in pocket . . . . | 10 00 00 |

| | |
|---|---|
| A Chattle Lease Under John Charlton Esq. of a Tenement Called ye Broad gates dated ye thirteenth of Augt 1716 . . . . | 20 00 00 |
| Security for . . . . . . . . . | 350 00 00 |
| things unseen and forgotten . . . . . . | 00 03 06 |
| Toto . . . | 433 05 10 |

## 162. Robert Roe

Of Hadley, clerk, taken by Rowland Cotton and Thomas Moreton on 5 August 1717 and exhibited on 20 December 1717.

*Imprs. in the House place*

| | |
|---|---|
| A Dresser with drawers in it and a pewter Frame . . . | 00 06 08 |
| ffourteen pewter dishes and a pewter Bason ten pewter plates a fflagon & other pewter and two brasse Candlesticks . . . | 01 10 00 |
| A little Table and Seven old Chairs . . . . | 00 05 00 |
| A Grate Fireshovell Tongs & other Iron wares . . . | 00 07 00 |
| One Iron Jack and two spits . . . . . | 00 10 00 |
| A warming pan and pair of bellows . . . . | 00 02 00 |
| Earthen ware of all sorts & Tinware . . . . | 00 03 00 |

*In the Parlour*

| | |
|---|---|
| One Chest . . . . . . . . . | 00 13 04 |
| One Ovall Table . . . . . . . . | 00 07 06 |
| Seven Chairs two stools one skreen and one Couch . . | 00 13 04 |
| A small silver Cup and six small silver spoons . . . | 01 10 00 |
| Lynnen and Nappery Ware . . . . . . | 02 00 00 |

*In the best Chamber*

| | |
|---|---|
| A ffeather bed with Bedsted blanketts Curtains bolster and furniture | 01 00 00 |
| Eight Chairs a looking glasse and Chest . . . . | 01 00 00 |

*In the Parlour Chamber*

| | | |
|---|---|---|
| A Pendulum Clock and case | . . . . . | 02 00 00 |
| A Feather bed and Truckle bed Bedstedds blanketts & furniture | . | 02 00 00 |
| A Joyn'd Chair one other Chair two little Tables a Chest boxes and other things . . . . . . . . | | 00 10 00 |

*In the Cellar and other places*

| | | |
|---|---|---|
| Barrells and brewing vessells | . . . . . | 00 15 00 |
| A Gold Ring . . | . . . . . | 00 10 00 |
| A parsell of old Netts | . . . . . | 00 05 00 |
| A Marmett a Cooler a Kettle and pot | . . . . | 01 10 00 |
| His wearing Apparrell | . . . . . | 01 00 00 |
| Things omitted and out of sight . | . . . . | 00 05 00 |
| | | 19 02 04 |

## 163. John Shipman

Of Wellington, blacksmith, taken by John Bradshaw and Thomas Macham on 14 June 1718 and exhibited on 3 October 1718. He died on 12 June 1718.

*In the house*

| | | |
|---|---|---|
| Tow Tables 3 ordinary Segg Chaires 4 Joyne Stools | . . . | 00 08 00 |
| one Dish Bench . . . . . . . | | 00 04 00 |
| one Screen . . . . . . . . | | 00 02 00 |
| Pewter dishes and plats . . . . . . | | 01 00 00 |
| one Iron Jack And 3 Litle Spits . . . . . | | 00 04 00 |
| one fire shoofell and Tonges . . . . . | | 00 04 00 |
| one Brass pott Iron pot and one Litle Ketle . . . | | 00 05 00 |

*In the parlor*

| | | |
|---|---|---|
| one Bed and Steeds with the furniture . . . . | | 01 10 00 |
| foure Chires & Litle Stand Table . . . . . | | 00 03 06 |

*In the Chambr over the house*

| | | |
|---|---|---|
| one bed and bed steeds and furniture . . . . | | 01 10 00 |
| 4 Chaires . . . . . . . . | | 00 03 04 |
| one Chest & Trunck and one Close Stoole . . . | | 00 05 00 |
| one old Press . . . . . . . . | | 00 01 06 |

*In the Roome over the Brewhouse*

| | | |
|---|---|---|
| 3 p of ornary Bedsteeds and flock Beds and Chaf Beds and Corse Blanketts . . . . . . . . | | 00 10 00 |

*In the kitchen*

| | | |
|---|---|---|
| one old furnace and a Litle Boyler . . . . | | 01 05 00 |
| Brewing vesells and a kneding Turnell . . . . | | 00 10 00 |
| A Second hand old malt mill . . . . . | | 00 05 00 |

## THE INVENTORIES OF WELLINGTON

*In the Cellar*
| | | |
|---|---|---|
| A Leaven Barrells Greate & Small . . . . . | 01 02 00 |

*In the Shops*
| | | |
|---|---|---|
| one p of Bellows and an old andvill 9 hamers . . . . | 01 10 00 |
| A p of Pinsons 3 p of Smyths Tongs and an old vice . . . | 00 03 04 |
| Iron 20 lb weight . . . . . . . . | 00 03 04 |

| | | |
|---|---|---|
| Too Pigs 1:7:0 42 Sheepe 06 00 00 and too old horses 02 00 00 one Cow 02 00 00 and a Colt 20 shillings in all . . . | 12 07 00 |

| | | |
|---|---|---|
| his waring Aparell 01 00 00 6 pair of sheets 01 05 00 A Table Cloth & napkins 00 10 00 and 2 spining wheels 3 - 0 in all . . | 02 18 00 |
| odd small maters omitted . . . . . . . | 00 02 00 |

|  |  |
|---|---|
|  | 26 16 06 |

### 164. George Smith

Of Wellington, labourer, exhibited on 7 October 1720. The appraisers are not named, and the inventory is undated. George Smith died on 12 June 1720.

*Inpris.*
| | | |
|---|---|---|
| One old horse 1 old Mare . . . . . . . | 01 10 00 |
| One old Cow . . . . . . . . . | 01 05 00 |
| One sucking Calf . . . . . . . . | 00 06 00 |

*In the House*
| | | |
|---|---|---|
| Three small pewter dishes 6 pewter plates, ten pewter spoons, 3 old pewter porringers 1 pewter pint . . . . . . | 00 05 00 |
| Two old Iron potts . . . . . . . . | 00 01 00 |
| One small brass Caldron, & 1 brass spoon . . . . | 00 01 04 |
| One Iron grate fireshovel & tongs, & other small Iron Ware . | 00 02 06 |
| 2 old wood formes 1 small table . . . . . . | 00 02 06 |
| One Churn 1 tub 2 firkins . . . . . . . | 00 04 00 |

*In the Chamber over the Buttery*
| | | |
|---|---|---|
| One flockbed steads blankets, & other small furniture belonging to the same . . . . . . . . . | 00 05 00 |
| 2 old Coffers 2 old Boxes . . . . . . . | 00 04 00 |
| Linnens of all sorts . . . . . . . . | 00 02 06 |
| Wearing Apparel . . . . . . . . | 00 06 00 |
| things forgotten . . . . . . . . | 00 01 06 |

|  |  |
|---|---|
|  | 04 16 04 |

## 165. Jane Eastop

Of Ketley Wood, Wellington, taken by William Eastop of Ketley Wood and John Bennett of Watling Street on 15 August 1720 and exhibited on 17 August 1720.

*Imp In the house place*

| | |
|---|---|
| 1 Long Table . . . . . . . . | 00 10 00 |
| 1 old Press & Cubard 1 Little Round Table & 1 form . . . | 00 11 00 |
| 1 Kneading Tub 1 Cheese Tub & other Wooden ware . . . | 00 04 06 |
| 1 Iron Grate fire shovel & Toungs . . . . . | 00 05 00 |

*In The Roome above The House*

| | |
|---|---|
| 2 old Bedsteads and ferniture 1 old Chest 1 old Cuffer . . . | 01 02 00 |

*Cattle*

| | |
|---|---|
| 1 Pide Cow & 1 Red Cow . . . . . . | 05 10 00 |
| 1 old cow 2 2 year old Heifers . . . . . | 01 10 00 |
| 1 Calfe of the yeare . . . . . . . | 00 10 00 |
| 1 year old heifer . . . . . . . | 00 15 00 |
| Totall . . . | 10 17 06 |

## 166. William Bradshaw

Of Wellington, taken by Robert Turner and William Bates on 13 December 1720 and exhibited on 27 April 1721. The house appears to be the same one described in the inventory of Mary Bradshaw (*190*) in 1735.

*Imprs. In the Chamber over the house*

| | |
|---|---|
| A Bed and Bedstead with its furniture . . . . . | 02 00 00 |
| 6 Chairs at 6d each . . . . . . . | 00 03 00 |
| A Chest at . . . . . . . . | 00 04 00 |
| An old Cupboard . . . . . . . | 00 01 00 |
| A Looking-glass . . . . . . . . | 00 01 00 |

*Item In the Chamber over ye Parlour*

| | |
|---|---|
| A Bed with its furniture . . . . . . | 01 00 00 |
| An old Flock bed . . . . . . . | 00 01 06 |
| A Trunk, 2 Coffers, & a Close stool . . . . | 00 05 00 |
| Linens of all sorts . . . . . . . | 02 00 00 |

*Item In the Parlour*

| | |
|---|---|
| A Bed with its furniture . . . . . . | 01 10 00 |
| An old Table and Chest . . . . . . | 00 10 00 |
| An old Cupboard & 1 old Chair . . . . . | 00 04 00 |

## THE INVENTORIES OF WELLINGTON

*It: In ye House place*

| | |
|---|---|
| 2 Tables, & 1 Fourm | 00 08 00 |
| 5 old Chairs, 3 Cushions & a Joynt stool | 00 03 06 |
| Another old Table | 00 01 06 |

*It: In the Kitchin*

| | |
|---|---|
| a Table, & Fourm | 00 03 00 |
| A Screen, and 4 old Chairs | 00 05 00 |
| A Jack, and 2 Grates | 00 14 00 |
| An iron Dripping pan and 2 Spitts | 00 03 00 |
| A dish-bench, and little Wheel | 00 08 00 |
| Pewter Dishes and Plates | 01 10 00 |
| A warming, and frying Pan Fire shovel, and Tongs, and a pair of Racks | 00 06 00 |

*It: In ye Brewhouse*

| | |
|---|---|
| an old Furnnace, & Boiler | 01 00 00 |
| Brewing Vessels of all sorts | 00 12 00 |
| A Gawn, and Pail | 00 01 06 |
| 3 Barrels | 00 06 00 |
| Another old Flock-Bed, and Bedsteads | 00 05 00 |
| Two Cows | 05 00 00 |
| A Colt | 02 00 00 |
| A Pig | 01 00 00 |
| Wearing Apparel | 01 00 00 |
| Stock of Leather and Shoes | 10 00 00 |
| Money in his pocket | 01 00 00 |
| Things omitted and not seen | 00 01 00 |
| | 34 07 00 |

### 167. Richard Glover

Of Ketley, Wellington, collier, taken by John Fowler, Joshiah Freeman and Gabriel Cleaton on 18 August 1721 and exhibited on 31 July 1722.

| | |
|---|---|
| Impr. One store swine | 01 00 00 |
| An Old Table board & a little Cubbard | 00 02 06 |
| ffive small Old Chairs | 00 01 06 |
| Seven little pewter dishes & 6 old spoons | 00 06 06 |
| Two Old pewter Quarts | 00 02 00 |
| A ffire Shovell and Tongs | 00 00 08 |
| Two Old Iron potts | 00 02 00 |
| An Old ffrying pan & an Old pair of potthooks | 00 01 06 |
| Two Old Axes & two Old Shovells | 00 03 06 |
| An Old Coffer & two Spining Wheels | 00 03 06 |
| Three Barrells & three Little Tubbs | 00 12 00 |
| Two pails, & a Small old Turnill | 00 01 06 |
| A Chest & an Old Trunk | 00 09 06 |
| An Old Joyn Beadstead & a truckell Bedstead | 00 07 00 |

| | | |
|---|---|---|
| Two Old Hurden Chaff Beds two Old Ruggs, & One Old thin Blankett | | 00 09 00 |
| Three pair of Old Hurden Sheets and a Little Table Cloth | . . | 00 09 06 |
| An Old Mill & pair of Old Bedsteads and an Old press . | . . | 01 00 00 |
| A Little Old Table board at ye trench Lane | . . . | 00 05 00 |
| Hemp in ye Rough, Tewter'd and Untewtered . | . . . | 00 06 00 |
| A Smal Iron ffurnice & a Wheelbarrow . | . . . | 01 05 00 |
| Three Old Share Evills | . . . | 00 02 00 |
| His Wareing Apparrell and Money in his Pockett | . . . | 01 05 00 |
| Things Out of Sight & fforgotten . | . . . | 00 01 06 |
| The Totall is . | . . | 08 17 08 |

## 168. George Cleaton

Of Wellington, labourer, taken by William Icke and Robert Turner on 24 March 1723 and exhibited on 8 April 1724.

Imprimis
*In the houseroom*
| | | |
|---|---|---|
| One Skreen one Cupboard . . . . . . . | . | 00 05 00 |
| four old pewter dishes five plates and earthenware | . . | 00 06 04 |
| one brass kettle and a Maslin kettle . . . . | . | 00 08 00 |

Item
*in the buttery*
| | | |
|---|---|---|
| one old barrell two firkins and an Iron pott | . . . | 00 03 09 |

*In the roome over the house*
| | | |
|---|---|---|
| one flock bed & bedding . . . . . . . | . | 00 10 00 |
| One little Chest a box two small Chaires 2 Coffers and a table . | . | 00 12 06 |
| Weareing Apparell & money in his pockett | . . . | 01 00 00 |
| | | 03 05 07 |

## 169. John Hampton

Of Horton, Wellington, yeoman, taken by Thomas Studley and William Hampton on 11 July 1723 and exhibited on 5 October 1723.

| | | |
|---|---|---|
| Seven Cowes . . . . . . . . . | . | 16 00 00 |
| ffour Bullocks . . . . . . . . | . | 12 00 00 |
| ffive Twinters . . . . . . . . | . | 10 00 00 |
| Three yearlings . . . . . . . . | . | 03 00 00 |
| ffive Rearing Calves . . . . . . . | . | 02 10 00 |
| One Mare and Colt . . . . . . . | . | 05 10 00 |
| ffive sheep and three Lambs . . . . . | . | 01 15 00 |
| One hogg . . . . . . . . . | . | 00 14 00 |
| One paire of Tumbrell wheels . . . . | . | 04 10 00 |
| One waine Wheel . . . . . . . | . | 01 05 00 |
| One plow One harrow & Implemts of husbandry | . . | 01 00 00 |
| Hay in ye Barn & hay & Corne on ye ground | . . | 39 00 00 |

## THE INVENTORIES OF WELLINGTON

*In the House place*

| | | |
|---|---|---|
| Eleven pewter Dishes | 00 16 00 |
| Six pewter plates & a brass warming pann | 00 06 00 |
| Three pewter spoons & a Candlestick | 00 01 00 |
| Three Brass Kettles & one Brass pott | 01 00 00 |
| Two Iron Potts Grate fireshovell & tongues | 01 00 00 |
| A Broach, Dripping pann, Candstick & Iron pestill | 00 01 06 |
| Two tables, one Joyn fforme & five wood Chaires | 00 10 00 |

*In the parlour*

| | |
|---|---|
| One ffeather bed and furniture | 02 00 00 |
| Two tables one press Cupboard one old skreen One Box and three old Chaires | 00 15 00 |

*In the Buttery*

| | |
|---|---|
| ffour Barrells one Churn one Kneading Turnell Three brewing Stunds & other wooden ware | 01 00 00 |

*In the Chamber over ye Parlour*

| | |
|---|---|
| One fflock Bed and furniture | 00 15 00 |
| One table & frame one old coffer & one old Chaire | 00 04 00 |

*In the Chamber over ye Buttery*

| | |
|---|---|
| One ffeather Bed and furniture | 02 00 00 |
| One Table one Chest and five old Boxes | 00 15 00 |

*In the Chamber over ye house place*

| | |
|---|---|
| ffifty Cheeses, wool, flax, one old spinning wheel and other wooden ware | 03 05 00 |
| One ffeather bed Bolster and Two Blanketts | 01 10 00 |
| Linnen of all sorts | 03 00 00 |
| Ready Money | 01 00 00 |
| Wearing Apparell | 00 10 00 |
| Things forgott and unappraised | 00 05 00 |
| Tot | 117 17 06 |

## 170. Tryphosa Barnes

Of Wellington, spinster, taken by Rowland Cotton and Samuel Currier on 22 October 1723 and exhibited on 1 November 1723.

*Imprinis*

| | |
|---|---|
| one bed & all belonging is in ye best roome | 01 10 00 |
| a box of linin in ye best roome | 00 10 00 |
| bookes in ye best roome | 00 02 06 |
| one cheire & window curtains in ye best roome | 00 00 07 |
| one bed a cheire & a chest in ye next roome | 01 00 04 |

*goods in ye dineing roome*

| | |
|---|---|
| 6 cheirs 2 round tables a glass some small pictures | 00 15 00 |

*goods in ye Kitchin*

| | |
|---|---|
| 6 puter dishes ten plates ten polingers two salts | 00 12 00 |
| a puter frame a warmeing pan & a jack | 00 10 06 |
| fireshovell & tongs fender & Spit a plate chafin dishe & flesh fork | 00 05 00 |
| 3 candlesticks a candle box two dregers & a baster | 00 02 00 |
| knives & forks three cheires & a table | 00 04 00 |
| 2 silver spoones | 00 12 00 |

*Shop goods*

| | |
|---|---|
| 20 yardes of remnants of linin of all sorts | 01 00 00 |
| remnants of crape for Shrowds | 02 00 00 |
| a counter boxes Shelves & a lookeing glass | 01 14 00 |
| a box of hard sope | 00 06 08 |
| remnants of lace a box of ferreling & ribbons & fans | 00 12 00 |
| 3 paire of small scales & waights & five paper boxes | 00 04 00 |
| thread & inkle & part of a pot of snuff | 00 06 00 |
| 2 small kettles two paills & a smoothing iron | 00 05 00 |
| 2 paire of sheets | 00 10 00 |
| a small barrell in ye Seller | 00 01 00 |
| a quilt for a bed & warein apparrell | 03 00 00 |
| book debts due to ye deceased | 03 11 05 |
| The sum is | 19 14 00 |

## 171. William Judgson

Of Wellington, innkeeper, taken by Thomas Studley and Thomas Sockett on 12 July 1725 and exhibited on 19 October 1725.

| | |
|---|---|
| Two Heifers & a Bullock | 07 10 00 |
| one Mare & Colt | 05 00 00 |
| Two Swine | 02 00 00 |
| Old Hay in ye Barn & Ricke | 04 00 00 |

*In the Stable*

| | |
|---|---|
| A Wheellbarrow & other effects | 00 08 00 |

*In the Brewhouse*

| | |
|---|---|
| One Furnace, one Malt mill Cooler & other Brewing Vessells one Iron Bowler two barrells & other effects | 04 10 00 |

*In the Buttery*

| | |
|---|---|
| Two Barrells & other effects | 00 10 00 |

*In the Milkhouse*

| | |
|---|---|
| One Churne & other effects | 00 02 06 |

## THE INVENTORIES OF WELLINGTON 359

*In the Cellar*
ffourteen Barrells . . . . . . . . 03 10 00
Ale Beer & Cyder therein & other effect . . . . 15 10 00

*In the New Parlour*
One Feather Bedd & Furniture . . . . . . 03 00 00
Clock & Case . . . . . . . . . 01 10 00
one Bag of Hops . . . . . . . . 02 00 00
one Table Skreen, one Joyn'd Form, Six Leather Chairs two Small
Tables & a warming Pan . . . . . . . 01 00 00

*In ye old Parlour*
One Feather Bedd & Furniture . . . . . . 02 00 00
One Table Skreen five old Chairs & an old Coffer . . . 00 06 00

*In the Chamber over ye Kitchin*
Two Feather Bedds & Furniture . . . . . . 04 00 00
one Hanging Press, two Chests one Trunk, six old Boxes & three
old Chairs . . . . . . . . . 01 00 00

*In ye Closett by ye sd. Chamber*
one Flock bedd & Furniture . . . . . . 00 10 00

*In the Crown Chamber*
Two Feather bedds & Furniture . . . . . . 10 00 00
Two large Tables one Chest some Chairs one joyn'd Forme one
looking Glass & other small matters . . . . . 02 10 00
one parcell of Hops . . . . . . . . 01 00 00

*In the Chamber over ye old Parlour*
one Feather Bedd wth its Furniture . . . . . 04 00 00
One Chest, six Chairs two Tables & other effects . . . 01 00 00

*In ye Garretts.*
Three ordinary Bedds & Furniture & one pair of Bedsteads . . 01 10 00
Corne . . . . . . . . . . 00 08 00
Oats . . . . . . . . . . 00 06 00
One old Bathing Tub & other effects . . . . . 00 05 00

*In the Kitchin*
ffourteen Pewter Dishes . . . . . . . 01 10 00
Thirty six Pewter plates . . . . . . . 01 10 00
Pewter Quarts Pints & other Pewter . . . . . 01 10 00
one Jack . . . . . . . . . 00 10 00
one Iron Grate & other Ironware . . . . . . 01 05 00
one Brass & one Iron Pott . . . . . . . 00 18 00
Two Brass Kettles . . . . . . . . 00 06 00
one Iron Marmlett . . . . . . . . 00 01 00
one Brass Morter Pestill brass Candlesticks & other Brassware . . 00 10 00

| | | |
|---|---|---|
| one Round Table one old wooden screen seven wooden Chairs Joyn'd stooles Small Table & other wooden ware | | 01 00 00 |
| one Iron Morter & Pestill & other effects. | | 00 08 00 |
| Linnens of all Sorts . | | 15 00 00 |
| Wearing Apparrell . | | 03 00 00 |
| Ready money | | 03 00 00 |
| Things forgotten | | 00 05 00 |
| | Tot | 109 18 06 |

## 172. William Barker

Of Watling Street, innholder, taken by Robert Bolas, John Bromley and John Bennett and exhibited on 19 October 1725. The inventory is undated.

Impris. in his dwelling house in Wattling Street aforesd. as followeth (viz)

### In the Kitchin

| | |
|---|---|
| One Jack . | 00 12 00 |
| 1 Iron Grate, Iron plate, Fire Shovell & 2 pair of Tongues | 00 08 00 |
| 3 Broaches & 1 Iron dreeping pan . | 00 05 00 |
| 1 Pair of Racks 2 Iron plates & 1 grid Iron | 00 05 00 |
| 1 Frying pan 1 warming pan 1 pudding plate 1 Tin Cover & 2 Tinn dreeping panns . | 00 05 06 |
| 2 Smootheing Irons, 1 Chopping knife; 1 pair of Bellowes & 6 Iron Candle Sticks . | 00 02 06 |
| 14 Pewter dishes 1 pewter saucer 18 pewtr Plates | 00 17 00 |
| 8 pewter porrengers 3 pewter Quarts 1 pewter Pint one half pint of do; 1 pewter Salte & Mustard pott; 1 brass pepperbox & 1 pewter Cupp . | 00 09 05 |
| 1 Pewter Tankard . | 00 01 06 |
| 1 Dish board Dress & Drawers 2 little Square Tables 1 joyned Stool & one Short Dresser . | 00 12 06 |
| 1 skreen or Seat | 00 02 00 |
| 3 Chairs . | 00 01 06 |

### In the Parlour

| | |
|---|---|
| 1 Clocke & Case . | 01 00 00 |
| 1 Chest 1 little Skreen 3 Tables 1 joynd Form 1 Cupp-Board & Glass Cage 5 Chairs . | 01 08 06 |

### In the Room over the Kitchen

| | |
|---|---|
| 2 Feather Beads & Flock Beads wth appts. | 02 10 00 |
| 1 Cooler 1 Chest 1 Table & 1 joyned Chair | 00 10 00 |

### In the Room over the Parlour

| | |
|---|---|
| 2 Feather Beads wth appts. 1 Table & 1 joyned Chair . | 03 05 00 |

*In the Room over the Stable*
2 Feather Beads wth Furniture 1 little wheel 1 Cradle & 1 joyned Form . . . . . . . . . .  02 15 00

*In the Room over the Celler*
1 Feather Bead wth appts. 1 little Chest & 1 Chair . . .  02 00 00

*In the Brewhouse*
1 Furnace & Boyler 1 Cooler 2 Stunds 1 Pale 8 Trenchers 1 Brass kettle & a sauce pan . . . . . . . .  01 01 00

*In the Celler*
4 Barrells 2 Hogs heads 2 little Barrells 2 of the large Barrells with ale in . . . . . . . . . .  03 08 00

*Item In the Out buildings*
2 Swine . . . . . . . . .  02 00 00
14 Horses wth Geerses . . . . . . .  38 00 00

Item. Corn growing in a Yard by the House . . . .  06 00 00

Item In Book debts . . . . . . . .  08 00 00

                        Tot . . .  74 18 05

## 173. Joshua Taylor

Of Wellington, dyer, taken by Thomas Sockett and Francis Hampton on 10 November 1725 and exhibited on 21 April 1726.

*Imprs. In the Brewhouse*
Two ffurnaces An other Brewing Vessells together with A Dyer's Press and other Dyer's Implements . . . . .  06 10 00

*Itm. In the Kitchin*
Eighteen Small peuter dishes Two dozen of puter plates Three small Brass potts, one dish bench . . . . . . .  03 00 00
One Table one fforme, one Grate one Purgatory A fire Shovell And Tongs one ffrying Pan one dreeping and Broaches and one Jack  01 10 00

*Item In the Roome over the Kitchin*
One Bed with all other ffurniture . . . . . .  05 00 00

*Itm In the Next Roome Adjoyning*
One Bed Six Chairs one Table, One Chest and One Chest of Drawers  04 00 00
Itm. One Horse . . . . . . . .  01 10 00

*Itm. In the Two Garrotts*
One Bed, one table, one Trunke and other Lumber . . .  01 10 00

*Itm. In the Shop*
One Hanging Press one Schreen one Table and other Lumber . . 01 00 00

*Itm. In the Cellar*
Barrells and Drinke . . . . . . . . 02 00 00

Itm. Linnens And wearing Apparell together with other Things forgotten and omitted . . . . . . 03 00 00

                                                                                                  29 00 00

## 174. Andrew Sockett, Snr.

Of Wellington, mercer, taken by William Massey and John Bradshaw on 21 November 1725 and exhibited on 21 April 1726.

*Impris. In the Workhouse*
| | |
|---|---|
| One Iron Furnace . . . . . . . . | 01 10 00 |
| Five tallow Tubbs . . . . . . . . | 01 10 00 |
| One Mold Table & Scraper . . . . . . | 00 05 00 |
| 18 dozn. of Candle-Rodds . . . . . . | 00 18 00 |
| One tallow seive and a Small Gaun & one Iron pan . . | 00 03 00 |
| one old Tallow Trough & two knifes . . . . | 00 02 06 |
| four Wooden Railes . . . . . . . | 00 02 00 |
| Candles: 14 dozn and a halfe at four shillings and six pence p dozn ; | 03 05 00 |
| Renderd Tallow 4: Hundred . . . . . | 06 00 00 |
| two Pack Saddles & 2 pair of Panniers . . . . | 00 10 00 |
| One Iron Beam herwingles and other Lumber . . . | 00 02 00 |

*In the Kitchen*
| | |
|---|---|
| One Iron Marment & other Brasse Furnace . . . | 01 10 00 |
| one pair of Iron Gobbetts . . . . . . | 00 02 06 |
| one Iron dreeping Pan . . . . . . | 00 01 04 |
| one frying Pan . . . . . . . | 00 01 00 |
| one Cupp-board . . . . . . . | 00 03 00 |
| one powdering tubb with a Covre . . . . . | 00 02 06 |
| one Brewing stund . . . . . . . | 00 03 00 |
| one Dogg wheel . . . . . . . | 00 01 06 |
| one half hoggshead 2 more att Betty Hansons one lent Dorothy Webb | 00 18 00 |
| 2 quarter Barrells one at Betty Hanson & the other at Will. Jennings one more & one other . . . . . . | 00 08 00 |

*In the Shopp*
ten Chests of Boxes and one Desk Eleven Drawers and one Box four Counters & one in Dan. Turnors Shopp . . . . . 00 10 00

*In the Little Chamber*
| | |
|---|---|
| One Chest a little Table 2 Trunks . . . . . | 00 12 00 |
| One Close stool Case . . . . . . . | 00 03 00 |

# THE INVENTORIES OF WELLINGTON

*In the room over the house*

| | |
|---|---|
| one Bead and steads and Furniture | 01 10 00 |
| one Side Table | 00 00 06 |
| one Sett of Drawers | 00 16 00 |
| one Cabbinett with Drawers | 00 04 00 |

*In the Chamber over the Shop*

| | |
|---|---|
| 20 Cane Chairs | 03 02 00 |
| one large Chest of Drawers | 02 06 00 |
| a side Table and Small Cabbinett | 00 08 00 |
| a large looking Glasse | 01 01 00 |

*In a Garrett*

| | |
|---|---|
| one Box | 00 02 00 |
| and in a by Room empty grocery Barrells & other Lumber | 00 04 00 |

*In the lodging Garrett*

| | |
|---|---|
| 2 Bedds and Beddsteads | 03 08 00 |
| one small Chest one little Box | 00 03 00 |
| one Pair of Beadsteads taken asunder and other Lumber | 00 06 00 |

*In another Garrett*

| | |
|---|---|
| a Spinning Wheel & little wheel Beddsteads taken down wires and other Lumber | 00 04 00 |

*In another Garrett*

| | |
|---|---|
| one Bead and Bead-steads and one Coffer and Chains of Iron and other Lumber three boards a wooden Beam a wire Riddle and other Lumber. a cutting Knife and Iron Casemt. and a Cast Chamber Grate | 00 12 00 |

*In the house*

| | |
|---|---|
| 20 Pewter Dishes large and small 19 Plates one Sallvre a Candlestick and one Tankard | 03 04 06 |
| a little Brasse Pott and little Massling kettle | 00 04 06 |
| and a little Flanders Kettle | 00 00 06 |
| two round Tables one warming Pan | 00 09 00 |
| one Iron Grate fire shovell & Tongues | 00 04 00 |

*In the Barn*

| | |
|---|---|
| Hay | 00 10 00 |
| The Mare and Colt | 02 10 00 |
| one Pigg | 01 00 00 |
| a large Beam & Scales weights with another Beam and other Scales | 01 00 00 |

| | |
|---|---|
| His wareing apparell & for things omitted | 01 00 00 |

*In the Room over the workhouse*

| | |
|---|---|
| An Ingene to cut tobacco & a Screw & all materials belonging thereto | 08 00 00 |
| | 51 01 04 |

## 175. John Turner

Of Arleston, Wellington, taken by Thomas Holland and William Podmore on 30 May 1726 and exhibited on 18 October 1726.

Imp:

| | |
|---|---|
| ffour Oxen and Six Bullocks | 30 00 00 |
| ffive Cows and one year old heifer | 15 00 00 |
| ffive Calves | 02 00 00 |
| One Mare | 05 00 00 |
| Thirteen Sheep & one Lamb | 02 10 00 |
| One wagon & two Tumbrells | 07 10 00 |
| Two Wain bodies with two paire of Riples & one old pair of Wheels | 02 00 00 |
| Plows & harrows wth yokes & Chaines | 01 05 00 |
| Corn & Hay in the barn | 04 10 00 |
| Two Store Pigs | 02 00 00 |
| Corn and Grain in the field | 50 00 00 |

*In the house place*

| | |
|---|---|
| One Clock two tables one dish bench one skreen one Jack & nine Joyn Stooles one Grate two fire shovells two pair of tongues wth other small thinges | 04 00 00 |
| It. Brass & Pewter four spits four chairs | 07 00 00 |

*In the little Chamber*

| | |
|---|---|
| One Bed two presses one Table Seaven Joyn Stooles and one old coffer | 02 00 00 |
| It. Two Beds one Press 2 Coffers 3 Boxes | 03 00 00 |

*In the Room over the little Chamber*

| | |
|---|---|
| Two Beds wth their ffurneiture one pair of Bedsteads two Chairs & one old Table | 03 15 00 |

*In the Room over the house place*

| | |
|---|---|
| One Bed wth its ffurneiture one hanging press two Chests three Tables seaven Chairs one Box a looking Glass | 04 05 00 |

*In the kitchen*

| | |
|---|---|
| One ffurnace wth brewing vessells one Cheese press | 02 00 00 |

*In the Buttery*

| | |
|---|---|
| ten Barrels | 01 10 00 |

*In the dairy*

| | |
|---|---|
| One Cheestub two pails two Gawns two Mits One Churn wth some other Wooden Vessels | 01 05 00 |

*In the Malt house*

| | |
|---|---|
| One Malt mill one Table leafe four spinning wheels | 00 15 00 |

THE INVENTORIES OF WELLINGTON

| | | |
|---|---|---|
| Money in his Pocket wth Wearing Apparell . . . . | 145 00 00 |
| Linnen wth thinges unseen or forgotten . . . . . | 05 00 00 |
| Totall . . . | 312 00 00 |

## 176. Mary Banger

Of Wellington, taken by John Bradshaw and John Rowley on 7 July 1726 and exhibited on 18 October 1726.

| | |
|---|---|
| Imprs. Three Small pewter Dishes . . . . . . . | 00 03 06 |
| Eleaven Small plates. . . . . . . . . | 00 04 00 |
| One Brass Ketle pot & an old bust sausepan An old brass Hand Candlestick A Masling Ketle . . . . . . | 00 05 00 |
| One Old Warming pan . . . . . . . | 00 01 06 |
| One Chest of Drawers Old ffashion . . . . . | 00 06 08 |
| One old Worm Eaten Table . . . . . . . | 00 02 06 |
| One Small Round Table . . . . . . . | 00 02 00 |
| ffour Old ffashion Lined pictures . . . . . . | 00 05 00 |
| One Dozen & a halfe of other pictures very small . . | 00 02 00 |
| One Old over worn Couch . . . . . . . | 00 03 00 |
| One Old bed & bowlster & all things thereunto belonging . . | 01 00 00 |
| ffour Old Worm Eaten Chaires . . . . . . | 00 00 06 |
| A very small paire of Tonges & A small ffire shovell & proker . . | 00 01 06 |
| One parcell of Lumber Stuff . . . . . . | 00 01 06 |
| Two Small Silver Spoons & A Silver pint . . . . . | 01 15 00 |
| Tot . . . | 04 14 08 |

## 177. William Icke

Of Leegomery, Wellington, taken by Robert Turner and John Hooper on 9 September 1726 and exhibited on 21 October 1726.

| | |
|---|---|
| Imprs. Seaventeen Cows and bullocks and 2 Calves . . . | 40 00 00 |
| three mares and a Colt . . . . . . . | 10 00 00 |
| Seaven Lambs and one Sheep . . . . . . | 00 18 00 |
| three piggs . . . . . . . . . | 02 10 00 |
| Barley, Pease and Oates . . . . . . . | 08 00 00 |
| hay and Chees . . . . . . . . | 12 00 00 |
| Rye and Muncorn . . . . . . . . | 04 00 00 |

*In the house place*
| | |
|---|---|
| Brass and pewter . . . . . . . . | 02 10 00 |
| two tables and a Dish bench . . . . . . . | 00 15 00 |
| a Jack and 2 spitts & some small Irons belonging to the fire place . | 00 15 00 |
| Six Chairs and old Clock and a Mortar . . . . . | 01 06 00 |

*In the Parlour att Lee*
| | |
|---|---|
| a bed and press 3 tables and a Stand . . . . . | 04 00 00 |

*In the Chamber Over ye Parlour*

| | |
|---|---|
| one bed and Furniture . . . . . . | 04 00 00 |
| two Chests with Linnens and three Chairs . . . . | 05 00 00 |

*In the Kitchen*

| | |
|---|---|
| a boiler and furnace . . . . . . . . | 02 05 00 |
| Brewing Vessells & a Cheese press and table . . . . | 01 00 00 |

*Over the house place*

| | |
|---|---|
| 2 beds and one Coffer . . . . . . . | 06 00 00 |

*Over the Kitchen*

| | |
|---|---|
| one bed . . . . . . . . . | 01 00 00 |
| a few other boards and Railes . . . . . . | 00 05 00 |
| Corn and Cheese in the house and Malt . . . . | 06 00 00 |
| Bacon and Butter . . . . . . . . | 01 00 00 |

*In the Cellar*

| | |
|---|---|
| Seaven barrells and a Wooden bottle . . . . . | 01 08 00 |
| Two old Carts and 2 tumbrells and a pr of Harrows . . | 04 00 00 |
| Coales and Old bookes . . . . . . . | 02 00 00 |

*In the Parlour at Kinnersley*

| | |
|---|---|
| Six Segg'd Chairs 12 wooden Chairs a table a Chest of drawers a Looking glass a small cubbard & a form . . . . . | 01 10 00 |

*In the house room*

| | |
|---|---|
| fiveteen pewter dishes a dish bench a Clock three spitts two dripping pans a Salt box a table a grate two fire shovels and tongs three Candlesticks four brass bosses two froggs a glass crate a fender a small Looking glass and twenty four plates . . . . | 04 00 00 |

*In the Kitchen*

| | |
|---|---|
| two brass potts a brass Kettle two marmitts a frying pan a Stund two barrells three Cheese mitts a milk boal a Cheese tub one Cooler three benches a wooden bottle a tun dish a Churn a Cheese press a pr. of Racks an ax a broom hook and bill . . . . | 01 10 00 |

*In the Roome Over the house*

| | |
|---|---|
| three feather beds Six blanketts and ruggs and Old Coffer a trunk a Joyn'd Stools and a half Strike . . . . . . | 03 00 00 |

*In the Room Over the Parlour*

| | |
|---|---|
| One bed with the furniture 2 Chests and 2 beds in them with Some Linnen two Chests more two Small tables a Trunk a flaskett and two basketts . . . . . . . . . | 04 00 00 |

*In the Cellar*

| | |
|---|---|
| three barrells one bench one iron Crow . . . . | 00 05 00 |

## THE INVENTORIES OF WELLINGTON

| | |
|---|---|
| Old Plate | 05 00 00 |
| three old Leases | 100 00 00 |
| One bond Debt | 20 00 00 |
| Wearing apparrell and Money in his pockett | 10 00 00 |
| Things Omitted and Not Seen | 00 10 00 |
| tot | 270 07 00 |

### 178. John North

Of Ketley, Wellington, taken by Robert Cleaton and Joseph Freeman on 2 November 1726 and exhibited on 18 April 1727.

| | |
|---|---|
| Imprimis ffour Cows two Twinter heifers 2 Calves | 14 10 00 |
| An old mare & two Coults | 07 00 00 |
| Therty sheep & Lambs | 05 00 00 |
| one Swin & two Store pigs | 02 10 00 |

*In the house*

| | |
|---|---|
| A Clock and Pewter | 02 15 00 |
| one Brass Kettle a warming pan & two potts | 00 12 00 |
| Tinn a 'ware | 00 01 00 |
| Two Spitts, 2 dreeping pans, an Iron furnis and old Jack | 00 18 06 |
| One Grate, fireshovell & Toungs, a marmit | 00 09 00 |
| Potgeales and other smal Iron things | 00 01 06 |
| Two Tables, Two furms, three stools, | 00 08 00 |
| Three Chaires, and a Glasscage | 00 02 00 |
| A little paire of Cooberts and a doz. & halfe of Trenchers | 00 02 06 |

*In ye Parlour*

| | |
|---|---|
| A Bed and furniture | 01 05 00 |
| An old hanging Press, a little Table, and Chests | 00 09 00 |
| An old Trunck a Little looking Glass a little case of drawers | 00 03 06 |
| A wooden Chaire a little box and a little old Grate | 00 01 06 |

*In the Buttery*

| | |
|---|---|
| Three Barrils a Press and a Cheese Press | 00 17 00 |
| A Churn and Brewing vessells | 00 07 00 |

*Over ye Parlour*

| | |
|---|---|
| One Bed and a little folding Bed | 01 10 00 |
| Two Boxes and a Chair | 00 01 06 |

*Over ye Stable*

| | |
|---|---|
| an old pair of Bedsteeds and 3 old wheels | 00 05 00 |
| Two old Turnils; and 3 old boxes | 00 05 06 |
| Two Straw wisketts | 00 01 03 |
| Lying | 02 00 00 |
| Impliments of husbandry | 00 15 00 |
| Books | 00 06 00 |

|  |  |
|---|---|
| Corn in the Barn | 01 10 00 |
| heay | 01 05 00 |
| Corn upon the Grownd | 01 10 00 |
| Wareing apparell and mony in the pockett | 02 00 00 |
| ffor Lumber and things not seen | 00 03 00 |
|  | 49 04 09 |

## 179. Richard Roe

Of Wellington, tailor, taken by John Bradshaw and Thomas Tudor on 17 February 1727–28 and exhibited on 23 April 1728.

*In the Workehouse & Chamber*

|  |  |
|---|---|
| A Chest and Linings given by his will to his sister Jane Allso Given the said Jane his sister A Bed and Steeds and all furniture theareunto Belonging | — — — |
| In the same Roome & workehouse one old chaor and 2 Cusions | 00 01 06 |
| Allso a Cofer and a Large Box | 00 06 00 |
| Allso an other old Coffer | 00 01 06 |
| Allso 2 other Little Boxes | 00 01 06 |
| Allso an ordinary Tuckle bed with ordnary Corse Bedding | 00 18 00 |

*In the House*

|  |  |
|---|---|
| one Iron marmett | 00 01 03 |
| Allso foure dishes and 2 plates | 00 05 10 |
| Allso one dish bench | 00 02 06 |
| Allso a litell Brass morter and pestell | 00 05 06 |
| Allso one old Chair & cushion | 00 01 04 |
| Allso one Table Board | 00 03 00 |
| Allso one Joyne stoole | 00 01 00 |
| Also 2 old Segon Chayars | 00 01 00 |
| Allso one Little Payle | 00 01 06 |
| Allso one Bench | 00 01 06 |
| Allso one other Little payle | 00 00 06 |
| Allso one Iron Grate Tonges fire shofell And other Iron Things | 00 07 00 |
| Allso one Little frying Pan | 00 01 00 |
| Allso an old paire of Bellowes | — — — |
| Allso 3 Little Shilfes to put glasses on | 00 01 00 |

*In the Buttery*

|  |  |
|---|---|
| Tow Small Barells 2 Small pudering Tubbs A Bole dish and Dish Crach | 00 04 00 |
| The deseaseds Apparell Given a way in his Life time | — — — |
| money In the deseaseds posession | 05 16 07¼ |

*Moneys due upon Bond*

|  |  |
|---|---|
| one Bond given by mr William Hayard in his Life Time to Richard Roe Deceased for the payment of | 20 00 00 |

THE INVENTORIES OF WELLINGTON

| | | |
|---|---|---|
| other Securityes to the value of . . . . . . | 67 | 00 00 |
| Booke debts to the pty deceased . . . . . | 05 | 00 00 |
| Things omitted 2s . . . . . . . | 00 | 02 00 |
| | 100 | 17. 04¼ |

## 180. Richard Hancox

Of Wellington, surgeon, taken by John Bradshaw and Thomas Ward on 14 April 1728 and exhibited on 25 April 1728.

*Imprs. In the Kitchen*

One Iron grate, and Iron Fendr. fire Shovel and Tongs one frying pan One pair of Links Six Iron Candlesticks Two Spitts One Jack one pair of bellows one Iron dripping pan 12 Small pewter dishes 18 pewter plates one dish bench Two Small Tables five Chairs One Spinning Wheels One Joynt Stool one looking glass one warming pan . . . . . . . . . . . 02 04 00

*In the Kitchen Chamber*

One Chest of drawers one Table Six Small Chairs and looking glass . 00 10 00

*In the Little Room*

Two feather beds & Steads Two Chairs and a Chest of Drawers . 02 03 03

*In the Cock Lofts*

One feather bed & Steads & furniture Two old Chairs one feather bed and furniture one Table & one Chair one Chest with Linnen in Two Small barrells . . . . . . . . 04 01 00

| | | |
|---|---|---|
| Wareing Apparell . . . . . . . . | 00 | 02 06 |
| thinges omitted & not seen being Lumber . . . . | 00 | 02 06 |
| | 09 | 03 03 |

## 181. John Bromley

Of Watling Street, Wellington, blacksmith, taken by Robert Bolas and Thomas Ward on 27 June 1728 and exhibited on 16 October 1728.

*Imprs. In the Turn pike house*

| | | |
|---|---|---|
| One Chaff bed & bedsteads with a Cover & a blankett . . . | 00 | 03 06 |
| One Small table with a drawer in it & one Small Square table . . | 00 | 02 06 |

*In the house place*

| | | |
|---|---|---|
| Twelve Small pewter dishes . . . . . . | 01 | 04 00 |
| thirteen old Batter'd plates . . . . . . . | 00 | 04 00 |
| a dish board . . . . . . . . | 00 | 03 06 |
| one old batter'd warming pan . . . . . . | 00 | 01 00 |

| | |
|---|---|
| one Ovall Table & 2 fforms. | 00 06 00 |
| Two Small Tables & 1 old Chair | 00 01 00 |
| Thirteen old Trenchers | 00 00 09 |
| One old Small grate ffire shovell and Tongs | 00 01 09 |
| One Tin Cover & Cheese Toster | 00 00 04 |
| One old Spinning wheel | 00 00 09 |

*In the room over the house*

| | |
|---|---|
| Two Joyn bed steads & Course bedding upon them &c. | 02 00 00 |
| One long Table one Chest one Coffer | 00 10 00 |

*In the Brewhouse*

| | |
|---|---|
| Two Small barrells two small tubs & 1 old Cooler One washing Turnell One pale & 2 small potts. | 00 05 00 |

*In the Shop*

| | |
|---|---|
| One pair of bellows, one old hanvill one vice & some old Tools | 01 01 00 |
| Two paire of old Scales | 00 10 00 |
| things omitted & not seen | 00 02 09 |
| | 06 18 02 |

## 182. John Moss

Of Wellington, shoemaker, taken by Robert Morris and William Cooper on 30 July 1728 and exhibited on 16 October 1728.

*In the Garrat*

| | |
|---|---|
| Leather | 00 10 00 |
| Wooden Cloggs | 00 01 00 |

*In the Chamber*

| | |
|---|---|
| Two beds & furnitures | 01 10 00 |
| Two tables | 00 02 06 |
| 4 boxes & 2 Coffers | 00 03 00 |
| 6 Chairs | 00 01 00 |

*In the house place*

| | |
|---|---|
| pewter of all Sorts | 00 06 00 |
| a dish bench | 00 02 06 |
| a folding table & 1 Skreen | 00 02 00 |
| Iron ware of all sorts | 00 02 06 |
| 1 Spinning wheel & 2 Chairs | 00 01 00 |

*In the Shop*

| | |
|---|---|
| 30 pair of Shoes | 03 10 00 |
| 5 Seates and tooles | 00 03 00 |
| things forgotten & omitted | 00 05 00 |
| | 06 19 06 |

## 183. Henry Adams

Of Wellington, shoemaker, taken by William Stanworth and John Adams on 9 March 1728-29, and exhibited on 8 April 1729. He died on 6 March 1728-29.

| | |
|---|---|
| goods in the house and Brass & pewter of all sorts . . . | 06 00 00 |
| goods in the parlour one table Chairs . . . . . . . | 01 00 00 |
| goods In The Roome over the parlour 2 Beds with their furnetur one Chest of drawers and Table & Chairs . | 08 00 00 |
| goods in th roome over the house 2 Beds & furniture one Chest one Table Two Trunks & Chairs . | 05 00 00 |
| Linnen of all sorts . . . . . . . . | 03 00 00 |
| a Stock of barly & Malt . . . . . . . | 20 00 00 |
| a Stock of Lether & Shoes in the Shop . . . . . | 12 00 00 |
| a Stock of Hay in the Barn . . . . . . . | 04 00 00 |
| five Cows . . . . . . . . . | 18 00 00 |
| 2 swine . . . . . . . . . . | 01 10 00 |
| Mony upon Bond . . . . . . . . | 100 00 00 |
| Mony & debts desperate . . . . . . . | 30 00 00 |
| The deceased wearing apparell & Mony in pockett . . . | 08 00 00 |
| Things omitted & forgotten . . . . . . | 00 10 00 |
| Totall . . . | 217 00 00 |

## 184. John Brown

Of Wellington, glover, taken by William Cookson and Thomas Smart on 20 December 1729 and exhibited on 30 April 1730.

| | |
|---|---|
| Imprs. 29 Duz: of Pelts . . . . . . . | 02 18 00 |
| 14 skins of Tan Leather . . . . . . . | 00 08 00 |
| 33 Caplins . . . . . . . . . | 00 11 00 |
| 41 Kyps & Calbe skins . . . . . . . | 02 01 00 |
| 5 Duz: of White leather . . . . . . . | 00 10 00 |
| 5 Horse Hydes . . . . . . . . | 00 15 00 |
| peices for Caplins & lacins . . . . . . . | 00 05 00 |
| 23 Duz: of Wash leather shipskins . . . . . . | 09 04 00 |
| 4 Duz: of Wash lamb skins . . . . . . . | 00 16 00 |
| 1 Duz: of Ash coulor gloves . . . . . . | 00 08 00 |
| 1 Duz: of wash leather Gloves . . . . . . | 00 06 00 |
| 1 Duz: of Childrens gloves . . . . . . . | 00 03 00 |
| 2 Duz of Childrens gloves & Mittins . . . . | 00 04 00 |
| 10 paire of Mittins for Women . . . . . . | 00 05 00 |
| 1 Duz: of Mens Mittins . . . . . . . | 00 06 00 |
| 3 Duz: of White skins . . . . . . . | 00 12 00 |
| 9 stone of Woole . . . . . . . . | 02 15 00 |
| Rubbidge peices of White Leather . . . . . | 00 10 00 |
| 2 Beds & 2 Bedsteads & 2 Boulsters with 2 Coverlets & 2 Blanketts . | 02 10 00 |
| Lynnen & pewter . . . . . . . . | 02 04 00 |

| | | |
|---|---|---|
| Wareing Apparell . . . . . . . | 01 10 00 |
| money . . . . . . . . | 100 00 00 |
| | 129 01 00 |

## 185. John Rowley

Of Wellington, taken by William Clarke and Francis Hampton on 12 January 1729-30 and exhibited on 29 April 1730.

*Imprs. In the Kitchen.*

| | |
|---|---|
| 12 pewter Dishes . . . . . . . | 01 04 00 |
| 14 pewter plates . . . . . . . | 00 07 00 |
| 3 pewter quarts 3 pints 4 porringers and some other Small pewter things . . . . . . . . . | 00 04 00 |
| A Dish bench 2 Little tables 5 Chairs an Old Skreen a glass Crate A bacon Cratch a Salt box 2 Cubbards . . . . | 01 02 06 |
| A Dripping pan an Iron grate a fire Shovell and a pr of tongs two Spitts a Jack and Some other Small things . . . | 02 05 00 |
| a flitch of Beef . . . . . . . . | 00 05 00 |
| A Warming pan a Little brass kettle an Iron pott a Marmett a pr of Scales . . . . . . . . . | 00 05 00 |

*In the Brewhouse*

| | |
|---|---|
| three Coolers 2 old tubbs two Little barrells with Alegar a Lading gaun with Some Other Small Wooden Vessells . . . | 03 00 00 |
| a ffurnace . . . . . . . . | 00 10 00 |
| A Sow and piggs . . . . . . . | 02 00 00 |

*In the parlour*

| | |
|---|---|
| eighteen Old pictures . . . . . . . | 00 05 00 |
| A Skreen a round table four Old Chaires 4 Little basketts two Old flasketts . . . . . . . . | 00 15 00 |

*In the room over the kitchen*

| | |
|---|---|
| A Bed with the furniture . . . . . . | 01 10 00 |
| two Chaires five old boxes . . . . . . | 00 07 00 |
| two Coffers a trunk a Chest . . . . . | 00 08 00 |

*In the room over the parlour*

| | |
|---|---|
| Two beds and bedstedds with the Furniture and one Other Old bed . | 05 00 00 |
| A Long table and foorm a Little table A Joyn'd Chest an Old Chaire . | 00 10 00 |

*In the room over the Shop*

| | |
|---|---|
| One Old bed and bedsteds one other pr of bedsteds a packell a Little Wheel with Some Other Small things . . . . | 00 12 00 |
| A Mare . . . . . . . . | 03 00 00 |
| hay . . . . . . . . . | 00 10 00 |

# THE INVENTORIES OF WELLINGTON

| | |
|---|---|
| Some druggs. | 05 00 00 |
| Hemp. | 00 10 00 |
| Muck and ffaggots. | 00 05 00 |

*In the Cellar*

| | |
|---|---|
| eleven barrells four whereof with Ale | 05 17 00 |
| potatoes with a few bottles. | 00 15 00 |
| Linnen and Yarn | 02 00 00 |
| a Sadle | 00 05 00 |
| A Lease | 15 00 00 |
| Wearing apparrell & Money in his pockett | 01 10 00 |
| ffor things Omitted and Not Seen. | 00 05 00 |
| tot | 53 06 06 |

## 186. William Cooper

Of Wellington, gent., taken by William Evans and Thomas Ward on 9 September 1730 and exhibited on 29 October 1730.

*Impr. In the Kitchen*

One Grate two pair of Tongs & 2 Fir shovels One haning plate one Iron dreping pan One Grid Iron One Iron purgatory One pair of Iron Racks three Smoothing Irons One Spitt One ffendr. Six brass Candlesticks & one Iron one Knarce One brass Skimmr. One Tin Skimmr. One Iron fflesh ffork One brass baisting apoon. One pestall One Iron Mortar One brass Mortar Eight Iron Skuers One pair of brass snuffers One Jack One ffrying pan One Fowling peice. On sword One bacon Cratch Six pewter dishes thirty pewter plates One pewter Tankard 3 pewter poringers three pewter Salts One warming pan One pewter Ladle One Tinn Cullindr One Tin Cover. One Tin apple Roaster One Tin Tunning dish One Tin peppr box & 1 Tin drudger| Four brass Kettles. One brass pott One Coppr pott & 1 brass Lid. Two Saucepans One Coppr. can One Clock & Case One dresser of drawers one Skreen two tables, One Salt box one Chafing dish two Joyn Chairs & 1 Stool One hand Saw One brush One Tin dripping pan.     08 00 00

*In the parlour*

Six Cain Chairs Six Leather Chairs One Table One Couch One Looking Glass Six large Glass pictures four small ones 2 Skonces four maps King Williams Speech in fframe One pewter standish     02 19 10

*In the Cellars*

Three horses Six barrells One bench One Table, Six Knives & Six fforks.     01 01 06

*In the Brewhouse*

Two Iron Marmotts One Coppr ffurnace One Iron boyler 2 brewing stunds One Close bowl One Tun dish One Search One hair sive two

large coolers 3 small Turnells One half strike One half peck, One
horse, two pales One Coppr pudding pan . . . . .    05 09 04

*In the Chambr over the Cellar*
One ffeather bed 2 blanketts One Quilt One Boulster & 1 pillow
bedsteads & courtains.
One Chest with Linnens in as follows:—
one douzen of french diapr Napkins a Table Cloth
One douzn of huckaback Napkins & Table Cloth
Ten plain fflaxen Napkins & Table Cloth
six Course Towells & three pair of pillow beers
Six pair of ffine fflaxen Sheets
One small diapr table cloth
One Stool . . . . . . . . .    09 10 00

*In the Chambr over the Kitchen*
One ffeather bed One boulstr four blanketts & quilt One pair of
Bedsteads & Courtains One Table three Chairs One Looking Glass .    04 07 00

*In the Chambr over ye parlour*
One ffeather bed boulstr two blanketts One Quilt bedsteads &
courtains three cain chairs One large cain chair Window Courtains
One Close Stool One Chest of drawers One large bible One pockett
pistoll twenty five bookes of several sorts . . . .    07 05 00

*At the Stair head*
One ffoulding bed steads ffeather bed One blankett Coverled &
Courtains . . . . . . . . . .    01 10 00

*In the Cock Lofts*
One ffeather bed two blanketts & Coverlid bedsteads & Courtains
two hanging presses One Little Coffer One Long wheel One small
wheele One pewter dish three barrells One childs ffendr. three Joyn
Chairs . . . . . . . . . . .    03 10 00

*In the Stable*
One mair: & hay in the ground . . . . . .    06 00 00

money in pockett & wearing Apparrell . . . . .    40 00 00
In Securitys . . . . . . . . . .   120 00 00
things omitted & not seen . . . . . . .    00 05 00

            Total .  . .   209 18 02

## 187. John Walford

Of Wellington, apothecary and surgeon, taken by John Fowler and
Peter Langley on 9 March 1730-31 and exhibited on 6 May 1731.

Imprs.
One Mare . . . . . . . . . .    04 00 00

# THE INVENTORIES OF WELLINGTON

| | |
|---|---|
| One Colt | 02 00 00 |
| a parcell of hey | 01 00 00 |
| for a Small pcell of ffitches. | 00 02 06 |

*In the room ovr the parlour*

| | |
|---|---|
| One bed bedsteads & all things belongeing to it, One Little Table One Chair One box & window Hangings | 01 05 00 |

*In the Room over the Shop*

| | |
|---|---|
| One Chest, One Trunk, two Small boxes and a Chest of drawers | 01 10 00 |

*In the Room ovr the Kitchen*

| | |
|---|---|
| One bed & all things belonging to it, One Chair & two boxes | 03 00 00 |
| a Little Table & 2 Chairs | 00 04 00 |

*In the Kitchen*

| | |
|---|---|
| Iron Ware | 00 15 00 |
| a dish board & pewter | 01 10 00 |
| One Table & 3 Chairs | 00 12 00 |

*In the Little Room*

| | |
|---|---|
| Two Small barrells & 2 brewing Stuns | 00 10 00 |
| a parcell of squar'd boards | 02 10 00 |
| For Linnen of all Sorts | 01 00 00 |
| Linnen yarn 14 pounds | 00 10 00 |
| 1 douzn of hemp | 00 05 00 |
| A Course hempen bed Tick. | 00 10 00 |
| 2 old fowling peices | 00 06 00 |
| One Old Sadle & 2 Rideing whips | 00 05 00 |
| One Still | 00 10 06 |
| Drugs, Counters & boxes & Instrumts in ye Shop | 30 05 07 |
| Booke debts | 05 00 00 |
| One boyler & pott | 00 03 00 |
| Waring Apparrell & money in pockett | 01 10 00 |
| Things omitted & not seen | 00 05 00 |
| Total | 59 08 07 |

## 188. Thomas Bryan

Of Wellington, farrier, taken by Charles Dixon and John Davies on 19 February 1731–32 and exhibited on 28 April 1732.

*Imprs. In the Kitchen.*

Eight pewter dishes Ten pewtr. plates two pewter porringers One long Table & two fforms two pewter quarts One pewter pint One pewter Salt One brass kettle One ffrying pan One Stund One grate Mill One Joynt Stool one half pewter pint One Iron Marmitt four brass Candle Sticks two Choprs two Spitts one Grate fire shovell & tongs, One ffrying pan One fflesh ffork & dripping pan three Chairs

|  |  |
|---|---|
| a pair of bellows One plate One Iron pott One Iron Mortar & one Iron pestall one brass Kettle . . . . . . | 01 08 02 |

*In the passage and Cellar*

|  |  |
|---|---|
| Two barrells One Spade One pick One Sherrwill and 1 pale . . | 00 09 00 |

*In the Chambr over the Kitchen*

|  |  |
|---|---|
| One Clock One long Table one oval Table two ffeather beds & steads and furniture & two pillows One Chest One Trunk One large press a parcell of hops ffive boxes one Looking Glass Six Sheets and Eight Napkins Six blanketts One Rugg two Joynt Stools & 1 Chair . . . . . . . . . | 07 05 06 |

*In the Cock Loft*

|  |  |
|---|---|
| three Coffers wareing apparrell . . . . . | 00 11 00 |

*In the Outhouse*

|  |  |
|---|---|
| One large Oval Cooler two Tabs One Churn and Staff two pair of weeding Tongs, hewd Timber . . . . . . | 00 15 00 |
| drink in ye buttery . . . . . . . . | 00 10 00 |
| things omitted & not seen . . . . . . . | 00 10 00 |

*In the ground and Out buildings*

|  |  |
|---|---|
| ffive Cowes . . . . . . . . . | 12 17 06 |
| hay in ye barn . . . . . . . . . | 02 00 00 |
|  | 26 06 02 |

## 189. The Revd. William Sockett

Of Wellington, exhibited on 2 November 1732. The appraisers are not named and the inventory is undated.

*Imprs. In the Kitchen.*

|  |  |
|---|---|
| Item a Dresser & pewter . . . . . . . | 01 05 00 |
| an old Table & Chair . . . . . . . | 00 07 06 |
| a Grate fireshovel & Tongs & an old Jack. . . . . | 00 14 06 |
| Two spits & other small Iron ware. . . . . . | 00 08 00 |
| a Driping pan & a warming pan . . . . . . | 00 03 00 |

*Item. In the passage from the Kitchen to the Stairs*

|  |  |
|---|---|
| one Table six Chairs & one looking glass . . . . | 00 13 06 |

*Item. in the room over the Kitchen*

|  |  |
|---|---|
| one bed & furniture . . . . . . . . | 02 15 00 |
| one Chest two Chairs & a small nest of Drawers . . . | 00 16 00 |
| one looking glass . . . . . . . . | 00 01 11 |

# THE INVENTORIES OF WELLINGTON

*Item. in the Chamber over the Passage*
| | |
|---|---|
| one old bed & furniture . . . . . . | 02 05 00 |
| one Chest & Cofer & Chairs . . . . . | 00 10 00 |

*Item. In the Garrett over the Kitchen*
| | |
|---|---|
| Two beds & furniture . . . . . . | 02 02 06 |
| one Cofer & press . . . . . . . | 00 06 06 |

*Item In the Garrett over the Passage*
| | |
|---|---|
| one old bed . . . . . . . . | 00 09 06 |
| An old Cofer Trunke & Close stool . . . . | 00 05 06 |
| five old Chairs . . . . . . . | 00 08 06 |
| Six pound of flax . . . . . . . | 00 03 00 |

*Item in the Brew house .*
| | |
|---|---|
| one furnace & old vessels for brewing . . . . | 01 04 06 |
| Two pots & a kettle & brass pan & 2 saucepans . . . . | 00 09 06 |

*Item In the Cellar*
| | |
|---|---|
| four barrels 3 small firkins two horses . . . . | 00 17 06 |

| | |
|---|---|
| Item. Two old Mares one of 'em blind & an old Cart . . . | 04 13 00 |
| Geers & Saddles & bridle . . . . . . | 00 12 09 |
| Two Store pigs . . . . . . . . | 00 18 00 |
| Books and wearing Apparrell . . . . . | 07 00 00 |
| Money in Pockett . . . . . . . | 00 06 05 |
| Sheets & Table Linnen . . . . . . | 04 03 09 |
| Things omitted . . . . . . . | 00 04 09 |
| | 34 06 01 |

## 190. Mary Bradshaw

Of Wellington, widow, taken by Robert Turner and Richard Lummas on 2 April 1735 and exhibited on 17 April 1735. The house appears to be the same one described in the inventory of William Bradshaw (*166*) in 1720.

*Imprs. In the Chamber over the house*
| | |
|---|---|
| a Bed & Bedsteds with furniture . . . . . | 02 00 00 |
| Six Chairs . . . . . . . . | 00 03 00 |
| a Chest . . . . . . . . . | 00 04 00 |
| an old Cupboard . . . . . . . | 00 01 00 |
| a Looking Glass . . . . . . . | 00 01 00 |

*Item in the Chamber over the Parlour*
| | |
|---|---|
| a Bed with its furniture . . . . . . | 01 00 00 |
| An old flock bed . . . . . . . | 00 01 06 |
| a trunk two Coffers & a Close Stool . . . . | 00 05 00 |
| Linnens of all sorts . . . . . . . | 02 00 00 |

*Item in the Parlour*

| | |
|---|---|
| a Bed with its ffurniture | 01 18 00 |
| an old Table & a Chest | 00 10 00 |
| an old Cupboard & an old Chair | 00 04 00 |

*Item in the house place*

| | |
|---|---|
| Two Tables & a form | 00 08 00 |
| five old Chairs 3 old Cushions & a Joyn Stool | 00 03 06 |
| another old Table | 00 01 06 |

*Item in the Kitchen*

| | |
|---|---|
| a Table & form | 00 03 00 |
| a Skreen & 4 old Chairs | 00 05 00 |
| a Jack & two Grates | 00 14 00 |
| One Iron dripping pan & two Spits | 00 03 00 |
| A Dish Bench & a little wheel | 00 08 00 |
| Pewter dishes & plates | 01 10 00 |
| A warming Pan a frying Pan a fire shovell pair of Tongs a pair of Racks | 00 06 00 |
| an old furnace & a Boyler | 01 00 00 |

*Item in the Brew House*

| | |
|---|---|
| Brewing vesseles of all sorts | 00 12 00 |
| A Gawn & Peal | 00 01 06 |
| Three Barreles | 00 06 00 |
| Another old flock bed & bedsteads | 01 05 00 |
| Wearing Apparrele | 01 00 00 |
| Money in Pockett | 01 00 00 |
| Things omitted & not seen | 00 01 00 |
| | 16 07 00 |

## 191. Benjamin Langley

Of Wellington, taken by Richard Lummas and John Adams on 12 March 1735-36 and exhibited on 22 March 1735-36.

*In the House Place*

| | |
|---|---|
| One Dish bench & furniture | 00 15 00 |
| One dozen of trenchers 4 Chairs one Grate one fireshovel one pair of Tonges one frying Pan | 00 07 06 |
| Basons & other Ticknall Ware | 00 01 00 |
| One Copper pot one Warming Pan | 00 05 00 |
| one Iron Pot | 00 02 06 |

*In the Room over the house*

| | |
|---|---|
| two Beds & Clothing to them | 02 10 00 |
| one Chest & one Chest of Drawers with the Linnens | 02 00 00 |
| Some small Boxes | 00 05 00 |
| Two Chairs | 00 01 00 |

## THE INVENTORIES OF WELLINGTON

*In the little room over the Buttery*
one bed & Hillings one coffer & empty bottles . . . . 01 02 00

*In the Buttery*
Barreles . . . . . . . . . 00 07 06
Spinning Wheels . . . . . . . . 00 05 00
Two Peals . . . . . . . . . 00 02 00

Wearing Apparrell . . . . . . . . 01 10 00

                                                                                                 09 13 06

### 192. Charles Stowers

Of Wellington, gardener, taken by George Chester and Andrew Childs on 7 February 1736-37 and exhibited on 22 April 1737.

Imprs. Pertaters . . . . . . . . 01 05 00
a Watter Pan . . . . . . . . . 00 01 00
a Garden Rake and Spade . . . . . . . 00 02 00
fflower Potes . . . . . . . . . 00 02 06
Glasses . . . . . . . . . 00 05 00
Plants . . . . . . . . . . 00 05 00
Seed beans . . . . . . . . . 00 02 00
Kittney beans . . . . . . . . 00 01 00
Small Seeds . . . . . . . . . 00 01 06
a Garden Line . . . . . . . . 00 00 04
axe and Hooke . . . . . . . . 00 01 06
His Wareing apparrell Money in his Pockett . . . . 02 00 00

                                                                                                  04 06 10

### 193. John Wright

Of Wellington, dyer, taken by John Cherrington and William Taylor on 4 April 1737 and exhibited on 4 November 1737.

*Imprs. In the Kitchen*
Ten Small Pewter diches & one duzen of Plates ffour quarts . . 01 00 00
The Pewter Shilf one Table one Grate and other ffurniture in the
said Kitchen . . . . . . . . 00 18 00

*In the Parler*
one Table one ffurm one Screen Six old Cheers . . . . 00 12 00

*In the Chamber Over the Kitchen*
One bed & bedstids and ffurniture . . . . . 01 10 00
One Chest One Littel Table Six Old Cheers One Small Looking Glass 00 15 00

*In the Chamber Over the Entery*
One Table One ffurm One Old bed and bedstids. . . . 00 18 00

*In the Garrett Over the Parler*
One bed and bedstids One Table Two ffurms One Old Cuffer . . 00 10 00

*In the Garrett Over the Kitchen Chamber*
One Small Table Two Wheels . . . . . . 00 05 00

*In the Seller*
Two Small Vessells full ffive Small Ones emty . . . 02 00 00

*In the Brewhouse*
One Iron ffurnice Two Tubs Two Coolers One Tuning dich One bowldich . . . . . . . . . 01 00 00

Linning and Waring apparrell . . . . . 00 08 00
Things Omitted and not seen . . . . . . 00 02 00

                                                                                                                            90 18 06

## 194. Jane Hartshorne

Of Wellington, widow of coal master, taken by Joseph Leake and James Ball on 10 April 1737 and exhibited on 4 November 1737.

In the House at Wellington.

*In the Maids Garretts*
2 Beds Bedsteads & appurtenances . . . . . 01 10 00
1 Coffer . . . . . . . . . 00 05 00
1 Closestool . . . . . . . . . 00 04 00

*In the mans Garrett*
2 Beds Bedsteads & Appts. . . . . . . 02 00 00
1 large spinning wheel . . . . . . . 00 02 06
1 pair of Earwinds . . . . . . . . 00 01 00
1 press Bedstead . . . . . . . . 00 02 00
a parcell of wheat . . . . . . . . 00 05 00

*In the Store Chamber*
a parcell of Flax . . . . . . . . 00 10 00
1 Flitchen of Bacon . . . . . . . . 00 10 00

*In Chamber over the Dining room*
2 Beds Bedsteads & appts. . . . . . . 07 10 00
1 Chest of Drawers . . . . . . . . 00 05 06
2 Chairs . . . . . . . . . 00 02 00

# THE INVENTORIES OF WELLINGTON

*In the room over the Kitchen*

| | |
|---|---|
| 1 Bed Bedsteads & appts. | 02 10 00 |
| 1 Chest of Drawers | 01 00 00 |
| 1 other Chest of Drawers | 00 05 06 |
| 1 Little Table | 00 02 00 |
| 1 Looking Glass | 00 05 00 |

*In the Landing place in the Garrett*

| | |
|---|---|
| 1 Chest wth Linnen | 02 00 00 |

*In the Landing place below*

| | |
|---|---|
| 1 Chest | 00 05 00 |
| 1 Little table | 00 01 06 |

*In the Best room*

| | |
|---|---|
| 1 Bed Bedsteads & apprts. | 05 00 00 |
| 1 truckled Bed & appts. | 01 00 00 |
| 1 Looking Glass | 00 02 06 |
| 1 Easey Chair | 00 10 00 |
| 1 small table | 00 01 06 |

*In the Dining room*

| | |
|---|---|
| 6 Cain Chairs | 00 12 06 |
| 1 large Ovell table | 00 07 06 |
| 1 small round table | 00 02 06 |
| 1 Arme Chair | 00 02 06 |
| a Corner Cupboard wth drawers under | 00 10 00 |
| 1 Silver tankard | 05 00 00 |
| 1 Silver pint | 02 00 00 |
| 2 silver Salts | 00 10 00 |
| 6 large silver spoons | 01 10 00 |
| 6 Tea spoons | 00 06 00 |
| some China & Glasses | 00 02 06 |
| 1 small Ovall table | 00 02 06 |
| 1 Stand | 00 01 00 |

*In the Parlor*

| | |
|---|---|
| 6 Chairs | 00 12 06 |
| 1 Tea table | 00 02 06 |

*In the Hall*

| | |
|---|---|
| 1 Clock | 02 00 00 |

*In the Kitchen*

| | |
|---|---|
| a jack | 00 12 06 |
| 1 Grate | 00 05 00 |
| several Iron things in the Chimney | 00 10 00 |
| 4 Brass Candlesticks | 00 05 00 |
| 2 Coffee potts | 00 04 00 |
| 1 pair of Stilliards | 00 04 06 |
| 3 Box Irons | 00 03 00 |

| | |
|---|---|
| 4 plate Irons | 00 04 00 |
| severall tin Things | 00 02 06 |
| 2 small tables | 00 04 00 |
| 5 Dozen of plates | 01 04 00 |
| 19 Dishes on Dishbench | 02 10 00 |

*In the Sellar*

| | |
|---|---|
| 1 Hogshead | 00 07 06 |
| 4 half Hogsheads | 00 12 00 |
| 2 quarter Vessells | 00 02 06 |
| 3 Barrells | 00 07 06 |
| 1 Ale fitt | 00 05 00 |

*In the Brewhouse*

| | |
|---|---|
| 3 Stunds | 00 07 06 |
| 2 Coolers | 00 05 00 |
| 1 Washing Tub | 00 02 00 |
| 1 Furnice | 00 05 00 |
| 1 Boyler | 00 02 06 |
| 3 pails | 00 02 06 |

*In the Malthouse*

| | |
|---|---|
| 1 Stund | 00 02 00 |
| 2 Barrells | 00 04 00 |
| 1 Maltmill | 00 15 00 |
| 2 Hogsheads | 00 10 00 |
| a quantity of Laths | 01 00 00 |
| some malt | 01 01 00 |
| a Malt Skreen | 00 05 00 |
| 6 Horses & Gears | 18 00 00 |

| | |
|---|---|
| The Lease of the Bank House | 25 00 00 |

In the House at the Bank

*In the Kitchen*

| | |
|---|---|
| 1 Grate | 00 15 00 |
| 1 par of Crans | 00 05 00 |
| 1 purgatory | 00 02 06 |
| 1 pair of Tongs & 2 fire shovells | 00 05 00 |
| 1 Defender | 00 02 00 |
| 2 Iron dripping pans | 00 10 00 |
| 2 Brass Candlesticks | 00 03 00 |
| 1 pair of Snuffers | 00 00 06 |
| 1 plateholder | 00 02 00 |
| 2 Cupboards | 00 05 00 |
| a Dishbench & Dresser | 01 00 00 |
| 13 pewter Dishes | 01 10 00 |
| 18 plates | 00 15 00 |
| 3 Broaches | 00 04 00 |

*In the Hall*

| | |
|---|---|
| 1 Table | 00 06 00 |
| 1 Clock Maps & Pictures | 01 10 00 |

# THE INVENTORIES OF WELLINGTON

*In the Parlor*

| | |
|---|---|
| 1 Glass | 01 00 00 |
| 2 Armd & 10 Chairs | 01 18 00 |
| 1 little table | 00 02 06 |
| 1 Stove Grate | 00 05 00 |

*In the Old Kitchen*

| | |
|---|---|
| 1 Grate | 00 05 00 |
| 1 Jack | 00 12 00 |
| 1 Table | 00 02 00 |
| 1 Skreen | 00 01 00 |
| 3 Chairs | 00 01 00 |

*In the room over the Old Kitchen*

| | |
|---|---|
| 1 Bed Bedsteads & Appts. | 02 00 00 |
| 1 Table & 1 Chest | 00 05 00 |

*In Men Servts. roome*

| | |
|---|---|
| 2 Beds & Steads | 01 10 00 |

*In roome over New Kitchen*

| | |
|---|---|
| 1 Looking Glass | 00 01 00 |
| 1 press | 00 04 00 |
| 1 Bed Bedsteads & Appts. | 02 10 00 |

*In Little room over the Hall*

| | |
|---|---|
| 1 Bed Bedsteads & Appts. | 01 00 00 |

*In the Best Chamber*

| | |
|---|---|
| 1 Bed Bedsteads & Appts. | 05 10 00 |
| 1 looking Glass & table | 01 00 00 |
| 1 Chest of Drawers | 00 05 00 |
| Pictures | 00 01 00 |

*In the Brewhouse*

| | |
|---|---|
| 2 Furnaces | 00 15 00 |
| 4 Brewing Vessells | 00 10 00 |
| 2 potts | 00 04 06 |

*In the Cellars*

| | |
|---|---|
| 10 Vessells | 01 00 00 |

In Dawley Field

*In Brandlee*

| | |
|---|---|
| 1 Gin & Horse Engine | 12 00 00 |
| Crippen's Ginn wth. out ropes | 04 00 00 |
| Walletts Ginn wth. ropes | 10 00 00 |
| Rushtons Ginn wth. ropes | 10 00 00 |
| Bayleys Do & ropes | 07 00 00 |

| | | |
|---|---|---|
| 6 Turn Barrells. 1 pr. ropes at Cleatons pitt & 3 pair of Feal Stakes . | 04 10 00 | |
| Trunks Lamps Water boukes & other materials . . . . | 00 15 00 | |
| a parcell of Iron Stone abt. 12 Doz. Gott by Walton . . . | 12 00 00 | |
| Stock of Coals ab. 102 Stacks at 2–3 p. Stack . . . . | 11 09 06 | |

### In Ketley Lordship

*In Hainses Wood*

| | |
|---|---|
| 16 Doz. of Ironstone at 3s 8 Doz. Mr. Ford haveing pd for Getting . | 17 08 00 |

*At Ketley*

| | |
|---|---|
| John Howles pitt. 17 st. of Coales at 2s 6d. . . . . | 10 02 06 |
| John Walkers 46 at do . . . . . . | 05 15 00 |
| Wm. Onions 4 at do . . . . . . . | 00 10 00 |
| Charles Wallett 309 at do . . . . . . | 38 12 06 |
| at Walletts pitt 2 Ginns one wth. ropes . . . . | 14 00 00 |
| at Howles pitt 1 Ginn & Ropes . . . . . | 08 00 00 |
| at Wm. Onionses do . . . . . . . | 07 00 00 |
| at Wm. Rawbones Junr. do . . . . . . | 04 00 00 |
| at John Walkers 2 Ginns one wth. ropes . . . . | 12 00 00 |
| At Wm. Rawbones Sen. 2 Turn Barrells Feal Stakes & ropes . . | 12 00 00 |
| At Walkers Lamp itt a Turn Barrell Feal stales . . . | 00 05 00 |
| Lamps Water bouks &c. . . . . . . | 02 00 00 |
| 1 Fire Engine Cast Barrells &c. . . . . . . | 200 00 00 |

### In Ld. Staffords Work

*In Hollyn Wood*

| | |
|---|---|
| 1 Ginn & Ropes . . . . . . . | 03 10 00 |
| Head Stakes & Turn Barrell & Ropes . . . . | 02 00 00 |

*At Snebshill*

| | |
|---|---|
| Prices pitt. 1 Ginn & Ropes . . . . . | 04 00 00 |
| 1 Ginn wth. out Ropes . . . . . . | 06 00 00 |
| Martins pitt Fealstakes Ropes & Turn Barrell . . . | 01 00 00 |
| the Royalty of 16 st. at 18d p. Stack . . . . | 01 04 00 |
| 1 Brass Barrell . . . . . . . | 10 00 00 |
| Tot | 546 14 00 |

**195. John Cherrington**

Of Wellington, dyer, taken by Andrew Powell and John Jennings on 21 February 1737–38 and exhibited on 28 April 1738.

*First of all in the Malthouse*

| | |
|---|---|
| 500 Strike of Malt at 4s. . . . . . . | 100 00 00 |
| 40 Strike of Barley at 2s 10d . . . . . | 05 13 04 |
| a Malt Screen. . . . . . . . | 00 14 00 |

# THE INVENTORIES OF WELLINGTON 385

a Maltmill, a hair cloth a Strike ½ Strike a peck & half peck . . 01 07 00
2 Ladders a spade a Shovel a scoop & Gatter . . . . 00 10 06

## In the Dyhouse

a punch Tub & Punch . . . . . . . . 00 10 06
4 Furnices . . . . . . . . . 14 00 00
8 Winces . . . . . . . . . 00 04 00
1 Press plate & Crows . . . . . . . . 10 10 00
5 pair of Sheers press boards & papers . . . . . 02 15 00
Fustick . . . . . . . . . 01 04 00
Red wood . . . . . . . . . 02 00 00
pott ashes . . . . . . . . . 02 10 00
Logwood & Sumack . . . . . . . . 00 14 00
Indigoe . . . . . . . . . 01 00 00
Gauls & allam . . . . . . . . 00 10 00
Tinetors . . . . . . . . . 01 10 00
4 Stone Cisterns . . . . . . . . 01 10 00
2 Large Cupboards & a Counter . . . . . . 02 00 00
Brewing Vessells & Barrells . . . . . . . 03 00 00
a Silver Cup & 10 Silver spoons . . . . . . 06 00 00
4 Looking Glasses . . . . . . . . 03 00 00
a Chest & a Chest & Drawers . . . . . . 02 07 00
2 Tables . . . . . . . . . 00 07 00
China . . . . . . . . . . 00 07 06
2 Coverd Stools . . . . . . . . 00 08 00
6 Beds & Bedding . . . . . . . . 26 00 00
a Map & Pictures . . . . . . . . 00 10 00
2 Large hanging presses . . . . . . . 01 10 00
Covvers & Boxes a pillion & 2 Wheels . . . . . 01 15 00
20 Chairs . . . . . . . . . 03 00 00
3 Tables . . . . . . . . . 00 13 00
2 Skreens & 2 Glass Cages . . . . . . . 00 16 00
29 Pewter Dishes 48 plates . . . . . . . 07 16 00
A large Spoon a rigg & Castors . . . . . . 00 05 00
4 Toasters a Cover & Cullinder . . . . . . 00 06 00
a Dish Board & Shelves . . . . . . . 00 16 00
Brass potts Kettles Saucepanns . . . . . . 02 05 00
A Lead Cistern & 2 Marmitts . . . . . . 00 08 00
a Clock & a Jack . . . . . . . . 03 10 00
Brass Candlestick & other Brass things . . . . . 01 00 00
a Dreeping pan a Warming pan & a frying pan . . . . 00 18 00
a Mortar & 2 pestills . . . . . . . . 00 06 00
2 Box Irons & 2 flatt ones . . . . . . . 00 08 00
a firegrate pitt Grate & fenders . . . . . . 01 15 00
fire Shovell & Tongs & two Cleavers . . . . . 00 12 00
2 Spitts . . . . . . . . . 00 02 00
House Linnen . . . . . . . . 07 00 00
Knives & forks . . . . . . . . 00 05 00
6 Doz of Bottles . . . . . . . . 00 06 00
Lumber . . . . . . . . . 00 10 00
Wearing Apparrell . . . . . . . . 03 00 00

Tot . . . 230 03 10

## 186. William Cleaton

Of Watling Street, Wellington, taken by Edward Jones and James Turner and exhibited on 28 April 1738. The inventory is undated.

*In the House*
1 Table two forms 8 chairs 2 screens 1 Jack, 2 spits 1 dripping pan 1 Grate, 1 fireshovel and tongs fender Plate & Purgatory 4 Candlesticks 1 Clock & warming pan . . . . . . 04 02 00

*In the best Parlor*
1 Bed and furniture . . . . . . . 04 00 00
1 ovel Table . . . . . . . . 00 08 00
1 Chest of Drawers 1 hanging Press . . . . 01 01 00
1 side board and 1 tub with other Lumber . . . 00 05 00

*In the little Parlor*
2 Beds & furniture . . . . . . . 03 00 00
1 Chest one table 1 Close stool 1 Coffer & other Lumber . 00 15 00

*In the Pantry*
one Cupboard 8 pewter dishes & 3 Plates. . . . 01 10 00

*In the Brewhouse*
One Furnace 2 Coolers 2 brewing Vessels 1 pair of Racks & other Lumber . . . . . . . . 02 12 00

*In the Stairhead Room*
Two beds & one Coffer . . . . . . 01 10 00

*Cheese Chamber*
123 Cheeses valued to . . . . . . 10 00 00
one pair of bedsteads . . . . . . 00 05 00

*In the little room over the House*
One bed & furniture . . . . . . . 00 15 00

*Small Beer in the Buttery*
2 Barrels 1 Pott 6 wooden bottles & other Lumber . . 01 10 00

*In the Cellar*
8 Barrels 2 two hogsheads the hogsheads full of Beer . 06 00 00
Two flitches of Bacon . . . . . . 02 00 00

*In the Chests*
Linnen and wearing Apparell with money in Pocket . . 12 00 00

*In the Work house*
1 Malt Mill . . . . . . . . 01 10 00

# THE INVENTORIES OF WELLINGTON

| | |
|---|---|
| 10 pair of Raiths | 01 05 00 |
| 10 Sett of Fillys | 03 00 00 |
| 8 Axel trees | 00 12 00 |
| 2 Strikes 2 Tubbs & other Husbandry Implements with other Lumber | 03 00 00 |

*In the best Stable*

| | |
|---|---|
| Six wagon horses valued to | 36 00 00 |

*In the old Stable*

| | |
|---|---|
| six wagon horses and mares | 30 00 00 |

*In the Folds*

| | |
|---|---|
| 3 Colts | 12 00 00 |
| 41 Sheep | 09 00 00 |

*In the Cowe Houses*

| | |
|---|---|
| 5 Cowes | 20 00 00 |
| Two 3 year old Heifers | 07 00 00 |
| 4 Twinters | 08 00 00 |

*In the Barn*

| | |
|---|---|
| 50 Thrave of Muncorn at 6s p Thrave | 15 00 00 |
| 100 Strike of Barley at 2s 6d p strike | 12 10 00 |
| Hay & Clover | 10 00 00 |

*In the Cart House*

| | |
|---|---|
| 3 old waggons | 12 00 00 |
| 2 old tumbrills | 05 00 00 |
| Plows horses and other Implements of Husbandry | 07 00 00 |
| Gears for 12 horses and Mares | 03 00 00 |

*In the Swine Sties*

| | |
|---|---|
| one fatt Swine & 3 Stores | 03 10 00 |

*In the Fields*

| | |
|---|---|
| 4 Calves 1 weaner Colte | 05 00 00 |

*In the House*

| | |
|---|---|
| 30 Strike of Oats | 02 05 00 |
| 10 Strike of Pease & Beans | 02 00 00 |
| 10 Strike of Muncorn | 01 10 00 |

*Corn upon the Land*

| | |
|---|---|
| 20 Strike of Muncorn | 03 10 00 |
| Total | 265 03 00 |

## 197. John Hicks

Of Wellington, baker, taken by John Adams and Thomas Felton on 31 July 1738 and exhibited on 26 October 1738.

*First. In the Kitchen*

| | |
|---|---|
| One Clock and Case . | 01 10 00 |
| 10 pewter dishes | 01 01 00 |
| 18 plates . | 00 12 00 |
| 11 pewter porrengers one pewter tankard one Chamber pott & other odd things . | 00 15 00 |
| One Dresser and Small Table | 00 05 00 |
| 3 Brass Kettles one warming pann and other brass Things | 00 05 00 |
| one Jack . | 00 05 00 |
| one Grate and Severall other Iron Things . | 00 05 00 |
| Chairs and Stooles and other odd things . | 00 02 00 |

*In the Chamber*

| | |
|---|---|
| 2 Beds bedsteads & furniture | 02 00 00 |
| 2 Chests and Linnen . | 01 00 00 |

*In the Shop*

| | |
|---|---|
| 2 Barrells and other wood things . | 01 00 00 |
| Faggotts . | 00 10 00 |
| things omitted . | 00 05 00 |
| Debts due and owing | 40 00 00 |
| Tot . | 49 15 00 |

## 198. William Lloyd

Of Wellington, currier, taken by William Hanworth, Stephen Winckle and Benjamin Harper in October 1738 and exhibited on 27 October 1738.

*House Place*

| | |
|---|---|
| One Dish Bench & Drawers . | 00 10 00 |
| 14 small pewter Dishes . | 01 05 00 |
| 2 Brass Kettles & a brass pott | 06 10 00 |
| 10 pewter plates & 7 porringers . | 00 05 00 |
| A Table & 2 forms . | 00 03 00 |
| 2 Iron potts & a brass Kettle | 00 02 06 |

*first Room*

| | |
|---|---|
| One Bed & all Things thereunto belonging | 01 05 00 |
| 3 Cofers a Chest a close stool & 2 boxes . | 00 12 00 |
| 3 Chairs a Table & a pr of Iron Gobbetts . | 00 06 00 |

*Second Room*

| | |
|---|---|
| 2 old Beds & an old Chest . | 01 00 00 |

*Shop Tooles*

| | |
|---|---|
| A pin Block & Board & Knives | 00 08 06 |

*Buttery*

| | |
|---|---|
| 2 Tubbs one Turnell & 2 Barrells . | 00 10 00 |
| Tot Sume . | 06 17 00 |

## 199. Ralph Boulton Leeke

Of Wellington, taken by Michael Betton and Charles Wright and exhibited on 25 April 1739. The inventory is undated.

*In the Kitchin*
| | |
|---|---|
| Four Douze and odd plates. | 02 00 00 |
| Twenty Two pewter Dishes | 02 00 00 |
| One Jack | 01 00 00 |
| One Grate Fender & Spitt one Fire Shovell & Tongs | 01 00 00 |
| Two cranes & purgatory one Dresser of Drawers | 01 00 00 |
| One plank & a Small Screen one Small Table | 00 07 00 |
| One iron Dripping pan 1 old pastee pan, 4 brass Candlesticks 1 plate Stand,1 Coffee pott. | 00 10 00 |
| 2 Fowling peices, 2 Blunder Bushes 2 Case of pistolls, odd Lumber. | 03 10 00 |

*In the Pantry*
| | |
|---|---|
| 1 table 2 Chairs 1 joint Stool 1 Small Mitt & or Lumber | 00 08 00 |

*In the Drawing Room*
| | |
|---|---|
| Four chairs. | 00 05 00 |

*In the Hall*
| | |
|---|---|
| Two Tables. | 00 07 00 |
| One Round Table One Writing Desk | 01 00 00 |
| Six Old Chairs | 00 10 00 |
| Three pictures | 00 10 00 |

*In the Little Parler*
| | |
|---|---|
| Three Chairs & a Little Table | 00 04 00 |

*In the Scullery*
| | |
|---|---|
| 1 Cast Boyler 3 Brass Pots 1 Brass Kettle 2 Tea Kettles. | 01 10 00 |
| One old Naptkin press and shelves. | 00 03 00 |

*In the Best Parler*
| | |
|---|---|
| Two Tables. | 00 15 00 |
| Eight New Chairs. | 01 10 00 |
| One fire Shovel Tongs and Fender. | 00 05 00 |
| One Looking Glass. | 02 00 00 |

*In the Small Room*
| | |
|---|---|
| one Bed & furniture. | 02 00 00 |
| Two Old Chairs 3 chests & 2 Truncks | 01 10 00 |

*In the Mans Garrett*
| | |
|---|---|
| One Bed & furniture | 01 00 00 |
| One Chest and a Small Couch | 00 05 00 |

*In the Maids Room*

| | | |
|---|---|---|
| One Bed and Furniture | . . . . . . . | 01 00 00 |
| Three Chairs and a cabinett | . . . . . . | 00 12 00 |

*In the Green Parlor*

| | | |
|---|---|---|
| Two beds and Furniture | . . . . . . . | 08 00 00 |
| Six joint Chairs 1 Elbow Chair | . . . . . . | 00 10 00 |
| 1 fire Shovel Tongs and a Looking Glass | . . . . . | 00 02 06 |
| A Little Table | . . . . . . . . | 00 01 00 |

*In the Blew Room*

| | | |
|---|---|---|
| One Bed and Furniture | . . . . . . . | 03 00 00 |
| Three pictures | . . . . . . . . | 00 10 00 |
| One Table & Two Chairs 1 Looking Glass | . . . . | 00 04 00 |
| One Clock on the Stairs and a Weather Glass | . . . | 04 00 00 |

*In the Brew House*

| | | |
|---|---|---|
| One Brass Kettle | . . . . . . . . | 00 08 00 |
| One Iron Furnace | . . . . . . . . | 01 00 00 |
| One Malt Mill | . . . . . . . . . | 00 05 00 |
| One Iron Grate | . . . . . . . . | 00 03 00 |
| Wooden Vessells | . . . . . . . . | 00 10 00 |
| One table & lumber over the Brew House | . . . . | 00 05 00 |

*In The Cellars*

| | | |
|---|---|---|
| 11 Vessells | . . . . . . . . . | 01 05 00 |

*In the Dairie etc.*

| | | |
|---|---|---|
| Three pair of Brass Scales & Weights | . . . . . | 00 15 00 |
| One old Churn | . . . . . . . . | 00 01 06 |
| Three milking Cows & Two Yerlings | . . . . . | 12 00 00 |
| 1 Horse | . . . . . . . . . . | 03 10 00 |
| A parcell of Hay | . . . . . . . . | 03 00 00 |
| A Small Studdy of Books | . . . . . . . | 20 00 00 |
| | Tot . . . | 110 14 00 |

## 200. John Bromley

Of Watling Street, Wellington, blacksmith, taken by James Turner and Roger Clayton on 10 June 1740 and exhibited on 23 October 1740.

*In the house*

| | | |
|---|---|---|
| One Grate one Purgatory fire Shovall & Tongs & one hanging plate a fender & an old Jack | . . . . . . . | 01 05 00 |
| One old Dresser of Drawers & a pewter frame eight old Dishes & 12 plates | . . . . . . . . | 01 05 00 |
| One old Mortar & a dripping pan | . . . . . . | 00 02 00 |
| One oval Table & an old skreen | . . . . . . | 00 07 00 |
| Half a Dozen of old Chairs & a Stool | . . . . . | 00 04 00 |

## THE INVENTORIES OF WELLINGTON

*In the Parlour*
| | | |
|---|---|---|
| One old little Table & 2 old Chairs . . . . . | 00 03 00 |

*In the Chamber over the House*
| | |
|---|---|
| Two Beds with Hangins & Bed Hillings being very old ones . . | 03 10 00 |
| An old oval Table an old Hanging Press & an old Box of Drawers . | 00 08 00 |
| One old Chest an old Trunk an old Box & 2 old Chairs . . . | 00 06 00 |

*In the Chamber over the Shop*
| | |
|---|---|
| One old Bed & Bedding one old Table one old Cofer & an old flock Bed . . . . . . . . . . | 00 15 00 |

*In the Buttery*
| | |
|---|---|
| Three old Barrells & 2 old Benches . . . . . | 00 05 00 |
| One Stand & one old Cooler . . . . . . | 00 04 00 |
| Two old Pails . . . . . . . . . | 00 01 00 |
| One old furnace & 2 old Potts . . . . . . | 00 15 00 |

*In the Shop*
| | |
|---|---|
| One old Anvill one old pair of Bellows one Vice Hammers & Tongs & Punches . . . . . . . . . . | 02 10 00 |

*In the Stable*
| | |
|---|---|
| One old blind Mare . . . . . . . . | 01 07 00 |

*In the Pig Stye*
| | |
|---|---|
| One Pig . . . . . . . . . | 00 12 00 |

*In the House*
| | |
|---|---|
| Linnen & wearing Apparell . . . . . . . | 01 05 00 |
| | 14 18 00 |

### 201. James Massey

Of Watling Street, Wellington, innkeeper, taken by Allen Pickering and James Turner on 6 October 1740 and exhibited on 23 October 1741.

*In the House*
| | |
|---|---|
| One Grate fire Shovel & Tongs & Iron Jack . . . . | 01 00 00 |
| Three Broaches & a fire plate & Frying pan & 5 Smoothing Irons & one Dripping pan . . . . . . . . | 00 10 00 |
| One Dresser of Drawers & Pewter & plates . . . . | 02 05 00 |
| Six Candlesticks 2 Hanging fire plate a Grid Iron & a Chopping Knife &c. . . . . . . . . . | 00 05 00 |
| A Screen two Little Tables three Stooles & fourteen Old Chairs . | 00 12 00 |
| A Brass warming pan & a Candlestick & some tinn ware & one little Copper pint . . . . . . . . . | 00 06 00 |

### In the parlour
Three Old Tables & a Screen & One Old Form On Chest & One Old Clock . . . . . . . . . . 01 18 00
A Lookeing Glass Some Old pictures Drinking Glasses & some white ware . . . . . . . . . . 00 05 00

### The Little room over the Celler
One Bed & all thinges belonging to it & one Little Old Chest . . 01 15 00

### In the Chamber over the house
Two feather beds & all things belonging to them & one old Chaff Bed & one Chest . . . . . . . . 02 16 00

### In the Chamber over the parlour
Two feather Bedes & all things belonging to them . . . 04 00 00

### In the Chamber over the Stable
Two feather beds & all things belonging to them & one Chest . . 05 10 00
Two Dozen of Napkins & Table Cloths & Six paire of Sheets . . 02 00 00

### In the Brewhouse
One Iron furnace & one Iron Boyler . . . . . 00 16 00
Three Brewing Stoondes & 2 Coolers . . . . . 01 00 00

### In the Ground Cellers
One hodgshead four half hodgesheads . . . . . 01 04 00
Drink in the Celler . . . . . . . . 04 00 00

### Small Beer Celler
Three Little Barrells & some Small Beer . . . . . 00 05 00
Some Old Bend ware three old pails & one Old Chirn . . . 00 05 00
Earthen Ware Quarts & pints & Old pewter quarts pints & porringers . 00 05 00
Things seen & unseen . . . . . . . 00 02 00
Wareing apparell & money in pockett . . . . . 01 00 00

### In the Fould
One Cow One Heifer & one Calf . . . . . . 05 10 00
Four Old Horses & Geering belonging to them . . . . 09 00 00
Three Swine & three Stores . . . . . . 04 00 00

### Implements of Husbandry
Two Old Tumbrells 2 Old Carts One plow & One pair of Harrows . 04 10 00

### In the Barn
Winter Corn . . . . . . . . . 08 00 00
A Small Stack of Barley . . . . . . . 11 00 00
Hay in the Barn & Tallents & Stable . . . . . 20 00 00

Tot . . . 93 19 00

The Deceased Dyed in Debt with rent & other Debts to severall persons £55.00.00

## 202. Robert Stanley

Of Wellington, stone cutter, taken by John Sambrook and William Taylor on 21 March 1740–41 and exhibited on 23 October 1741.

*Imprs. In the House Place*

| | |
|---|---|
| One Dishbench and Pewter Two Small Tables . . . . | 01 00 00 |
| Imprs. Six Cheirs Two Small Brass Kettles One Grate and Tonges . | 00 05 00 |

*Imprs. In the ffur. Room*

| | |
|---|---|
| One Bed One Chear Two Small Boxes . . . . . | 01 00 00 |

*Imprs. In the Room Over the House*

| | |
|---|---|
| One Bed One Table One Chest & Linnen. Two Chears One Small Glass . . . . . . . . . . . | 01 00 00 |

*Imprs. In the Room Over the Buttery*

| | |
|---|---|
| an Old Bed and a Old Wheel . . . . . . | 00 05 00 |

*Imprs. In the Kiching*

| | |
|---|---|
| One Pail One Turnell One Brewing Tub . . . . . | 00 03 00 |

*Imprs. In the Buttery*

| | |
|---|---|
| Two Barrells and a Salt Box . . . . . . . | 00 02 06 |
| Imprs. an old Horse . . . . . . . . . | 00 17 00 |
| Imprs. Waring apparell & Things Not Seen . . . . | 01 00 00 |
| Imprs. Working Tools . . . . . . . . | 00 02 00 |
| Impr. Sum Stone un Worked . . . . . . . | 00 15 00 |
| Totall . . . | 06 09 06 |

## 203. William Webb

Of Wellington, taken by Peter Colley and Peter Massey on 17 December 1741 and exhibited on 29 April 1742. The Forester Rent Roll for 1719 (S.R.O. 1226/297) shows Webb leasing the Talbot in Wellington and two crofts.

*In ye Kitchin*

| | |
|---|---|
| 24 Pewter Dishes at 2/3 p Dish . . . . . . | 02 14 00 |
| 4 Doz. plates at 5s p Doz. . . . . . . . . | 01 00 00 |
| 7 pints 4 Quarts 2 Tankards . . . . . . . | 00 10 00 |
| 3 pewter Chamber Potts 3 Salts 3 pollengers . . . . | 00 07 00 |
| Clock and Case . . . . . . . . . | 02 00 00 |
| a Jack . . . . . . . . . . . | 01 01 00 |
| 2 driping pans, 4 Broaches 1 pair of Gobbotts 1 Grate Fire Shovel, Tongs 7 Candlesticks 2 plates a Fender purgotory Grate and 2 Smoothing Irons . . . . . . . . . | 02 07 06 |

Tin War 1 puding plate 2 Covers & 1 Cullender 1 Doz patty pans
1 Tun Dish . . . . . . . . . .  00 04 00
1 Warming pan . . . . . . . . .  00 03 00
a Dress of Drawers a Screen a Ovil Table 1 Form 6 Cheirs a Joint
Stoole . . . . . . . . . . .  01 08 00
1 Iron Beam and Scales & Hedging Bill . . . . .  00 10 00
1 Glass decanter & small Glasses . . . . . .  00 01 00

*In the parlor*

a Hanging press a Table 2 Forms 6 Cheirs and a Stand . .  01 07 00
a Fire Shovel and Tonges . . . . . . .  00 01 06

*Room over parlor*

1 Bed . . . . . . . . . . .  02 07 06
a Table a Form a Chest & 4 Chairs . . . . .  00 10 00

*Room over ye Buttery*

2 Beds and all things belonging . . . . . .  03 05 00
2 Chests 2 Coffers 2 Chairs & a weell . . . . .  00 12 00
Linning 4 Table Cloths 2 Doz Napkins 6 pair of Sheets and some
other Linning . . . . . . . . .  03 04 00

*In the Room over ye Shop*

2 Beds and all things belonging except one pair of Steds . .  02 10 00
a Table 1 Chest 3 Chairs & an old folding screen . . .  00 17 00

*Room over ye back Kitching*

1 Bed and all things belonging . . . . . .  03 05 00
an Ovill Table and 9 Chairs . . . . . . .  00 11 00
Picktures . . . . . . . . . .  00 01 06

*Room over the Fore Kitching*

1 Bed and all things belonging . . . . . .  04 00 00
an Ovil Table and 9 Chairs . . . . . . .  00 15 00
1 Chest of Drawers . . . . . . . . .  01 15 00

*In the Closet By*

1½ Doz Bottles of Cyder . . . . . . .  00 08 00
a Little Table . . . . . . . . . .  00 01 00
a Looking Glass Window Curtains & pictures . . .  00 09 00
a pair Tongs Fire Shovell and Fender . . . . .  00 02 06

*In the Garratt*

23 cwt. of Cheese . . . . . . . . .  35 00 00
Salt . . . . . . . . . . .  06 08 00
Hops . . . . . . . . . . .  06 05 00
Butter . . . . . . . . . . .  04 00 00
Lard . . . . . . . . . . .  00 10 00
1 pair Hampatts 2 Doz. Empty Bottles Tubbs & other Lumbr. .  00 10 00

*in ye Fold*
| | | |
|---|---|---|
| 8 Piggs | | 06 08 00 |
| Hay in the Barn | | 08 00 00 |
| Coals | | 01 00 00 |

*In the Brewhouse*
| | | |
|---|---|---|
| 3 Coolleres 3 Mash Tuns 1 Guile Tun 3 Barrels 2 pails and a Furnis | | 03 11 06 |

*in the Malt House*
| | | |
|---|---|---|
| Dry Malt 160 Bushels on the floor and kiln 35 Bushels | | 39 00 00 |
| 6 Baggs | | 00 05 00 |
| a Screen 2 Malt Mils ½ Strike 2 Malt Shovels | | 02 15 00 |
| 19 Flitches of Bacon | | 15 00 00 |

*in the Shop*
| | | |
|---|---|---|
| a pair of Small Scales Weights and Stilliards | | 00 05 00 |
| 2 Cupboards | | 00 08 00 |

*In the Back Kitching*
| | | |
|---|---|---|
| 2 Small Iron Boiler 2 Grates 2 Iron potts a Brasn pott an Iron Kettle a Lanthorn 2 Tups and an old Cupboard | | 01 05 00 |

*in the Buttery*
| | | |
|---|---|---|
| Drink 16 Strike's Brewing | | 03 08 00 |
| 9 Casks | | 02 00 00 |

*In the Buttry by the House*
| | | |
|---|---|---|
| 44 Strikes Brewing of Drink | | 09 07 00 |
| 13 Casks | | 02 12 00 |

*In the Field*
| | | |
|---|---|---|
| One Mare | | 01 01 00 |

*at Wenlock*
| | | |
|---|---|---|
| 17 Lb of Old Cheese | | 01 03 00 |
| 117 Lb of New do | | 01 10 00 |
| one Flitch of Bacon | | 00 14 00 |

| | | |
|---|---|---|
| a Note of hand | | 21 02 00 |
| Book Debts Money in the House and Waring Apparals | | 65 00 00 |
| Other things unseen & forgot | | 00 01 06 |
| Totall | | 276 13 06 |

## 204. William Davis

Of Ketley Brook, Wellington, weaver, taken by Thomas Onions and William Taylor on 20 July 1742 and exhibited on 14 October 1742.

*In the House Place*

| One Dish Bench five small Dishes one Dozen of Plates . . . | 00 12 00 |
|---|---|
| Six Trenchers & a little brass Kettle . . . | 00 01 06 |
| A warming pan two Tables a form & three Chairs . . . | 00 03 00 |
| One Grate fire Shovell & Tongs . . . . . | 00 01 06 |
| One small Iron Pott . . . . . . . | 00 01 00 |

*Up Stairs*

| Two old Beds & Bedsteads two old Cofers one old Trunk & Linen . | 02 05 00 |
|---|---|

*In the Shop*

| Three old Looms & Geers . . . . . . . | 01 10 00 |
|---|---|
| Two Barrells one Turnel one Pail . . . . . | 00 05 00 |
| One Cow & Calf . . . . . . . . | 02 10 00 |
| Wearing Apparell . . . . . . . . | 01 00 00 |
| Things not seen . . . . . . . . | 00 02 06 |
|  | 08 11 06 |

## 205. Robert Harper

Of Wellington, shoemaker, taken by D. Brearley on 8 October 1742 and exhibited on 14 October 1742.

*In the Garratts*

| Leather . . . . . . . . . | 01 15 00 |
|---|---|
| one Table . . . . . . . . | 00 03 06 |
| one Malt Mill . . . . . . . . | 00 10 00 |
| one Bed Stead . . . . . . . . | 00 05 00 |
| 3 Doz: wood Heels and other Lumber . . . . | 00 05 06 |

*In the room over the Kitching*

| 1 Chest of Drawers . . . . . . . | 01 10 00 |
|---|---|
| 1 Bed . . . . . . . . . | 01 10 00 |
| 1 ovill Table . . . . . . . . | 00 05 00 |
| 10 Framed pickturs . . . . . . . | 00 05 00 |
| 2 boxes & 1 Trunk . . . . . . . | 00 03 00 |

*In the room over the Shop*

| one Bed . . . . . . . . . | 00 15 05 |
|---|---|
| one Chest . . . . . . . . . | 00 04 06 |
| Hops . . . . . . . . . . | 00 10 00 |

*In the Parlor*

| 1 Screen . . . . . . . . | 00 03 00 |
|---|---|
| 9 Cheires . . . . . . . . | 00 03 00 |

*In the Kitching*

| 1 Dresser and pewter . . . . . . . | 02 00 00 |
|---|---|
| 2 Little Tables . . . . . . . . | 00 04 00 |
| 5 Old Cheirs . . . . . . . . | 00 01 03 |
| a Little old Screen . . . . . . . | 00 01 07 |
| one Grate Tongs & Shovel and other Small necessares . . | 00 10 00 |

## THE INVENTORIES OF WELLINGTON

*In the Celler*
6 Casks . . . . . . . . . 00 18 00

*In the Brewhouse*
one Furnes . . . . . . . . 00 10 00
3 Tubs . . . . . . . . . 00 08 06
one Sirce . . . . . . . . . 00 00 06

*In the Shop*
18 pair of Shoes . . . . . . . 02 02 06
one pair of Boots other Small Necessaries . . . 00 07 08
Book Debts and waring Aparel . . . . . 03 01 06

                  18 15 03

### 206. John Mansell

  Of Wellington, glover, taken on 11 March 1742–43 and exhibited on 15 April 1743. The appraisers are not named.

| | |
|---|---|
| 3 Dozn & 6 Ground Sheeps 10 more Wash Leather skins | 01 10 04 |
| 20 Shamey linings at 4d p skin | 00 06 08 |
| 21 tan sheep at 22d p skin | 00 04 04½ |
| 3 Dozn tand Lambs & 3 22d p skin | 01 00 00 |
| four Dozn & nine Coarse Tand | 00 03 00 |
| 2 Dozn Whit Rubbing Skins at 10d p Dozn | 00 10 00 |
| 200 Slink pieces | 00 05 04 |
| 16 pair of Hedge Mittings | 00 01 08 |
| 10 pair of Tand Gloves unfinished | 00 05 00 |
| 29 pair of Ws Ordnary Black Gloves | 00 05 00 |
| 11 pair of Coars Mitts at 9d | 00 02 09 |
| 12 pair of Womans Tand Gloves at 4d | 00 04 00 |
| 8 pair of Womans Black Gloves | 00 02 08 |
| 11 pair of Womans White Mitts | 00 03 08 |
| 13 pair of Womans White Sheep Gloves at 3d p pr | 00 03 06 |
| 9 pair of Girls White Mitts | 00 01 06 |
| 10 p of Ordinary White at 3d pr | 00 02 06 |
| 5 pair of Small Tand Mitts | 00 00 10 |
| 8 pair of Womans Coarse Ash Colour'd Gloves | 00 02 10 |
| 7 pair of top tand Gloves | 00 03 06 |
| 3 pair of Sheep Mens | 00 00 06 |
| 5 pair of Small Mens Ash Coloured Gloves | 00 04 08 |
| 14 pair of Mens Black Gloves | 00 03 00 |
| 12 pair of Womens Black Gloves | 00 05 06 |
| 17 pair of Mens White Gloves | 00 05 08 |
| 9 pair of Mens White Lamb Gloves | 00 03 09 |
| 19 p of Childrens Mitts & Gloves | 00 03 02 |
| 2 pairs of Mitts unfinished Lamb | 00 00 02 |
| 3 pair of Coarse Boys Gloves | 00 00 04 |
| 187 pelts in the Limes | 00 15 06 |
| Lumber Goods to Value | 01 10 00 |
| for old bedding & old furniture above stairs | 01 10 00 |
| | 14 02 07½ |

## 207. William Briscoe

Of Ketley Brook, Wellington, yeoman, taken by William Taylor and Thomas Sockett on 22 July 1745 and exhibited on 10 April 1746.

*Imprs. In the House Place*

| | | | |
|---|---|---|---|
| Six Small pewter Dishes and ffour plates . | 00 | 11 | 06 |
| Six Eartan plates . | 00 | 00 | 08 |
| Two Brass Ketels . | 00 | 08 | 00 |
| One Screen . | 00 | 02 | 00 |
| One Grate fire shovells and Tonges and Spitt . | 00 | 02 | 06 |
| Two Chaiers . | 00 | 01 | 04 |
| One Wheele . | 00 | 01 | 06 |
| One Littell Table . | 00 | 01 | 06 |

*Imprs. In the Little Room*

| | | | |
|---|---|---|---|
| One Turnell One Barrell One Pail and Other Lumber . | 00 | 06 | 00 |

*Imprs. up Stares*

| | | | |
|---|---|---|---|
| Two Old Beds and Bedstides . | 01 | 10 | 00 |
| One Chest . | 00 | 03 | 00 |
| One Small Pigg . | 00 | 07 | 00 |
| One Old Cow . | 02 | 00 | 00 |
| Lumber and Warring apariell . | 00 | 10 | 00 |
| | 06 | 05 | 00 |
| In debt . | 01 | 10 | 00 |
| Totall . | 04 | 15 | 00 |

## 208. Francis Peate

Of the Seven Stars, Wellington, taken by Roger Sockett and Thomas Freeman on 12 December 1746 and exhibited on 16 December 1746-47.

First.

| | | | |
|---|---|---|---|
| Two Cows . | 04 | 10 | 00 |
| Five Twinters . | 03 | 05 | 00 |
| one Calf . | 01 | 00 | 00 |
| part of a Bay of Barley & pease . | 01 | 10 | 00 |
| Some Straw . | 00 | 04 | 00 |
| Oats in the Straw over the Cowhouse . | 01 | 10 | 00 |
| Hay . | 03 | 00 | 00 |
| Wheate in the Straw . | 03 | 03 | 00 |
| Harrows & plow . | 00 | 15 | 00 |
| one Cart Body . | 00 | 05 | 00 |
| Tumbril & Wheels . | 01 | 00 | 00 |
| Cart & wheels . | 03 | 03 | 00 |
| Horses Gearing . | 00 | 16 | 00 |
| one Hive of Bees . | 00 | 02 | 00 |

# THE INVENTORIES OF WELLINGTON

*In the Kitchen*

| | |
|---|---|
| Grate Nigards fire Shovell & tongs fender Grid Iron & fire plate | 00 10 06 |
| one Jack three Spitts & Gobbetts | 01 00 00 |
| ffrying pan dreeping pan & Haster | 00 03 00 |
| One Iron Stand flesh fork one plate with shares Clever one Iron pele Leasy Back three Candle Sticks 1 pair of Snuffers | 00 04 06 |
| thirteen pewter dishes | 01 06 00 |
| twelve plates | 00 06 00 |
| one Quart pint two Gills & one porenger all pewter | 00 01 00 |
| one dishebench | 00 05 00 |
| one Clock & Clock Case | 01 05 00 |
| one Warming pan & Briler | 00 04 00 |
| one long table & forme | 00 05 00 |
| three screens | 00 03 00 |
| two little tables | 00 01 00 |
| two Chairs & a Stoole | 00 01 00 |
| one looking Glass | 00 00 08 |

*In the Brewhouse*

| | |
|---|---|
| one furnice & Boiler | 01 15 00 |
| one maslaine pott one Iron pott two Brass Kettles | 00 07 06 |
| one malt mill | 00 07 06 |
| four Tubbs | 00 08 00 |
| two Coolers | 00 04 00 |
| one fferkin one Barrell two tubbs & one Tunning Dish | 00 09 00 |
| one Chopper | 00 00 10 |

*In the Milkhouse*

| | |
|---|---|
| three woodden Bottles & two Churns | 00 03 00 |
| one Cheese press | 00 05 00 |
| four strike of Malt | 00 10 00 |
| three pailes & one Chese tubb | 00 05 00 |

*In the Cellar*

| | |
|---|---|
| Ten Barrells | 02 00 00 |
| Ale & Beer | 03 00 00 |
| horses & Benches | 00 04 00 |
| one mitt | 00 01 00 |
| six Glass Bottles | 00 00 06 |
| Nine Stone of Hemp | 01 02 06 |

*In the parlour*

| | |
|---|---|
| one ffeather Bed Chaff Bed ffeather Bolster one Blankett one Rugg Hangings Bedsteads & a carpet | 02 02 00 |
| one little feather Bed & rugg & Bedsteads | 00 10 00 |
| one Close Stoole | 00 03 00 |
| one long table & forme | 00 05 00 |
| one little round Table | 00 01 06 |
| Six Chairs | 00 03 00 |
| one Cubbard & Glass Cage | 00 03 00 |
| pictures & Bottles | 00 02 06 |

### In the parlour Chamber

| | | |
|---|---|---|
| two feather Beds bolster & four Blanketts two ruggs two pair of Bedsteads with Hangings & appurtenances | 03 | 00 00 |
| one Chest one form & Chair | 00 | 05 00 |

### In the Kitchen Chamber

| | | |
|---|---|---|
| one long table & forme | 00 | 03 00 |
| one long Spinning wheel | 00 | 01 06 |
| one Barrell | 00 | 02 06 |
| one horse pad & two pillian Cloaths | 00 | 05 00 |
| one Chaff Bed bedsteads &c. | 00 | 03 00 |

### In the little room over the part of the Brewhouse

| | | |
|---|---|---|
| one feather Bed Blanketts & all appurtenances | 05 | 00 00 |
| one Chest | 00 | 07 06 |
| one hanging press | 01 | 01 06 |
| one Chest of Drawers | 00 | 12 06 |
| one round table | 00 | 01 06 |
| one Cabinett | 00 | 04 00 |
| three slippings of Yarne | 00 | 03 00 |
| forty eight Bottoms of Yarne | 00 | 10 00 |
| one painted sheet & Bedquilt | 00 | 05 00 |
| two pair of Sheets one table Cloath | 00 | 12 00 |
| one remant of New Cloath | 00 | 15 00 |
| two Course table Cloaths | 00 | 04 00 |
| one lumber in several roomes not before specified | 00 | 08 00 |
| one other feather bed &c. | 00 | 17 06 |
| | | |
| two Anvells & two pair of Bellowes | 05 | 00 00 |
| 11 pair of tongs | 00 | 04 00 |
| punches & seats | 00 | 01 06 |
| Bicken & Voice | 00 | 06 00 |
| Shears | 00 | 01 06 |
| 7 Hammers & pinsors | 00 | 05 00 |
| Butterys | 00 | 00 06 |
| three Bolsteets | 00 | 00 06 |
| one Dogg | 00 | 00 03 |
| Wearing Apparell | 00 | 10 00 |
| Tot | 65 | 19 03 |

## THE INVENTORIES OF WROCKWARDINE

**209. John Smith**

Of Admaston, Wrockwardine, weaver, taken by William Smith and William Dawe on 25 May 1654 and exhibited on 18 September 1661.

| | | |
|---|---|---|
| Imp. one barren cow | 01 | 10 00 |
| It. one two yeare ould heifer | 01 | 06 08 |
| It. one yearelinge heiffer | 00 | 18 00 |
| It. 3 Sheepe | 00 | 09 00 |
| It. Corne growinge on the grownd | 02 | 00 00 |
| It. all the brasse & pewter & Iron ware in the house | 02 | 00 00 |
| Itt. trinedling ware | 00 | 10 00 |
| It. 2 tables & one frame & one forme one cheere loose boardes & Shilfes | 00 | 13 04 |
| It. house hould provision | 00 | 10 00 |
| It. bed stides | 00 | 06 00 |
| It. 2 feather beds 2 flock beds and all furniture belonginge thereunto | 02 | 00 00 |
| Itt. all the linnin in the house | 01 | 10 00 |
| It. 3 loomes & 9 woollen geeres & 23 linnin geeres and the warping trough & barre | 04 | 00 00 |
| It. his wearinge Apparell | 00 | 13 04 |
| It. all thinges not seene & forgotten | 00 | 02 06 |
| Some | 19 | 09 10 |

**210. Roger Pemberton**

Of Leaton, Wrockwardine, yeoman, taken by James Smith, Thomas Roe, Thomas Smith, Thomas Laurence, Roger Roe and Edward Pemberton on 10 June 1661 and exhibited on 30 April 1662. He was buried on 21 May 1661.

| | | |
|---|---|---|
| Imprimis oxen, kyne, yonge beasts and calves | 120 | 00 00 |
| Item. horses mares and colts | 36 | 00 00 |
| Item. sheepe & lammes | 30 | 00 00 |
| Item. swyne | 05 | 13 04 |
| Item. pullen & poultrey | 00 | 06 08 |
| Item. corne & malt in the house | 110 | 00 00 |
| Item. corne of ye grounde | 43 | 06 08 |
| Item. brasse & pewter | 16 | 00 00 |
| Item. dreepinge pans broaches grates & other iron ware | 02 | 10 00 |
| Item. bedsteads bedds beddinge and furniture | 38 | 13 04 |
| Item. lynnens & lynnen yarne | 28 | 00 00 |
| Item. table Boards & formes | 05 | 03 04 |
| Item. Chests and Coffers | 03 | 06 08 |
| Item. Chayres Stooles & cushions | 02 | 00 00 |
| Item. hoggsheads barrells stunds and trynnen ware | 05 | 06 08 |
| Item. waynes ploughes yoakes Chaynes and all other implements of husbandry | 13 | 06 08 |

# THE INVENTORIES OF WROCKWARDINE 403

| | | |
|---|---|---|
| Item. his wearing apparrell & cloth in ye house to have made him clothes . . . . . . . . | 20 00 00 | |
| Item. muck & compost . . . . . . | 02 00 00 | |
| Item. debts and leases sperate . . . . . | 134 00 00 | |
| Item. debts desperate . . . . . . | 80 00 00 | |
| Item. one malt myll . . . . . . . | 02 00 00 | |
| Item. plate . . . . . . . . | 06 00 00 | |
| Item. whyttmeate . . . . . . . | 08 00 00 | |
| Item. sythes . . . . . . . . | 00 10 00 | |
| Item. all thinges forgotten & upappised . . . . | 00 05 00 | |
| The whole some is . . | 1,112 00 00 | |
| from wch ye £80 desperat debt being deducted ye rem is . . | 1,032 00 00 | |

## 211. Thomas Cope

Of Allscott, Wrockwardine, miller, taken by Roger Roe and George Cheshire on 16 January 1666–67 and exhibited on 8 May 1667. He was buried on 4 January 1666–67.

| | |
|---|---|
| Imprs Brass & pewter . . . . . . . | 01 10 00 |
| Item One Iron pott, & one morter . . . . . . | 00 05 00 |
| Item Tables, fformes, stooles & Chaires . . . . | 00 10 00 |
| Item One Chest, one Coffer & one Box . . . . | 00 06 08 |
| Item Two old ffeather beds wth ye Bedding thereunto belonging . | 01 00 00 |
| Item One Bedstead & a Trundle bedstead . . . | 00 07 00 |
| Item Linens & other Napery ware . . . . . | 01 00 00 |
| Item ffour Cowes, one Bull & three Heifers . . . | 11 00 00 |
| Item ffive Horses & two Colts . . . . . | 10 00 00 |
| Item ffive Swine . . . . . . . | 02 00 00 |
| Item Beefe, Bacon, & other household pvision . . . | 01 10 00 |
| Item Hay . . . . . . . . | 02 00 00 |
| Item Pullon & poultry . . . . . . | 00 05 00 |
| Item Trinnen ware . . . . . . . | 00 10 00 |
| Item His wearing Apparell . . . . . . | 02 00 00 |
| Item Things fforgotten . . . . . . | 00 04 00 |
| Totall . . . | 34 07 08 |

## 212. Hercules Felton

Of Nash, Wrockwardine, taken by Edward Pemberton of Wrockwardine, Thomas Smith of Admaston, Philip Howle of Orleton and William Daw of Admaston on 29 March 1668 and exhibited on 29 July 1668. He was buried on 24 March 1667–68.

| | |
|---|---|
| Impri the lease of the house &c for & during the life of Elinor ffelton vid: . . . . . . . . | 18 00 00 |
| It three Cowes & three Calves . . . . . | 07 00 00 |
| one Incalfe Cow . . . . . . . | 02 06 08 |
| Six barren Cowes & one heifer . . . . . | 11 10 00 |

| | |
|---|---|
| three bullocks & one bull | 06 16 08 |
| two yearling calves | 00 17 00 |
| ffive Horses & Colts | 11 00 00 |
| Two swine | 00 14 00 |
| nine couple of ewes & lambs | 02 14 00 |
| Sixteen yearling sheep & weathers | 03 10 00 |
| Hay | 01 00 00 |
| Hemp | 00 05 00 |
| Corne in the house | 00 05 00 |
| Corne in the barne | 02 10 00 |
| Compost | 00 10 00 |
| Corne in the feild | 05 00 00 |
| Bees | 00 10 00 |

*In the house*

| | |
|---|---|
| Bacon & beefe | 01 00 00 |
| Two brasse & two iron potts | 00 16 00 |
| brasse vessels of all sorts | 00 13 04 |
| Pewter of all Sorts | 00 15 00 |
| one small table board & bench | 00 03 04 |
| one Iron dreeping pann one fire shovell & tongues, one grate & one paire of copboards | 00 10 00 |

*In the lower Chamb*

| | |
|---|---|
| One waiscott bedsteed & one truckle bed | 00 08 00 |
| one Chest one Cupboard two ioyned stools & one form | 00 13 04 |
| Linnen of all sorts | 05 00 00 |
| three fetherbeds with their furniture | 03 10 00 |
| two small coffers & one little box | 00 05 00 |

*In the other Chamb*

| | |
|---|---|
| one chaffe bed with furniture | 00 05 00 |
| Butter & Chease | 01 00 00 |
| All the wooden vessels | 01 00 00 |
| one Cart & all implements of husbandry | 02 00 00 |
| Wearing apparell | 01 10 00 |
| Poultry | 00 03 04 |
| All things forgotten | 00 02 06 |
| | 94 03 02 |

## 213. Thomas Smith

Of Admaston, Wrockwardine, yeoman, taken by Edward Mytton, Edward Pemberton Senr., Edward Pemberton Junr., and John Warter on 19 May 1670 and exhibited on 30 May 1670. He was buried on 6 May 1670.

| | |
|---|---|
| Imprs. Six Oxen | 30 00 00 |
| item. Twelve Cowes | 34 00 00 |
| Item. Seven two year olds | 14 00 00 |

## THE INVENTORIES OF WROCKWARDINE

| | |
|---|---|
| Item. ffoure yearlings | 05 00 00 |
| Item. Weaning Calves five | 02 10 00 |
| Item. Two Mares & two Colts | 10 00 00 |
| Item. ffive Swine & 3 Shuts | 03 00 00 |
| Item. Sheep | 12 00 00 |
| Item. Corn & Mault in ye house | 25 00 00 |
| Item. Corne in ye ffield both winter & lent tillage | 30 00 00 |
| Item. ffoure standing Beds & two Truckle Beds wth their furniture | 20 00 00 |
| Item. Pewter of all sorts | 07 00 00 |
| Item. Brass vessels of all sorts | 05 00 00 |
| Item. Iron ware of all sorts for ye use of ye house | 02 00 00 |
| Item. Table boards longer & lesser wth ye formes belonging to ym | 02 00 00 |
| Item. Stooles & Chaires | 01 00 00 |
| Item. Three presses, two Chests one Desk, & Coffers of all sorts | 03 00 00 |
| Item. Thirteene Silver Spoones | 05 00 00 |
| Item. Linnens of all sorts | 20 00 00 |
| Item. Cheese & other prvision for ye house | 05 00 00 |
| Item. Wooden vessels & other utensils for ye house | 02 10 00 |
| Item. Two stone cisternes | 01 00 00 |
| Item. Two ffowling Guns | 01 00 00 |
| Item. Waines & other Implemts of husbandry | 15 00 00 |
| Item. A lease of ye premises for one & twenty years after his decease | 200 00 00 |
| Item. An Assignement of other Lands for two lives | 60 00 00 |
| Item. His waring apparell | 05 00 00 |
| Item. Things omitted | 01 00 00 |
| The totall | 519 00 00 |

### 214. Ralph Pearce

Of Long Lane, Wellington, taken by William Cope, Edward Pemberton Senr., and Thomas Laurence on 1 June 1671 and exhibited on 17 October 1671. He was buried on 27 April 1671.

| | |
|---|---|
| Imp. ffoure Kine | 10 00 00 |
| Itm. one little Gray mare | 02 00 00 |
| Itm. ffive Eawes & lambes & Three sheepe of a yeare ould | 01 10 00 |
| Itm. one little Swine | 00 08 00 |
| Itm. Two little iron potts | 00 05 00 |
| Itm. Three little brasse kettles and one Skellett and a little scummer | 00 13 04 |
| Item. Three small pewter dishes, one little saucer, one pewter Candlesticke and one brasse candlesticke and six pewter spoones | 00 04 00 |
| Item. one short Table in the house Two chaires and woodden vessells of all sorts | 00 06 08 |
| Itm. one short broach a little ffrying pan & a paire of pott geales | 00 01 06 |

*Itm. In the loft over the house*
| | |
|---|---|
| one paire of Joyned bedsteades with the furniture thereto belonging a little chest and an ould coffer | 01 00 00 |

*Itm. In the loft over the shop*
| | |
|---|---|
| Two low paire of bedsteades with theire furniture and an ould coffer | 00 10 00 |

| | | |
|---|---|---|
| Itm. Linnens of all sorts | . . . . . . . | 01 00 00 |
| Itm. New Cheese in the house | . . . . . . | 00 06 08 |
| Itm. Three Loomes for a weaver for all theire appurtenances | . . | 02 00 00 |
| Itm. his wearing apparell | . . . . . . . | 00 15 00 |
| Item. Two hens & a cocke | . . . . . . . | 00 01 00 |
| Itm. All things fforgotten | . . . . . . | 00 05 00 |
| | Tot . . . | 19 06 02 |

## 215. Thomas Binnell

Of Allscott, Wrockwardine, yeoman, taken by William Cope, Roger Roe and Thomas Roe on 7 October 1678 and exhibited on 8 October 1678. He died on 1 August and was buried on 3 August 1678.

*Imprmis In the hall*

| | | |
|---|---|---|
| Two Table boards 2 fformes 2 Skreenes, 2 Chairs, 2 dreepinge panns 1 warminge panne, 1 Iron grate 1 fir shovell 1 paire of Tonges & 1 plate | . . . . . . . . | 01 18 08 |

*Item in ye Parlor*

| | | |
|---|---|---|
| Two Table boards & 1 Carpett, 1 fforme, 1 ffeather bed & ye furniture thereunto belonginge & 2 Cushions | . . . . | 01 16 00 |

*Item in ye Inner Chamber*

| | | |
|---|---|---|
| One bedd & ffurniture | . . . . . . . | 00 06 08 |

*Item In ye Buttery*

| | | |
|---|---|---|
| 5 Barrells | . . . . . . . . | 00 07 06 |

*Item In ye Chamber over the parlor*

| | | |
|---|---|---|
| One bedd & furniture One Chest, & one Joyned presse | . . . | 02 00 00 |
| Item: Lynnens & Napry ware | . . . . . . | 01 00 00 |
| Item: Brasse & pewter | . . . . . . . | 03 00 00 |
| Item: All manner of Trynnen ware | . . . . . | 00 15 00 |
| Item: In ready money | . . . . . . . | 00 15 00 |
| Item: Three Lammes | . . . . . . . | 00 08 00 |
| Item: The decedents wearinge apparrell | . . . . . | 03 00 00 |
| Item: All things forgotten | . . . . . . | 00 05 00 |
| | | 15 12 04 |

## 216. Thomas Roe

Of Wrockwardine, taken by Richard Wicksteed, John Newton, Phillip Howle and John Carver on 6 December 1679 and exhibited on 21 April 1680. He was buried on 7 December 1679.

# THE INVENTORIES OF WROCKWARDINE

*Impr. In the parlor*
one gine bead in the parlor wth furniture thereunto belonginge . 02 00 00
A table borde a forme a carpit and a preese . . . . 01 12 00

*Itm. In the Chamber over the parlor*
one beadstide a preese tow Chaeres . . . . . 02 00 00

*Itm. In the Chamber over the buttrey*
one bead and furniture a Chest a Box . . . . . 01 10 00

*Itm. In the Chamber over the house*
one bead with the furniture a deaske a chere . . . . 03 10 00

*Itm. In the Chamber over the entrey*
one bead and a Couffer . . . . . . . 00 15 00

*Itm. In the Chamber over the kiching*
one standing bead and a truckell bead wth thire furniture . . 01 10 00
Itm. three Couffer and a Cheare . . . . . . 00 12 00

*Itm. In the Stoure Chamber*
the Chease . . . . . . . . . 06 00 00

*Itm. In the house*
a drawinge table a side table a forme foore stoules tow scrines
one chere six cussings and a Carpit . . . . . 03 00 00

*Itm. In the kitchinge*
a table borde a Cubbort . . . . . . . 00 05 00
Itm. The brase . . . . . . . . 06 00 00

*Itm. In the Chamber over the grond seler*
a table bord and Cubbort . . . . . . . 00 11 06
Itm. All the pouter . . . . . . . . 03 10 00
Itm. All manner of linnings . . . . . . . 10 00 00
Itm. All maner of Trinnige ware . . . . . . 04 00 00
Itm. All maner of Irne ware . . . . . . . 02 00 00

*Itm. In the backe house*
a kneadinge trecke tow witing stonds . . . . . 01 00 00

Itm. The bidgest youcke of Ozen . . . . . . 09 00 00
Itm. The second youcke of Ozen . . . . . . 08 00 00
Itm. The bullockes . . . . . . . . 07 00 00
Itm. The tow steres . . . . . . . . 03 10 00
Itm. The teene kinne . . . . . . . . 20 00 00
Itm. The five yearlings . . . . . . . 05 00 00
Itm. The Six Kavles . . . . . . . . 04 00 00
Itm. The therty shippe . . . . . . . 03 10 00
Itm. The swine . . . . . . . . 04 14 00

| | |
|---|---|
| Itm. All maner of graine thraisted and unthraisted with the haye and the corne that is sowed . . . . . . | 54 04 00 |
| Itm. Waines Plowes harror with all the Impluments belonginge to husbentry . . . . . . . . | 12 00 00 |
| Itm. Three twinter kowlts one yeare ould coult and a sucking coult . . . . . . . . . . | 09 10 00 |
| Itm. A grey mare . . . . . . . . | 04 05 00 |
| Itm. A Baye mare . . . . . . . . | 03 10 00 |
| Itm. The Blacke horse . . . . . . . | 03 00 00 |
| Itm. his wearinge Apparell . . . . . . . | 05 00 00 |
| Itm. Thinges unprized and forgotten . . . . . | 02 00 00 |
| Itm. Deabts oweing to the deseaced upon band . . . | 05 13 06 |
| Itm. Other deabts lent upon worde . . . . . | 03 06 00 |
| the tot . . | 203 08 00 |

### 217. Francis Hawkins

Of Charlton, Wrockwardine, taken by George Colley and George Brooks on 16 December 1679 and exhibited on 16 January 1679-80. He was buried on 1 December 1679.

| | |
|---|---|
| Imprimis Three oxen pricd . . . . . . . | 11 10 00 |
| Item Seaven cowes . . . . . . . . | 17 10 00 |
| Item Three Three yeere ould Bease . . . . . | 06 10 00 |
| Item ffoure Two yeare ould Bease. . . . . . | 06 00 00 |
| Item Three yeere ould Bease & a weaning coult . . . | 04 00 00 |
| Item one mare . . . . . . . . | 02 10 00 |
| Item Thirtie foure Sheepe . . . . . . . | 04 10 00 |
| Item ffive swine . . . . . . . . | 04 00 00 |
| Item Rye in the Barne . . . . . . . | 10 00 00 |
| Item Barlie . . . . . . . . . | 12 00 00 |
| Item pease & oates . . . . . . . . | 05 00 00 |
| Item Hay . . . . . . . . . | 05 00 00 |
| Item Corne in the ffield . . . . . . . | 08 00 00 |
| Item A waine & Tumbrill wth Iron Bound wheles & other implemts of husbandrey . . . . . . . . | 07 00 00 |
| Item Two Joyned Beds wth other Bedsteeds . . . . | 02 00 00 |
| Item Three ffetherbeds & two fflock Bedds wth other furniture belonging to them . . . . . . . . | 15 00 00 |
| Item Tenn pare of Sheetes wth napkins . . . . . | 04 00 00 |
| Item Two Chests & Three coffers . . . . . . | 01 10 00 |
| Item Two presses & a screene . . . . . . | 02 00 00 |
| Item Table Boards Bonches & formes . . . . . | 01 10 00 |
| Item Three Brasse pots & three Brasse kettels wth sume other brasonweare . . . . . . . . . | 05 00 00 |
| Item One duzon of pewter dishes two candlestickes wth sume other pewter . . . . . . . . . | 02 00 00 |
| Item Two Ironpotts a dreeping pan wth Broches calbots grate & other necessaries . . . . . . . . | 01 13 04 |

## THE INVENTORIES OF WROCKWARDINE 409

| | |
|---|---|
| Item A weeting fatt brewing stund & other trinenware . . . | 02 00 00 |
| Item A mault mill . . . . . . . . | 01 10 00 |
| Item Cheese & Butter . . . . . . . | 02 10 00 |
| Item Baken in the house . . . . . . | 01 10 00 |
| Item Bible & other Bookes . . . . . . . | 01 00 00 |
| Item Mondeyes due by Bond . . . . . . | 300 00 00 |
| Item moneyes oweing wthout Bond . . . . | 05 00 00 |
| Item things forgotten . . . . . . . | 00 05 00 |
| Item the testators wearing apparell & moneyes in his porse . . | 03 00 00 |
| | 454 18 04 |

### 218. Elizabeth Bullock

Of Wrockwardine, spinster and schoolmistress, taken by William Cope and Robert Pemberton on 10 June 1681 and exhibited on 14 June 1681. She was buried on 7 June 1681.

| | |
|---|---|
| *Imp In the loft which was the place where shee kept schoole in* one Trucklebed with the furniture thereunto . . . . | 01 00 00 |
| Itm In the same Roome one little table Three buffet stooles & a low ioyned stoole with a drawer Two Greene Chaires seven benches & four little stooles . | 00 10 00 |
| Itm In the same Roome one brasse pot three little iron pots one very little kettle one boxe to hold salt a paire of bellowes one grate a paire of pothookes a paire of tounges a fire shoulv one plate to warme drinke on before the fire a paire of Pot Geales and a ffrying pan . . . . | 01 00 00 |
| *Itm In her lodging Chamber* one Joyned Bedstead with the furniture thereunto belonging . . | 05 00 00 |
| Itm In the same Chamber one little table on Livery table with a drawer One Livery Cupboard one Chest one ould Trunke Two Deskes one being a little one a coffor two dale boxes and foure little baskets one Glasse cratch . | 02 00 00 |
| Itm In the same Chamber one warming pan Eight dishes of pewter some little & some larger three saucers & one pewter Chamber pot one pewter Candlesticke a dozen of pewter spoonee a dozen of trenchers A looking glasse and three Jugs with blue spots with other earthenware . . . | 01 06 00 |
| Itm In the same Chamber Three paire of flaxen sheetes & one od one one seven paire of hempen & Canvise sheetes ffifteene napkins for Comon servine one Table Cloath and six Pillows beares and six Towells . . . | 04 00 00 |
| Itm ffine Linnen Cloath unmade and a piece of blue linnen . . | 01 00 00 |
| Itm ffor wearing apparell of all sortes both linen and wollen & a peice of rough woollen Cloath to make a petticote . . . | 03 06 00 |
| Itm ffor bookes of all sortes . . . . . . | 01 00 00 |
| Itm money in the house . . . . . . . | 14 00 00 |
| Itm money upon bond . . . . . . . | 30 00 00 |
| Itm All things fforgotten . . . . . . . | 00 10 00 |
| | 64 13 04 |

## 219. Eleanor Newe

Of Wrockwardine, taken by William Hall,* Thomas Juson, Robert Crump and Richard Viggers on 6 October 1681 and exhibited on 5 October 1681.

*Imprs. In the Parlor*

| | | | |
|---|---|---|---|
| one standing bed one feether bed two boulsters one under bed and beding thereunto belonging . . . . . . | 02 | 00 | 00 |
| It. one joyned press one old table board one beare hoggs head two halfe barrells one range of wainescott shilives and two coffers praised at . . . . . . . . . | 02 | 08 | 06 |
| It. Linne yearen in the same roome praised at . . . . | 01 | 00 | 00 |
| It. benches shilves and stooles at . . . . . | 00 | 09 | 00 |
| It. A fire grate a pair of tongues pott gailes a large back plate for ye fire and two broaches . . . . . . | 00 | 18 | 04 |

*It. In the milkhouse and butterey*

| | | | |
|---|---|---|---|
| milk vessells on rinling tubb 5 shelves & 12 Cheeses . . . | 00 | 11 | 00 |
| It. One brass pan three littell bras kettles one brass pott, two littell dreeping panns, one Iorn pott and other small thing praised at . | 01 | 12 | 06 |

*It. In the littell chamber*

| | | | |
|---|---|---|---|
| one paire of bedsteeds A feether bed and bed hillings one littell Coubbard one Cuffer a littell bentch and one narrow shilfe praised at . . . . . . . . . . | 01 | 04 | 04 |

*It. In the Chamber ov' ye littell roomes*

| | | | |
|---|---|---|---|
| flax and hemp ready tewtand and old implements for husbandry . | 01 | 00 | 00 |
| It. A mattock pike forks A beame for waits and other old Iorne . | 00 | 03 | 00 |
| It. one Reath or stock for A cart wheel . . . . | 00 | 01 | 00 |

*It. In ye Chamber ovr the house*

| | | | |
|---|---|---|---|
| one paire of bedsteeds one feether bed and beding thereto belonging praised at . . . . . . . . . | 01 | 00 | 00 |
| It. A trickle bed old bed stides A beare barrell plow timber and wheele timber 4 spade trees and two littell spining wheeles &c. . | 00 | 18 | 00 |

*It. In the store chamber*

| | | | |
|---|---|---|---|
| Nine and forty cheeses . . . . . . . | 02 | 02 | 00 |
| It. fell wool old vessells and two coffers . . . . | 00 | 13 | 00 |
| It. trainan ware and vessells of all sorts . . . . | 00 | 08 | 00 |
| It. one Iorne pestell an Iorn wedg sev' iorn Chissels and other iorn implements . . . . . . . . | 00 | 03 | 00 |
| It. one pannell or pad . . . . . . . | 00 | 01 | 08 |
| It. Pewter of al sorts one puding plate one brass skimer & a brass candlestick . . . . . . . . . | 00 | 13 | 00 |
| It. one Large kneeding tubb or mott . . . . . | 00 | 05 | 00 |
| It. Linnoens viz five paire of hemp sheets two paire of canvas one paire of flaxen sheets 15 napkins a table cloth & other napry . . | 01 | 13 | 00 |
| It. one young mare and an old mare . . . . | 03 | 00 | 00 |

It. Eight cowes two three yeare old beasts two twinters and the
calves of this year . . . . . . . . 22 03 04
It. one store swine praised att . . . . . . 00 12 00

*In the barne*
of Rie 5 mesures or strikes at 4/- per strike . . . . 01 00 00
Barley 12 strikes or mesures 2/- per strike . . . . 01 04 00
It. Oates and dregge 25 strikes 1/2 per strike . . . . 01 09 02
It. Muck manuer or Compost praised at . . . . . 00 13 00
It. Hay and other Fodder . . . . . . . 05 00 00
It. Poulterey as gees and oth' pullen . . . . . 00 01 00
It. things not seene And forgotten. . . . . . 00 02 02
It. the Testes wearing Apparrell disposed off in her lifetime . . — — —

                                                                                                                                                            55 03 08

## 220. Thomas Barker

     Of Pains Lane, Wrockwardine Wood, taken by Thomas Smith,* John Cox and John Watkiss and exhibited on 31 March 1682. The inventory is undated.

Imprimis. one owld Cowe at . . . . . . . 02 00 00
Im. one younge Cowe at . . . . . . . 02 10 00
Im. one twinter heefer at . . . . . . . 01 05 00
Im. one molte mille at . . . . . . . 01 00 00
Im. of hard Corne: 12 stricke at . . . . . . 01 08 00
Im. ye fother unspend . . . . . . . 00 10 00
Im. ye mucke in ye fowld . . . . . . . 00 02 06
Im. husbantree towles one crow 3 axes tow wedges and other nesessaries usfull . . . . . . . . . 00 05 00
Im. other Imelmentes of husbandtrey . . . . . 00 00 08
Im. one Iron poot & one marment one litell kettell of brass and zellet . . . . . . . . . . 00 07 08
Im. one broche and Cobates and pestell . . . . . 00 02 08
Im. one grate one pare of toonges pot gealls and howkes . . 00 05 00
Im. pwter: 3 dishes one candellstick one flagon 3 spownes . . 00 03 06
Im. one Cwbarte one tabelle one fowrme. . . . . 00 10 00
Im. one Chaf bed and one fether beed with bedstedes and hillines to them with pillowes & bolstores . . . . . . 01 01 03
Im. linen sheetes: 4 pare: and all other linen shifts and other things ther belownginge . . . . . . . . 00 15 08
Im. some hempe on doz dresed . . . . . . 00 05 00
Im. for all lumber ware . . . . . . . 00 04 03
Im. his waringe aparell . . . . . . . 01 01 04
Im. for thinges forgotten or unpraysed . . . . . 00 02 08

                                                                                                                                                            14 00 02

## 221. Edward Dawe

Of Wrockwardine Wood, yeoman, taken by Richard Ball, Richard Higgins and Richard Vickers,* on 7 November 1683 and exhibited on 13 January 1683-84.

| | |
|---|---|
| Impris. six Cowes | 11 10 00 |
| Itm. three twinter heifers | 05 00 00 |
| Itm. four yearling heifers | 04 00 00 |
| Itm. three reareing calves | 01 10 00 |
| Itm. one mare | 03 00 00 |
| Itm. one sowe and six pigs | 01 10 00 |
| Itm. five sheep | 00 17 00 |
| Itm. Corne in the house and in the barne and one the ground | 08 00 00 |
| Itm. hay in the barne | 01 00 00 |

*Itm. in the Parlour*

| | |
|---|---|
| one Table board, one Cubbard, two ioyned formes and three chaires | 01 10 00 |
| Itm. in the chamber over the Parlour | |
| one ioyned beddstedd and feather bedd and all things thereunto belonging | 00 03 00 |
| Itm. two chests | 00 13 04 |

*Itm. in the chamber over the house*

| | |
|---|---|
| one bedd | 00 05 00 |

*Itm. in his own chamber*

| | |
|---|---|
| one bedd and all things thereunto belonging | 02 00 00 |
| Itm. Butter and cheese | 00 13 04 |
| Itm. hempe and flax and hempe seed | 00 07 00 |
| Itm. five barrells, two kneading Turnells and a little Stund and a churne, and a cheese tubb, peales and all other trinnen ware | 01 07 00 |
| Itm. two coffers and two shelves | 00 03 00 |
| Itm. a cradle and a dishboard, and a little table board and one chaire | 00 05 00 |
| Itm. one iron marment | 00 03 00 |
| Itm. a warming pan | 00 04 00 |
| Itm. brass and pewter | 01 18 00 |
| Itm. linnens of all sorts | 01 15 00 |
| Itm. all manner of iron ware | 00 10 00 |
| Itm. implements of husbandry ware | 00 02 00 |
| Itm. his wearing apparell and money in his purse | 02 10 00 |
| Itm. any thing forgotten unpraised | 00 05 00 |
| Totall sume | 48 18 02 |

## 222. Thomas Cooper

Of Long Lane Wrockwardine, taken by Rowland Langley, Samuel Machen* and Richard Powis Senr., on 29 September 1684 and exhibited on 10 October 1684. He was buried on 14 September 1684.

# THE INVENTORIES OF WROCKWARDINE

| | |
|---|---|
| Impris one bed & furniture belonge to it . . . . | 01 10 00 |
| Item three coffer and one Trunke . . . . . | 00 06 06 |
| Item one birding gunn . . . . . . ; | 00 10 00 |
| Item one trebble Vyall & Case . . . . . | 00 10 00 |
| Item one Cowe and a heifer . . . . . | 02 10 00 |
| Item one Coult . . . . . . . | 02 10 00 |
| Item the Reversion of two Leases chared with severall Anuities . | 05 00 00 |
| Item his wearing Apparell and Money in his pockett and Linnens . | 02 10 00 |
| Total . . . | 15 06 06 |

## 223. Phillip Howle

Of Wrockwardine, taken by Robert Pemberton, John Barker, John Carver* and Thomas Laurence on 17 July 1685 and exhibited on 10 November 1685. He was buried on 28 June 1685.

| | |
|---|---|
| Imp Three mares and one nag . . . . . . | 08 13 04 |
| Itm ffour kine . . . . . . . | 08 06 08 |
| Itm Two yeare ould beasts & a weaned calfe . . . | 02 10 00 |
| Itm Tenn sheepe and three lambes . . . . | 01 13 04 |
| Itm A sow and seven pigs . . . . . . | 00 15 00 |
| Itm Corne growing upon the ground . . . . | 08 00 00 |

*Itm In the house*
one table board, one bonch one dishboard one ioyned stoole and two chaires . . . . . . . . . — 00 10 06

*Itm. In the parlour*
one short ould table one ould chaire one glasse cratch one Joyned bedstead with hangings Two fether beds two bolsters, one blanket & a rugge . . . . . . . . — 03 00 00

*Itm. In the Buttery nexte the Streete*
one large barrell and foure little ones . . . . — 00 13 04

*Item In the milkehouse*
one safe four shelves and ffive mitts for Milke . . . — 00 10 00

*Item In the booting house*
one kneading mitt one churne, a hogshead & an ould barrell . — 00 06 08

*Itm In the kitchin*
one grate one fireshouvell one paire of Tounges, a paire of Cobirons, two spitts, one dropping pan one morter & pestill two paire of pot geales four chaires, a Stoole & a shorte dresser . . . — 00 16 06

*Itm In the malthouse*
one vessell to water barley in, one haire cloath & a skreene to try malt with one long spinning wheele & two short ones . . — 01 10 00

*Itm In the Chamber where the servant man lodgeth*
one low bedstead & the furniture thereof . . . . 00 05 06

*Itm In the loft over the parlour*
one bedstead with the bed and furniture thereto, in the same loft a hanging presse two coffers one short table, one ould chaire and a ioyned stoole. . . . . . . . . 02 03 04

*Itm In the loft ovr.*
the two low bedstead & the furniture thereunto two little ioyned chests two dale boxes and three ould chaire bottomed with segs . 01 10 00
Itm Linnens of all sortes . . . . . . . 07 02 06

*Itm In the storechamber*
a frame to beare cheeses upon seven shelves for that use & the cheeses thereon & a few fleeces of wooll . . . . 01 10 00
Itm Brasse & Pewter one iron furnace and three little iron potts . 03 02 06
Itm Pailes to milke in, Two vessells to make cheese therein with the other woodden ware . . . . . . . 00 06 08
Itm One handmill & a cheesepresse in ye same roome . . 01 01 06
Itm An ould Cart, an ould Tumbrell two ploughs one paire of plough irons, one harrow, & gears for the horses with other implements of husbandry . . . . . . . . 03 03 04
Itm A small Cisterne to hold wash. . . . . . 00 02 06
Itm his wearing Apparell . . . . . . . 03 00 00
Itm Hempe fflax and linen yarne . . . . . . 00 16 00
Itm The lease of the house . . . . . . . 04 10 00
Item Bees in the Garden . . . . . . . 00 06 08

Tot . . 66 05 10

## 224. Thomas Smith

Of Wrockwardine, webster, taken by Peter Langley, John Warter the elder and Thomas Laurence on 29 June 1687 and exhibited on 19 October 1687. He was buried on 23 June 1687.

Imp. ffive kine and Two weaning calves . . . . . 11 00 00
Itm Two heifers one Two yeares ould and the other of a yeare ould . . . . . . . . . . 02 03 04
Itm An ould mare and a yeare ould colt . . . . 04 06 08
Itm six Ewes & lambes & seven young sheepe . . . 02 12 06
Itm Two little swine. . . . . . . . 00 13 00
Itm Corne growing in the ffeild . . . . . . 03 02 06

*Itm In the dwelling house*
one little brass pan one kettle one skellet seven pewter dishes one plate one ould pewter kanne one Candlestick & a salt & an ould brasse pot . . . . . . 01 05 00
Itm one large iron pot, & an other little one, an iron Morter & pestill, a spit, a little paire of cobirons, a dreeping panne, a frying

THE INVENTORIES OF WROCKWARDINE 415

| | | | |
|---|---|---|---|
| panne, a little ould grate, Two fire shovells, a small paire of fire Tounges & Two pare of pot Geales & some iron skures. . . | 01 | 13 | 04 |
| Itm A short Table with a Joyned frame, one Joyned forme, one Joyned Chaire two rush ones a little ould skreene & a paire of bellowes . . . . . . . . . | 01 | 00 | 00 |
| Itm Pailes for milke & water & other vessells of wood . . . | 00 | 08 | 06 |

*Itm In the Buttery*

| | | | |
|---|---|---|---|
| ffive barrells foure Glasse bottles . . . . . . | 00 | 10 | 00 |

*Itm In the little Chamber*

| | | | |
|---|---|---|---|
| one Joyned Table, A little Mitt a vessell to coole wort in, one little ould stoond . . . . . . . . . | 00 | 06 | 00 |

*Itm In the little house on the backside*

| | | | |
|---|---|---|---|
| a cheese presse a kneading vessell & an ould stoond to keepe wash . | 00 | 03 | 04 |

*Itm In the loft over the house*

| | | | |
|---|---|---|---|
| one ould Joyned bedstead & the furniture thereto, one Truckle bed with its furniture, a short side table, one Joyned Chest, Two little ould coffers & a whisket made of straw . . . . | 03 | 13 | 04 |

*Itm In the store chamber*

| | | | |
|---|---|---|---|
| an ould Truckle bed & the bedding thereto, A small parcell of new cheeses . . . . . . . . . | 00 | 13 | 06 |
| Itm Linnens of all sorts . . . . . . . | 02 | 03 | 04 |
| Itm his wearing apparell . . . . . . . | 01 | 06 | 08 |

*Itm In the shop*

| | | | |
|---|---|---|---|
| Two loomes with theire Geares and a warping trough & a little wheele . . . . . . . . . | 02 | 02 | 06 |

*Itm In the loft over the shop*

| | | | |
|---|---|---|---|
| one ould Truckle bed three ould coffers two ould whisketts . . | 00 | 10 | 00 |
| Itm the boords & ioyce which make the loft . . . . | 01 | 02 | 06 |

*Itm In the little chamber adioyning to the shop*

| | | | |
|---|---|---|---|
| one vessell to salt meate in, a few bouches & some other vessells usefull for making of cheese . . . . . . | 00 | 05 | 00 |
| Itm Debts sperate by bond & otherwise . . . . . | 23 | 01 | 06 |
| Itm Debts desperate . . . . . . . . | 06 | 00 | 00 |
| Itm Two paire of homes & Trases an ould axe, a bill a broome hooke, an ould packe saddle, a spade & a picke & some other small necessaries for use about the house . . . . . | 00 | 06 | 08 |
| Itm A little spinning wheele . . . . . . . | 00 | 01 | 06 |
| Tot . . | 70 | 11 | 04 |

## 225. Thomas Ball

Of the Moss, Wrockwardine Wood, yeoman, taken by Richard Shelton, Richard Rycroft, Edward Bould* and William Cartwright on 13 April 1688 and exhibited on 20 April 1688.

*Imprs. In the house*
| | | |
|---|---|---|
| On Table prized . . . . . . . | 00 | 10 | 00 |

*In the Parlor*
One Large Table one Chest one skreen one Chair on pair of Bedsteads all prized . . . . . . . . 02 10 00

*In the Chamber over the house*
one halftester bed one truckled bed Two Coffers prized . . 00 10 00

*In the Chamber over the Parlor*
one paire of Bedsteds one Chest on Trunk one Glass cage one Large Bible prized . . . . . . . . ; 01 00 00

*In the ould house*
Two Little Tables 4 Joyne stooles one press prized . . . 00 10 00

*In the Roome over the ould house*
| | | | |
|---|---|---|---|
| one paire of Bedsteads . . . . . . . | 00 | 02 | 06 |
| Bedding of all sorts . . . . . . . | 03 | 00 | 00 |
| Brass and Pewter of all sorts . . . . . . | 01 | 15 | 00 |
| Iron ware of all Sorts . . . . . . . | 02 | 00 | 00 |
| Wooden ware of all sorts . . . . . . . | 02 | 10 | 00 |
| | | | |
| Three heiffers . . . . . . . . | 06 | 00 | 00 |
| one Twinter Colt . . . . . . . . | 01 | 10 | 00 |
| Sheep prized . . . . . . . . . | 01 | 10 | 00 |
| Corne upon the Grouns . . . . . . . | 04 | 00 | 00 |
| | | | |
| Linnen of all sorts . . . . . . . . | 01 | 10 | 00 |
| A Mault Mill . . . . . . . . . | 01 | 00 | 00 |
| | | | |
| ffour horses or Mares . . . . . . . | 04 | 00 | 00 |
| Implements of husbandry . . . . . . . | 02 | 00 | 00 |
| Wareing Apurrill and Money In his purse prized . . . | 04 | 00 | 00 |
| All other things omitted or out of Sight prized . . . | 00 | 05 | 00 |
| due upon Bond . . . . . . . . | 16 | 00 | 00 |
| | | | |
| Sum . . | 56 | 02 | 06 |

## 226. Thomas Laurence

Of Clotley, Wrockwardine, yeoman, taken by Edward Mytton, Thomas Wood, William Pemberton and Thomas Bate on 27 April 1688 and exhibited on 17 October 1688. In his will dated 13 August 1687 he left his property to his wife Anne. It included a tenement in Clotley Wood leased to Richard Lockley and houses and gardens in New Street, Wellington. He was buried on 19 April 1688.

| | |
|---|---|
| Imp 5 oxen & 2 bullocks at | 28 00 00 |
| Ite & Cowes & a Bull | 23 00 00 |
| Ite 4 yeare olds at | 04 00 00 |
| Ite 1 old Mare & colt one 3 yeare old colt & one 2 yeare old colt | 10 00 00 |
| Ite one younge mare at | 05 00 00 |
| Ite 9 ewes & lambes & 14 younge sheepe | 06 00 00 |
| Ite 5 rearinge calves | 01 13 04 |
| Ite 2 swyne | 02 00 00 |
| Ite Corne in the Barne | 02 10 00 |
| Ite Corne in the house & Mault at | 03 10 00 |
| Ite Corne uppon the Grownde | 10 00 00 |
| Ite Oates & pease uppon the ground | 04 00 00 |
| Ite one old wayne & Tumbrell with the Implements of husbandry | 08 00 00 |
| Ite one Mault Mill & a whisk at | 02 00 00 |
| Ite Brasse & pewter of all sortes | 07 00 00 |
| Ite one Jack dreeping pannes cobirons broaches with all other sortes of Iron ware | 04 00 00 |
| Ite in the Parlor one bed with ye furniture & a Clock | 04 10 00 |
| Ite in the house one table with one cubbord and stooles at | 01 00 00 |
| Ite in the Chamber over the house Bedding & furniture | 04 00 00 |
| Ite in the little Chamber one Bed with furniture &c | 02 00 00 |
| Ite in the Greene Chamber one & furniture &c | 05 00 00 |
| Ite in the Kitchen Chamber one Bed & furniture | 02 00 00 |
| Ite Hogsheads Barrells with all sortes of wooden ware | 03 00 00 |
| Ite Linnen & Linnen yarne with wearinge Apparell | 20 00 00 |
| Ite one Chattle Lease valued at three yeares Rent | 90 00 00 |
| Ite ready Money in the house | 20 00 00 |
| Ite debts sperat | 54 10 00 |
| Ite debts desperat | 12 00 00 |
| Ite one silver box & two little dishes | 01 00 00 |
| Ite Bookes of all sortes | 01 00 00 |
| Ite Lumber & thinges fforgotten | 02 10 00 |
| | 342 13 04 |

## 227. John Binnell

Of Allscott, Wrockwardine, yeoman, taken by Edward Mytton, Edward Russell and William Pemberton on 18 February 1688-89 and exhibited on 17 April 1689. He was buried on 10 February 1688-89.

| | |
|---|---|
| Imprs. | |
| Corne on ye grownd | 10 00 00 |

| | |
|---|---|
| six Cowes | 12 00 00 |
| Two Oxen | 05 05 00 |
| ffive twinter beasts | 06 05 00 |
| Three yearling beasts | 01 10 00 |
| Three Horses | 07 00 00 |
| 40 sheep | 08 00 00 |
| Implements of Husbandary of all sorts | 07 10 00 |
| Corne & Hay in ye Barne | 08 00 00 |
| 4 swine | 01 05 00 |
| Timber ready falne | 02 00 00 |

*In ye Hall*

| | |
|---|---|
| one long Table 2 fformes 1 side Table a forme 1 schreen 1 joyned chaire two joyned stooles 1 cupboard 1 nursing stoole & 1 carpett | 02 10 00 |

*In ye parlor*

| | |
|---|---|
| 4 chaires 1 side Table 1 other table 2 Joyned stooles 1 Carpett & 3 cushions | 00 10 00 |

*In ye passage Chamber*

| | |
|---|---|
| Brasse & pewter of all sorts | 08 10 00 |
| In ye same Chamber 1 Cupboard & 1 Table board | 00 12 00 |

*In ye Chamber over ye Parlor*

| | |
|---|---|
| 1 ffeather bed & bolster wth ye ffurnituer 1 joyned Bedstead & 1 Truckle bedstead | 02 10 00 |
| In ye same Chamber 1 Presse 1 side Table 1 Chest 1 Joyned chaire & 1 Trunke | 02 10 00 |

*In ye Chamber over ye Hall*

| | |
|---|---|
| 1 ffeather bed & furniture one Joyned Bedstead 1 Chest of Drawers one round Table one Large Trunke one Chest one little Table six chaires of calves skin on Twiggen chaire one Deske 2 stands & one looking glasse | 10 00 00 |
| Plate in ye same Roome | 02 10 00 |
| Linnen of all sorts | 10 00 00 |

*In ye Staire head chamber*

| | |
|---|---|
| one ffeather bed and ffurniture one Joyned Bedstead & presse 1 coffer 1 little Trunke 2 boxes & 3 flasketts | 02 10 00 |

*In ye servants Chamber*

| | |
|---|---|
| 1 truckle bed & furniture | 01 00 00 |
| Corne & Mault in ye house | 03 00 00 |
| Wooden ware of all sorts | 04 00 00 |
| Iron ware of all sorts | 02 10 00 |
| Beef Bacon & other household provisions | 05 00 00 |
| Books & wearing Apparell | 06 00 00 |
| Hemp & fflax | 01 00 00 |

THE INVENTORIES OF WROCKWARDINE

one saddle one pillion & one Gun . . . . . 01 00 00
Muck & Compost wth Lumber & things not seen . . . 02 00 00

              Tot . . 137 17 00


## 228. Sarah Cornes

  Of the Street Way, Wrockwardine, widow, taken by Andrew Hotchiss and exhibited on 23 June 1690. The inventory is undated. She was buried on 29 November 1691.

a Table and forme . . . . . . . . 00 05 06
1 cheare . . . . . . . . . 00 00 06
a fire shouell tongues and grate . . . . . 00 02 00
a brandert . . . . . . . . . 00 00 06
2 broaches and a paire of cobberts and dreepinge pan . . . 00 02 10
a brase pan . . . . . . . . . 00 03 00
a brase cettle . . . . . . . . . 00 00 06
a brase pott . . . . . . . . . 00 02 06
a plate . . . . . . . . . . 00 00 04
pouter . . . . . . . . . . 00 03 06
2 stondes . . . . . . . . . 00 03 00
2 barrells . . . . . . . . . 00 03 00
a bucket . . . . . . . . . . 00 00 04
a paile . . . . . . . . . . 00 00 09
a coouler . . . . . . . . . 00 02 00
a churne . . . . . . . . . . 00 01 00
a cubbert . . . . . . . . . 00 03 00
2 wheels . . . . . . . . . 00 01 00
2 counes . . . . . . . . . . 00 04 00
a neared petty coat and wastcoate . . . . . 00 01 00
a stuff petty coate and a cloth petycoate . . . . 00 01 00
a paire of shuse and stockinges . . . . . 00 01 00
a hat . . . . . . . . . . 00 00 06
6 napkines . . . . . . . . . 00 02 06
7 paire of sheets and 1 od . . . . . . 00 15 00
3 eles of cloth . . . . . . . . 00 03 00
a bible . . . . . . . . . . 00 03 00
2 cuffers . . . . . . . . . 00 02 00
a trunke . . . . . . . . . 00 02 00
2 bed steads . . . . . . . . . 00 04 00
a friinge pan . . . . . . . . . 00 00 04
shifts . . . . . . . . . . 00 05 00
a pillowe bear and boulster . . . . . . 00 02 00
2 glases and a cup . . . . . . . 00 00 04
a pikil . . . . . . . . . . 00 00 02
a mattocke and a broum hoocke . . . . . 00 01 00
2 bod rickes . . . . . . . . . 00 07 00

                    04 09 03

## 229. Robert Fenn

Of Wrockwardine Wood, taken by Allen Pickerell, Richard Vickers and George Goulbourne on 19 January 1693-94 and exhibited on 24 April 1694. He was buried on 12 January 1693-94.

| | |
|---|---|
| Two Cowes at three pound ye cow . . . . . | 06 00 00 |

*Item. in ye Chamber*

| | |
|---|---|
| Two Chests one press one Table board one Joyne Bedstead and feather bedd & one Chaire . . . . . . . | 03 00 00 |

*Item. in ye Chamber over ye house*

| | |
|---|---|
| two standinge bedds one flocke bedd & one Chaffe bedd Coverletts and blanketts and hillings att . . . . . | 01 10 00 |

*Item. In ye house or hall where they live*

| | |
|---|---|
| Brass and pewter of all sorts . . . . . . | 01 00 00 |
| Item. one Table board one Joyne forme one Joyne press and two Chaires . . . . . . . . . . | 00 13 04 |
| Item. Wooden ware of all sorts . . . . . | 00 10 00 |
| Item. one Grate firepan & Toungs & all Iron Ware . . | 00 05 00 |
| Item. Linnige of all sorts three pair of hempton sheetts three paire of Hurden sheetts napkins & Towells . . . . | 01 00 00 |
| Item. Corn in ye barn & corn in ye house . . . | 01 10 00 |
| Item. Earthen Ware of all sorts . . . . . | 00 00 08 |
| Item. Wearinge Aparrell & money in his pockett . . . | 01 00 00 |
| Item. things forgott and not Apraised . . . . | 00 05 00 |
| Sume . . | 16 14 00 |

## 230. William Pemberton

Of Leaton, Wrockwardine, gent., taken by Roger Pemberton, John Evans and Roger Sockett on 24 March 1693-94, and exhibited on 28 March 1693-94.

*Imprs. In the Hall*

| | |
|---|---|
| one Table Board and fframe and two fformes Three joyned Screenes, one joyned Chaire and two other chaires and one nursing Stoole, one brass morter and two iron pessells one Iron Grate, fire shovell and Tongs, one Smootheing Iron . . . . . . | 01 10 00 |

*Item In the parlor*

| | |
|---|---|
| one ffeather bed, ffeather Bolster one blankett, one Coverlett one paire of sheetes one joyned Bedsted and Curtains and Vallens, one old Table and fframe and one fforme, one old Carpett one joyned press cubboard one livery Table & one pewter dish one Coffer, one pewter Chamber pott, two Diaper Towells . . . . | 02 05 00 |

## THE INVENTORIES OF WROCKWARDINE

*Item In the Buttry*

| | |
|---|---|
| one little Table, one old joyned Cubboard, Six Pewter dishes, two pewter Candlesticks, one pewter pollenger One brass pott, two Searches one haire sieve and other Trumpery . . . . | 01 00 00 |

*Item In the Kitchin*

| | |
|---|---|
| one old Brasse ffurnace, two large brass pans three old brasse kettles one Marmlett one litle brasse pan two little brasse pans one posnett one Skellett one little kettle three iron spitts one iron grate one warmeing pan one brewing stund one large Mitt Three pailes one Churne two Tubbs one pewter Bason one pewter gun and one pewter pollinger Two dozen of Trenchers one Dozen of Bottells one paire of Iron Racks one paire of Cobberts . . . . | 02 10 00 |

*Item in the New Chamber*

| | |
|---|---|
| one joyned Bedsted ffeather bed bolster and other Apptences one joyned Chest one Coffer a Dozen and halfe of coarse Napkins Two old Trunks Six paire of course Sheetes one Livery Table one Childs Chaire and two basketts . . . . . . | 02 00 00 |
| one joyned Chest in the Spare . . . . . . | 00 05 00 |

*In the farther Chamber*

| | |
|---|---|
| Three joyned Bedsteds two ffeather beds and one Chaffe Bed three blanketts and three Coverletts two Coffers one old Cradle one old Truckle Bed . . . . . . . . | 02 00 00 |

*Item In the Chamber over ye house*

| | |
|---|---|
| Two ffeather beds one old Chest and one Livery Table . . . | 01 05 00 |

| | |
|---|---|
| Item Hardcorne and Barley. . . . . . . | 03 00 00 |
| Item Two Mares and one Colt ffoure Cowes and Three Calves . . | 14 00 00 |
| Item one Sow and Seaven Shutts and hay . . . . | 02 05 00 |
| Item one Waine and Implements of husbandry . . . . | 01 10 00 |
| Item Two wheeles and three Barrells . . . . . | 00 08 00 |
| Totall . . | 33 15 00 |

## 231. Richard Mountford

Of Bratton, Wrockwardine, yeoman, taken by Robert Richards, Thomas Lowe and William Newton on 13 July 1694, and exhibited on 2 October 1694. In his will dated 1 March 1689-90 he left his whole estate, apart from some small legacies, to his wife Alice (*233*). He was buried on 7 July 1694.

| | |
|---|---|
| Imprs. Two Oxen . . . . . . . . | 10 00 00 |
| Seaven Cowes and one Bull. . . . . . . | 22 00 00 |
| Two Twinter heifers and two Twinter Bullocks . . . . | 08 00 00 |
| Three yeare old Calves . . . . . . . | 03 00 00 |

| | |
|---|---|
| Eight Sheepe | 01 12 00 |
| Two Mares and one Sucking Colt | 08 00 00 |
| one yeare old Colt | 02 00 00 |
| Two Swine | 01 15 00 |
| Nyne Geese | 00 04 06 |
| one waine two paire of wheeles and other Implements of husbandry | 06 00 00 |
| Corne growing on ye ground | 12 00 00 |
| The value of the Lease to continue for one Anncient Life | 30 00 00 |
| Two ffeather beds | 02 00 00 |
| Three other Beds | 01 10 00 |
| ffive blanketts and twelve paire of sheetes | 02 00 00 |
| Bedsteds | 01 10 00 |
| Two dozen of Napkins | 00 10 00 |
| Two Table Cloathes | 00 05 00 |
| One Joyne press 2 Quoffers one Chest Three Tables one Boxe one Joyne fforme two Chaires & three Joyne Stooles | 01 10 00 |
| Brass and pewter | 01 10 00 |
| one Iron pott Grate, ffireshovell Tongs and other Iron ware | 00 15 00 |
| All sorts of wooden ware as Barrells Stunds &c. | 01 00 00 |
| Whitmeate | 02 10 00 |
| debts sperate and desprate | 60 00 00 |
| wearing Apparrell and ready money | 03 00 00 |
| Things not seene omitted or fforgotten | 00 05 00 |
| | 184 16 06 |

## 232. Thomas Latham

Of Allscott, Wrockwardine, yeoman, taken by John Laurence, John Warter and John Smith on 28 June 1698 and exhibited on 7 October 1698. He was buried on 21 June 1698.

| | |
|---|---|
| Imps. Corne on the grounde | 12 00 00 |
| Foure cows | 10 00 00 |
| Three two yeare olds | 04 10 00 |
| ffour yearelings | 04 00 00 |
| Three horses | 06 00 00 |
| A Twinter Colt | 02 10 00 |
| Thirty Sheepe | 06 00 00 |
| Tenn Lambs | 01 05 00 |
| Implements of husbandry of all sorts | 03 10 00 |
| Three Calvs | 01 10 00 |
| Two Swine | 01 00 00 |

*In the hall*

| | |
|---|---|
| one long table 2 forms 1 side table & form 1 screen 1 joyn chair 2 joine Stools 1 cupboard 1 nursing stool and one carpett | 02 10 00 |

*In the parlour*

| | |
|---|---|
| three chaires one side table one other table two joine stools and three cushions | 01 00 00 |

*In the passage chamber*
brass and pewter of all sorts . . . . . . 06 00 00

*In the same chamber*
1 cupboarde & one Table board . . . . . 00 10 00

*In the chamber over the parlour*
1 feather bed bolster with the furniture one joyned bedd and one
Truckle bedstead . . . . . . . . 02 10 00

*In the same chamber*
1 press 1 sidetable A chest one joyned chaire and 1 trunk . . 02 10 00

*In the Chamber over ye hall*
1 feather bed and furniture one joyned bedstedd one chest of
Drawers one round table 1 larg trunk one chest one little table
Six chairs 1 twiggen chaire 1 desk two stands and one looking
glass . . . . . . . . . . 10 00 00
Linen of all sorts . . . . . . . . 10 00 00

*In the Stairehead chamber*
1 feather bed & furniture one joined bedstead & press on Coffer one
little trunk twoo boxes and three flaskits. . . . . 02 00 00

*In the Servants Chamber*
one truckled bed and furniture . . . . . . 01 00 00

Wooden Ware of all sorts . . . . . . . 04 00 00
Iron Ware of all sorts . . . . . . . 02 00 00
Books and wearing apparell . . . . . . 04 00 00
Hemp and flax and yarn . . . . . . . 00 10 00
Muck and Compost with Lumber and things not seen . . 02 10 00
                                                                         103 05 00

## 233. Alice Mountford

Of Bratton, Wrockwardine, widow of Richard Mountford (*231*), taken by Richard Powis Senr., Edward Silcox and Thomas Lowe on 7 February 1698-99 and exhibited on 27 April 1698. The parish register notes 'about the beginning of November (1696) was John, a bastard child of Alice Mountford of Bratton, baptised', but her burial is unrecorded.

Imprimis. Seven Cowes at 3 pound a peice . . . . 21 00 00
Item. Two Oxon at 8 pounds . . . . . . 08 00 00
Item. Three twinters at fortey shillings apice . . . . 06 00 00
Item. Six younge bese more . . . . . . 07 00 00
Item. Two mares at 5 pounds a pice . . . . . 10 00 00
Item. one wening Coult at 1 pound . . . . . 01 00 00

| | | | |
|---|---|---|---|
| Item. five shipe at 4 shillinges a pice | 01 | 00 | 00 |
| Item. Two Store Swine at 8: Shilling apice | 00 | 16 | 00 |
| Item. for poltrey | 00 | 02 | 00 |
| Item. for harde Corne in ye barne | 06 | 00 | 00 |
| Item. for barley | 05 | 00 | 00 |
| Item. for oates in ye barne | 00 | 10 | 00 |
| Item. for pese in ye barne | 01 | 00 | 00 |
| Item. for hay | 03 | 00 | 00 |
| Item. for Corne upon ye Ground | 05 | 00 | 00 |
| Item. for one wayne & tow pare of wheles and All other Implements of husbandray | 03 | 00 | 00 |
| Item. for malte 5: strick | 01 | 00 | 00 |
| Item. for whitmeate | 02 | 10 | 00 |
| Item. for bras & pewter | 11 | 05 | 00 |
| Item. for tow Iron pots | 00 | 10 | 00 |
| Item. for tow bedes & bedstides with all the forniture | 03 | 10 | 00 |
| Item. for linenes | 02 | 00 | 00 |
| Item. for tow table bordes & 2 Coffers & one Chest | 01 | 10 | 00 |
| Item. for barrells & other Couperey ware & for Cheres & Stoles | 01 | 05 | 00 |
| Item. for Grate & fier shovell & tonges & pot houckes | 00 | 03 | 00 |
| Item. the value of ye lease to Containe for one ould life | 15 | 00 | 00 |
| Item. bets sperate and desperate | 26 | 00 | 00 |
| wareing aperill & redey monney | 20 | 00 | 00 |
| thinges not seene omited or forgotten | 00 | 05 | 06 |
| Totall is | 155 | 16 | 06 |

## 234. Thomas Binnell

Of Clotley, Wrockwardine, yeoman, taken by William Turner, Walter Marigold and George Churme on 24 November 1700 and exhibited on 9 April 1701. He was buried on 10 November 1700.

| | | | |
|---|---|---|---|
| Imp his wearing Apparrell & money in his purse | 02 | 06 | 08 |
| It Bedsteads bedds and Bedding | 07 | 04 | 06 |
| It Tables fourmes presses stooles & chaires | 01 | 13 | 04 |
| It Coffers and Chests | 00 | 16 | 00 |
| It Brass and pewter | 02 | 07 | 00 |
| It Llinnens | 01 | 17 | 00 |
| It hemp and Flaxe | 01 | 19 | 00 |
| It Corne & hey in ye Barne and corne & Mault In the house | 16 | 00 | 00 |
| It Cowes oxen & other younge catle | 42 | 00 | 00 |
| It horses and sheepe | 22 | 10 | 00 |
| It Swine | 03 | 00 | 00 |
| It Implements of husbandry | 01 | 18 | 06 |
| It Iron Ware | 00 | 15 | 06 |
| It one Chattall Lease | 70 | 00 | 00 |
| It things unnominated & forgotten | 00 | 10 | 00 |
| | 174 | 17 | 06 |

## 235. William Charlton

Of Charlton, Wrockwardine, yeoman, taken by Richard Astley junr. of Harpswood and Johanthan Brooke on 19 September 1704 and exhibited on 28 April 1705. He was buried on 22 August 1704.

| | | | |
|---|---|---|---|
| Imprs. Eight Oxen . . . . . . . . | 31 | 00 | 00 |
| Item fiveteen cowes. . . . . . . . | 37 | 10 | 00 |
| Item Teen Two yeare oulds . . . . . | 20 | 00 | 00 |
| Item Two Bulls . . . . . . . . | 04 | 00 | 00 |
| Item Seven yearlings . . . . . . . | 07 | 17 | 00 |
| Item Seven Caules . . . . . . . . | 03 | 10 | 00 |
| Item Eight Horses and Coultes . . . . . | 22 | 00 | 00 |
| Item Ninety seven sheep . . . . . . | 11 | 00 | 00 |
| Item One and seventy Piggs . . . . . | 09 | 05 | 00 |
| item Poultry of All Sorts . . . . . . | 01 | 00 | 00 |

*Item In ye Hall*
one Long Table two formes one Press one Screen one Clocke . .    03 10 04

*Item In ye Seller*
Hoggsheds & Six Barrells . . . . . . . .    01 05 00

*Item In ye Buttrey*
two littell tables two Dosson & a half of Glas Bottels . .    10 08 00

*Item In ye Parlor*
two Beeds & one pare of Bedstids one Table five Joyne Stooles Six Chaires one Joyne Press one Coffer . . . .    07 08 00

*Item In ye Chamber over ye Parlor*
one Beed & Bedstids one Coffer one Box. . . . .    02 15 00

*Item In ye Chamber over ye kitching*
| | | | |
|---|---|---|---|
| three pare of Bedstids one Beed one Cheste three Coffers and one Box . . . . . . . . . . . | 03 | 10 | 00 |
| Item The Servants Beeds . . . . . . . | 01 | 10 | 00 |
| Item All Sorts of Linnings . . . . . . . | 10 | 00 | 00 |
| Item Hemp & flax drest and undrest . . . . | 03 | 10 | 00 |
| Item Cheese in the House . . . . . . . | 08 | 08 | 00 |

*Item In ye kitching*
| | | | |
|---|---|---|---|
| one Table one bench four spinning Wheeles one Salt Box Six Stooles one dish crate one Glas crate and other small things . . . | 01 | 04 | 00 |
| Item Brass and Pewter of All Sorts . . . . | 04 | 15 | 00 |
| Item All in ye millck house. . . . . . . | 01 | 00 | 00 |
| Item Coupperiware in ye Brewhouse of all sorts . . . | 01 | 10 | 00 |
| Item Iron Ware of all Sorts . . . . . . | 02 | 00 | 00 |
| Item Beefe & Bacon provision for the house . . . | 01 | 00 | 00 |

| | |
|---|---|
| Item Corne in the house | 02 14 06 |
| Item haigh and Clover in the Barne | 10 00 00 |
| Item Corne & Graine of all Sorts | 67 00 00 |
| Item Waines & Tumbrills & other Imployments of husbandry | 14 00 00 |
| Item Muck & Compost | 05 00 00 |
| Item The Reversion of a Lease from Jonathan Row | 80 00 00 |
| Item due upon a morgag from William Pemberton | 100 00 00 |
| Item the decesed wareing apparill and moneys in pockett | 11 00 00 |
| Item All things fforgotten | 00 05 00 |
| totall | 491 11 04 |

## 236. Daniel Pucksley

Of Wrockwardine Wood, webster, taken by Hugh Delves and Robert Pucksley on 6 January 1704-05 and exhibited on 23 January 1704-05.

Imps.
| | |
|---|---|
| one Cow | 02 00 00 |
| two loomes warpings trough & gears & tooles belonging to his trade | 02 00 00 |
| Beds one Hive | 00 05 00 |
| Bedsteds Bedding & Napere ware | 00 10 00 |
| Brass & pewter | 00 16 00 |
| two Iron Marmots one pall | 00 05 00 |
| two tables two fformes | 00 18 00 |
| one Cubart | 00 10 00 |
| one Chest 3 coffers 2 Boxes | 00 06 08 |
| one kneadeing Turnell | 00 03 00 |
| one grate & all Iron ware | 00 03 04 |
| Hempe yarne & wheeles | 01 03 04 |
| Butter & Cheese | 00 04 00 |
| his weareinge apparell | 00 15 00 |
| out of sight | 00 01 00 |
| toto | 09 06 04 |

## 237. Jane Scholefield

Of Wrockwardine, spinster and schoolmistress, taken by John Smith and John Grice on 31 January 1704-05 and exhibited in February 1704-05. She was buried on 19 January 1704-05.

*Imprs. In her lodging roome over ye house*
| | |
|---|---|
| one standing Bed one feather Bed one Chaff Bed two Boulsters & two pillows one Blankett one Rugg wth hangings Round | 02 18 00 |
| Item one little Bed wth one feather Bed two Blanketts & on Boulster | 00 12 00 |
| Item Truncks & Boxes two of each one little table one little Desk & one dressing Box | 00 09 00 |

# THE INVENTORIES OF WROCKWARDINE

| | | |
|---|---|---|
| Item one Trunck one Coffer two little Boxes and one looking Glass . . . . . . . . . . | 00 05 06 |
| Item The Chimney Dress . . . . . . . | 00 01 00 |

*Item In ye other Roome over ye house*

| | |
|---|---|
| one Standing Bed one fflock Bed one Chaff Bed one feather Bolster one Blankett one Rugg wth Hangings . . . . . | 01 00 00 |
| Item one other Trindell Bed one feather Bed one Boulster one Blankett one Rugg with Hangings . . . . . . | 01 15 00 |
| Item one Chest . . . . . . . . | 00 04 00 |

*Item In the Chamber over ye Schoole*

| | |
|---|---|
| one standing Bed one feather Bed one fflock Bed one feather Boulstr: one fflock Boulstr: two ffeather pillows two Blanketts and one Quilt . . . . . . . . | 03 10 06 |
| Item one Trindell Bed one feather Bed one fflock Bed one feather Boulster one Blankt Two Ruggs wth Hangings . . . . | 00 04 00 |
| Item one Chest & one Box . . . . . . . | 00 04 00 |
| Item one Pilling . . . . . . . . | 00 05 00 |

*Item In ye Schoole*

| | |
|---|---|
| Six Benches Three Stools . . . . . . . | 00 01 06 |

*Item In ye Dwelling House roome*

| | |
|---|---|
| one press two tables one forme two Joynd Chears Six Black chears & Six Small chears . . . . . . . . | 00 16 10 |
| Item Three paire of fflaxen Sheets Ten paire of Hempn Sheets ffoure fflaxen pillow Beers and Three Course pillow Beers . . | 03 06 02 |
| Item Three window Curtains one vallance . . . . | 00 01 06 |
| Item nine Table Cloths two Dozen & Seven Napkins and one Dozen of Towells . . . . . . . . . | 00 10 06 |
| Item Pewter of all Sorts . . . . . . . | 01 19 00 |
| Item Tinn ware 2s 6d Brass ware 15s Iron ware £1 15s 0d . . | 02 12 06 |
| Item Wooden & Trinen ware £1 9s 0d & 2 Dozen of Glass Bottles 2s . | 01 11 00 |
| Debts upon Sperialty . . . . . . . | 05 07 06 |
| Debts wthout sperialty . . . . . . . | 19 19 02½ |
| Books waring apparell both linnen and woollen . . . . | 17 00 00 |
| Things unseen unthought of and forgotten . . . . | 00 05 00 |
| Sum Totall . . | 64 18 08½ |

## 238. Joseph Cope

Of Allscott, Wrockwardine, millner, taken by John Smith and Joshua Calcott on 19 February 1704–05 and exhibited on 28 April 1705. He was buried on 18 February 1704–05.

| | |
|---|---|
| Imps Cattell of all sorts . . . . . . . | 10 00 00 |
| Item Horses . . . . . . . . . | 07 10 00 |
| Item Sheepe . . . . . . . . . | 01 00 00 |
| Item Corne . . . . . . . . . | 04 00 00 |

| | | |
|---|---|---|
| Item Piges | . . . . . . . . . | 02 00 00 |
| Item Linnens. | . . . . . . . . | 01 10 00 |
| Item Beding . | . . . . . . . . | 03 00 00 |
| Item Chests and Coffers | . . . . . . . | 00 10 00 |
| Item Bras and Pewter | . . . . . . . | 01 00 00 |
| Item Ironware of all sorts | . . . . . . | 00 10 00 |
| Item Wooddess Vessells | . . . . . . | 00 10 00 |
| Item Tables Benches and stooles | . . . . . | 00 10 00 |
| Item The deceseds waring apparell | . . . . | 01 10 00 |
| Items All things forgotten | . . . . . . | 00 03 00 |
| | totall . . | 33 13 00 |

## 239. Richard Vickers

Of Wrockwardine Wood, yeoman, taken on 23 February 1704–05 and exhibited on 30 April 1705. The appraisers are not named. He died on 18 February 1704–05 and was buried on 20 February 1704–05.

*Imps. Ye house place*
One Table, one fform, one skreen, one Dish bench and three Chairs . 00 10 00
ffour Pewter Dishes and a Tankard, ffive spoons and one Little Brass pot and a skellet . . . . . . . 00 10 00

Item one Iron Pott, one Little Brass Kettle, one Little Grate and ffire shovell and Tongues one ffrying pan: a little back and one Little Iron marmott . . . . . . . . 00 10 00

*The Parlour*
One pair of Bedsteads and ffeather Bed with fittings thereunto belonging one Press and one Coffer one Little Table and Two Chairs . . . . . . . . . . . 01 10 00

*Chamber over ye Parlour*
One pair of Bedsteds and fflockbed a small parcell of Flax and Hemp and ffour Cheeses . . . . . . . 00 12 00

*Ye house Chamber*
Item A pair of Joynd Bedsteads and fflock Bed and all belonging to it a small quantity of Beef and Bacon one Coffer and Three pair of sheets . . . . . . . . . 02 00 00

*The Buttery*
Item Too Little Barrells one stund a Little Churn, one small Kneading Turnell one pail and one Little Gawn . . . . . 00 10 00

*Corn and Cattle*
Item ffour Little Cowes too of them very ancient, ffour small Heifers and too Calves . . . . . . . 15 00 00

Item Too Aged Horses and old Gears for to Carry Coals withall . 02 10 00

## THE INVENTORIES OF WROCKWARDINE 429

| | |
|---|---|
| Item a few small Implements of Husbandry . . . . | 00 10 00 |
| Item A small quantity of Barley in the straw and a Little parcell of Hay . . . . . . . . . . | 03 00 00 |
| Item Corne on the ground . . . . . . . | 01 00 00 |
| Item The Muck . . . . . . . . | 00 06 08 |
| Item his wearing Apparrell and money in his pockett . . . | 02 00 00 |
| Item his funerall Charges . . . . . . . | 02 00 00 |
| Sum tot is . . | 32 08 08 |

### 240. Thomas Icke

Of Trench Lane, Wrockwardine Wood, labourer, taken by William Icke on 30 April 1708 and exhibited on 30 April 1708. The parish register records the burial of Thomas Icke senr. of the Trench Lane, carpenter on 27 August 1707.

| | |
|---|---|
| Imps. Two kine sold at . . . . . . . | 03 08 00 |
| Itm. Two Heifers sold at . . . . . . . | 01 08 00 |
| Itm A Little pigg . . . . . . . . | 00 10 00 |
| Itm One old press . . . . . . . . | 00 04 00 |
| Itm Two Little old tables . . . . . . . | 00 02 00 |
| Itm An Iron Possnett . . . . . . . | 00 01 00 |
| Itm An old Iron broken pott . . . . . . | 00 00 04 |
| Itm An old bed . . . . . . . . | 00 02 00 |
| Itm for Lumber . . . . . . . . | 00 04 00 |
| | 05 10 02 |

### 241. Edward Bold

Of Trench Lane, Wrockwardine Wood, yeoman, taken by Edward Dawes and Edward Currier on 2 July 1708 and exhibited on 4 May 1709.

| | |
|---|---|
| Imps. one Brass pann three Brass Kettles one brass pott . . | 00 14 00 |
| Itm one Spitt one paire of Tongs one paire of pot gales . . | 00 01 00 |
| Item one Iron pott and one driping pann . . . . | 00 02 00 |
| Item one Table Board and one fforme . . . . | 00 04 00 |
| Item one Chaire and one Stoole . . . . . | 00 00 08 |
| Item Linnens of all sorts . . . . . . | 00 06 08 |
| Item Three Beds and ffurniture . . . . . . | 01 18 00 |
| Itm one chest one Quoffer and one cupboard . . . | 00 10 00 |
| Item wooden ware of all sorts . . . . . . | 00 10 00 |
| Itm one Maslin Kettle and pte of one Dishboard . . . | 00 01 00 |
| Item two Spinning Wheeles. . . . . . . | 00 03 00 |
| Item one candlestick and two Salts . . . . . | 00 01 00 |
| Item one leafe of a Table and one Quoffer . . . . | 00 02 00 |
| Item things not seene omitted or forgotten . . . . | 00 02 00 |
| Item One Brass pott one little Brass Kettle . . . | 00 02 00 |
| | 04 17 04 |

## 242. Richard Lummas (or Lomas)

Of Pains Lane, Wrockwardine Wood, master collier, taken by William Dawes* and Richard Poole on 4 September 1711 and exhibited on 16 October 1711. He was buried on 28 August 1711 when the parish register described him as a yeoman. In his will made on 25 August 1711 he left all his property to his wife, after whose death his leasehold land in Eyton was to go to his son Richard, and his property at Pains Lane to his son John.

| | |
|---|---|
| Imprs. three cows one 3: years old heafer and one twinter | 14 00 00 |
| one mare | 05 00 00 |
| Seavon Sheep and two Lambs | 01 10 00 |
| Four store piggs | 01 10 00 |
| Four bigg Swine | 05 00 00 |
| Corne of all sorts | 15 10 00 |
| Hay valued att | 03 00 00 |
| one Joyne press | 00 12 00 |
| one screene six chaires 1 Littell table | 00 08 00 |
| one bedsteds 2: fether beds with all the furniture belonging to them | 05 00 00 |
| one Littell table & five chaires | 00 07 06 |
| one table one form | 00 03 00 |
| one Joyne bed one truckoll bed | 04 00 00 |
| one chest two boxzes one coffer and one trunk | 01 00 00 |
| one Joyne bed with the furniture | 05 00 00 |
| one other bed & all things belonging to it | 02 00 00 |
| one press and one Chest | 00 15 00 |
| two coffors | 00 10 00 |
| one table two Joyne Stooles Six Chairs two Joyne forms | 01 00 00 |
| Twenty Eight pewter dishes together with all other pewter one brass pott two warmeing pans and six brass kettells | 02 00 00 |
| two Iron furnaces foure Iron potts two Littel marmolets | 03 15 00 |
| two fir shovels two pairs of tongs two spitts two grates pot Racks two frying pans with all other small iron things | 00 15 00 |
| two Dreeping pans | 00 06 08 |
| Drink in the Celler | 04 00 00 |
| Linnes of All sorts | 04 15 00 |
| Wooden ware of All sorts | 02 10 00 |
| one Steele mill | 01 00 00 |
| Implements of Husbandry | 02 00 00 |
| weareing Apparrell and money in his purss | 02 10 00 |
| things forgotten and not Apprized | 00 05 00 |
| Totall is | 93 14 02 |

## 243. Joshua Calcott

Of Allscott, Wrockwardine, taken by John Evans and Thomas Binnell on 17 April 1714 and exhibited on 3 May 1714. The parish register records the burial of Mr. Joshua Calcott of Allscott and his daughter Esther on 19 April 1714.

THE INVENTORIES OF WROCKWARDINE                               431

Imprs.
| | | |
|---|---|---|
| Eleven Cowes and a Bull . . . . . . . | 42 00 00 |
| Six working Bullocks . . . . . . . | 22 00 00 |
| Six Two year old Beasts . . . . . . . | 09 00 00 |
| Five year olds . . . . . . . . | 05 00 00 |
| Three Mares and two Horses and one two year old Colt . . | 20 00 00 |
| Eleven Sheep . . . . . . . . . | 05 00 00 |
| Eleven Swine . . . . . . . . . | 05 10 00 |
| Hard Corne upon the Ground . . . . . . | 10 00 00 |
| Lent Graine . . . . . . . . . | 20 00 00 |
| Old corne and Hay . . . . . . . . | 10 00 00 |
| Implemts of husbandry . . . . . . . | 04 00 00 |
| Brass and Pewter and Iron ware . . . . . . | 03 10 00 |
| Beding of all sorts . . . . . . . . | 10 00 00 |
| Linnen of all sorts . . . . . . . . | 02 00 00 |
| His wearing Apparel . . . . . . . . | 06 00 00 |
| One Clock . . . . . . . . . | 05 00 00 |
| Things unseen and forgotten . . . . . . | 03 00 00 |
| Total . . | 182 00 00 |

## 244. Allen Pickering

Of Pains Lane, Wrockwardine Wood, taken by Christopher Pickering and Thomas Taylor* and proved on 4 March 1714-15. The inventory is undated.

Impris.
| | |
|---|---|
| Six horses and mares at . . . . . . . | 13 00 00 |
| The Wagon and all the Traces and one great Chaine and all materials belonging to the Wagon and horses . . . . . | 05 00 00 |
| Wearing Apparel and money in his pocket . . . . | 01 00 00 |
| For things seen and unseen . . . . . . . | 00 10 00 |
| | 19 10 00 |

## 245. William Ball

Of Quob Pool, Wrockwardine Wood, collier, taken by William Dawes and Christopher Pickering on 28 May 1717 and exhibited on 1 June 1717. In his will made on 17 May 1717 he left his dwelling house at Quob Pool and his share in 'the coalworks' to Richard, his eldest son, his house at the Trench and the land adjoining to his second son, Richard, and 'Pixley's house and garden, the Synderhill Copy and Edward Fenn's house and garden' to William, his third son.

*Imp In ye which was in his house place of ye Quobb poole*
| | |
|---|---|
| All beding and all beLonging to it . . . . . . | 01 11 06 |
| Itm All pewter . . . . . . . . | 00 05 04 |
| All wooden ware wt: in and wt: out of all sorts . . . . | 01 09 00 |

| | | |
|---|---|---|
| All ye Linin . . . . . . . . | 00 06 08 | |
| All Iron ware wt: in & wt: out of all sorts . . . . | 00 16 00 | |
| The Brass . . . . . . . . . | 00 02 00 | |
| Tow Cowes and one yeare ould heyfor . . . . | 05 15 06 | |
| Three Mares . . . . . . . . . | 07 00 00 | |
| The Corne upon ye ground . . . . . . . | 01 06 06 | |
| His Debts . . . . . . . . . | 02 00 00 | |
| His warin Apparill and Money in pockitt . . . . | 01 10 00 | |
| All Things Omitted and out of sight . . . . | 00 10 00 | |
| | **22 12 06** | |

## 246. John Yarsley

Of the Oaken Gates, collier, taken by Roger Sockett and John Sockett on 3 July 1719 and exhibited on 7 October 1719. All the probate documents refer to Oakengates, none of them naming a parish. The Wrockwardine parish register records the marriage of John and Judith Yarsley on Ascension Day 1680 and the birth of their son in March 1680-81.

| | |
|---|---|
| ffour Cows . . . . . . . . . | 09 00 00 |
| one hogg . . . . . . . . . | 00 10 00 |
| Twelve Ewes & Twelve Lambs . . . . . . | 03 00 00 |
| Eight yeare old sheep . . . . . . . | 01 04 00 |

*In the house place*

| | |
|---|---|
| ffour pewter dishes . . . . . . . . | 00 06 00 |
| 3 porrengers one plate & other small Iron potts . . . | 00 02 00 |
| Two Small Caldrons & two Small Iron potts . . . | 00 04 00 |
| one Grate ffire Shovell & Tongues. . . . . | 00 05 00 |
| one Iron peal a paire of Racks & one Broach . . . | 00 02 00 |
| one Flesh Forke & one old Tinn dreeping pan . . . | 00 00 09 |
| one Long Table one Joyne Forme & a Joyne Chaire . . | 00 05 00 |
| Three old Chaires & one old Joyne stoole . . . | 00 00 08 |

*In the parlour*

| | |
|---|---|
| one ffeather Bed bedstead & 2 Blanketts & other Furniture belonging to the same . . . . . . . . | 01 10 00 |
| one Chest & one Coffer . . . . . . . | 00 04 00 |
| one old Long Table & one old Joyne fforme . . . | 00 03 00 |

*In the Buttery*

| | |
|---|---|
| Two ffirkins & one old Churne . . . . . . | 00 01 06 |
| one old small pewter dish & two old Benches . . . | 00 00 09 |

*In the Chamber over the house*

| | |
|---|---|
| one old ffeather Bed one old fflck Bed 2 Bedsteads one Truckle bedstead and Blanketts . . . . . . . | 00 15 00 |
| one Chest one old Coffer & one old Cradle . . . | 00 03 00 |

# THE INVENTORIES OF WROCKWARDINE 433

| | | |
|---|---|---|
| Linnen of all sorts | 01 00 00 |
| Weareing apparrell & money in pockett | 00 15 00 |
| Things omitted & Forgotten | 00 05 00 |
| | 19 16 08 |

## 247. John Barker

Of Pains Lane, Wrockwardine Wood, yeoman, taken by Samuel Winnall and John Ringley on 24 December 1721 and exhibited on 1 January 1721–22.

| | |
|---|---|
| Three old Cowes and 2 geese | 07 00 00 |
| Hay in the barn | 01 10 00 |

*In the Hous place*

| | |
|---|---|
| 8 small pewter dishes | 00 08 00 |
| 6 pewter porringers and one pewter tankerd | 00 03 00 |
| one pewter Chamber pot and 18 pewter spoons | 00 02 00 |
| Two old iron Marmallets one iron and one old brass pott, one small Calldron | 00 04 06 |
| Two iron broaches one iron dripping pan one grate fire shovel and tonges and other iron ware | 00 05 00 |
| Two Small table and one join'd forme and other wooden ware | 00 05 00 |

*In the buttery*

| | |
|---|---|
| Three small barrels and kneading and churn | 00 07 00 |

*In the Parlor*

| | |
|---|---|
| one hanging press, one old Cupboard one pair of bedsteads and one brewing vessel | 01 00 00 |

*In the two Chambers over the hous place*

| | |
|---|---|
| Two old feather beds and sheets & blankets &c belonging to the same | 02 00 00 |
| One old Coffer and one large Spinning Wheel | 00 01 00 |

*In the Chamber over the parlor*

| | |
|---|---|
| One old feather bed with Sheets & blankets | 01 10 00 |
| Two Chests and Two boxes | 00 05 00 |
| Linnen of all sorts | 01 05 00 |
| Wearing Apparel | 00 05 00 |
| Ready money | 00 06 00 |
| Thinges forgotten and unpraisd | 00 03 00 |
| Tot | 16 19 06 |

## 248. Thomas Bold

Of Trench Lane, Wrockwardine Wood, taken by Thomas Higgins and Edward Currier on 14 July 1722 and exhibited on 2 October 1722.

| | |
|---|---|
| Imprs. Too Cows | 04 10 00 |
| Itm one too year old Heifor | 02 05 00 |
| Itm Too Rearing Calfes | 01 04 00 |
| Itm Too Hoarses | 04 00 00 |
| Itm Corne one The Ground | 03 00 00 |
| Itm Too Beds and Bedsteeds whith all the furniture belonging to them | 01 10 00 |
| Itm Tables Stooles Chests Cobards Chairs and all sorts of Joyners weare | 01 02 00 |
| Itm pewter of all sorts | 00 05 00 |
| Itm Iron ware of all sorts | 00 06 08 |
| Itm one Brass kettle | 00 01 00 |
| Itm Coopers ware of all sorts | 00 10 00 |
| Itm Linins of all sorts | 00 10 00 |
| Itm wearing aparill and money in pockett | 00 10 00 |
| Itm Things omitted or forgotten | 00 05 00 |
| | 19 18 08 |

## 249. William Cheshire

Of Admaston, Wrockwardine, gent., taken by Richard Allsop and Charles Fairchild on 14 January 1725–26 and exhibited on 21 April 1726. He was buried on 12 January 1725–26.

*In the Hall*

| | |
|---|---|
| one long Table & one round do | 00 17 00 |
| one little Table | 00 02 00 |
| one Form & one Skreen | 00 06 00 |
| Six Wainscott Chairs | 00 12 00 |
| one Clock and Brasse for a Grate | 01 00 00 |

*In the Parlour*

| | |
|---|---|
| one large & one small round Table | 00 16 00 |
| nine leather Chairs | 01 07 00 |
| one pair of hand Irons for the Grate | 00 04 00 |
| one Couch | 00 06 00 |
| 15 Pictures | 00 05 00 |

*In the Study*

| | |
|---|---|
| one Table and Bookes | 01 00 00 |

*In the Pantry*

| | |
|---|---|
| one Dozen pound of Hemp & ½ dozen of Flax | 00 07 00 |
| Two Cupp-boards and one small Table | 00 07 00 |
| Twenty-four Trenchers Glasses & Tickneyware | 00 05 00 |

one Straw Whiskett & two Pasty peales . . . . 00 05 00
one old Churn . . . . . . . . 00 06 00

*In the Passage*
one hairpad . . . . . . . . . 00 02 06
one Chair . . . . . . . . . 00 02 00
one Saddle one Pillion and Cloth . . . . . 00 14 00
Netts . . . . . . . . . . 00 04 00

*In the Dairy*
Two Flitches of Bacon . . . . . . . 02 00 00
one Churn & Staffe & one Cheese Tubb . . . . 00 07 00
Four wooden Bottles . . . . . . . 00 04 00
Six Cheese Fetts . . . . . . . . 00 04 00
Milk panns and Stoan Potts . . . . . . 00 01 06
one Block . . . . . . . . . 00 00 06
one pair of Wooden Scales and Weights one Pair do . . 00 02 00
one pair of Yaringles . . . . . . . 00 00 06
Three Shelves . . . . . . . . 00 01 06
1 Frying Pan & one Strawe Tubb . . . . . 00 02 03

*In the Kitchen*
One Bowler . . . . . . . . . 00 04 00
Thirty one pewter Dishes & one Cheese Plate . . . 05 10 00
Three Dozen and five Plates . . . . . . 01 05 00
Four Salvers twelve Porringers . . . . . . 00 08 00
one Tankard Seven Brasse Candlesticks . . . . 00 11 00
Four Brasse Potts and three Brasse bottles . . . . 03 06 00
Two Iron Dreeping Panns . . . . . . . 00 15 00
one Jacke & six Spitts . . . . . . . 01 10 00
one Pair of large Racks one Pair of Small do . . . 00 05 00
Eleven Knives and eleven Forkes . . . . . 00 04 00
five Sillver Spoons . . . . . . . . 02 00 00
Two watering Panns . . . . . . . 00 02 06
one Pair of Garden Sheers . . . . . . 00 01 06
Two Tinn Covers . . . . . . . . 00 00 08
one large Grate . . . . . . . . 00 16 00
one Brass and one Iron Frogg . . . . . . 00 02 06
One Tinn Pasty Pann and one Tinn do . . . . 00 01 04
one little Brasse Porter and Pestill . . . . . 00 03 00
Four Fire-Shovells and three pair of Tonges . . . 00 07 06
one warming Pan . . . . . . . . 00 03 00
Two flatt Irons & one Box Iron & heaters . . . 00 02 00
Three Iron & one small Brasse candlestick . . . . 00 01 06
Two chopping knives and one Flesh Fork . . . 00 02 06
one Cleaver . . . . . . . . . 00 00 08
one Skewer Frame & twelve skewers . . . . 00 02 00
one Skreen one Table and Drawers . . . . 00 07 00
one large Table and Form . . . . . . . 00 06 00
Three Chairs and three joyned stooles . . . . 00 02 00
one long Gaun . . . . . . . . 00 10 00
one Hatchett . . . . . . . . . 00 01 00
one Birdspit . . . . . . . . . 00 00 06

| | |
|---|---|
| A Glasse-Cage and Glasses . | 00 02 00 |
| one wooden Morter and Pestill . | 00 01 00 |
| Three Pewter Salts . | 00 00 06 |
| one Tunning Dish . | 00 00 02 |
| one Pair of Nigards . | 00 01 06 |
| one chafeing Dish . | 00 00 06 |

*In the Scullery*

| | |
|---|---|
| One Cheese-Presse and three pales . | 00 07 06 |
| Two Gauns and a Seay—& one Possnett . | 00 02 06 |
| One Sauceppann and two Turnells . | 00 03 04 |
| Two Iron Kettles . | 00 06 00 |
| Four Noggins and six Trenchers . | 00 01 00 |
| One Cullinder and four Spoons . | 00 00 06 |

*In the Cellar*

| | |
|---|---|
| Four Beer Vessells 5 halfe Hoggs-heads Five Smaller Barrells & one Powdering Tubb and Horses . | 03 02 06 |

*In the Parlour Chamber*

| | |
|---|---|
| Three Feather Bedds, two pair of Bedd-steads one presse Bead, three Bolsters four Pillowes one Quilt one Coverlidd Six Blanketts and two pair of Hangings . | 08 00 00 |
| One Pair Chest of Drawers . | 00 10 00 |
| one Small Table and one large looking Glass . | 00 12 00 |
| one Easy Chair and one water Stand . | 00 03 06 |
| one Peice of new Hurden Cloth: 20 Elne . | 00 18 06 |
| Three Trunks and a Close-Stool and pann . | 00 05 06 |
| one Straw Whiskett and a dressing Box . | 00 03 06 |

*In the Chamber over the Parlour*

| | |
|---|---|
| Two pair of window Curteins . | 01 00 00 |

*In the Chamber over the Pantrey*

| | |
|---|---|
| Two pair of Beddsteads and two feather Bedd three Blanketts and a Coverlidd . | 02 10 00 |
| One Chest one Trunk and one Chair . | 00 07 00 |
| One little round Table . | 00 01 06 |
| one Spinning wheel and one Hopper . | 00 02 00 |

*In the Dairy Chamber*

| | |
|---|---|
| One pair of Beddstead Hangings Feather Bedd Bolster Counterpinn and 5 Blanketts . | 05 00 00 |
| One pair of window Curtains . | 00 05 00 |
| One Chest and one Chest of Drawers . | 01 00 00 |
| eight Cain Chairs . | 01 05 00 |
| one Fender and one little Table . | 00 04 00 |
| one looking Glasse . | 00 08 00 |

*In the Kitchen Chamber*

| | |
|---|---|
| one pair of Beddsteads one Feather Bedd & Bolster two Blanketts and a Coverlidd . | 02 10 00 |

# THE INVENTORIES OF WROCKWARDINE

one hanging Presse one Chest . . . . . . 00 15 00
Three Trunks and a Stand . . . . . . . 00 10 00
one Small Table one close stoole & Pan . . . . 00 05 00
one looking Glasse . . . . . . . . 00 01 06

*In the Closett*

Four Small Trunks and four Boxes . . . . . 00 04 00
Three Dale Boxes . . . . . . . . 00 01 06

*In the Porch Chamber*

One pair of Beddsteads Feather Bedd & Bolster one Blankett &
Coverlidd . . . . . . . . . 01 00 00
One Side Saddle . . . . . . . . 00 05 00
one Small Chest & one Trunk . . . . . . 00 02 00

*In the Passage*

one large Chest . . . . . . . . 00 15 00

*In the Fellowes Chamber*

Two Beddstead one Flock Bedd two Blanketts and one Chest . . 01 10 00

*In the Bakehouse*

One Malt Mill . . . . . . . . . 00 06 00
Three Brewing Stunds . . . . . . . 00 13 00
One large cooler and kneading Turnell . . . . . 00 10 00
One Sive and one search one Cend buckett . . . . 00 01 06
Two Bowl Dishes, three wooden Horses . . . . . 00 02 00
Two Peales one wert Ladder . . . . . . 00 01 06
Two Stone Cisterns one Furnace . . . . . . 03 06 00
One Moulding Bench . . . . . . . 00 01 00
Feathers . . . . . . . . . 01 00 00

*In the Chamber over*

One Hair Cloth . . . . . . . . 00 05 00
One large witch and Malt . . . . . . . 03 00 00
Two Trine of Fellys . . . . . . . . 00 14 00
One Malt Skreen . . . . . . . . 00 05 00
Six plow Beams . . . . . . . . 00 03 00
Ten Tutor Slates . . . . . . . . 00 02 06
Thirteen Axtle Trees . . . . . . . 01 06 00
Four flitches of Beef hanged . . . . . . 00 12 00

*In the Grainery*

Seventy four Cheeses . . . . . . . 04 10 00
White pease 2 3/4 str. . . . . . . . 00 09 00
Two Strike of Rye . . . . . . . . 00 07 00
Ten Strike of Pease £1-5s Corne 5s . . . . . 01 10 00
Eight Sives & a Riddle 4s 6d wisketts and 1 str of wheat 6s . . 00 10 06
Plow Timber £2 waggon rope 2s Baggs 5s . . . . 02 07 00

| | £ s d |
|---|---|
| Eight Cowes | 31 10 00 |
| Two Bullocks | 06 10 00 |
| Four Sterks | 07 00 00 |
| Eight Calves | 09 00 00 |
| Eight Horses Mares and Colts | 29 00 00 |
| A Rick of Oats | 09 00 00 |
| A Rick of Wheet | 20 00 00 |
| A Rick of Hay | 05 00 00 |
| A Stack of White Pease | 05 00 00 |
| Thirty three Sheep | 03 00 00 |
| A Fatt Pigg | 02 08 00 |
| A Sow | 01 05 00 |
| Five Store Piggs | 03 05 00 |
| Barley in the Barn | 20 00 00 |
| Rye in the Barn | 07 00 00 |
| Grey Pease in the Barn | 03 10 00 |
| A Small parcell of Clover | 00 10 00 |
| A Waggon | 08 00 00 |
| Cart and Wheels | 02 00 00 |
| The Hay over the Cow-House | 02 00 00 |
| Part of a Rick of Fodder | 00 10 00 |
| Tumbrill and Wheels | 01 11 00 |
| Tumbrill body and Draughts | 00 13 04 |
| Wain Body and Cart Body | 00 10 00 |
| Plowes and Harrowes | 00 15 00 |
| Hay in the carthouse Talents | 03 00 00 |
| Gearing for five Horses | 01 05 00 |
| One Pannell | 00 01 06 |
| Two Scythes Cather & four waping hooks | 00 04 00 |
| Three Spades Seven Pikevills & Muck-fork | 00 08 00 |
| Three Stone Pigg Troughs & two wooden do | 00 07 00 |
| Grindle Stone and Wheelbarrow | 00 02 00 |
| Corn Sowed in the Ground | 06 00 00 |
| Muck in the Fold | 01 00 00 |
| Hemp and Flax | 00 10 00 |
| Thirty Seven Slippins of Hemptn Yarn | 01 04 00 |
| Noggon Yarn | 00 05 00 |
| Old Iron and odd things forgott and not herein inserted | 01 00 00 |
| Three Stone of Wool | 00 15 00 |
| Wearing Apparell and money due | 09 00 00 |
| Six Thousand of Tyle | 03 00 00 |

*Linnens*

| | |
|---|---|
| Two dozen and a half of Diaper Napkins | 01 05 00 |
| One large Table-Cloath one long do and 2 little do | 00 18 00 |
| One Towell Diaper | 00 01 06 |
| Nine pair of fine Sheets | 04 10 00 |
| Two dozen of Flaxen Nappkins | 00 12 00 |
| Two flaxen Table-Cloaths | 00 06 00 |
| Eighteen Pillow Bears | 00 08 00 |
| Three Huggabag Table Cloaths and ten Nappkins | 01 00 00 |
| Two Long Table Cloaths | 00 05 00 |
| Twenty Paire of Sheets | 02 10 00 |

| | | |
|---|---|---|
| One Dozen and a halfe of course Nappkins . . . . | 00 06 00 |
| Half a Dozen of course Table-Cloaths . . . . . | 00 02 00 |
| Tot . . | 308 00 03 |

## 250. Elizabeth Blackshaw

Of Leaton, Wrockwardine, taken by John Langley and Matthew Cross* on 9 November 1727 and exhibited on 25 April 1728. The parish register records the burial of Mrs. Elizabeth Blackshaw on 12 November 1727.

*Imprs. In her own Lodging Room*

| | |
|---|---|
| one Bed with ffurniture belonging to it . . . . . | 02 00 00 |
| In the Same Room one Chest and one Trunke . . . . | 00 09 00 |
| Three pewter dishes . . . . . . . . | 00 05 00 |
| Linnen of All sorts . . . . . . . . | 04 00 00 |
| Rent due at Her death . . . . . . . | 12 00 00 |
| Money at Interest . . . . . . . . | 80 00 00 |
| Wearing Apparell . . . . . . . . | 03 10 00 |
| | 100 04 00 |

## 251. Thomas Binnell

Of Allscott, Wrockwardine, yeoman, taken by John Smith and Thomas Calcott on 11 March 1727-28 and exhibited on 25 April 1728. He was buried on 3 March 1727-28.

| | |
|---|---|
| Imprs. all ye goods in ye house place . . . . | 04 00 00 |
| all ye goods in ye parlor . . . . . . . | 04 10 00 |
| all ye goods in Chamber over ye house . . . . | 20 00 00 |
| all ye Cheese and other things in yt room . . . | 04 00 00 |
| all ye goods in ye Roome at ye Staire head . . . | 04 00 00 |
| all ye goods in ye parlour Chamber . . . . . | 04 10 00 |
| all ye goods in ye Little Chamber . . . . . | 01 00 00 |
| all ye goods in ye passage . . . . . . | 08 00 00 |
| all ye goods in ye Drink Butterey . . . . . | 02 00 00 |
| all ye goods in ye Brue house . . . . . | 04 00 00 |
| all ye goods in ye Garret . . . . . . | 01 00 00 |
| all ye goods in ye Entry . . . . . . | 00 05 00 |
| all ye Cowes . . . . . . . . | 26 05 00 |
| all ye heifers . . . . . . . . | 04 10 00 |
| all ye Calves . . . . . . . . | 04 00 00 |
| all ye Horses and a Colt . . . . . . | 20 00 00 |
| all ye Swine . . . . . . . . | 01 10 00 |
| all ye Corne in ye Barne . . . . . . | 03 00 00 |
| all ye Corne on ye Ground . . . . . . | 11 00 00 |
| all ye Implements of husbandry . . . . . | 12 00 00 |
| all his wareing Apparel & money in pockit . . . | 03 00 00 |
| Tot . . | 144 00 00 |

## 252. Robert Hawkins

Of Charlton, Wrockwardine, taken by William Hall and Richard Steventon on 10 November 1729 and exhibited on 30 April 1730. He was buried on 8 November 1729.

| | |
|---|---|
| Imprs. four Oxen | 20 00 00 |
| Eight heaifers | 21 10 00 |
| Six Cowes | 21 00 00 |
| Two Mares | 11 00 00 |
| One Colt | 02 10 00 |
| Two Swine | 05 10 00 |
| Sixteene Sheep | 03 00 00 |
| five yeard Olds | 10 00 00 |
| three Store Swine | 02 18 00 |
| Seven Calfes | 07 00 00 |
| Winter Corne | 15 00 00 |
| Barley | 15 00 00 |
| Peases | 02 00 00 |
| Oates | 04 00 00 |
| hay | 05 00 00 |
| Clover Seed | 02 00 00 |
| fetches | 00 10 00 |
| Implements of husbandry | 06 00 00 |
| furniture in ye Kichen | 04 00 00 |
| furniture in ye parlor | 03 10 00 |
| The Roome over ye parlor | 03 00 00 |
| The Roome Over ye kichen | 03 00 00 |
| The Buttrey | 01 00 00 |
| The Store Chamber | 04 00 00 |
| furniture in ye malt house | 03 00 00 |
| Wareing Apparill And money in ye purse | 15 00 00 |
| Totall is | 190 18 00 |

## 253. William Icke

Of Trench Lane, Wrockwardine Wood, taken by John Hooper and Richard Watkiss on 17 April 1731 and exhibited on 4 May 1731. He was buried on 27 March 1731.

Imprimis.
| | |
|---|---|
| Two cowes one yeare old | 06 00 00 |

*Item. goods in ye house place*
| | |
|---|---|
| Six pewter dishes one table two chears one grate and tongues | 01 05 00 |

*Item In the Shop*
one table and pres and working tooles . . . . . 01 03 00

*Item. In the buttrey*
two Barils & a chorn . . . . . . . 00 04 06

*Item. In the roome over the House*
one bed and one chest . . . . . . . 01 09 00

*Item. over the Shop*
two old beds and one chest. . . . . . . 02 05 00

Item. waring Apparill and money in his pocket . . . 02 05 00

           Sum is. . 14 11 06

## 254. John Smith

 Of Allscott, Wrockwardine, yeoman, taken by G. Colley, John Phillips* and Thomas Blackmore on 3 March 1731-32 and exhibited on 28 April 1732. He was buried on 27 February 1731-32.

*Imprimis in ye houseplace*
2 Jacks 6 Spitts 2 Racks at . . . . . . . 01 10 00
Item a Marment 1s, fireshovel & Tongs 1s and four Candlesticks at 6d . . . . . . . . . . 00 02 06
Item a Grate a Cleever 2 Plates a Skimmer and three fleshforks at . 00 05 06
Item Pothooks 2 Smoothing Irons 1s and a Pair of Bellows at 4d . 00 01 04
Item a hacking knife Chafeing Dishes toster . . . . 00 01 00
Item 2 Guns 8s, a Cupboard of Books 2s 6d . . . . 00 10 06
Item 2 Screens 6s, 4 Chairs & 2 Join stools at 2s, 3 Tables & 3 Forms at 10s . . . . . . . . . 00 18 00
Item a Cupboard & Glasses 1s, 7 Pewter dishes . . . 01 01 00
Item a Long Wheel at 1s 6d, Beef and Bacon at 1 li, a Looking Glass 6d . . . . . . . . . . 01 02 00
Item 2 Pewter Candlesticks & a Grater 3d, 6 Twiggen Rings at 6d . 00 00 09
Item a pudding plate 1s, a Mustord pot 1d . . . . 00 01 01

*Item in ye Parlour*
ye Clock & Case . . . . . . . . 02 00 00
Item a Chest at 9s, a Cupboard at 6s . . . . . 00 15 00
Item 2 round Tables 6s, Six Chairs and a Stool at five shillings . 00 11 00
Item a Cupboard & Box 1s a Looking glass and Pictures at 3s . . 00 04 00
Item Glasses & Teapotts 2s, a Small Desk 6d . . . . 00 02 06
Item Small Drawers & Books 2s, a Fireshovel and Tongs at 2s . . 00 04 00

*Item in ye Passage*
67 lb of Pewter at 7d . . . . . . . 01 19 01
Item 21 plates and 2 dishes at . . . . . . 00 09 00

| | | |
|---|---|---|
| Item 60 lb of Brass at 9d p lb | 02 05 00 |
| Item a press 4s, 2 Pillions 2 old Saddles and Pillion Cloths at 6s | 00 10 00 |
| Item 2 Dripping pans 6d, an old warming pan & a Brazen Spoon 1s | 00 07 00 |
| Item 2 Barrels & a Small Box at | 00 05 00 |

*Item in ye Milk Buttery*
2 Sides of Bacon in ye Salt 16s, a Bench and Earthen Vessels 1s 6d .   00 17 06

*Item in ye Drink Buttery*
10 Barreles 2 Small Turnells & 2 Tunning dishes at  .  .  .   01 15 00

*Item in ye best Room*

| | |
|---|---|
| 2 Bedds 2 Bolsters 5 Pillars 6 Blankets 2 paire of Sheets & all ye furniture belonging to ye 2 Beds at | 07 00 00 |
| Item 6 Seg Chairs at 3s, ye Elbow Chair and 4 Cushions at 4s . | 00 07 00 |
| Item a Chest of Drawers 10s a Looking Glass 5s . | 00 15 00 |
| Item a Trunk 4s, a Livery Table 1s, a press 4s. | 00 09 00 |
| Item a Chest a Table & Close Stool at | 00 10 00 |
| Item Pictures & Whiteware at | 00 01 00 |
| Item Windowhangings at 1s 6 pair of Flaxen Sheets at £1 10s . | 01 11 00 |
| Item 8 pair of hurden sheets at 16s & 3 Dozen & 8 of ye best Napkins at 2 li 4s. | 03 00 00 |
| Item a fine Table cloth 5s, 3 pillows beers at 2s . | 00 07 00 |
| Item 9 Course Tablecloths & 11 Napkins . | 00 14 06 |
| Item a Saddle & a pair of Leathern Baggs at 10s & a Whip & Vidor at 1s . | 00 11 00 |

*Item in ye Parlour Chamber*

| | |
|---|---|
| one Ioin Bed wth feather Bed & Sheets 2 Blanketts & a Coverlid with hangings at | 03 10 00 |
| Item one Bedstead wth 2 feather Beds one Bolster one pair of sheets one Blanket wth Green hangings at | 02 15 00 |
| Item 2 Chests at 11s a hanger 3s, 3 Chairs and one stool at 2s . | 00 16 00 |
| Item a Sidesaddle & old Bridles at 5s and hangings for ye Windows at 6d . | 00 05 06 |

*Item in ye Passage Chamber*

| | |
|---|---|
| a Join Bed & all belonging to it at . | 01 15 00 |
| Item a hanging press at 10s a coffer Chest and Desk at 10s | 01 00 00 |
| Item a Cupboard Table at 2s 6d and 51 pound of Iron at 4s 3d | 00 06 09 |

*Item in ye Cheese chamber*

| | |
|---|---|
| 2 hundred and a half of Cheese at 2li ye Shilves that they stand on at 8 shillings . | 02 08 00 |
| Item a Whisket of Malt at 8s, 3 Chilves at 1s & 3 Baggs at 2s . | 00 11 00 |
| Item 12 lb of hops 12s, 2 Baskets and Linning Yarn at 4s a Coffer at 1s . | 00 17 00 |

*Item in ye further Garret*

| | |
|---|---|
| 30 Strike of Barley at 2s p Strike . | 03 00 00 |
| Item 2 Barrels and a Whisket at | 00 05 00 |

## THE INVENTORIES OF WROCKWARDINE

*Item in ye Garret at ye Stairhead*

| | | | |
|---|---|---|---|
| Join Bedsteads wth furniture & 2 old Chairs . . . . | 01 | 11 | 00 |
| Item 2 Bolsters & a Chaff Bed . . . . . | 00 | 03 | 00 |

*Item in ye Malthouse upon ye Withering floor*

| | | | |
|---|---|---|---|
| 8 Strike of Malt at . . . . . . . | 01 | 00 | 00 |
| Item a Steel Mill at 5s, a Tub a Churn & all ye Lumbryware belonging to ye Withering floor at 10s . . . . . | 00 | 15 | 00 |
| Item 2 Packhill & 2 Cartropes . . . . . | 00 | 07 | 00 |

*Item on ye Coming floor*

| | | | |
|---|---|---|---|
| 2 Cheese presses at 15s, 3 coolers at 10s . . . . | 01 | 05 | 00 |
| Item 10 Strike of Barley in Baggs . . . . . | 01 | 00 | 00 |
| Item 5 Strike of Moncorn at . . . . . | 00 | 10 | 00 |
| Item 4 Tubs at 7s, 3 old Barrels at 4s and a Stone Malt Mill at 2s 6d . | 00 | 13 | 06 |
| Item a kneading trough at 1s 6d, 8 Baggs 12s . . . | 00 | 13 | 06 |

*Item in ye Kitchen*

| | | | |
|---|---|---|---|
| 3 Tubs at 7s a boyler & Furnace 10s, Cheesevats and Benches and a hacking Block at 1s 6d . . . . . . | 00 | 18 | 06 |
| Item 3 Skellits a fireshovel & Tongs . . . . | 00 | 03 | 06 |
| Item 3 Hillock rakes at . . . . . . | 00 | 00 | 06 |

*Item in ye Entrey*

| | | | |
|---|---|---|---|
| a Cheese Tub 5 pails 2 Gaurns & a bole Dish at . . . | 00 | 09 | 00 |
| Item 5 Spades 2 Axes 2 Broomhooks 2 Bills and a Mattock at . | 00 | 10 | 00 |
| Item a Marmit & kettle 3s, 2 pothooks 2 Maids 2 sausepans a Backband 1s 6d, 5 Bottles a Churn and Turnell at 5s . . . | 00 | 09 | 06 |
| Item a little Table & Scales at . . . . . | 00 | 01 | 00 |

*In William Bithem's House*

| | | | |
|---|---|---|---|
| Item in ye Parlour Join Bedsteads and a press Cupboard at . . | 01 | 00 | 00 |
| Item in ye Buttery a little Firkin at . . . . . | 00 | 01 | 06 |
| Item in ye Houseplace a Table at . . . . . | 00 | 03 | 06 |
| Item in ye best Room Join Bedsteads . . . . | 00 | 07 | 00 |
| Item out of Doors a Washstone and Trough at 7s 6d a Grindlestone at 1s . . . . . . . . . | 00 | 08 | 06 |

*In the Schoolhouse*

| | | | |
|---|---|---|---|
| Item a long Table and Form and 3 Stools at 10s 6d, a Little Table & Chair 3s . . . . . . . . | 00 | 13 | 06 |
| Item out of Doors 19 Sheep 5li 4 houses 11 li . . . | 16 | 00 | 00 |
| Item 4 Calves & a Year old Colt . . . . . | 05 | 00 | 00 |
| Item 4 two Year olds at 7 li 10s, four Cows & 3 Calves at 12 li . | 19 | 10 | 00 |
| Item 3 heifers at 8li 6s, 2 sows 1 & 12 at 1 li at 18s . . | 10 | 03 | 00 |
| Item Hay 1 li, ye Corn in ye Barn at 1 li 15s . . . | 02 | 15 | 00 |
| Item Clover seed 12s, a fan & sives 3s 9d . . . . | 00 | 15 | 09 |
| Item a Wheel barrow & Pig troughs . . . . | 00 | 03 | 00 |
| Item a Wagon and 2 Tumbrells at 7 li 10s & a Ox harrow at 18s . | 08 | 08 | 00 |
| Item 2 pair of small harros 12s, 2 ploughs 8s . . . | 01 | 00 | 00 |
| Item Gearing for 4 horses at . . . . . | 01 | 04 | 00 |

| | |
|---|---|
| Item a Coffer in ye Stable 2s, a washstone 3s | 00 05 00 |
| Item ye Corn on ye Ground at | 09 00 00 |
| Item Wearing Apparel and Money | 05 00 00 |
| Things Omitted and forgotten | 00 10 00 |
| | |
| Reced. of Will Bithen | 17 17 09 |
| the Michaelmas Rent | 17 00 00 |
| | |
| Recd. Tho: Taylor rent for Michas Rent | 01 00 00 |

## 255. John Brown

Of Wrockwardine, taken by Roger Roe and Peter Massey on 23 September 1732 and exhibited on 2 November 1732. He was buried on 19 September 1732.

| | |
|---|---|
| Impris. | |
| Ten Cowes and a Bull | 27 00 00 |
| 4 heyfers | 08 00 00 |
| 6 Twinter heyfers | 09 00 00 |
| 4 Calves | 03 10 00 |
| 4 horses & 2 Colts | 17 00 00 |
| 4 Swine & a Sowe & piggs | 05 00 00 |
| 24 Sheep | 05 00 00 |

*Item In ye house place*

| | |
|---|---|
| Brass and pewter of all sorts | 02 00 00 |
| A Dishboard & 3 old chairs. | 00 05 00 |
| a Jack a Driping pan & 2 Broaches | 00 07 00 |
| An Iron pott 2 Candlesticks a Grate ffireshovel & Tongs | 00 15 00 |

*Item In the Parlor*

| | |
|---|---|
| A Table a Chest Bedsteads & hangings & a small Grate. | 01 00 00 |

*Item In ye Garrett*

| | |
|---|---|
| A parcell of Cheeses. | 08 00 00 |

*Item In ye Room over ye houseplace*

| | |
|---|---|
| A Bed & furniture | 01 10 00 |
| A Coffer a Straw Wiskett & Close Stoole. | 00 04 00 |

*Item In ye parlor Chamber*

| | |
|---|---|
| A Chaf Bed 2 Wisketts 3 little Wheels & 1 long Wheel 2 pads & a small parcell of Wooll | 01 00 00 |

*Item In ye best Chamber*

| | |
|---|---|
| One Bed & furniture & 1 Bed Tick | 03 15 00 |
| A Chest a Box a Little Table & 7 Chairs | 01 00 00 |
| Linnen of all sorts | 04 00 00 |

THE INVENTORIES OF WROCKWARDINE 445

*Item In the Buttrey*

| | | |
|---|---|---|
| 5 Barrells 2 Wooden Bottles & a little Salting Mitt | . . . | 00 18 00 |
| 2 Cheese presses 2 Mitts & a brewing Stund | . . . . | 01 04 00 |
| A Cheese Tub a Churn 4 pails & other Wooden Whare | . | 00 12 00 |
| Tickney Whare of all sorts . . . . . . . | | 00 02 00 |

*Item In ye Malt house*

| | | |
|---|---|---|
| A Stone Wheting ffet 2 Malt Mills & a Malt Shovel a Tuter & a half strike . . . . . . . . . . . | | 01 05 00 |
| A Whiskett & plough Timber . . . . . . | | 00 02 06 |
| A Washstone & 3 stone pig Troughs . . . . | | 00 06 00 |
| An Old Waggon a Tumbrell and other Imploymts of husbandry | . | 06 00 00 |
| An old Ladder & Grindle stone . . . . . | | 00 03 00 |
| hey & corn of all sorts . . . . . . | | 21 00 00 |
| Books Whareing Apparell and money in his pockett | . . | 02 10 00 |
| Things unseen & forgott . . . . . . | | 00 01 06 |
| | Tot . . | 132 00 00 |

## 256. Richard Ball

Of the Quob Pool, Wrockwardine Wood, collier, taken by Richard Watkiss and John Hayward on 2 April 1735 and exhibited on 16 April 1735. He died on 26 March 1735. He was the son of William Ball (*245*).

| | | |
|---|---|---|
| Impris. | | |
| All the Goods in ye House Place and furniture belonging to it . | . | 02 00 00 |
| All the Goods in the Roome over the House . . | | 00 10 00 |
| All the Goods in the New House and Belonging to it | . . | 01 10 00 |
| All the Goods in the Parlor . . . . . . | | 02 00 00 |
| All the Goods in the Roome Over the Parlor . . | | 01 00 00 |
| All the Drink in ye Seller and the Vessels in the Seller . | . . | 02 10 00 |
| All the Goods in ye Kitchin ye furnace and all other vessells | . . | 01 05 00 |
| | | |
| The Horses and Mares . . . . . . | | 05 00 00 |
| One Cow and Calve and Heifer . . . . . | | 03 10 00 |
| The Sheepe . . . . . . . . | | 06 01 00 |
| The Corne one ye Ground . . . . . . | | 01 00 00 |
| The 2 pigs . . . . . . . . | | 00 15 00 |
| The things Omitted & out of sight . . . . | | 00 05 00 |
| The Wareing Apparel & Money in Pockitt . . | | 01 10 00 |
| All ye Goods in ye Roome over ye New House . | . . | 00 10 00 |
| | Tot . . | 29 06 00 |

## 257. John Pemberton Senr.

Of Wrockwardine, gent., taken by Peter Massey on 21 July 1735 and exhibited on 30 October 1735. He was buried on 15 July 1735.

| | |
|---|---|
| Item, One Bed and ffornitude belonging to it | 02 10 00 |
| Three Cheeres | 00 06 00 |
| one Chest | 00 07 00 |
| Ten Trenchers | 00 03 00 |
| Three goold Rings | 01 05 00 |
| Six Pare of Sheetes | 01 16 00 |
| Six Pilloes beeres | 00 06 00 |
| fforteen hand towels | 00 08 00 |
| one Dosen of Napkins | 00 10 00 |
| one pillow | 00 01 00 |
| one Silver pinte | 01 10 00 |
| one Small Silver cup. | 00 07 06 |
| Waring Aparell and Money in pocket | 04 00 00 |
| things fforgot | 00 10 00 |
| | 13 10 06 |

## 258. Peter Langley

Of Leaton, Wrockwardine, gent., taken by William Massey and Francis Hammersley on 21 July 1735 and exhibited on 15 November 1735. He was buried on 10 July 1735.

*Goods in the Parlour*

| | |
|---|---|
| 1 Doz of Cane Chairs 2 Elbow | 01 10 00 |
| 2 plain tables, & 1 tea table, 1 large Glass corner Cupboard 2 large Pictures | 01 03 00 |
| A pair of blow bellys & Maps & small pictures | 00 05 00 |

*In the Room over the Parlour*

| | |
|---|---|
| 2 Beds & furniture | 04 00 00 |
| 2 small Tables | 00 03 00 |
| The Hangings of the Room | 00 18 00 |
| 2 Bed quilts & 1 new Blanket | 01 04 00 |

*The Room over the Kitchen*

| | |
|---|---|
| the Best Bed & furniture | 04 10 00 |
| 2 other Beds & furniture | 03 01 00 |
| 1 hanging press, 1 close Stool 2 old trunks 1 old table leaf | 01 05 00 |
| An old Chest of Drawers & Glass | 00 15 00 |
| A Clock & Case | 02 02 00 |

*In the Kitchen*

| | |
|---|---|
| 6 Leather Chairs | 01 04 00 |
| The Dish Bench & pewter | 04 16 00 |
| 3 pair of Brass Candlesticks & snuffers & old Brass | 01 00 00 |
| The Jack, Spits, driping pans & Gobbotts | 01 05 00 |
| The grate, tonges, fireshovels fender, purgatory & other odd things belonging to the fireplace | 01 05 00 |
| The Counter a little table 2 old Chairs & o stool, 2 little Wheels | 01 05 00 |
| A Coffee Mill & Tea board | 00 03 00 |

# THE INVENTORIES OF WROCKWARDINE

| | |
|---|---|
| A study of Books | 00 10 00 |
| A Brass Mortar & a Marble Mortar. | 01 00 00 |
| for Linnings | 03 11 00 |
| Barrels & brewing vessels | 02 00 00 |
| Iron furnace | 01 01 00 |
| A Brass furnace & Copper Still | 01 10 00 |

*In the Pantry*

| | |
|---|---|
| a Little Boyler a small tub & old pail | 00 05 00 |
| A Bacon Cratch | 00 03 00 |
| the silver plate | 20 00 00 |
| Half a Doz of silver hafted knives & forks & case | 03 00 00 |
| An old Mare & Colt | 03 00 00 |
| An old Horse | 02 05 00 |
| A 3 year old Colt | 03 00 00 |
| A Chair & harness | 03 00 00 |

Goods delivered to Mr. John Cherrington Jnr. valued or appraised at £15.03.00 which being paid for is added at the bottom

| | |
|---|---|
| Rents due from Thos. Felton | 27 00 00 |
| for wearing Apparell & Cash | 24 10 00 |
| for things omitted & unseen | 00 05 00 |
| | 128 03 00 |

An Account of the goods & Chattells (in this Inventory omitted & overlooked by the Appraisors) given by Eliz. Langly Widow & Administratix of Peter Langly deceased followth to wit:

| | |
|---|---|
| A Chest & Portmanteau Bag with old Curtains belonging to one Bed | |
| 2 pair of Hemp Sheets & one table cloth | 05 00 00 |
| An old fish net | 00 04 00 |
| A hair Cloth | 00 15 00 |
| A small Stone trough | 00 02 06 |
| Part of an old Bed Stead | 00 06 00 |
| A small quantity of quart & pint glass bottles | 00 07 00 |
| two Cheeses | 00 03 06 |
| part of a flitch of Bacon | 00 07 00 |
| About five strike of Malt | 01 16 00 |
| One strike & half of Meal | 00 05 00 |
| One old Barrel | 00 02 00 |
| A Damask table Cloth | 00 15 00 |
| Eighteen Ells of Hemp cloth | 01 07 00 |
| Ten pounds of Hemp yarn | 00 12 00 |
| Half a Doz of old knives & formks a sasifras knife & Bench | 00 04 00 |
| One half Hogshead of small beer | 00 08 00 |
| A small quantity of China Delf & flint glasses | 01 07 00 |
| Two Lignum Vita Castors | 00 02 06 |
| A Eight Round Ladder | 00 03 00 |
| One Doz: of tin patty pans, two tin plates & Cover | 00 03 00 |
| five strainers or searchers | 00 02 06 |

| | | |
|---|---|---|
| one Iron pot three small old Brass potts & three Covers | 01 00 00 |
| A screw cock for a vessell & Basson Stand | 00 03 06 |
| A chopping Blox, & two Shelves in the Cellar | 00 03 06 |
| four Basketts one Bottle Bing a small number of ordinary Gally potts | 00 06 06 |
| A worm Tub, a Salve Box & five Doz of viol Corks | 00 06 06 |
| two hanging Locks & 2 large door Locks | 00 04 04 |
| two old Brushes 2 Rolling pins 1 Spade & one herb press | 00 05 10 |
| one Bed & Bolster being very ordinary 2 foot mattings & one Coffer | 00 16 00 |
| 1 hammer six pound of Lead & one of Brass weights | 00 02 00 |
| 2 Lanthorns, a nail passer an old rotten watering pan a small quantity of nails 2 pair of small scales & a keel | 00 08 00 |
| 2 Books Declincourt upon Death & Beaumont psyche | 00 08 00 |
| A Hair line & Hooks & 2 ells of coarse Cloth & a Batch Bag & trowell | 00 04 04 |
| A pair of green Kidderminster Curtains & a folding Screen & grate | 01 05 00 |
| Two old Chairs omitted by the Appraisors | 00 02 00 |
| A linne Bag & a half strike of Beans | 00 01 06 |
| An old stand Candlestick | 00 00 08 |
| omitted by the Appraisors as by my Calculation appears the Sum of 30£ due from Thos. Felton on Account of Rent exceeding the 27£ in this Inventory expressed | 30 00 00 |
| A bottle Rack being a very old one | 00 00 08 |
| A Shoe Iron | 00 00 04 |
| A Bed in the Hands of Mrs. Ellen Langly | 03 00 00 |
| Cash Charrington £15.3d. included & in the Inventory expressed Reced since the Death of the sd Peter Langly & in his life time to him due | 42 10 09 |
| | 95 01 09 |

## 259. Robert Allen

Of the Long Lane, Wrockwardine, joiner, taken by Allen Pickering and Francis Rodenhurst on 2 January 1737-38 and exhibited on 28 April 1738. He was buried on 30 December 1737.

*Imprmis The goods in the House place*

| | |
|---|---|
| A grate one paire of tongs and fire shovel ye Clock and Skreen ye Jack the Pewter Nine Dishes and Sixteen plates and on Brass pan One Brass a little one Dozen of trenchers one Dreeping pan One warming pan | 03 10 00 |

*Item The Goods in the Butterey*

| | |
|---|---|
| five Barrels and one Churn and two tubs | 00 15 00 |

*Item The goods in the Chamber over ye house place*

| | |
|---|---|
| two beds and all belonging to them and a Chest and one coffer | 01 10 00 |

| | |
|---|---|
| Item The tools in the Shop | 00 10 00 |
| Item The Cheese Press | 00 07 00 |
| Item Three cheirs & two guns and One Coffer and One ffurnace | 00 14 00 |

THE INVENTORIES OF WROCKWARDINE 449

| | |
|---|---|
| Item Two pots and One table and form two Broaches a frying pan fire plate and Morter . . . . . . . . | 01 00 00 |
| Item The winter Corne . . . . . . . | 00 10 00 |
| Item The pease and the Oats and Barley . . . . . | 03 10 00 |
| Item ffour cowes . . . . . . . . | 06 00 00 |
| Item Two two yeare olds and three yeare olds . . . . | 03 10 00 |
| Item ffour Horsese and Mares . . . . . . | 08 00 00 |
| Item Two Swine . . . . . . . . | 01 10 00 |
| Item Implymts. of Husbandry One Carte three pare of tracese . | 02 10 00 |
| Item Things Omitted and Oute of sight . . . . . | 00 02 00 |
| Item Wareing Apparell and Money in pockit . . . . | 01 00 00 |
| tot . . | 34 18 00 |

## 260. Jonathan Dabbs

Of the Long Lane, Wrockwardine, yeoman, taken by Allen Pickering and Thomas Blest on 4 March 1737–38 and exhibited on 16 April 1738. He married Jane Davis on 9 January 1737–38 and was buried on 28 February 1737–38. The many uses of 'and' in the first paragraph are correct readings and not misreadings of 'one'.

*The goods in the House place*

| | |
|---|---|
| ye grate ye tongs ye pot Gales pudding pan ye Pestell flesh hooke. Ballese frying pan two pots and a marmant and kettle and Ladle 3 Chairs 2 Pails and Gaun and Piggin and Dish and table and Dish Bench five pewter dishes and two Pollenchers 18 spoons 2 Chess fits tuning dish five plates some few Bottles and tickney ware Glasson ware Heire sive and Lantern . . . . . . | 01 00 00 |

*The Butterey ye goods yt are in it*

| | |
|---|---|
| and Axe and Broom Hooke sickles a maddock and Pick 2 Barrels a Churne a paire of scales a flock Bed a paire of sheets 2 Blankits and paire of Bedsteeds some few Milk pans and Steans . . . | 00 10 00 |

*Item ye Chamber Over the House*

| | |
|---|---|
| Two paire of Bedsteads and a feather bed and two blankits a paire of Sheetes and Caft Boulster 2 paire of sheets and one sheet and two table Cloths One Napkin 3 Coffers and Boxe two Mark baskits and two stuns a Little wheele and a Big wheele and Evile a trunke . . | 01 05 00 |
| Item. A ffliching of Bacon and of pt ffliching . . . . | 00 10 00 |
| Item. five Cows and one Calve . . . . . . | 07 05 00 |
| Item. Two 3 yeare olds Heifer . . . . . . | 02 00 00 |
| Item. Three 2 years olds Heifers . . . . . . | 02 05 00 |
| Item. Two Reareing Calves . . . . . . . | 01 00 00 |
| Item. One Mare . . . . . . . . | 01 10 00 |
| Item. The corne one ye ground . . . . . . | 00 05 00 |
| Item. And one Pig . . . . . . . . | 00 07 00 |

| Item. Things omitted out of sight | 00 01 00 |
|---|---|
| Item. Three strike of Corne and 2 strike barley | 00 10 00 |
| Item. Money in pockit and wareing Apparell | 00 10 00 |
| | 18 18 00 |

## 261. William Binnell

Of Clotley, Wrockwardine, taken by Joseph Grice, Robert Turner and Charles Stilgoe on 7 July 1740 and exhibited on 23 October 1740. He was buried on 2 July 1740.

| Inprimis. 4 Bullocks and 2 splaid Haifors | 20 10 00 |
|---|---|
| 12 Cowes | 36 00 00 |
| 4 Mares | 11 00 00 |
| 2 Coults | 03 10 00 |
| 6 too year ould Cattle | 10 10 00 |
| 5 Yearlings | 05 00 00 |
| 6 Caulves | 03 00 00 |
| 8 score Sheep | 23 00 00 |
| 8 Swine | 03 10 00 |
| Goods in ye house | 03 00 00 |
| In the Parlor | 01 00 00 |
| The Roome over the Parlor | 06 00 00 |
| The Roome over the House | 04 00 00 |
| In the Chiching | 01 10 00 |
| Inflaments of Husbanttree | 08 00 00 |
| Winter Corn on the Grown | 15 00 00 |
| Lent Grain on the Grown | 30 00 00 |
| Wareing Aparril and Money in his Purs | 02 00 00 |
| things unseen and Forgotten | 00 05 00 |
| | 186 15 00 |

## 262. Richard Fenn

Of the Quob Pool, Wrockwardine Wood, taken by Allen Pickering and George Oliver on 2 March 1741–42 and exhibited on 28 April 1742.

*The Goods in ye House Place*

| The tongs and Grate and ffire Shovel ye Disbench and pewter and Clock and ye ffurnitude belonging to ye House place | 03 00 00 |
|---|---|

*The Goods in ye New House*

| The tongs and Grate And Disbench and Pewter and Table and the ffurnitued belonging to ye New House place | 02 00 00 |
|---|---|

*The Goods in ye Parlor*

| A Table and forms a bed Cubbard and ye ffurnitude Belonging to ye Parlor | 02 00 00 |
|---|---|

## THE INVENTORIES OF WROCKWARDINE

*The room over ye New House*
Two Little Beds . . . . . . . . 00 10 00

*The room Over ye Parlor*
One Bed and ye ffurnitude belonging to ye Roome over ye Parlor . 01 '10 00

*The Ground Seller*
Three Barrels . . . . . . . . . 00 06 00

*The back House*
A ffurnice And Brueing Studs And Cooler . . . . 00 12 00

The Sheepe . . . . . . . . . 05 00 00
Two Cows . . . . . . . . . 04 10 00
ffour three yeare Old Heifers . . . . . . 08 00 00
ffour two yeare old Heifers . . . . . . 05 00 00
Two year old Calves . . . . . . . . 01 10 00
One pig . . . . . . . . . 00 12 00
Three Horses and Mares and ye Heareing . . . . 03 00 00
Things Omitted and Out of Sight . . . . . 00 02 00
Money in pockit and wareing Apparrel . . . . 01 00 00

                                                                                 tot . . 38 12 00

### 263. Abigail Binnell

Of Clotley, Wrockwardine, widow, taken by Joseph Grice, Robert Turner and Peter Harding on 14 October 1743 and exhibited on 6 April 1744. She was buried on 11 October 1743.

Imprimus.
Six Oxce Beasts . . . . . . . . 20 10 00
aleven Cow Beastes . . . . . . . . 33 00 00
fouer mares . . . . . . . . . 11 00 00
five Cowltes . . . . . . . . . 10 00 00
Tow Calving Hefefers . . . . . . . 06 00 00
Fouer Two year oulds . . . . . . . 06 00 00
Eight Calves . . . . . . . . . 05 00 00
Eight Scower Shipe & lambs . . . . . . 23 00 00
Ten Piges . . . . . . . . . 05 00 00

Goods In the House . . . . . . . . 03 00 00
Goods In the Parlor . . . . . . . . 01 00 00
Goods in the Roome over ye Paror . . . . . 06 00 00
Goods In the Roome over ye House . . . . . 04 00 00
Goods In the Chichen . . . . . . . 01 10 00

Implements of Husbandry . . . . . . 08 00 00
Winter Corne In ye Barne . . . . . . . 10 00 00
Barly In ye Barne . . . . . . . . 21 10 00

| | | |
|---|---|---|
| Pease & oates. | | 10 00 00 |
| Waring aparill & money In ye Purse | | 02 00 00 |
| Things forgoten & unseene. | | 00 05 00 |
| | | 186 15 00 |

### 264. Thomas Calcott

Of Allscott, Wrockwardine, taken by Joseph Grice and Samuel Elsmere on 30 June 1744 and exhibited on 6 August 1744. He was buried on 23 June 1744.

*Imprs.*

| | | |
|---|---|---|
| 18 Cows 1 Bull & a Calf valued at 4 lib each the Calf included | | 76 00 00 |
| 6 Twinters £3.7s.0d. each | | 20 02 00 |
| 7 Year olds £1.15s.0d. each | | 12 05 00 |
| 12 Large Pigs 18s each | | 10 16 00 |
| 2 Lean Sows | | 01 00 00 |
| 7 Little Pigs 7s each | | 02 09 00 |
| 9 Little Pigs 2s 6d each | | 01 02 06 |
| 32 Ewes & a Tup 6s each | | 09 18 00 |
| 32 Lambs 4s 6d each | | 07 04 00 |
| 13 Weathers 8s each | | 05 04 00 |
| 3 Mares & 1 Horse 6 Lib each | | 24 00 00 |
| 1 Mare | | 07 00 00 |
| 1 Mare & 2 Colts | | 08 08 00 |
| 9 Rearing Calves | | 04 10 00 |

*Implements of Husbandry*

| | | |
|---|---|---|
| 1 Waggon | | 10 00 00 |
| 1 do | | 07 00 00 |
| 1 Tumbrill & Wheels | | 02 05 00 |
| 1 Plough & 2 paire of Irons. | | 02 10 00 |
| 2 pair of Harrows | | 01 01 00 |
| 1 Old Tumbrill & 2 old pair of Wheels | | 00 11 06 |
| 7 pair of Traces & Backbonds | | 01 05 00 |
| 2 Cranks | | 00 02 06 |
| 2 Cart Saddles &c. | | 00 13 00 |
| 5 Collars & 7 pair of Homes | | 01 04 06 |
| 5 Bridles & 1 old Bridle | | 00 11 06 |
| 2 Iron Backbonds | | 00 02 00 |
| A Saddle & 4 Bridles | | 00 15 00 |
| 3 Old Pads | | 00 03 00 |
| 3 Waggon Ropes | | 00 09 00 |
| 2 old Corn Coffers | | 00 05 00 |
| A Winnowing Fan & Frame | | 00 05 00 |
| 2 Tuters | | 00 14 00 |
| a pair of Scales | | 00 01 04 |
| 6 Stone Troughs & Grindstone | | 00 14 00 |
| A Wheelbarrow | | 00 01 06 |
| 2 Ladders | | 00 02 00 |
| 4 Spades | | 00 03 00 |

| | |
|---|---|
| A Bottle Cratch | 00 08 00 |
| A Watering pan | 00 00 02 |
| 2 Mauls & 3 Wedges a Mattock Crow & Hatchet | 00 06 00 |

*Over the Stable*

| | |
|---|---|
| A Skreen | 00 14 00 |
| a Malt Mill | 00 10 00 |
| a half Strike & a peck | 00 02 06 |
| a Grate Niggard 2 Racks & old Iron | 00 15 00 |
| 5 Wire Sieves & Riddles | 00 06 00 |
| 2 other Sieves | 00 00 04 |
| a pealing Iron | 00 05 00 |
| 60 Strikes of Malt at 2s 3d.. | 06 15 00 |
| 12 Strikes of Wheat at 2s 8d | 01 12 00 |
| 4 Strikes of Rye | 00 05 04 |
| 8 Strikes of Oats | 00 10 00 |
| 12 Old reaping Hooks | 00 02 00 |
| 1 Hopper | 00 00 06 |
| Bags | 01 00 00 |
| 3 pair of weeding Tongs 2 Dung hooks 1 Draining knife 2 Evills | 00 05 06 |
| Rakes & Pikell | 00 05 00 |
| 3 Corn Shovells | 00 01 09 |
| Corn in the Barn unthres'd valued to | 03 15 00 |
| Clover old & new valued to. | 17 00 00 |
| Old Hay valued to | 04 00 00 |
| New Hay valued to | 02 05 00 |
| Flax & Hemp Undress'd & Dress'd | 23 00 00 |

*Tilling on the Ground*

| | |
|---|---|
| Corn | 15 00 00 |
| Barley | 24 00 00 |
| Oats | 01 16 00 |
| Pease | 10 17 06 |
| Flax | 30 00 00 |

*Goods in the Kitchen*

| | |
|---|---|
| 1 Jack & Chain | 01 00 00 |
| 5 Spitts | 00 05 00 |
| 4 Brass Candlesticks & pair of Snuffers | 00 04 06 |
| 2 Fireshovels 3 pair of Tongs | 00 05 00 |
| 5 Iron Candlesticks | 00 02 06 |
| 2 Flesh Forks 1 Basting Spoon 1 Egg Spoon | 00 01 00 |
| 2 plates with a Doz of Iron Skuies. | 00 00 06 |
| 2 Choppers a Pestill & Mortar 2 Iron potlids | 00 04 08 |
| 5 Iron Dreeping pans | 00 10 00 |
| 2 plates 1 cast plate & Creeper | 00 03 00 |
| 1 Fender 2 Hand Iron 4 Hooks 2 Cranes wth Links & 3 pair of Pothook | 00 10 00 |
| 3 Iron plates to hang before the Fir 1 Box Iron to heat Smoothing Iron 1 Tossing pan & Chafing Dish | 00 06 00 |
| 3 Guns & 2 Brace of Pistols | 01 17 06 |

| | | |
|---|---|---|
| 1 Iron Wax Candlestick 1 Iron Stand to warm plates 2 Frying pans & 1 pitt grate. | 00 | 08 06 |
| 1 Dark Lanthorn a Salt Box & pair of Bellows | 00 | 00 06 |
| 2 Brass Skimmers 2 Brass Kettles 2 Saucepans 1 Copper Pot 1 Copper Tea Kettle & Iron Tea Kettles a Tin Coffea Pot a Tuning Dish a Tin Broiler Baster Drudger & Grater | 00 | 13 06 |
| Earthen Ware sevll. sorts | 00 | 02 06 |
| 2 Dressers & Drawers to one | 00 | 12 00 |
| 1 Clock & Case | 02 | 10 00 |
| Pewter 135 lib at 7d p lib | 03 | 18 09 |
| Plate Shelves | 00 | 02 00 |
| 1 Table | 00 | 04 00 |
| 7 Chairs | 00 | 03 00 |

*In the Parlour & Closet*

| | | |
|---|---|---|
| 2 Tables | 00 | 09 06 |
| 6 Leather Chairs | 00 | 12 00 |
| a Little Chest of Drawers | 00 | 01 00 |
| a Hand Bell & Coffea Mill | 00 | 02 06 |
| Earthen Ware. | 00 | 01 00 |

*Smoaking Room*

| | | |
|---|---|---|
| a Couch 6 Chairs little Table & 6 Pictures | 00 | 15 00 |

*In the Pantry*

| | | |
|---|---|---|
| a Table & a Napkin Press | 00 | 05 06 |
| 5 Shelves | 00 | 01 06 |
| 14 Knives & Forks & Basket | 00 | 03 00 |
| 1 Lanthorn 2 Butterboxes 10 pattypans | 00 | 01 02 |

*Brewhouse & Milkhouse*

| | | |
|---|---|---|
| 18 Cheesefits. | 00 | 13 00 |
| 2 Cheese presses wth Troughs | 01 | 01 00 |
| 2 Cheese Tubs | 00 | 08 00 |
| 5 Wooden Bottles 2 Churns | 00 | 15 00 |
| 4 Stunds & 1 Whey Tub | 00 | 19 00 |
| 2 Cans & 2 Buckets | 00 | 04 00 |
| 5 pails & a pair of Scales | 00 | 07 00 |
| a Great Mill 1 Search 3 Seeths & Trea | 00 | 01 08 |
| 2 Lanthorns & a Table | 00 | 02 06 |
| 3 Axes & 2 Bromhooks | 00 | 04 00 |
| 3 Iron pots & 2 Washing Tubs | 00 | 06 08 |
| 2 Lading Buckets & 5 Boal Dishes. | 00 | 02 00 |
| 2 Boilers & Iron Oven Lid | 01 | 15 00 |
| 1 Cullender 22 Trenchers Milk Seeth 3 Chees Ladders | 00 | 03 00 |
| a pair of Gibbers 2 peels | 00 | 04 00 |
| 2 Brass pans & a Salting Mitt | 01 | 10 00 |

*In the Cellar*

| | | |
|---|---|---|
| 4 Hogsheads 11 Barrels 2 Droppers & Tundish | 03 | 14 00 |

## Room over the Parlour

| | | |
|---|---|---|
| 1 Chest of Drawers & little Dressing Tables | . . . . | 00 09 06 |
| 4 Stone of Wool at 11s p Stone . | . . . . | 02 04 00 |

## Little Room at the Stair Head

| | | |
|---|---|---|
| 1 Bed & Furniture 1 Glass & 3 Shelves | . . . . | 02 03 00 |
| Book . . . . | . . . . | 01 01 00 |

## Room over the Kitchen

| | | |
|---|---|---|
| 3 Beds & all belonging | . . . . . | 06 05 00 |
| 2 Chests . . | . . . . . | 00 06 06 |
| 1 Chest of Drawers . | . . . . . | 00 09 00 |
| 2 Little Desks a Close Stool & Child Chair | . . . | 00 03 06 |

## Room over the Pantry

| | | |
|---|---|---|
| 2 Beds wth Furniture & 1 Chest . | . . . . | 03 04 00 |

## In the Cheese Chamber

| | | |
|---|---|---|
| 1 Chest 2 Coffers 2 Barrells | . . . . | 00 07 06 |
| 4 Spinning Wheels 1 Pail 5 Baskets 1 Reel 1 pair of Yarwings & other Lumber . . . . . . | | 00 05 00 |
| a Chafer . . . . . . . . | | 00 05 06 |
| 86 old Cheese . . . . . . . | | 10 10 00 |

## Over the Milkhouse

| | | |
|---|---|---|
| 3 Beds & Furniture . . . . . . . | | 01 10 00 |

## In the Malthouse

| | | |
|---|---|---|
| 35 New Cheese . . . . . . . | | 03 10 00 |
| 4½ Strike of Pease . . . . . . . | | 00 06 09 |
| a Malt Shovel . . . . . . . . | | 00 01 04 |
| a Casting Net . . . . . . . . | | 00 06 08 |
| | | |
| Linnen of all Sorts belonging to the House | . . . | 00 15 00 |
| Another parcell of Linnen as was designd for the Children | . | 01 05 00 |
| Household Provisions . . . . . | . | 02 10 00 |
| Wearing Apparell & Money in Pociett . | . . . | 03 00 00 |
| | | 435 08 07 |

Debts due to Thos. Calcott
| | | |
|---|---|---|
| Mr. Clerk of the Rea . . . . | £150 00 00 | |
| Mr. Clerk of the Wheatley . . . | 30 00 00 | |
| Unpaid of his Wife's Fortune . . | 100 00 00 | |
| Svll Debts bad & good as is Exprest in the Intestates Book . . | 57 11 03 | 337 11 03 |
| | | 772 19 10 |

A Lease Living in Allscot for on Life wch is Settled on the Intestates Widow

### 265. Jonathan Hawkins

Of Charlton, Wrockwardine, yeoman, taken on 7 April 1747 and exhibited on 9 October 1747. The appraisers are not named. He was buried on 28 March 1747.

| | |
|---|---|
| Imprs. Eight Cows & Calves | 28 00 00 |
| 1 Bull & Barren Cow | 05 00 00 |
| five Mars & one horse | 21 00 00 |
| One two Year old Colt | 03 10 00 |
| one Year old Colt | 03 00 00 |
| five two Year olds | 11 02 06 |
| Six year olds | 06 15 00 |
| five three year olds | 15 00 00 |
| Twenty three Couples of Sheep | 09 01 00 |
| Twenty three Barren Sheep | 06 00 00 |
| Two Sows & Piggs | 04 09 00 |
| four Stor Pigs | 03 00 00 |
| Winter Corn on the Ground | 23 00 00 |
| Pease on the Ground | 06 00 00 |
| oats on the Ground | 04 00 00 |
| Corn to thrash | 07 00 00 |
| Barley in the House | 02 00 00 |
| Implements of husbandry of all sorts | 12 00 00 |
| Furniture in the Kitchen | 03 10 00 |
| furniture in the Little Parlour | 02 00 00 |
| The Room over the Little Parlour | 02 10 00 |
| The Room over the Kitchen | 02 10 00 |
| In the Cellar | 03 00 00 |
| In the big Parlour over the Cellar | 01 00 00 |
| In the Room over the big Parlour | 01 01 00 |
| In the Store Chamber | 02 00 00 |
| furniture in the Small House | 03 00 00 |
| Books wearing apparel & money in the Pocket | 02 00 00 |
| Things forgotten & not seen | 00 02 00 |
| | 191 09 06 |

# GAZETTEER OF PLACE NAMES MENTIONED IN THE INVENTORIES

Grid references are all from square SJ. For townships, parishes and other sizeable areas a reference is given which will enable the place to be readily identified on the 1:50,000 Ordnance Survey map, sheet 127, Stafford and Telford.

|  |  | Grid reference |
|---|---|---|
| Admaston | Township in Wrockwardine | 632130 |
| Allscott (Alscot, Arlscot) | Township in Wrockwardine | 623130 |
| Arleston (Arlston) | Township in Wellington | 662102 |
| Aston (under the Wrekin) | Township in Wellington | 613097 |
| Brandlee | Part of Great Dawley | 681075 |
| Bratton | Township in Wrockwardine | 634141 |
| Bullocks Brook | Now Beanhill Brook in parish of Wrockwardine | 641130 |
| Charlton | Township in Wrockwardine | 596112 |
| Cheswell Grange (Cheshill) | Farm in Lilleshall parish | 717167 |
| Clotley | Township in Wrockwardine | 634103 |
| Cluddley (Cluddlease) | Township in Wrockwardine | 632103 |
| Croppings | Farm in Little Dawley | 666060 |
| Dawley (Daulley) | Parish | 687065 |
| Dawley Field | Collieries in Great Dawley township | 687065 |
| Dawley Green | Area which is now High Street, Dawley | 685074 |
| Dawley Magna | Parish and township | 687065 |
| Dawley Parva | *See* Little Dawley | |
| Donnington (Donington, Dunnington) | Township in Lilleshall | 710140 |
| Donnington Wood | In Lilleshall parish and Donnington township—woodland remained until early 19th century | 710121 |
| Dothill | Township in Wellington. Shrunken due to emparking by 1660 | 645130 |
| Eyton (upon the Weald Moors) | Partly in Wellington, partly separate parish | 651148 |
| Finney | Area in Little Dawley | 675053 |
| Frame | Fields, now Doseley quarries, in Little Dawley | 676069 |
| Hadley | Township in Wellington | 672120 |
| Hadley Park | In Wellington parish and Hadley township | 677135 |
| Hainses Wood | In Ketley | Location unknown |
| Hem | Farm in Shifnal | 730059 |
| Hinks | Farm in Lilleshall parish | 797168 |
| Hollinswood | Area on borders of Malins Lee township in Dawley and Priorslee chapelry | 702094 |
| Holywell (Lane) | Squatter settlement in Little Dawley | 678059 |
| Honnington (Hunnington) | Farm in Lilleshall parish | 723150 |
| Horton | Township in Wellington | 685145 |
| Ketley | Township and manor. Township in Wellington parish. Manor extends into Wombridge | 675110 |
| Ketley Bank House | House in Wombridge portion of Ketley, also known as The Bank House | 680103 |

| | | |
|---|---|---|
| Ketley Brook (Kettle Brook) | In Wellington parish, Ketley township | 670111 |
| Ketley Wood | In Ketley township | Location unknown |
| Lane, The | In Wellington parish, probably Street Lane | |
| Lawley | Township in Wellington | 670085 |
| Leaton | Township in Wrockwardine | 614114 |
| Leegomery | Township in Wellington | 668130 |
| Lilleshall (Lilishall, Lylleshall) | Parish | 729152 |
| Lilleshall Heath | On northern boundary of Lilleshall parish | 724165 |
| Lilleshall Lodge | Hunting Lodge in Lilleshall park | 720124 |
| Lilleshall Manor | Now the Old Hall, Lilleshall | 727150 |
| Little Dawley | Township in Dawley | 682060 |
| Little Wenlock | Parish | 647068 |
| Long Lane | Squatter settlement in Wrockwardine parish | 610150 |
| Lubstree Park | Now a farm in Lilleshall parish | 696156 |
| Madeley | Parish | 695043 |
| Malins Lee | Township in Dawley | 698090 |
| Middle Leasow | In Little Dawley township | Location unknown |
| Moss, The | Part of Wrockwardine Wood | 704122 |
| Muxton (Muxon) | Township in Lilleshall | 715144 |
| Nash (Ness) | Township in Wrockwardine, now deserted | 629116 |
| Oakengates | Roadside settlement on borders of Wombridge Shifnal and Wrockwardine Wood | 700110 |
| Pains Lane (Paynes Lane) | Crossroads settlement on borders of Lilleshall, Wrockwardine Wood and Shifnal, known since the 1850s as St. George's | 706108 |
| Pawn Hatch | Field, in Dawley parish | 678075 |
| Pool Hill | Area in Dawley | 681069 |
| Preston upon the Weald Moors | Partly in Wellington, partly a separate parish | 681153 |
| Preston Brockhurst | Township, partly in Shawbury, partly in Moreton Corbet | 538247 |
| Quob or Quom Pool | Area north of present Oakengates town centre | 696107 |
| Ridges, The | Field in Dawley, site of a mill and subsequently of the Lightmoor ironworks | 679053 |
| Ruckley | In Wellington parish | Location unknown |
| Seven Stars | Inn on Watling Street, in Hadley township | 676110 |
| Shawbirch | Crossroads in Wellington parish | 646135 |
| Snedshill (Snebshill) | Part of the chapelry of Priorslee in Shifnal parish | 703103 |
| Stoney Hill | In Little Dawley township | 667058 |
| Street Grange | *Als.* Watling Street Grange, farm at the southern extremity of Lilleshall parish | 722113 |
| Street Lane (Street Way) | Name used for the Roman Watling Street throughout the district | — |
| Trench Lane | Squatter settlement along Wellington-Newport road on borders of Eyton and Wrockwardine Wood | 695130 |
| Uppington | Parish | 597094 |

# GAZETTEER

| | | |
|---|---|---|
| Walcot | Detached township, Wellington parish | 595119 |
| Walcot Waste | In Walcot township | 582114 |
| Wappenshall | Township in Wellington | 664144 |
| Watling Street | Roman Road passing through the district en route from London to Wroxeter | 659110 |
| Watling Street Demesne | An area, in effect a township, in Wellington parish | 660111 |
| Wellington | Parish and township | 651117 |
| Wilmore Grange | Farm in Lilleshall parish | 739158 |
| Wheat Leasows | In Wellington parish, now Wheatley Grange | 672138 |
| Woodhouse | Farm in Lilleshall parish | 729119 |
| Woodseaves | Township in Market Drayton parish | 686310 |
| Wrekin | Part of Wellington parish adjacent to the hill | 630092 |
| Wrockwardine | Parish and township | 625120 |
| Wrockwardine Wood | Detached township, Wrockwardine parish | 699118 |

Gazetteer compiled by Mr. J. Pagett

# GENERAL GLOSSARY

**Alcuin/Alkemy.**—Antimony.
**Alegar.**—Malt vinegar.
**Alum/Allam.**—Potassium (or Sodium or Ammonium) Aluminium Sulphate, used in dyeing as a mordant, and also in tanning.
**Andirons.**—Moveable iron plates used to contract the fire area in a grate.
**Apparitor.**—The servant or attendant of a civil or ecclesiastical officer, or sometimes just a servant.
**Appennes/Apptences.**—Appurtenances.
**Apporn.**—Apron.
**Ark.**—A bin for meal.
**Axeltree/Axtree.**—The fixed bar on the rounded ends of which the wheels of a vehicle revolve.

**Backbands.**—A strap passing over a cart saddle and supporting the shafts of a vehicle.
**Badstaff.**—Probably a staff used in a butter churn.
**Bag.**—A measure, particularly of hops, usually 2½ cwt.
**Balles/Ballow.**—Bellows.
**Barefoot wheels.**—Wheels without an iron rim.
**Bason.**—Basin.
**Bear/Bere.**—A pillow case.
**Beckhorn.**—A small anvil, or the pointed end of an anvil.
**Bellys.**—Bellows.
**Bickhorn/Bicken.**—*See* beckhorn.
**Bill (hook).**—A heavy knife or chopper with a hooked end.
**Bing/Bin.**—A receptacle for corn or meal, a manger.
**Bird spit.**—A spit for cooking poultry or game birds.
**Blanquit.**—Blanket.
**Blood strike.**—Meaning unknown. Some kind of blacksmith's tool.
**Bole.**—A bowl.
**Bolting vessell.**—A receptacle for sifting.
**Bonch (many variations).**—A bench.
**Booting house.**—Meaning uncertain. Possibly a workshop.
**Bouch/bouk.**—Bucket.
**Brandard.**—Brand-iron, i.e., Andiron.
**Briscote.**—Brisket (of beef).
**Broach/Broche/Brooch.**—A narrow tapering iron rod or pin, especially the rod on a spit.
**Bromhook/Broom Hook.**—A tool for clearing undergrowth, particularly brooms.
**Buffet stool.**—A low stool or foot stool.
**Bushell.**—A measure, particularly of grain, and usually 56lb. The Shropshire bushell of wheat or barley was sometimes expressed as 9½–10 gallons.
**Butt.**—The thicker or hind part of a skin or hide.
**Butt.**—A cask containing 126 gallons, usually of wine. Alternative of pipe.

**Cage.**—A cupboard with an open front.
**Calbot.**—Cob-iron.
**Calldron.**—Cauldron.
**Cambrell.**—*See* Gambrell.
**Cann/can.**—A vessel for holding liquids, not necessarily of metal.
**Cantell.**—Fragments or remnants.
**Canvass.**—A coarse form of linen.

# GENERAL GLOSSARY

**Cap.**—Cop. A cover for a waggon.
**Caplin.**—The leather hinge on a flail.
**Carbine.**—A gun, shorter than a musket, used especially by cavalrymen.
**Card.**—A tool for combing wool or flax before spinning.
**Caslin.**—An inferior type of calf skin.
**Caster hat.**—A hat made of beaver fur (in 16th century), later used or one of rabbit skin.
**Castor.**—A vessel with a perforated top for containing pepper or drugs.
**Cettle.**—Kettle.
**Chafer.**—A small dish containing hot ashes or charcoal for heating food.
**Chafing dish.**—A dish to contain food to be placed on a chafer.
**Cheeks.**—The sides of a grate
**Chestub/Chesvat/Cheswit.**—Cheese tub or vat.
**Chiching.**—Kitchen.
**Chims.**—Chimes.
**Chorn.**—Churn.
**Church.**—Probably form of Search.
**Cidderminstr.**—*See* Kidderminster.
**Clansing sieve.**—Probably a cleansing sieve.
**Clift.**—Probably 'cleft' or cut timber.
**Close bouke/pan.**—A bucket or pan for placing under a close stool.
**Close stool.**—A commode.
**Clote leather.**—Meaning uncertain.
**Coaffer.**—Coffer.
**Cobbert/Cob-iron.**—Irons which supported a spit. Usually two iron bars with knobs at one end which rested on the back of the grate. Sometimes used to mean Andirons, and sometimes a kind of cradle for firewood. *See also* Dogs.
**Cobbert.**—Corruption of cupboard. Meaning usually evident from context.
**Cockloft.**—The space between the uppermost ceiling of a house and the roof, sometimes used loosely to mean an attic or garrett.
**Cog.**—One of the short handles on the pole of a scythe.
**Cooler.**—An oval tub, particularly one used to cool the wort in brewing, or in the dairy to receive the warm milk from the pail. *See also* Turnell.
**Coopery/Cooperie ware.**—Goods like barrels, etc., made by a cooper.
**Cop.**—The cover for a waggon.
**Copsole.**—A wedge for keeping the coulter of a plough in its place at the proper angle to the beam.
**Corve.**—Originally a basket, hence a basket used to bring coal from a pit, later a waggon used in a mine.
**Costrell.**—A small keg or barrel for carrying drink to the field, or simply a wooden bottle.
**Couching floor.**—A floor on which grain was spread in order to germinate, particularly as used in malting, or in the preparation of woad for dyeing.
**Coupery/Cowperie ware.**—*See* Coopery ware.
**Counterford/Countersat.**—Counterfeit, an item made of a base metal looking like a precious one.
**Covre.**—Cover.
**Crab mill.**—A mill for crushing crab apples to make cider.
**Crank cart.**—Probably one which is out of repair.
**Cratch.**—A wooden frame, rack or flight of shelves, or a rack for feeding animals.
**Creeper.**—A small iron dog, of which a pair would be placed between the andirons in a grate. Alternatively a small iron frying pan with three legs.
**Crow.**—Crow bar.

Cuschin.—Cushion.
Cwbarte.—Cupboard.

Dale.—Deal, i.e., softwood.
Damnified.—Damaged.
Desperate (debts).—Debts of which there was little hope of recovery.
Diaper.—A linen fabric mainly used for table cloths, hand towels, etc.
Dicker.—A parcel or lot of ten hides or skins.
Dixnary.—Dictionary.
Dizlee.—Perhaps an adze.
Docking iron.—A tool for docking the tails of horses.
Dog.—A type of clamp.
Dogs.—Bars which supported the ends of logs on a wood fire, or on which a spit turned. Originally ornamented with dogs' heads. See also Cobbert.
Dog wheel.—A treadmill wheel revolved by a dog, used especially for working a spit.
Dozen.—A measure for minerals, particularly of iron ore.
Dredge.—A mixture of grains, most commonly oats and barley sown together.
Dripping pan/dreeping pan.—A pan put under a revolving spit to catch the fat.
Drudger.—Dredger (for flour, etc.).

Earling.—Yearling.
Earwingles.—See Yarwingles.
Ell.—A measure of cloth, usually 45 inches. A Shropshire ell was 48 inches, but it seems likely that most references in these inventories are to standard ells.
Envill.—Anvil.
Ewer.—A pitcher with a wide spout, particularly for carrying water for washing.

Fat.—Vat.
Feal stakes.—Some kind of surface equipment at a coal mine, but the exact meaning is uncertain. A feal heap is a spoil tip.
Felloe/Felly/Filly;—A segment of the exterior rim of a wheel.
Fetches/Fitches.—Vetches.
Fire Slice.—Fire shovel.
Firkin.—A small cask, usually 8 gallons of ale or 9 gallons of beer.
Fither.—Feather.
Flag(s).—Rushes, reeds or coarse grass.
Flagene/Flaggon.—Flagon.
Flanders Chest.—A chest highly ornamented in the Flemish style.
Flasket.—A long shallow basket with a handle at each end, or an oval washing rub, or a small barrel for taking beer to the harvest field.
Flitch/Flitchen.—A side of an animal, salted and cured.
Float.—Flute.
Fother.—Fodder.
Fowling piece.—A gun for shooting wild fowl.
French wheat.—Buck wheat.
Fring.—Fringe, ornamental bordering.
Frog.—A utensil found in fireplaces. Meaning uncertain, but possibly a corruption of Furgon, an oven fork or poker.
Furnace/furnes/furnis.—A large metal pot, particularly one used for brewing or boiling.
Fustick.—A dyeing material. Old fustick, derived from *Chlorphora Tinctoria* gave yellow with alum as mordant, olive with copper. Young fustick, from *Cotinus Coggyria* gives orangy brown with alum as mordant.

Gales/Geals/Goals.—A swing crane over a kitchen grate.

# GENERAL GLOSSARY

**Galls.**—Morbid excrescences on leaves and young twigs of certain types of oak tree, used in dyeing. Aleppo galls were the best and contained up to 60 per cent. tannic acid.
**Gally pots.**—Gallipots—small, glazed earthenware pots.
**Gambrell.**—A bent piece of iron used by butchers for hanging meat.
**Gaun.**—A ladle, particularly used for dispensing milk, in origin one that held a gallon.
**Gears.**—Harness for horses, or for use with a loom.
**Gilt.**—A young female pig.
**Ginn.**—A horse gin used for winding a pit.
**Girth.**—Strap of leather or cloth placed around horse to secure saddle or pack.
**Gonn.**—*See* Gaun.
**Gobbards/Gobirons/Gubburns.**—*See* Cob-irons.
**Grey peas.**—Runcival or field peas.
**Grindle stone.**—Grindstone.
**Guileing tub/vat.**—A vat in which the wort in brewing is put to work after the yeast has been added.
**Gun.**—particularly if a 'pewter gun', a gaun.

**Hack.**—A tool rather like a pick-axe or hoe.
**Hacking knife.**—Tool used in kitchen. Meaning uncertain.
**Hackle.**—*See* Heckle.
**Hackney saddle.**—One for use in ordinary riding.
**Haigh.**—Hay.
**Hair cloth.**—A coarse oven fabric made from horse hair and used for drying malt over a kiln. Possibly also used for a cloth employed in cheesemaking.
**Halbeard/Halberd.**—A combination of spear and battle axe.
**Halter.**—Strap or rope with a noose by which a horse is led.
**Hamber.**—Hammer.
**Hames.**—*See* Holmes.
**Hampatts.**—Meaning uncertain. Perhaps a form of 'hamper' or possibly hand-pats for butter.
**Handles.**—Wooden devices in which teasels were set for raising nap on cloth.
**Hanging press.**—A wardrobe.
**Hanglesses.**—Hengels or hangers, pieces of chain on a chimney breast from which utensils were hung on pot hooks.
**Hanvil.**—Anvil.
**Haster.**—A stand or screen for concentrating the heat of a fire.
**Hayfor.**—Heifer.
**Headstand.**—The part of a bridle which fits around a horse's head.
**Head stakes.**—The head stocks at a mine.
**Healing.**—A covering.
**Heckell/Heckle.**—An implement for combing flax or hemp.
**Hedge mittens.**—Perhaps thick leather mittens for hedging.
**Heifer.**—A cow from her first year until she has a second calf.
**Hempen.**—A fabric made from hemp.
**Heriot.**—A feudal due paid to the lord of the manor on the death of a tenant.
**Hilling.**—A bed quilt or cover.
**Hillock rakes.**—Perhaps for raising piles of hay in hay-making.
**Hogg/Hog sheep.**—A young sheep not yet shorn.
**Hogshead.**—A large cask, with capacity for 48 gallons of ale or 54 gallons of beer.
**Holland.**—A fine linen fabric, originally made in the Netherlands.
**Holmes/Homes/Hames.**—Curved pieces of wood fastened to or forming the collar of a draught beast.

**Hookaback.**—*See* Huckaback.
**Hopper.**—A basket in which a sower carries his seed.
**Horises.**—Horses.
**Horse.**—A stand for barrels or shelves.
**Horn.**—A thimble used in conjuection with a knife.
**Huckaback/Huggabag.**—A linen fabric with the weft threads thrown up alternately to make a rough surface, as in towelling.
**Hurden/Horden.**—A coarse linen cloth made from the hurds, the pieces of flax or hemp separated by combing with a heckell.

**Idle.**—Empty or useless.
**Imelments/Impellments.**—Implements.
**Iorne.**—Iron.
**Ioyne.**—*See* Join.

**Jack.**—A machine for turning a spit.
**Jack windlass.**—A windlass with two chains and wheels at top and bottom for lifting, capable of being worked by one man.
**Join/Joyne/Joynt.**—Usually furniture made by a joiner.
**Joined bed.**—Usually one with a canopy and tester.
**Joined stool.**—Usually one with turned legs held by rails above and a stretcher below.

**Kanne.**—Can.
**Kavle.**—Calf.
**Keave/Keeve.**—A large tub for fermenting beer.
**Keaving/Keeving Table.**—Probably a stand for a keave.
**Kettle/Kettel/Ketele.**—Often an open cooking pot or pan.
**Kidderminster.**—Carpet, or carpet-like material made at Kidderminster.
**Kindyr.**—Meaning uncertain. Possibly a corruption of Kinderkin.
**Kine.**—Cows—usually the milking cows in a herd.
**Kilderkin/kinderkin.**—A cask holding 16 gallons of ale or 18 gallons of beer.
**Kimnel.**—An oval tub for scalding a pig, salting bacon, washing butter or keeping whey. A powdering tub.
**Kip.**—A bundle of hides of young beasts, usually a specific number, but the number varied from place to place.
**Kiver dish.**—A dish with a cover.
**Kiverlett/Kiverlid.**—Coverlet.
**Kneading tub.**—One for kneading dough or butter.
**Kowle.**—Colt.
**Kymes.**—Meaning uncertain. Part of a harrow.
**Kyp.**—*See* Kip.

**Lacein.**—Probably a leather cord on which a sword was hung.
**Ladder.**—A flight of shelves, particularly for storing cheese.
**Lame/Lamme.**—Lamb.
**Lanthorn.**—Lantern.
**Lasts.**—Wooden models of feet on which boots and shoes are shaped.
**Lather.**—Ladder.
**Laund iron.**—Laundry iron, i.e., a smoothing iron.
**Lent corn.**—Spring wheat.
**Lent grain.**—Spring barley, oats or peas, but not, usually, wheat.
**Lent Tillin/Lentilling.**—Spring-planted crops.
**Lignum vitae.**—Resin from the Guaiacum tree from the West Indies and Central America and the drug from it.

# GENERAL GLOSSARY

**Livery cupboard.**—A small cupboard, often with fronts and sides of turned balusters, originally for the storage of the bread and wine which people took to their sleeping rooms.
**Livery table.**—A table, often a large side table, or one on which a livery cupboard might be put.
**Loom.**—An implement or tool of any kind, an open vessel like a bucket or tub used in a dairy or brewhouse, as well as a machine for weaving.
**Low bed.**—A truckle bed.
**Lowm.**—Loom.

**Madder.**—Ground root of *Rubia Tinctorum* used for producing red dye.
**Maid.**—A clothes horse.
**Malt mill.**—A hand-operated mill for grinding malt before brewing.
**Mandrell.**—A pick, sharp-pointed at each end, used in getting coal.
**Mantle.**—An overcoat.
**Marmalade/Marmalett.**—A diminutive form of a marmite.
**Marmite/Marment/Marmit.**—A large cooking pot, usually of iron.
**Maslin (kettle).**—A kind of brass. Often a maslin kettle is simply a pan used for boiling fruit or ham of ordinary brass or tinned copper.
**Maslin.**—Mixed grain, muncorn or dredge.
**Mattock.**—A kind of pick-axe with one end of the blade arched and flattened at right angles to the handle.
**Mather.**—Madder.
**Matt/Mat.**—A thick sheet, often made of rushes, laid on cords stretched across a bed frame, under the mattress.
**Maul.**—A heavy hammer.
**Maundrell.**—*See* Mandrell.
**Meat.**—Of good quality, or possibly a utensil used for cooking meat.
**Micksen.**—*See* Mixen.
**Midden.**—*See* Mixen.
**Mitt.**—A dairy vessel.
**Mittings.**—Mittens.
**Mixen.**—A fold for keeping manure or compost.
**Molt.**—Malt.
**Moulting board.**—A board on which dough is kneaded or moulded.
**Muncorn.**—Mixed grain, often wheat and rye sown together.

**Nail passer.**—A gimlet or bradawl.
**Napery ware/Napparies.**—Table linen.
**Nare.**—Perhaps a 'Nave', a prop to support the shaft of a loaded cart, but reading in *9* is certainly Nare.
**Neat.**—A calf.
**Niggard.**—A false bottom for a grate, intended to reduce fuel consumption.
**Nine.**—An indefinite period between a week and a fortnight.
**Noggin.**—A small drinking vessel, sometimes holding a quarter of a pint.
**Noggon/Noggen.**—Coarse flax or hemp.

**Offals.**—Waste cuts of leather.
**Ornary.**—Ordinary.
**Oundyrons.**—*See* Andirons.
**Ovr.**—Over or overhead.

**Packnell.**—Probably a pack saddle.
**Pack Saddle.**—A saddle for supporting the load to be carried by a pack animal.
**Pad.**—*See* Panel.

**Panel.**—A piece of cloth placed under a saddle to protect a horse's back from being chafed. Also a kind of saddle, particularly a wooden saddle for asses.
**Parcel.**—A quantity, often a small quantity, of certain things.
**Pasty plates/pans.**—Plates or pans for cooking pasties or pies.
**Patty pan.**—A tin in which small pies, pasties or tarts are baked.
**Peale/peel.**—A long-handled implement with a broad, flat end, to draw bread from an oven. Sometimes a corruption of pail.
**Peck.**—The raw skin of a sheep.
**Pestall.**—Pestle.
**Peuter.**—Pewter.
**Pide.**—Pied.
**Piggin.**—A small wooden vessel or pail with one stave longer than the rest to serve as a handle.
**Pike-Evell/Picknell/Pickerell.**—A pitchfork.
**Pillion.**—A saddle, especially a light one for a woman, or a special cushion attached to the rear of an ordinary saddle to enable a second person to ride a horse.
**Pillow beer.**—Pillow case or slip.
**Pin block.**—A tool used by a currier.
**Pinsons.**—Pincers.
**Pipe.**—A cask, containing 126 gallons, usually of wine. A butt.
**Pollenchers.**—*See* porringers.
**Polraikes.**—Probably the head of a rake, *cf.* the 'poll' or head of an axe or pick.
**Porket.**—A small or young pig or hog.
**Porringer.**—A basin, especially one used for porridge.
**Portmanteu Trunk.**—A trunk used for clothing.
**Posnet/Posernet.**—A small metal cooking pot with a handle and three feet.
**Potlinks/Potlings.**—The chain on which a pot hook was suspended, sometimes including the hook itself.
**Pottender/Pottinger.**—*See* Porringer.
**Poutter.**—Pewter.
**Powdering Tub.**—A tub for salting or pickling meat.
**Press.**—A cupboard usually a large one with shelves. A hanging press is one in which clothes could be hung, i.e., a wardrobe.
**Proker.**—Poker for a fire.
**Pullen.**—Poultry.
**Purgatory.**—A receptacle for ashes beneath or in front of a fire.
**Puter.**—Pewter.
**Puission/Pvission.**—Provisions.
**Pwdring Tub.**—*See* Powdering Tub.

**Quishions.**—Cushions.
**Quoffer.**—Coffer.

**Racks.**—A pair of iron racks in which spits were kept when not in use.
**Rathe.**—A rail on a cart.
**Redwood.**—Generic name covering the 'soluble' red dye woods, Brazil wood and Campeachy wood, and the 'insoluble' Sandalwood, barwood and camwood.
**Reele.**—A device used for spinning without a wheel, or a receptacle for yarn spun on a wheel.
**Riddle.**—A sieve.
**Rindle/Ringling.**—*See* Runlet.
**Ripple.**—A set of rails added to a cart or waggon to increase its carrying capacity when loaded with hay, alternatively the iron rim on a cart wheel.

## GENERAL GLOSSARY

**Rubber file.**—A tool used to take the scale off red hot iron.
**Runlet/Rundlett/Rundle Tub.**—A cask of varying capacity, particularly for wine, or for holding the wort when brewing, or a circular wooden trencher.
**Sack.**—A measure, particularly of hops, usually reckoned to equal 4 bushells in Worcestershire.
**Saddle Tree.**—The framework of a saddle.
**Safe.**—A ventilated cupboard for meat.
**Salve.**—Ointment.
**Sasafras/Sasufrax/Saxifrage.**—The dried bark of the tree *Saxifraga granulata* from North America, used as a medicine.
**Sasepan.**—Saucepan.
**Sawsere.**—Saucer.
**Scowstowne.**—Perhaps a scouring stone.
**Screwplate.**—A plate with threads on it, used by smiths, etc.
**Scuers.**—Skewers.
**Scummer.**—*See* Skimmer.
**Searce/Search.**—A sieve or cloth made of bristles used in the diary, or a tool used for nicking wrought iron or steel.
**Seat/Set.**—The piece of leather pegged or sewn to the boot as a foundation for the heel.
**Seedness.**—A sowing of a certain crop.
**Segg chair.**—One made of or with a seat of basketwork.
**Settles/Settle/Settlas.**—A raised shelf or frame of brick or wood for supporting barrels or milk cans.
**Shamey.**—Chamois.
**Share-evill/Sharevill/Sherwill.**—Shovell.
**Sheers.**—Shears, particularly large ones used for cutting nap on cloth.
**Shilf.**—Shelf.
**Ship.**—Sheep.
**Shipon.**—*See* Slipping.
**Shoat/Shot/Shut.**—A young weaned pig, or an idle, worthless person.
**Sie bole.**—A bowl for use with a searce for straining liquids, especially milk.
**Sierce/Sirce.**—*See* Searce.
**Sithe.**—Scythe.
**Sistern.**—Cistern or trough.
**Skels.**—Scales.
**Skimmer/Skimer/Skummer.**—Either an iron implement for taking the ash from the hearth, or, more commonly, a metal spoon for taking fat from a boiling pot, or for use in the diary.
**Skreen.**—Screen.
**Skuers.**—Skewers.
**Slay.**—Instrument used in weaving to beat up the weft.
**Slice/Schlice.**—*See* Fire Slice.
**Slink pieces.**—Probably skins from aborted calves or from weak, sickly beasts.
**Slippen/Slippon/Slipping.**—A skein or hank or yarn.
**Snead.**—The shaft pole of a scythe.
**Specialty.**—Corruption of Sperialty.
**Sperate/Sperialty.**—Debts of which there is hope of recovery.
**Stack.**—A measure, particularly of coal, usually 4 cubic yards or 25 cwt.
**Stall (of bees).**—A hive.
**Stean.**—An earthen ware vessel with two handles or ears, used for storing liquids or butter.
**Steel mill.**—A device for producing a spark by rotating a steel disc against a flint.

**Steel yard/Stilliard.**—A balance with unequal arms. The item to be weighed is attached to the shorter arm, and a counterweight is slide along the longer one until equilibrium is reached, the position indicating the weight of the object. Used particularly for meat.
**Sterk.**—A young bullock or heifer, one or two years old.
**Still.**—A stand for a barrel or tub, or the apparatus for distilling.
**Stoan.**—Stone or stoneware.
**Stock.**—The hub of a wheel.
**Stone.**—A measure, particularly of wool or yarn, usually 14lbs., but in Herefordshire 12lbs.
**Stone horse.**—An uncastrated male horse or stallion.
**Store pig.**—An animal acquired for fattening.
**Stund/Stound/Stond.**—An earthenware jar.
**Suck.**—The part of a plough which cuts through the slice of earth cut out by the colter from below.
**Sumack.**—A preparation of the *rhus* species for a black dye, or for use in tanning.
**Surcingle.**—A girth for a horse.
**Sway pole.**—A crane over a fire.
**Syth (Cog).**—Scythe. A cog is one of the short handles on the pole of a scythe.

**Tallet/Tallent/Tallant.**—A hay loft.
**Tallet Poles.**—The poles supporting a hay loft.
**Tancot.**—A tankard.
**Tand.**—Tanned.
**Taw.**—*See* Tow.
**Tenters.**—Structures over which cloth was hung with weights to be stretched.
**Tester.**—The canopy over a bed.
**Tewtaw.**—An implement for breaking hemp or flax.
**Thrave.**—A measure of straw, etc., usually either 12 or 24 bundles.
**Thripples/Thrillbells.**—The chain tugs leading from the collar of a horse to the shafts of a cart or waggon.
**Thrum.**—Cloth with tassells or a fringe of threads left at the side.
**Tick.**—The case in which flock, feathers, chaff, etc., were put to make a bolster or mattress.
**Tinetor.**—Tenter.
**Tickney/Ticknall.**—Coarse earthenware, especially that made at Ticknall in Derbyshire.
**Toster.**—An iron plate used for toasting.
**Tow.**—The coarse yarns separated from hemp or flax by heckling.
**Towed yarn.**—Flaxen or hempen yarn from which the tow has been removed.
**Towles.**—Towells, or tools.
**Traces.**—A pair of ropes, chains or leather straps by which the collar of a draught animal is connected with the splinter bar or swingletree attached to a cart or implement.
**Trainen.**—*See* Treen.
**Trases.**—Traces.
**Trea/Try.**—A sieve or screen for sifting.
**Treen/Trenen/Trine.**—Wooden ware.
**Trencher.**—A thin, flat wooden plate.
**Tressell.**—Trestle.
**Trindleware.**—Treen ware.
**Truckle/Trundle/Trindle.**—A low bed, usually on wheels, often kept out of use beneath a standing bed.

# GENERAL GLOSSARY

**Trumper.**—Rubbish, or items of little or no value.
**Trynen ware.**—*See* Treen ware.
**Tumbrell.**—A two-wheeled cart, especially for muck.
**Tun.**—A vessel, holding 252 gallons, usually of wine.
**Tundish/Tuning Dish.**—A shallow wooden vessel with a hole in the bottom used as in funnel in brewing or in a dairy.
**Tup.**—A ram, or the head of a hammer.
**Turn barrell.**—Winding apparatus at a mine.
**Turnell.**—A large oval tub, especially used for salting meat, kneading bread, or putting under a cheese press.
**Turkey work.**—A woollen material woven in the same way as a Turkish carpet.
**Twiggen/Twiggon.**—Made of twigs, wicker, rush, or basket work.
**Twinter.**—A two-year-old beast, usually a cow, which has lived for two winters.
**Tynnen.**—Made of tin or tin plate.

**Vallants/Vallans/Valens/Vallians.**—Vallence, a border of hanging drapery round a bed.
**Verdigriss/Verninice/Vergine.**—A greenish substance used in dyeing, formed by the action of acetic acid on copper.
**Vetches.**—The bean-like fruit of a leguminous plant of genus *vicia*.
**Verginals.**—A keyed musical instrument set in a box or case without legs.
**Voice.**—vice.
**Voyder.**—A waste basket.
**Vyall.**—A viol, a musical instrument with 5, 6 or 7 strings, played with a bow.

**Wadfat.**—Woad vat.
**Wafering/Waffring Iron.**—A leather tie or rope particularly for binding a load to the back of a cart.
**Wainscote.**—Pannelling, either lining a wall, or incorporated in a chair or a screen.
**Wallett.**—A bag for holding provisions, etc., with a receptacle at each end for use either on foot or with a horse.
**Wayneing.**—Weaning.
**Wayte.**—Weight.
**Weather/Wether.**—A male sheep, usually castrated.
**Which/Whisk/Wich.**—A wooden bin for grain, etc.
**Whiskett.**—An osier basket used in the garden or for feeding cattle.
**Whitemeat.**—Dairy produce.
**Whiteware.**—Earthenware, probably of good quality and white in appearance.
**Wimble.**—A gimlet or auger drill, particularly used in mining. Also a hay-trusser's tool, but probably not in this collection.
**Wings/Whings.**—The iron side pieces of a grate.
**Winns.**—Winch.
**Wisscote.**—*See* Whiskett.
**Worm tub.**—A tub used in distilling.

**Yarwingles/Yarwinds.**—An appliance for winding a skein of yarn into a ball.
**Yearne ware.**—Earthenware.
**Yorne.**—Yarn.
**Yronware.**—Iron ware.

# GLOSSARY OF SPECIALISED TERMS USED IN MERCERS' INVENTORIES

*(Where relevant, earliest recorded use given in O.E.D. is in brackets)*

**Alamode.**—A thin, light, glossy, black silk (1676).

**Annel seed.**—Aniseed: seeds of *Pimpinella Anisum*. Used as a carminative, and in oil of anise. Sometimes confused with dill.

**Board string twist.**—Meaning uncertain.

**Bone.**—From its position in Johnson's inventory it should be tobacco, but O.E.D. gives no such use of this word. Bone dry is the form in which tobacco is imported so this is the most likely meaning. The value precludes most of the obvious meanings such as dice, whalebone, bobbins.

**Bone Lace.**—Lace made with bobbins, which were often made of bone. But it is not the same as bobbin lace since both are listed in Cowcher (1574).

**Brode.**—Broad. The next entry (narrow) makes this meaning clear.

**Buckram.**—Linen cloth stiffened with gum or paste (1436).

**Bugle cuffs.**—Bugles were tube-shaped glass beads, usually black, used to decorate wearing apparel. So, cuffs adored with, or resembling bugles.

**Caddis, Cadour, Cadias, Caddeaux.**—A word with which the appraisers had great difficulty. A worsted yarn, or ribbons used for garters and girdles. There are other definitions, but the position of all the entries makes this meaning almost certainly the one intended (1580).

**Caddows.**—Blanketting or blankets. Wilkes, 1670, had some on his bed (1579).

**Calamanco.**—A glossy woollen stuff originally from Flanders, twilled and chequered in the warp, so that the checks are seen on one side only. Much used in the 18th century for waistcoats and breeches (1598).

**Calico.**—Originally imported, but by 1600 also made in England. A plain, often white, unprinted cotton, coarser than muslin. In 1748 used by Joseph Wayman of Ludlow for a quilt. By 1680 it was also printed and glazed.

**Callome.**—*See* Galloon.

**Camlet.**—Originally a costly oriental fabric. Later a substitute made of various combinations of wool, wilk, hair, cotton or linen. John Wright, 1703, had a camlet hood. Joseph Wayman, 1748, Ludlow, used it for bed curtains (1400).

**Cantaloons.**—A woollen stuff manufactured in the West of England. A wide range of quality. Johnson's cost 10d. per yard, but Coley had it at 4d. (1711).

**Canvas.**—(1) A coarse, unbleached cloth made of hemp or flax. In this sense used for sheets by Robert Langley, 1661, Lilleshall (1260).

(2) An unbleached cloth woven on regular meshes for tapestry work. In some inventories called cusion canvas (1611).

Wright's was probably (1), but Johnson's could be (2), or else a cloth made in imitation of Nankeen, a naturally yellow cotton from Nanking. Other mercers also had yellow canvas.

**Cards.**—Not for carding wool, but playing cards. The entry in Wright's inventory makes this certain, and the context of Johnson's entry makes it extremely probable. Mercers commonly stocked playing cards, but they also sometimes stocked wool cards. Both sorts were much the same price so can be confused.

**Carrow seeds.**—Probably caraway seeds: the seeds of *Carum carni* used as a carminative and for flavour.

**Clock lines.**—The cords carrying the weights in a pendulum clock.

**Cloth.**—Plain wove woollen fabric as opposed to twill. Used for black breeches, dark coat and breeches, and black waistcoat by William Poyner, 1715, Dawley. Elizabeth Judgson, 1715-6, Wellington, had green cloth chairs.

# GLOSSARY OF SPECIALISED TERMS

**Cloves.**—Dried flower buds of *Caryophyllus aromaticus*. Used as a pungent spice and to make oil. The spice came from the Moluccas and was still a Dutch monopoly in 1700.

**Coloured.**—Sometimes it means 'as opposed to white', but more often it meant 'patterned or of more than one colour'.

**Construeing book.**—The Offices of the Shrewsbury School bailiffs laid down what books were to be used in the school, between 1578 and 1798. The same regulations applied at Ercall School, in which case the local mercers might well have stocked *The Dialogues drawn out of Tulley's Office,* and *Ludovicus Vives by Thomas Ashton sometyme cheif schoolmaster.*

**Coronation tape.**—Carnation-rose coloured. It was fashionable for haberdashery, but found only once used on a fabric.

Shakespeare, *Love's Labour Lost,* III, i, 46, 'How much carnation tape may a man buy?'

**Coventry Blue.**—A type of blue thread made at Coventry and used for embroidery (1581).

**Crape.**—Johnson's *Dictionary* gives 'a Sort of thin worsted stuff of which the dress clergy is sometimes made'. Probably what Wright had though there are other meanings (1682). It is more likely though that Wright stocked it for the same reason as Tryphosa Barnes, i.e., woollen shrouds which were compulsory after 1678.

**Cravat.**—The wearing of cravats became fashionable in France during the 17th century in imitation of the linen scarves worn around the neck by Croatian mercenaries. Of lace, linen or muslin, edged with lace and tied in a bow. In *Love in Wood,* 1672, William Wycherley suggests that it was possible to buy them ready made.

**Crown Hood.**—The other hoods are all differentiated by the materials from which they were made. There seems to be no possible meaning of crown that would fit in with this. Possibly 'in the shape of a crown' is what is meant.

**Currens.**—Currants. Originally raisins of Corinth. Small seedless raisins from the Levant.

**Diaper.**—A linen fabric with a patterned weave, by the 17th century, often not particularly expensive. Used for napkins and other table linen.

**Dimity, Dimothy, Timothy.**—A stout cotton cloth, woven with raised stripes and fancy figures. Used undyed for beds and hangings and sometimes for garments (1440).

**Drugget.**—A kind of stuff, all of wool, or half wool and half silk or linen. Used for a black coat by William Poyner, 1715, Dawley (1580).

**Ducape.**—A plain wove, stout, silk fabric of softer texture than Gros de Naples. Its manufacture was introduced to this country by French refugees in 1685 (1678).

**Dyed.**—*See* text.

**Ell.**—A variable measure, usually 45 inches. Comparing the prices of similar fabrics in the two units suggests that this was the case in this area. During the 17th and 18th century it seems to have been used only for some linens, mainly those used for bedding.

Long ell—A cloth (woollen), not a different length.

**Ferret.**—A stout tape, commonly made of cotton, but also of silk. Used among other things for garters (1649).

**Filling lace.**—Possibly a piece of lace to make decent a low-cut gown, or to fill a slashed sleeve, etc., but it follows an entry of 'open tapes' which suggests a connection. It could also be an abbreviated form of filletting. A fillet was originally a head band to keep a headdress in position, but later was often ornamental.

**Flannel, Flannen (perhaps also Lanill).**—Possibly from the Welsh 'gwlanen'. It was an open, woollen stuff of loose texture, usually without nap (1503).

**Flatting trough.**—Presumably for soaking and flattening the rolled-up hands of dried tobacco prior to stripping and fermenting. If this is what it was for, then it was not the only method of doing this, as Moore, a much bigger tobacco processer had a flatting mill.

**Flaxen.**—The product of the flax plant, *Linun usitatissimum*, which also produced linseed. Quality of flaxen cloth was variable, since it depended on the skill of the retter and the energy of the heckler. Much was sold unbleached when it was called brown. The best quality plainwove was called Holland, *q.v.*

**Flowers of Sulphur, Fflos: Sul:.**—A pure form of sulphur used medicinally as a laxative and sudorific, and as an ingredient of ointments, especially for skin diseases.

**Footings.**—Frills, ruffles, the narrow strip of lace sewn to the edge of the material and to which the main decorative edging lace is attached.

**Frieze.**—A coarse woollen cloth, with a nap, usually on one side only (1418).

**Fustian.**—A coarse cloth made from flax or cotton. Used by William Poyner, 1715, Dawley, for a 'frock'. In the 19th century, 'Ffustian jackets' was a term commonly used to mean the working classes. Many mercers had Bolton fustian and pocket fustian (1200).

**Galloon.**—Very varied spelling. Its use as a verb meaning 'to dress the hair with gold bands or ribbons' goes back to the 12th century. From the 17th century used for a narrow, close-woven ribbon or braid of gold, silver or silk (or copper according to Johnson's inventory), for trimming articles of apparel. Stored with the laces (1604).

**Gauze.**—A very thin transparent fabric of silk, linen or cotton (1561).

**Gemece Pepper.**—*See* Pepper—Jamaica.

**Gimp, Gympe.**—Silk, worsted or cotton twist with a cord or wire running through it (1664).

**Ginger.**—(White). The scraped root, often artificially bleached, from Jamaica. (Black). The unscraped root from the East Indies.

**Grains.**—Grains of Paradise or Guinea Grains, the capsules of *Amomum meleguetta* from East Africa. Used as a spice and a medicine. Sometimes confused with Cardamom.

**Gum.**—Too many possibilities to guess which is the most likely. Among other things used as a stiffener. Often confused with rosen, but not in Wright's case since he had both.

**Hard wax.**—Sealing wax, often made of beeswax and lac.

**Head roll.**—Presumably needed to make up one of the complicated head dresses fashionable in the 17th century. Most of the mercers stocked the separate parts needed. Justice also seems to have had some for sale ready made-up.

**Hemp, hempen.**—*Cannabis sativa*. A vigorous annual plant which it is now illegal to grow as it is the source of the drug Cannabis. The male and female organs are found on separate plants and the quality of fibre produced from the two is very different. In the 17th century the staminate or male plant was believed to be the female because the flowers were more conspicuous and the fibres finer. The produce from this male barren plant was called fimble, and, because it was ready for harvesting first, summer hemp. The coarser, female plant was called male, carl, steel or winter hemp. The two varieties explain the variation in price found in the household inventories. The residues after the fibre had been prepared (for this *see* text) included a tarry substance which burns well. The tow or very coarse fibres could be spun on a special distaff and woven into a rough cloth called hurden (*q.v.*) or used for ropes and sacking. Wright's hemp was probably fimble but not of an especially high quality. Johnson's hempen cloth was almost certainly a coarse variety as its value is well below that given in several household inventories.

**Holland.**—Linen fabric, originally Holland cloth, because it originally came from there. When unbleached called brown Holland. Mentioned in many inventories for bed and table linen and clearly of far better quality than other linens and therefore extremely expensive (1427).

**Hood.**—Justice's inventory makes it clear that it is for women. Probably the fashionable French hood in which there was a front band, depressed over the forehead and raised in folds and loops over the temple. A 'set hood' was probably an arrangement of ruffs and pleats. The meaning of 'Crown hood' is uncertain.

**Hookes and Eyes.**—Another entry that the appraisers had trouble spelling. The early mercers had two varieties for breeches (clearly larger) and unspecified small ones. By the turn of the century most mercers only had a few.

**Hops.**—A native plant, growing freely in the hedges, also a cultivated plant harvested in September, so perhaps Wright's stocks were low. Cobbett in *Cottage Economy* calculated that the average household used about 274 gallons a year. Wright's hops were sufficient for about four households. Clearly he was not Wellington's only supplier! Possibly many people still drank their ale unhopped. Richard Leeke, 1690, Wrockwardine, a collier, had 1cwt., i.e., more than Wright.

**Hornbrook.**—A board on which was written the alphabet, sometimes the digits, the Lord's Prayer and some simple spellings. The surface was protected with a thin layer of horn.

**Huckaback.**—A stout linen fabric so woven that the surface was rough. Used for towels (1690).

**Hurden, Harden.**—A very coarse cloth made from the refuse of flax or hemp. Used for sheets and other linens. It could also mean hemp generally and carl hemp in particular. Usually used in the Telford inventories to distinguish the poorer of two qualities of hempen cloth found in a house.

**Inkle.**—A kind of linen tape, or the thread from which it was made (1541).

**Kenting, Ghenting.**—Probably both are the same, a fine linen cloth originally from Ghent (1700).

**Kersey.**—A coarse, narrow cloth, woven from long wool and usually ribbed. Contrasted with 'cloth' and 'broadcloth' since the piece was shorter and narrower (1390).

**Kive.**—A large vat, also used for brewing, with a bottom drain, used in the preparation of tobacco, though for exactly which part of the process is not clear.

**Lace Pepper.**—Probably lack pepper, i.e., inferior or black pepper. Seventeenth-century writers seemed rather inclined to use 'ce' when 'ck' would have been correct. Wright has white pepper followed by the cheaper lace pepper which supports this reading.

**Lamp Black.**—A pigment consisting of almost pure, finely divided carbon, made by collecting the soot produced by burning oil.

**Lanill.**—Probably flannel, *q.v.*

**Leading Strings.**—Strings with which children could be guided and supported when learning to walk.

**Lining.**—Often just a mis-spelling of linen. Not so in Wright's inventory where it is listed among the woollens and is a material for linings and underwear.

**Linings.**—Items of underwear worn one on each leg.

**Linsey.**—More correctly linseywoollsey. A mixed facbic of wool and linen, or inferior wool. Used for furnishings and clothing for the poorer classes (1483).

**Looplace.**—Picot. An ornamental edging to lace (1630).

**Lutestring.**—A glossy silk fabric (1661).

**Mace.**—Dried outer covering of nutmeg.

**Mild.**—Milled, i.e., pressed, rolled and fulled.

**Mixt.**—Mixed, i.e., not pure wool.

**Molasses.**—A thick black treacle that drains from the sugar, about half the price of the cheapest sugar. Used in cooking (for things like gingerbread) and in medicine. Brimstone and treacle was a favourite country laxative into this century.

**Muslin.**—General name for the most delicately woven cotton fabric, used for women's dresses (1609).

**Nans thread.**—Nuns thread, a fine white sewing cotton sometimes called ounce thread (1766).

**Necklace.**—Probably a lace or ribbon for the neck. See William Poyner, 1715, Dawley.

**No thread.**—Possibly Nuns thread or knotting thread. Knotting was fancy work similar to tatting, and according to Addison in 1712, much in fashion.

**Open tape.**—Probably open work, *but see* 'filling lace'.

**Osnaburg.**—Ozembrigs, a kind of coarse linen, originally from Osnabruck (1545).

**Outnall.**—Linen thread (1662).

**Pace board, pasteboard.**—There was a headdress called a 'paste' because it was fashioned from pasteboard or cardboard. Most mercers had stocks of this among their haberdashery.

**Packthread.**—Stout thread or twine used for sewing or tying up packs. The position in Justice's inventory does not support this meaning there.

**Paper—Cap, white cap.**—A kind of wrapping paper. The use of 'cap' in the words like 'foolscap' does not start until the 19th century.

**—A Pound.**—Also stocked by Glover, who kept it with his brown cap paper near the Scales. 'Pound' has meanings near to 'pack up' and it also can mean to 'weigh'. Whatever the derivation it appears to refer to packing paper.

**Pepper.—White and Black.**—As now, prepared from the fruits of *Piper nigrum*.

**—Lace.**—Probably 'lack' or inferior. *See* Lace.

**—Gemace.**—Probably Jamaica pepper, i.e., Allspice.

**Persian silk.**—A thin, soft silk, used for linings (1696).

**Pgin galloon.**—Clearly an abbreviated form of the word. Another mercer had p'ging, where the abbreviation is clear and indicates a word such as 'parging'' To parge is an obsolete form of 'parget'. 'Pargeting' can mean covering or decorating a surface of any kind though originally it referred to plasterwork.

**Pipes.**—Probably clay tobacco pipes, already being manufactured in Broseley in the 17th century, and in Wellington by Evans.

**Pitch.**—Obtained from boiling tar. A local product.

**Plain, Plains.**—A cloth similar to flannel mainly from Wales (1600).

**Powder Horn.**—For carrying gunpowder, normally made from an ox or cow horn.

**Primer.**—A text book.

**Prunella.**—A strong stuff, originally silk, later worsted, formerly used for graduates, clergymens' and barristers' gowns, later for the uppers of women's shoes (1656).

**Quines.**—From the context in Justice's inventory it must be an article of clothing or for use in making garments.

**Raisins of the Sun.**—Sun-dried grapes.

**Res: Sol:.**—Abbreviated form of *Reslings solis*. See above.

**Rosin.**—A solid residue after the distillation of oil turpentine from crude turpentine. Often confused with gum.

**Ruffells.**—A strip of lace or other fine material gathered on one edge and used as an ornamental frill, especially at wrist, breast or neck.

**Sagathy.**—A woollen stuff, sometimes mixed with a little silk. Most of the quotes in the O.E.D. associate it with druggets and camlets. William Poyner, 1715, Dawley, used it for a grey coat (1707).

**Sarsenett, Sarsnet.**—A very fine, soft, silk material used for linings and dresses (1463).

**Satin.**—A silk fabric with a glossy surface on one side produced by a method of weaving by which the threads of the warp are caught and looped by the weft only at intervals (1366).

**Seeds.**—Almost certainly Caraway seeds which were grown as a field crop in Essex and elsewhere on heavy soils. Fennel and dill seeds, similar types of plant another possibility. These would all be very cheap. Wormseed, also stocked by mercers and apothecaries, was much more expensive and should not be considered here.

**Serge.**—A very durable, twilled cloth of worsted or a warp of worsted and weft of wool, mainly used for clothing, but Joseph Wayman, 1748, Ludlow, had red, serge, bed curtains. Thomas Jones, 1692, Wellington, and William Poyner, 1715, Dawley, had black waistcoats of serge (1386).

**Shalloon.**—A closely-woven material used chiefly for linings (1678).

**Shamy Skins.**—A kind of soft, pliable leather, or wash leather. Originally chamois skins.

**Sleeves.**—A separate garment. See William Poyner, 1715, Dawley.

**Statute galloon, lace, etc.**—Indicating a unit of measurement or weight fixed by parliamentary statute.

**Stay Tape.**—A stay lace for lacing a woman's stays, but also used by tailors for binding the edge of a fabric.

**Stirrups.**—A kind of footless stocking with a strap under the foot, also the strap itself. In this case it must be the stockings.

**Stomacher.**—A kind of waistcoat worn by men, or, as is more likely here, an ornamental covering for the chest worn by women.

**Stone Blue.**—A mixture of indigo with starch or whiting, used in laundrywork.

**Stript.**—Striped.

**Stuffs.**—A cloth with no nap or pile, usually light in weight made of worsted, silk or a mixture. A speciality of Norwich. They were often dyed, patterned or printed.

—**Kidderminster.**—O.E.D. considers that K. stuffs and K. carpets are identical, but all the quotes given for 17th century describe stuffs as a double cloth the two being of contrasting colours interwoven with each other and used for hangings and carpets in the sense that the word was used then. K. stuffs were quite clearly not carpeting in the modern sense. William Langley, 1689, Wellington, used it for curtains (1670-1).

**Sugar—Fine.**—Once refined, a poor grade also called powder.
  **—Brown.**—As above. It was in this state that sugar was imported so it is often identified by place of origin, which appears to have affected the price.
  **—In.**—Probably an abbreviation for Indian.
  **—Brown Candy.**—Double refined. Probably what we would call lumps. Often called 'suckit', which indicates its use.
  **—Triple Refined, Loaf.**—Hard all better qualities of sugar not stocked by the Wellington mercers.
  **—Bastard.**—The very lowest grade made from the refuse of previous boilings.

**Tabby.**—A general term for silk taffeta, apparently originally striped but afterwards applied also to silks of uniform colour waved or watered (1638).

**Taffeta.**—A name applied at different times to different fabrics. In the 17th century it always seem to have referred to silks, often used for ribbons. One feature commonly mentioned is the use of warp and weft of different colours.

**Tammy.**—A fine worsted cloth of good quality often with a glazed finish, much mentioned in the 17th and 18th centuries, but obsolete by 1850 (1665).

**Temple Wires.**—'Temples' were ornaments of jewellery or needlework worn by women at the side of the forehead, but apparently only prior to 1650. More likely these wires were needed for the fashonable French hoods. *See* Hood.

**Tooling.**—By its position in Justice's inventory it ought to be some kind of thread.

**Tow.**—There are several meanings. It can mean flax before it is scutched, and also the heckled fibres ready for spinning. Some of the entries like 'yarn and tow' suggest that it is used in this sense in North Telford. Also means the refuse left by heckling which could be used for the manufacture of hurdens or for sacking or rope.

**Twind.**—Read tied. *See* Cravat.

**Twist.**—A fine silk thread used by tailors, hatters, etc., but also thread generally made of two or more filaments wound round one another.

**Vermillion.**—A fabric dyed with vermillion. (L. Roberts, Treas. Traffick 33. 1641. 'They buy cotton wooll in London and perfit it into Fustian, vermillions and other such stuffs.')

**Wash Balls.**—A ball of soap (sometimes perfumed or medicated) used for washing the hands and face and for shaving. The best were made in Bologna (*see* Evelyn's *Diary*, May 1645.).

**Whisk.**—A neckerchief worn by women in the latter half of the 17th century.

**Whited bro:.**—White brown thread. Thread was normally listed as black (i.e., dyed black) and brown (i.e., unbleached). White brown must be bleached linen thread.

**Worsted.**—Cloth, but also the yarn from which it is made. Here the yarn is meant, a well twisted yarn made from longstaple wool, combed to lay the fibres parallel.

# INDEX OF SUBJECTS AND PLACES

Figures in italics (e.g., *84*) refer to inventories. Other figures refer to pages in the Introduction.

Admaston: 13, 78, *87*, *209*, *212*, *213*, *249*
Agriculture: 72-90
'Alkemmy': 43, *107*, *115*, *130*
Allscott: 13, 50, 64, 78, *211*, *215*, *227*, *232*, *238*, *243*, *251*, *254*, *264*
Alum: 60
Andirons: 104
Antimony: 43 (*see also* 'Alkemmy')
Apley: 12, 14
Apothecaries: 26-27, 41, 54, *160*, *180*, *187*
Appraisers: 60-10, 28, 49, 52
Arable farming: 83-89
Arleston: 12, 25, *175*
Aston: 12, *81*, *154*

Bacon: 103
Bags: 85, 112
Bakers: 64-65, *197*
Bark: 44-45
Barley: 84-85, 111-12
Barrels: 67, 110
Basting spoons: 104
Bays: 32
Beans: 85-86. 97
Beds and bed linen: 36-37, 98-99
Beef: 103
Beer: 68-69, 111-13
Bees: 6, 39-41
Bewdley: 25
Bibles: 100
Bills: 89
Bird Calls: 102
Bishop's Castle: 44, 81, 101, 109
Blacksmiths: 14, 16, 65-66, 68, 72, *18*, *33*, *90*, *108*, *116*, *124*, *133*, *150*, *163*, *181*, *188*, *200*, *208*
Boards: 17
Bodkins: 102
Boilers: 104, 112
Bonds: 18-19
Books: 26
Bottles: 102-03
Bows: *36*
Bowls: 100, *119*
Boxes: 91, 95-98
Box irons: 108
Bran: 56
Brandlee: 70, *194*
Brass: 106-07
Bratton: 13, 78, *231*, *233*
Brewing: 23, 43, 45, 68-69 71, 111-14
Bricks: 17, *110*

Bridgnorth: 19-21, 44, 48
Bringewood: 107
Bristol: 40-41, 61
Broaches: 104
Broom hooks: 89
Broseley: 3, 70
Building materials: 17
Bulls, bullocks: 76
Butchers; 64, *113*
Butter: 78, 80, 110-11, 114
Buttons: 34

Cages: 95-96
Calves: 74, 76, 103
Candles, candlemaking: 25-26, 39, 41, 108-09, *174*
Carpets: 92-93
Carpenters: 66-67, 91, 114, *19*, *24*, *45*, *50*, *109*
Carriers: 68-70, *82*, *186*
Caster hats: *107*
Cattle: 72-78, 83, 88-89
Chafing dishes: 105
Chairs: 93-94
Chamber pots: 108
Charcoal: 11, 27
Chattell leases: 17-18
Charlton: 13, *217*, *235*, *252*, *265*
Cheese: 17, 71, 77-78, 80, 105, 109-10, 113-14
Cheshill Grange: *58*
Chests: 91, 95-98
Chester: 21, 31, 48, 50, 59, *15*, *28*
Chimes: 100, *144*
China: 102-03, *100*, *110*, *115*, *195*
Chopping knives: 106
Cider: 113, *154*, *177*, *203*
Cleavers: 106
Clergymen: 43, 70, 110, 119, *156*, *162*, *189*
Clocks: 100-01, 114
Close stools: 108
Clothiers: 64
Clothing: 34-35, 65, *16*, *142*, *144*
Clotley: 13, *226*, *234*, *261*, *263*
Clover: 85-86, 113
Cloves: 29-30
Cluddley: *158*
Coal: 65, 70-72, 103, 109, 111, *12*, *26*, *73*, *156*, *194*, *239*, *245*
Coalbrookdale: 11, 73, 104
Coats of arms: 99-100, *8*, *110*
Cob-irons: 104

Cock lofts: 17
Coffee: 113–14, 77, *199*, *258*, *264*
Coffers: 95–98
Colours (of fabrics): 33–35, 56–61
Coolers: 110
Coopers and coopery ware: 67, 109–12
Copper: 107, 112
Copperas: 60–61
Cordwainers, corvisors: 47, *94*, *103*, *125*, *149*
Corves: 67, *19*
Couches: 95
Coventry: 25
Crabs: 113, *9*, *81*
Cranes: 104
Cream: 110
Creepers: 104
Croppings, The: 22
*Crown*, inn: 68–69, *146*, *159*, *171*
Crudgington: 22
Cucking, Sussex: 25
Cullinders: 106
Cupboards: 95–98
Curriers: 45–47, *198*
Cushions: 95
Cutlery: 107, *147*, *195*, *249*, *258*, *264*

Dairy farming: 71, 73–78, 113
Dairies: 17, 103, 109–11
Dawley: 11, 70, 76
Desks: 95–98
Desperate debts: 18
Diaper: 35
Dictionaries: 100, *85*, *126*
Dining rooms: 16, *12*, *118*, *148*, *194*
Dishboards: 95–96
Dissenters: 23–25
Dogs: 66, 83
Dog wheels: 38, *174*
Donnington: 11–12, *52*, *64*, *69*, *76*, *77*, *79*
Dothill: 12, 14
Drawing rooms: 17, *199*
Dredge: 84
Dressers: 96–98
Dripping pans: 104
Drugs: 26, 43, *160*, *185*, *187*
Dubbing boards: 49
Ducks: 83, *5*, *9*, *42*, *109*
Dyes, dyeing, dyers: 26, 33, 47–61, *84*, *98*, *121*, *127*, *173*, *193*, *195*

Earthenware: 102
Easy chairs: 94, *194*, *249*
Elbow chairs: 94
Ellesmere: 48, 58, 101
Esquires: *148*
Ewers: 71, *87*

Fabrics: 32–38
Faggotts: 65, 109, *185*, *197*

Farming: 72–90
Fastenings (of clothes): 34
Feltmakers: 65, 82, *134*, *136*
Fenders: 104
Fimble: 36
Finney, The: *14*
Fire irons: 103–04
Fish, fishing: 83
Flagons: 106
Flatting troughs: 38
Flax: 43, 61–63
Flutes: 100, *144*
Forks: 107–08
French Wheat: 84
Frying pans: 105
Fuel: 6, 65
Fullers, fullers earth: 50, 64
Furnaces: 104, 112
Furnishings: 90–108
Furnishing fabrics: 35, 92–93
Fustic: 56, 58

Galls: 56, 60
Gambrels: 64
Gardeners: *192*
Gauns: 101, 106, 110
Gears: 63
Geese: 83, *3*, *5*, *36*, *42*, *117*
Gentlemen: 26, 72, *8*, *17*, *22*, *65*, *77*, *118*, *135*, *144*, *154*, *161*, *186*, *230*, *249*, *257*, *258*
Gins: 194
Ginger: 29–30
Glass (cases or cages): 96, 102–03
Gloves, gloving: 44–46, *85*, *89*, *184*, *206*
Gold: 101-02
Grates: 103–05
Grocery: 27-29
Guile tuns: 112
Guns: 101, *92*, *93*

Haberdashery: 27, 34
Hacking knives: 106
Hadley: 12, 22, 66, *106*, *114*, *130*, *150*, *151*, *152*, *162*
Hair cloths: 112
Hair sieves: 110
Halberds: 101, *8*, *49*, *104*
Handles: 49–50
Hands (of tobacco): 38
Hangings: 99
Hard corn: 84
Harrows: 86–88
Harpswood: *235*
Hatchetts: 106
Hatters: 65
Hay: 75–77
Hazlewoods Living: *22*
Heifers: 76
Hemp: 36, 47, 61-63

## INDEX OF SUBJECTS AND PLACES

Hem, The: 26
Heriots: 19
Herrings: 28
High Ercall: 87
Hinks, The: 54, 55, 94
Hollinswood: 194
Holywell Lane: 11, 72, 21
Honey: 40-41
Honnington: 11, 53
Hooks and eyes: 34
Horses: 65, 69-70, 82-83, 88
Horton: 12, 102
Hosiery: 27-28
Houses: 14-17
Huckaback: 35
Husbandmen: 16, 72, 3, 29, 97
Hutches: 97, 9

Indigo: 54-57
Industrial Revolution: 1-2
Inns: 16, 68-70, 146, 147, 159, 171, 172, 201, 203
Investments: 18-19, 23, 31, 90, 114
Iron, iron ore: 70-72, 194
Irons (smoothing): 108

Jacks: 104
Jackfield Ware: 102
Joiners: 259

Keepers: 101, 36, 44, 63
Ketley: 5, 12, 52, 70-71, 101, 138, 143, 165, 178, 194, 204, 207
Ketley Bank House: 70, 194
Kettles: 104-06
Kidderminster stuffs: 35, 47, 93
Kitchens: 103-08
Kummels: 112
Kynnersley: 7, 13, 20, 177

Labourers: 16, 72, 14, 46, 51, 153, 158, 164, 168, 240
Ladders: 110
Lard: 203
Lawley: 12, 25
Leases: 17-18
Leather trades: 44-47
Leaton: 13, 210, 230, 250, 258
Leegomery: 12, 18, 51, 78, 87, 91, 109, 177
Lent grain: 84
Lichfield (diocese and record office): 2-3, 6, 10, 31; (city): 7, 19, 21, 26, 40, 41, 48-51, 100
Lilleshall: 11-12, 14, 44, 61, 64, 76, 78, 80, 85-86
Linens: 26, 33, 36-37, 51, 61-63
Literacy: 9-10
Little Wenlock: 18, 102, 100, 109
Livery tables and cupboards: 92

London: 25, 26, 31, 52, 58
Long Lane: 13, 67, 214, 222, 259, 260
Looking glasses: 99
Looms: 63-64, 110, 112
Ludlow: 19, 20, 31, 44, 48, 50, 101

Madder: 56-58
Madeley: 3, 70. 8, 30
Malins Lee: 11, 71, 12, 17, 18
Malting: 23, 43, 44, 49, 50, 56, 68, 69, 99, 111-12
Manchester: 34
Maps: 44, 99
Market Drayton: 62
Market tolls: 24, 26
Marmites; marmalades: 105
Mash tuns: 112
Maslin: 84
Maslin kettles: 106
Mathematicians: 44, 100, 74
Mercers: 20-41, 113-14, 107, 112, 126, 132, 144, 161, 170, 174
Miners, mining: 25, 70-72, 82, 114-15, 11, 12, 20, 21, 167, 242, 245, 246, 256
Mills, millers: 12, 52, 65, 37, 78, 95, 111, 138, 211, 238
Mitts: 105, 110
Money: 17-19
Montrose: 34
Mordants: 56-59
Mortars and pestles: 31, 105-06
Mortgages: 18
Moss, The: 225
Muck: 89-90
Museums: 1
Music: 100
Mustard pots: 106
Muxton: 11, 44, 67, 68, 47, 51, 59, 60, 64, 66, 67, 68, 71, 74

Nailers: 145
Nantwich: 21
Nash: 13, 212
Newport (Salop): 20, 48, 101, 64
Niggards: 103
Nursing chairs: 94

Oakengates: 14, 246
Old Hall (Wellington): 70, 194
Open fields: 12-14, 23, 113
Orleton: 13, 14, 212
Oxen: 88-90, 113
Oxford: 15

Pack Saddles: 70
Pains Lane: 13, 220, 242, 244, 246
Paper: 27
Pasty and patty pans: 105
Pawn Hatch: 67, 24
Peas: 84-86

Penkridge: *15*
Pepper: 29-30, 106
Pewter: 101-02, 106
Pickells: 89
Pictures: 99-100
Pigs: 81-82, 110
Physicians: *9*
Pipes, pipemakers: 28, 38, 68, *122*
Pistols: 101
Pitch pans: *60*
Ploughs: 86-88
Points: 34
Pokers: 103
Pool Hill: 67, *19*
Porkets: 81
Porringers: 106
Posnetts: 105
Potatoes: 86, *185, 192*
Pot geals and hooks: 104
Pot ash: 61
Pottery: 102
Poultry: 6, 83
Presses (cupboards): 95-96; (cheese): 110
Preston on the Weald Moors: 12, 43, 99
Priorslee: 3
Probate inventories: locations, etc.: 2-3; characteristics: 3-6
Professions: 41, 43-44
Property: 17-19
Pudding plates: 105
Pumps: 82

Quob Pool: *245, 256, 262*

Railways: 67
Raisins: 29
Razors: *135*
Ricks: 76-77
Rindletts: 111-12
Ropes, ropemakers: 67-68, *96, 194*
Ruckley: *141*
Rundletts: 111
Rye: 84-85. 113

St. George's: 13 (*see also* Pains Lane)
Salt: 28, 103, 106, 110, *58, 224*
Salvers: 106
Scales: 30-31, 100
Schools, schoolteachers: 24, 43-44, *218, 237, 254*
Screens: 99, 112
Sculleries: 17, *26, 199, 249*
Scythes: 89
Securities: 18-19
Segg chairs: 94
Servants: 4, 17, 98-99, *39*
*Seven Stars*, The: 66, 68, *208*
Shearing boards, shears: 49, 50
Sheep: 36-37, 99
Shifnal: 3, 12, 14, 25, 66, *101*

Shoes, shoemakers: 47, 114, *123, 157, 166, 182, 183, 205*
Shots, shoats, shuts: 81
Shrewsbury: 19, 21, 25, 26, 31, 32, 48, 50, 51, 52, 66, 101
Sickles: 89
Sidbury: *30*
Sieve bowls: *9*
Silks: 20, 27
Silver: 101-02
Skates: 100, *49*
Skelletts: 105
Skimmers: 105, 110
Skinners: *89, 264*
Sleds: 88, *17*
Smoking: 17, 38 (*see also* Tobacco)
Snedshill: *194*
Snuff: 38-39
Soap: 28
Spermacetti: 28
Spices: 26-30
Spinning, spinning wheels: 61-63, 71-72
Spits: 104
Spoons: 107
Squatting: 11, 14, 67, 114
Stationery: 27
Steam engines: 71, *194*
Steel Yards: 100
Stone cutters: 68, *202*
Stools: 94-95
Store chambers: 17
Store swine: 81
Street Way, Lane: 14
Stunds: 112
Sugar: 27-28, 39, 41, 42
Sumach: 56, 60
Surgeons: *see* apothecaries
Surveying: 44, 74
*Swan*, The: 68, *147*
Swords: 101, *49, 82*
Syllabub cups: 106, *110*

Tables: 91
Tailors: 65, *129, 140, 179*
Tallants: 76, *80*
Tanning: 44-47, *95, 111*
Tapestries: 99
Tar: *13*
Tea: 113-14, 77, *148, 194, 258, 264*
Teasles: 49
Telford: 2
Tenters: 49-50
Testers: *9*
Thatchers: 72, *51*
Thoroughfare trade: 14
Threshing: 86
Thrum: *9*
Tickney Ware: 102, 110
Tiles: 17, *110*
Time: 100-01

# INDEX OF SUBJECTS AND PLACES

Tin: 107
Toasters: 105
Tobacco: 24-26, 28, 38-39, *174*
Tokens: 25, 31
Tools: 89
Tow: 36
Trench Lane: 5, 13, *240, 241, 245, 248, 253*
Trenchers: 102, 107
Trinen ware: 109-10
Truckle beds: 98-99
Trunks: 91
Tumbrels: 86-87
Tundish: 110
Turkeys: 83, *71*
Turkey work: 35, 43, 47, 94
Turnells: 105, 110, 112
Turnips: 86, *84, 128*
Turnover (of mercers' shops): 31
Turnpike roads: 11, 14, 65-66, *181*
Twinters: 76

Uppington: *9*

Vats: 53-55, 110, 112, *84, 98*
Verdigris: *46, 66*
Vetches: 85-86
Viols: 100, *222*
Violins: 100, *144*
Virginals: 100, *8*

Waffering irons: 105
Waggons: 86-88
Wainscot: 99
Walcot: 12, 65, *85, 138*
Walnut tree (Muxton): 47
Warehouses: 30
Warping troughs: 63
Washing: 108
Watches: 101, *16, 17, 147*
Watling Street: 12, 13, 14, 65, 68-69, 82, *96, 147, 172, 186*
Wax: 41
Weald Moors: 13, 52, 101
Weather Glasses: 77, *154*

Weaving, weavers, websters: 15-16, 61-64, 72, 77, 114, *7, 10, 52, 72, 75, 105, 151, 152, 204, 209, 224, 236*
Weighing: 100
Wellington: 10, 12, 19-20, 26, 65, 101, 113
Welsh cloth: 32, 50-51
Wem: 31
Whalebone: 28
Wheat: 83-85
Wheat Leasows: *88*
Wheels: 86
Wheelwrights: 67, *57*
Whistons: *62*
Whitesmiths: 66, *131*
Winches: 53
Winnowing: 86
Woad: 49, 52, 54-57, *84, 98*
Wombridge: 3, 12, 14, 43
Women: 4, 8, 90
Wooden ware: 107, 109-10, 112
Woodseaves: *62*
Wool: 81
Woollens: 32, 33, 50, 51
Worcester: 21, 27
Wrekin: 12, *81, 117*
Wrockwardine: 13, 77, 78, 80, 82, 85-86
Wrockwardine Wood: 13, *220 221, 225, 229, 236, 239, 240, 241, 242, 245, 247, 248, 253, 256, 262*
Wroxeter: 51, 52

Yarwingles: 63
Yearlings: 76
Yeomen: 72, *1, 9, 26, 30, 31, 36, 38, 40, 47, 52, 53, 54, 56, 58, 60, 62, 73, 80, 87, 91, 130, 137, 141, 169, 207, 210, 213, 215, 221, 225, 226, 227, 231, 232, 234, 235, 239, 241, 242, 247, 251, 254, 260, 265*

## INDEX OF NAMES

This index *does not* include the names of people whose inventories are published in this collection (*see* complete list, pp. 119-159) unless they are referred to in the Introduction or appear in an inventory in another context. References in the Introduction are indexed only when significant new information is revealed. The index *does* include the appraisers of all the inventories published, with a brief summary of the other occasions on which appraisers of the same name acted, and any person mentioned in the texts or preambles of inventories.

Figures in italics (e.g., *242*) refer to INVENTORIES. Other references (e.g., 67) are to PAGES in the Introduction. A set of brackets shows that the individual(s) of that name acted as appraiser; the first number gives the number of occasions, the dates, the time span, the initials, the parish of the deceased (D=Dawley, L=Lilleshall, W=Wellington, R=Wrockwardine). The following numbers in italics show the inventories published in this volume. An asterisk denotes more than one mention in the inventory.

Thus: Sockett: Andrew, 25, 26, 31, 38, 39 (18; 1670-1725; W) *106, 107\*, 109, 128, 136, 157*; i.e., the name Andrew Sockett is mentioned in the Introduction on pp. 25, 26, 31, 38, 39, it appears as an appraiser on 18 inventories between 1670 and 1725, all in Wellington, of which six are published here as Nos. *106, 107, 109, 128, 136, 157*, and the name Andrew Sockett appears twice in number *107*.

Adams: John (8; 1728-46; W), *183, 191, 197*; William (2; 1676-84; W, R), *102*
Adney: William (1), *79*
Allsop: Richard (1), *249*
Ambler: ——, *107*
Ankers or Ankret: Arthur (4; 1671-1710); D, L, W), *14*
Apley: Richard (1), *58*
Arden: George, 7 (5; 1716-32; D), *21, 26, 28*
Ashwood: William (1), *8*
Assley: Richard (1), *235*

Bache: Thomas (1), *154*
Ball: James (1), *194*; Richard, *245* (3; 1660-83; W, R), *221*; William, *245*
Banks: William, 111
Barkham: Edward, *150*
Barnes: Tryphosa, 26, 27, 38

Barrett: Ralph (2), *40, 95*; Thomas (3; 1718-24; D), *19, 20*; ——, 25
Basnet: Thomas (1), *59*
Bassett: Richard (3; 1686-1729; L, W), *54*
Bate: Mary, 74; Thomas, 72; (1) *226*; William (4; 1670-1720; W), *87, 166*
Baxter: Francis, *104*
Bayley: Francis (3; 1665-80; W), *88*; ——, *194*
Beaumont: Joseph, 100, *258*
Beddow: Andrew (1) *149*; John, 85
Bell: William, 7
Bellis: Richard (2; 1720-1; D, W), *17*
Benbow: George (1), *71*
Bennett: Humphrey (6; 1661-80; W), *84*; John (4), *82, 90\*, 165, 172*; Roger (1), *109*; Samuel (11; 1676-1701; W, R), *90\*, 92, 93, 99, 113, 137*; Thomas (4; 1659-93; W), *82, 90*

482

# INDEX OF NAMES

Besford: Edward, 82, 83
Betton: Michael (1), *199*; Richard (1), 113
Bickley: Thomas (1), *110*
Bingley, *see* Ringley
Binnell: Thomas (9; 1657-1726; W, R), 96, 243; ——, *148*
Binton: Richard, 54
Birch: William, 7, 26, 27, 43, (1), *126*
Birchwood: Robert (1), *84*
Bithem: William, 254
Blakemore: Thomas (1), *254*; William (1), *48*
Bolas: Robert (4; 1725-30; W), *172, 181*
Bold: Edward (1), *225*
Booksley, *see* Pucksley
Bowdler: John, 31
Boycott: Elizabeth, 44; Francis (1), *9*; William, 44; ——, *66, 124*
Boyden: Thomas, 260
Bradborne: Thomas, 7 (3; 1671-75; L), *39, 40*; Walter (8; 1690-1724; L), *72*
Bradshaw: John, 6 (15; 1658-1728; W), *100, 110, 112, 118, 163, 174, 176, 179, 180*; Rowland (4; 1695-1739; W), *125*; William (8; 1702-43; W), *125, 153*
Brearley: Da. (2; 1740-42; W), *205*
Bridgin: Thomas (1), *29*
Bridgwood: Richard (3), *3, 5, 6*
Broadhurst: Walter (7; 1679-1704; L), *46, 48, 62*
Bromley: John (3; 1705-49; W, R), *172*
Brooke: George (8; 1661-1716; L, W, R), *85*; Jonathan (1), *235*; Samuel (1), *85*
Brookes: James (1), *80*
Brown: Richard (6; 1662-76; W, R), *83, 86*
Broxton: Nicholas, 69 (1), *150*
Bullock: Thomas (1), *48*
Burton: Richard, 54
Buttery: George (2; 1679-82; W), *100*
Byrd: —, *119*

Calcott: Joshua (1), *238*; Thomas, *264*, (1), *251*
Campbell: John, 61
Cartwright: William, 44 (5; 1657-1716; L, R), *41, 69, 225*
Carver: John (3; 1679-85; R), *216, 223*
Charlton: family, 17; Francis, *83*; John, *161*; Jonathan (1), *55*; William (2; 1690-98; L, R), *55*
Cheese: William (2; 1678-92; L. W), *116*
Cherrington: John, 49, 52, 53, 54, 57, 58, 61, *258*\* (3; 1721-37; W), *193*
Cheshire: George (1), *211*

Chester: George (1), *192*
Childs: Andrew (1), *192*; Thomas (1), *30*
Chirme: George (1), *234*; John (1), *15*; Thomas (2; 1676-85; D, R), *7*
Clark: Edward (2), *81, 117*; Michael (4; 1676-94; W), *91, 123*; William (1), *185*
Cleaton: Gabriel (11; 1672-1721; W), *108, 120, 167*; John, *150*; Joseph, *84* Robert (1), *178*; Roger, *127*, (3; 1690-1740; W, R), *200*; William (2; 1703-07; W), *147*; ——, *194*
Clerk: ——, *264*\*
Clowes: Richard (5; 1659-66; D), *1, 2, 4*
Cludde: family, 13
Cole: James (1), *153*
Colley: George (4; 1679-1731; L. R), *53, 217, 254*; James (1), *53*; Peter (1), *203*
Cooke: William (1), *116*
Cookson: William (5; 1685-1729; W), *105, 114, 151, 184*
Cooper: William (3; 1712-28; W), *182*
Cope: John, 64; William (4: 1671-81; R), *214, 215, 218*
Corbett: family, 17; Sir John, *83*; Robert, 25; William (8; 1681-1729; L, W), *68, 71, 75, 97*
Cornes: Sarah, 35
Cotton: Rowland (3; 1679-1723; W), *162, 170*
Cowcher: Thomas, *21, 27*
Cox: John (1), *220*
Crippen: Ann, *14*; John, *14*; ——, *194*
Cross: Matthew (1), *250*
Crowther: Richard, 7 (6; 1671-76; L), *38, 42, 43, 52*
Crudgington: George (1), *114*
Crump: Robert (1), *219*
Currier: Edward (3; 1705-22; R), *241, 248*; Samuel (1), *170*
Cuxson, *see* Cookson

Dabbs: Jane, 260
Dager: widow, 260
Dale: James (1), *56*; John (2), *104, 105*; Lewis (10; 1671-1735. L), *38, 41*
Dalley: ——, *107*
Darby: Abraham, 72, 115
Darrall: Andrew (1), *9*; Daniel (1), *21*; Edward, 16, 72, 115; Richard (3; 1659-65; D), *1, 3*; William (1), *6*
Davids: Eleanor (1), *101*
Davis: John (2; 1731-37; W), *188*; Robert (1), *33*; Silvanus, 10, Venus, 260
Dawes: Edward (1), *241*; Thomas (1), *102*; William (17; 1654-1740; L, W, R), *89, 209, 212, 242, 245*

Deacon: Samuel (1), *158*
Dicken: Thomas, 10 (1), *103*
Dixon: Charles (1), *188*
Dolves: Hugh (1), *236*
Doughty: William, 26 (2; 1700-08; W), *132*
Drelincourt: Charles, 100, *258*
Duddell: Dorothy, *24*; John, 67 (1), *23*
Dunn: Thomas, 110
Dunton: Joshua, 7 (8; 1662-79; W), *83, 86*

Eastop: William (2; 1666-1720; D, W), *5, 165*
Edwards: Thomas (1), *30*
Ellis: Richard, *93*
Ellesmere; Samuel (1), *264*
Embry: William, 10
Evans: John (7; 1672-1719; L, W, R), *72, 230, 243*; William (7; 1683-1730; W), *101, 186*
Eykin: Richard (7; 1676-1718; L), *43, 50*
Eyton: family, 6; John, 35

Fairchild: Charles (1), *249*
Felton: Elinor, *212*; Thomas, *258\** (3; 1729-38; W, R), *197*
Fenn: Edward, *245*; Robert, 8
Fewtrell: William, 8.
Field: John, 43; Miles, *54*; Timothy, *148* (15; 1686-1716; W, R), *108, 118, 131, 134, 149*
Fieldhouse: Thomas, 82
Fisher: Joseph (2), *32, 34*
Flemming; Edward (1), *48*
Floyd: William (1), *149*
Ford: Richard, 71; ––, *194*
Forester: family, 6, 23, 23, 37, 69, *203*
Fosbrook, *see* Holbrook
Fowler: John (4; 1721-30; W), *167, 187*
Francis: John, *109* (3; 1665-1701; W), *136*
Freeman: Alan (6; 1684-1717; L, W), *104*; Jos. (7; 1721-45; W), *167, 189*; Thomas, *101* (14; 1677-1749; W), *120, 143, 152, 208*

Garbett: Francis (2; 1600-1702; W), *139*
Gaywood: Thomas (2; 1701-07; L), *64*
Golbourn: George (1), *229*; John (1), *108*
Goldsmith: Thomas (1), *220*
Gough: John (1), *12*
Greenell: John (2; 1684-86; L), *51*
Grice: Elizabeth, 78; John (12; 1672-1704; W, R), *126, 139, 141, 237*; Joseph, 78 (6; 1714-44; W, R), *261, 263, 264*
Griffiths: John (1), *91*; Thomas (1), *111*

Grosvenor: John (2; 1689-98; W, R), *110*

Hall: John (6: 1681-1708; W), *146*; Richard (4; 1715-27; D, W), *15*; William (5; 1663-1729; L, R), *219*
Hammersley: Francis (1), *258*; William (5); 1676-1737; L), *45, 76, 79*
Hampton: Francis (3; 1725-29; W), *173, 185*; William (1), *169*
Hanson: Betty, *174*
Hanworth: William (1), *198*
Harding: Peter (1), *263*
Harper: Benjamin (1), *198*; Dorothy, *260*; Thomas, 7, 84 (5; 1659-67; L, W), *32, 82*; William (1), *144*
Harrington: Andrew (1), *131*; George (3; 1699-1700; W), *129, 130*; Richard (3; 1677-81; W), *97*
Hartshorne: Jane, 70-1, 114; Richard, 4, 70-1, 115; Walter, 71, 72, 77
Haughton: Henry, 43, (4; 1675-87; L), *40, 47*
Hawkins: ––, *71*
Haynes: John, *127*; ––, *194*
Hayward: John (1), *256*; William, *135, 179*
Higgins: Richard, 64 (6; 1676-1721; D, L. W. R), *11\*, 221*; Thomas, 6 (9; 1666-1731; D, L. W. R), *11, 77, 248*
Hill: E, (1), *23*; Job (1), *155*: John, 39 (4; 1681-1748; W, R), *97*; Mary, *155*
Hillin: John, 39
Holbrook (possibly Fosbrook): John (1) *19*
Holland: George (3; 1675-83; W); *101*; Thomas (1), *175*
Holmes (also Hulmes): John (9; 1661-1701, D, L), *13, 33, 40, 41, 49, 52*; Robert (5; 1683-96; L),*56*
Hooper: John (5; 1725-41; W, R), *177, 253*
Hotchkiss: Andrew (1), *228*; Francis (1), *154*; John (3; 1668-99; L, W), *94*
Howle: Humphrey (1), *89*; John, *194\**; Philip (4; 1662-84; W, R). *83, 212, 216*; Thomas, *260* (6; 1668-1709; L, W, R), *48, 130, 219*
Hughes: Thomas (3; 1686-1706; L, R), *63*
Hulmes, *see* Holmes
Husband: John (3; 1676-79; L), *43, 46*
Hussey: Joseph (1), *31*

Icke: Roger (5; 1665-80; W), *95*; Timothy (1), *107*; William, 6 (13; 1687-1723; W), *109, 148, 152, 156, 168, 240*

# INDEX OF NAMES

Inson, see Juson
Ison: James (2; 1709-14; W, *158*

Jackson: Richard, *129*; William (1), *125*
James: John (5; 1693-1727; L, W), *67, 68*
Jebb; Thomas, 78
Jennings: John (1), *195*; William, *174*
Jerningham: Family, Earls of Stafford, 71, *194*
Jewson, see Juson
Johnson: Jane, 8; Joshua, 7, 22, 23, 26, 28, 30, 31, 32, 33, 34, 38, 39, 41; Richard, *83*; Robert, 22, 23, *160* (1), *103*
Jones: Edward (1), *101*; R., 6 (5; 1670-75; W), *89*; Richard (9; 1660-1732; D, W), 7, *94, 196*; Thomas, *104*; William (10, 1670-1735; D, W), *123, 124*
Jordan: Richard (9; 1676-1716; D, W), 7, *13, 138*
Judgson: family, 68-9; John (6; 1609-1705; W), *132, 140*
Juson (*also* Jewson): Thomas (5; 1681-1700; W, R), *130, 219*
Justice: Margaret, 20-22, 26, 28, 31, 32, 38, 39

Kanadine: Thomas (5; 1695-1712; W), *140, 142, 145*
Keen, William (1), *18*
Kerby: William (1), *16*
Kervin: Ann, 25
Key: John, 65; Robert (5; 1681-98; L, W), *54, 102*

Lancashire: Robert, 7
Langley: Elizabeth, 8 (10, *258\**; Ellen, *258*; John (1), *250*; Peter (2), *187, 224*; Ralph (1), *101*; Rowland, *222*; William, 7, 43
Lathe: Richard (7; 1673-1703; L, W), *99*
Lawrence: Charles (1), *27*; Hugh (4; 1676-83; L), *45, 49*; John (7; 1688-1729; W, R), *121, 232*; Thomas (13; 1659-1732; L, W, R), *81, 89, 96, 210, 213, 223, 224*
Lea: Richard (1), *154*
Leeke: John, 7 (1), *160*; Jos 1 (1), *194*; Mary, 23; Thomas (7; 1677-1704; L, W), *49, 61, 62*; ——, *157*
Lennox: John, 14
Leveson: Sir Richard, *32*
Leveson-Gower: family, 6, 11, 12, 17, 44
Lewis: Catherine, *160*
Light: Robert (2; 1711-48; L), *80*; Thomas (1), *50*
Littlehales: Ralph (1), *16*
Littleton: Richard (1), *161*

Lloyd: Thomas (2; 1676-1703; W), *90*
Loch: James, 11, 14, 17
Lockley: Richard (3; 1676-85; L), *44*; Thomas, 12 (2; 1692-1729; L, R), 56
Lowe: Thomas, 78 (9; 1686-1715; L, W, R), *54, 231, 233*
Lummas: John, *242*; Richard, *242* (5; 1723-38; W), *190, 191*

Machin (Machem): Samuel (1), *222*; Thomas (2; 1718-24; W), *163*
Maddox: William, *142*
Mannering: John (2; 1671-72; W), *88*
Mansel: John, 46 )3; 1684-86; L), *51, 54*; Walter, *44*
Marigold: Walter, *104* (7; 1666-1715; W, R), *234*; William, 40
Martin: ——, *194*
Massey: Peter (12; 1713-44; W, R), *203, 255, 257*; William (9; 1722-41; W, R), *174, 258*
Meeson: John (4; 1731-46; D), *31*
Middleton: ——, *119*
Minnion: John, 78
Minshall: Mary, 52; William (1), *87*
Mitton: Edward (\*; 1669-97; W, R), *213, 226, 227*; Robert (1), *85*
Moreton: Thomas (1), *162*
Morris: James, *107*; Robert, 23, 26 (3; 1716-28; W), *182*
Moulton: Thomas (5; 1663-1732; L, R), *35*
Mountford: John, *233*; Richard, 10

Newell: Thomas (11; 1671-1716; L, W), *67, 148*
Newton: John (3; 1679-88; W, R), *216*; Thomas (5; 1659-87; D), *1, 4*; William, 6 (6; 1683-1700; D, W, R), *112, 231*
North: Catherine, *110*
Norton: Thomas (1), *139*

Old, John, *64, 104*
Oldfield: James, 21, 27, 39
Oliver: George (2; 1728-41; R), *262*; ——, *260*
Onions: Michael, *22*; Thomas (1), *204*; William, *194\**
Ore, Francis (7; 1671-91; W, R), *97, 101*; Samuel (1), *141*
Orme: Francis (1), *111*
Orrel: Thomas (2), *92, 93*
Owen: Thomas (1), *151*; William (1), 58

Palin: Richard (1), *98*
Palmer: Mary, *129*; Thomas, 36
Payne: Charles (1), *123*

Pearce: William, 6, 7, *155*
Peate: George, 66, *150*; John, 66; Robert (3; 1693-94; W), *122*
Pemberton; Edward (10; 1659-79; W, R), *81, 87, 210, 212, 213\*, 214*; J. (3; 1700-13; W, R), *132*; Robert (4; 1679-85; R), *216, 218, 223*; Roger (1), *230*; William 235 (4; 1682-89; R), *226, 227*; —, *119*
Penson: Thomas, 82; William (4; 1661-87; L), *33, 50*
Peploe: Ann, *28*; Jane, *3*; John, *3*; Nathan, *3* (2, 1715; D, W), *159*; Podmore, 9, *28* (6; 1666-1710; D), *5, 8, 14*; Samuel, *15, 28*; Thomas, *3*; William, *3*
Perkins: William, 49
Phillips: family, 32; Elinor, 25; John (1), 254; Richard 25; William 25 (9; 1666-1711; W), *87, 98, 103, 126*; —, *119*
Pickerell: Alan (almost certainly Alan Pickering, q.v.) (1), 229
Pickering: (see also Alan Pickerell), Alan, 7, 9, 10 (21; 1680-1741; L, W, R, also Kynnersley), *99. 201, 259, 262*; Christopher (3; 1714-17; R), *244, 245*
Picksley: (see also Pucksley), —, *245*
Pococke: Richard, 102
Podmore; John (1), 2; Sarah,26; William, 85 (2), *98, 175*
Poole: Richard (11; 1665-1716; D, L, W, R), *56, 147, 242*
Powell: Andrew (1), *195*; Thomas, *104*
Powis: Richard (6; 1672-92; W. R), *118, 222, 233*
Poyner: William, 35
Price: —, *194*
Pucksley (see also Picksley): Daniel, 40; Robert (1), *236*
Puller: Francis, 47

Rabison: —, *148*
Randle: John (1), *137*
Ravenall: John (1), *97*
Rawbones: William, *194*
Reynolds: John (2; 1711-20, W), *154*; Pelham (1), *17*; Robert (2; 1696-1910; L), *69*; William (1), *148*
Richards: Daniel, 89; John (5; 1661-88; D), *2, 3, 6*; Richard, *160*; Robert (6; 1679-1727; R), *231*
Richardson: Mrs., *107*
Ringley (possibly Bingley): John (1),*247*
Robotham: Richard (1), *69*
Rodenhurst: Francis (1), *259*; Richard, *126*
Roe: Ann, *26*; Jane, *179*; Jonathan,

Roe, Ann—*continued*
235; Roger (20; 1657-1739; D,W, R), *12, 210, 211, 215, 252, 255*; Thomas (6; 1661-1746; D, W, R), *210, 215*
Rogers: Elizabeth, *160*; John, 27, *160*
Rowley: John (1), *176*; Richard (3; 1663-1727; L, W), *35*; Thomas (2; 1682-1730; W, R), *99*
Royston: William (11; 1680-1745; L), *47, 59, 64, 66*
Ruckson: Francis (2; 1675-1747; D, W), 29
Rushbury; James (3; 1690-1715; W, R), *146, 159*
Rushton: —, *194*
Russell: Edward (2), *85, 227*
Rycroft: Richard (2), *7, 225*

Salt: Thomas (1), *61*
Salter: William (1), *111*
Sambrook: John (2; 1740-42; W, R), *202*
Sandys: Thurstan (5; 1705-1716; W), *157, 161*
Scot: —, *107*
Seamoore: —. *107* (possibly Timothy Seymour, Shrewsbury mercer)
Shelton: family, 7, 78; Andrew (11; 1675-87; L, W), *40, 41, 44, 47, 50, 95*; Eleanor, *64*; Joan, 73; John (2; 1675-1717; L), 73; Philippa, *64*; Richard, *64* (10; 1661-1734; L, R), *33, 38, 42; 43, 76, 225*; Robert, 9, *64* (4; 1663-1700; L), *37, 57*; William, *64, 73* (7 + 1 for Shoton; 1685-1716; L), *66, 71*
Shenton: John, 31
Sicall: John (1), *150*
Silcox: Edward (1), *233*
Sillitoe: John (2; 1705-1731; L, W), *77*
Simmonds: John, *104* (1), *143\**; Richard (6; 1681-1705; L, W), *55*; William, *55*
Skitt: John (1), *156*
Slaney (possibly Staney): Jonas (1), *20*
Smalridge: Ann, 49, 50, 51, 53, 54, 55, 57, 59, 60
Smart: Jane, 52; John, 49, 50, 52, 53, 54, 57; Richard, 52; Thomas (2; 1729-36; W), *184*
Smith: Jacob (1), *18*; James (2; 1661-69; R), *210*; John (17; 1669-1730; D, W, R), *22, 232, 237, 238, 251*; Richard, *260*; Thomas (12; 1657-1728; W, R), *101, 210, 212*; William, *260\** (6; 1654-1704; L, W, R), *209*; —, *107*

# INDEX OF NAMES

Smitheman: John (1) *100*; Thomas (1) *114*
Sockett: Andrew, 25, 26, 31, 38, 39 (18; 1670–1725; W), *106, 107\*, 109, 128, 136, 157*; John (2; 1719; W, Oakengates), *246*; Mary, 35; Robert (1), *208*; Roger (11; 1693–1719; D, W, R, Oakengates), *12, 121, 128, 145, 230, 246*; Thomas, 25, *157* (8; 1725–43; W), *171, 173, 207*; William, 25, 43 (1), *160*
Southall: Vincent (3; 1700–27; W), *134*
Spearman: John, 10 (14; 1663–1747; L. W), *47, 63, 68*
Spruce: Nathaniel (1), *122*
Stafford, Earls of, *see* Jerningham
Stanworth: Henry, 10, 47; William (1), *183*
Steed: John (1), *4*
Steventon: John, 64 (4; 1661–1729; L, W), *54*; Mary, *58*
Stilgoe: Charles (4; 1675–1740; W, R), *89, 117, 261*
Studley: Thomas (3; 1718–25; W), *169, 171*
Suttons: Thomas (1), *78*
Swift: Thomas (3; 1676–1716; D, W), *7, 91*
Swinnerton: Richard (1), *25*

Tart: Thomas (1), *94*
Taylor: John, 47, 80 (2), *78, ˙124*; Thomas, *254* (2; 1714–19; D, R), *244*; William (5; 1737–47; W), *193, 202, 204, 207*
Thrapp: Samuel (1), *82*
Tildesley: Thomas (1), *65*
Tipton: William (2; 1676–79; D), *9*
Tudor: Thomas (1), *179*
Turner: Daniel, *174*; James (7; 1734–44; W), *196, 200, 201*; Margaret, *see* Justice; Margaret; Robert,*157*, 11); 1720–44; W, R), *166, 168, 177, 190, 261, 263*; Thomas (13; 1700–29; L), *57, 65, 66, 70, 73, 75*; William, 85, *109* (9; 1669–1700; W, R), *86, 94, 95, 130, 234*; ––, *119*

Vickars: John, 7; Richard, 8 (4; 1680–93; R), *219, 221, 229*

Wade: John (1), *99*
Walker: John, 44, 69, *194\**; Roger, *119* (6; 1674–91; W), *113, 115*
Wallett, Charles, *194\**
Wallis: Elizabeth, 8

Walton: ––, *194*
Ward: Robert, *84*; Thomas (10; 1705–31; L, W), 74, *144, 180, 181, 186*
Warter: John (10; 1670–1701; W, R), *213, 223, 224, 232*
Watkiss: George (3; 1664–1704; W, R), *252*; John (3; 1675–1704; W, R), *141, 220*; Richard (3; 1731–41; R), *253, 256*; William (1), *138*; ––, *107*
Webb, Dorothy, *174*; Edward (2; 1683–99; W), *129*; William, 77
Wellington: Grace, *22*; John, *22*; Martha, *22*; Richard, *22*; Susannah, *22*; Thomas, *22*
Wheeler: George (1), *137*
Whitmore: Henry (2), *58, 62*; John (1), *36*; Margaret, *36*
Whittingham: Edward (2), *26, 28*; Robert (3; 1671–81; L, W), *88*; Thomas, 82 (6; 1684–1725; D, W), *104, 105, 151*
Wickstead: Charles (1), *74*; Richard (3; 1679–77; D, L, R), *216*; Thomas (5; 1675–89: L), *48*
William III: *186*
Williams: Godfrey (2; 1720–12; L), 70; John, *260*
Windsor (*also* Winshurst): Ralph, 10 (2), *49, 51*; Thomas, 6, 9, 10, 83, *39* (14; 1661–1720; L), *32, 33, 34, 36, 37, 38, 52*
Winkle: Stephen (1), *198*
Winnall: Samuel (1), *247*
Winshurst, *see* Windsor
Wood: Henry, *43*; Thomas (1), *226*
Woolley: John (6; 1697–1739; D), 22, 25, 27; William (3; 1694–1708; L), *64, 66*
Wootton: Edward (1), *60*; John (1), *60*
Worrall: John (1), *34*; William (2; 1676–86; L), *39*
Wright: Adam, 6 (9; 1677–1705; W), *97, 106, 112, 115*; Andrew, *109*; Ann, 34, 111; Anna, 23, 24; Benjamin, 23–5, 26, 28, 30, 31, 32, 33, 34, 38, 39 (2; 1662–84; W), *103*; Charles (5; 1702–43; W), *199*; Francis, 23, 39, 52, 53, 58, *109, 119* (1), 64; John, 52 *109*; Kervin, 24; Margaret, 24, *109*; Mary, *109*; Thomas, 50, 51, 52, 53, 56, 57, 58, 59, 60 (2), *60, 69*

Yarsley: Judith, *246*
Yates: Richard (2; 1705–08; W), *142*
Young: Arthur, 56, 61, 62